Years of Russia, the USSR and the Collapse of Soviet Communism

second edition

DAVID EVANS & JANE JENKINS

HODDER
EDUCATION

Hachette's policy is to use papers that are natural, renewable and recyclable products and made from wood grown in sustainable forests. The logging and manufacturing processes are expected to conform to the environmental regulations of the country of origin.

Orders: please contact Bookpoint Ltd, 130 Milton Park, Abingdon, Oxon OX14 4SB. Telephone: +44 (0)1235 827720. Fax: +44 (0)1235 400454. Lines are open 9.00a.m.–5.00p.m., Monday to Saturday, with a 24-hour message answering service. Visit our website at www.hoddereducation.co.uk

First published in 2001 by
Hodder Education,
An Hachette UK Company,
338 Euston Road,
London NW1 3BH.

This second edition first published 2008.

Impression number   5 4 3 2
Year   2012 2011 2010 2009

The front cover shows Stalin, 1930s © Hulton Archive/Getty Images, and Lenin proclaiming Soviet power, Petrograd, 1917 © BPK

Typeset in 10pt Minion by Fakenham Photosetting Limited, Fakenham, Norfolk
Printed in Malta

A catalogue record for this title is available from the British Library.

ISBN 978 0 340 96661 7

Contents

Back drop.

⁓ ACKNOWLEDGEMENTS ⁓

The Publishers would like to thank the following for permission to reproduce material in this book:

The Alliluyeva Trust, for extracts from *Twenty Letters to a Friend* by Svetlana Alliluyeva (Harper & Row, 1967) used on pages 366, 373; **Cambridge University Press**, for extracts from *Russia, Revolution and Counter-Revolution 1917–1924* by John Daborn (Cambridge University Press, 1991) used on pages 199, 201, 220; for an extract from *The Russian Landed Gentry and the Peasant Emancipation of 1861* by Terence Emmons (Cambridge University Press, 1968) used on page 40; **Gabriel Earl Music (ASCAP)**, for the lyrics to "Happy Birthday, Leonid Brezhnev" by Joan Baez used on page 450; **HarperCollins Publishers**, for an extract from *The Life and Times of Grigorii Rasputin* by Alex De Jonge (Fontana Collins, 1983) used on pages 182–183; for extracts from *The Russian Revolution 1899–1919* by Richard Pipes (Fontana, 1990) used on pages 205, 217; **David Higham Associates**, for an extract from *The Twilight of Imperial Russia* by Richard Charques (Oxford University Press, 1958) used on page 96; **History Today**, for an extract from "Alexander II's Reforms, Causes and Consequences" by Carl Watts, *History Review*, Number 2 (December 1998) used on page 47; **Lawrence & Wishart**, for extracts from *Works* by Josef Stalin (Lawrence & Wishart, 1952) used on pages 103, 125, 249, 271, 275, 291, 301; **Orion Publishing Group**, an extract from *One Day in the Life of Ivan Denisovich* by Alexander Solzhenitsyn (Penguin Books, 1970) used on pages 363–364; **Oxford University Press**, for extracts from *Endurance and Endeavour: Russian History 1812–1986* by J. N. Westwood (Oxford University Press, 1973) used on pages 4–5, 84, 135–136; for extracts from *The Russian Empire, 1801–1917* by Hugh Seton-Watson (Oxford University Press, 1967) used on pages 29, 30, 53, 96–97, 165, 175; **Palgrave Macmillan**, for an extract from *Stalin's Economic Policy* by Malcolm Falkus (Macmillan, 1986) used on pages 289–290; for extracts from *The Russian Revolution and the Soviet State 1917–21* by M. McCaulay (Macmillan, 1975) used on pages 219, 220; **Pathfinder Press**, for an extract from *From Lenin to Stalin* by V. Serge (Monad Press, 1937) used on page 256; **Pearson Education**, for an extract from *Russia* by E. Acton (Longman, 1986) used on page 34; for an extract from *Russia in the Age of Modernisation and Revolution* by Hans Rogger (Longman, 1983) used on page 182; **University of Chicago Press**, for extracts from *Serfdom and Social Control in Russia: Petrovskoe, a Village in Tamboo* by S. L. Hoch (University of Chicago Press, 1986) used on pages 7–8, 9; for extracts from *Readings in Russian Revolution* by T. Riha (University of Chicago Press, 1964) used on pages 49, 71; **University of North Carolina Press**, for a table from *Stalinist Planning for Economic Growth, 1933–52* (University of North Carolina Press, 1980) used on page 284; **Yale University Press**, for extracts from *A Source Book for Russian History from Early Times to 1973*, edited by G. Vernadsky (Yale University Press, 1972) used on pages 7, 22–23, 29, 34, 196, 198.

The publishers would like to thank the following for permission to reproduce the following copyright illustrations in this book:
Akg-images pages 65, 349; Betmann/CORBIS pages 89, 109, 453 left, 453 right; bpk Berlin pages 364, 365 top; © Sergei Chirikov/epa/CORBIS page 467; Viktor Drachev/AFP/Getty Images page 468; Henry Guttman/Getty Images page 314 right; © Hulton Archive/Getty Images pages 286, 403; © Hulton-Deutsch Collection/CORBIS pages 93, 262 right, 345, 369; Keystone/Getty Images page 422; The David King Collection pages 25, 68, 96 right, 110 left, 110 right, 145 left, 145 right, 261 right, 283 left, 283 right, 303, 365 centre left, 365 centre right, 370; Cartoon for the PID by Kem 1939, courtesy of Alexander and Richard Marengo page 330; Private Collection/Archives Charmet/The Bridgeman Art Library page 395; © Punch Limited/Topfoto pages 168, 331, 381; © 2006 RIA Novosti/Topfoto pages 288, 366; © 2005 Roger-Viollet/Topfoto page 262 left; Society for Cooperation in Russian and Soviet Studies pages 30, 314 left; SOLO Syndication page 387; Three Lions/Getty Images page 441; Topfoto.co.uk pages 96 left, 129; Peter Turnley/CORBIS page 456.

Every effort has been made to trace and acknowledge ownership of copyright. The publishers will be glad to make suitable arrangements with any copyright holders whom it has not been possible to contact.

Preface: How to use this book

In 1916, Henry Ford in an article in the *Chicago Tribune* famously wrote, 'History is more or less bunk,' and Augustine Birrell was no more complimentary when he described history as 'That great dust-heap'. The dismal Voltaire saw history as being 'nothing more than a tableau of crimes and misfortunes.' Others have been kinder and more constructive. Emerson's view was that, 'There is probably no history; only biography,' and Thomas Carlyle agreed when he wrote 'History is the essence of innumerable biographies.' It was left to Samuel Taylor Coleridge to truly identify the value of this study when he wrote – 'If men could learn from history, what lessons it might teach us.' So much for history, what then of examinations? As long ago as 1820, the clergyman, Charles Caleb Colton, wrote 'Examinations are formidable even to the best prepared' – little has changed!

Although the introduction of a two-tier system of examinations, Advanced Subsidiary and Advanced Level (AS and A2), has brought changes in syllabus content and methods of assessment, the skills required to achieve success remain largely the same – the ability to analyse, evaluate, interpret and use different types of historical sources, the ability to use historical concepts by developing an argument or writing an account, and the ability to communicate clearly and concisely. To these has been added a synoptic dimension which we will consider later. The skills required in the use of sources and essay writing remain the same.

1 ⌒ USING SOURCES

We study history to find out about the past. Not merely what happened but also why it happened and what were its consequences. To do this it is necessary to find evidence. On almost every historical topic there is a vast amount of source material that can be used to build up an overall picture. The sources may be primary or secondary. Primary sources may take the form of written documents, eye-witness accounts and photographs; secondary sources may written accounts based on research interpretations and opinions, illustrations, maps, diagrams, cartoons and sometimes, statistics. Different sources provide different types of evidence and the first task of a historian is to assess usefulness by judging their reliability. Is the source genuine? To what extent is it likely to be biased?

AS and A1 examinations use many types of sources. The questions you will be asked may be based on a single source, two sources or many (multi-) sources. Some may be original or primary sources representing the views of contemporary historians whilst others will represent the views expressed in the publications of writers and historians that may challenge the earlier interpretation and evaluation. Remember too that historians seldom agree and that sources may represent conflicting points of view. The documentary exercises that accompany the chapters in the book are designed to help you develop the skills needed to assess evidence and help you to comment on their value and reliability. The questions have been chosen to test your ability to:

● recall and/or select and use historical knowledge and terminology in order to demonstrate understanding of the historical content covered by the chapter
● evaluate and interpret source material, both primary and secondary and of various types
● extract the relevant information needed to answer the question
● distinguish between fact, opinion and fiction
● detect bias, gaps and inconsistencies in the source material, place it in context
● compare and reach conclusions based on the evidence provided by the sources.

2 ↩ ADVICE ON ANSWERING DOCUMENTARY EXERCISES

The documents you may be asked to consider may be extracts from books and documents as well as visual material such as pictures, illustrations, maps, cartoons and statistics. Statistics may appear in numerical form or in graphical form such as column graphs and pie charts. If the questions are structured, the chances are that the mark for the sections will be progressive with the highest mark reserved for the last. This means that your answer will need to be more extensive and probably require you to refer to all the sources. You are also sometimes invited to include your own background knowledge.

QUESTIONS BASED ON AN UNDERSTANDING OF THE TEXT

You might be asked to explain the meaning of a particular word or phrase. If this is the case, a simple dictionary definition may not be sufficient. It is usually necessary to explain the meaning within the context of the source and your answer should be designed to indicate your understanding of the source. Keep your answer as brief as possible and do not, unless you are asked to do so, include additional background information. In this type of question it is possible to waste a great deal of time by providing unnecessary detail.

QUESTIONS REGARDING THE AUTHORSHIP OF A DOCUMENT

Authorship, sometimes referred to as the 'provenance' of a source, involves you to consider:

- who actually wrote the source?
- was he a person with a depth of knowledge and able to provide reliable information about the subject or was he merely expressing a personal opinion?
- did the author have a particular reason or motive for writing in that way? In other words, was he biased or even lying?

Remember even a biased source may have some value since, even though it may be one-sided, it will illustrate an attitude and may provide useful background information.

QUESTIONS BASED ON INFORMATION IN THE DOCUMENT ABOUT PEOPLE, TIME, PLACES AND IDEAS

This is a form of comprehension in which you will be expected to show an understanding of the meaning of documents or a comparison of themes and arguments. You might be asked to comment on what is written and then work out what the author really meant. This will require you to 'read between the lines' – to discover a meaning that is not directly expressed but implied.

QUESTIONS REGARDING THE ATTITUDE(S) THAT THE DOCUMENT MIGHT REVEAL

You may be asked to comment on the tone of the language used in the document. Some sources may reflect the feelings of the author and show one of a range of emotions such as anger, hatred, prejudice, excitement, pleasure and sympathy. Again, it may be necessary for you to 'read between the lines'. One of the clues to detecting prejudice or bias is to consider whether the author selected the information deliberately in order to give it a particular slant. Is it propaganda and deliberately intended to be misleading or biased? Is the document complete or is it selective with sections left out? Is it intended to make a specific impression on the reader/listener and so have an impact on his thinking? Remember that a personal view may be unwittingly biased. On the other hand, the author may have a poor memory or he may actually have intended to misguide his readers/listeners with an intended falsehood.

QUESTIONS REGARDING THE RELIABILITY OF A SOURCE

This involves detecting the presence of bias, statements that are assumptions or simply long accepted if fallacious points of view. At times, all of us show bias and either purposely or unwittingly give a coloured or distorted personal view in order to get out of trouble or to make an impression. Again, as long as this is recognised, this type of bias does not always diminish the value of the source. Even if the source is an out-and-out lie, the writer must have had a reason for misleading his readers.

QUESTIONS NECESSITATING EVALUATING A SOURCE

Such questions are designed to make you state whether the source:

- is of considerable or limited value
- is significant or of relatively little importance
- is complete or is deficient with gaps and inconsistencies
- is fact or unsubstantiated opinion
- is of vital importance to an historian or is mere trivia.

3 ⌐ ESSAY QUESTIONS

Most history questions fall into one of three categories: list, significance or discussion.

- List questions require an investigation of causes, effects and consequences and will tend to start with phrases such as 'Account for...', 'For what reasons...' or 'With what results...'.
- Significance questions require you to decide upon the relative importance of factors and are introduced with such phrases as 'How valuable...', 'How important ...', 'To what extent ...' or 'How effectively ...'.
- Discussion questions are likely to begin with such phrases as 'Do you agree that ...', 'With what justification can it be claimed that...' or 'Comment on the view that...'. Such questions can also begin with a quotation followed by 'Discuss this view of ... ', 'How valid is this assessment of ... ', or 'How satisfactory is this explanation of ... '.

Examples of all the questions detailed above are provided at the end of the chapters.

Writing successful essays

Before you even start **make sure that you have read the question correctly**. Failure to answer the question as set is one of the main reasons why candidates fail to achieve their expected grades. Some advise you to prepare an answer in outline, a skeleton answer, before you begin writing. This can prove useful but do remember that it can be very time consuming.
A good essay should aim to achieve:

- balance – make sure that you tackle all aspects of the question
- breadth – use plenty of sources. Quote freely from your notes, textbooks and other relevant works that you may have studied
- depth – consider each point in full and support your argument with solid factual evidence.

Your answer should be divided into three parts – introduction, development and conclusion.

INTRODUCTION

This should outline the main theme or points to be considered in your essay. Set the scene and state your argument briefly. By relating it directly to the wording of the question, your answer will be less likely to become irrelevant and develop into an excessive narrative. A word of warning, some feel that a flamboyant or dramatic opening statement will impress the examiner. This is not always the case!

DEVELOPMENT TO INCLUDE ARGUMENT AND ANALYSIS

This is the main section of your answer in which you develop the points made in your introduction. Here you develop your argument and offer explanations and supporting evidence. You can also use your detailed knowledge, refer to sources and try to achieve a balance between analysis and detail. Write in well constructed paragraphs and constantly refer back to the question to make sure that what you are writing is relevant.

CONCLUSION

Here you should again refer to the introduction and make sure that the points mentioned have been adequately dealt with. Your conclusion should not simply be a summary of the content and argument used in your essay. It should be used to tie together the main themes and put the issues you have raised into a wider perspective. The conclusion should be brief and indicate that your argument is completed.

The general description of an essay likely to attain the highest marks/grade is:

- it should use accurate historical knowledge suitably deployed and displaying no factual errors, omissions or misconceptions
- it should be well focused and relevant throughout
- it should use an evaluative/analytical approach
- it should develop an argument that is well presented and supported
- it should be well constructed with the use of clearly defined sentences and paragraphs
- it should contain the minimum of grammar, punctuation and spelling errors.

Examiners are not impressed by:

- flannel, verbiage and chatty-type answers
- answers that merely repeat notes
- 'I'll tell you all I know-type answers' – whether it is relevant or not
- answers which are largely narrative and where the main issue raised by the question is covered in the final paragraph
- answers that contain significant omissions
- poor standards of literacy. If you are going to use historical terms – agrogorod, kolkhoz, perestroika, zhdanovshchina – or historical names – Alliluyeva, Dzerzhinsky, Khrushchev, Pobedonostev – learn to spell them correctly
- inaccurate dates
- the use of slang or witticisms.

4 ⌐ SYNOPTIC QUESTIONS

The word synoptic comes from the Greek synopsis and means to take an overall or general view. A synoptic-type question will require you to draw together your knowledge of an extended period of history, usually 100 years, and be able to show your understanding of the political, economic, cultural and social characteristics of that period. The questions will most likely follow an on going theme. You will be required to use a range of historical concepts to present an argument. To do this, you will be required to:

● **recall**, identify from the content of your study that which is relevant to the topic or theme
● **communicate**, indicate your mastery of that knowledge and understanding in a clear manner
● **understand**, show your ability to interpret and indicate that you have an understanding of the important characteristics of the historical
● **interpret**, show evidence of your ability to evaluate and use different types of sources
● **explain**, be able to evaluate interpretations of historical events
● **identify**, from the content of your study recognise evidence of change and continuity
● **assess**, indicate the importance or significance of events, individuals, ideas and attitudes in their historical setting
● **make judgements**, provide historical explanations and evaluate evidence and show your understanding of historical theories.

The questions may be structured, take the form of an open-ended essay or be based on a range of sources. The sources used may be primary or secondary and may cover areas of historical debate. In which case you will need to bear in mind the basis upon which the authors of the sources reached their conclusions. Some topics covered by this book that might be used as the basis of synoptic questioning are included at the end of Chapter 15 (see page 472).

5 ⌐ MAKING NOTES

These advice sections at the ends of the chapters will help you to develop your key skills of research and analysis based upon the content and themes explored in the chapters. The guidelines below will help you break down the information by asking questions about the various elements. You are also encouraged to make use of the bibliographies to carry out further research and so develop your own ideas and form judgements.

● Locate the relevant sections of the chapter and refer to the written or visual evidence.
● Skim-read the located section to establish an overall picture, context and the main ideas of the arguments or interpretation. This has the advantage of focusing attention on relevant material and ensures efficient reading.
● Then, using the questions shown under headings, organise your notes on the main themes covered in the chapters, leaving out detail that adds nothing to the understanding of the main points identified.

Imperial Russia by 1855

INTRODUCTION

By the middle of the nineteenth century Russia embraced a vast Empire that covered almost one-sixth of the earth's land area with around 200 different nationalities. In February 1836 Lord Dudley Stuart speaking in the House of Commons said of Russia, '(it) is often mentioned as being great, but let the House consider for a moment what Russia is. The emperor of Russia rules over an extent of territory in Europe greater than all the rest of Europe put together, and this was joined by a tract of country by dominions in Asia, three times as great as the possessions of Russia in Europe'. It had the strength of being continuous and compact but it was in the words of the Russian writer, Gogol, a 'hard land, whose overpowering landscape reduced men and their works to insignificance. Towns and villages were like little dots'. Its frontiers extended 6000 miles from Vladivostok on the Pacific coast to the Russo-German frontier in the west and nearly 3000 miles from the Arctic Sea to the Persian frontier in the south. Apart from the high mountain ranges along the southern frontiers and the chain of low hills of the Ural Mountains that separate European Russia from Siberia, the country was one large open plain that occupied two-thirds of the country. The North was mainly forest-land with open steppes where the climate ranged from extreme cold in winter to brief, hot, mosquito-laden summers. Parts of south and central Russia were very fertile but in other areas the soil was barren. It had rich natural resources of iron ore in the Urals, coal, oil and other minerals but it lagged far behind the rest of Europe in making use of its great resources. Its people, who in the main lived in the European provinces of Russia, the Ukraine, Byelorussia, Poland and the Caucasus, were backward and suffered at the hands of their rulers.

1 ～ THE NATURE OF RUSSIAN SOCIETY

A *Population size and distribution*

Russia in the mid-nineteenth century was a country of long-established traditions and was backward by European standards. It was sparsely populated; with 94% of its people living in small isolated villages and engaged in farming. In 1840 the ratio of villagers to townspeople was 11 to 1 whereas in England it was 2 to 1 and in France 5 to 1. During the

average

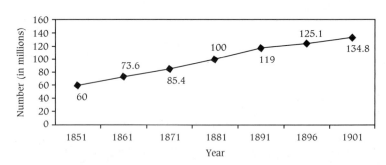

DIAGRAM 1

Growth in Russia's population 1851–1901

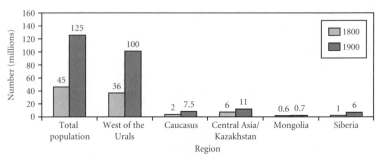

DIAGRAM 2

Regional population of the Russian Empire in 1800 and in 1900

Nationality	Number (in millions)
Great Russians	44.3
Ukrainians	17.8
Polish	6.3
Jews	4.0
Turkic	10.8
Finns	2.8
Germans	1.4
Latvians and Lithuanians	2.5
Estonians	1.0
Armenians	0.9
Georgians	1.0

TABLE 1

Major nationalities of the Russian Empire according to the 1895 census (in millions)

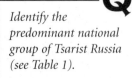

Identify the predominant national group of Tsarist Russia (see Table 1).

See Map 1 on page 3.

course of the nineteenth century the population grew from 45.6 million in 1800 to 69 million in 1851 and 125 million by 1900. The greatest areas of growth were the central agrarian regions, New Russia, and the Lower Volga to the south and the northern and southern Urals to the east. The percentage of those who lived in towns was small, at 6% in 1861 rising very slowly to 15% by 1896. St Petersburg, the capital of the tsars, was the largest town with 500 000 closely followed by Moscow, while the other towns of Riga, Warsaw, Odessa, Kishinev, and Saratov were much smaller. Towns functioned as administrative and marketing centres rather than for industrial purposes.

The Empire was composed of different nationalities, cultures, and religions. Some of its people were primitive tribesmen living in small and remote villages, over 50% were not ethnic Russian while about 20–25 million were Muslim, with another 5 million Jews. Jews suffered from discrimination. They were confined to the 15 provinces of Pale, were not allowed to own or work the land, and were subjected to anti-Jewish riots from 1881 onwards. The most loyal and ruthless supporters of the empire were the Cossacks, who lived on the steppes of the Ukraine. They were a free and originally democratic military brotherhood, called the *Host*, composed mostly of runaway serfs, who lived on the borderlands of the Russian Empire. They had lived from pillage but as the Empire became more settled they turned to farming. They had the reputation of being excellent fighters and had been given special privileges in return for military service. By the nineteenth century they had been absorbed into the Tsarist army. Nationalism became an increasingly important issue amongst Russia's national groups, particularly in the frontier provinces, and in Poland where attempts at *Russification* provoked rebellion and suppression in 1831 and again in 1863.

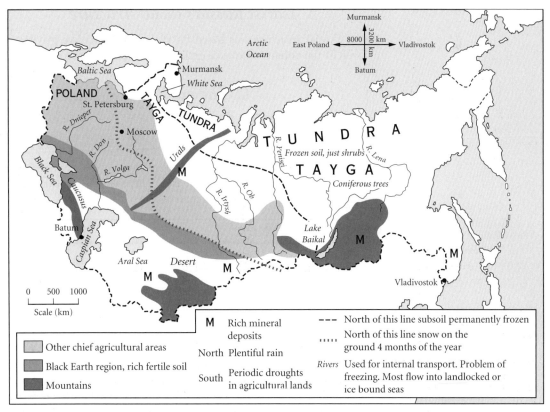

MAP 1 *Soil and climate of Russia*

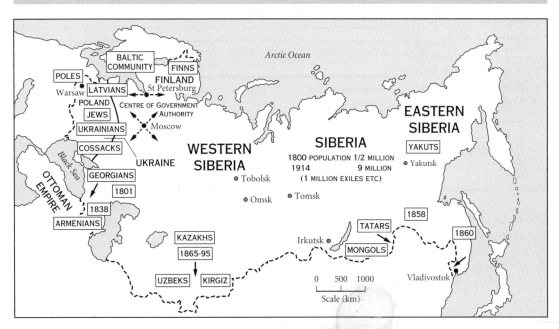

MAP 2 *Regional divisions of Tsarist Russia*

B *Tsarist Russia's social structure*

Russia's social structure was based on ranks with extensive privileges enjoyed by the nobility who were excluded from paying taxes.

C *The nobility*

In 1858 there were about one million nobles of whom 247 000 belonged to the Russian hereditary nobles while many of the others were Polish. The census of 1858–9 showed that there were 90 000 serf owners of whom only 18 500 owned more than a 100 serfs each, or '*souls*' as they were defined in the census. There were wide variations within their ranks as the following tables show.

TABLE 2
Russia's social structure early nineteenth century

Classes	%
Non-productive (educated classes)	
Nobility including the ruling group	1.1
Military	5.0
Officials of various kinds and *Raznochintsy* (people of mixed rank) (predominantly urban)	3.7
Clergy	1.1
Merchants	0.5
Total	**11.4**
Productive (peasants and urban working classes/small traders)	
Meshchane (urban working class and small traders)	3.7
State peasants	32.7
Landlords' serfs	50.7
Free people (mainly Cossacks)	0.6
Other categories of peasants	0.9
Total	**88.6**

TABLE 3
Serf-owning landlords in European Russia 1858–9

Landlord group	Number in group	Number of serfs owned by each member	Percentage of total serf owners
Grand seigneurs	1032	Over 1000	1.1
Gentry	1754	501–1000	2.0
Gentry	15 717	101–500	18.0
Impoverished gentry	30 593	21–100	35.1
Impoverished gentry	38 173	Average 7	43.8

Q

What was the basis of a noble's wealth?

This extract from P. Kropotkin, *Zapiski revolyutsionera*, 1966, quoted in J.N. Westwood, *Endurance and Endeavour Russian History 1812–1986*, OUP, 1987, illustrates the views of the nobility.

At that period the wealth of a landowner was measured by the number of 'souls' he possessed. 'Souls' meant male serfs, women did not count. My father was a rich man, he had more than 1200 souls in three different provinces ... In our family there were eight persons, sometimes ten or twelve; fifty servants in Moscow and sixty or so in the country did not seem too many ... The dearest wish of every landowner was to have all his requirements supplied by his own serfs. All this was so that if a guest should ask, 'What a beautiful-tuned piano! Did you get it tuned at Schimmel's?' The landowner could reply, 'I have my own piano-tuner'.

Q

How typical of the nobility was this landowner's lifestyle? (See Table 3.)

This state of affairs arose out of the inheritance law that divided a property amongst all the male heirs on the death of the noble. The effect of this was to ruin families; a problem aggravated by the absence of alternative sources of income since there was an excess of nobles compared with posts in the bureaucracy.

KEY ISSUE

Relationship between nobles and serfs.

Apart from the obligation not to kill, damage, or injure their serfs, landlords had extensive powers and few legal controls. They:

- controlled the lives of their serfs including marriage and sale
- could demand feudal dues in the form of labour, money, and goods
- controlled the distribution of land, including dispossession that reduced a serf to the role of household servant
- had unrestricted powers to punish including flogging or exile to Siberia
- could demand any money earned by a serf as taxation.

Despite these opportunities to exploit their serfs it was in the self-interest of landlords to use their powers sensibly. Cruelty nevertheless existed.

The grand seigneurs formed the ruling elite who formed the basis of the autocracy of the Tsar. Their extravagant and luxurious lifestyle revolved around their country estates and town houses in Moscow or St Petersburg or their visits to various European health resorts. Politically they involved themselves in court intrigues and schemed for positions in foreign affairs. They dominated the army, controlled the guard regiments at the palace and the top positions in the bureaucracy.

Below the ruling elite were those nobles who worked as government officials and were dependent on a salary. By the mid-nineteenth century, their number and importance had grown so that there were 12 civil servants per 1000 people. They were beginning to develop into a professional, disciplined inner group around the Tsar who governed with the help of eight ministries, including War, Finance, and Internal Affairs. Amongst their duties were the important functions of tax collection, maintenance of law and order and acting as provincial governors. Nobles also controlled the officer ranks of the army.

D *The middle class*

Given the absence of a significant growth of towns or industry it follows that this group played a minor role in society. It was composed of small shopkeepers, entrepreneurs (those responsible for organising production), as well as those who worked in a clerical capacity as government officials at central and provincial level. In 1850 there were about 114 000 such officials, of whom 32 000 were purely clerical. The group also included merchants and those who formed Russia's 'intelligentsia' (those who were learned). Some were very wealthy though they had no political power, nor could they own serfs. They resented the economic privileges of the nobility. They were little affected by European influences, but the government sought their advice on financial, taxation, and economic issues. Their numbers and influence increased in the second half of the century with the growth of industry and towns.

More difficult to define was the intelligentsia, a small and underprivileged group in a society where 90–95% of the population were illiterate in 1850. Many were the children of priests. They filled the ranks of teachers, doctors, government statisticians, and experts. They were paid a salary, often small, and enjoyed some privileges depending on their wealth, status, and power. They became increasingly critical of the Tsarist regime, its restrictions on free speech and press, and its emphasis on birth and wealth. Some joined revolutionary groups that plotted to overthrow the system.

E *Peasants*

The vast majority of Russia's productive population were peasants. Few were free and their status depended on region, type of serfdom and master:

1 State serfs – were those who lived on private estates owned by the State, Church or Tsar. Those who paid a fixed cash sum to state officials were called *Obrok*. They were to be found in the less fertile northern regions where it was more profitable to demand money rather than labour. In 1858 the number of state serfs was estimated at 19 379 631.

2 Privately owned serfs or *Barshchina* were those serfs who had to pay the landlord's feudal dues with their labour, usually for 3 days a week or more at harvest time. This was demanded by right and tended to occur in areas where farming was profitable, such as the Black soil regions. In other areas where the land was not so fertile, peasants might be required to make payments in cash or goods. Since serfs had to pay whatever the landlord demanded they could find themselves having to make all three-type payments. They were worse off than state serfs were since they had less control over their lives.

3 Household serfs worked as maids, butlers, cooks, coach-drivers or gardeners. In 1858 they numbered 724 314 and were the most exposed to landlord control. They had no land and were not paid a money wage but were given board and lodge.

Soviet historians have estimated that feudal dues by the nineteenth century could account for between one-third to two-thirds of the labour and income of a peasant family. The latter also had to pay state taxes that could take the form of a direct tax affecting 1 in 25 males. This was army recruitment and it was particularly harsh. Prior to 1830 recruits had to serve for 25 years but this was then reduced to 15. At the end of service a serf was given his freedom but this was not as generous as it sounded. Mortality was high and those who survived were separated from home and village. Wives of serfs called up for service were legally declared widows and allowed to remarry. Peasants also paid indirect taxes through their purchase of vodka.

Serfs were free to farm the land given to them for their own use and they controlled village life. The village community was known as the *Mir*, more than a half had between 50 and 300 people.

The following is from a description of the Russian commune by a German traveller Haxthausen, 1843, quoted in G. Vernadsky (ed.), *A Source Book for Russian History from Early Times to 1917*, Yale University Press, 1972.

> The facts here described constitute the basis of the Russian communal system one of the most remarkable and interesting political institutions in existence and one that undeniably possesses great advantages for the social condition of the country. The Russian communes show an organic coherence and compact social strength that can be found nowhere else and yield the incalculable advantage that no proletariat can be formed so long as they exist with their present structure. A man may lose or squander all he possesses but his children do not inherit poverty. They still retain their claim upon the land by a right derived not from him but from their birth as members of the commune. On the other hand it must be admitted that this fundamental basis of the communal system the equal division of the land is not favourable to the progress of agriculture which ... under this system could for a long time remain at a low level.

Q

To what extent did peasants benefit from the commune?

Its economy was based on agriculture, particularly the growing of grain and rye, though there were also rural crafts. It was self-sufficient for, apart from growing their own food, villagers made their own clothes, tools, and furniture and built their houses. Any surpluses were sold to pay taxes and feudal dues. Families had their own remedies for illness – often vodka-based – though each village also had a healer, a *znakharka*, whose herbs were paid for in kind – bread, eggs or cloth. There were local markets where peasants bought their vodka, salt for curing, and metal goods such as ploughshares.

Land was worked as a whole to take account of periods when peasants had to provide feudal dues of labour service. It was organised on an open field basis – the arable fields were divided into strips and each family was allotted their share across the three fields though this could be altered to take account of changing circumstances. Given the absence of artificial fertilisers, they allowed one field to lay fallow every year.

An insight in to working the land from S.L. Hoch, *Serfdom and Social Control in Russia: Petrovskoe, a Village in Tamboo*, University of Chicago Press, 1986.

> As a consequence of the extremely short growing season – five and a half to six months instead of the eight to nine months in Western Europe – under the three-field system the harvesting of winter and spring cereals and the ploughing and sowing of the winter field all came in quick succession within the span of six weeks. From mid-July to the end of August was the harvest season ... an agonising period of activity demanding that numerous tasks be accomplished simultaneously. A work team, or *tiaglo*, of husband and wife together proved

the best allocation of labour resources. A single male simply could not complete all the necessary field work if he were to allow the cereals to mature fully yet avoid the danger of an early frost.

There thus emerged in Russia a clear differentiation of field labor by sex. During the harvest season, women used sickles to cut rye, winter wheat, if any, and sometimes oats, while the men reaped the other spring cereals with scythes. Winter crops could not be cut with a scythe because it knocked too many seeds off the stock, but this was not a problem with less ripe spring cereals. The women then tied the grain into sheaves for drying, and the men began ploughing the winter field. While they sowed the next year's rye crop, the women started to cart the sheaves from the fields assisted by their husbands if time permitted. In general, ploughing, harrowing, cutting hay, and harvesting with a scythe were men's field work; tending the kitchen garden and hemp field, raking hay, cutting stalks with a sickle, tying them, and transporting them to the threshing floor were women's field work. A partnership was essential.

Q

How did the method of farming affect the division of labour between men and women in the Tambov province?

TABLE 4

Distribution of work activities

Work activities	Adult male	Boys	Adult women	Girls
Domestic work	5.7	4.5	40.2	25
Crafts/trades	32.5	17.6	13.7	14
Livestock	7.5	5.1	13.4	2.8
Agriculture	27.5	14.7	20.4	8.8
Unused time	26.8	58.1	12.3	49.4

Q

To what extent did age and sex influence the distribution of work activities within the family?

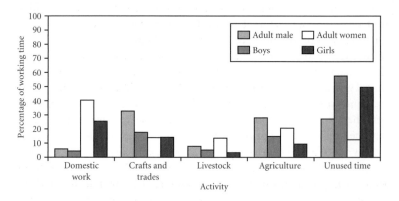

DIAGRAM 3

Distribution of work activities

Members of the village had a strong sense of community. They elected their village officials though the latter were responsible to the landlord. These officials administered the common lands, supervised the collection of state taxes, made provision for the aged, sick and orphaned and provided for education. Decisions at the *Mir* assembly were arrived at by common agreement though they were often controlled by the priest or a rich peasant **kulak**.

Life was very hard. Conditions in peasant homes were primitive, and crowded as highlighted in the following description of the interior of peasant huts in the village of Petrovskoe in the early nineteenth century. This extract is by S.L. Hoch from his book *Serfdom and Social*

kulak Russian for 'fist' so named from their apparently greedy make up.

Control in Russia: Petrovskoe, a Village in Tamboo, University of Chicago Press, 1986.

> Inside the huts the air was fetid from animal and fowl excreta. The walls and ceiling were covered with soot and ash. Smoke especially in the morning when the stove was lit filled the top half of the *izba*. In the evening soot from the *luchinas* stung the eves. The dirt floor was always damp and in the spring and autumn it was muddy. It was impossible to keep cockroaches out of the food; they even became a symbol of abundance and material wealth and a sign of good luck. In fact when moving to a new home the head of the household would bring a few roaches with him and let them loose. These were the conditions under which all the serfs lived for at least a third of the year.
>
> In contrast the warm months brought considerable relief from the squalor of the hut and the psychological effect must have been substantial. Livestock of course was moved outside. The stove was heated less often and in summer was used only for cooking. More hours of sunlight reduced the need for *luchinas*. Animal dung were removed from the hut though with warm weather came the stench of decomposing manure piled in the yard.

Q

How does this source challenge the idealisation of rural life that was so common in writing about rural Russia?

By the middle of the nineteenth century the family was declining in size as sons started to set up their own homes. Children were seen as economic assets. Not only was more land allotted to large families, but also there was a larger labour force. Children who were not needed to work on the land could be sent to work in factories to earn extra cash. Children also represented security against old age since they took care of the aged members of the family. The importance of children in peasant economy led to a high level of marriage, for girls, usually at the age of 24. Infant mortality was high with 50% of children dying before the age of five and 45% before their fifth birthday. Those who reached their fifth birthday could expect to live to 40 years and those who survived to 20 could expect to live to their fifties.

Peasants were exposed to unpredictable rises and falls in harvests and famine, which occurred in 1820, 1833, 1839, 1845, 1855 and 1859. In almost every year in one part of the empire there was an outbreak of peasant violence due to shortages. Estimates of the numbers of such disturbances vary but one source claims that there were at least 400 during each 5-year period following 1826, and from 1844 to 1849 the number rose to 605. Although not large they were followed by a large flight of peasants to the frontier, and by passive resistance by those who remained.

KEY ISSUE

Peasant disturbances.

F *Industrial workers*

This was not a clear-cut group. It included town labourers but some of these were strictly speaking peasants sent to work in factories, driven off the land by the shortage of agricultural land, particularly in central Russia. Growth in population led to increased demand for goods as well as a bigger labour force, but industry suffered from lack of capital and technical skills, mainly in the textile and metallurgic areas. Labourers were employed in the gold, silver, copper, and coal mines of Siberia and in the growing iron industry in the Urals. By the beginning of the nineteenth century Russia had become the world leader in iron production, and the European leader in silver. Industrial workers were under the control of the Tsar, and his officials since most of the heavy industries were in governmental hands. Private industrialists were generally members of the nobility who had acquired their factories as a reward for good service.

Workmen were ill-treated and overworked. They were paid low, and sometimes irregular, wages and expected to work long hours. Complaints to St Petersburg led to some attempts to improve workers' conditions by trying to restrict the night work of minors, regulating wages by state officials or an infrequent confiscation and transfer of ownership of whole factories. These rarely met with success, in some cases the worker had died before his complaint was addressed. Thousands escaped to Siberia or along the southern frontiers. Those who remained resisted by mass refusal to work, go-slow, disobedience, violence and heavy vodka consumption.

> **KEY ISSUE**
>
> *Workers' grievances.*

2 ⌁ THE NATURE OF TSARDOM

For four centuries the central state power in Russia was personified in one man, the Tsar, who claimed unrestricted power. The strength of his character and his personality were fundamental to the successful running of the state as highlighted when the weak Nicholas II became Tsar in 1894. Tsardom was based on the three principles of 'Orthodoxy, Autocracy and Nationality', which were promoted by journalists, courtiers, and priests.

A *Orthodoxy*

By Orthodoxy was meant faith in God, the divine will of the Tsar, and with it the Russian Orthodox Church. This led to a ruthless suppression of rival Catholic and **Uniate Churches** in the countries controlled by Russia, such as Poland and the western borderlands. The Church was the defender of the Tsar and once a year, until the reign of Tsar Alexander II (1855–81), priests declared a curse on all those who did not acknowledge that the tsars of Russia were divinely appointed.

> The **Uniate Church** was founded in 1596 to attract the Slavic and Orthodox peoples of the Ukraine and Byelorussia to Poland and Roman Catholicism. It recognised the authority of the Pope but services were carried on in the Slavic languages.

B *Autocracy*

Fear of challenges to the empire, both from peasant rebellions within, and hostile neighbours outside, had led the ruling class to unite around an autocratic ruler who enjoyed total power. Nobles recognised that their privileged position depended on the Tsar.

The following is from a memorandum on autocratic government by Prince Bezborodko, 1799, quoted in M. Raeff (ed.), *Plans for Political Reform*, Prentice-Hall Inc., 1966.

Russia is an autocratic state. Its size, the variety of its inhabitants and customs and many other considerations make this the only natural form of government for Russia. All arguments to the contrary are futile and the least weakening of autocratic power would result in the loss of many provinces, the weakening of the state, and countless misfortunes for the people. An autocratic sovereign if he possesses the qualities befitting his rank must feel that he has been given unlimited power not to rule according to his whim but to respect and implement the laws established by his ancestors and by himself; in short having spoken his law he is himself the first to respect and obey it so that others may not even dare to think of evading or escaping it.

> **Q**
>
> *What were the duties and responsibilities of an autocratic state and its ruler?*

The Tsar was not controlled by any institutional or legal checks, a Parliament or elections. Everyone in the state was expected to provide service in various forms based on land except the nobility. Each province and village was expected to provide conscripts for the army, which was used to police the empire. A personality cult developed around the Tsar who was seen as a 'father' protecting his subjects.

C *Nationality*

Nationality was interpreted in several ways:

1 A union of the Russian Orthodox Church with autocracy to make the Russian nation. The Russian Church became a national church in 1453 when Byzantium (or Constantinople as it was called, and now modern-day Istanbul) fell to the Muslim Turkish Empire. In 1721 it came under the control of the Tsar's government represented by the Most Holy Directing Synod and was then a symbol of Russia's nationality.

2 *Russianism* based on the belief that Russia's history and geography gave it its individual character, different beliefs, ambitions, and outlook signified by serfdom. Tsars who felt strong links with Germany opposed supporters of Russianism who argued that the German dominated Baltic provinces should be Russianised. These divisions gave rise to the Slavophiles and Westernisers, who debated Russia's future direction in the 1840s (see Section 4).

3 ⌁ THE NATURE OF TSARIST GOVERNMENT

A *Administrative bodies*

Although he was an autocratic ruler with no legal or constitutional restraints on his power, the Tsar had three main bodies who advised:

1 An *Imperial Council of Ministers* chosen from the rich landowners; who had the responsibility of preparing, but not initiating, legislation. Its number varied from 35 to 60 nobles with a large subordinate staff. Tsars did not have to follow its recommendations and often issued decrees without reference to it. Nevertheless, the council survived until the 1905 Revolution, when it then became the second chamber of the new parliament or *Duma*.

2 A *Committee of Ministers* that grew from 8 to 14 by 1900. It was a collection of individual heads of department who combined an advisory with a supervisory function. Each minister also ran his own department – finance, interior, army, education, and war. They were appointed by, and held office at the Tsar's pleasure and could be dismissed by him at a minute's notice. They had the power to issue ministerial decrees that were approved by the Tsar and had the force of law. The committee was not a ministry with collective responsibility and its members often held contrary views. It did not exercise a co-ordinating role over the other bodies but survived until 1906 when it was reorganised as the council of ministers.

3 The *Senate*, founded in 1711, supervised the activities of these two bodies, though the practice of tsars taking control meant that it did not play a leading political role. Alexander II eventually reformed it into the Supreme Court of the Empire in 1864.

Tsars made use of the '*Third Section*' responsible for the political police. Its agents controlled the regular bureaucracy and every aspect of society. It acted independently of the law, and became virtually a state within a state. Its presence not only encouraged rivalry with other government agencies, but also espionage, and the use of agent provocateurs within the groups of revolutionaries. Tsars also made use of specially composed committees for specific purposes, or trusted individuals who were given special powers – to report, negotiate or make decisions, who were outside the ordinary machinery of government.

Ruling group	Size (000s)	Percentage
Nobility	1000	71
Officials	114	8
Intelligentsia	50	4
Merchants/ middle class	246	17
Total	1410	100

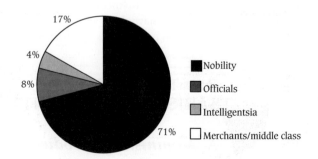

DIAGRAM 4 *Structure of the Ruling group in 1850*

B *The bureaucracy*

The bureaucracy manned central and provincial government. It encouraged the development of a professional educated civil servant, mostly drawn from noble ranks or from the junior ranks of the army or priests' sons.

C *Censorship*

By the middle of the nineteenth century Russia had vigorously suppressed free speech. Secret police had always existed but by the start of Alexander II's reign in 1855 the Third Section of the Imperial Chancellery had turned Russia into a police state. The law was applied in all its severity to control the people and full use was made of executions, imprisonment, exile, and flogging as well as restricting foreign travel. Strict censorship was introduced to fight the growth of nationalist and liberal ideas. A variety of agencies – ecclesiastical, security police, any department of state administered it. There was also a committee responsible for the censorship of censors. People were exposed by informers, and arrested on suspicion. In some cases the censorship ban was ludicrous and unfair – newspaper articles could not include the word 'serf', a cookery book could not refer to 'free air' because this sounded too revolutionary. Individual writers were closely watched, and held in custody for days or weeks. Under such conditions writers, such as Dostoevsky and Tolstoy, used fiction to discuss social issues as well as to inform public opinion of what was going on.

D *Financing of Tsarist Government*

Financing of Tsarist Government came from two sources, feudal dues and taxation, both direct and indirect. Peasants bore the burden since the nobility and clergy were exempt from the payment of the direct money tax, the poll tax. In the main 88.6% of peasants and urban working classes and small traders provided 90% of the revenue to finance not only the costs of government but also the privileged and luxurious life-style of the Tsar, his royal court, and his nobles.

Types of taxes	Income (percentage)
Direct tax (poll tax and obrok)	25
Tax on vodka	30
Tax on salt	5
Custom duties	18
Other	22

TABLE 5
Income of the Russian Government in 1846

> **Q**
> *What were the most important sources of government revenue (see Table 5)?*

Different areas of spending	Expenditure (%)
Loans	17
Army and Fleet	45
Imperial Court	7
Ministry of Finance	13
Ministries of Justice and Education	4
Other	14

TABLE 6
Expenditure of the Russian Government in 1846

> **Q**
> *What appeared to be exceptional in terms of the different areas of spending by the Russian state?*

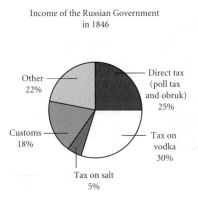

Income of the Russian Government in 1846

Other 22%
Direct tax (poll tax and obruk) 25%
Customs 18%
Tax on vodka 30%
Tax on salt 5%

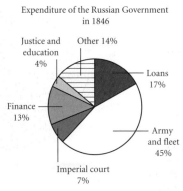

Expenditure of the Russian Government in 1846

Justice and education 4%
Other 14%
Loans 17%
Finance 13%
Army and fleet 45%
Imperial court 7%

DIAGRAM 5
Income and expenditure of the Russian Government in 1846

4 ⌐ ROLE OF THE ARMY

The Russian army at one million was the largest, and most expensive to maintain in Europe enjoying the reputation of never having lost a battle.

About one-third of the peacetime army was used to man military colonies created in the early nineteenth century in the provinces of St Petersburg, Novgorod, Kherson and Kharkov where soldiers and their families spent an over-regimented existence devoted to farming and soldiering. They were given special privileges – exemption from taxation, in return for a life in uniform, but every aspect of their life was controlled including marriage and children were brought up as soldiers. These colonies came to resemble prison camps and provoked revolts that were brutally suppressed.

KEY ISSUE

Abuses in the army.

- The army suffered from inadequacies in its recruitment, provisioning and administration. Apart from its units of Cossack soldiers, its rank and file was composed of an annual recruitment of between 1% and 2% of eligible males between the ages of 20 and 35.
- It had inferior weapons, insufficient ammunition and low morale.
- Mortality rates were high that led eventually to the military reforms associated with the reign of Alexander II (see pages 44–5).
- The aristocracy, who bought commissions for sons, controlled the High Command of the army.
- Corruption and embezzlement existed at all levels. Regimental commanders spent less than the approved budget on food; officers employed conscripted men as labour for their own purposes; or raided cash from the regimental cash; while doctors or engineers falsified costs and pocketed the difference. In every case it was the ordinary soldier who suffered.

By 1855 military service by peasant recruits with good reputations had been reduced from 25 to 15 years, but proposals to reduce service to 5 years in the interests of achieving a small, professional and less expensive force, was rejected by the nobility. They feared that such a system would lead to a long-term emancipation of male serfs because of the custom of giving serfs their freedom on completion of military service.

5 ⌐ DEVELOPMENT OF A REVOLUTIONARY TRADITION

Throughout the three centuries of Romanov history, the regime experienced challenges to its authority in the form of riot, mutiny, and rebellion. A number of issues encouraged the spread of a revolutionary movement.

A *Popular unrest*

Most revolts by peasants, Cossacks, and military colonists were due to serfdom and forced labour. Violence ranged from illegal timber cutting to the destruction of crops and the murder of landowners and bailiffs. These disturbances were typical of the food riots that characterised eighteenth century society in other parts of Western Europe. They were spontaneous, short-lived, leader-less and often confined to the locality. They were rebellions of the belly motivated by hunger and resentment rather than a politically inspired campaign to change society. They posed more of a threat to individual noble families than to the Tsar. It would be incorrect to see these peasant protests as the beginnings of the revolutionary movement that occurred in the second half of the nineteenth century. Intellectuals did not yet appeal to the illiterate peasantry.

B *The challenge of intellectuals*

By the middle of the nineteenth century three main issues had emerged in Russian society that were fiercely debated by its small group of intellectuals:

KEY ISSUE
Debates on Russia's

1 The relationship between the individual and the autocracy.

2 The relationship of Russia to Europe.

3 The gulf between the upper and lower classes centring on the question where did Russia's future lie?

By the 1840s issues surrounding the future development of Russia were beginning to merge in the debates between two broad groups of intellectuals who were termed Slavophiles and Westernisers.

COMPARISON OF SLAVOPHILES AND WESTERNISERS

Similarities	*Differences*
Both groups: <ul><li>were influenced by European philosophers</li><li>shared a love of Russia</li><li>feared the incompetence of the existing Russian government and agreed it was unsatisfactory,</li><li>idealised the peasant and wanted their emancipation</li><li>defended the *Mir* and the commune as a specifically Russian institution that could be used as the basis for future development</li><li>pressed for reform especially social but also some form of consultative representative institution.</li></ul>	<ul><li>Slavophiles regarded themselves as non-political and were conservative in outlook in contrast with the Westernisers who believed that future development would be based on a class struggle within a capitalist system.</li><li>Slavophiles emphasised 'Slavic' values of togetherness (*sobórnost*), the unity of the Tsar and people that had been broken by Peter the Great whereas the Westernisers valued western ways including industrialisation and urbanisation.</li><li>Slavophiles were devout Christians and believed in Orthodoxy; Westernisers were non-believers who were opposed to the idea of a state religion.</li><li>Slavophiles opposed individualism because it was associated with freedom; Westernisers valued the rights of the individual including democracy.</li></ul>

KEY ISSUE

*Development of
Pan-Slav ideas.*

Some Slavophiles sponsored Pan-Slav ideas to unify all Slav peoples into one empire that would be based at Constantinople (*Tsargrad*). Such ideas were potentially dangerous since they challenged the maintenance of traditional regimes such as Austria, Turkey, and Prussia who had Slav peoples within their empires. The desire to return to the purity of old Russian society and its traditions interfered with *Russification* policies in the non-Orthodox parts of the empire. Tsars, who tended to marry into German ruling families, preferred the Westernisers though this was complicated by their challenge of ortho-doxy, autocracy and nationalism. Most of the Slavophiles and Western-isers belonged to a small group of intellectuals, who spoke only to this small group, and were hardly known to the illiterate workers and peas-ants. As a political programme, their work had little immediate effect. Nevertheless, their influence was enormous, for their ideas were carried into the universities and from there spread among the teachers of future generations.

6 ⌐ EDUCATION

By mid-nineteenth century Russia's educational system was based on a Ministry of Education that divided the country into six regions, that subsequently grew to 15 by 1914. Each was under the control of a curator, who was in close touch with the Ministry of Education, and who was a member of the Central School Board. A comprehensive state system of education existed based on four types of schools that were headed by the universities:

1 Universities, located at Moscow, St Petersburg, Dorpat (that taught in German and served the Baltic provinces), Vilna (that catered for the Poles of Lithuania), Kazan and Kharkov. The curriculum was controlled and based on Theology, Church History and Church Law while Russian and Slavic History were introduced at Moscow and St Petersburg.

2 *Gimnazii*, renamed in 1849 as *realschulen* or *Realgimnazi*, were higher 7-year secondary schools serving the towns.

3 County schools provided 3 years of schooling at district, *uezd* level.

4 Parish schools formed the base of the educational pyramid pro-viding a 1-year elementary course. They relied on the charity of landowners and the church for their money so that there were many parishes that had no schools.

5 Church and military schools, private boarding schools for nobles at Moscow, Nizhnii, Novgorod, and Penza existed alongside state schools.

The regime feared that education would lead to the dangerous spread of ideas and so kept its masses ignorant. Few of the 21.7 million serfs or even the 3.4 million town people who formed a large part of the 60 million population in 1851 were educated.

Date	Number of university students	Number of Gimnazii	Number of county schools	Number of parish schools
1832	2153	64	393	552
1842	3488	76	445	1067

TABLE 7
Educational progress between 1832 and 1842

7 ✑ RUSSIAN EXPANSION

A *The 'moving' frontier*

Between 1646 and 1914 Russia's territory and population grew at a faster rate than that of any other European country being exceeded only by the United States. It was said by Sir D.M. Wallace that, 'an insignificant tribe, or collection of tribes, which, 1000 years ago, was confined to a small district near the sources of the Dnieper and the Western Dvina, has grown into a great nation with a vast territory stretching from the Baltic to the Northern Pacific, and from the Polar Ocean to the frontiers of Turkey, Persia, Afghanistan, and China'.

By 1850 Russia was generally regarded as the greatest of the European land powers having expanded her frontier outwards in a number of movements:

● a general northeastwardly direction between 1580 and 1650 that took her from the Urals to the Pacific leading to the settlement of the great Siberian plain by peasant colonists
● north-westerly movement into the Baltic and North Sea that gave Russia control of Finland and the Arctic port of Archangel; the Baltic

Date	In Europe and Caucasia	In Asia
1725	1 738 000	4 092 000
1800	2 014 000	4 452 000
1855	2 261 250	5 194 000
1897	2 267 360	6 382 321

TABLE 8
Size of Russian Empire 1533–1914

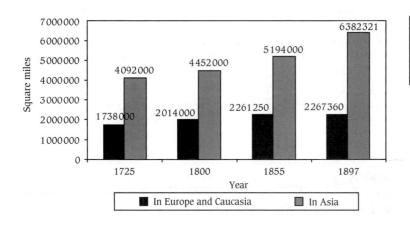

Q

Which region saw greatest growth in the Russian Empire?

DIAGRAM 6
Growth in size of Russian Empire 1725–1897

provinces, the German dominated Estonia, Latvia, and the more Polish orientated Lithuania and Riga, dominance over Sweden, and annexation of the Ukraine and two-thirds of Poland

● eastwards across the Siberian plain via the rivers, then after 1689, across the Bering Strait into North America, annexing Alaska and eventually halting 60 miles north-west of San Francisco in what was then a Spanish colony

● southwards to the Black and Caspian Seas that brought Russia control of the Caucasus. This region, though populated by Armenians and Georgians, was both geographically and politically part of Muslim Persia and Turkey until it was given to Russia in 1829. The Armenians had their own Christian Church and had welcomed becoming a part of the Russian Orthodox Church in the hope of being protected against the occasional bouts of persecution by its Muslim neighbours.

By the end of the eighteenth century Russia had three great ports – at Archangel, St Petersburg and Azov but other western powers prevented her acquiring Constantinople on the straits of the Dardanelles that would have given her control of the passage from the eastern Mediterranean into the Black Sea. As a result she continued with her drive

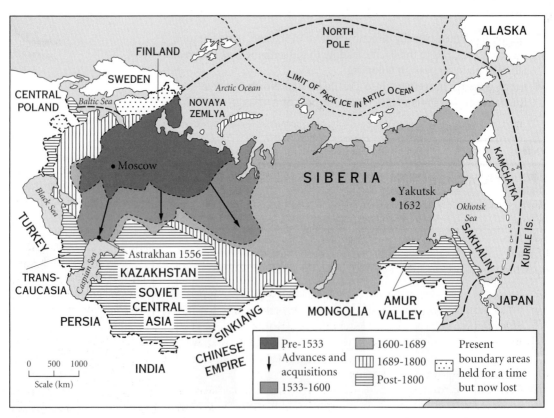

MAP 3
Growth of the Russian Empire 1533–1914

across Asia to gain an ice-free port there. This explains her two 'drives' in the nineteenth century.

● From the Black and Caspian seas into central Asia 1865–85.
● From Siberia into the Amur Valley and from there onto Manchuria from 1850–60.

Territories were acquired either by conquest, treaty or economic colonisation.

> See Map 3.

B *Motives for expansion*

These can be summarised as:

1 Strategic – the push to the Black Sea was motivated by the need to strengthen the southern borders and end the raids by Crimean Tartars, who seized thousands of Russian prisoners for sale into slavery in Istanbul. Expansion in the Caucasus and Central Asia stemmed from fear that otherwise the Caucasus would fall to Turkey or Persia and Central Asia to Britain.

2 Economic-expansion towards the Baltic Sea was motivated by the need for a warm-water port to promote economic and cultural ties with the West. Siberia had been settled to tap its vast natural resources of land and minerals, while the drive towards the Far East and Central Asia was spurred on by the opportunities to obtain raw materials, oil and raw cotton, and markets. Russia built the Trans-Caspian railway to transport these goods as well as for strategic defence. By the 1860s, when serfs had their freedom, relative over-population in the central black earth, the Ukraine, and middle Volga settlements persuaded increasing numbers to migrate from these provinces.

C *National identity versus* Russification

The lands acquired by the Russian Empire by the middle of the nineteenth century had brought different nationalities under the control of the tsar. The percentage of Russians declined but, despite the fact it consisted of many races, the Russian Empire was unified. A number of principles lay behind the relationship between Russia and her nationalities:

1 Respect of the *status quo*, whereby the central government left intact local laws and institutions. Local circumstances and the level of loyalty shown determined the amount of self-rule.

2 Broad co-operation of the regime with non-Russian nobility who would be used to govern the new territories, such as occurred in the case of the Left-Bank Ukraine.

3 Creation of certain advantages in the legal status of non-Russians as compared with that of Russians. Apart from Jews, this was often better for the non-Russians. However, even Jews were not made slaves or serfs or recruited into the army and they had taxation privileges.

Russification was the policy of forcing subject peoples to accept Russian language, religion, culture, as well as legal, administrative and judicial systems in place of their own.

Status quo means keeping existing systems/state of affairs unchanged.

4 Free availability of government posts to non-Russians who accounted for 16% in 1850 and 23% of the Russian army by 1868.

5 Maintenance of a higher standard of living in minority regions compared with that for Russia along with a lower levy of taxes.

Response to Russian control varied.

● Peoples with a tradition of statehood, such as Poland, resisted Russian annexation and revolted in 1830 and again in 1863.
● Regions, such as Finland, with no statehood experience developed and peaceful existence side by side.
● Religious and cultural links were also significant. Orthodox Armenia, Georgia, Ukraine, Byelorussia and Moldavia shared the same experience and there were few problems whereas the conquest of the Caucasus and central Asia led to a long drawn out holy war with heavy casualties.
● The manner in which the country was absorbed was also important. Military conquest created more problems than peaceful acquisition through treaty. Finland accepted incorporation, Poland resisted and events there were to have a great influence on the hardening of the regime's attitudes towards its national minorities in the second half of the nineteenth century.

8 ➝ BIBLIOGRAPHY

A bibliography for Chapter 1 covering the themes introduced in this chapter appears on page 120.

9 ➝ STRUCTURED QUESTIONS

A *This section consists of structured questions that might be used for discussion or written answers as a way of expanding on the chapter and testing understanding of it.*

1. (a) Explain what is meant by 'autocracy'.
   (b) What were the main features of government at central and local level by 1855?
2. (a) Explain what is meant by 'nationality'.
   (b) What were the main principles governing Russia's treatment of its nationalities up to 1830?
3. (a) Explain what is meant by 'serfdom'.
   (b) What were the main strengths and weaknesses of the *Mir*?

10 ➝ MAKING NOTES

Read the advice section about making notes on page ix of the Preface: how to use this book, and then make your own notes based on the following headings and questions:

A *Division of Russian society*
1. What was the relationship of rural to town population by 1850?
2. How far did this relationship change between 1861 and 1896?
3. What effect did this relationship have on the economy?
4. Identify the dominant national groups in the Russian Empire.
5. Explain the system of 'ranks' in Russian society.
6. What was the importance of the ranking system?

B *The nature of serfdom*
1. What was the status and role of serfs in society?
2. What was the main difference between the obrok and the Barshchina?
3. What do you understand by 'feudal dues'?
4. To what extent were the peasants exploited by (a) noble landlords and (b) the state?
5. What was the *Mir*?
6. How was village life organised?
7. In what respects did the system of land organisation (a) benefit and (b) disadvantage peasants?
8. How did the peasantry react to their condition?
9. What were the main problems arising from the communal system?
10. What arguments could be put forward to defend the commune against its critics?

C *The industrial workers*
1. What was the status and role of the industrial workers in society?
2. What were the main grievances of those who worked in the towns?
3. How did the workers react to their condition?

D *The nature of Russian government*
1. What was the significance of the position of the Tsar?
2. Explain the meaning of (a) orthodoxy, (b) autocracy and (c) nationality.
3. What was the membership and role of each of the following: (a) Imperial Council, (b) Committee of Ministers and (c) the Senate?
4. What were the main sources of (a) income and (b) expenditure of the regime?

E *The role of the army*
1. What were the main sources of recruitment?
2. What were the main abuses suffered by the rank and file?

F *Development of a revolutionary tradition*
1. What was the scale of peasant disturbances?
2. What were the main characteristics of peasant disturbances?
3. How serious a challenge did they present to the regime?
4. What do you understand by the term '*intelligentsia*'?
5. What were the main issues discussed by Russia's intellectuals?
6. What do you understand by each of the following terms: (a) Slavophiles and (b) Westernisers?

7. To what extent did they agree in their view of the regime?
8. What was the significance of their debate for the future direction of Russia at home and abroad?

G *Extent of the Russian Empire by 1855*
1. What was the extent of the Russian Empire by 1855 in terms of its frontier to the northeast, the Baltic and North Sea and southwards to the Mediterranean?
2. What were the main motives of the regime in extending its frontiers?
3. To what extent had the regime been successful in achieving its foreign policy goals by 1855 in its southward movement to the eastern Mediterranean?
4. What were the main principles adopted by the regime for governing its nationalities?
5. What do you understand by the term '*Russification*'?

11 ⌐ DOCUMENTARY EXERCISE ON THE NATURE OF SERFDOM IN THE 1840s

Study the description of the Russian commune by the German traveller, Haxthausen in 1843 and then answer the questions that follow:

The following information was given to us concerning the division of land in the village communes. The principle is that the whole of the land (tillage, meadows, pasture, woods, streams, and so on) belongs to the population of a village community regarded as a whole, and in using these communal possessions every male inhabitant has a right to an equal share. This share is therefore constantly changing; for the birth of every boy creates a new claim, and the shares of those who die revert to the commune. The woods, pastures, hunting grounds, and fisheries remain undivided and free to all the inhabitants; but the arable land and meadows are divided equally, according to their value, among the males. This equal division is of course very difficult, as the soil differs in quality, and portions of it maybe distant or inconveniently situated. The difficulties are great; nevertheless the Russians overcome them easily. There are in each commune skilful land surveyors, who, competently, with insight acquired from the traditional habits of the place, execute the work to the satisfaction of all. The land is first divided, according to its quality, position, or general value, into sections, each possessing on the whole equal advantages. The sections are then divided into as many portions, in long strips, as there are shares required, and these are taken by lot. This is the usual plan, but each region, and frequently each commune, has its local customs ...

The facts here described constitute the basis of the Russian communal system one of the most remarkable and interesting political institutions in existence and one that undeniably possesses great advantages for the social condition of the country. The Russian communes show an organic coherence and compact social strength that can be found nowhere else and yield the incalculable advantage that no proletariat can be formed so long as they exist with their present structure. A man may lose or squander all he possesses but his children do not inherit poverty. They still retain their claim upon the land by a right derived not from him but from their birth as members of the commune. On the other hand it must be admitted that this fundamental basis of the communal system the equal division of the land is not favourable to the progress of agriculture which ... under this system could for a long time remain at a low level.

SOURCE A
From G. Vernadsky (ed.),
A Source Book for
Russian History from Early
Times to 1917.
Yale University Press, 1972.

1. *What principle was applied to land ownership in the village community?*
2. *What measures were taken to ensure fairness in land ownership?*
3. *Is it possible to tell whether Haxthausen approved of the commune? Support your answer by full reference to the source.*
4. *Did the peasants benefit from the communal system?*
5. *What evidence is there to suggest that the communal system would be favoured by socialists?*
6. *What evidence is there to suggest that the communal system acted against the long-term interests of the Russian economy?*
7. *How valuable is this source for a historian studying the nature of serfdom on the eve of emancipation (when surfs gained their freedom)?*

Alexander II – 'Liberator' or Traditionalist? 1855–81

ALEXANDER NIKOLAEVICH, 1818–81, EMPEROR OF ALL RUSSIA 1855–81

Crowned in the Cathedral of the Moscow Kremlin on 26 August 1856, Alexander's reign seems to be a contradiction. Known as the 'Tsar Liberator', he is associated with a number of important reforms, notably the abolition of serfdom, as well as changes in national, military and municipal organisation. He introduced local councils, and law courts, increased the provision of education, reformed finances and encouraged economic development. He also rethought foreign policy whereby Russia avoided overseas expansion and concentrated on strengthening its borders. In 1867, he sold Alaska and the Aleutian Islands to the United States. His greatest foreign policy achievement was the successful war of 1877–8 against the Ottoman Empire, resulting in the liberation of Bulgaria and annulment of the conditions of the Treaty of Paris of 1856, imposed after Russia's defeat in the Crimean War. This extensive record of 'Great Reforms' stood in marked contrast to the repression of his father's reign. The western historian, Terence Emmons has regarded them, as 'probably the greatest single piece of state-directed engineering in modern European history before the twentieth century'. However they did not solve the problems facing Russia in the second half of the nineteenth century or silence the mounting tide of criticism and opposition. Alexander's attempts to modernise were restricted by his refusal to surrender his autocratic powers. Prior to becoming tsar he did not show any liberal leanings. He had no general programme when he embarked on his reforms. Moreover, his liberal approach was short-lived. After the first attempt on his life on 4 April 1866 by a young student activist, Dmitri Karakozov, he became more conservative though the general trend throughout his reign was towards change. One Russian historian has said of Alexander's reforms that they were designed not to 'improve the lot of the people, develop the principle of elective representation, or lay the foundations of a state ruled by law…but to entrench the autocracy, strengthen military power, and expand the empire for the sake of Russia's greatness as Alexander II and his closest associates understood it', Larisa Georgievna Zakharova, '*Emperor Alexander II, 1855–1881*, in the *Emperors and Empresses of Russia* (eds Donald J. Raleigh, M.E. Sharpe, 1996). This view is also taken by his English biographer, W.L. Mosse, who wrote of Alexander that, 'he proved himself not only a disappointing 'liberal' – if indeed that term can be applied to him – but more seriously an inefficient autocrat'. Far from silencing critics of the regime, protests mounted, along with attempts on his life. On 1 March 1881, Alexander died after two bomb attacks in St Petersburg by members of the revolutionary organisation 'The National Will'. The Cathedral of the Resurrection on Blood was built on the site of the murder.

1 ～ ALEXANDER II: A TSAR IN THE MAKING

A *Alexander's background and training*

The eldest son of Emperor Nicholas I, he came to the throne at the age of 36 on 19 February 1855. He was, according to one of his biographers, W.L. Mosse, 'perhaps the best prepared heir-apparent ever to ascend the Russian throne'. Alexander's education had been based on a

PICTURE 1 Alexander II, *portrait as a young man*

special 'Plan of Instruction' for 12 years of schooling which gave him a well-rounded education that included Russian and world history, natural science and languages – French, German, Polish and English.

He completed his education with a 7-month tour, by coach, of 30 Russian provinces that included a visit to Siberia, the first by a member of the Imperial family. He followed this with a 16-month tour of the leading countries of Western Europe 1838–9 during the course of which he met the 15 year old Princess Marie of Hesse Darmstadt, whom he subsequently married in 1842. On his return from his tour, Alexander was given a number of responsible posts by his father including membership of the Council of State, 1841 and Committee of Ministers, 1842 as well as being recognised as Nicholas's deputy during the Tsar's absence. He was also chairman of the committee responsible for building the St Petersburg–Moscow railway. He held a number of military titles and posts as well as a number of important civil appointments. He was made chairman of two Secret Committees on Peasant Affairs in 1846 and the Secret Committee on Household Serfs, 1848 though he defended the existing order.

B *Alexander's personality*

A. White, a secretary in the American embassy, described Alexander in his 1905 autobiography as 'tall, like all the Romanovs, good-looking and with a very distinguished bearing, but he had much less of his father's majesty and was completely devoid of the latter's misplaced severity'. He had a sound and practical mind combined with a sense of duty to improve the well-being of his people. He recognised the necessity to free the serfs, promote economic growth and modernise the armed forces and government. However, he had limitations as a reformer. One of the ladies in waiting at the royal court, A.F. Tiutcheva, has left a very perceptive evaluation of Alexander II in her diary entry for January 1856. The following extract is from A.F. Tiutcheva's diary for this date and is quoted in D.J. Raleigh and A.A. Iskenderov (eds), *The Emperors and Empresses of Russia*, M.E. Sharpe.

Q *What, according to Tiutcheva, were Alexander's limitations as a reformer?*

The Tsar is the best of men. He would be a wonderful sovereign in a well-organised country and in a time of peace ... But he lacks the temperament of a reformer. The empress lacks initiative as well. ... They are too kind, too pure, to understand people and to rule them. They do not have the energy or the impulse to take charge of events and direct them as they see fit; they lack passion. ... Without realising it himself, he has become involved in a struggle with powerful forces and dreadful elements he does not understand. ... They (the royal couple) do not know where they are going.

Apart from differences of outlook on the necessity for reform, Alexander was his father's son in other respects. He was a firm conservative and accepted the traditional view of his duty to uphold the principles of autocratic government followed by his father. He refused to consider even the possibility of a Russian constitution for 25 years. To some he seemed even more of a conservative at a time when public opinion was beginning to make itself felt and even a Russian autocrat could no longer behave as he pleased. Alexander's determination to preserve his autocratic authority was revealed in a conversation with Otto Von Bismarck, then Prussia's ambassador to Russia, on 10 November 1861. In response to a question about the possibility of a constitution and liberal institutions in Russia, Alexander II said:

> The people see their monarch as God's envoy, as their father and all-powerful master. This idea, which has the force almost of religious feeling, is inseparable from their personal dependency on me, and I am inclined to think that I am not mistaken. The crown gives me a feeling of authority; to forgo it would be to damage the nation's prestige. The profound respect that the Russian people have accorded the throne of their Tsar from time immemorial, arising from an innate feeling, cannot be dismissed. I would not hesitate to curtail the government's authoritarianism if I wanted to bring representatives of the nobility or the nation into it. God knows where we will end up regarding the question of the peasants and landowners if the Tsar's authority is insufficient to exercise decisive influence.

Q

What were Alexander's reasons for rejecting a Constitution?

The above is from Alexander II's conversation with Otto Von Bismarck, then Prussia's ambassador to Russia, on 10 November 1861, quoted in D.J. Raleigh and A.A. Iskenderov (eds), *The Emperors and Empresses of Russia*, M.E. Sharpe.

2 ∽ ALEXANDER THE TSAR 'LIBERATOR'

TIMELINE

1855	Alexander II becomes tsar
1856	Treaty of Paris ends the Crimean War. Alexander warns that serfdom must be abolished 'from above'
1857	Secret Committee of Ministers is set up to begin the process of freeing the serfs
1858	Ministers have to submit their reports to special commissions of the State Council, who will return them to the ministers with comments before they are presented to the tsar
1861	The Secret Committee becomes public as the Main Committee. Serfdom is abolished. A Commission is set up to look into reform of the legal system.
1862	Public budgets improve the system of auditing. A Ministry of Finance and state bank are created; tax collection is removed from the hands of private financiers and a large government staff is organised to deal with taxpayers
1862–74	Army and Navy are reformed
1863	Second Polish revolt occurs. Popular education is extended with more schools being opened in the countryside and secondary schools being allowed to admit women. Universities are given greater freedom

1864	Local government is reformed with the introduction of the *zemstva* (s. *zemstvo*).
	The judiciary is reformed
1865	Censorship is relaxed
1866	First assassination attempt is made on the tsar by Karakozov. State serfs are emancipated on more favourable terms to those belonging to the nobles. The *Zemstva's* right to tax is limited
1867	Restrictions are imposed on the *Zemstva's* right to publish their proceedings without the permission of administrative officials
1870	Municipal reform occurs with the introduction of the *Duma*, (pl. *Dumy*)
1872	Press Law provides for the transference of offences committed by the press from the jurisdiction of the courts to the Council of Ministers. Offences against the state, punishable by loss of rank, are transferred to a special session of the Senate unless the tsar decides to refer them to the Supreme Criminal Court
1873	Censorship laws are tightened
1874	Military service is reformed. Populist critics of the regime publish '*Going to the People*'
1875	Universal military liability is introduced
1877	Regulations on the conduct of troops during public disorders are introduced
1877–8	The Russo-Turkish war is fought
1878	Congress of Berlin imposes a diplomatic defeat on Russian ambitions to extend its control and influence in the Balkans at Turkey's expense. Cases involving public disobedience to civil authorities are removed from the jurisdiction of the normal criminal courts. Alexander appeals to all estates to defend public safety/social groups against the revolutionaries
1879	Alexander appoints the governor-generals of Moscow, Kiev, Warsaw, Kharkov, St Petersburg and Odessa as 'regional military dictators' with the power to use any measure necessary, including exile, to maintain peace in educational institutions. Security Law bans the sale of firearms. Police are armed with guns. Provincial governors are given the power to intervene in the affairs of the *Zemstva*
1880	Powers of provincial governors over the *Zemstva* are repealed *Zemstva* are invited to submit proposals for reform of local administration
1881	Alexander gives his approval to the setting up of a commission composed of representatives from the *Zemstva* and towns with consultative powers to examine legislative bills before submission to the State Council (Alexander III subsequently rejected this proposal). Alexander II is assassinated

A   *Forces for change*

Alexander had no sympathy for radical or liberal ideas, but he recognised that some improvements were necessary to preserve his autocratic system of government. He took a leading role in the reforms associated with the 1860s appointing reform-minded ministers to carry out his instructions. He was supported by a number of the leading members of his family who had liberal ideas. His brother, the Grand Duke Constantine supported emancipation of the serfs but even more important was his aunt, the liberal Grand Duchess Elena (Helen) Pavlovna. She was well respected in Russian public life helped by her work for soldiers during the Crimean War. Her palace was a meeting place for leading liberals such as Nicholas Alexevich Milyutin (1818–72), who was made assistant Minister of the Interior in 1859. With the support of other liberal-minded nobles and officials who now came into public office with the new reign, he was the main driving force behind some of the key reforms until his dismissal in 1861. There were a number of other forces for change at work apart from those within the Imperial circle.

Force for change	Main features
Personal	Alexander II was seriously aware of the weakness of the Russian state. His recognition of the necessity to introduce reforms was crucial in an autocracy where the tsar held ultimate power to over-rule opposition from powerful vested interests. He quickly signalled his intentions by ending restrictions on the most 'dangerous' and radical groups in the country. He lessened the restrictions on university entrance so that a broader social range of students could attend, including those from the Raznochintsy. Restrictions on foreign travel were relaxed which opened the way for circulation of more foreign and Russian language publications by political exiles. In a speech to the nobility in Moscow on 30 March 1856, he made it clear that 'the existing system of serf owning cannot remain unchanged. It is better to abolish serfdom from above than to wait for the time when it begins to abolish itself from below. I ask you, gentlemen, to think of ways of doing this. Pass on my words to the nobles for consideration (quoted by G. Vernadsky (ed.), *A Source Book for Russian History from Early Times to 1973*. New Haven, Conn., Yale University Press, 1972).
Political – legacy of the Crimean War	The Crimean War revealed the weaknesses, and corruption, of leadership of the army. The latter depended on the loyalty of serfs who had been compulsorily enlisted but the hardship experienced by so many encouraged a more critical attitude. This ill feeling expressed itself in an increase in agricultural disturbances and riot. The shock of Russia's defeat in the Crimean War raised questions regarding the efficiency of the Russian army. It had lost its superiority over the French and English armies. Military advisers, such as General Dmitri Milyutin, later Minister of War, 1861–81 and a firm supporter of emancipation, warned Alexander that reform of the army was impossible while serfdom survived. He warned the tsar in 1867, 'thanks to the army, Russia became a first-class European power and only by maintaining the army can Russia uphold the position it has acquired'. However 'serfdom does not permit us to shorten the term of service nor to increase the number of those on indefinite leave so as to reduce the number of troops on hand' (quoted by Lionel Kochan and R. Abrahams, *The Making of Modern Russia*, Penguin 1983). The war also revealed the inadequacy of Russia's communications. It was recognised that railways were crucial for a speedy deployment of troops as well as for dispersal of goods. Poor distribution of grain had in the past led to local shortages to the detriment of landlord and serf. An improved transport system would help Russian cereal growers to compete in a world market. This would encourage the development of a commercialised system of farming once serfdom was ended. Transport meant increased mobility and migration of people to expanding areas of production whereas serfdom tied peasants to the village.
Moral	Various groups had expressed concern about the welfare of peasants under serfdom. In 1842 Nicholas I had declared to the Council of State, 'there can be no doubt that serfdom in its present situation in our country is an evil … (It) cannot last for ever … The only answer is thus to prepare the way for a gradual transition to a different order' (quoted by H. Seton-Watson, *The Russian Empire, 1801–1917*, OUP, 1967).
	The minority of landowners who supported emancipation were partly influenced by a concern for the welfare of the peasants as well as the economic deficiencies of serfdom. The Slavophile landowner, A.I. Koshelyov wrote a memorandum to the tsar early in 1858, in which he presented the argument that it was morally wrong for a landowner to own other

(continued overleaf)

PICTURE 2

*Russian Landowners and their
Serfs, Gambling for Souls, from
G. Doré,* Histoire de
la sainte Russie, 1854, *Mansell
Collection. A French caricature
shows a contrast with the idyllic
picture of rural life generally
shown in Russian sources*

Force for change	Main features
Moral (continued)	human beings like possessions and that such ownership demoralised the landowner. 'This measure is more necessary for the welfare of our class itself than for the serfs. The abolition of the right to dispose of people like objects or like cattle is as much our liberation as theirs for at present we are under the yoke of a law that destroys still more in us than in the serfs any human quality' (quoted by H. Seton-Watson, *The Russian Empire, 1801–1917*, OUP, 1967).
Economic	Criticism that serfdom was economically inefficient had been prevalent since the 1760s. Early nineteenth century educated Russians argued that free wage labour was more productive than forced labour because workers would lack the motivating influence of wages being determined by market forces. The benefits of free peasant labour had been demonstrated in Siberia, a fact brought out in the accounts of a Scottish visitor to the region in 1864. 'It was probably the growing prosperity of Siberia and the marked superiority of the population there, that induced the government to emancipate the serfs of Russia proper' (quoted by J. McManners, *Lectures in European History, 1789–1914*). The arguments of this group of pro-reformers were not supported by the great mass of provincial nobility who were ignorant of free labour principles. Serfdom, as we have seen from Chapter 1, had shown itself to be adaptable in terms of allowing some peasants to engage in paid work. Provincial opinion was more concerned with the social and political dangers of maintaining serfdom particularly peasant unrest. In the 1840s, Benckendorff, Head of the Secret Police, warned Nicholas I that, 'the whole mood of the people is concerned with one aim – emancipation … Serfdom is a powder keg under the state, and

TABLE 9

*Serfs mortgaged by owners
1820–59*

Year	Serfs mortgaged (millions)	Percentage of all serfs
1820	1.8	20
1830	4.5	37
1842	5.6	50
1855	6.6	61
1859	7.1	66

is the more dangerous because of the fact that the army itself consists of peasants. ... It is better to begin gradually, cautiously, than to wait until the process is started from below by the people themselves' (quoted in David Christian, *Imperial and Soviet Russia: Power, Privilege and the Challenge of Modernity*, Addison-Wesley Longman, 1986).

Serfdom was blamed for the rising debt contracted by nobles to finance their extravagant western lifestyles. By 1859 landlords had mortgaged 66% of their serfs as security for loans from the State Loan Bank. The State was also suffering from a decline in its revenues from the taxes paid by peasants, the poll tax and the obrok, in relation to its income from the tax on vodka. By 1855 the government was 54 million roubles in debt. To offset this, the nobles and the State increased their demand for grain causing famine among the peasantry who had been left with insufficient reserves.

General

The number of peasant disturbances increased from the 1840s leading to the Third Section reporting on rumours amongst serfs that, 'they expect a liberator, whom they call Metelkin', who will sweep (nobles) away' (quoted in H. Seton-Watson, *The Russian Empire, 1801–1917*, OUP, 1967). By 1859 the country faced a prospect of a peasant war, which was particularly worrying for rural nobles living on remote country estates, and the provincial governors and gendarmes.

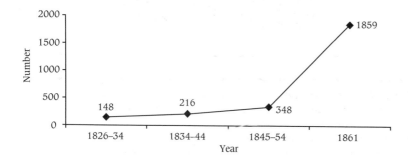

DIAGRAM 7
Number of peasant disturbances 1826–61

B *Main stages in the emancipation of the serfs*

Alexander appointed a secret committee in January 1857 to examine the issue of emancipation of the serfs under the chairmanship of Alexei Fedorovich Orlov, the strongly conservative president of the Council of State.

ALEXEI FEDOROVICH ORLOV (1786–1861)

PROFILE

Descended from a favourite of Catherine the Great, he had, 'that half-European, half-Asiatic lordly arrogance that had so recently produced among us a kind of powerful magic charm'. He had started his career as a soldier and policeman in the French Wars, 1805–14 and had participated in the suppression of various disturbances in Nicholas I's reign. He spent 12 years on the mission to Istanbul 1844–56, before becoming Head of the Third Section 1856–8. He resigned in 1861 due to illness.

KEY ISSUE

What were the main issues discussed by the committee?

The committee, composed of land-owning nobles and pro-emancipators made little progress. It spent months reading reports sent from the ministry of the interior and wasting sessions in discussing trivial matters. Alexander in a sense of frustration had his brother the Grand Duke Constantine, who was forceful and quick-tempered, join the committee in August to help speed up the process.

The tsar instructed the committee to explore a number of questions whether:

1 land owners should retain ownership of the whole of their land
2 emancipated serfs should be protected in their right to use part of the land
3 land owners should receive compensation only for such land as they granted to the peasants or also for the sacrifice of their rights over the persons of their serfs.

In November 1857 Alexander drew up a procedure based on the Nazimov rescript. This was prompted by a request from the representative, General V.L. Nazimov, of the landowners of Lithuania to free their serfs without land. He rejected this request in favour of serfs being allowed to keep their homesteads and buy them from their former lords within a stated period. They were to be allowed to rent land sufficient for their needs and be organised into communes. This reply, the Nazimov rescript, laid down the principles of emancipation. Nobles were instructed to set up provincial committees to collect evidence and eventually, after discussions, to present an emancipation plan to the tsar. Some of these regional committees could not agree and sent in majority and minority reports.

The publication of the rescript led to discussions in the press and opinion quickly divided.

1 The majority of the nobles were concerned to retain their economic and judicial control over their serfs.
2 Conservative opponents to reform argued that the security of the tsar and hence the state would be endangered.
3 Radical reformers proposed that the peasants should be given complete freedom and ownership of the land they held at the time of emancipation.

KEY ISSUE

What main arguments were expressed during the public discussions?

Alexander's response to these debates was to tighten censorship laws relating to the emancipation question. Landowners' fears of a peasant rebellion were well founded. During 1858 disturbances broke out in Estonia causing one of the pro-reform committee members to warn that 'if we deprive the peasants of the land we will set Russia alight'. Alexander was forced to intervene in the discussions. He closed the provincial assemblies and put the final stages of the process in the hands of an Editorial Commission of 38 members that was a subcommittee of the Main Committee. Reformers, led by Nicholas Alexevich Milyutin, dominated the commission that was made up of members of the bureaucracy and experts.

NICHOLAS ALEXEVICH MILYUTIN (1818–72)

PROFILE

He was one of the enlightened bureaucrats appointed by Alexander to carry out the preparations for the end of serfdom. His uncle, the liberal reformer Kiselyov, who had been in charge of state peasants 1834–56, had been an early influence. He had been a bureaucrat from 1835 becoming responsible for the reorganisation of St Petersburg municipal government in the late 1840s. His reputation as a radical meant that Alexander initially distrusted him but he had powerful patrons in the form of the minister of the interior, Lanskoy, and the Grand Duchess Elena. He was made deputy minister of the interior in the autumn of 1858 and became the main driving force behind emancipation. Between 1859–61 he was chairman of the commission for *zemstvo* local government reform until he was dismissed in 1861 for his liberalism. On that occasion Alexander II said, 'I am sorry to part with you, but I must. The nobility describe you as one of the reds' (W. Mosse, *Alexander II and the Modernisation of Russia*, English Universities Press, 1970). In 1863 he drafted reforms for *Russifying* Poland and became State-Secretary for Polish Affairs 1864–7 until he retired due to ill health. Two other leading supporters of reform joined him, his brother Dmitri, Minister of War, 1861–81 and Michael Reitern, Minister of Finance 1862–78.

There was bitter hostility between landowners and bureaucrats on the Editorial Commission. Two groups emerged:

1 Pro-reform group composed of noble landowners, which wanted a peaceful settlement of the serf problem in the interests of Russia's national greatness. They had little influence in St Petersburg.
2 'Red Party', composed of officials, writers, and journalists, who were more numerous and powerful. They were a formidable group in St Petersburg, but with sympathisers in the provinces.

The commission's work was concluded in October 1860 at which time several principles had been agreed:

KEY ISSUE

The emancipation.

- Abolition of serfdom was agreed in principle.
- Landowners retained ownership of the land.
- Peasants would be allowed to buy their houses and the surrounding land, *usad'ba* worked by them at the time of emancipation and would have access to further land to meet their needs.
- Peasants were to pay *obrok* or labour service for 2 years before becoming emancipated.
- Peasants were to make annual payments to buy their land.
- Peasants would be put under the control of the peasant commune, the *Mir*, whose powers would be strengthened though landlords would keep their policing powers.

● Peasants' land would not be secured at the expense of the land-owners, but that the latter would be compensated for loss of land but not for loss of rights over their serfs.

The final proposals were approved and on 19 February the statutes were signed whereby 'the serfdom of peasants settled on estate owners' landed properties and of household serfs, is abolished forever'. Alexander had achieved, without bloodshed, a most momentous reform, which challenged the traditional structure of Russian society that had rested on the landowner. It brought Russia into the modern age.

The following is from Alexander II's Speech to the Council of State, January, 1861, quoted by G. Vernadsky (ed.), *Source Book for Russian History*, Yale University Press, 1972.

Q

Why did Alexander II consider the 'liberation of the serfs ... to be a vital question for Russia'?

Why would 'further delay be disastrous to the state'?

Is it possible to tell whether Alexander was sympathetic to the condition of the serfs? Explain your answer with reference to the source.

How convincing is Alexander's claim that 'the approach to the matter was made on the initiative of the nobility itself'?

Assess the value of this speech to an historian studying the emancipation of the serfs.

> The matter of the liberation of the serfs, which has been submitted for the consideration of the State Council, I consider to be a vital question for Russia, upon which will depend the development of her strength and power ... I have another conviction, which is that this matter cannot be postponed...
>
> For four years now it has dragged on and has been arousing various fears and anticipations among both the estate owners and the peasants. Any further delay could be disastrous to the state.... Although the apprehensions of the nobility are to a certain extent understandable, ... (I) shall never forget that the approach to the matter was made on the initiative of the nobility itself...
>
> I hope, gentlemen, that on inspection of the drafts presented to the State Council, you will assure yourselves that all that can be done for the protection of the interests of the nobility has been done. If, on the other hand you find it necessary in any way to alter or to add to presented work, then I am ready to receive your comments; but I ask you only not to forget that the basis of the whole work must be the improvement of the life of the peasants, – an improvement not in words alone but in actual fact
>
> My late father was continuously occupied with the thought of freeing the serfs. Sympathising completely with this thought, already in 1856 while in Moscow I called the attention of the leaders of the Moscow nobility to the necessity for them to occupy themselves with improving the life of the serfs, adding that serfdom could not continue forever and that it would therefore be better if the transformation took place from above rather, than from below.'

In this next extract from E. Acton, *Russia*, Longman, 1986, the author assesses the emancipation process.

axiomatic self-evident.

> The government's overriding concern to ensure domestic stability ruled out the possibility of landless Emancipation. It was axiomatic that peasant agriculture must not be jeopardised that the peasantry

must remain closely bound to the land and that the spectre of a restless landless proletariat must be avoided. The sharp rise in disturbances between 1857 and 1859 underlined the dangers of an excessively harsh settlement. Nevertheless while the statute was taking shape the nobility were able to reduce the quantity and quality of land in peasant hands and to extract limited amendments to the legislative proposals. In acquiescing the government was well aware that the final terms would provoke peasant hostility and took suitable precautions. In the capital the police told employers to work their men to the point of exhaustion the day before the terms were to be made known in order to leave them too weary to protest. The statute was promulgated during Lent in the hope that abstention would find the peasants in subdued mood. The military were fully alerted and when the village priest read out the details the police were in attendance to stifle the groans of disbelief with which they were met. Throughout the Tsar had made abundantly clear his wish to damage the position of the nobility as little as was compatible with social order and with the parlous condition of the State Treasury. In doing so he avoided confrontation: the State continued to be guided by a primary concern for the interests of the landed nobility.

> **Q**
>
> *In what ways might Acton use the evidence of Alexander's speech to the Council of State to support his conclusions on (i) reasons for emancipation, (ii) Alexander's concern to have the support of the nobles, (iii) Alexander's concerns for the peasants, (iv) Alexander's concerns to balance the interests of the serf and the landowner.*
>
> *Why, according to Acton, did the government fail to protect the interests of the nobles?*

C *Implementation of reforms*

Abolition of serfdom did not happen immediately, but was phased in over a period of years. It was a gigantic task; at the time of emancipation about 50 million of the 60 million inhabitants of European Russia were peasants of one kind or another. Of these 23 million were the serfs of nobility and gentry, with fewer than 20 million being state peasants while the remainder belonged to other categories of serfs or non-serf peasants. The main problem lay with the landlords' serfs. Recognising the complexity of the land settlement and that it would vary between regions, the government provided for it to be phased in over a period of 2 years though in fact it took over 20 years for the whole process to be completed.

Phase	Main features
1 1861–63	● Twenty-three million landlords' serfs were given their freedom that removed them from the controls previously exercised by their owner. They controlled their own lives, could marry, travel, and have legal status. However, to avoid misunderstanding and to protect public and private interests, they were compelled to remain under the control of their lord for two years. ● The landlord kept the land he had farmed for himself. In future this would be worked by hired labour, usually his ex-serfs. ● The serfs were allowed to keep their own cottages and the surrounding area known as the *usad'ba*, but had to buy the other land they had worked. However, their small, scattered strips were not consolidated and since the meadows, pasture and woodland reverted to the landlord their customary rights to these areas actually declined. This was particularly the case in the rich fertile areas of the Black soil and middle Volga provinces, where the pressure for land was most acute. Here the serfs were worse off after emancipation.

(continued overleaf)

Phase	Main features
1 (continued)	• The communal open fields went to the *Mir* for use by all the ex-serfs. The peasant was still tied to the *Mir*. It continued to distribute the allotments, regulate the dues of each individual and to accept joint tax responsibility for all members. If a peasant left his village he surrendered all rights to the common land. • For the first two years peasants had to keep paying all the feudal dues they had paid before the reform and the landlord was not allowed to change their nature or extent. In return, the peasants were to continue farming the land they had used before. • During this two-year period inventories were drawn up identifying the land used by peasants along with their feudal dues and that claimed by the landlord.
2 *Started in 1863 but did not have a specific end date.*	• The ex-serfs remained in a state of 'temporary obligation'. • Communal courts replaced nobles' legal control over the peasants. They were managed by ex-serfs under the supervision of government officials and a peace officer who was a member of the nobility. • Arrangements were made for the distribution of land between landowner and peasants and for the size of the redemption payments.
3 *No fixed date*	• The final stage began once the agreement had been reached on the transfer of land. • Provision was made for the peasants to spread the repayment of the government loan over a 49 year period in the form of 'redemption payments'. • These payments became a form of direct taxation and were roughly equal to the amount that had been paid in feudal dues prior to emancipation. • Usually the land was over valued to the benefit of the landowner and to the disadvantage of the peasant. The latter found themselves burdened with debt aggravated by the continuing payment of the poll tax till 1886. • Once peasants had reached this final stage in the negotiations their legal and economic ties were transferred from the landlord to the commune and the government.

The government was concerned that emancipation should be phased in peacefully and that private and public interests should be protected. To prevent confusion, it introduced an administrative structure to implement these changes. *Volosts* were a unit of local administration set up in the 19 February 1861 decree consisting of between 300 and 2000 people living in a number of villages, with its own law courts and administered by an assembly of representatives.

D *Effects of emancipation*

HISTORIANS' DEBATE

Differing views of the effects of emancipation

Historians have varied in their assessment depending on whether they have taken a humanitarian, economic or political perspective.

Humanitarian

M.S. Anderson, *The Ascendancy of Europe 1815–1914*, 2nd edn, Longman, 1985.

Anderson views the events of 1861 as a moral improvement, claiming that 'the grant of individual freedom and a minimum of civil rights to twenty million people previously in bondage was the single greatest liberating measure in the whole history of Europe.'

J.N. Westwood, *Endurance and Endeavour; Russian History 1812–1986*, OUP, 1973.

Westwood's assessment of Alexander II was that 'with the possible exception of Khrushchev, no Russian ruler brought so much relief to so many of his people as did Alexander II, autocratic and conservative though he was'… 'Despite its imperfections the Emancipation was an enormous step forward'.

Economical

Historians have disagreed on the economic impact.

Martin McCauley and Peter Waldron, *The Emergence of the Modern Russian State 1855–1881*, Macmillan, 1986.

They have pointed to the decline in the size of peasants' agricultural holdings; by on average 4% though this loss was considerably higher in the more fertile regions. Peasants in the Steppe provinces saw a 23.3% decline and those in the Ukraine, 30.8%. There was an insufficient supply of fertile land for distribution that affected both the peasantry and nobility.

Alexander Gerschenkron, *The Beginnings of Russian Industrialisation*, Soviet Studies, 1970.

He argues that emancipation delayed economic development due to the introduction of internal passports to regulate the movement of peasants in their district. This restriction prevented the development of a mobile labour force. In addition, the debt incurred by peasants to make the redemption payments reduced their purchasing power and hence the volume of internal demand.

M.E. Falkus, *The Industrialisation of Russia*, Macmillan, 1972.

He rejects the view that internal passports were restrictive. He argues that large numbers were issued and that there was an increase in labour supply as a result of the loss in land ownership by so many peasants. Moreover the long time scale adopted to make redemption payments made these another form of the rent that had been previously paid to landlords.

Political

W. Mosse, *Alexander II and the Modernisation of Russia*, English University Press, 1970.

They stress the limitations of the administrative, judicial, military, even financial reforms that followed in the wake of 1861. Commissions, often working in isolation prepared these reforms. However, they were weakened by rival or hostile influences. They argued that Alexander missed the opportunity to build a new Russia because of his determination to preserve his autocratic inheritance. He also failed to provide central co-ordination. According to this line of interpretation 'Alexander in the end succeeded after immense labours in making of the new Russia an incomplete and uncomfortable dwelling where friends and opponents of innovation felt almost equally ill at ease' (quoted by W. Mosse).

E *Summary of main effects of emancipation*

Social group	Gains	Losses
Peasants	● Given freedom from noble interference and control of their lives. ● End to feudal dues and payments in kind ● Some peasants increased land holding. ● Freed from fear of being forced to do military service ● *Mir*'s powers strengthened, represented local autonomy. ● Freedom to move both within Russia and emigrate, usually to Germany or America. ● A new class of rich peasant emerged, the Kulaks, who developed as private owners and were resented by the peasants.	● Overall loss of land. ● Need to rent additional land at higher prices. ● Over-valuation of land one source estimating that ex-serfs paid on average 134% of the free market price for their land ● Increased debt as redemptions payments were spread over 49 years but government failed to keep its promise of helping to fund these payments. ● Higher tax burden. ● Still subject to special communal courts, the *volosts*, so did not have full citizen rights. ● *Mir* tended to replace the gentry in terms of controlling the lives of peasants and their independence. It allocated the small parcels of land, organised the dues and had responsibility for the payment of taxes and redemption payments on a village basis. ● *Mir*'s regular reallocation of land based on changing family circumstances discouraged peasants from improving their land so that farming became based on an extensive rather than intensive basis. ● Subsistence farming made peasants more vulnerable to famine. ● Long-term decline in the average size of peasant holding or *nadiel* as the result of the right of each male child born in the *Mir* to land. ● Loss of privileges and protection. ● Remained tied to the village by redemption payments. ● Loss of security with removal of landlord protection. ● Discontent continued. Peasants felt disappointed and disillusioned and many rioted. The Ministry of the Interior reported 647 riots in the first four months of 1861, 1159 for the whole year affecting 1176 estates and requiring the army to restore order on 337 estates.

Sir Donald Mackenzie Wallace, *Russia on the eve of War and Revolution*, C.E. Black (ed.), Random House, 1961, in which an English traveller commented on peasants' loss of security.

If the serfs had a great many ill-defined obligations to fulfill [under serfdom], such as the carting of the master's grain to market…they had, on the other hand, a good many ill defined privileges. They grazed their cattle during a part of the year on the manor land; they received firewood and occasionally logs for repairing their huts; sometimes the proprietor lent them or gave them a cow or a horse when they had been visited by the cattle plague or the horse stealer; and in times of famine they could look to their master for support. All this has now come to an end. Their burdens and their privileges have been swept away together, and been replaced by clearly defined, unbending, unelastic legal relations. They now have to pay the market price for every stick of firewood that they burn, for every log that they require for repairing their houses, and for every rood of land on which to graze their cattle. Nothing is now to be had gratis. The demand to pay is encountered at every step. If a cow dies or a horse is stolen, the owner can no longer go to the proprietor with the hope of receiving a present, or at least a loan without interest, but must, if he has no ready money, apply to the village usurer, who probably considers twenty or thirty per cent as a by no means exorbitant rate of interest.

Q

What privileges were lost by serfs after emancipation?

What was the implication of this loss?

What is the value to a historian of eye-witness accounts by foreign observers?

Year	Size of peasant holding	
	Central industrial region	*North-eastern region*
1860	4	8.4
1880	3.3	5.2
1890	2.6	3.3

TABLE 10 *Decline in the average peasant holdings 1860–90 (in dessyatiny)* *(1 dessyatina = 2.7 acres = 1.09 hectares)*

Region	Before emancipation	After emancipation	Change (%)
Less fertile region (15 provinces)	13 944 000	13 390 000	−4
More fertile black soil and eastern provinces (21)	14 016 000	10 709 000	−23.6
Russian Poland	7 737 000	10 901 000	40.9

TABLE 11 *Peasant land holdings before and after emancipation (in dessyatiny) (1 dessyatina = 2.7 acres = 1.09 hectares)*

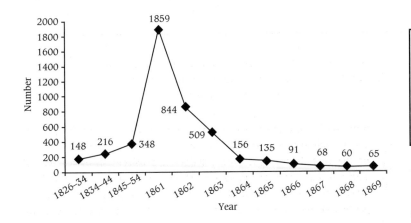

Q

What evidence is there to support the view that 'the peasants felt that they had gained something from emancipation'?

DIAGRAM 8 *Number of peasant disturbances in Russia 1826–69*

Social group	Gains	Losses
Land-owners	● Some increased the size of their estates. ● Compensated for loss of rights over serfs with increased local administrative powers through the *zemstva*.	● Many became poorer. ● Loss of legal ownership of their serfs and the compulsory feudal dues that were paid in labour, goods or in some case money. ● Loss of land – in some cases up to a third. ● Redemption payments used to repay old debts. ● Political and economic power and influence declined in local affairs. Led some liberal-minded landowners to demand the introduction of elected local government assemblies, and an independent judiciary with power to prosecute corrupt officials and freedom of the press. Alexander refused such demands. ● Power over conscription declined necessitating military reforms to establish a reserve peasant army. ● Majority of gentry remained conservative and resentful of change. Some employed estate managers but others sold and moved to towns.

Year	Amount of land held
1867	87
1882	71
1911	43

TABLE 12 *Decline in land ownership by the nobles (in million dessyatiny) (1 dessyatina = 2.7 acres = 1.09 hectares)*

From the Petition to Tsar Alexander II by the Tula gentry, December 1861, quoted by Terence Emmons, *The Russian Landed Gentry and the Peasant Emancipation of 1861*, Cambridge University Press, 1968.

Q

Why, according to the gentry, had 'the legislation ... so far proven unsatisfactory' from the perspective of:
(i) relationships
(ii) prosperity of the gentry
(iii) prosperity of the state.

What aspects of their argument were most likely to appeal to the state?

The legislation ... has so far proven unsatisfactory. The difficulties and conflicts of interest arising from it disturb the economy, sow destructive discord between peasant and landowner and cause incalculable harm to agriculture. The Gentry deprived of more than half of the land belonging to them in exchange for a direct money payment, which does not correspond to its value, are unable to receive income from the land remaining to them because the obligatory labour of free men is unthinkable and in view of the surplus allotment of land to the peasants hired labour is unprofitable. As a result the quantity of grain on the market has decreased and will decrease still more in the future. A loss to the state is inevitable and taking into consideration the rapid destruction of the forests which the landowners are incapable of reserving and the destruction of many factories and various other industrial enterprises for whose continuation there are no means, the damage to the economic strength of the state will be immediate. The Gentry class that has always preceded all other classes on the path to enlightenment and goodwill will through no fault of its own come to complete ruin.

Social group	Gains	Losses
General	<ul><li>Old abuses questioned.</li><li>New local government structure introduced based on the *zemstva*.</li><li>Decline of labour services encouraged the spread of a money economy and businesslike initiatives.</li><li>More questioning attitude encouraged amongst nobles and peasants.</li><li>New spirit of enterprise fostered amongst some.</li><li>Encouragement given to growth of railways, banking, industry and cities.</li><li>Removal of nobles' legal powers necessitated legal reforms.</li><li>Growth of liberalism amongst some sections led them to press for further reforms.</li></ul>	<ul><li>Technical backwardness of agriculture emphasised.</li><li>Increased sense of resentment felt by nobles and peasantry benefited the increasing number of intellectuals who challenged autocracy</li></ul>

F *Administrative reforms*

The abolition of the legal and judicial control of the gentry over their serfs required a new system of local government. Alexander appointed a Commission in 1860 under the chairmanship of the liberal reformer, N.A. Milyutin, soon to be replaced by Petr Valuyev, Minister of the Interior.

The Commission decided on a system of elected rural local councils, known as *zemstva* (singular: *zemstvo*) at district and provincial level elected by three separate electoral colleges – for nobles, townspeople and peasants. The nobility dominated the *zemstva* allowing them to preserve their local authority as compensation for their losses of 1861. The *zemstva* were given limited powers to approve local community projects, such as road, prisons, public health, poor relief education and industrial construction. Other areas of local government, such as powers to levy state and local taxes, appoint officials, and maintain law and order remained with the governors appointed by the tsar. Similar elected councils for the towns were established in 1870 with the introduction of the *Dumy*.

Liberal hopes that these governmental reforms would lead to a national assembly were defeated by Alexander's refusal to surrender his autocratic control. He was supported by:

1 **Reactionary** landowners who feared a loss of their social privileges.

2 High officials who wanted to preserve their power and prestige.

3 Progressives, both within and outside the government, who feared that a National Assembly would be dominated by the landowners who would block social progress wanted to delay change until the masses were educated enough to take part in an assembly of the people. Until that time arrived they were prepared to stay with autocracy.

A **reactionary** is one who is opposed to progress and reform.

KEY ISSUE

To what extent did the zemstva benefit from these reforms?

The *zemstva*, for all their limitations, provided for local initiative in place of administrative control. Westwood observed that their local knowledge 'enabled them to do a good job, where a St Petersburg official would have failed'. They became critical of the regime as they became more concerned with local issues, particularly in the field of education, and welfare. Liberal minded teachers, doctors and scientists were appointed who became a focal point for further reform later in the nineteenth century.

Zemstva had a number of weaknesses that limited their effectiveness. Dominated by the nobility, they spread slowly with the result that by 1914 only 43 of 70 provinces had introduced them. Accounting for an average 41% of the voters to *uezd* assemblies they dominated the percentage of seats in the *zemstva* which allowed them to continue to run local affairs to their advantage.

TABLE 13 *Percentage distribution of seats in* zemstva *institution 1865–7*

1865–7	Nobles	Merchants	Peasants	Priestly families
District/Uezd	42	10.5	38	6.5
Provincial	74	11	10.5	4

Most were not interested in their responsibilities particularly when provincial governors had the power to reverse those *zemstva* decisions they considered 'contrary to the laws and to the general welfare of the state'. Westwood has written of the *zemstva* that their success 'demonstrate that the people were indeed capable of looking after their own affairs'. The failure to follow up this success with a corresponding widening of public participation in central government meant that there was no concerted effort to make a success of the new institutions. This failure was also apparent with the new judicial system of 1864.

G *Judicial reforms*

The judicial system inherited by Alexander II was chaotic, arbitrary, secret and cruel leading to the setting up of a committee of officials from the Ministry of Justice. They were ordered to work out 'those fundamental principles, the undoubted merit of which is at present recognised by science and the experience of Europe, in accordance with which Russia's judicial institutions must be reorganised' (quoted by W. Mosse, *Alexander II and the Modernisation of Russia*, English Universities Press, 1958). Over the next 3 years the Council of State and Alexander considered its proposals before giving their approval in 1864 followed by their introduction in 1865 by new regional courts.

KEY ISSUE

How did Alexander II propose to reform the main abuses in the judicial system?

Crimes by high officials were taken out of the jurisdiction of local courts and tried by special procedures. In 1872, a special bench of the Senate tried crimes against the state while the Ministry of the Interior was given the power to banish to other parts of the country anyone regarded as dangerous or politically suspicious. Ecclesiastical courts and courts martial were excluded from the 1864 law.

Abuses	Reforms
● Different courts for separate classes at local level ● Cases could be transferred between them leading to years of delay	● Equality before the law ending the system of separate courts for separate estates (classes) ● New lower courts, *volost*, to replace serf owner as local magistrate
● Unqualified and often illiterate judges ● Court secretaries, who wrote down decisions, exercised great power	● Judges to be better trained ● Justices, elected for three years by local councils
● Police had a judicial role; they not only investigated crimes but also in some cases imposed punishment, usually fines	● Separation of judicial and administrative powers making for a more independent judiciary
● Bribery and abuse of power were encouraged due to low salaries paid to police and judges ● Villages carried legal responsibility for offences committed by a member; and could be liable to pay fines	● Judges to be better paid ● Judges to be removable by government
● The accused never saw the judges; evidence was submitted in writing and considered according to a rigid guideline of rules based on its acceptability, e.g. a confession, or collaborating statements of two independent witnesses ● Bribery of witnesses ● Accused had no opportunity to challenge evidence ● The lower the social rank of the individual the more difficult to achieve justice	● Evidence to be considered in the open, and a defence counsel allowed ● Trial by jury for criminal cases ● Trial of petty cases by Justices of the Peace ● Public tribunals ● Simplification of court procedure to speed up decisions ● Accused had the right of appeal to a conference of justices of the peace at provincial level ● Press coverage of cases
● Savage sentences and punishments	● Flogging to be reduced ● Offences carried a reprimand, fines (up to 300 roubles) and prison sentences of 3 months to a year

The system of justice established by these reforms, considered good, fair and less corrupt, made a major contribution to the modernisation of Russia. According the H. Seton-Watson, 'it raised general moral and even political standards'... 'for a long time the court-room was the one place in Russia where real freedom of speech prevailed, and its main champion was the lawyer'. Alexander's reforms helped promote a climate based on rule of law. The court of the justices of the peace was one of the most valuable new judicial institutions.

KEY ISSUE

What were the beneficial effects of these reforms?

KEY ISSUE

What were the limitations of these reforms?

The new system had numerous imperfections. There was a shortage of trained lawyers in the early years and they were still influenced by the government who controlled their promotion prospects. The bureaucracy continued to intervene so that trial by jury was not universally enforced; it was excluded in Poland, the western provinces and the Caucasus. The separate *volost* courts for the peasantry kept them outside the judicial system emphasising their existence as a separate group and preventing equality before the law. Apart from the peasantry other groups remained outside the new system: government officials, priests, military, critics of the regime and revolutionaries. The latter group continued to be harassed by the secret police of the Third Section (not abolished until 1880), and to face the risk of arbitrary administrative arrest and in the 1870s trial by special courts.

H *Military reforms*

KEY ISSUE

In what respects did Milyutin's reforms end class privilege in the army?

Reform of the army was made necessary by two events: defeat of Russia in the Crimean War 1854–6 and the abolition of serfdom that affected conscription of the rank and file. Responsibility was put in the hands of Dmitri Milyutin, Minister of War, 1861–81 who aimed to remove the abuses that had become apparent during the Crimean campaign. Recognising the necessity for greater efficiency and fairness, he showed little regard for established privileges introducing a number of radical reforms over a 20-year period:

1 Modern weapons, such as rifles and screw-driven, ironclad steamships, were introduced to make Russia more competitive with her European rivals. Greater emphasis was put on engineering including the construction of strategic railways to improve transport, provisioning and medical care of troops.

2 The officer corps was given proper training with the introduction of military colleges, which admitted non-noble recruits. Promotion became more open to make leadership more effective. Privates were allowed to rise to officer rank on grounds of merit alone.

3 Administration was improved with the introduction of 15 regional commands. The Military Code was reviewed and changes were introduced in military courts procedure.

4 Dmitri Milyutin's most significant change was in the system of enlistment. He had criticised serf-based conscription and had pressed for the 1861 abolition. He aimed to create a smaller, more professional and less expensive army by:
   - ending the practice of drafting convicts into the army
   - ending military colonies
   - reducing the size of annual conscription to 100
   - reducing the length of service to 15 years' active service and ten years 'leave' in the reserves
   - extending liability to military service to all classes, including nobles, at the age of 21
   - improving morale by reducing the number of offences that carried capital punishment and abolishing flogging.

His reforms were opposed by the nobility and merchants who disliked the prospect of service in the ranks. They used the press, public discussions and private influence with the tsar to prevent the enlistment reforms being introduced but Alexander gave his royal assent in 1874 and they became law in 1875.

Reduction in the length of military service during peacetime was cheaper than keeping a large standing army of a million men. This was a significant saving in government expenditure when the army and navy had accounted for 45% of spending in the 1846 Budget. A smaller more professional and less class-ridden army developed and was soon put to the test in 1877 when Russia found herself at war with Turkey. The latter was defeated, though it took longer than expected, even though Turkey was in decline. In other respects however, Milyutin had restored Russia's international reputation. The army also developed a trained reserve that could be readily mobilised when required. Incentives to encourage a more educated recruit helped the spread of literacy; two to three million soldiers were educated in the 1870s–90s.

Despite efforts to make the system fairer, people could still be represented by substitutes and officers remained heavily aristocratic. The army was still based on peasant conscripts so that high levels of illiteracy amongst the recruits reduced the effectiveness of training. This was evident in the wars fought by Russia in the later nineteenth and early twentieth centuries. She only defeated the Turks after months of bitter fighting 1877–8 and suffered a humiliating defeat by Japan 1904–5 and Germany 1914–17. Problems of supply and provisioning as well as leadership remained.

KEY ISSUE
What were the beneficial effects of these reforms?

KEY ISSUE
What were the limitations of these reforms?

I *Education*

The standard of teaching improved as responsibility was transferred from the Church to the new *zemstva* in 1864. Popular education was widely extended:

- Schools were declared open to all classes and the number of primary schools in the countryside grew from 8000 in 1856 to 23 000 in 1880. Their curriculum aimed to 'strengthen religious and moral notions and to spread basic knowledge'.
- Secondary schools grew both in terms of numbers and in an extension to include women (1864) resulting in a doubling of numbers to 800 000 during the 1860s. Secondary schools were open to 'children of all estates, without distinction of profession, or religious belief' of their parents. Their curriculum was extended so that *gimnazii* could focus either on a study of the classics, (Latin and Greek), or modern subjects (natural science and drawing). All secondary schools taught divinity, history, geography, Russian language and literature and mathematics.
- Universities were given greater independence in 1863, though this was short-lived. Revolutionary disturbances in the 1870s led to the re-introduction of state supervision.

University numbers grew from 3600 to 10 000 as did revolutionary activity. According to one historian, 'the efforts of Tsarism to survive, and reform in order to conserve, inevitably increased the numbers of the educated and potentially critical' (T. Kemp, *Industrialisation of Nineteenth Century Europe*, 1969).

The government retained the right to veto university appointments and to ban student organisations particularly after the reactionary disturbances. In 1861 many universities were closed and students were prosecuted for criticising the regime.

> **KEY ISSUE**
>
> *What were the beneficial effects of these reforms?*

J *Censorship*

Censorship was re-organised and relaxed though with limited success:

- 1862 censorship was moved to the Ministry of the Interior
- 1863 prepublication codes were reduced resulting in the publication of liberal ideas and anything that was not considered dangerous to the regime
- 1865 the Press was allowed to discuss government policy
- foreign publications were allowed into Russia but their sale was subject to political approval
- editors were given more freedom over what they could publish.

However, publishers remained uncertain of where responsibility lay with the survival of separate ecclesiastical and military censorships while the regime retained control over what was written and read.

The relaxation of censorship encouraged a growth in the number of books and of political journalism. The number of books published grew from 1020 in 1855 to 1836 in 1864 and 10 691 by 1894, the latter number was equal to the combined British and American output. Public opinion became more educated especially as the judicial reforms led to more openness in the conduct of trials. However, growth in criticism provoked a counter-reaction in the 1870s and tight censorship returned (see Section 4 below).

K *Financial and economic reforms*

> **KEY ISSUE**
>
> *Main features of Count Michael Reutern's financial reforms, 1862–78*

Reutern attempted to improve the auditing of accounts and the collection of revenue but there was no real tax reform. Russia's currency, the rouble, was not stabilised and a third of government expenditure went to repay old debts. Foreign trade, banking and a planned railway network were also encouraged but with mixed success. Government guarantee of an annual dividend attracted foreign investors and the amount of track and traffic grew. This boosted fuel, metallurgy and engineering industries along with grain producers but few railway lines proved profitable.

TABLE 14 *Growth in Russian railways during Alexander II's reign*

Year	Mileage	Freight traffic (million tons)
1866	3 000	3
1883	14 700	24

Period	Annual volume (in million poods)
1861–5	76
1876–80	257

TABLE 15 *Increase in Russian grain during Alexander II's reign (1 pood = 36 lb = 16.36 kg)*

3 ⌁ ASSESSMENT OF ALEXANDER II'S REFORMS

Study the collection of sources below and answer the questions that follow:

The great reform laws of 1860–5 altered the structure of the empire fundamentally, but years were to elapse before their practical effect was fully felt. Officials learned only gradually to work cooperatively within the new system, and the state machinery as well as the minds of the masses had to be adjusted to radically changed circumstances. In the meantime the progressives, belonging to all classes of the population, became impatient. Socialist tendencies increased, and in 1863 a revolt occurred in Poland that was suppressed with unnecessary brutality. In 1866, in a growingly tense atmosphere, an attempt on the life of Alexander II, the 'Tsar Liberator' was made.

SOURCE A
From Walther Kirchner, Russian History, Harper Perenial/Harper Collins, 1991.

Russian intellectuals interpreted Alexander's reforms as an attempt to perpetuate the existing political system. Historical opinion has for the most part agreed with this assessment. Florinsky, for example, has suggested that the reforms were nothing more than 'half-hearted concessions on the part of those who (with some exceptions) hated to see the disappearance of the old order and tried to save as much of it as circumstances would allow. The response of the Russian intelligentsia was the Populist 'going to the people' in 1874. When this failed, propaganda gave way to terrorism, which culminated in the assassination of Alexander II in 1881. Although it did not achieve its objective of igniting a revolution in Russia, Populism was nevertheless significant. It made a start in developing the political consciousness of the people and its terrorist actions inspired later insurrectionists. The Social Revolutionaries, descendants of Populism, were the most important insurgent group at the turn of the century.

When Alexander II became Tsar in 1855, the Russian state was in desperate need of fundamental reform. The programme of reforms introduced by him was radical in comparison with previous Russian experience, but it did not go far enough. The government's commitment to modernise Russia through a process of westernisation was moderated by its concern to perpetuate the interests of its ruling social class. This approach alienated the Russian intelligentsia and, in so doing, undermined the stability of the regime, compelling it to rely on repression for its preservation. This strategy succeeded for some time, but in the long term it was likely to achieve precisely the opposite of its intended effect.

SOURCE B *From Carl Watts,* Alexander II's Reforms, Causes and Consequences, *History Review, December 1998, number 32, in which the author assesses the impact of Alexander II's reforms.*

Q

Using the evidence of the two sources, what do you consider to have been Alexander's main aims in sponsoring reform?

How successful were Alexander's reforms?

What can you learn from the sources of the reasons for growth in opposition to the regime?

'The Tsar Liberator' was a victim of the unresolved conflict between social reform and the doctrine of political autocracy' (H. Seton-Watson, Decline of Imperial Russia, 1964). *Using the evidence of the sources, how far would you agree with this interpretation of Alexander and his reforms?*

4 ～ THE GROWTH OF A REVOLUTIONARY MOVEMENT

A *Who were the revolutionaries?*

Alexander's reforms failed to satisfy his critics among the liberal and socialist ranks. With the relaxation in press censorship, liberals, radical students and a growing body of socialists openly discussed liberal and radical political ideas in the 1860s, the lead being taken by radical journalists. A number of manifestos were published which all contained the same grievance. 'The sovereign has betrayed the hopes of the people, the freedom he has given them is not real and is not what the people dreamed of and need'. They also agreed that their aim was that, 'we want all citizens of Russia to enjoy equal rights, we do not want privilege to exist, we want ability and education, rather than birth, to confer the right to high position, we want appointments to public office to follow the elective principle' (G. Vernadsky *et al.* (eds), *A Sourcebook for Russian History from Earliest Times to 1917*, Yale University Press, 1972). In 1862 a group of student radicals published the manifesto '*Young Russia*' in which they argued that revolution was the only solution.

The following is from this student revolutionary manifesto, *Young Russia*, 1862, quoted by G. Vernadsky *et al.* (eds), *A Sourcebook for Russian History from Earliest Times to 1917*, Yale University Press, 1972.

KEY ISSUE

'*Young Russia*'.

Society is at present divided into two groups that are hostile to one another because their interests are diametrically opposed. The party that is oppressed by all and humiliated by all is the party of the common people. Over it stands a small group of contented and happy men. They are the landowners ... the merchants ... the government officials – in short all those who possess property either inherited or acquired. At their heart stands the Tsar. They cannot exist without him or he without them. If either falls the other will be destroyed ... This is the imperial party. There is only one way out of this oppressive and terrible situation which is destroying contemporary man and that is revolution – bloody and merciless revolution ...

Q Which social groups were identified as members of the imperial party?

KEY ISSUE

The organisation.

The most important of the student revolutionary groups was the *Organisation*, started in 1863 at Moscow University with the aim of moulding public opinion to accept a general rebellion. There was a high level of peasant and student unrest and disturbances during the 1860s including a failed attempt on Alexander's life in 1866. These revolutionary developments divided educated Russian society. Many liberals abandoned their liberalism and became either conservative nationalists or radicals. Alexander blamed the educational system for encouraging the spread of seditious ideas. He replaced the liberal reformers and progressives who had carried through the 'Great Reforms' with outspoken reactionaries. They recommended a strengthening of the police, tighter control of universities and the press and an extension of the policy of *Russification* of nationalities, policies that characterised the last 15 years of Alexander's reign.

B *The Populist movement*

Despite its policy of repression revolutionary activity continued in the 1870s in the form of the Populist movement, the *Narodniks* (name derived from *v narod* 'To the people') and the *Narodnaya Volya* (*The People's Will*). Both posed a real threat to the regime. The Populists aimed to achieve their ideal of a perfect society based on the peasant and the village commune. Between 1873 and 1874, 2000–3000 educated Populists from the nobility and intelligentsia decided to 'Go to the People'. They visited peasant villages to share in the 'true' life of the peasant and to educate them to rise up in rebellion against the tsar and establish a Populist State. An account of the experiences of one Populist, Catherine Breshkovskaya, the daughter of a noble and later a founder of the Socialist Revolutionary Party, is given below. This extract is from her memoirs in which she describes her experiences as a Populist in the town of Smela, a centre of the sugar-beet industry, quoted in T. Riha, *Readings in Russian Civilisation*, University of Chicago Press, 1964.

> **KEY ISSUE**
>
> *The People's Will.*

> To the request that he (an old man whose hut room she shared) help me in my revolutionary propaganda in Smela the old man answered: 'I have no strength left. I have been cruelly punished. One soldier stood on one arm, another on the other, and two on my legs. I was beaten, beaten until the earth was soaked with blood. That is how I was flogged. And that did not happen merely once or twice. I was exiled to Siberia, came back, and began all over again; but I can't do it any more.'
>
> [Other peasants] made no protest against my proposal to prepare the soil for a general revolt; but it was evident that the recent punishments (after the 1861–3 uprisings) had made a terrible impression on them. They said as one man: 'If everyone agreed to rise at the same time, if you went around and talked to all the people, then it could be done. We tried several times to rise. We demanded our rights to the land. It was useless. Soldiers were sent down and the people were punished and ruined.'

> **Q**
>
> *How useful is this source for accounting for failure of the Populists to rouse the peasants to rebel?*

The peasants viewed the Populists with deep suspicion; and either beat them up or reported them to the police. Populism had failed. Two major trials of 243 young revolutionaries were held in 1877–8 (see Section 6C below). Those who escaped arrest or who had escaped from their place of 'administrative exile' kept the revolutionary movement alive.

C *Divisions in the Populist ranks*

Some decided that revolution would not come from the conservative and traditional peasants. They turned their attention to the ideas of Karl Marx and to revolution based on the industrial workers. Other groups retained faith in the peasants but tried a new approach. One such group was known as '*Land and Liberty*', *Zemlya I volya* that appeared in 1876. After their experiences in the early 1870s they recognised the need for a strong central organisation that enforced discipline through its ranks if they were to succeed against the state machine of repression. H. Seton-Watson has described what emerged as the 'first revolutionary party in Russia'. Its leaders developed a highly organised system of central and local command which included a section dealing with escapes from prison of arrested members, assassinations of government officials as revenge for ill treatment of revolutionaries and the discovery and punishment of traitors or police spies. Support for the revolutionaries grew as discontent increased with Russia's involvement in war against Turkey in 1877–8. They continued the ideal of 'Going to the people' but learning from the failure of the mid-1870s, they adopted a different approach. This was based on revolutionaries, dressed in peasant clothes, going to work in villages as doctors, teachers or skilled workmen, helping to organise them to resist tsarist officials and landlords. It was apparent however that the peasants would not stage a revolution from below and by 1879 the Land and Freedom movement had died away.

It was at this point that division appeared in the ranks of the revolutionaries over the future direction of the revolutionary movement and the methods to be pursued.

1 *Black Partition*, *Chorny peredyel*, led by Plekhanov, centred their activities on the condition of the peasantry whose interests they aimed to advance through political reform and mass agitation rather than violence.
2 *People's Will*, *Narodnaya Volya* believed in political terrorism and directed all their attention on the assassination of the tsar which was successfully achieved on 1 March 1881, when Alexander was fatally injured in the second of two bomb attacks.

This division brought Populism to an end.

D *Significance of Populism*

Its methods had proved to be very expensive not only in money but also in membership, many of whom were arrested after each outrage. Its activities had alienated many members of the public who had accepted its arguments but not its methods. However, it should not be dismissed as a complete failure. It succeeded in promoting a political awareness in many people and its ideology and actions influenced later generations of revolutionaries particularly the **Socialist Revolutionaries**.

KEY ISSUE

The growth of political terrorism.

Socialist Revolutionaries were committed to democratic socialism. They believed in the right of people to govern themselves. As heirs to the Populists they attached importance to peasant organisations, which accounts for the support they gained from sections of the peasantry. They played a role in encouraging peasant discontent.

5 ⌐ THE REGIME TAKES A REACTIONARY TURN — 1865

It is generally acknowledged that 1865–6 was a watershed, not only in politics but also in the personal life of Alexander. His eldest son died while his wife, whose health was shattered by tuberculosis, retreated into a private life. Alexander alienated leading members of his family when he embarked on a relationship with a young princess, Catherine Dolgorouky, who 'alone could give him a new life'. She was given private apartments in the Winter Palace; four children were born to the relationship before they were eventually married a year before his assassination. Close liberal members of his family who had encouraged Alexander to pursue his programme of reform lost influence. Grand Duke Constantine and Grand Duchess Helen found it increasingly difficult to obtain an audience with the tsar.

In politics, the golden age of reform was coming to an end. Alexander found himself under pressure from the right and the left. He rejected reformist demands for a general assembly of elected representatives from throughout Russia to discuss the common needs of the entire state. Extreme conservatives wanted a break on further reform, a view supported by Alexander after the failed attempt on his life. His interest in, and commitment to, reform declined as he became increasingly exhausted by criticism from all sides.

KEY ISSUE

Significance of 1865–6.

PICTURE 3
Tsar Alexander II, Princess Catherine Dolgorouky and their elder children, George and Olga, c. 1879

6 ↷ ALEXANDER THE TRADITIONALIST

A *Ministerial changes*

Alexander replaced his liberal reforming ministers with conservatives including Count Peter Shuvalov, who was made chief of police in charge of the Third Section (1866–74). His appointment heralded the return to a conservative atmosphere and a policy of repression.

B *Educational reforms*

<table>
<tr><td>KEY ISSUE</td></tr>
<tr><td>What were the effects of these reforms?</td></tr>
</table>

Alexander's reactionary Minister of Education, Count Tolstoy, (not the well-known author) blamed the university curriculum for the spread of revolutionary ideas. Subjects that encouraged independent thought, like history, science, modern languages and even Russian, were replaced with Mathematics, Latin, Greek and Church history. At the same time a few extreme left publications were closed down. In 1871, a formal division was made between schools, called *gimnaziya*, that concentrated on a classical education and modern subject schools, called 'real schools'. Only *gimnaziya* students could progress to university while students from 'real schools' went on to higher technical institutions. Despite these reactionary policies Tolstoy's educational policy did show some liberal aspects. He increased the number of teacher training colleges and although he disapproved, he had to accept Moscow University's decision to organise lectures for women.

Extension in the provision of education is evident in the substantial increase in schools as shown by the following table:

TABLE 16
Growth in educational provision 1863–81

Year	Number of gimnazii	Number of students	Number of 'real schools'
1863	94	31 132 (boys)	N/A
1876	203	52 455	23
1881	270	Less than 50 000 (includes girls)	79 (17 484)

<table>
<tr><td>Why did the number of students in gimnazii decline? Q</td></tr>
</table>

Students moved to Switzerland to study a wider curriculum and also to listen freely to professional agitators and anarchists. Others found themselves either expelled from the universities for revolutionary activities or recalled home from abroad as part of the regime's *Russification* policy. The net result was the same. There was an increase in the number of disenchanted intelligentsia; socialists, Populists and many joined the ranks of the revolutionaries.

C *The 'Shuvalov era'*

A conservative with a military and police background, Shuvalov had opposed Alexander's reforms of the 1860s. He brought other reactionary conservatives into office who supported increased use of rule by decree, use of military courts to try cases of political violence, a tightening up of censorship including banning some periodicals, student co-operatives and processions. These measures had some effect in the later 1860s, though the few liberals who remained in office, such as Nicholas Milyutin, opposed them. A diary entry for 31 December 1873 reveals Milyutin's bitter feelings:

The following is an extract from Nicholas Milyutin's diary entry of 31 December 1873, quoted by Hugh Seton-Watson, *The Russian Empire 1801–1917*, OUP, 1967.

> For me 1873 passed like a dark cloud; only sad impressions are left of it. In no preceding year did I endure so much unpleasantness annoyance and failure. The intrigue begun long ago against me grew to full maturity and unfolded in all its ugliness.... Everything is done under the exclusive influence of Count Shuvalov who has terrified the emperor with his daily reports about frightful dangers to which allegedly the state and the sovereign himself are exposed.... Under the pretext of protection of the emperor's person and of the monarchy Shuvalov interferes in everything and all matters are decided in accordance with his whisperings. He has surrounded the emperor with his people; all new appointments are made at his instructions ... Such is the **milieu** in which I am condemned to operate. Is it possible for one man to fight against a whole powerful gang? What a devastating and disgusting contrast with the atmosphere in which I entered the government 13 years ago! Then everything was striving forwards; now everything is pulling backwards. Then the emperor sympathised with progress, he was moving forward; now he has lost confidence in everything be created, in everything that surrounds him, even in himself.

milieu environment.

Q *What main pressures were experienced by Milyutin and other liberally inclined ministers?*

Revolutionary activity increased between 1873 and 1877 leading to the arrest of 1611 Populists, 15% being women, some of who died in prison from ill treatment. Two major public trials were held: 'trial of the 50' who belonged to the Moscow group of young revolutionaries and 'trial of 193', amidst intense propagandist activity. Relatively 'mild' sentences were passed provoking the regime to send those freed into administrative exile in Siberia.

Social group	Number
Noble	279
Non-noble official	117
Priest	197
Merchant	33
Jew	68
*Meshchane	92
*Peasant	138

TABLE 17
Social composition of the revolutionaries tried 1877–8 (refers to legal status not actual occupation and probably represented children of city workers)*

D *Signs of relaxation of repression 1880*

Shuvalov's appointment as ambassador to London in 1874 removed the main reactionary associated with repression and opened the way for liberals to regain influence. Conservatives were replaced by more liberal ministers particularly Loris-Melikov, who headed a Supreme Commission set up in 1880 to consider reform to meet the revolutionary challenge. Loris-Melikov abolished the Third Section and transferred its functions to the Police.

Loris-Melikov realising that the *zemstva* expected reform proposed a plan for a limited involvement of elected persons in legislation based on an administrative and a financial commission, composed of appointed experts. Alexander was assassinated before the government's plans could be published. The hopes of revolutionaries that his death would be followed by a collapse of the regime were not realised. Despite the presence of revolutionary forces there had never been the practical possibility that they could seize power. There was never a crisis in the affairs of the ruling body; the bureaucracy, police and army remained loyal. It was only when the loyalty of the armed forces was lost as a consequence of humiliating defeat in war that the revolutions of 1905 and 1917 became possible. In the case of 1905 it was only a partial loss and that is one of the reasons for the successful recovery of the regime; in 1917 it became permanent forcing Tsar Nicholas II to abdicate.

7 ⌐ RUSSIAN EXPANSION

Alexander expanded into Central Asia acquiring Turkestan, Tashkent, and Samarkand which established Russia on the eastern shores of the Caspian Sea. A substantial portion of the ruling group and of society as a whole thought that such expansion would make it possible for the country to restore its military and political prestige after its defeat in the Crimean War, but the policy brought her into conflict with England.

8 ⌐ RUSSIA'S RELATIONS WITH THE WEST

A *Relations with France*

Russia's friendship with France in the late 1850s and early 1860s, after the hostilities of the Crimean War was short-lived. Relations between the two powers became strained due to French sympathy for the Poles during their second revolt against the Russian regime in 1863. This strain was intensified as a result of Alexander II's growing support for France's enemy, Prussia. In 1870, Alexander refused to respond to the appeals of the French government for help and protection when it was threatened by a Prussian invasion. The tsar made clear his Prussian sympathies, even though a substantial portion of Russian society and its ruling bureaucracy did not share them.

B *Relations with Prussia*

To some extent, Alexander's attitude toward Prussia was influenced by a number of considerations:

1. He hoped that a Franco-Prussian War would force France into accepting a reopening of the Dardanelle and Bosphorus Straits to Russian warships.
2. He had strong personal and family sympathies with the King of Prussia, who was his uncle. Russia remained neutral when Prussia went to war against France's neutrality, but sent Russian officers, doctors, and field hospitals to serve in the German army. Alexander II, in supporting Prussia against France, did not recognise the threat implied to Russia in the formation of a strong, militarised, neighbouring power.

C *Relations with Austria*

Reconciliation with Austria-Hungary was also achieved. Russia, Germany and Austria-Hungary formed the Three Emperors' League in October 1873.

D *Relations with Turkey*

In the late 1860s, Pan-Slavism became identified with Russian nationalism and expansionism. Amongst the minority Slav people it promised security, the brotherhood of equal Slav nations – Catholic and Protestant as well as Orthodox. As far as Alexander and his advisers were concerned their attitude towards Russia's relations with Slav minorities in the declining Turkish Empire was more cautious and conservative. Ambitions to extend Russian control in Constantinople and the Black Sea region continued as did encouragement of subject nationalities to oppose Turkish rule.

In 1875 trouble broke out again in the Balkans with revolts in Bosnia and Herzegovina followed by Russian intervention in 1877 on behalf of the Slav peoples of the Balkans to protect them against Turkish cruelties. In the war that followed Russia had some successes but the substantial gains she made in the first treaty of San Stefano that followed were reversed by an international congress called by Britain in Berlin (see Map 4).

1. Turkey would lose most of her territory in Europe.
2. A new large state of Bulgaria was created stretching from the Danube to the Aegean.
3. Armenia and Bessarabia were given to Russia.
4. Austria received Bosnia and Herzegovina.
5. Serbia and Montenegro were made independent.

Britain refused to recognise these arrangements because Bulgaria would have fallen under Russian influence. The issue was referred to another

MAP 4

The Balkans – territorial arrangements at San Stefano, 1878

MAP 5

The Balkans – territorial arrangements at the Congress of Berlin, 1878

international conference in Berlin, 1878, though many of the points in dispute were settled in a series of secret agreements that Britain signed with Russia, Austria and Turkey before the congress met.

The Congress of Berlin was dominated by the British Prime Minister, Disraeli, who was opposed to any suggestion of an increase in Russia's power (see Map 5).

- The 'Big Bulgaria' of San Stefano was divided into three:
  (a) The south and west, Macedonia, was returned to Turkey.
  (b) The north became independent as Bulgaria but under the influence of Russia.
  (c) The southern region was returned to Turkey.
- Britain was given Cyprus.
- Russia kept her gains in Bessarabia.
- Bosnia Herzegovina continued to be administered by Austria.
- Serbia and Montenegro remained independent but lost some land.

KEY ISSUE

Significance of the Russo-Turkish War 1877–8.

1 Britain had succeeded in propping up the Turkish Empire though unrest continued. The Christian Balkan League declared war against Turkey in 1912 and events in this region eventually provoked outbreak of a European war in 1914.

2 The Congress also laid the foundations for the future hostility between Austria and Russia and of suspicion between Germany and Russia.

3 Russia's gains had been drastically reduced. Russia's obvious diplomatic defeat increased the government's difficulties at home. The upsurge of patriotism roused by the war to free the Slavs succeeded in silencing the regime's critics only temporarily. When terror was revived the tsar had become the target.

9 ⌐ BIBLIOGRAPHY

A general bibliography for Russia under the tsars appears on page 120 of Chapter 4.

Specific resources on Alexander II include: Mosse, *Alexander II and the Modernisation of Russia*, English University Press, 1970 and a number of articles in publications specifically aimed at VI formers – Peter Neville, *Tsar Alexander II Liberator or Traditionalist?* Modern History Review, vol. 9, issue 1, September 1997, Carl Peter Watts, *Alexander II's Reforms*, History Review, Number 32, December 1998; David Moon, *Defeat in War Leads to Rapid Russian Reforms: Benefits Undermined by Restrictions*, New Perspective, vol. 1, number 1, September 1995.

10 ⌐ STRUCTURED AND ESSAY QUESTIONS

A *This section consists of structured questions that might be used for discussion or written answers as a way of expanding on the chapter and testing understanding of it.*

1. (a) What was Alexander II's attitude towards liberal demands for reform?
   (b) To what extent were liberal reformers successful in achieving their demands for reform in the 1860s?

2. (a) What main criticisms were directed against serfdom?
   (b) How far were these criticisms answered by the 1861 Emancipation Edict?

3. (a) What do you understand by the term 'serfdom'?
   (b) Why was it abolished?

4. (a) What were the *zemstva*?
   (b) To what extent were they effective?

5. (a) What were the main abuses in the administration of justice?
   (b) How far were these removed by the judicial reforms of 1865?

6. (a) What were the main features of Dmitri Milyutin's reforms as Minister of War?
   (b) How effective were these reforms?

7. (a) Who were the Populists?
   (b) To what extent did they succeed in achieving their aims?

8. (a) Why did the regime experience a turning point in 1865–6?
   (b) To what extent was there a return to repressive policies?

9. (a) What were the main features to Pan-Slavism in the 1860s?
   (b) How successful was Alexander II in furthering Russian interests in the Balkans?

B *Essay questions.*

1. Examine the condition of Russia at the accession of Alexander II.

2. To what extent did Alexander II succeed in his attempts to modernise Russia?

3. 'The emancipation of the serfs and Alexander II's other reforms made little difference to Russian politics and society? Discuss.

4. Why did the reforms introduced by Alexander II fail to satisfy liberal and socialist elements in Russia?

5. To what extent does Alexander II deserve the title 'Tsar Liberator'?

6. 'He worked to abolish serfdom and remove poverty and privilege … he deserved a better fate' (Lionel Kochan, *The Making of Modern Russia*).
   How valid is this interpretation of the attempts of Alexander II to solve the problems of the Russian peasantry?

7. Why did the reforms of Alexander II not make him a more popular tsar?

11 ~ MAKING NOTES

Read the advice section about making notes on page ix of the Preface: how to use this book, and then make your own notes based on the following headings and questions.

A *Alexander II's personality and attitude as tsar*
1. What was his attitude towards his role as tsar?
2. What were his strengths and weaknesses as a reformer?

B *Abolition of serfdom*
1. 'Serfdom was becoming a dire threat to both domestic and foreign security' (E. Acton, *The Tsarist and Soviet Legacy*, 2nd edn, Longman, 1995). What were the main reasons for the abolition of serfdom? In your answer refer to the role of each of the following:
   (a) Alexander II
   (b) political issues including the legacy of the Crimean War
   (c) economic criticisms of serfdom
   (d) moral arguments of various reform groups
   (e) general issues relating to security of the state and peasant disturbances.
2. Outline the work of the Secret Committee (renamed Main Committee January 1858) set up to discuss emancipation. In your answer refer to each of the following aspects:
   (a) membership
   (b) issues discussed
   (c) main stages
   (d) arguments of abolition opponents
   (e) implementation of emancipation.
3. What were the main effects of emancipation in terms of gains and losses on each of the following:
   (a) peasants
   (b) landowners
   (c) *Mir*
   (d) local administration?
4. How have historians interpreted the effects of emancipation?

C *Administrative reforms*
1. What were the main criticisms directed against the administration of Russia?
2. What was the *zemstvo*?
3. What were its main powers?
4. How effective were the *zemstva*?
5. What were their main limitations?
6. Why did Alexander II refuse to grant reformers' demands for a representative assembly?

D *Judicial reforms*
1. What were the main abuses in the judicial system by 1861?
2. How did Alexander II's government propose to reform the judicial system?
3. What were the beneficial effects of these reforms?
4. What were the limitations of these reforms?

E *Military*
1. In what respects did Milyutin's reforms end class privilege in the army?
2. What were the beneficial effects of these reforms?
3. What were the limitations of these reforms?

F *Education and Censorship*
1. What were the main features of Alexander II's educational and censorship reforms between 1861–6?
2. What were the beneficial effects of these reforms?
3. What were the limitations of these reforms?

G *Financial and economic reform*
1. What were the main features of Reutern's financial reforms?
2. How successful were these reforms?

H *Assessment of Alexander II's reforms*
1. To what extent was Alexander II successful in achieving his aims for reform?
2. Identify the main forces opposed to reform.
3. To what extent were Alexander II's reform policies in conflict with his doctrine of political autocracy?
4. Were Alexander II's reform policies doomed to fail?

I *The growth of a revolutionary movement*
1. Who were the revolutionaries?
2. What were the aims of the Populist movement?
3. How successful were they in achieving their aims?
4. What was the significance of the Populists among the ranks of revolutionaries?
5. What do you understand by political terrorism?
6. What factors promoted its growth?

J *The regime takes a reactionary turn 1865*
1. Why was 1865–6 regarded as a turning point for the regime?

K *Alexander the Traditionalist*
1.   What do you understand by the phrase the '*Shuvalov* era'?
2.   What were the main features of the repression adopted by 1865–80?
3.   To what extent was the policy of repression challenged by Loris-Melikov's reform proposals?

L *Russian expansion*
1.   How successful was Alexander II in furthering Russian interests in each of the following regions:
     (a) Asia
     (b) Balkans?

M *Foreign policy*
1.   What changes occurred in Russia's relation with each of the following:
     (a) Austria
     (b) Prussia
     (c) France
     (d) Britain?

12 ⤳ PLANNING AN A2 TYPE ESSAY

Revise the advice section about writing essays given on pages xii in the Preface: How to use this book. The following is an example of a significance type of essay shown in the title: How successful was Alexander II in solving the problems facing Russia during his reign?

This question requires you to identify the problems facing Russia in 1855 and then assess how far they were solved during his reign with some comment on events subsequent to 1881. You will need to know about Russia's economic, social and political structure, Alexander's attitude as tsar and the effect of his policies at the time and subsequently. An appreciation of the deep-seated obstacles to success is also relevant to indicate that failure was not entirely due to Alexander.

There are two possible approaches to planning your answer. One approach is to identify the problems and then the policies of the regime with some reference to success at the end. The pitfall to this approach is that you write two 'mini-essays' and fail to make a thorough assessment. The second approach is to identify a problem, discuss the policies to deal with it and then assess the value and limitations/effectiveness/gains/losses linking such assessment not only back to the problem but also to its future significance.

Essay planning sheet: significance essay

Title: How successful was Alexander II in solving the problems facing Russia during his reign?

Introduction: Perception of Alexander II's reign as a progressive period compared with the repression of his father, Nicholas I's reign. Alexander's major reforms of the 1860s appeared to be transforming Russia from a medieval to a modern state, but these were only half successful as a result of the return to repression in the 1870s.

Para.	Problem	Policies	Assessment of success
1	Stagnation in agriculture – could not compete with cheap grain produced in new countries, such as America. Serfdom was no longer profitable and the nobles who governed the serfs were bankrupt.	Process of the emancipation of the serfs – including special administrative arrangements – the *volost*.	Gains and losses to the peasants and to the nobility. Effect on level of riot and popular disturbances by peasants. Effect on agriculture – the economic structure of society remained relatively unchanged – dominance of the *Mir* – continuing backwardness carried on after 1881.
2	Backwardness of the economy and society affected the ability of the regime to raise sufficient income to support its European and expansionist role. The general backwardness of society had revealed itself in the defeat of the Crimean War.	The reforms of Reutern – building of railways to improve communications and help increase trade and hence revenue.	Victory in the Russo-Turkish war 1877–8. Expansion in Asia.
3	Increasing bureaucracy and a collapsing system of government led to demands by liberal reformers for a more representative government. Also need to remove some of the more glaring abuses in the administration of justice.	Extensive programme of reform of local government – *Zemstva*, of the army by Milyutin and judicial reforms.	Beneficial effects of these reforms but also limitations. *Zemstva* not given adequate authority and they did not develop into representative institutions. Problems that remained – the autocratic basis of government. Noble dominance of the bureaucracy – resisted radical reform proposals.

Para.	Problem	Policies	Assessment of success
4	Growing unrest amongst the peasantry and criticism from the intelligentsia had led to increasing repression. Alexander II saw a threat to the authority of the tsar if he did not renew the Russian state through 'reform from above'.	Relaxation of censorship controls – temporary	Change after 1866 – growth of populism and political terrorism – underlying problems remained – Alexander II's main aim – reform to preserve autocracy – so that radical reform was beyond the power and intention of the regime – lesson not lost on would be reformers.

Conclusion: Alexander II's reforms helped prolong the life of the regime though he did not solve its underlying problems. In the longer term the new course he had adopted would conflict with Russian traditions and lead eventually to the death of the tsarist order in 1917.

3

Alexander III and the age of reaction and counter-reform 1881–94

ALEXANDER ALEXANDROVICH, 1845–94, EMPEROR OF ALL RUSSIA 1881–94

As the second son, Alexander III, had not been groomed for tsardom, but pursued an army career until he was 20 when he then became heir presumptive on the death of his elder brother, Nicholas, in 1865. He had supported the nationalist opposition that had opposed many of Alexander II's views and reforms. His disapproval of his father's policies had been motivated not only by ideological differences on the issue of reform, but also by criticism of his father's relationship with, and subsequent marriage to, Princess Catherine Dolgorouky. His reign, which was marked by 13 years of peace and stability, saw a return to repression of political opposition and a conservative social policy. His domestic policy was particularly harsh, directed not only against revolutionaries but other liberal movements. His concern to preserve autocracy also led him to encourage a state-led, forced industrialisation programme that strengthened capitalism.

1 ⌐ ALEXANDER III AND HIS SUITABILITY FOR TSARDOM

A *Alexander III's personality*

According to one Russian biographer, Valentina Grigorievna Chernukha, he was a limited, unfit ruler whose 'personality dominated the statesman in him' and whose policies were doomed from the start, and pushed Russia further along the path to revolution. Known as 'Little Bulldog' within his family, they did not consider him to be fitting material for statesmanship and on the death of his brother, the heir, his aunt, the Grand Duchess Helen, had suggested that the crown should

See Picture 4 on page 65.

PICTURE 4
Portrait of Alexander III,
British Museum

pass to his younger brother, Vladimir. Alexander had had no preparation for ruling having been left 'almost entirely to his own devices during his childhood and young manhood'. He was not very intelligent, was slow to learn, and had a very inadequate knowledge of history, literature, economy and law. He was interested in all things military and by the time he became the heir he was a colonel, and *hetman* or leader of all the Cossack troops.

B *Alexander's training*

At the age of 20 his education was taken over by amongst others, the deeply conservative Konstantin Pobedonostsev (see page 67).

During the 15 years that he spent as heir presumptive, Alexander III represented the nationalist opposition of the political right. He opposed his father's reform policies, though never openly, on a number of occasions before he became tsar:

1 He disagreed with Alexander II on the issue of treatment of Russia's nationalities, particularly the Poles. He did not see the need either to reconcile Russia's nationalities to Russian rule or to consider European opinion of Russia. He was totally committed to a policy of *Russification* that was eventually to be speeded up during his time as tsar (see page 74).

2 He supported the continuing presence in government of ministers in favour of a policy of harsh repressive measures against political extremists whereas Alexander II tried to keep them out of state affairs when the country was peaceful.

> **KEY ISSUES**
>
> *Differences between Alexander, and his father, the 'Tsar Liberator'.*

3 Alexander III supported those nobles who opposed Milyutin's plans to liberalise the army and his recruitment changes of 1874 (see page 44).

4 He was in the 'party of action' in the events leading to the Russo-Turkish war of 1877–8 when Alexander II was concerned to avoid conflict.

5 Alexander III stressed the positive features of Russia's past that his father worked to end. They disagreed on the issue of judicial reforms that were acknowledged to be among Alexander II's most important work. Alexander III made it clear that he would revise them once he became tsar.

Alexander III increasingly became the focal point for other reactionaries while even those who did not support his ideas recognised that the future of Russia lay with him. Those ministers whom he had personally chosen were assured of his support and they in turn respected him.

C *His attitude as tsar*

Alexander made it very clear at the beginning of his reign that he would never permit limitations on autocratic rule. His father's assassination had confirmed his hostility to reform. He was determined to re-enforce the authority of the tsar and to stamp out political opponents who posed a challenge. He rejected any suggestion of a western style parliamentary institution in the belief that it was foreign to Russia's tradition and history and was not wanted by the peasants. His belief that he had a mystical bond with the Russian peasants gave a Populist element to his rule. His conservative reactionary views were supported by the ministers he chose to advise him, particularly Konstantin Pobedonostsev and Count Dmitri Tolstoy. He was a strong supporter of Russian nationalism and Pan-Slavism and was determined to reverse the pro-German policy that had been adopted by his father and grandfather. There was a modernising element to his policies but his state-led industrialisation programme was motivated more by his concern to preserve autocracy and strengthen Russia as a great power.

2 ⌐ ALEXANDER III – THE REACTIONARY TSAR

A *Appointment of ministers and advisers*

Alexander began his reign with a proclamation announcing his determination to rule as an autocrat. This was followed by the appointment of conservative advisers, the most significant being Konstantin Pobedonostsev, Procurator of the Holy Synod, responsible for church affairs. He was known behind his back as the 'Black Tsar' and even Alexander was not totally uncritical declaring that 'one could freeze to death just listening to him all the time'.

KONSTANTIN POBEDONOSTSEV (1827–1907)

He was tutor in legal matters to Alexander III and Nicholas II and exercised great influence as the champion of orthodoxy, autocracy and nationality. He had been a critic of Alexander II's liberalising policies and an opponent of democracy. In 1860–5 he was professor of Civil Law at Moscow University and was a member of the commission that prepared the judicial reforms of 1863. He became Procurator of the Holy Synod 1880–1905 and from then on his views became more fixed.

He was passionately intolerant of other faiths and as a nationalist he was hostile to minorities in the Empire. He was critical of Alexander II's liberalising policies and in his *Reflections of a Russian Statesman*' (1898) he attacked parliamentary government as 'the great lie of our time'. He believed that he represented true Russians and was an important influence on re-enforcing Alexander III's conservative reactionary support for the principles of orthodoxy, autocracy and nationality. He genuinely believed that liberals were a threat to tsarist authority and blamed them for the political extremism and death of Alexander II. He supported a policy of repression and even came to criticise the legal reforms he had helped sponsor in the 1860s. In a memorandum sent to Alexander III in 1885, he attacked the separation of judicial and executive powers, argued for greater control of barristers by the courts and advised the abolition of trial by jury. He supported policies that would return Russia to a police state.

Pobedonostsev persuaded Alexander II to govern with the advice of a small body of experienced ministers. Serving as a Prime Minister, he influenced Alexander to appoint conservative reactionary ministers, who shared his conservative views.

B *Main features of 'counter-reform' policies 1881–95*

Alexander began his reign by publicly hanging the five agents of the *People's Will* who had taken part in his father's assassination. Many aspects of Russian life subsequently experienced repression, including judicial organisation, the government, education of the Jews and Russia's nationalities. The emancipation of the serfs remained but the peasants came under the closer control of officials while agriculture stagnated. These policies led to a deep hatred of Alexander by Jews, Germans, revolutionaries, nationalities and those who broke from the Orthodox Church. Yet, Alexander was unique amongst the tsars in that he preserved peace throughout his reign, apart from some minor fighting in central Asia. In that respect it could be said that he deserved the title 'peacemaker'. However, he undoubtedly laid the foundations for the 1917 revolution.

AN OVERVIEW OF THE MAIN FEATURES OF ALEXANDER III'S COUNTER-REFORMS

Political (central government) and internal security

Main features	Effects
● 1881: Defeat of proposals for constitutional reform after a series of conferences.	● Indicated that Alexander III had no intention of 'completing the great reforms of Alexander II which remained unfinished'. He had every intention of preserving autocratic rule. ● Reforming ministers resign.
● Statute Concerning Measures for the Protection of State Security, 1881, or more generally the Law on Exceptional Measures gave the government far-reaching powers to interfere with civil liberties. If the situation was considered to be sufficiently critical, a Commander-in-Chief could be appointed to set up military police courts, confiscate property and arrest, imprison or fine people, remove elected officials and suppress publications. ● Formation of the *Okhrana*.	● The 1881 Law was used in some regions until the 1917 revolution. ● Revolutionary groups were weakened for a decade and activists were forced into exile. ● Alexander's reign appeared to be peaceful and stable but this was due more to a rigid system of repression based on executions and exile to Siberia rather than to a solution of their grievances.

Okhrana were the secret police concerned with preservation of public order.

PICTURE 5 *'Russian Civilisation', forced labour in Siberia*

George Kennan, *Siberia and the Exile System*, 1891. In 1885, George Kennan, who had lived in Russia as a young man, returned to the empire to carry out a report on the prison system.

Marching parties of convicts three or four hundred strong leave Tomsk for Irkutsk weekly throughout the whole year and make the journey of 1040 miles [1660 kilometres] in about three months ... Each prisoner receives five cents a day in money for his subsistence and buys food for himself from peasants along the road who make a business of furnishing it ... No distinction is made between common convicts and political convicts except that the latter if they are nobles or belong to one of the privileged classes receive seven and a half cents a day instead of five and are carried in carts instead of being forced to walk.

Q

How useful is this source for revealing the size and scope of opposition under Alexander III?

Political (local government) and internal security

Main features	Effects
● Publications critical of the regime could be suspended indefinitely and editors prevented from publishing anything else.	● Nobility continued to decline despite the introduction of the Land Captain.
● 1887: Defeat of attempts to assassinate Alexander by a group of student protestors. Followed by executions including Lenin's older brother, Alexander Ulyanov.	● The peasantry resented being put under the authority of the Land Captain supervised by the Ministry of the Interior. They were prevented from developing self-government.
● 1884: Recommendations of Kakhanov Report that the *volost* should be responsible for all classes rejected.	● Increased bureaucratic control and number of officials.
● 1889: Office of *volost* justice of the peace abolished and their duties were transferred in the towns to city judges appointed by the Ministry of Justice and in the rural areas they were shared between the *uezd* member of the provincial assembly and a new officer – the Land Captain. The latter, drawn from the ranks of the local nobility, was elected by the provincial governor subject to the approval of the Ministry of the Interior.	● Local self-government continued but was subject to constant interference by central government. The latter stifled local initiative in all aspects of its work including any attempts to improve people's welfare.
	● The *zemstva* concentrated on improving local services including roads, fire-fighting and education.
	● Slow pace to improvements in the cities and these were confined to the main streets while the outlying parts were neglected in terms of street cleaning and lighting.

Main features	Effects
• 1890: *Zemstva* Act changed the way in which membership was elected. This was determined by three electoral colleges that were dominated by the landowners while peasant representation was reduced and made indirect. *Zemstva* were under the disciplinary control of the Ministry of the Interior. • 1892: Municipal Government Act restricted, and thereby reduced, the electorate in the towns to owners of immovable property over a certain value.	• Increase in the number of trained experts particularly doctors, teachers and engineers employed by the *zemstva* and cities. These were mainly young idealists who wanted to bring improvements to the people despite being poorly paid. They tended to be liberal or socialist in their political outlook and came to form an important group in favour of political reform. They were also active in cultivating a professional identity, which expressed itself in the formation of professional organisations. They regarded themselves as part of the intelligentsia rather than government officials.

Education

Main features	Effects
• 1882: Higher courses for women were to be gradually closed. • 1884: University Statute replaced that of 1863. It established state control over the universities in an attempt to stamp out riots, such as had occurred in 1882 in St Petersburg and Kazan. • 1886: Final closure of higher courses for women. • 1887: Increase in university fees to exclude all but the wealthy. • 1887: Fees in *gimnazii* were raised to keep out students from lower social ranks. This exclusion was emphasised in Delianov 'Cooks' Circular' of	• Increase in the powers of government appointed inspectors who were made directly responsible to the curators. • University rectors, deans and lecturers were appointed by the Minister of Education rather than as in the past by the academic university boards. • Students were banned from belonging to student groups. • Reforms brought peace to the universities until 1887 when there was a fresh outburst of rioting. • Students continued to organise themselves in unofficial regional societies known as *zemlyachestva*. Their activities

1887 that stated that the secondary schools should exclude 'children of coachmen, servants, cooks, washerwomen, small shopkeepers and persons of similar type. Excepting for gifted children, it is completely unwarranted for the children of such people to be brought out of the social environment to which they belong'.

● 1888: Vocational schools were set up.

● 1890: New *gimnazii* curriculum reduced the amount of time spent studying Latin and Greek.

● The church was given more control over primary education and was encouraged to set up church schools in the parish.

were co-ordinated by a central committee known as the Union Council, the *soyuzny sovet*. By the end of the 1890s individuals active in illegal political movements used the Council to encourage student unrest.

● Between 1892 and 1895 the number of children in *gimnazii* fell from 65 751 to 63 863 while the percentage of children of nobles and officials increased from 47 to 56%. However, the number in real schools rose from 17 500 to 26 000. Church schools increased from 4064 to 31 835. At the time of the 1897 census only 21% of the population were literate. The government believed that peasants should receive the minimum of education since it encouraged dangerous ideas.

Judiciary

Main features	Effects
● 1885: Minister of Justice was given increased disciplinary powers over the judiciary.	● Legal reforms of Alexander II's reign were reversed, but not totally.
● 1887: Minister of Justice was given the power to order a trial to be held in camera to protect 'the dignity of state power'.	● Increased government interference in the law courts.
● 1887: Term of service on *volost* courts was increased to three years.	● Judges became liable to dismissal.
● 1889: Crimes against state officials were to be heard in special courts without a jury.	● Trial by jury undermined.
● 1889: *Volost* justices were abolished and cases heard by them were transferred to the state appointed Land Captain.	
● 1889: Minister of Justice was given the power to appoint town judges instead of justices.	

Religion

Main features	Effects
• 1883: Dissenters were not allowed to build new centres of worship, wear religious clothes outside their church, or engage in religious propaganda. Any attempt to convert a member of the Orthodox church to a dissenting religion was punished by exile to Siberia. • 1894: *Stundism*, an evangelical sect, that had emerged in the Ukraine, about 1858, was declared 'an especially dangerous sect' and its prayer meetings were banned.	• Pobedonostsev's policies to enforce Orthodoxy became associated with Alexander III's policy to *Russify* his nationalities. It caused resentment and encouraged the growth of nationalist movements.

3 ↪ ALEXANDER III'S REFORMS

AN OVERVIEW OF THE MAIN FEATURES OF ALEXANDER III'S REFORMS

Political

Main features	Effects
• 1882: Kakhanov Commission set up to consider reform of administration at *Volost* and village levels (abolished in 1885). • Proposed to reconvene a *zemsky sobor*, an Assembly of the Land. • *Zemstva* continued to carry out improvements in the village.	• Rejection of any prospect of constitutional government – autocracy upheld. • Some growth in the provision of primary education.

Social

Main features	Effects
Gains made by peasantry • 1881: Law to end 'temporary obligation'. This reform had been prepared by Loris-Melikov.	• The 1881 Law was applied to 37 'internal provinces' of European Russia affecting about 15% of former serfs. Allotments were made compulsory and redemption payments were reduced.

Gains by the peasants

- 1883: Peasants' Land Bank gave peasants cheap credit to buy land though this had the danger of indebtedness. But it did increase substantially the share of the total land owned by peasants.
- 1883–6: Abolition of poll-tax.
- Inheritance tax placed a larger share of the financial burden on wealthy and privileged classes.
- Reduction in village authority over peasants with introduction of right of appeal to higher courts.

Gains by the nobles

- 1885: Nobles' Land Bank.

Gains by the workers

- 1882: Child labour was regulated and working hours were reduced.
- 1882–90: Laws to provide for compulsory education for young factory children.
- Reduction in hours worked by women at night.
- Reduction in unjust fines.
- Reduction in payment in kind instead of money.
- Factory inspectors appointed to enforce legislation and to supervise labourers' living and working conditions.

Despite good intentions to improve the conditions of rural and urban workers the reforms had limitations. This was partly due to the

- Rapid increase in population which increased the number of poor (see page 2).
- Corruption that meant the laws were not fully applied.
- Introduction of Land Captains and the increase in indirect taxes checked progress in the villages.
- Development of industry in the towns led to poor living conditions as houses were built quickly and cheaply but were still insufficient to meet demand. Families lived together in large sleeping halls and drunkenness, filth and immorality were commonplace.
- Poor health of town population as a result of the evils of town living but also long hours remained. In 1897 the average expectation of life at birth was 32 years.
- Whole families worked in the factories so that the care and education of children were neglected.

Religion

Main features	*Effects*
<ul><li>1883: Dissenters, except **skoptsy**, were allowed to have passports, to engage in commercial and industrial activities, hold minor office and hold religious meetings in their homes.</li><li>1893: Priests were paid a salary by the State.</li></ul>	

skoptsy (meant castrates) and was a religious sect whose members deprived themselves of their manhood.

4 ∽ ALEXANDER III AND THE POLICY OF *RUSSIFICATION*

Russification that had been apparent during the 1870s became the official policy under Alexander III as advisers committed to such a policy became more influential in government circles. His successor, Nicholas II continued with his policies until 1917. These were directed towards ensuring that 55% of the Empire's population (according to the 1897 Census), that was made up of nationalities lost all trace of their identity and became Russian in terms of their language, culture, religion, legal system and ruling elite. Education was geared to making nationalities loyal subjects of the tsar and the Russian nation. This included conscription into the Russian army to help in defence of the empire. This vigorous *Russification* policy was supported by

KEY ISSUE

Supporters of a Russification policy.

1 bureaucrats drawn from noble landowning families, who believed in order and uniformity
2 soldiers who were concerned with security issues particularly on Russia's borders in the Baltic, Bessarabia and Transcaucasia
3 orthodox priests, especially the Procurator of the Holy Synod, Konstantin Pobedonostsev, out of a sense of religious intolerance.

Policies were pursued which reflected growth in an increasingly aggressive national consciousness re-enforced by a more reactionary brand of Slavophilism (see page 15). These included attempts at complete unification of Western lands and the Trans-Caucasus (1860s), the Baltic provinces (1880s) and Finland (1890s) as well as the attack on the privileged status of Baltic Germans (since 1890s). A number of factors help to explain this shift in policy:

A *Factors promoting a more vigorous Russification policy*

1 The Polish revolts of 1830 and 1863 led Alexander III and his advisers to become disillusioned with the earlier liberal policy based on peaceful integration. They concluded that only a firm approach with the nationalities could guarantee survival of a united state. Some historians have described this attitude as the 'Polish syndrome'; a fear that liberal policies would lead to revolt and belief that repression would bring peace.
2 The widespread emergence of national liberation movements, which gained momentum in the 1860s with the emergence of national liberation movements in different parts of the Russian Empire. These emerged at different times reflecting the different 'age' or maturity of the country concerned. The Russian government's hope that it could halt the development of nationalist movements by taking a firm line had mixed results. They succeeded in slowing down nationalist movements amongst young nations between 1864 and 1905. However, among the Finns, Poles,

Lithuanians and Armenians as well as of Muslims on the Middle Volga, *Russification* policies acted as a stimulus to revolutionary movement that demanded independence. Non-Russians played a role disproportionate to their numbers, for example Latvians were 7.45 times more active than Russians, as shown in the following table:

TABLE 18
Nationality of exiled revolutionaries in 1907–17

Nationality	% Among the exiled	% Among the population	Ratio of % among the exiled to % among the population
Russians	43.5	43.5	I
Poles	17.6	6.2	2.84
Jews	15.8	3.9	4.05
Latvians	8.2	1.1	7.45
Ukrainians	4.2	12.5	0.34
Georgians	2.3	1.1	2.09
Armenians	1.9	0.9	2.11
Estonians	0.6	0.8	0.75
Byelorussians	0.4	4.6	0.09
Lithuanians	0.2	1.3	0.15
Others	5.4	0.2	0.22

Q

Identify (i) the most and (ii) the least active of revolutionaries.

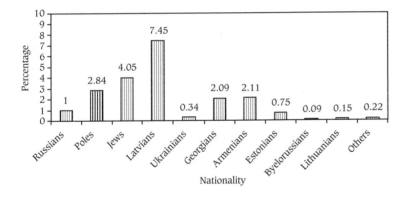

DIAGRAM 9

B *Russia's treatment of her Jewish population*

By the start of Alexander III's reign there were 5 million Jews who were confined to the area known as the Pale which consisted of Lithuania, Poland, the southwestern provinces including the Ukraine and White Russia. Their position had always been uneasy and they were subject to repeated persecution and violence as a result of the widespread resentment of their commercial and financial activities and position as moneylenders. There had been some relaxation during Alexander II's liberal phase but this had been short-lived. He had allowed certain groups – wealthy Jews, who paid more than a 1000 roubles in tax each year, university graduates and skilled craftsmen – to settle anywhere in the Empire, but this moderate policy was reversed after the 1863 Polish revolt. They were considered by some to have been responsible for the revolt and anti-Semitic literature appeared, some of which was state financed. Hostility against the Jews increased in the 1870s:

- Jewish schools were closed
- restrictions were placed on the civil rights of Jews in the revision of town government in 1870. They were disbarred from holding office as mayor and membership on town councils was restricted to a third of the total.

The presence of Jews amongst revolutionary and nationalist groups in non-Russian parts of the Empire, along with the claim that they had been involved in the assassination of Alexander II, sealed their fate. Alexander III sanctioned a policy of savage persecution that continued under Nicholas II to 1917:

1   A series of pogroms broke out affecting 12 cities in 1881 and continued in another four cities in 1883. These were organised by the influential Holy League, an extreme nationalist and anti-Semitic organisation that had the support of Pobedonostsev and other high-ranking government officials. Activities took the form of armed gangs of men breaking into shops and houses in the Jewish parts of towns burning and looting property as well as beating, raping and killing anyone they encountered. It was claimed that these pogroms were the 'spontaneous demonstration of an outraged people' but in fact the men who took part had been well prepared. They had been indoctrinated with anti-Semitic propaganda, were often amply supplied with alcohol and were transported into the affected areas by train. Local authorities rarely took action against them since they had the protection of the Ministry of the Interior. Alexander III was persuaded by his advisers that the Jews were 'social parasites, demoralising every community into which they penetrated – a species of human vermin whom every government should seek to destroy for the general good' (Charles Lowe, *Alexander III of Russia*, Heinemann, 1895). However, Alexander III did not approve of the activities of the Holy League and it was banned in 1882.

2   The 'Provisional or Temporary Rules' were issued in 1882. These banned Jews from:
    - settling in rural areas, even inside the Pale, or from owning or managing land
    - holding any administrative office, or becoming a lawyer
    - running schools or printing books in Hebrew
    - marrying a Christian unless he gave up his religion
    - having the right of appeal against any court sentence.

KEY ISSUE

Main features of 'Provisional or Temporary Rules'

The Rules were intended to be temporary but lasted until 1917. Alexander believed that the Jews' condition was 'preordained by the Gospels' and that they deserved punishment because they had crucified Christ. Few in government challenged this persecution apart from the liberal Michael Reutern. A commission was set up in 1883 to examine the status and position of Jews in Russian society and to make recommendations to revise the laws governing their position. It advised that Russia's Jews should be treated as Russians and not foreigners, that 'the system of repressive and discriminating measures must give way to a graduated system of emancipatory and equalising laws'. Nothing came of these recommendations.

Anti-Semitism had become securely established in government and society, particularly in areas that had a large Jewish population, such as the Ukraine and Lithuania resulting in escalation of policies between 1887 and 1893:

- 1887: the *Numerus clausus* set down quotas for Jews attending university
- 1889: persons of 'non-Christian persuasion' could only practise law with the permission of the Minister of Justice but this was not granted in the 10 years following the decree
- 1890: saw the deportation of foreign Jews from Russia and of Russian Jews from outside the Pale
- 1891: Alexander II's law of 1865 that had allowed Jewish craftsmen to settle beyond the Pale was repealed resulting in 2000 being deported from Moscow
- 1892: Municipal reform restricted representation of Jews on town councils within the Pale to not more than 10% of membership
- 1894: Jews were banned from selling spirits which became a state monopoly. This had been one of the few remaining important sources of income.

They had some success – Jewish businesses that had set up in the rural areas had to be sold at low prices while in the towns there was some decline in their trade, and hence profits. Jews who had settled beyond the Pale were forced to leave. Pogroms became a regular feature of Russian life, especially under Nicholas II who had a deep-rooted hatred of Jews. They occurred on an ever widening scale in 1903, 1905, 1906 and 1907 and provoked criticism in Britain and the United States. An estimated 225 000 ruined Jewish families left Russia for western Europe or the United States and South America during Alexander III's reign, while 2 million fled between 1914 and 1917 when they were treated as spies during World War I. They took with them a deep hatred of tsardom that would influence other nations to condemn Russia.

Those Jews who remained in Russia contained a large number of the intelligentsia and they became increasingly attracted to socialist and revolutionary ideas. There were large numbers of Jews amongst the Populists in the 1870s, while in the 1880s and 1890s interest shifted to Marxist socialism with its ideas of class warfare and the inevitability of revolution that would lead to the overthrow of tsarism. The year 1897 saw the formation of the General Union of Jewish Workers in Russia and Poland, the *Bund*, which was to play an important role in the development of a social democratic movement. It encouraged strikes and demonstrations against Russian autocracy as well as promoting the

KEY ISSUE

Escalation of policies 1887–93.

KEY ISSUE

To what extent were the regime's antisemitic policies successful?

idea of revolution amongst the people during the last years of Romanov rule. Russian Jews also became supporters of the Zionist movement that promoted the development of a Jewish nationalist identity.

5 ⌐ ECONOMIC CHANGE AND ITS SOCIAL IMPLICATIONS

Another one of the lessons learnt from the Crimean War was the need to modernise not only society but also the economy if Russia was to compete as a great power on equal terms with the more advanced industrial economies of the west, particularly Britain and Germany. There was also the need for Russia to develop her own resources rather than rely on foreign imports. The continuing backwardness of agriculture also showed the need to develop alternative sources of wealth. The military motivation for industrialisation meant that the initiative was taken by the State rather than by private individuals.

A *Main factors promoting Russia's economic development*

Railways were significant in opening up the vast open spaces of Russia that could not be exploited by a suitable river or coastal navigation. They were used for colonising and for developing iron and coal industry in the Ukraine which became the major producer of iron. Railways made possible development of the oil-producing region of Baku on the Caspian Sea that was linked to the ports of the Black Sea. In its turn railway construction became an important customer of the iron and steel industries, accounting for 60% of total production by the 1890s. The cotton textile industry also benefited from the coming of the railways, both in terms of opening up new areas for the cultivation of raw cotton as well as finding new markets in Asia for the finished cotton goods. Apart from developing industry, they made possible more extensive cultivation of the Black Earth Zone and the steppe as well as extending Russian trade in the Far East. Some landowners became entrepreneurs, introducing hired labour, and modern farming techniques to expand production of wheat for the growing export markets of Odessa. These developments helped promote social change.

The need for a money economy had been fairly limited prior to the emancipation of the serfs. In a peasant based economy dealings took the form of services and payments in kind except in the case of the government which needed cash to pay for its growing military commitments. After the emancipation of the serfs in 1861 rural society was forced to develop a cash-based economy which led to social changes as relationships previously based on status and custom gave way to those based on contract and law.

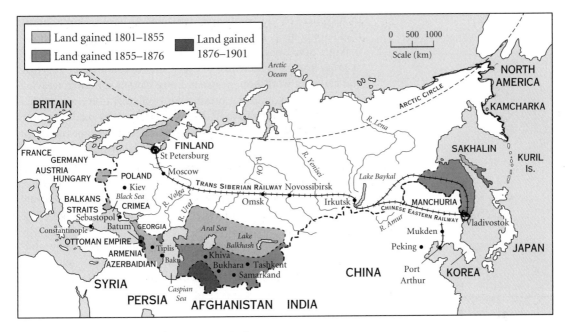

MAP 6 *Trans-Siberian and Chinese Eastern Railways*

B *Main features of Russia's industrial organisation prior to 1890s*

Prior to the 1890s and the intervention of Sergei Witte, the regime had no clear strategy for industrial development. There were three types of industrial enterprises:

1. State, 'proprietary' factories provided manufactures essential for national security, such as armaments and army clothing, saltpetre, gunfounding, and sailcloth, arms. Labour for these state-run factories was drawn from peasants on State and Crown lands, that were frequently attached to a factory for life and were sold with it, supplemented by prisoners of war, beggars, criminals, orphans and the wives of soldiers on service. Raw materials, such as wool, for the textile industries were obtained instead of taxes. The main problem in these state factories was the relatively low quality of the work carried out.

2. 'Estate' factories, were developed in the eighteenth century by some nobles on their estates who used the labour of their serfs. Nobles who had no factories would sell or hire out their manufacturing serfs for service elsewhere. On the emancipation of the serfs the freed workers gave up working in the nobles' factories which were either sold, or died out, but some survived in the cotton and distilling industries.

3. 'Domestic', '*kustar*' industries developed alongside the estate factories. Peasants taught the craft skills acquired in the estate factories

to members of the family who remained at home. Home industries sprang up as a winter occupation in weaving, spinning, boat-making. Some peasants formed co-operative associations, known as *artels,* for the production of every kind of manufactured article and started a workshop, *svietetka.* Every kind of spinning, weaving and metal work, and the production of almost every article that could be made out of wood, bone or leather, was made in those *svietetka.* Some of peasant families progressed to become merchant manufacturers and contributed to the development of a middle class.

4 Private enterprise existed in only one industry prior to 1850 – cotton. It developed in St Petersburg and the district around Moscow, attracted by the availability of the rivers Oka and Volga that connected the district with the south and east while the forest region to the North provided both fuel and labour. The river Volga carried supplies of raw cotton from the Levant and Persia and when wood became scarce it carried naphtha oil.

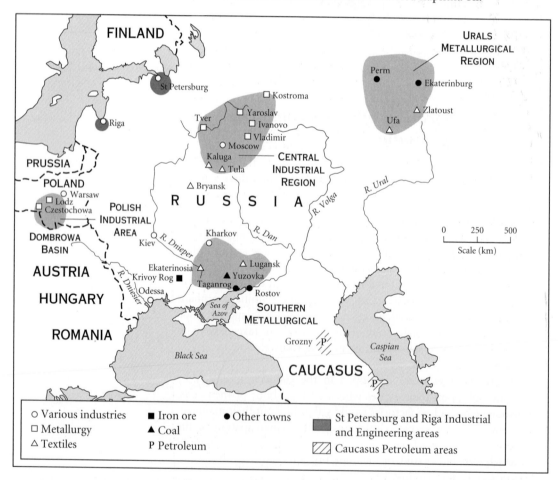

MAP 7 *Russia's economic development*

By 1860 there were 800 000 peasants engaged in domestic industry and 860 000 in factories. Both these areas of employment expanded by 1913 at the same rate of 275% to three million respectively.

C *Contribution of Sergei Witte to Russia's industrialisation*

Sergei Witte, the minister responsible for Russia's drive towards modernisation in the 1890s, was a representative of the new breed of businessmen that were appearing in Russia in the closing years of the nineteenth century.

SERGEI YULYEVICH WITTE (1849–1915)

Born in Tiflis, the capital of Georgia in 1849, he was the son of a German or Dutch father while his mother was the daughter of a governor whose family was well known Pan-Slavists. He spent his early years in the Caucasus in the environment of minor provincial nobility. He graduated from Odessa University with a degree in Mathematics and entered government office in the service of the Governor-General in 1871 working for the Odessa Railway until 1877. When the company was sold to private business he remained as manager and made friends with leading capitalists including some who were Jewish. He became famous in 1883 with the publication of his book on railway tariffs that established his reputation as an expert on railway administration. This led to him being offered in 1889 responsibility for developing a new railway department within the Ministry of Finance. He established a reputation as an able and competent administrator and in 1892 was promoted to be Minister of Communications and then six months later, Minister of Finance 1892–1903. He subsequently became chairman of the Committee of Ministers 1903–6 and was one of the few ministers who had the power to partly choose his own cabinet.

Witte was, according to Hugh Seton-Watson, 'One of the outstanding statesmen of the nineteenth century, a brilliant organiser and a man of broad ideas'. He was in many respects an outsider in terms of his social background, his career in business and railway administration, and his marriage to a Jewish divorcee. Inevitably he had critics amongst the aristocracy some of whom played a role in his dismissal in 1903. There was a certain contradiction in his political thinking. He was a firm supporter of autocracy and admired Alexander III, but he also recognised the urgent need of Russia to modernise. He eventually abandoned his opposition to Parliamentary democracy and in 1905 supported the movement for political and constitutional reform that he saw as the complement to his economic modernisation. Witte was made the first Prime Minister in 1905 and succeeded in floating a loan of £80 million in Britain and France, which freed Nicholas II from dependence on the Duma. He lost Nicholas's favour and was replaced by a reactionary. He never held office again and was an opponent of the 1914 War.

Witte gained the support and loyalty of Alexander III, as evidenced by his rapid promotion in 1892. His great financial skill succeeded in keeping the tsars from bankruptcy, especially by borrowing money from France, a policy that gave his critics the opportunity to accuse him of being too subservient to foreign capitalists. He was a faithful supporter of tsarism and had a good working relationship with Alexander III. This was based on Witte's admiration of Alexander for having secured a peaceful period for Russia and Alexander III's willingness to delegate authority to Witte. The latter's admiration for Alexander III is clearly shown in Witte's Memoirs in which he described Alexander as a tsar who was above 'all selfish interests that prevail among ordinary mortals, above all the egotistical and material interests that so often corrupt the human heart. (He) recognised that Russia could be made great only when it ceased being an exclusively agricultural country. A country without strongly developed industry could not be great.' There was also a personal motive for Witte's support of the regime. In the view of Theodore H. Von Laue, 'what perhaps endeared autocracy most to Witte at least in the reign of Alexander III was that under its firm protection a man could do a good job. Witte was an autocrat in his own right. Autocracy … favoured men of his type. What he wanted was a secure position from which to direct the affairs entrusted to him. Under Alexander Ill, the last Romanov who made his will felt throughout the government, he could do his job with the efficiency that comes from the possession of a delegated share of absolute power' (Theodore H. von Laue, *Sergei Witte and the Industrialisation of Russia*, Colombia University Press, 1974).

KEY ISSUE

Witte's policies.

He argued that if Russia did not modernise and become an industrialised country she would run the risk of becoming a colony as had occurred in the case of the Chinese Empire. He believed that the State should provide the means – transport, markets, money, to achieve industrial growth, but that private businessmen would take responsibility to develop industries and trade.

1 Home industries were protected against foreign competition by high import duties imposed in 1887 and again in 1891. The metal industry benefited most, as did the Moscow textile industry whereas textile producers in St Petersburg found that they had to pay more for their supplies of raw cotton by sea. Higher tariffs also increased government revenue.
2 Foreign investors, especially French and Belgian, were encouraged to invest in Russian industry.

3 A new rouble was introduced in 1897 linked to the gold standard in the hope of increasing investors' confidence. The rouble's value was fixed against other countries' currencies and was made freely convertible to gold in the hope that this would produce a more stable rouble and end the wild fluctuations of previous years.

4 Indirect taxes were raised to achieve a reserve of gold.

5 Railways, financed by foreign capital, were constructed to provide easier access to raw materials and to markets for finished goods. Witte's greatest achievement was the Trans-Siberian Railway and the Chinese Eastern Railway through northern Manchuria. The Trans-Siberian Railway, started in 1892, and completed as a single track by 1904, connected Moscow with Vladivostok on the Pacific. This was a massive undertaking covering a distance of 6000 km and had important economic and strategic advantages. It led to the economic development of western Siberia and a government sponsored plan for encouraging peasant migration from the over-populated European Russia. Siberia proved attractive to the more enterprising peasants; it had never experienced serfdom and government control was less repressive. Under State encouragement it became an important supplier of grain, meat, butter for the markets of Moscow and St Petersburg as well as for England and Germany. In the eastern half the railway was used to transport troops and supplies to support Russia's Empire in the Far East.

See Map 6 on page 79.

Effects of Witte's policies

1 There was increased foreign investment rising from 26% in 1890 to 41% by 1915, but this was achieved at the cost of mortgaging revenue. By 1900, 20% of the budget was used to service the foreign debt, ten times as much as was spent on education. The number of foreign companies rose from 16 in 1888 to 269 in 1900. Witte's critics attacked him for over-dependence on foreign investment and loans.

2 Railways stimulated exports and foreign trade as a result of the lowering of transport costs. Russia's main customers were Germany, Britain and the Netherlands while China supplied tea and the United States raw cotton. The expansion of the railways also contributed to government revenue in terms of income earned from freight charges and passenger fares.

Year	Imports	Exports	Balance
1880	622.8	498.7	–
1890	406.6	692	+
1900	626	716	+

TABLE 19

The Russian balance of trade 1880–1900 (in millions of roubles)

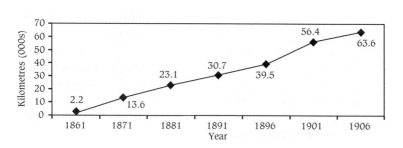

DIAGRAM 10

Expansion in railway track construction 1861–1906

Year	St Petersburg	Moscow
1881	928 000	753 500
1890	1 033 600	1 038 600
1897	1 264 700	1 174 000
1900	1 439 600	1 345 000
1910	1 905 600	1 617 700
1914	2 217 500	1 762 700

TABLE 20

Growth of population in Russia's two main cities 1881–1914

Year	Coal	Pig iron	Oil	Grain
1860	0.29	0.31	–	–
1870	0.68	0.33	0.03	–
1880	3.24	0.42	0.5	34
1890	5.9	0.89	3.9	36
1900	16.1	2.66	10.2	56
1910	26.8	2.99	9.4	74

TABLE 21

The tsarist economy: annual production (million tons)

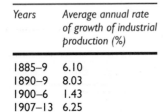

Years	Average annual rate of growth of industrial production (%)
1885–9	6.10
1890–9	8.03
1900–6	1.43
1907–13	6.25

TABLE 22

Rates of industrial growth, 1885–1913

3 Existing industries expanded and new ones developed. Coal, iron and oil industries developed rapidly, especially in the Ukraine, a centre of heavy metallurgical industry. The Caucasus region grew with development of its oil wells in Azerbaijan and manganese deposits in Georgia. Textiles continued to expand and to be the biggest industry in terms of its workforce, though there were changes in the relative significance of production areas. St Petersburg declined in relation to Moscow and Poland. A Russian engineering industry developed in St Petersburg along with centres in Moscow, the Baltic provinces and some centres in the south, to build the engines and wagons required by the railway industry.

4 Russia's average annual growth rate was higher than that of any other industrial country by the 1890s; (though this percentage was distorted by the fact that growth was from a lower base). Between 1894 and 1913, European Russia's national income grew by 50% which was comparable with France's 52%, Germany 58% but lower than that of Britain (70%) and Austria's 79%.

5 Industrialisation encouraged increased co-operation both between industrialists and between industrialists and the government.

6 Industrial production in all industries, apart from sugar factories and vodka distilleries, became more concentrated in larger factories. Domestic, *kustar* industries survived and continued to grow.

7 Witte's policies encouraged a further merging of rural and urban lifestyles. Increasingly peasants between the ages of 20 and 40 worked outside the village and then retired to their allotment of land and families.

8 Witte's industrialisation led to great social strains:
   ● the increase in import duties and indirect taxes in the 1890s reduced still further the already low standards of living suffered by the masses following a famine in 1891. The latter, caused by drought and crop failures, was the worst of the nineteenth century and resulted in the deaths of nearly half a million peasants from hunger between 1891 and 1892.

- Witte's policies added to people's suffering, a fact that provided ammunition for his enemies to attack his policies. Although a law of 1897 shortened hours of work, conditions remained unhealthy and dangerous.
- Workers in factory and mining industries were protected by an inspectorate and in some cases medical care but they still had a miserable existence.
- The Russian factory order was brutal: the foreman had the power to pay, punish, discipline and sack his workers. The latter bitterly resented their low pay and working conditions.
- Although housing conditions varied between regions they tended to be universally bad. Workers were crowded together in wooden barracks with little ventilation or light, and with anywhere from two to seven families crowded together in family. Workers lived in one room which was divided into several cubicles separated from each other by boards. There was little privacy and people lived surrounded by noise and filth, but the increasing demand for living space as new peasant families moved into the towns forced up rents. These urban poor had little sense of belonging and proved to be easily responsive to the ideas of revolutionaries in Nicholas II's reign. They were joined by thousands of unskilled, casually employed or unemployed people who also flocked to the towns.
- Accidents were frequent in the metallurgical factories as indicated in Table 23.

Year	Deaths	Injuries
1890	245	3 508
1904	556	66 680

TABLE 23

Witte was very aware of these hardships but gambled that industrialisation would eventually lead to improved living standards before workers and peasants found them impossible to accept any more. He failed in the face of severe famine in the central Volga area 1898–9 and an industrial slump in 1899. Events were set in motion that led to the 1905 Russian Revolution.

See page 133.

6 ∽ THE END OF ALEXANDER III'S REGIME

Alexander III's failure to leave his son a secure inheritance was the inevitable consequence of the policies of the regime. Although he had kept peace it was at the expense of building up resentment amongst the masses and the growing class of intelligentsia. Critics of the regime had been forced to flee abroad and they swore revenge on the tsarist regime.

7 ∽ BIBLIOGRAPHY

A bibliography for Imperial Russia appears at the end of Chapter 4 on page 120.

8 ⌒ STRUCTURED AND ESSAY QUESTIONS

A *This section consists of questions that might be used for discussion or written answers as a way of expanding on the chapter and testing understanding of it.*

1. (a) What were Witte's main aims for the Russian economy?
    (b) How successful were Witte's modernisation policies for the Russian economy?
2. (a) Why did Russia embark on a programme of industrialisation in the 1890s?
    (b) How successful was the programme of industrialisation of Russia?
3. (a) What is meant by 'Russification'?
    (b) To what extent did the policy benefit Alexander III's regime?
4. (a) What political problems did Alexander III inherit?
    (b) How successfully did Alexander III solve these problems?

B *Essay questions.*

1. To what extent does Alexander II deserve the title 'Tsar Persecutor'?
2. To what extent was Russian industrialisation a triumph for the economy but a disaster for tsarism?
3. To what extent does Alexander III deserve the title 'Tsar Peacekeeper'?

9 ⌒ MAKING NOTES

Read the advice section about making notes on page ix of Preface: How to use this book, and then make your own notes based on the following headings and questions.

A *Alexander III's personality and attitude as tsar*

1. What was his attitude towards his role as tsar?
2. What were his strengths and weaknesses as tsar?

B *Alexander III's main policies of reaction and repression*

1. What were the main features of repression in government, internal security, justice and education?
2. What was the effect of Alexander III's policies of counter-reform?

C *Alexander III's main policies of reform*

1. What were the details of Alexander III's social and economic reforms?
2. What was the effect of these reforms?

D *Policy of Russification*

1. Identify those individuals and groups who supported a *Russification* policy.
2. What were the main factors leading to a more aggressive *Russification* policy?
3. What were the main features of *Russification*?

E *Russia's industrialisation programme*
1. What were the factors promoting economic development?
2. Briefly explain the contribution of each of the following to Russia's industrial development: (a) state, proprietary industry; (b) estate industries; and (c) '*kustar*'.
3. What were the reasons for the 'great spurt'?
4. What were the details of Witte's policies?
5. What were the effects of industrialisation on (a) the economy and (b) the masses and social life?

10 ⌐ AN AS EXAM-TYPE EXERCISE

Study the collection of sources relating to the economic growth of Russia from 1880 to 1900 and then answer the questions, which follow.

Date	Coal	Pig iron	Oil	Grain
1880	3.2	0.42	0.5	34
1890	5.9	0.89	3.9	36
1900	16.1	2.66	102	56

SOURCE A
Figures in the table show changes in industrial production in Russia (in millions of tonnes).

It was in the 1880s that the government changed its initial attitude of hostility to industrialisation. Industrial development, slightly stimulated by emancipation and, far more so, by the growth of the railways, was already occurring, but it was the government's commitment to that process which helps explain the big upsurge.

SOURCE B
From John Hite, Tsarist Russia 1801–1917, *Causeway Press, 1989.*

The Tsarist government's motives were military rather than economic. It is true that the capitalists (financiers and factory owners) did well out of the industrialisation, but it was not the government's intention to create a new capitalist class. The Tsar and his ministers viewed industrialisation as a means of improving the military might of the Russian Empire.

SOURCE C
From Michael Lynch, Reaction and Revolutions: Russia 1881–1924, *Hodder & Stoughton, 1992.*

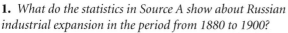

1. *What do the statistics in Source A show about Russian industrial expansion in the period from 1880 to 1900?*
2. *How does the statistical evidence of Source A support the view expressed in Source B of Russian economic growth after 1880?*
3. *Using the evidence of the sources and your own knowledge, what role was played by the State in the transformation of the Russian economy between 1881 and 1900?*

4

Nicholas II – the last years of the autocracy 1894–1905

NICHOLAS ALEXANDROVICH, 1868–1918, EMPEROR OF ALL RUSSIA 1894–1917

Nicholas II has tended to be viewed as a man with a tragic fate; the last representative of a dynasty whose collapse he did much to bring about. Whereas his father had kept Russia free from war, his son was less careful. Within ten years of his accession he had involved the country in an ill-advised attempt at expansion into the Far East that led to war against Japan resulting in total humiliation. The event precipitated revolution in Russia and the demand for liberal constitutional reform. Instead of learning from the experiences of 1904–5 Nicholas subsequently involved Russia in World War I that broke out in 1914. Yet again Russia suffered humiliating defeat against Germany and its allies in 1914–17, ending in a second revolution and the murder of himself and his whole family in the summer of 1918. The latter event could have been avoided if Britain had been prepared to grant political asylum.

1 ⌐ NICHOLAS II AND HIS SUITABILITY FOR TSARDOM

A *Nicholas II's personality and training*

At just over 1.67 metres in height. Nicholas II has been described by his critics as small in body as well as in mind. He did not possess the 'commanding character proper in a ruler'. He was naturally reserved and sensitive and possessed great personal charm though this was associated by his enemies with weakness and indecision. He hated unpleasant disagreements and was known by some contemporaries as 'Nicholas the Pacific'. He often kept his own views to himself rather than become involved in an argument even to the point of agreeing to a course of action that he had no intention of following. His tutor, Pobedonostsev, considered Nicholas impatient with 'general problems' and capable of evaluating 'the impor-

PICTURE 6 *The Russian Imperial family, 1914.* Seated left to right: Grand Duchess Olga, Tsar Nicholas II, Grand Duchess Anastasia; The Tsarevich Grand Duke Alexis; Grand Duchess Tatiana. Standing Grand Duchess Marie; Empress Alexandra

tance of a fact only in isolation, without relation to the rest, without any link to the total of other facts, events, tendencies'. For his part Nicholas admitted that he found 'it difficult to focus his mind'. These characteristics earned Nicholas the reputation of being a weakling and not very intelligent. However, he could be obstinate when he had decided on a course of action.

B *Nicholas II's attitude as tsar*

Nicholas II shared many of the views of his father and tutor Pobedonostsev. The latter was credited with having taught Nicholas to 'fear any innovation'. He started his reign with the firm intention of strictly following his father's policies rather than pursuing a particular policy programme of his own apart from support for the principles of expansion of Russian influence in the Far and Middle East and a refusal to retreat. He believed that he had a divine right to rule and a religious obligation to preserve the autocracy. He considered it his duty to pass on to his son the authority he had inherited from his father. He believed that the existing system was essential to the general welfare. He rejected the principles of popular representation and even the idea of a united government. He was not even prepared to call the Council of Ministers, preferring to receive his ministers' reports face to face in private to prevent any possibility of them uniting against him. He ignored the sound advice of his ministers and when he intervened in the running of the country he usually made things more difficult. He was opposed to making changes on the grounds that tsars had always had 'unity and trust'. Even though he was forced to make concessions for representative government in 1904 under the threat of revolution he subsequently cancelled this when he believed the danger to have passed. It was his failure to keep his promises that contributed to his downfall.

2 ⌁ NICHOLAS II AND HIS MINISTERS

A *Appointment of ministers and advisers*

During the early part of his reign Nicholas II continued with some of the Chief ministers and officials of his father's reign and their policies. Almost all the existing ministers remained in their posts. Konstantin Pobedonostsev, Procurator-General of the Holy Synod, continued to exercise great influence during the first part of the reign till 1905 while Sergei Witte remained Minister of Finance until he was dismissed in 1903 as a result of a political difference. The most able minister to hold the post of Minister of the Interior and Chairman of the Council of Ministers between 1906 and 1911 was Petr Arladievich Stolypin who was concerned to preserve the position of the tsar against the many challenges to autocracy.

PETR ARLADIEVICH STOLYPIN (1862–1911)

He was a landowner who spent his early years in provincial government as Governor of Grodno and then of Saratov, on the Volga. The latter was the scene of some of the worst peasant disturbances in 1905 and Stolypin took a harsh line against peasants and workers. It was his action in 1905 that brought him to the attention of Nicholas II who made him Minster of the Interior and Chairman of the Council of Ministers in 1906. He was a complex, controversial figure whose role in the history of Nicholas' reign has been the subject of some debate amongst historians. Some have seen his policies between 1906 and 1911 as the beginnings of change which had it continued might have saved the regime from revolution and collapse. Leonard Shapiro (*Russian Studies*, Collins Harvill, 1968) has commented that

> no other figure in the modern history of Russia has aroused so much controversy. By the left, he is generally dismissed as a savage butcher who hanged peasants and workers ... To the extreme right he became a hateful figure, whose policy of reform and attempt to work with the *Duma* or parliament were a threat to the principles of autocracy ...
>
> For his many admirers he has posthumously become the wisest statesman that Russia ever had, who could, had he been given time, have saved Russia from war and revolution, and have effected a peaceful transformation of the country on moderate and modern lines.

The moderate left hated Stolypin as the man who dissolved the first two attempts at representational government, the *Duma* and changed the electoral law. He also faced strong opposition from the upper ranks of the bureaucracy, and the majority of the Emperor's inner circle. He survived the hostility of his enemies only so long as he had Nicholas' support and protection. The latter was prepared to provide this while he felt that his interests were being served but by the time of Stolypin's assassination on 1 September 1911, during celebrations to mark the unveiling of a monument to Alexander II, the inevitability of his dismissal was being debated.

In some respects hostility from the left and revolutionaries was unfair for Stolypin showed genuine concern for the condition of the peasants. In many respects he was a counterpart to Witte for he was concerned with the development of agriculture. He was a political conservative and a nationalist whose attitude can best be summed up as suppression first and then reform. He wanted to derevolutionise the peasantry by removing some of their more glaring grievances and creating a system of private peasant ownership. He believed that his programme would take 20 years but in fact he had only five years before an assassin's bullet killed him during a performance of the Kiev Opera. Given the conservatism of the Russian peasant it is doubtful whether his agricultural policy would have succeeded.

B *Changes in the structure of the ruling elite*

Class	Size 1850		Size 1900		Increase (%)
	000s	*%*	*000s*	*%*	
Nobility	1000	71	1800	55	+80
Officials	114	8	500	15	+339
Intelligentsia	50	4	400	12	+700
Merchant/ 'Bourgeoisie'	246	17	600	18	+144
Total	c. 1410	100	c. 3300	100	+134

TABLE 24 *Changes in the structure of the ruling group, 1850–1900*

The changes were observed by P.N. Milyukov in 1903 (quoted by T. Riha, *Readings in Russian Civilisation*, University of Chicago, 1964).

What must be mentioned first is the enormous growth of the politically conscious social elements that make public opinion in Russia. The gentry still play a part among these elements, but are by far not the only social medium of public opinion, as they were before the emancipation of the peasants. Members of the ancient gentry are now found in all branches of public life: in the press, in public instruction, in the liberal professions, not to speak of the state service, and particularly the local self-government. But it would be impossible to say what is now the class opinion of the gentry. The fact is that the gentry are no longer a class; they are too much intermingled with other social elements in every position they occupy, including that of landed proprietors.

Q

Identify the social group that saw a relative decline.

Identify the group that saw the largest change.

What were the potential dangers for Nicholas arising from the increased number of intelligentsia?

Q

What had happened to the nobility by 1900?

What was the effect of this change on the role they played in government?

The merchants, intelligentsia and officials who were now part of the ruling elite made new demands on the regime to consider their interests.

C *Instability in government*

See pages 113–15.

Nicholas' failure to have a particular domestic policy programme created disorganisation in the functioning of government. The political climate was changing under the impact of mounting social pressures and the activities of different revolutionary groups. Divisions appeared over tactics and policy to deal with the challenge to autocracy. Rivalry and differences developed within government on such issues as government response to meet the rising level of strikes and public disturbances. Witte favoured the traditional Tsarist policy of repression employing more policemen and calling in the army to suppress disturbances. The Ministry of the Interior responsible for domestic security supported the policy advocated by the head of the Moscow Security Police, General Sergei Zubatov of 'divide and rule' to win over the workers even if this meant allowing trade unions to operate under police control.

The increasing troubles of the reign were reflected in the rapid change of ministers during 1894–1917:

TABLE 25
Ministerial changes 1894–1917

2	Chairmen of the Committee of Ministers (office abolished 1905)
8	Chairmen of the Council of Ministers
15	Ministers of the Interior
7	Ministers of Justice
8	Ministers of War
7	Naval Ministers
9	Procurators of the Holy Synod
11	Ministers of Education
6	Ministers of Finance

D *The role of the tsarina, Alexandra Feodorovna*

There has been some debate as to whether Alexandra took an active part in dealing with state matters from the very beginning of the reign or whether it was later after she had completed ten years of numerous pregnancies. She shared Nicholas' belief that it was his sacred duty to preserve the autocracy. Alexandra was well educated and intelligent but she lacked social skills, tact and good health. She did not get on with her mother-in-law who had precedence as the Dowager Empress and Alexandra was initially isolated at court until she had learnt Russian. She was aware of her unpopularity both at court and amongst the people. Cold and remote, she was inclined to live in a world of her own and made few friends. She was ambitious for her husband and was suspicious of any attempts by the 40 relatives who made up the royal family to encroach on Tsarist absolutism. Inevitably she made mistakes and more importantly enemies. She acted as an advisor even on issues outside her interests and convinced Nicholas' that he must assert himself as tsar 'by the grace of God' and 'father to his people'. She influenced his decisions and actions in governing the state and when difficulties arose she pressed him to be firm, forceful and make no concessions to the forces of liberalism or democracy. Her influence was not always in Nicholas' best interest. This was particularly evident during the war years when he insisted on taking the post of supreme commander-in-chief accompanying the Russian army to the battlefront even though 'his overall spiritual make-up was least suited for that of supreme military commander'. Sharing a belief in Divine guidance they put their faith in mystics or holy men who promised that they could cure the young Tsarevich Alexis, who suffered from **haemophilia**. The most notorious to gain ascendancy was Grigory Rasputin, a Siberian peasant who arrived at court in October 1906.

haemophilia is a condition that stops the blood from clotting causing excessive bleeding or internal haemorrhaging when the sufferer is cut or receives a heavy blow.

E *The role of Grigory Efimovich Rasputin*

Born in 1869 at Pokrovskoye, a village in the foothills of the Ural Mountains, he grew up to be an 'aggressive, drunken and smooth lecher'. He had appeared before the courts on several occasions accused of horse stealing and drunken behaviour. He abandoned his wife and children and travelled over 2000 miles to the Verhoturye Monastery in Greece to escape the anger of his fellow villagers. Here he is credited with having experienced a spiritual awakening leading to his decision to give up drinking, smoking, eating meat and womanising. He learnt to read Church Slavonic.

On his return to Russia, he became a self-styled monk priest who travelled the country preaching, visiting holy places, and claiming to have great powers to heal and make predictions. He is credited with having had near hypnotic fascination for all those with whom he came into contact in spite of his 'obscene personal habits, dirty beard and foul body smell'. He had excessive energy, indulging in drunken orgies and loose living and becoming involved in scandalous scenes in public that made him a national scandal. His closeness to the Imperial family provided a weapon to the political opponents of the Tsar. Stolypin had attempted to warn Nicholas of the irreparable damage Rasputin was inflicting on the reputation and prestige of the Imperial family. Nicholas is reported as having replied, 'I know and believe, Petr Arladievich, that you are sincerely devoted to me. Perhaps everything you are telling me is the truth, but I ask you never to speak to me again about Rasputin'. All of Rasputin's defects were ignored by Alexandra who regarded him as a *starets*, a man of God who had the power to hypnotise the Tsarevich to stop his bleeding and keep her son alive. In 1912, Alexis had a severe internal haemorrhage and appeared to be on the point of death. He was given the last rites and Rasputin was sent for. Within two days of his arrival the young Tsarevich improved and recovered within a year. His position was assured and Alexandra defended him against his critics even those within the royal family. He was the only person close to the tsar's family who was capable of calming and restraining her nervousness. Wild rumours circulated of his power and relationship with the tsarina (see Picture 8 and Case study) and these gave added power to revolutionaries who worked to undermine respect for autocratic power among the people. It was claimed that he had the power to appoint and

PICTURE 7
Grigory Rasputin, Radio Times Hulton Picture Library

dismiss ministers and other high officials. In fact his power to influence appointments was probably greatly exaggerated. His significance lay in the damage done to the image and reputation of the Imperial family as his presence at the royal court developed from a private scandal into a major political issue. He was a divisive influence at court. He was a firm believer in monarchy and hostile to the representative assembly, the *Duma,* that was imposed on Nicholas in 1905. He urged her to encourage her husband to enforce strict autocratic rule at a time when concessions were required. His influence at court was strongest after 1915 when the tsarina headed the 'Rasputin Party' and he was partly responsible for making some of the poor appointments. Set against this group were leading members of the royal family and government. Stolypin fell from power for urging an investigation into Rasputin's conduct and a respected theologian, Bishop Hermogen of Saratov, a member of the Holy Synod, was exiled for his criticism of the favourite. The Russian nobility were particular critics since they felt that their traditional role as advisers to the monarchy was being by-passed. The problem of Rasputin was eventually solved by his death at the hands of a small group of conspirators. It included Yusupov, a homosexual and a member of the Imperial court, who had been introduced to Rasputin by his father in the hope that he could be 'cured', and also Purishkevich, a politician of the extreme right and Grand Duke Dmitri Pavlovich.

F *Case study – personal relationships at the Russian court*

(a) *Diary entry for Sunday 29 August 1915*
For the first time the press has attacked Rasputin. Hitherto the censorship and the police had protected him against newspaper criticism. It is the *Boursse Gazette,* which has opened the campaign.

(b) *Diary entry for Friday 27 August 1915*
In spite of the strict secrecy enjoined by the Emperor, his decision to take command of the army has already leaked out among the public.

The news has produced a deplorable impression. It is objected that the Emperor has no strategic experience, he will be directly responsible for defeats the danger of which is only too obvious, and lastly he has the 'evil eye'.

(c) *Diary entry for Tuesday 12 October 1915*
Has Rasputin the same power over the Emperor as over the Empress? No, there is a material difference. As regards relations between Alexandra Feodorovna and the Staretz (Rasputin), she lives in a kind of hypnosis. Whatever opinion or desire he expresses she acquiesces and obeys at once. In the case of the Tsar the fascination is much less passive and complete. He certainly thinks Grigory is a ... Man of God but to a large extent he retains his liberty of judgement in dealing with him, and he never allows him the initiative. This comparative independence of mind is particularly marked when the Staretz intervenes in a political matter ...

SOURCE A
From Maurice Paléologue, An Ambassador's Memoirs, *vol. II.*

In the rear, the political situation was getting more and more critical. The summoning of the Duma had been postponed and postponed; the aged Premier, Goremykin, was afraid to meet it and as one now knows it was for this reason, and by the wish of the Empress, that he was displaced (February 1916). It was she who chose his successor directly on the recommendations of Rasputin.

I was bound for General Mishchenko who was in charge of an extensive section of the lines in the marshes ... There was a considerable staff and when I arrived they were just expecting back an ADC whom Mishchenko had sent to Petrograd to find out why all the supplies were going wrong. The officer returned during my visit; his account was very simple; everything was now in the hands of Rasputin who was the tool of every kind of profiteer. The rear was by now putrefying fast.

SOURCE B *From Bernard Pares, My Russian Memoirs, 1931.*

Extracts from *Letters from Alexandra to the tsar, Nicholas*

1915

No hearken unto our Friend (Rasputin). He has your interest at heart – it is not for nothing that God sent him to us – only we must pay attention to what he says ...

Forgive me but I do not like the choice of the Minister of War (General Polivanov) ... is he not our friend's enemy, as that brings bad luck ... He regrets you did not speak to him more about all you think and were intending to do and speak about with your Ministers and the changes you were thinking of making ...

Now, before I forget, I must give you a message from our Friend, prompted by what he saw in the night. He begs you to order that one should advance nearer Riga, says it is necessary otherwise the Germans will settle down so firmly for the winter that it will cost bloodshed and trouble to make them move ...

I always remember what our friend says and how often we do not enough heed his words ... When he says not to do a thing and one does not listen one sees one's faults always afterwards

9 November 1916

Our Friend says that Sturmer can remain still some time as President of the Council of Ministers as that one does not reproach him so much, but all the row began since he became Minister of Foreign Affairs which Grigory realised in summer and told him then already that this will be your end.

SOURCE C *From A.F. Kerensky, The Road to Tragedy, Hutchinson, 1935.*

SOURCE D *Two images of Grigory Rasputin, 1869–1916.* **PICTURE 8** *(Left)* *The Tsar and Tsarina in the Clutches of the Evil Monk,* Ullstein Bilderdienst. **PICTURE 9** *(Right) Nicolas, Rasputin and Alexandra,* David King Collection).*

SOURCE E
Richard Charques, The Twilight of Imperial Russia, *Oxford University Press, 1958.*

A determining psychological factor in what followed was the religiosity of the Empress. It was the increasingly superstitious religiosity of an ailing and neurotic woman. Before she had given birth to a son and heir in the summer of 1904 Rasputin had had a predecessor of sorts, himself the latest in a line of miracle workers, in a French-born mystico-medical quack named Philippe. Now after the birth of a son and heir who suffered from the incurable disease of haemophilia, the empress, her health worsening was racked by anxiety for his life. Awkward and unhappy in public and resentful of her lack of popularity, she saw scarcely anyone outside her family or the narrowest court circle. From the first she discovered in Rasputin not only an inspired vessel of Orthodoxy but also the embodiment of peasant devotion to the crown. Next came the discovery, which is supported by apparently reliable evidence from several quarters, that he could stop the Tsarevich's bleedings when the doctors had failed. It was clear to her that Rasputin could be no other than an instrument of divine Providence. As such the doors of Tsarkoe Selo were open to him.

The correspondence between the Imperial couple, published after the revolution, shows that he placed great confidence in her judgement, and that she attached importance to the views of Rasputin. Whether it is right to conclude that in Nicholas's absence the empress managed, or mismanaged, the political leadership of the Empire, and that her choice of advisers was determined by Rasputin is perhaps more doubtful. The frequent references to 'Our Friend's' approval or disapproval of individuals may prove only that the empress consulted him, not necessarily that his preferences were accepted in all cases by the Tsar, still less that the political initiative came from Rasputin. Apologists for the last emperor maintain that he made up his own mind on the merits of every case, as he saw them, and argue that the legend of the power of Rasputin was created by his enemies, who deliberately exploited the minor misdeeds and discreditable character of the Siberian sectarian in order to smear the reputation of the Imperial family. The least that can be said is that the facts, which were known in 1915–1916, and the further facts which became known later, lend some plausibility to the theory of Rasputin's influence. At the time it was widely believed.

SOURCE F
Hugh Seton-Watson, The Russian Empire 1801–1917, *Oxford, 1967.*

Study Sources A, B and C

1. *What claims do two contemporaries, Paléologue and Pares, make that Rasputin had a powerful influence in Russian politics?*
2. *To what extent does Alexandra's correspondence with her husband, Nicholas, support the views expressed by the authors of Sources A and B?*
3. *What evidence is offered that Rasputin had powerful friends?*

Study Source D – Pictures 8 and 9

4. *What images have the two artists in Picture 8 adopted to emphasise relationships between Rasputin and the Tsar and Tsarina at the royal court?*
5. *What was likely to be the impact of the propaganda posters on the reputation of the Imperial monarchy?*
6. *How reliable are these posters for an historian studying attitudes towards the Tsarist regime in the early years of the twentieth century?*

Compare Sources A, B and C with the two posters in Source D

7. *To what extent does the evidence of Sources A, B and C support the claims made by the artists in the two propaganda posters in Source D (Pictures 8 and 9) with reference to the relationship between*
   a) *Rasputin and Alexandra?*
   b) *Rasputin and Nicholas II?*

Study Sources E and F

8. *How have historians explained Rasputin's hold over Alexandra?*
9. *Was Rasputin's influence as real as it appeared to contemporaries?*

3 ↜ MAIN FEATURES OF THE LAST YEARS OF AUTOCRATIC GOVERNMENT 1894–1904

A *Sergei Witte and industrial growth*

The early years of Nicholas' reign continued to reflect the two-sided policy that had characterised the last years of Alexander III. These were based on efforts to speed up the country's industrial and financial growth and ensure for the future a stable, conservative, agrarian Russia dominated by the nobility.

The country's economy was developing at a rapid rate with the help of Witte's adoption of the gold standard in 1897 which attracted further foreign investment. By 1914 one-source estimates that foreigners owned 47% of Russian securities, excluding mortgage bonds. There were obvious dangers in linking the Russian economy so closely to the performance of foreign economies as became evident in the slumps of 1900 and 1903 but the country was sound financially, profits were good. By 1914 the empire was the fifth largest industrial power and the fourth largest producer of coal, pig iron, and steel while only Texas rivalled the Baku petroleum fields. The economy grew at a very good rate of 8.5% between 1908 and 1914, even though weak areas remained – in the chemical, electrical and machine-tools industries. A consumer-based industry was also beginning to develop – cars, textiles, which remained the biggest single industry, and food processing. Factories sprang up on agricultural land on the outskirts of cities, a railway network spread to more and more new industrial regions, mines and ports. Population continued to grow including in the two major cities of St Petersburg and Moscow.

DIAGRAM 11

Performance of the Russian economy, 1890–1916

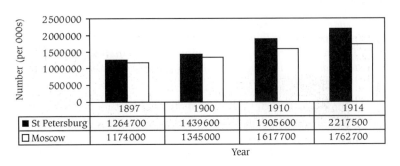

Year	1897	1900	1910	1914
■ St Petersburg	1264700	1439600	1905600	2217500
☐ Moscow	1174000	1345000	1617700	1762700

(a) Growth in population of St Petersburg and Moscow, 1897–1914

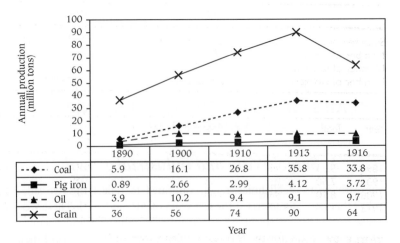

		1890	1900	1910	1913	1916
--◆--	Coal	5.9	16.1	26.8	35.8	33.8
—■—	Pig iron	0.89	2.66	2.99	4.12	3.72
−▲−	Oil	3.9	10.2	9.4	9.1	9.7
—✕—	Grain	36	56	74	90	64

(b) The Tsarist economy: annual production (million tonnes) 1890–1916

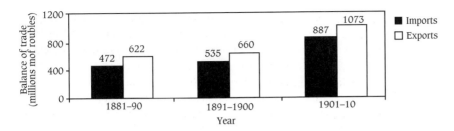

(c) *Russian balance of trade, 1881–1910*

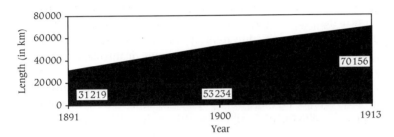

(d) *Growth of Russian railways, 1891–1913*

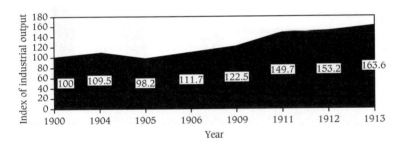

(e) *Industrial output in the Russian Empire, 1900–13*

TABLE 26
Growth in the Russian economy between 1908 and 1914

	1908	1914
State revenues	2 billion roubles	4 billion roubles
Number of banks	1146	2393
Number of factories	22 600	24 900
Number of workers	2.5 million	2.9 million

Year	Total index	Total agriculture	Population	Urban population	Volume of grain exports	Railways (length)	Iron	Government revenue
1896	5.33	1.96	1.70	4.25	6.47	17.95	5.33	3.36
1901	7.50	1.81	1.83		7.40	25.64	9.67	4.41
1906	8.10	1.89	1.99		7.25	28.91	9.00	5.57
1913	11.65	3.09	2.32	6.96	7.83	31.91	14.00	8.38

TABLE 27   *Index numbers of economic growth, 1896–1913*

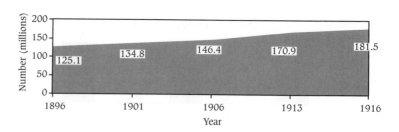

DIAGRAM 12

*Population growth in
Russia, 1896–1916*

According to some historians the 'great spurt' forward in Russia's industrialisation was achieved at the expense of agriculture. It has been claimed that capital was channelled into industry rather than being invested in improving cultivation of the land by introducing modern machinery and farming methods. As a result of this neglect land was farmed extensively rather than intensively. This low efficiency in farming meant that agriculture found it increasingly difficult to meet the demands of the rapidly rising population. The latter grew from 125 millions in 1896 to 181.5 million by 1916 with an increasing percentage moving to the towns (from 15% to 18%) (see Diagram 12). Blame was placed on:

KEY ISSUE

*Developments in
agriculture.*

- the peasants, who it was claimed were lazy and drunk, and who were discouraged from carrying out improvements because of the periodic redistribution of land
- the *Mir* for its failure to show a sufficient sense of responsibility.

More recent research has challenged the suggestion that industrial progress was achieved at the expense of agricultural decline. Figures now indicate that there was an annual rise of 9% in investment between 1891 and 1913. Two major areas of Russian agriculture – grain, especially wheat and rye, and cattle witnessed expansion between 1891 and 1913. Grain production grew from 36 to 90 million tonnes, particularly in the Ukraine, southern Russia and western Siberia, while the number of cattle rose from 25 to 32 million in European Russia. This increase not only fed the expanding population but also enabled Russia to become the largest cereal exporter in the world. Russian agriculture also began to become more varied. Potatoes and dairy products were produced for the market, especially in Poland and the Baltic States, while sugar beet was grown in the Ukraine and cotton in Turkestan. These improvements had temporary setbacks at times of bad weather. There were serious famines in 1891–2, affecting the Volga region, and in 1911, but these occurrences did not halt either the continuing rise in population growth or the fall in mortality. The number of people who died per thousand of the population fell from 37 per thousand in the period 1871–5 to 29 per thousand for 1906–10 (European Russia) and 27 per thousand by 1913 (all territory). On the evidence of these developments it is now claimed that 'the prospect of further progress in the Russian Empire's agriculture as a whole grew strong', though in making this claim historians are playing the game 'what if'. There are serious limitations to such as approach.

B *Social discontents*

Russia's peasants suffered from misery and famine with a third dying of diphtheria, typhus, of hunger from hardship. Thousands migrated either to America or to work on the land in Germany. By the 1890s it had become evident that

- population growth had increased the demand for land leading to land hunger, high price for land and smaller holdings
- redemption payments had left peasants heavily mortgaged and poverty-stricken
- periodic redistribution of land by the *Mir* discouraged improvements and increased peasants' sense of insecurity
- bad harvests and the severe famine of 1891–2 had increased their sense of grievance
- taxation burden had become too heavy
- agricultural methods remained backward due to limited application of new technology
- illiteracy remained high
- gentry continued to exploit peasants renting out land in return for money, crop or labour payments. Few were prepared to help the peasantry.

Peasants responded to their condition by rioting spontaneously though these were confined to the local area. They saw a solution to their problems through gaining gentry land, especially the areas that had been lost at the time of emancipation. As literacy spread, especially amongst those soldiers who returned to the village after serving their term, they began to be influenced by revolutionary propaganda. A new generation, which had not known the slavery of serfdom, had grown up since 1861 and they were no longer prepared to accept their condition without protest.

The peasant unrest in 1898 was documented in the extract below, quoted by L. Kochan, *Russia in Revolution 1890–1918*, Granada, 1966.

> In certain provinces, predominantly southern and south-eastern, there has recently emerged a series of peasant disorders in the form of systematic damage to the landowners' fields and meadows, together with the driving away of cattle under the protection of men armed with sticks, staves and pitchforks, and attacks on the landowners' watchmen and guards or considerable illegal timber-cutting in the landowners' woods and brawls with the foresters. When the guards seize the peasants cattle, the peasants, hoping to free it, often moving by whole villages, carry out armed attacks on the buildings and farmhouses of the landowners and divide up the working and even the living quarters, attacking and wounding servants and guards.

By 1904 there were rural disturbances throughout the country which reached a peak in the 1905 peasant rebellion.

KEY ISSUE

Condition of the peasants.

Q

What methods did the peasants adopt to draw attention to their grievances?

How serious was their threat to public order?

In what respects
had peasant unrest
become more serious
by 1905?

Q

Petition by landlords experiencing peasant unrest in 1905 in the province of Penza, quoted by D. Floyd, *Russia in Revolt 1905,* Macdonald, 1969.

> Country houses are being burnt and looted; agitators go round in army uniforms; there is no protection; few troops; we urgently beg you to place more army units and Cossacks at our disposal; we implore help, otherwise, the province will be utterly devastated.

It was not until the 1905 revolution that the regime attempted to resolve these long-standing problems. The initiative, as we will see in a later section, was then taken by Pietr Stolypin (see page 162).

The problems that had materialised under Alexander III with the development of the working class in the towns continued to be ignored by Nicholas II. Initially they had been passive out of fear of losing their jobs but during the course of the 1890s they were targeted by the different revolutionary groups who used them as a weapon in their own battle with the regime. In 1896 and 1897 Lenin and his small revolutionary group, the Bolsheviks, organised strikes amongst the St Petersburg textile workers securing for them a maximum 11.5 hour working day. This was the first time that workers' strike committees appeared, called *soviets*. The working class became increasingly more rebellious. The number who went on strike reached a peak for the decade in 1899 affecting 97 000 workers. They demanded

KEY ISSUE

*Condition of the
factory workers.*

- higher wages
- shorter working day
- improved working conditions
- the right to organise trade unions.

Witte responded by recruiting more police, calling out the army, 19 times in 1893, 50 times in 1899 and 522 times in 1902. They declared martial law in affected areas, which gave the army the power to hold quick trials of arrested strikers and carry out an immediate death sentence. This policy earned Witte the nickname of 'the hangman', but it did not curtail industrial unrest as evidenced by the high number of strikes that continued to occur (see Table 28).

Witte's repressive policy was criticised within government, especially by those opposed to public disorder. In 1901 the Ministry of the Interior instructed General Sergei Zubatov, the Head of the Moscow Security Police to pursue a policy of reconciliation. It was based on conceding some of the workers' demands in the hope of taking away the appeal of the revolutionaries. Zubatov argued that it was safer for the regime if it allowed trade unions to develop under the general control of the police. Between 1901 and 1903 he organised several large trade unions and allowed them to hold meetings, discussion groups and lectures with the purpose of promoting non-violent methods to campaign for workers' demands. Unions organised social clubs and plans were drawn up to introduce workers' welfare schemes.

Year	Number of strikes
1905	13 995
1908	892
1910	222
1911	466
1912	2 032
1913	2 404
1914	3 574

TABLE 28
Frequency of strikes, 1905–14

KEY ISSUE

*Zubatov and
'revolutionary*

Zubatov's policy appeared to be working but its success alarmed industrialists. When the unions took advantage of police sponsorship to organise a series of strikes in 1903 in the oilfields of the Caucasus and the industrial regions of the Ukraine, this gave his enemies the weapon to secure his dismissal.

Students and teachers continued to be a potentially disruptive element with disturbances breaking out in February 1899. The regime responded by expelling students from university for taking part in disorders and drafting them into the army for the period of their expulsion. State control was tightened over the universities and this was a cause of irritation along with student obligation to wear uniforms, poor financial assistance and postgraduate unemployment. Openings in the state bureaucracy and the railways were limited so that many frustrated students went into the 'free' professions of law and medicine or into the provincial *zemstva*. They joined the ranks of the rapidly expanding intelligentsia that provided many of the leaders of the revolutionary movement whose demands ranged from democratic reform to overthrow of the Tsarist regime. In the case of Russia's nationalities, students joined in the demand for independence.

A newspaper article by Josef Stalin, 1901, *Works*, Lawrence & Wishart, 1952.

> Groaning are the oppressed nationalities and religions in Russia, among them the Poles and Finns... Groaning are the unceasingly persecuted and humiliated Jews, deprived even of those miserable rights that other Russian subjects enjoy the right to live where they choose, the right to go to school, etc. Groaning are the Georgians, the Armenians and other nations who can neither have their own schools nor be employed by the State and are compelled to submit to the shameful and oppressive policies of Russification... Groaning are the many millions of Russian sects who want to worship according to the dictates of their own conscience rather than to those of the Orthodox priests.

KEY ISSUE

Student activity.

Q

What, according to Stalin, were the grievances of minorities in Russia?

Some of the more extreme opponents of the regime contributed to the wave of political terrorism that returned in the opening years of the twentieth century. Following the assassination of two leading ministers police controls were tightened in an unsuccessful attempt to repress disorder. Two thousand political assassinations were carried out by one of the revolutionary groups, the Social Revolutionaries between 1901 and 1905. Even the murder of his uncle could not persuade Nicholas to grant democratic reform. Many of her ruling elite turned to the new ideologies that were making headway in the early twentieth century – liberalism, socialism and nationalism – as a rival to autocracy. Behind an appearance of quiet loyalty many of the intelligentsia were increasingly regarding autocracy as out of date and in need of replacement by representative government.

See page 113.

4 ∽ THE CHALLENGE OF RIVAL IDEOLOGIES

A *Main features of Russian Liberalism*

Liberalism is defined as the belief in individual rights of freedom of speech, the rule of law and participation by the people in government. In western countries it was adopted during the course of the nineteenth century by the emerging middle class who challenged control of political power based on birth and possession of land. The absence of a middle class of any significant size meant that it had less relevance for Russia. The main supporters of this ideology were those nobles who believed that Russia's future lay in her adopting western ways. They succeeded in attracting the support of individuals drawn from the lower aristocracy, intellectuals, factory owners and traders.

See page 15.

Liberals had initially been encouraged by Alexander II's liberal reforms of the 1860s, though he eventually rejected proposals for consultative government based on the *zemstva*. *Zemstva* liberals wanted to improve public welfare and believed that a central representative body was necessary to achieve consultation between central government and the people's spokesmen. They did not believe in universal suffrage but consultation between the tsar and people, as advocated by the Slavophiles. The moderates, dominated by the nobility, were prepared to co-operate with the autocracy in the hope that the tsar would grant such reforms. Demands to this effect were made by the Tver provincial *zemstva* in 1895. Nicholas' dismissal of the request for an advisory body in 1895 as a 'senseless dream' did not discourage *zemstva* liberals. They organised congresses and campaigning for the introduction of an advisory body based on the principle of elections from 1896 onwards, though not all were prepared to wait for the regime to grant reform. A more radical group emerged from the expert officials drawn from the professions, such as lawyers and teachers, who were employed by the *zemstva*. By the end of the nineteenth century they were known as the **Third Element** and demanded abolition of corporal punishment, the introduction of universal primary education, and an end to peasants' separate legal status. The moderates continued to campaign for reform through the *zemstva*.

Third Element was a radical group composed of expert officials from the legal and teaching professions employed by the *zemstva*.

Both groups aimed for political reform but the radicals were also concerned with social issues arising from the condition of the peasantry. They organised revolutionary banquets addressed by speakers who attacked the government and demanded political and constitutional reform. Radical Liberals gained majority support at a meeting of *zemstva* representatives in 1904 reflecting the more radical trend of Liberalism. As such it also attracted the support of socialists though the two differed on the question of tactics for the liberals were not prepared to use revolutionary violence. Liberals did not have much political influence, although they contributed to the momentum for change 1904–5.

Assessment of Liberalism by a Marxist historian, Isaac Deutscher, *Prophet Armed, Trotsky: 1879–1921*, 1970, page 152.

> The economic preponderance of the state the numerical weakness of the middle classes the predominance of foreign capital in industry the absence of a middle class tradition all combined to make Russian bourgeois liberalism still born.

Q

What, according to Deutscher, were the main weaknesses of Russian Liberalism?

B *Main features of Russian Socialism*

Russia's revolutionary parties owed their ideas to Karl Marx.

KARL HEINRICH MARX (1818–83)

Marx, the most influential social and political thinker of the nineteenth and twentieth centuries, was born in Trier, Germany. He was the son of a prosperous middle class lawyer of Jewish origin who had adopted Christianity. He followed his father's example and studied Law at Berlin University but became interested in philosophy and history. After graduating, he became a journalist and editor of *Rheinische Zeitung* in Cologne but was forced to leave Germany because of his political ideas. He moved to Paris in 1843 where he came into contact with Socialists and with the industrial poor. He believed that under the right leadership the oppressed industrial classes would rise in revolution and would bring in a new type of society. He met the wealthy industrialist, Friedrich Engels, 1820–95, with whom he maintained a lifetime friendship. He was expelled from Paris in 1844 and joined Engels in Brussels where he started to develop his ideas. Marx was never a clear thinker and it was Engels who clarified his ideas into a comprehensive system. He joined the Communist League and was commissioned with Engels to write the *Communist Manifesto,* in 1848, which became the clearest and most concise explanation of communism.

He returned to Germany in 1848 when liberal revolutions broke out in various countries of Europe, but he was forced to flee abroad when his newspaper was suppressed. He arrived in London where he remained for the rest of his life being buried in Highgate cemetery. He lived in poverty in Soho at a time when the worst effects of industrialisation – town slums, exploitation of workers in sweatshops and factories were all around him. Three of his six children died from the poor public health conditions and poverty he experienced. He had no employment and was dependent on his rich friend Engels for money. He spent his time at the British Museum studying capitalism. He completed his three-volume history, *Das Kapital* in the 1860s though only the first volume was published in his lifetime, in 1867. Between 1864 and 1872 he devoted much of his time to spreading his ideas of communism through the First International.

The *Communist Manifesto* began with a warning, 'a spectre is haunting Europe – the spectre of communism', and then went on, 'the history of all hitherto existing society is the history of class struggles … Let the ruling classes tremble at a communist revolution. The proletarians have nothing to lose but their chains. They have a world to win. Workers of the world unite'. Marx saw communism as the inevitable outcome of history, which was a series of class struggles. He believed that all societies would experience the same stages of development but not at the same time:

Stages:

1   A period of primitive communism characterised by the absence of any government, class structure and few goods.

2   The Feudal stage was based on absolute monarchy and a landed aristocracy, both of whom were supported by the dues and labour services of peasants who worked the land. Trade and industry existed along with an emerging middle class of merchants who were intent on changing society in order to gain greater freedom and a share of political power. Absolute monarchy and dominance by the landed interest would eventually give way to dominance by industry and trade which represented the capitalist stage.

3   Capitalism, which was the age of parliamentary democracy, based on middle class or bourgeoisie liberal ideas. The middle classes, especially industrialists, were the dominant social group, while the working class, or proletariat, formed the mass of the population. According to Marx, as industry expanded the working class would increase and develop a socialist consciousness. They would become revolutionary as they became aware of their increasing exploitation at the hands of their employers. Factory owners were seen as money-grubbing individuals who seized the profits that came from the work of the workers who were the wealth creators. This state of affairs would eventually lead to a socialist revolution and the fourth stage.

4   Socialism, which Marx defined as the 'dictatorship of the proletariat', would eventually replace Capitalism. Industrial workers, who owned the means of production – factories, machines and land – would create a new society designed to meet the needs of the people. There would be greater equality in society and a breaking down of class and class privilege. Industry would be fully developed and its products more evenly distributed. Marx did not consider the peasantry to be important in achieving this stage since it was only after a society had industrialised that a revolution would occur in the hands of the industrial classes. This stage of socialism would be marked by a gradual transition to the final stage of development, Communism, where the state played a very limited role.

5   Communism would be based on a totally equal society where no classes existed and everything was distributed fairly amongst the people on the principle of 'from each according to his ability, to each according to his needs'.

At each stage one class dominated the rest through its control of the means of production but eventually the oppressed would finally manage to overthrow those who were holding back their progress. This meant that each system was replaced once it had outlived its usefulness until in the final stage of the class struggle, the workers (proletariat) would overthrow the capitalist classes (the bourgeoisie and aristocracy) and following a revolution, a classless, socialist-based society would emerge.

Friedrich Engels in his funeral oration of Marx in 1883 said of him that he 'was above all else a revolutionary. His real mission in life was to contribute in one way or another to the overthrow of capitalist society and of the state institutions which it had brought into being, to contribute to the liberation of the present-day proletariat, which he was the first to make conscious of its own position and needs ... His name will endure through the ages and so also his work'.

The problem for Russian Marxists was that Russia had not experienced industrialisation. At the time that Marx was writing the country was still essentially feudal based on the peasantry and aristocracy. He made only three references to Russia in his great work *Das Kapital*, believing that the socialist revolution would occur in an industrialising nation such as Britain or Germany. The domination of foreigners in Russian investment and expertise led him to believe that a proletarian revolution would not occur in Russia until it had industrialised. This idea was unacceptable to the Populists who wanted to preserve the commune as the basis for a Communist society. Marx gradually changed his ideas as his expected socialist revolution in the west failed to appear. By 1882 he came around to the viewpoint that 'Russian common ownership of land may serve as the starting point for a communist development' (Preface to 1882 Russian edition of the *Communist Manifesto*). Russia's subsequent industrialisation in the 1890s raised new issues amongst Russian Marxists that the capitalist phase of her historical development had begun, a view not shared by all.

Georgi Plekhanov (1856–1918) was the 'Father of Russian Marxism'. He began his political life as a Populist but eventually abandoned support of the peasantry in favour of the urban workers whom he believed would be the prime movers of revolution in Russia. He knew Marx and translated the *Communist Manifesto* into Russia. He became a Social Democrat in the 1880s founding the Group for the Emancipation of Labour abroad. He was a major Marxist thinker influencing revolutionaries though he had little effect on the Russian labour Movement. He believed that revolution would come in two stages. First there would be a democratic-bourgeois revolution against Tsarism, which would get rid of the dominance of the landed nobility. This would enable capitalism to develop fully and would produce a large proletariat (working class), which would make the second stage, a socialist one, possible. However, as capitalism was in its infancy in Russia in the 1880s, it might be a long time before there was a socialist revolution. As the Russian proletariat was both small and backward, the intelligentsia would have to organise and rouse the workers. Plekhanov was a founder of the first Russian

KEY ISSUE

Relevance of the ideas of Karl Marx for Russia.

revolutionary Marxist organisation in 1883, which in 1898 merged with other groups to form the Social Democratic Workers' Party.

Despite his importance in introducing Marx's ideas into Russia, Plekhanov played no active role within the country itself. In 1880 he was forced into exile in Geneva, Switzerland where he remained till 1917. Responsibility for spreading Marxism belonged to Russia's intellectuals in the 1870s, then to university students in the 1880s and it was well established by the time of Marx's death in 1883. Intellectuals went amongst the workers though co-operation was limited both by workers' distrust and a conflict of aims. Leadership of the Marxist movement in Russia eventually fell into the hands of Vladimir Ilyich Ulyanov (Lenin) who adapted Marxist ideas into a plan of action.

PROFILE

VLADIMIR ILYICH ULYANOV (LENIN) (1870–1924)

Born in Simbirsk on the River Volga into the intelligentsia, his father had progressed from physics teacher to Chief Inspector for Elementary schools, a move that gave the family gentry status and prosperity. Lenin grew up in a family of six children with a father who was respectable, conservative and devout and a self-educated but talented mother. He showed a gift for languages, history, geography and literature at school, where he gained a reputation for 'unusual carefulness and industry' and 'systematic thought'. He was influenced by a number of contemporary socialists including his older brother, Alexander, who was the leader of a group of St Petersburg ex-student terrorists who had plotted to assassinate Alexander III. Despite the impact of his subsequent execution in 1887 on the family's reputation, Lenin was permitted to attend the University of Kazan in 1887. Within four months he was expelled for his participation in student disorders and during the next ten years, until his exile to Siberia, he gradually evolved his own revolutionary ideas influenced by Populist and Marxist ideas. These included his belief that the intelligentsia were vital as leaders of the working class if they were to develop Socialist ideas and that, if necessary, violence was permissible as a political weapon. In 1891 he graduated as an external student from St Petersburg University and for six years practised law, first in Samara in the middle Volga region and then St Petersburg. He spent most of his time working with fellow revolutionaries in underground Marxist clubs and establishing his leadership of the St Petersburg Marxists, known as the *Elders*. He worked amongst the city's factory workers, many of whom were ex-peasants, and wrote leaflets for striking workers. In 1894 his work, *What are the Friends of the People?* was published in which he argued for the setting up of a Russian Social Democrat party. In the summer of 1895 he toured Europe and, in Geneva, he met Plekhanov and other Social Democrats in exile who were impressed by his energy and organisational skills. On his return to St Petersburg in the autumn he spent the next three months writing pamphlets, and organising a strike. It was at this time that he met and forged a close political alliance with Julius Martov who was to play a leading role in the latter Russian Social Democratic party. In December 1895 Lenin and Martov with other associates were arrested on the evidence of an informer and sent to prison without trial. After fourteen months he was sentenced to exile in Siberia where he remained for three years and it was here that he took the name of Lenin from the river Lena. He sent for a fellow activist, Nadezhda Krupskaya, to join him and they were married. They lived in comparatively free and comfortable conditions. Their home became a centre of activity for other political exiles; Lenin wrote his first book, *The Development of Capitalism in Russia* and planned the setting up of a Social democratic Party. When he heard that a Congress of revolutionaries meeting in Minsk in 1898 had set up a Russian Social Democratic Labour Party (RSDRP) with a Central Committee, he wrote his *Project for Our Party's Programme.* At the end of his term he went into exile in Switzerland, then England and was joined by Krupskaya. The next 17 years were spent writing, including articles for the revolutionary newspaper, *Iskra* (The Spark), which he founded with Julius Martov. Lenin used this party newspaper to explain his interpretation of Marxism and planning for the Russian revolution to fellow party members. When it came in February 1917, Lenin, who was in Switzerland, was taken by surprise and he did not arrive in Russia until the April. He led the second revolution in October and became the first leader of the new state till his death in 1924.

PICTURE 10

Lenin with other members of the League for the Liberation of Labour, Radio Times Hulton Picture Library (Lenin is seated in the middle and Martov is to his right)

During his 17 years in exile Lenin maintained contact with the underground network of revolutionaries in Russia and sent copies of *Iskra* and other revolutionary literature. This was distributed in factories and public places and support gradually grew amongst the workers. Propaganda posters were also used by the Social Democrats to mould public opinion to their view of society. Picture 11 uses a wedding cake as a model to convey their message of the structure of power in the Imperial monarchy. Picture 10 is a variant of the same message.

PICTURE 11 *Structure of Russian Society pre-1914,* Novosti Press Agency. *Structure of Power in the Imperial Monarchy pre-1914.* The comments from top to bottom are 'They dispose of our money', 'They pray on our behalf', 'They eat on our behalf', 'They shoot at us', 'We labour for them'.

PICTURE 12 *Structure of Russian Society pre-1914,* Novosti Press Agency. *Social Democratic Party propaganda postcard 1901.* The comments from top to bottom are 'We reign over you', 'We govern you', 'We mystify you', 'We shoot you', 'We eat you', 'To live in freedom, to die in struggle'.

Q

What images has the Social democratic Party adopted to emphasise abuses in Russian society?

Which aspects of the postcard were likely to appeal to different groups of people and why?

What was likely to be the impact of the propaganda postcard on the reputation of the Imperial monarchy?

How reliable is this postcard for an historian studying attitudes towards the Tsarist regime in the early years of the twentieth century?

However, divisions appeared amongst Russian Marxists not only over the tactics and direction of the struggle to achieve a socialist state, but also over the dominance of some individuals. The final break came over the issue of who had the right to membership of the Social Democratic Party. Lenin argued that a small group of strong willed and well-disciplined professional revolutionaries drawn from the ranks of the intelligentsia could achieve revolution. An elected Central Committee would make all decisions and impose unity and discipline, vital if Tsarism was to be overturned. It was not necessary for them to be elected by the workers who lacked political awareness. In the first issue of *Iskra* 1900 he had written that 'organise, not only in benefit societies, strike funds and workers' circles, but organise also in a political party, organise for the determined struggle against the autocratic government and against the whole of capitalists society ... We must train people who shall devote to the revolution not only their spare evenings, but also the whole of their lives ... If we have a strongly organised party, a single strike may grow into a political demonstration, into a political victory over the regime. If we have a strongly organised party, a rebellion in a single locality may spread into a victorious revolution' (V.I. Lenin, *Collected Works,* Lawrence & Wishart, 1959). Lenin also disagreed with the faction known as the *Economists* who believed that the revolutionary movement should concentrate its efforts on improving the condition of the workers including the achievement of higher wages, formation of trade unions and co-operative societies rather than on fighting Tsarism. These divisions became obvious at the second Russian Social Democratic Party Congress in 1903, police broke up (the first in 1898 in Minsk). The *Economists* were defeated but the Social Democrats also divided on the issue of party organisation. Lenin quarrelled with his colleague, and co-editor of *Iskra,* Martov over the issue of leadership and membership of the party.

Martov believed that Lenin was aiming to become dictator of the party and there were fierce exchanges between the two friends ending in Congress being required to vote on the nature of the party. Lenin's supporters were in the majority and became known as the 'majoritarians' or *Bolsheviki* and his opponents the 'minoritarians' or *Mensheviki* led by Julius Martov. The latter subsequently became the majority group when Plekhanov split with Lenin whose dictatorial style of leadership he opposed though the formal break between the two leaders did not occur till during the World War I. Lenin wanted to turn it into a civil war while Plekhanov supported the war effort. When Plekhanov returned to Russia in March 1917 he became a committed opponent of the Bolsheviks condemning their seizure of power in the October revolution. Lenin left *Iskra's* editorial board and set up his own organisation, the Union of Committees of the Majority, with its own central bureau and newspaper, *Vperyod* (*Forward*).

> **KEY ISSUE**
>
> *Divisions in Russian Marxist ranks.*

> **Q**
>
> *Using the chart below, explain briefly the main differences between the Mensheviks and the Bolsheviks.*

Main areas of difference	Menshevik	Bolshevik
Revolution	Russia not yet ready for proletarian revolution until the bourgeois had occurred first	Bourgeois and proletarian stages could be merged stage into one
The party	Mass organisation with membership open to all revolutionaries	Tight-knit organisation of professional revolutionaries and restricted membership
Discipline	Open, democratic discussion within the party with decisions arrived at by votes of members	Authority to be exercised by the Central Committee of the party which Lenin described as 'democratic centralism'
Strategy	Alliance with all other revolutionary and bourgeois liberal parties Support of trade unions in pursuing better wages and conditions for workers	Rejection of co-operation with other parties Dismissed struggle for improved conditions as playing into hands of bourgeoisie Aimed to turn workers into revolutionaries

From Michael Lynch, *Reaction and Revolutions: Russia and 1881–1924*, Hodder & Stoughton, 1992.

C *Main features of Leninism*

'Without a revolutionary theory, there can be no revolutionary movement' (Lenin).

Lenin stressed the importance of the party in achieving revolution. In 1902 Lenin set forth his ideas in a pamphlet *What is to be Done?* In this he argued, amongst other things that 'the history of all countries shows that the working class, solely by its own forces, is able to work out merely trade-union consciousness'. By which he meant that workers would often be satisfied with economic gains, such as better working conditions and higher pay, whilst working within the capitalist system. For Lenin the most important thing was to smash capitalism and for this 'a strong organisation of revolutionaries' was required. His formula for a revolutionary party was based on

1 a stable organisation of leaders to ensure continuity and leadership
2 a small, tightly knit group of professional revolutionaries able and willing to carry through revolution and who had to accept orders from the Party leadership without question
3 a need to restrict membership to escape detection under a police state with an elaborate network of spies and informers who could easily infiltrate and make the movement useless
4 a broad base of mass support to form the rank and file of the movement.

Lenin also developed rival views to Marxism in terms of his views on the strategy of the revolutionary struggle. In *Two Tactics of Social Democracy*, written in 1905 he rejected those Marxist who claimed that the bourgeoisie were the natural leaders in an anti-Tsarist revolution, as he thought they would betray the revolution and seek a compromise with the ruling class. He argued that the working class, in alliance with the peasants, must lead the revolution. When the tsar was overthrown there would be a 'provisional government' with the workers taking part. This would then be followed by a clash between the *bourgeoisie*, who would have become concerned to defend their revolution, and the workers, who, with the support of fellow working class revolutions in Europe, would be successful. In this way the time taken to close the gap between the *bourgeois* and socialist revolutions, which Lenin's critics claimed might be long, would be shortened dramatically.

D *Main features of Russian Nationalism*

See Table 18 and Diagram 9: Nationality of exiled revolutionaries in 1907–17, on page 75.

Nationalism grew, as we have already noted, under the impact of Alexander III's more aggressive *Russification* policy, a serious development when 55% of the population of the Empire belonged to Russia's nationalities. The peoples of the Ukraine, the Caucasus, Poland, the Baltic States and Finland demanded greater cultural and political independence and many joined the ranks of the revolutionaries. In the case of Finland hostility against the regime peaked in the assassination of the Governor-General of Finland.

The appearance of these rival ideologies was dangerous for Tsarism as the growing numbers of the intelligentsia had the power to control the press and mould public opinion. Faith in the tsar, however, still remained unshaken in 1894, though this was to change in the next ten years.

5 ∽ FORMATION OF PARTIES AND REVOLUTIONARY GROUPS

The apparent peace and calm of Russia in 1894 concealed increasing support for liberal and revolutionary ideas. More extreme secret revolutionary groups were gaining momentum pledged to an overthrow of the whole Tsarist system and committed to political assassinations.

MAIN OPPOSITION TO TSARDOM 1894–1914

Main features	*Social revolutionaries (SRs)*
Origins	Appeared in 1901 Grew out of the nineteenth century Populist movement comprising '*Land and Liberty, Black Partition*', and '*People's Will*'.
Leadership	The intellectual Victor Chernov (1901)
Composition	Peasantry 50% of membership were urban working class or proletariat and artisans
Aims	Demanded redistribution of land to peasantry Supported the commune as a form of agrarian socialism Called for a Constituent Assembly whereby groups governed themselves
Tactics	Made use of – Propaganda – Discontent in the countryside – Political assassinations – Strikes
Activities	1901–5 anarchists committed political assassinations including Plehve 1904, Grand Duke Sergei 1905, Stolypin 1911 and 2000 government officials Influential in 1905 Peasant Union Congress Participated in the *Dumas* after the 1905 Revolution
Effectiveness	Developed a wide base First national congress December 1905 and drew up a programme based on aims 1906 claimed to have 50 000 members with a further 350 000 influenced by party aims 30 representatives in second Parliament, or *Duma* Undermined by police agents who infiltrated the party, but weakened by disagreements over tactics Split into anarchists and revolutionaries

See page 49.

See page 50.

(continued overleaf)

Main features	Social revolutionaries (SRs)
Effectiveness (continued)	Anarchists, wanted to continue with the terrorist methods adopted by '*The People's Will*' Revolutionaries were more moderate and were prepared to co-operate with other groups to achieve an immediate improvement in conditions for peasants and workers The SR leader, Victor Chernov, joined the provisional government in 1917, but fled to the United States after the second October Revolution by the Communists who suppressed the SRs

Main features	Social Democrats (All Russian Social Democratic Labour Party, RSDLP): 1. Mensheviks, 2. Bolsheviks
Origins	Founded in Minsk in 1898
Leadership	Drawn from middle and upper classes – Plekhanov, founder of Russian Marxism – Lenin, leader of Bolsheviks – Martov, leader of Mensheviks – Trotsky, President of St Petersburg Soviet, 1905
Composition	Industrial workers or proletariat Peasantry
Aims	Broad agreement on overthrow of Tsarism and the introduction of Socialism but differences had emerged by 1903 over tactics and strategy
Tactics	Small secret groups known as 'cells' Study groups Propaganda amongst workers Demonstrations and strikes
Activities	Organised wave of industrial strikes and unrest 1890s, and 1896–7 in St Petersburg December 1905 Bolsheviks organised the unsuccessful Moscow rising Contributed to 1914 St Petersburg strike but not able to control events
Effectiveness	Spread Marxist ideas of socialism and revolution Claimed to have 40 000 members in 1904, 150 000 in 1906 1906 SDs elected to second *Duma* 1910 Published official newspaper, *Pravda*, with 40 000 circulation Infiltrated by police informers and double agents and weakened by internal squabbles after split of 1903. Majority became known as radical Bolsheviks who grew 1912 onwards Minority formed the Mensheviks who drew their support from new legal trade unions Danger of over-exaggerating their influence – strikes would have occurred anyway

See pages 110–11.

Main features	Liberals: 1. Octobrists, 2. Kadets
Origins	Grew out of the *Zemstva* liberals 1902 League of Liberation 1904 Union of Liberation 1905 Moderate Octobrists, radical Constitutional Democrats (KD or Kadets) 1908 Progressists
Leadership	Shipov, *Zemstva* leader Pavel Milyukov, Kadet leader Guchkov, Rodzianko, Octobrist leaders
Composition	Not a large base of support due to failure to attract mass support Gentry and professionals employed by *Zemstva* assemblies Intellectuals especially at university level Some factory owners and merchants
Aims	Constituent Assembly to provide for democratic freedoms and civil liberties including abolition of class differences, freedom of speech and press, equality before the law, a constitution, and improvements in social conditions
Tactics	Peaceful propaganda and legal means such as meetings of *Zemstva* leaders starting in 1896 Use of Law societies to discuss liberal ideas Moderate pressure on government
Activities	Banqueting campaign and support for strikes in 1905 Moderate liberals supported Nicholas during the crisis year 1905 and helped him to recover his position Vyborg protest 1906
Effectiveness	Kadets formed largest group in *Duma* Activities confined to a few large cities Government refused to respond to demands for peaceful liberal reform prior to crisis of 1905 Limited support amongst masses who were attracted by socialism meant that liberalism overcome Liberals were compromised by their concern on the one hand to persuade the regime to grant constitutional changes while at the same time not provoking a revolution, which would destroy society

6 ⌐ THE RUSSO-JAPANESE WAR, 1904–5

When the regime was eventually faced with crisis the challenge came as a result of events abroad rather than domestic issues.

A *Events in the Far East prior to 1904*

See Map 9 on page 118.

Russia expanded her Empire in the Far East for strategic and economic reasons. One of the reasons for building the Trans-Siberian Railway had been to help her establish her domination over Northern China and expand into Korea. The vast Chinese Empire was in decline and a target for the colonising countries of Europe – Britain, France, Germany and Russia along with the United States of America and Japan, who were all concerned to gain a share of the rich trade and commercial centres along the south coast. Between 1858 and 1860 Russia acquired 400 000 square miles of Chinese territory, and followed this up with development of the port of Vladivostok. Occupation of the island of Sakhalin brought her into conflict with Japan, which was not settled until 1867, when it was agreed that Russia and Japan would have common rights of

MAP 8 *The Far East, 1850–90*

the island. This agreement was ended in 1875 when Japan gave her rights Sakhalin to Russia in exchange for the Kuril Islands. A treaty of friendship was signed which brought peace between the two countries till 1895. Russia proceeded to settle the island of Sakhalin with convicts and exiles, 30 000 by 1900.

Russia came into conflict with Japan again following the Sino-Japanese war of 1894–5. Japan, resentful of Russia's success in building railways and penetrating Chinese territory attacked and defeated China. The latter was then forced to make substantial commercial and territorial concessions to Japan, including the highly valuable warm-water Port Arthur. Russia and the other European powers reacted immediately declaring that this threatened peace in the Far East. Japan, keen to negotiate rather than fight, gave up her claim to Port Arthur, and three years later (1898), Russia extracted a lease of 25 year on the Liaotung Peninsula and the right to build a railroad to Port Arthur. Control of the latter freed Russia from total dependence on Vladivostok that had been iced for part of the year as well as offering a base for further expansion into Korea, regarded as a Japanese sphere of interest. By 1901 Russian troops were also occupying Manchuria to protect her interests there. The Japanese resented Russia's action and increased influence in the region. In 1902, Japan strengthened its position by agreeing a treaty with Britain, the Anglo-Japanese Alliance. As relations between Russia and Japan deteriorated further, Japan sent a mission to St Petersburg to try to calm the situation and find a solution. This mission was rudely received and sent home, and on 8 February 1904 the Japanese attacked Port Arthur. They appeared to be the aggressors but, in fact, they had been provoked into war.

B *Russian motives leading to war, 1904*

The initial impetus for Russia extending her Far Eastern interests into Korea was partly a combination of strategic and economic motives with a sense of foreign adventure and big power politics. Pressure for an

Q *What, according to this 1904 Japanese cartoon, was Russia's motives in 1904?*

PICTURE 13
Nicholas's Ambitions in the Far East, 1904–5, a Japanese cartoon mocks the Tsar

aggressive policy had come from a group of cavalry officers, admirals and courtiers who had successfully overcome the opposition of Sergei Witte, and General Kuropatkin. They supported proposals for a rather vague business venture in Korea proposed by a retired cavalry captain, Bezobrazov. He had planned to form a private company there, move Russian soldiers disguised as workmen into the Liaotung peninsula and take control of the area. Nicholas II, who believed that he was wresting Korea from the 'yellow peril' agreed to finance the venture. There was however, a powerful domestic motive shown by Vyachestav Plehve, his Minister of the Interior 1902–4 and some of his associates. They saw a successful war in the Far East as an opportunity to divert people's attention from deteriorating conditions at home and increasing violence. Plehve advised the tsar to embark on a 'little victorious war to stem the tide of revolution'. He thought that a 'war would distract the attention of the masses from political questions' since victory would increase Nicholas' prestige and popularity.

C *Japanese motives leading to war, 1904*

Japan's main concerns were strategic and economic. She had been excluded from a strategically important area, which she had wanted to acquire as a destination for her surplus population, coal and cotton

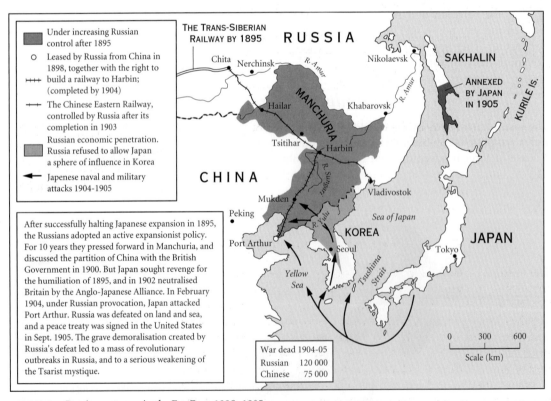

Under increasing Russian control after 1895

o **Leased by Russia from China in 1898, together with the right to**
+++ **build a railway to Harbin; (completed by 1904)**

--- **The Chinese Eastern Railway, controlled by Russia after its completion in 1903**

Russian economic penetration. Russia refused to allow Japan a sphere of influence in Korea

◄— **Japanese naval and military attacks 1904-1905**

THE TRANS-SIBERIAN RAILWAY BY 1895

RUSSIA

SAKHALIN

ANNEXED BY JAPAN IN 1905

KURILE IS.

Chita Nerchinsk *R. Amur* Nikolaevsk

Hailar Khabarovsk *R. Amur*

MANCHURIA

Tsitihar Harbin

CHINA

R. Sungari

Mukden Vladivostok

Peking Sea of Japan

R. Yalu KOREA JAPAN

Port Arthur Seoul Tokyo

Yellow Sea *Tsushima Strait*

After successfully halting Japanese expansion in 1895, the Russians adopted an active expansionist policy. For 10 years they pressed forward in Manchuria, and discussed the partition of China with the British Government in 1900. But Japan sought revenge for the humiliation of 1895, and in 1902 neutralised Britain by the Anglo-Japanese Alliance. In February 1904, under Russian provocation, Japan attacked Port Arthur. Russia was defeated on land and sea, and a peace treaty was signed in the United States in Sept. 1905. The grave demoralisation created by Russia's defeat led to a mass of revolutionary outbreaks in Russia, and to a serious weakening of the Tsarist mystique.

War dead 1904-05	
Russian	120 000
Chinese	75 000

0   300   600

Scale (km)

MAP 9 *Russian response in the Far East, 1895–1905*

exports in return for providing her with wheat, rice and beans. She had also been excluded from Port Arthur whereas Russia was expanding her influence through the construction of banks, provision of credit and experts. There was also a military and prestige element. Japan's victory against Russia had not been expected. Asian people had dared to challenge a great European Power and won – the boost to her prestige and reputation was significant.

D Battles of Mukden, February 1905 and Tsushima, May 1905

The war was, from the Russian point of view, a disaster. On land, Japanese troops took Port Arthur and inflicted heavy defeats on the Russian armies along the Yalu River, on the border between Manchuria and Korea, and at Mukden. The Russian soldiers fought brave enough but were badly led. They suffered heavy casualties and thousands were taken prisoner.

At sea, the Russian fleet at Port Arthur was destroyed, and to replace it the Russians sent their Baltic fleet to the Far East. In the North Sea, the Russian ships mistook some British trawlers for Japanese torpedo boats and opened fire. The incident irritated the already hostile British government. In May 1905, the Japanese fleet, under the brilliant Admiral Togo, virtually destroyed the whole of the Russian fleet in the Straits of Tsushima.

With Russian forces humiliated on land and at sea and the Japanese content with their achievements during the brief war, both sides agreed to accept reconciliation, and delegates of both countries met at Portsmouth, New Hampshire (USA) to discuss the terms of the treaty.

E The Treaty of Portsmouth, 1905

Under this treaty:

Treaty of Portsmouth was negotiated at Portsmouth in America.

1 Japan gained Port Arthur, southern Manchuria and the southern half of the island of Sakhalin
2 Korea was recognised as being within Japan's sphere of influence.

F Significance of the Russo-Japanese war

The Russo-Japanese conflict had been an imperialist war fought on the territory of two undefended, neutral countries, Korea and China, by two warlike nations seeking to expand their 'spheres of influence'. It was also the first instance in modern history of an eastern country defeating a western power, an event that had a great effect on Asian attitudes and Asian nationalism. But, in fact, the war served to show the backwardness of Russia compared to Japan who had embarked on a programme of industrialisation and westernisation in the nineteenth century. The war had revealed the inefficiency, weakness and corruption of the Tsarist State. As news of the fall of Port Arthur and the humiliating defeats at Mukden and Tsushima leaked through to the Russian people, their despair quickly turned to anger. The situation was made worse by an economic slump that led to food shortages in the cities affecting the industrial workers. Once again resort was made to violence – workers went on strikes, revolutionaries assassinated the Minister of the Interior, V.K. Plehve in July 1904 and liberals organised political banquets. This was the immediate context to the 1905 Revolution, which will be studied in the next chapter.

7 ⌇ BIBLIOGRAPHY

E. Crankshaw, *The Shadow of the Winter Palace – The Drift to Revolution 1825–1917*, Penguin, 1978; David Christian, *Imperial and Soviet Russia: Power, Privilege and the Challenge of Modernity*, Addison-Wesley Longman, 1986; Terence Emmons, *The Russian Landed Gentry, and t he Peasant Emancipation of 1861*, Cambridge University Press, 1968; M.T. Florinsky, *The End of the Russian Empire*, New York: Collier Books, 1961; Lionel Kochan & R. Abrahams, *The Making of Modern Russia,* Harmondsworth: Penguin 1983; Martin McCauley & Peter Waldron, *The Emergence of the Modern Russian State 1855–1881*, Macmillan, 1986; Martin McColgan, *Russia 1881–1921: From Tsarism to Communism*, Longman, 1994; R. Pipes, *Russia under the Old Regime*, Penguin, 1987; R. Sherman, *Russia 1815–81*, Hodder & Stoughton, 1991; Hugh Seton-Watson, *The Russian Empire 1801–1917*, OUP, 1967; J.N. Westwood, *Endurance and Endeavour; Russian History 1812–1986*, OUP, 1973.

8 ⌇ STRUCTURED AND ESSAY QUESTIONS

A *This section consists of structured questions that might be used for discussion or written answers as a way of expanding on the chapter and testing understanding of it.*

1. (a) Explain briefly the aims of the Liberals.
   (b) To what extent did they succeed in attracting the support of the masses?
2. (a) Explain briefly Marx's views on revolution?
   (b) In what ways did Lenin adapt Marxism to fit conditions in Russia before 1914?
3. (a) Why did Russia and Japan go to war in 1904?
   (b) What part did Russia's defeat play in the outbreak of revolution in 1905?
4. (a) How extensive was industrialisation in Russia by 1905?
   (b) What was the social cost of industrialisation?

B *Essay questions.*
1. Why did the first 10 years of Nicholas' reign end in protest and revolution by 1905?

2. To what extent would you agree with the claim that 'repression and reaction were the distinctive features of Nicholas II's rule to 1905'?
3. 'An unnecessary adventure carried out with incompetence and failure and having disastrous consequences for Russia'. Consider this view of the Russo-Japanese war 1904–5.
4. To what extent was war with Japan 1904–5 a disaster for both the government of Nicholas II and for his people?
5. How far and for what reasons was there a build-up of an effective revolutionary movement in Russia 1894–1905?
6. Analyse the opposition movement, which developed within Russia during the first ten years of Nicholas II's reign.
7. What political ideas, both Western and Russian, influenced the various political groups which developed in Russia in opposition to Nicholas II during the ten years before 1905?

9 ᘐ MAKING NOTES

Read the advice section about making notes on page ix of Preface: how to use this book, and then make your own notes based on the following headings and questions.

A *Nicholas II's personality and attitude as tsar*
1. What was his attitude towards his role as tsar?
2. What were his strengths and weaknesses as tsar?
3. What methods did he adopt to 'uphold the principle of autocracy?

B *Nicholas II's methods to uphold the principle of autocracy*
1. Appointment of key ministers – leading personalities and their attitudes.
2. The role of the tsarina, Alexandra Feodorovna.
3. The role of Rasputin.
4. Reasons for instability in government.

C *The Russian economy*
Using the statistical evidence for the performance of the Russian economy 1894–1914 (Diagrams 11(a)–(e) and 12 and Tables 26 and 27), and your own knowledge of the economic developments of the period, to what extent would you agree with each of the following interpretation:

Interpretation 1   'Until the onset of war in 1914 the Russian economy was developing into a modern industrial state'.
Interpretation 2   'Relative to developments in other countries the Russian growth was too limited to provide a genuine industrial base'.

Record the evidence for each interpretation using the chart below to organise the results of your evaluation. I have included some examples as a starting point for your own selection.

Interpretation	Evidence
1. 'Until the onset of war in 1914 the Russian economy was developing into a modern industrial state'.	● Increased industrial production ● Growth of labour force ● Growth of foreign investment
2. 'Relative to developments in other countries the Russian growth was too . limited to provide a genuine industrial base'.	● Predominance of a rural economy ● 80% of population were peasants ● Only 6.96 of population lived in towns ● Survival of the principle of autocracy – that looked to the past, based on a traditional peasant society rather than a modern industrial state with varied social classes who demanded a share in government

D *Social discontents*
1. Identify the grievances of different groups in society.
2. What action did each group adopt to draw attention to their grievances?
   Use the following chart with its accompanying exemplar to record your evaluation:

Social Group	Grievance	Action
Industrial workers	Long hours Low pay Poor living and working conditions Activities of supervisors Absence of trade union protection Activities of infiltrators and use of army to break strikes Absence of political representation	Strikes Demonstrations Acceptance of revolutionary ideas Soviets
Peasants		
Middle class (including students)		
Gentry		
Army		
Nationalities		
Political parties		

E *Growth of rival ideologies*

This section requires you to examine the impact of Western ideas on Russian society. In each of the three ideologies – Liberalism, Marxism and Nationalism – you need to be familiar with origins, aims, composition, relevance for Russia and political effectiveness. Use the following chart to record your information:

Main features	Liberalism	Marxism	Nationalism
Origins			
Aims			
Composition (i) Leadership (ii) Rank and file			
Relevance to Russian society			
Political effectiveness			

F *Karl Marx*
1. What were the main influences on Karl Marx?
2. What were the main ideas expressed in the *Communist Manifesto?*
3. What was the significance of Marx and his ideas?
4. What was the relevance of Marx's ideas for Russia?
5. Outline the growth of Marx's ideas in Russia and the role of Plekhanov.

G *Main features of Leninism*
1. What were the main influences on Lenin's emergence as a revolutionary?
2. To what extent did Lenin depart from conventional Marxist ideas?
3. What were the main points of difference between
   (a) Plekhanov and Lenin?
   (b) Martov and Lenin?
4. What was the outcome of these differences in 1903?
5. What were the main differences between the Mensheviks and the Bolsheviks?
6. Summarise Lenin's views on each of the following:
   (a) Nature of Party.
   (b) Strategy.

H *Formation of parties and revolutionary groups*

This section requires you to examine the growth of parties including their link with Western and Russian historical developments. In each of the three main political groupings – Social Revolutionaries, Social Democrats and Liberals – you need to be familiar with origin, leadership, composition, aims, tactics, activities and effectiveness. Use the following chart to record your information:

Main features	Social revolutionaries	Social Democrats	Liberals
Origins			
Aims			
Composition (i) Leadership (ii) Rank and file			
Tactics			
Activities			
Political effectiveness			

I *Russo-Japanese war 1904–5*
1. Summarise Russian aims in the Far East prior to 1904.
2. Why was Japan a rival?
3. Motives of each of the following for going to war in 1904:
    (a) Japan.
    (b) Russia.
4. Main features of war 1904–5 and Russian defeats.
5. Main terms of Treaty of Portsmouth.
6. Significance of the war on the position of
    (a) Nicholas II.
    (b) Russian society.
    (c) Troops.

10 ⌐ A DOCUMENTARY EXERCISE ON THE IMPACT ON RUSSIAN SOCIETY OF THE RUSSO-JAPANESE WAR

Study the collection of sources and then answer the questions, which follow:

In January 1904, in this context – a strike-prone working class, an impoverished peasantry, widespread contempt for the law, unremitting political hostility, an alienated intelligentsia of students, liberals and professional men – war broke out between Russia and Japan.

The years 1904–6 brought into the open political arena a four-fold force of vast hostility that left incurable scars on the body of the autocracy. Workers, peasants, liberals and national minorities (especially Poles, Finns and the Baltic peoples) moved en masse, though without coordination. None of these forces was new, but never had they overlapped so closely. They put Tsarism to an unprecedented ordeal. It withstood the attack and fought back. Yet the truth of Trotsky's dictum could not be denied, 'the revolution is dead, long live the revolution'!

The war met a mixed reception. But it did at least, if only provisionally, do something to still the voice of opposition. Government-organised demonstrations in its favour helped to encourage the waverers. By directing the call-up away from the more revolutionary-minded larger towns and industrial centres, the government hoped to prolong the relatively favourable atmosphere. Only in the borderlands – Finland, Poland and the Caucasus – were there major symptoms of disaffection and hostility to the war. But continuous military failure – all the more unwelcome in that it was so unexpected – quickly shook the government. The war became a catalyst that brought about an ever-deeper internal crisis. Each major Russian defeat in the Far East unleashed tremors thousands of miles to the west.

SOURCE A
From Lionel Kochan, Russia in Revolution, *Weidenfeld & Nicolson, 1966.*

Inadequate food and the absence of any kind of sanitary measures whatsoever are causing infectious disease to spread among the troops. These unbearable conditions are still further aggravated by the absence of anything like decent housing and clothing. Worn and weary, the troops are dying like flies. And this is after thousands have been killed by bullets ...

All this is causing unrest and discontent among the troops. The soldiers are awakening from their torpor, they are beginning to feel that they are human, they no longer blindly obey the orders of their superiors, and often greet their upstart officers with whistling and threats ...

The Tsarist autocracy is losing its main prop – 'its reliable troops'.

SOURCE B
From Josef Stalin, Works, *Lawrence & Wishart, 1952, vol. 1.*

Study Source A

1. *What, according to Source A, was the situation in Russia when war broke out in 1904?*
2. *Identify the four main forces which emerged between 1904 and 1906 in hostility to autocracy?*
3. *To what extent were these forces a serious challenge to Tsarism?*
4. *What part was played by the war of 1904–5 in undermining Tsarism?*

Study Source B

5. *Why, according to Stalin, was 'the Tsarist autocracy losing its main prop'?*

Study Sources A and B

6. *Using the two sources and your own knowledge, to what extent was war with Japan 1904–5 a disaster for the government of Nicholas II?*

5

Nicholas II – death of the Romanov dynasty

The year 1905 was a landmark in the history of the Romanov dynasty. It witnessed Nicholas' failure to keep the promise he made at the time of his coronation that he would, 'maintain the principle of autocracy just as firmly and unflinchingly as it was preserved by my unforgettable dead father'. In the aftermath of an event in St Petersburg, known as *Bloody Sunday* which occurred in the January, Nicholas was forced to agree to the setting up of a representative Assembly, the *Duma*. According to one historian, 'the 1905 Revolution in Russia was the first major confrontation of the conflicting forces at work in Russian society as the country moved into the twentieth century – the forces of autocracy and reaction on the one hand, and the forces of popular discontent on the other. It was a clear warning of the strength of the forces working against the Tsarist regime, but it was a warning which was scarcely heeded by those who were in a position to act effectively'. As we have already noted a situation existed by the beginning of 1905 in which there was widespread discontent against the government. This was the product of deterioration in the condition of life of the masses, an increase in strikes and increased political activity. The political banquets held by the Liberals in November 1904 had led many to expect political change. To this was added a sense of depression brought on by news of Russia's defeat at the hands of Japan, regarded as a second-rate Asian power. Many critics regarded Nicholas' government as weak and ineffectual whose only guarantee was its ability to mishandle the situation. This was demonstrated in its response to increasing disorder, which was to apply further repression. The number of secret police was increased, thousands of protestors, many of whom were industrial workers, were detained in prisons and penal colonies, and armed troops were deployed in villages and industrial centres. Sergei Witte's comments in his diary on the revolutionary crisis of 1905 observed that: (Sergei Witte's diary entry for 1905, quoted by J. Taylor, *Russia in Revolution, 1974*)

Q

What does Witte identify as the reasons for the disturbances of 1905?

A general feeling of profound discontent with the existing order was the most apparent symptom of the corruption with which the social and political life of Russia was infested ...

The student recognised no law. As for the workers they were concerned with filling their stomachs with more food than had been their wont ... Finally the peasantry, the majority of the Russian people, were anxious to increase their holdings ...

The government had lost its power to act, everybody was either doing nothing or moving in different directions, and the authority of the regime and of its supreme bearer was completely trampled down ...

1 ⤳ *BLOODY SUNDAY* 9/22 JANUARY 1905

A *Immediate events leading to Bloody Sunday*

The immediate events leading up to *Bloody Sunday* were an industrial dispute at the Putilov metal works in St Petersburg arising from the dismissal of three workers who were prominent members of a trade union, the Assembly of Factory Workers. A strike, supported by most of the 13 000 workers, was called which spread within days to other factories involving a total of 111 000 workers (by the 8/21 January). The dispute was a test of strength for the Assembly of Factory Workers, which had been introduced in 1903 as an officially sponsored union under the government policy of 'revolutionary socialism'. This was the setting up of trade unions apparently to defend workers' interests and voice their grievances, but actually to divert their revolutionary spirit and keep them under control. The initiative for both the setting up of the union and its subsequent activity was taken by Father Georgi Gapon, an orthodox priest, and *Okhrana* double agent who had developed a sense of commitment to improving workers' wages and conditions. The government responded to the January strikes by sending out large numbers of troops to guard essential public services including gasworks and electricity generating stations. Father Gapon decided to lead a peaceful deputation on Sunday 9/22 January to petition the tsar, who was believed to be at the Winter Palace in St Petersburg, for better distribution of food and work and for a constituent assembly. This decision suggests that the workers' still had faith in the tsar and blamed his ministers for having kept him ignorant of the state of affairs. This is confirmed by a letter Father Gapon wrote to Nicholas a day before the march in which he said, 'Sire, Do not believe the Ministers. They are cheating Thee in regard to the real state of affairs. The people believe in Thee. They have made up their minds to gather at the Winter Palace tomorrow at 2 p.m. to lay their needs before Thee ... Do not fear anything. Stand tomorrow before the people and accept our humblest petition. I, the representative of the working men, and my comrades, guarantee the inviolability of Thy person'. They believed that once Nicholas saw the demonstration he would concede their demands immediately.

See page 102.

Gregorian calendar
Pre-Revolutionary Russia used the old style Julian calendar of 46 BC, while the rest of the world followed the 'New Style' calendar of Pope Gregory, introduced in 1582 but adopted by different countries at different times. After 1918 the Russians used the latter. There was a difference of 13 days between the two calendars so 9 January on the **Julian calendar** was 22 January on the 'New Style'.

B *The working class petition of 9/22 January 1905*

Part of the Petition of the Workers' presented to the tsar, Sunday 9 January 1905, quoted by D. Floyd, *Russia in Revolt 1905 – the First Crack in Tsarist Power*, Macdonald, 1969.

Who were the petitioners?

What request had they made to their employers before the workers went on strike?

What had been the workers 'other demands'?

What complaints did the workers direct against Nicholas' officials?

What did the workers' regard as the solution to their grievances?

What does the tone of the Petition tell you about the attitude of the people to the tsar?

Sire:

We, working men and inhabitants of St Petersburg, our wives and our children and our helpless old parents, have come to You to seek truth, justice, and protection.

Sire: we have no more strength. Our endurance is at an end. We have reached that terrible moment when death would be better than the prolongation of intolerable sufferings ... Therefore we have stopped work and told our masters that we shall not start again until they comply with our demands. We ask but little. We want only what is indispensable for life ...

Our first request was that our employers should discuss our demands with us, but this they refused to do ... They regarded as illegal our other demands: reduction of the working day to eight hours, the fixing of the wage rates in consultation with us, investigation of our grievances against the factory managements, an increase in the daily rate for unskilled working men and women to one rouble, the abolition of overtime, medical attention to be given carefully and considerately, and the construction of factories in which it is possible to work without risk of death from wind, rain and snow ...

We have been in bondage, with the help and co-operation of Your officials. Anyone who dares to speak up in defence of the interests of the working class and the ordinary people is gaoled or exiled ... Government by bureaucracy has brought the country to complete ruin, involved it in a shameful war, and is leading further towards disaster ... Popular representation is essential. Capitalists, workers, bureaucrats, priests, doctors, and teachers – let them all choose their own representatives.

Let them all have a free and equal vote, and for this purpose order the election of a constituent assembly on the basis of universal suffrage ... But if You do not give these orders or respond to our pleas, we shall die here in this square in front of Your palace. We have nowhere else to go and there is no point in our going. There are only two paths ahead for us: one leading to freedom and happiness, the other to the grave. Let our lives be a sacrifice for suffering Russia. We do not offer this sacrifice grudgingly but gladly.

C *Events of the day*

A massed crowd of 20 000 men, women, children and elderly assembled at five or six points in their Sunday clothes and, carrying banners,

PICTURE 14 *A painting of* Bloody Sunday, *Father Gapon and his followers, Radio Times Hulton Picture Library*

marched in columns to the Winter Palace, arriving at two o'clock in the afternoon. Father Gapon who wanted the deputation to look like a religious procession led one column while other clergy led the other columns and the marchers sang hymns and carried religious icons and portraits of the tsar. Such processions were a common sight in the city of St Petersburg and attracted no attention from bystanders. The authorities reacted by placing columns of armed soldiers of the city's regiments at key points in the city suburbs, including the Narva Arch, which celebrated Russia's victories over Napoleon I's invasion of 1812. It was here that the marching columns met the armed police and troops and were ordered to halt. When this was ignored an armed detachment of Cossack cavalry galloped into the crowd and broke them up.

The crowd regrouped and continued the advance only to find that the Cossacks then used their knouts, then the flat of their swords and finally they fired. The strikers in the front ranks fell on to their knees and begged to be allowed to pass, protesting that they had no hostile intentions. Their pleas were ignored and the troops continued to fire. The dead and injured were carried away and Father Gapon fled into hiding. As news of the events spread other people joined the marchers, who continued with their original objective – the Palace Square – and once again the troops opened fire. Various accounts exist of the events though they differ in their details of the day reflecting different authorship, and bias.

200 000 workers moved to the palace.

'They were dressed in their Sunday best, the grey and old ones and the young; the women went along with their husbands.

Fathers and mothers led their little children by their hands. Thus the people went to their Tsar'.

Hearken, hearken, peasants!

Let every word engrave itself on your hearts ...

All the streets and squares, where the peaceful workers were to march, were occupied by troops.

'Let us through to the Tsar!' the workers begged.

The old ones fell on their knees.

The women begged and the children begged.

'Let us through to the Tsar!' – 'And then it happened!'

The guns went off with a thunder ... The snow reddened with workers' blood.

Tell all and sundry in what way the Tsar has dealt with the toilers of St. Petersburg ...

Peasants, at your meetings tell the soldiers, the people's Sons who live on the people's money, that they dare not shoot at the people.

ACCOUNT 1

Leon Trotsky, a Marxist revolutionary describes the events of Bloody Sunday, *quoted by B. Pares,* Russia and Reform, *Constable, 1907.*

To-day, at about 10 a.m. workers began to gather at Narva Gates, in the Vyborg and Petersburg districts, and also on Vasilievsky Island at the premises of the Assembly of factory Workers, with the aim, as announced by Father Gapon, of marching to Palace Square to present a petition to the Emperor. When a crowd of several thousand had assembled in the Narva district. Father Gapon said prayers and then together with the crowd, which had at its head banners and icons stolen from a Narva chapel as well as portraits of Their Majesties, moved off towards the Narva Gates where they were confronted by troops. Despite pleas by local police officers and cavalry charges, the crowd did not disperse but continued to advance ... Two companies then opened fire, killing ten men and wounding twenty ... A little later about 4000 workers who had come from the Petersburg and Vvborg districts approached the Trinity Bridge. Father Gapon was also with them. A volley was fired into the crowd, killing five and seriously injuring ten. Towards 1 p.m. people began to gather in the Alexander Garden, over-flowing out of the garden itself into the adjoining part of Palace Square. The cavalry made a series of charges to disperse the crowd, but as this had no effect a number of volleys were fired into the crowd. The numbers of dead and wounded from these volleys is not known as the crowd carried off the victims. The crowd then engulfed Nevsky Prospect and refused to disperse: a number of shots were fired, killing sixteen people, including one woman.

ACCOUNT 2

Report of the Head of St Petersburg police to Director of Department, 9/22 January 1905, quoted by M. McCauley, Octobrists to Bolsheviks: Imperial Russia, 1905–1917, *Edward Arnold, 1984.*

1. *What evidence is there in Account 1 to suggest that it was a peaceful demonstration?*
2. *How did the Police Chief in Account 2 attempt to discredit the reputation of the marchers?*
3. *To what extent do the two commentators agree in their account of the events of the day?*
4. *Which account do you consider the more useful and why?*
5. *Which account do you consider the more reliable and why?*
6. *What do you think were the aims of each commentator in his account of the day?*
7. *How did the different aim for which each account was written help to explain the differences between them in style and in content?*

There is no reliable record of the total number killed and injured on the 9/22 January. Official figures admit to 130 killed and 450 wounded but this only concerned those dealt with by the authorities and the estimate is far too low. A group of journalists later produced a list of 4600 people dead and wounded in the day's battles.

D *Significance of* Bloody Sunday

The regime had re-affirmed its strength but at a cost. It was recognised by some politicians that the event had damaged its reputation both abroad and at home. Count Kokovtsov, Assistant (1904–5) and then Finance Minister 1906–14 and Chairman of the Council of Ministers 1911–14, recalls: 'the impression it created abroad was tremendous, and this just as I was negotiating for two independent loans, one in Paris and the other in Berlin'. The greatest damage was to Nicholas' reputation at home though he seemed oblivious of this. When he came to make an entry in his diary for 22 January he made only a very brief reference to the events before passing on to record family happenings. 'A painful day! There have been serious disorders in Petersburg because some workmen wanted to come up to the Palace. Troops had to open fire in several places in the city; there were many killed and wounded. God, how painful and sad! Mama arrived from town; straight to Mass. I lunched with all the others. Went for a walk with Misha (Michael). Mama stayed overnight' (Marc Ferro, *Nicholas II: the Last of the Tsars*, Penguin, 1990).

Father Gapon, who had been a supporter of autocracy, denounced Nicholas as a traitor to his people. Any illusions that the people may have had that Nicholas would support them when he heard of their grievances was totally destroyed by the brutal action of the police and army. In the words of one foreign observer, 'the present ruler has lost absolutely the affection of the Russian people, and whatever the future may have in store for the dynasty, the present tsar will never be safe in the midst of his people' (Report of the United States consul in Odessa, quoted by L. Kochan, *Russia in Revolution 1890–1918*, Granada, 1966). Marxist revolutionaries, such as Trotsky, recognised the significance of the events of 9/22 January but as proof that the working people were an effective political force. His claim that 'the revolution has come' was both over-optimistic and rejected by the leader of the Bolsheviks, Lenin.

Reporting the events of *Bloody Sunday* in his newspaper, *Vperyod*, on the 31 January 1905 (No. 4, Geneva), Lenin wrote:

Q

Why, according to Lenin, did the 'Government deliberately allow the strike movement to develop'?

To what extent was the government successful in its deception?

Most important historic events are taking place in Russia. The proletariat has risen against Tsarism. The Government has driven the proletariat to the uprising. Now, there is hardly room for doubt that the Government deliberately allowed the strike movement to develop and a wide demonstration to be started in order to bring matters to a head, and to have a pretext for calling out the military forces. Its manoeuvre was successful. Thousands of killed and wounded – this is the toll of Bloody Sunday, January 22, in Petersburg … The revolution is spreading. The government is already beginning to waver. From a policy of bloody repression it is trying to pass to economic concessions and to save itself by throwing a sop, by promising the nine-hour day. But the lesson of Bloody Sunday must not be forgotten. The demand of the rebellious Petersburg workers – the immediate convocation of a Constituent Assembly on the basis of universal, direct, equal and secret suffrage – must become the demand of all striking workers.

E *Reaction of Nicholas II and his government*

General Dmitri Trepov, Governor General of St Petersburg, persuaded Nicholas that he should appease the working people by meeting representatives of the factories to assure them of his concern for their welfare. He agreed on condition that 'sensible men were selected'. Trepov's men and the factory inspectors made the selection to the disgust of the radicals within the factory who refused to have anything to do with the delegation. On being presented to Nicholas the delegates were given a short sermon in which he 'forgave them' and then sent down to the kitchens for food and drink before being sent home. Far from pacifying the people Nicholas' action merely served to increase their opposition. Nicholas now added to his mistake of having been absent for *Bloody Sunday* by failing to realise the seriousness of the revolutionary situation that developed. Within weeks the Governor General of Moscow, Nicholas' uncle, Grand Duke Sergei Alexandrovich, was assassinated.

2 ⌐ DEVELOPMENT OF
A REVOLUTIONARY MOVEMENT
JANUARY TO OCTOBER 1905

A *Causes of the revolution*

The issues that led to revolution have already been covered so they are just briefly summarised below:

Long-term	Short-term	'Trigger' factor
● Grievances of the industrial workers of long hours, poor living and working conditions, low pay.	● Economic slump leading to unemployment, increased poverty and hardship.	● Events of *Bloody Sunday*.
● Peasant discontent arising from burden of redemption payments, low productivity and profitability of land, taxation burden, insufficient land and high taxes.	● Series of bad harvest led many peasants to default on their mortgage; payments.	● Nicholas made a number of mistakes: he was absent from the Winter Palace on the 9/22 January, he failed to realise the seriousness of the situation and he made few concessions in the vital first few days.
● Middle-class resentment at exclusion from share in government, feeling of ill will against an incompetent government.	● Food shortages caused by harvest failures and war against Japan.	
● Student uprisings and over-reaction of police.	● Regime's failure to ensure a fair distribution of food.	
● Nationalities' resentment of imposition of Russian language, culture and religion and lack of regard for their demands for self-rule.	● Development of political parties and rival ideologies with leaders who were prepared to push for political change.	
● Impact of regime's repressive policies.	● Activities of Plehve as Minister of the Interior who made use of the secret police, the *Okhrana* and 'police socialism'.	
	● Frustration of *zemstva* liberals at activities of local civil servants who resented their suggestions for change led to the *zemstva* becoming more political. Ban on *zemstva* holding National Congresses led to 'banquets' or social gatherings that became an opportunity for demands for political reform – held in November 1904.	

B *Main stages to the 1905 Revolution*

At the end of January Nicholas was warned by one of his ministers that, despite his success in dealing with the events of *Bloody Sunday*, agitation remained and that he could not rely on the loyalty of his troops.

Yermolov, Agriculture Minister, discusses with Nicholas about the use of troops, January 1905, quoted by David Floyd, *Russia in Revolt 1905: The First Crack in Tsarist Power*, Macdonald, 1969.

Q

How serious was the situation confronting the regime in 1905?

What was the basis of Yermolov's warning to Nicholas?

On 9 January the soldiers certainly carried out the very difficult task which fell to their lot to fire on a defenceless crowd. The unrest, which started in Petersburg, has now spread to most of the towns of Russia and everywhere they have to be put down by force of arms. So far this is proving possible and the soldiers are doing their duty. But what shalt we do when disorder spreads from the towns to the villages when the peasants rise up and when the slaughter starts in the countryside? What forces and what soldiers shalt we use then to put down a peasant revolt, which will spread across the whole country? And in the second place…Your Majesty can we be sure that the troops who have now obeyed their officers and fired into the people but who come from that very same people and who even now are in contact with the population who have heard the screams and curses hurled at them by their victims can we be sure that they will behave in the same way if such incidents are repeated?

Subsequent events were to prove that Yermolov had been accurate in his predictions. Between January and October 1905 a revolutionary situation developed in which the different sections and interest groups in Russia united in opposition to the regime – an unprecedented event.

KEY ISSUE

Main events January–October 1905.

January –February

In the aftermath of Bloody Sunday, a general strike broke out in St Petersburg leading to an outbreak of protest strikes throughout the Empire.

Peasant disturbances spread quickly through the Kursk province into the Volga region and most of the Black earth provinces.

Mass political strikes by workers, students and teaching staff occurred throughout 1905 spreading to Moscow and many Russian cities and then outwards to all parts of the Russian Empire. Resentment against Russification policies provoked rebellion in the Ukraine, Poland, the Baltic States, Finland, the Caucasus. Jews played an active part in the unrest. Witte reporting on the disturbances of 1905 made specific reference to the grievances felt by some of Russia's nationalities when he wrote, 'seeing this great upheaval, (they) lifted their heads and decided that the time was ripe for the realisation of their dreams and desires. The Poles wanted autonomy, the Jews wanted equal rights, and so on. All of them longed for the destruction of the system of deliberate oppression that embittered their lives. And on top of everything, the army was in an ugly mood.'

Over a quarter of a million troops were required to keep order in Poland alone where fighting broke out on the streets. Martial law was proclaimed in the Baltic States where there was virtual civil war. The Russian army was seriously stretched between fighting a war with Japan, policing the nationalities and suppressing domestic disturbances.

Soldiers mutinied in the garrisons at Vladivostok, Tiflis, Tashkent and Warsaw.

February   A member of the Social Revolutionary Party assassinated Grand Duke Serge Alexandrovich.

Nicholas instructed his Minister of the Interior, Bulygin, to draw up plans for an elected assembly, chosen by the people 'to take part in the preliminary consideration of projects of law'.

March   Georgia declared itself an independent state.

On the 3rd March the tsar issued a reform programme which included plans for a consultative body, the State Duma, but this was too little too late.

May   The Japanese sank in one afternoon, the Baltic fleet, which had sailed half-way round the world.

The first **Soviet** appeared in the textile town of Ivanovo, east of Moscow. This was a strike committee whose members were elected from all the town's workers. It owed its idea to the peasant commune. Soviets appeared to other towns.

> **Soviet** is Russian word for advice or counsel.

June   On the 14th sailors mutinied on the battleship Prince Potemkin in the Black Sea and were briefly joined by the St George. This was the first significant show of disloyalty in the armed forces that always had been one of the main supporters of the regime. A survivor of the battle of Tsushima, A. Zaterty, recalled in 1907 some of the grievances felt by sailors (from J.N. Westwood, *Endurance and Endeavour; Russian History 1812–1986*, OUP, 1973).

These noblemen's sons, well cared for and fragile, were capable only of decking themselves out in tunics with epaulettes. They would then stick their snouts in the air like a mangy horse being harnessed, and bravely scrape their heels on polished floors, or dance gracefully at balls, or get drunk, in these ways demoralising their subordinates. They didn't even know our names. Corporal punishment was forbidden on paper only, for decency's sake: 'the sailors were beaten for all kinds of reasons, and often. It was considered the natural order of things. There was no way of complaining... We were compelled to eat rotten biscuits and stinking decaying meat while our officers fatted themselves with the best food and drank the most expensive wines'.

Urged on by several revolutionary activists the sailors killed many of the officers and took control of the ship. They sailed around the Black Sea bombarding Odessa, killing 2000 and threatening other southern ports. They sought sanctuary in Rumania where they sank the ship... The regime, fearful that mutiny would spread through the

Q

Identify the main grievances of the sailors of the Prince Potemkin?

What was the significance of the mutiny?

fleet ordered that no action should be taken against the *Prince Potemkin*. The mutiny was a severe blow to the confidence and prestige of the navy ministry, to the regime's prestige abroad as well as encouraging the revolutionaries into believing that southern Russia would revolt. The fears of the regime proved to be well founded – between June and July there were ten mutinies in the army and navy – though soldiers continued to suppress disorders.

June–July Trade unions were formed illegally reflecting the failure of the police and army to keep control.

Liberal members of the professions joined together the Union of Zemstva and Union of Liberation to form themselves into a 'Union of Unions', presided over by Pavel Milyukov. They argued that 'all means are admissible in the face of the terrible menace contained in the very fact of the continued existence of the present government: and every means must be tried'. They appealed to 'all groups, to all parties, all organised unions, all private groups and we say with all our strength, with all the means at our disposal, you must hasten the removal of the gang of robbers that is now in power, and put in its place a constituent assembly' (Declaration of Union of Unions, quoted by L. Kochan, *Russia in Revolution 1890–1918*, Granada, 1966). They demanded a constituent assembly and became known as the Constitutional Democrats or Kadets with Milyukov elected as their president in 1907.

In July the newly formed Peasants Union held a Peasant Union Congress at which it demanded that, 'private property in land should be abolished … The land should be considered the common property of the whole people'. The Peasants Union later joined Union of Union.

Peasants had embarked on a wave of protest that was spontaneous in many places but not completely uncontrolled or unorganised. They drove the landowner and his family and servants off the farm before setting fire to the farm buildings and then seizing the land for redistribution by the commune in equal plots among the peasants. The burning of buildings prevented the landlord from returning to his land or of Cossack soldiers having a billet if they were sent out to suppress peasant disturbances. According to a newspaper report of rural disturbances for the central provinces of Russia (quoted by David Floyd, *Russia in Revolt 1905: The First Crack in Tsarist Power*, Macdonald, 1969):

Hundreds of buildings worth several millions of roubles have been destroyed. All the buildings have been razed to the ground in (some) enormous estates. Many houses have been burnt down without reference to the relations which had existed between the peasants and the landowners or the latter's political views. The farms of ... well known *zemstvo* liberals, have suffered along with the rest.

June–July   University students went on strike and made university buildings available for public meetings. These became significant for organising unrest. At a student congress in Vyborg in 1905, students declared that: 'students must mobilise their forces in the powerful towns and create the possibility of using higher education institutions for revolutionary agitation and propaganda in the broad masses of the people and undertake measures to organise student fighting squads so that the students, when necessary, can join the general political strike and armed uprising' (quoted by L. Kochan, *Russia in Revolution 1890–1918*, Granada, 1966).

Writing of the crisis of these months Milyukov commented on the change in the relationship between the government and the opposition forces. He warned that (Pavel Milyukov, *Russia and its Crisis, 1905*)

Russia is passing through a crisis; she is sick and her sickness is so grave as to demand an immediate and radical cure. Palliatives can be of no use; rather, they but increase the gravity of the situation. To pretend that all is right in Russia, except for a few 'ill-intentioned' persons who are making all the fuss, is no longer ridiculous it is criminal. Upon quite peaceful and law-abiding citizens, who never shared in any political struggle, and never had any definite political opinions, the feeling begins to dawn that the system of self-defence practised by the government precludes general progress and the development of private initiatives, just as forty years ago progress was precluded by the further existence of serfdom ... Increased and unified as they are, the forces of opposition are still not strong enough to replace the government by a violent overthrow. But they are strong enough to make the use of violence continuous, and by increasing this to preclude any further peaceful work of civilization. No form of government can survive ... which possesses no moral force and is obliged to carry all its orders into execution by mere material force.

> **Q**
> *Why, according to Milyukov, had the time arrived for 'an immediate and radical cure'?*

consultative national assembly meant one that had no real power but existed merely to give advice, which could be rejected.

August   News arrived of Japan's defeat of Russia.

Nicholas tried to stop rioting by promising an elected but purely consultative national assembly based on a high property qualification, which excluded most workers, all

Jews and women. Peasants would elect 43%, landowners 33% and towns 23%. This assembly could eventually evolve into a representative body such as that demanded by the zemstva. Had he offered this in January it might have been accepted but by August opposition had grown too large and too angry and the Kadets rejected the offer.

September   On the 19th printing workers went on strike and workers in Moscow and St Petersburg quickly copied this.

October   On the 7th railway workers went on strike and within a few days Russia was faced with its first general strike. There were too few troops to suppress disorders and take over the running of essential services including transport. The following is from a report by the French consul in Kharkov, October 1905 (quoted by L. Kochan, *Russia in Revolution 1890–1918*, Granada, 1966).

Q

What was the impact of the general strike in Kharkov?

Identify the different groups who took part in the strike.

How effective was the action taken by the authorities?

In Kharkov, in the Ukraine, work stopped everywhere: on the railways, in all factories, workshops, in shops of all types, in the University, in all schools, in all administrative offices, even the telegraph offices … the whole population was on the streets, either as sightseers or as demonstrators. From the evening, people began to ransack arms stores and to smash the windows of the large stores and conservative journals. On the 24th, students directed by lawyers, doctors and teachers and helped by workmen and Jews, seized the district neighbouring the University and set up ten barricades made of heavy oak planks, telegraph and telephone poles, electric light standards and large paving stones. The rioters seized the law courts where the archives were and threw them into the streets.

All the police could do was organise a poor demonstration at one rouble a head, with a portrait of the emperor and the national flag. This demonstration failed pitifully before the student's revolvers – they tore the Tsar's portrait and the flags to shreds …

October   St Petersburg workers set up a Soviet in the Technical Institute with Leon Trotsky, a Menshevik, as Chairman. The committee, which was dominated by the intelligentsia, soon acquired more power than the city government. It co-ordinated the activities of Soviets in other cities so that the regime was faced with a united opposition for the first time. Many employers supported the strike, even paying their workers half pay.

In the middle of October unrest spread to the heart of government when officials employed in the Treasury and all the Ministries along with employees of the State bank went on strike.

Between the 15 October and the end of 1905 there were at least 211 mutinies affecting a third of the army in

European Russia, which extended to soldiers on the Trans Siberian Railway returning from the Russo-Japanese War. They were motivated by the belief that imperial authority had collapsed and that a collapse of discipline would result.

By the middle of October it was obvious that government was near to collapse and that concessions had to be made for it to survive. Nicholas was alarmed and, overcoming his dislike, he summoned the moderate Sergei Witte whom he thought might be able to restore order. Witte had recently returned from America where he had been involved in peace negotiations with Japan. He described the mass urban unrest in October, the press came out without any supervision or respect for the law. The municipal railways were on strike, almost all traffic on the streets had ceased, street lighting was no more, the inhabitants of the capital feared to go out on the streets at night, water supplies were cut off, the telephone network was out of action, all railways to St Petersburg were on strike (L. Kochan, *Russia in Revolution 1890–1918*, Granada, 1966).

He feared 'when the army returned home after all its failures it would join the revolution and then everything would really collapse'. In a series of meetings two possible courses of action were discussed before Witte persuaded Nicholas to accept his recommendations ... Writing to his mother at this time Nicholas implied his reluctance to accept his minister's advice but recognised that it was 'the only way out at the present moment'. Part of Nicholas II's letter to his mother in 1905 (quoted by R. Tames, *The Last of the Tsars: The Life and Death of Nicholas and Alexandra*, Pan, 1972) is given below.

See page 81.

We very often met in the early morning to part only in the evening when night fell. There were only two ways open:

To find an energetic soldier to crush the rebellion by sheer force. There would be time to breathe then but as likely as not one would have to use force again in a few months, and that would mean rivers of blood and in the end we should be where we started.

The other way out would be to give the people their civil rights, freedom of speech, and Press, also to have all the laws confirmed by a State *Duma* or parliament – that of course would be a constitution.

Witte defends this energetically. He says that while it is not without risk, it is the only way out at the present moment. Almost everybody I had an opportunity of consulting is of the same opinion ... He ... drew up a Manifesto (in October). We discussed it for two days and in the end, invoking God's help, I signed it ... My only consolation is that such is the will of God and this grave decision will lead my dear Russia out of the intolerable chaos she has been in for nearly a year.

Q

What was Nicholas' preferred course of action?

Why did Nicholas accept Witte's course of action?

What concessions did Nicholas make to the people?

C *Outcome of the 1905 Revolution*

The regime was forced to make a number of major political concessions between October 1905 and April 1906. Each concession was prefaced by a reference to end 'the rioting and agitation in the capitals' and the 'troubles that have broken out in the villages' and to restore order. He expressed concern with the welfare of his subjects and called on 'all true sons of Russia to remember their duty to their homeland, to put a stop to unprecedented unrest and together, to devote all their strength to the restoration of peace'.

The October Manifesto appeared to offer the people considerable concessions:

KEY ISSUE

The October Manifesto.

- civil liberties rights of 'free citizenship', and 'freedom of person, conscience, speech, assembly, and union'
- introduction of a consultative assembly or State *Duma*, with legislative powers elected by a broad franchise that would include social groups that had previously had no elected rights.

The Manifesto extended the earlier proposals Nicholas had made in August since the assembly was given the right to share in the making of laws and to supervise the legality of government. It was this last provision that ended Nicholas' autocratic powers. However the word 'consultative' is revealing since it implied that Nicholas could ask for advice but he was under no obligation to accept the views expressed. He refused to consider the radical liberals and socialists demand for a constituent assembly elected by direct, equal and secret universal suffrage that would draw up a constitution for the country.

Further concessions followed in the 3rd November Manifesto 'to better the conditions… of the peasant population' which continued with the fiscal reforms that had been introduced in 1902 and 1904. Remaining redemption payments were reduced from 1 January 1906, and discontinued altogether after 1 January 1907. The resources of the Peasant Land Bank were increased so that it could offer better terms for loans, to help the peasant with little land to buy more.

Nicholas' new constitutional system was published in the Fundamental Laws of the Russian Empire on the 23 April 1906. In re-affirming the powers of the tsar and his determination to maintain autocracy, the Laws indicated that Nicholas had learned nothing from the events of 1905. It was laid down that the tsar continued to have the power to:

1 hold supreme autocratic power by divine right
2 exercise law-making power in conjunction with the Council of the Empire and the Imperial *Duma*
3 approve the laws, and without his approval no law could come into existence
4 hold all governmental powers in their widest extent throughout the whole Russian Empire
5 appoint and dismiss the president of the Council, the ministers themselves, and the heads of the chief departments of administra-

tion, as well as all other officials where the law did not provide for another method of appointment and dismissal. Ministers were responsible to him alone and even if the *Duma*, by a two-thirds majority, passed a vote of censure on the government, the government did not have to resign

6   declare war and approve a peace settlement

7   rule by decree during periods when the *Duma* was not in session.

D *Response of different groups to Nicholas' concessions*

Nicholas' concessions effectively split the various interest groups that had united in opposition to him by October 1905. The October Manifesto met a mixed response amongst the Liberals. Those on the right of the Party immediately accepted its terms relieved that the revolution was over. Moderate Liberals re-organised to form a new party, the Union of 17 October, more appropriately known as the *Octobrists* with Alexander Guchkov as their leader and a daily newspaper, *Golos Moskvy.* The Liberal left wing had formed themselves into a rival party, the Constitutional Democrats, *Kadets*, earlier in the month. Led by Pavel Milyukov and Petrunkevich, they criticised the Manifesto for its failure to provide for an elected constitutional assembly with its own constitution. They were determined to continue with the constitutional struggle though they had no desire for revolution and so were prepared to accept the concessions as a starting point for further reforms. They accepted the regime's suppression of mutinies in the army and navy and working class strikes between October and December 1905.

> **KEY ISSUE**
>
> *Liberal response.*

The 3rd November Manifesto met one of the most pressing demands of the peasants – an end to redemption payments, though not immediately as they hoped but phased out over a 2-year period. Many had joined the 1905 revolution because they feared that the government would repossess the land of mortgage holders who had defaulted on payments as a result of the hardships caused by the series of bad harvests. The government recognised this fear and hoped that it could 'derevolutionise' the naturally conservative peasantry with the 3rd November concession. This did not happen immediately because some peasants interpreted the Manifesto as a right to seize the land that they considered to be theirs by custom but which had been reclaimed by the gentry at the time of emancipation. The number of peasant disturbances rose during the spring and summer 1906 the peasants burnt the landlord's houses and a number of Governors and police were killed. These disturbances reached a peak in November and December but then declined as Stolypin's agricultural reforms took effect.

> **KEY ISSUE**
>
> *Peasant response.*

What is perhaps most interesting is the impact of the November Manifesto on the rank and file in both the army and the navy, many of whom were peasants. According to J. Bushnell, they interpreted the November Manifesto as permission to ignore authority and indulge in expressions of resentment. Between October and December 1905

KEY ISSUE

Response of the rank and file in the army and navy.

mutinies in the army reduced the regime's effective control over the cities and blocked communication between Siberia and Manchuria. Loyal army units were hampered from returning to the two capitals to deal with unrest. The most famous incident was the mutiny at Kronstadt naval base in the Baltic 26–27 October which was put down with force only after 26 men were killed and another 107 injured. Other mutinies followed at Sebastopol in the Black Sea fleet, and Vladivostok between the 30 and 31 October (J. Bushnell, *Mutiny amid Repression: Russian Soldiers in the Revolution of 1905–06*, Bloomington: Indiana University Press, 1985). The mutineers acted in unison with either whole units mutinying or none. They usually confined their action to the presentation of a petition demanding improvements in conditions and they always expressed loyalty to the tsar. By November 1905 mutinies in the army had led to a situation where the government failed to have control of ten of the Empire's nineteen largest cities, including Moscow. This meant that the regime's situation remained desperate until with the help of loyal Cossack troops, it brutally suppressed mutinies in the army in December 1905. The inborn loyalty of the army became apparent in December when rank and file soldiers who had been mutineers a few days earlier were used to suppress a Bolshevik led uprising in Moscow with great bloodshed. Despite this, the army remained unreliable; there were 200 mutinies during the course of 1906, mainly between April and July when the *Duma* was in session, affecting more than 20% of army units.

KEY ISSUE

Working class response.

The industrial workers, who had gained valuable experience of political action, were not satisfied by Nicholas' concessions. Their expectations are best expressed by the claims of the St Petersburg factory metal workers when they went on strike in October 1905. They declared, 'we proclaim a political strike, and we will fight to the last for the summoning of a Constituent Assembly on the basis of universal, equal, direct and secret suffrage to introduce a democratic republic in Russia' (Trotsky 1905). They very quickly realised that their few gains were illusory. The guarantee of civil rights – of freedom of speech, and assembly and the legalising of trade unions was widely ignored by the regime when it sought to re-establish its control in November and December of 1905. The St Petersburg *Soviet* continued with its protest and on the 1 November 1905 called the second general strike in support of the rebellion of the Kronstadt sailors. The proclamation declared, 'the government continues to stride over corpses. It puts on trial before a court-martial the brave Kronstadt soldiers of the army and navy who rose to the defence of their rights and of national freedom. It put the noose of martial law on the neck of oppressed Poland. The Council of Workmen's Delegates calls on the revolutionary proletariat of Petersburg to manifest their solidarity with the revolu- tionary soldiers of Kronstadt and with the revolutionary proletarians of Poland through a general political strike, which has proved to be a for- midable power, and through general meetings of protest'. However, the *Soviet* increasingly met with little response and on the 5 November called off its strike. Unrest and strikes continued until 3 December when all members of the St Petersburg *Soviet*, including Trotsky, were arrested (he was sent to a remote Arctic penal colony), and the *Soviet* was closed by troops. This was followed by the suppression of the Moscow *Soviet* which had declared its intention to get rid of the tsar.

3 ⌐ REASONS FOR TSARIST SURVIVAL AND RECOVERY

'The lesson of 1905 was that as long as the Tsarist government kept its nerve and the army remained basically loyal, the forces of opposition would not be strong enough to mount a serious challenge' (Michael Lynch, *Reactions and Revolutions: Russia 1881–1924*, Hodder & Stoughton, 1992).

In October 1905 Nicholas II's regime appeared to be on the point of collapse; by the end of 1906 he was once again in firm control. He had achieved this recovery by a combination of concessions, which effectively split the previously united opposition, and by force, but there were other factors in his favour:

- He benefited from the inherent disunity of the opposition. The alliance of different social groups challenged the traditional division between Russia's educated elite and its illiterate peasants and workers. They had different aims for taking action in 1905 and were united only by a common cause against Nicholas II.
- No clear or capable leadership emerged to co-ordinate activities for most of the revolutionary activists, particularly Lenin (who did not return until December 1905), were abroad; apart from Trotsky who emerged as leader of the St Petersburg *Soviet*. His Marxist views on revolution alienated other groups who had no intention of achieving a revolution in terms of an overthrow of the political structures of power since this carried with it the danger of an accompanying social revolution.
- The mass protests were more outbreaks of rage with the intention of forcing concessions rather than revolutionary actions to replace government. This limited purpose explains the reluctance of middle-class liberals to go too far and their willingness to accept the October Manifesto, which satisfied their immediate needs. In that respect the Manifesto helped to 'take the fire' out of the revolutionary movement. Peter Struve, who was a Marxist prior to joining the Kadets in 1905, voiced the feelings of many when he said, 'Thank God for the tsar who has saved us from the people'. But even among the masses there was the same narrowness of purpose. Amongst the industrial classes use of the strike weapon declined as they suffered from lack of wages and there was little support for using violence, apart from in Moscow. Pacified by the promise of political reform and civil liberties, they began to return to work forcing the St Petersburg *Soviet* to call off the General Strike on 21 October. When further general strikes were called in November there was little

response and that of 1 November was called off after 4 days (on the 5). In the case of the peasants their disturbances were part of a generalised discontent, which had been more prominent in 1902–3 than in 1905. Their participation in 1905 added to the alarm of the government, but they were not a major threat and they were willing to be bought off by the November Manifesto.

● Nicholas benefited from the loyalty of the army as a whole and its willingness to destroy the *Soviets*. Where mutinies had occurred in the armed forces these had been confined and did not continue when the war against Japan came to an end. Loyal units that had been stationed in Manchuria returned to deal first with the St Petersburg *Soviet*, whose headquarters was stormed followed by the arrest of its leaders in the next few days. Even more violence was used against the Moscow *Soviet* to end the strike it had called on the 10th December. A considerable number of strikers were killed in the fighting and in the summary executions, which followed while thousands more were rounded up and sent to Siberia. Willingness on the part of the regime to take such harsh action ended revolutionary activity in the towns. The troops were then sent out to restore order in the villages so that order had been restored by January 1906 apart from some outbreaks of indiscipline amongst the troops in St Petersburg, Moscow, Kiev and other centres and mutiny on the Sebastopol. Revolutionaries who had not been arrested fled abroad.

PICTURE 15
The Revolution of 1905 – cartoon reflecting contemporary comment on the events. 'Now at last my people are free', says the tsar, BPC Library

PICTURE 16
The Revolution of 1905 – cartoon reflecting contemporary comment on the events. 'The Tsar as the Angel of Peace'

PICTURE 17 *The Revolution of 1905 – cartoon reflecting contemporary comment on the events. 'In this world there is a Tsar. He is without pity. HUNGER is his name'*, The David King collection

PICTURE 18 *The Revolution of 1905 – cartoon reflecting contemporary comment on the events. The Voter, by Ezha*, The David King collection

● In addition to the army and the police, the regime made use of frightened right-wing forces who came forward after the October Manifesto to defend the monarchy. They organised themselves into gangs, known as the *Black Hundreds*, and during the course of November and December attacked revolutionaries, students and nationalist Poles, and Finns but most of all Jews. The Jews had been a prominent group amongst the revolutionaries and this provoked a resurgence of the anti-Semitic feeling that had always been present in Russian society. The worst excesses took place in Odessa where over 500 Jews were killed and property destroyed. In many cases the police and army remained aloof and made no attempt to intervene to protect civil liberties.

Q

What message is conveyed in terms of the methods employed by Nicholas' regime to deal with the rioters?

Comment on the usefulness and reliability of these cartoons as a commentary on the events of 1905.

A *Significance of the 1905 Revolution*

The Revolution of 1905 was in fact no revolution at all. But the Tsarist régime did not emerge from the events of 1905 entirely unscathed. Russia was no longer an autocracy but, on paper at least, a constitutional monarchy, and, though the radicals had been defeated, there were still large sections of liberal opinion in the country which wanted to see the promises of the October Manifesto put into practice (David Floyd, *Russia in Revolt 1905: The First Crack in Tsarist Power*, Macdonald, 1969).

The Revolution had not resulted in the overthrow of the Russian monarchy or the Tsarist social system. The industrial workers had taken the lead and the Revolution had occurred in spite of, rather than because, of the revolutionaries. This fact has led some historians to challenge whether 'revolution' is the right term to apply to the events of 1905 especially as Nicholas succeeded in re-establishing his autocratic control within a year by means of fierce repression and executions. Once he had secured his position it was doubtful whether he would allow the liberals to consolidate the gains they had made in the October Manifesto. The subsequent history of the *Duma* and Nicholas' success in undermining its legislative challenge alienated many liberals in the years between 1906 and 1917. Led by Kerensky they carried through the first revolution in February 1917 that forced Nicholas to abdicate both on his and his son's behalf. In that respect the events of 1905 have been interpreted as a 'dress rehearsal for the real revolution of 1917'.

See page 205.

4 ⌁ THE AGE OF THE *DUMAS* 1906–17

A *Introduction*

Many historians generally regard Russia's experiment in constitutional monarchy as the regime's last chance of reforming itself to ensure survival. Unfortunately this was not the view of Nicholas II who in many respects was the author of his own ultimate downfall. He had been prevailed upon by Witte to agree to some of the moderate liberal demands as part of a wider strategy of dividing opponents in order to re-establish autocratic control. However he had no intention of keeping to his concessions and his opponents learnt a great from the experience. If the October Manifesto been given proper support from all sides, and if the *Duma* been allowed to work more effectively, then Russia might have been transformed to such an extent that the 1917 Revolution could have been avoided. In the view of one historian, 'the October Manifesto provided a framework within which the Russian state and Russian society should have found it possible to reduce the tension dividing them. This it failed to accomplish. A constitutional regime can function properly only if government and opposition accept the rules of the game: in Russia, neither the monarchy nor the intelligentsia was prepared to do so. Each regarded the new order as an obstacle, a deviation from the country's true system, which for the monarchy was autocracy and for the intelligentsia, a democratic republic. As a result, the constitutional interlude, while not without achievements, was largely wasted – a missed opportunity which would not recur' (R. Pipes, *The Russian Revolution 1899–1919*, Collins Harvill Press, 1990).

In 1912 rural literacy as an average of 12 European provinces was 39.8% men and 24.8% women.

B *Attitudes towards the* Duma

Constitutional government was a difficult challenge in a country with such a high level of illiteracy and a history of autocratic rule. As a Western system of government the Russian people had no experience, or expertise, in making it a success and the challenge was made the more daunting because the Ministers appointed by Nicholas who were responsible for making democracy work had no appetite for the task.

Nicholas had no intention of handing over any of his power to the people. He had agreed to the October Manifesto only to buy time and to split the opposition in order to re-establish his control. Once the rebellious groups had been suppressed he refused to take his concessions seriously. His view was that he 'had created the *Duma*, not to be directed by it, but to be advised', and he set out to ensure that that would be the case. Even before the elections were held for the first *Duma* he made a number of amendments, despite Witte's strong opposition, which seriously reduced its rights and powers.

See page 140.

He changed the existing State Council, into an upper chamber sitting alongside the *Duma* and having equal rights over the passing of legislation which would still require the imperial agreement. The new State Council would be equally divided between ministers appointed by Nicholas and those elected by the *zemstva* and professional classes. The *Duma* was deprived of any control over the expenditure of the Imperial court or of the army and navy. Finally he timed the publication of the Fundamental Laws to coincide with the meeting of the first *Duma*. Avoiding the term 'Constitution', he re-affirmed that, 'the Emperor of Russia has supreme autocratic power. It is ordained by God himself that his authority should be submitted to, not only out of fear but out of a genuine sense of duty'. He justified his decision on the grounds that if he was 'convinced that Russia wanted me to abdicate my autocratic powers, I would do that, for the country's good. But I am not convinced that is so' (Marc Ferro, *Nicholas II: The Last of the Tsars*, Penguin, 1991).

KEY ISSUE

Attitude of Nicholas II towards the Duma.

Witte shared Nicholas' lack of enthusiasm and is reported to have replied to one British observer, Sir Bernard Pares when questioned about the October Manifesto and its promise of a constitution, that he had 'a constitution in my head but as to my heart, I spit on it!' 'And he spat on the floor … These views were shared by the various right-wing organisations that were gathering strength, such as the Union of the Russian People, the Union of the Russian Land, and the Russian Orthodox Committee, all of which enjoyed support from the Church and sometimes the police. However, Witte's disapproval of Nicholas' amendments attracted bitter criticism from the right wing.

KEY ISSUE

Attitude of Witte towards the Duma.

His resignation coincided with the publication of the Fundamental Laws. His departing comment, which he later recorded in his 1921 *Memoirs*, provides an interesting insight into the limited prospects of success for constitutional monarchy. 'It soon became clear to everyone concerned that the position of the dynasty and of the régime generally was not as insecure as had appeared at first. The revolutionary ardour of the educated proved to be but intellectual itching and the result of idleness. As early as January 1906, I told the Grand-Duke Nikolai Nikolayevich that as soon as I had contracted the (*French*) loan and evacuated Manchuria I would resign my post, for the reason that I found it impossible to play the part of a screen for men and measures

I was opposed to. I did not wish to be a cat's-paw for General Trepov and the Grand-Duke Nikolai, or a shield for the *Black Hundreds*. I resigned in April' (Count Sergei Witte, *Memoirs* Heinemann, 1921). Nicholas who had never forgiven him for pressurising him to issue the October Manifesto accepted claiming that he remained 'unalterably well-disposed towards you and sincerely grateful'. It was reported that Alexandra, who had never been on good terms, gave a sigh of relief as her only comment on the news of Witte's resignation'.

Both the Social Democrats and the Socialist Revolutionaries (SRs) had no faith in the intentions of the tsar and his advisers and had no expectations that the monarchy would honour its promises. The SRs preferred 'direct action' or terrorism by their own organisations, and along with the Social Democrats, decided to boycott the elections to the first *Duma*. This decision split the SRs and a breakaway group formed the People's Socialist Party and its candidates, some of whom were peasants, stood for election. They were known as **Trudoviks**. Although they had felt a sense of despair with Nicholas' reneging of his October concessions, the liberal Constitutional Democrats, or *Kadets* with the support of the *Octobrists* were determined to make a parliamentary régime work under popular control.

> **KEY ISSUE**
>
> *Attitude of the various political parties towards the* Duma.

> **Trudovik** derived from Trudovaya Gruppa meaning Labour group.

C *Electoral system*

During meetings to discuss election procedures, Nicholas wrote that he found the conferences 'very serious and tiring', but details of the election system were finally published in February 1906 with voting to take place in March 1906. The election campaign that followed was hampered by new regulations intended to control the holding of public meetings. The pro-reformists had hoped that the electoral system would be universal, equal, secret and direct but Nicholas turned down 'very firmly' suggestions that there should be a general election based on universal suffrage with the rebuttal, 'God knows why these gentlemen let their imaginations run so wild'.

There would be elections for two chambers:

1 The upper chamber, known as the Council of State, totalling 196, was composed equally of elected and appointed members. The elected members totalling 196, were chosen by the Church, provincial *zemstva*, nobility, universities and business organisations.

2 The lower chamber, known as the State *Duma*, totalling nearly 500 had its deputies elected in separate electoral colleges, according to class and property. The five largest cities directly elected its members but elsewhere deputies were chosen indirectly. All men over the age of 45 were given the vote, but only very few, landowners with estates of more than 400 acres, were able to vote directly. Peasants voted indirectly in two stages, since they first voted for members of the *volost* assemblies and the later chose the official voters.

The property qualification for voting meant that only very few factory workers had access to the ballot box. Representation in terms of the distribution of seats amongst the constituencies tended to favour the peasant/rural areas in the government expectation that more conservative candidate would be returned. The system of voting gave 31% of the vote to the relatively small class of landowners, while the biggest group, the peasants had 42% and the town 27%. However imperfect, the system provided for some representation of the people including the nationalities. Of the 500 deputies, 412 represented the provinces of European Russia, while Poland had 36 deputies, the Caucasus 29 and the remaining 23 were allocated between Siberia, Central Asia and the Far East.

The first two *Dumas* were far more radical than Nicholas had expected or planned, particularly the second, which was attended by the Social Democrats. On the 3rd June 1907, Stolypin, who had become Minister of the Interior in April 1906, dismissed the second *Duma* and issued a new electoral law under the powers granted to Nicholas in the Fundamental Laws. His failure to obtain the consent of the *Duma* was a breach of the Laws so that Stolypin's action can be seen as a *coup d'etat*. This enormously restricted the franchise and gave added representation to the landowners and peasantry. A contemporary German observer estimated that under the new franchise it took 230 landowners, or 1000 wealthy business people, or 15 000 lower middle class voters, or 60 000 peasants or 125 000 urban workers to elect a deputy. This had the effect of reducing the number of men who could vote to one in six so that the peasants and working class were almost excluded. In addition representation of the hostile minorities, particularly the Poles, was significantly cut. This revision produced a third *Duma* with a greatly increased extreme right and right of centre grouping to the disadvantage of those parties on the left and more favourable to the regime so that it lasted for its full term of office. The impact of the two electoral systems on the composition of the four *Dumas* is shown in Table 29 and its accompanying profile of the main political parties. The complexity of the party system has led to different interpretation of party alignments giving rise to differing figures.

KEY ISSUE

Election procedures for the third and fourth Dumas.

TABLE 29
Composition of the four Dumas *1906–17*

Main party/political grouping	First Duma	Second Duma	Third Duma	Fourth Duma
Extreme left				
SDs Mensheviks	18	47	0	0
SDs Bolsheviks	0	0	19	15
SRs	0	37	0	0
Trudoviks	136	104	13	10
Moderate left				
Kadets	182	91	54	53
Progressists	27	28	28	41
Conservatives				
Octobrists	17	42	154	95
Right-wing and nationalist groups				
Rightists	8	10	147	154
National parties	60	93	26	22
Others	0	50	0	42
Total	448	518	441	432

> **Q**
>
> *Using the evidence of the table and its accompanying profile*
> **1.** *Identify the parties whose vote remained*
> ● *stable,*
> ● *rose,*
> ● *fell.*
> **2.** *How did the distribution of seats influence the attitude of each of the four* Dumas *to the autocracy?*
> **3.** *How do you account for the change in the distribution of seats amongst the parties?*
> **4.** *What effect did the composition of each* Duma *have on its effectiveness to achieve a constitutional government?*

D *Composition of the four* Dumas *1906–17*

PROFILE OF PARTIES AND POLITICAL GROUPINGS IN THE FOUR *DUMAS* 1906–17

Social Democratics (SDs)
Bolsheviks

Russian Social Democratic Labour Party – Bolsheviks gained a majority by September 1917 supported Lenin's view of a narrow centralised party of professional revolutionaries, in place of a broad-based workers' party. They drew their support not only from factory workers but also from a large section of poor peasants. Lenin rejected any suggestion that his party should be represented in the first and second *Dumas* on the grounds that 'the demand to appoint a ministry responsible to the *Duma* only serves to fortify constitutional illusions and to corrupt the revolutionary consciousness of the people. The Imperial *Duma* is an unsuitable institution for realising and ensuring the victory of the revolution. Only an all-popular Constituent Assembly elected by universal, equal, direct and secret ballot of all the citizens without distinction of sex, religion or nationality, and possessed of the full extent of state power – only it is capable of bringing about complete freedom'.

He had changed this view by the time of the third and fourth sessions although the Bolsheviks remained a small and insignificant group until October 1917. Most notable leaders were Trotsky and Lenin.

SDs Mensheviks

Russian Social Democratic Labour Party – Menshevik was composed of Marxian Socialists who believed that society must progress by natural evolution towards socialism, which meant that Tsarism should be replaced by a bourgeois state before the working class could conquer political power. This led them to oppose the November revolution. They rejected Lenin's view of a narrow centralised party of professional revolutionaries, in favour of broad-based workers' party. The Party, which drew its membership from the ranks of the intellectuals, most influential during the second *Duma* but ceased to have any representation in the third and fourth *Dumas*.

Social Revolutionaries (SRs)	This was the party of the peasants and of the fighting organisations with their terrorists who carried out political assassinations. It was divided by internal feuds and became a major competitor of the Bolsheviks. It took part in the Provisional Government of February 1917 through the presence of Alexander Kerensky and Victor Chernov. It opposed the latter Bolshevik seizure of power although one part of it the Left SRs joined the Bolsheviks briefly. Both left and right wings of the SRs were suppressed in March 1918.
Trudoviks	*Trudoviks* (Labour Group) were those members of the Social Revolutionaries who stood as *Trudoviks* (labourists) after the main party had decided to boycott elections to the first *Duma*. Numerically a small Party composed of intellectuals, the leaders of the cooperative societies, and conservative peasants. They claimed to be Populist Socialists and supported the interests of the lower middle class, such as clerks, and shopkeepers. They were a significant group in the first and second *Dumas* but thereafter declined. By the time of the fourth *Duma*, they were composed largely of peasant representatives and were led by Alexander Kerensky when the revolution of February 1917 broke out, at which time he became a member of the Socialist Revolutionary Party, SRs. The *Populist Socialists* were a nationalistic party and included Peshekhanov, and Chaikovsky.
Kadets	They were called after the initials of its name, Constitutional Democrats. Its official name was 'Party of the People's Freedom'. Under the tsar the Party was composed of Liberals from the propertied classes and was the great party of political reform. When the revolution broke out in February 1917 the *Kadets* formed the first Provisional Government. The *Kadet* Ministry was overthrown in April because it declared itself in favour of Allied war aims, including those of the tsar's Government. As the revolution became more concerned with the transfer of property ownership and restructuring of society, the *Kadets* grew more and more conservative. Its leaders included Milyukov, Vinaver, and Shatsky. The Party eventually split in 1917 and the *Group of Public Men*, was formed in Moscow. Delegates from the *Group of Public Men* were given offices in the last Kerensky Cabinet. The *Group* declared itself non-partisan, although its intellectual leaders were men, such as Rodzianko and Shulgin. It was composed of the more 'modern' bankers, merchants, and manufacturers, who realised that the Soviets must be fought by their own weapon – economic organisation. Typical of the *Group* were Lianozov and Konovalov.
Progressists	They were a party of businessmen, industrialist and *zemstva* activists who were more reformists than their equivalents in the *Octobrists*.
Octobrists	They date from the Union of 17 October 1905 and were formed by P.A. Heiden, A.I. Guchkov, M.V. Rodzianko, D.N. Shipov and N.A. Khomiakov. Its name refers to the date on which the tsar granted a constitution based on the State *Duma*. They were a conservative constitutional party and were a powerful group in the third *Duma* 1907–12. After the Second Revolution of November 1917, they ceased to exist openly and its members either worked underground, or joined the *Kadets*, as the *Kadets* came by degrees to stand for their political programme.

Rightists

They consisted of a number of individual groups who represented a range of conservative views from right of centre to extreme right.

National parties

These were composed of Independent Nationalists who represented the different nationalities of the Empire – Poland, the Caucasus, Siberia, Central Asia and the Far East. There were also Russian Nationalists who were mainly gentry landowners from the Western border provinces of the Empire. The latter group supported the Tsarist regime since they were concerned to preserve the unity of the Russian Empire.

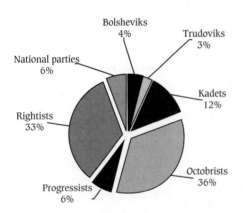

(a) Composition of the first Duma 1906

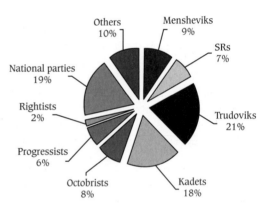

(b) Composition of the second Duma 1907

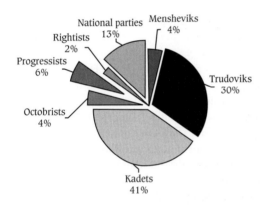

(c) Composition of the third Duma 1907–12

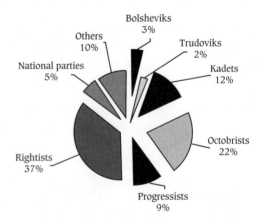

(d) Composition of the fourth Duma 1912–17

DIAGRAM 13 *Four pie charts showing changing composition of the four Dumas 1906–17*

E *Main features of the* Dumas *1906–14*

There were four *Dumas* between 1906 and the outbreak of the first revolution in February 1917. The distribution of seats amongst the parties ensured that the first *Duma* would be radical in its approach and demands, reflecting the radical views of the peasants and urban classes. This created a situation, which did not make a successful relationship with the autocratic Nicholas. The *Kadets*, who were the major group in the first *Duma*, were committed to a programme of extensive reform. It included

KEY ISSUE

First Duma
1st April–June 1906.

- land reform with compensation for landowners
- progressive income tax based on the principle of ability to pay
- health insurance for workers at employers' expense
- election of factory inspectors by the workers.

Even more radical was the second largest group, the *Trudoviks*, who shared the SRs programme of

- socialisation of land whereby it was taken out of private ownership and transferred to the State with no compensation to owners. The State would then divide the land amongst peasant families on the basis of 'labour ownership'
- federal structure of government for the Russian Empire with full national self-determination for the non-Russian peoples. This had implications for religious dissenters, Jews and nationalities who had been struggling for rights and freedoms since the 1880s.

Nicholas' ministers, who had all been chosen for their commitment to the autocracy, were hostile to such a programme. Goremykin, Minister of the Interior, informed them that their demands were 'inadmissible' while Nicholas is reported as having said, 'curse the *Duma* it is all Witte's doing'. Inevitably there was a lack of communication between the regime and the *Duma* whose members felt only anger. In its brief history of 2 months there was bitter quarrelling over the issues of redistribution of landed estates, a general political amnesty, factory reform, Poland and the rights of the Jews led Nicholas to dissolve the assembly. When the *Duma* issued what amounted to an illegal proclamation appealing for the people's support for agrarian reform this gave the government the excuse to dissolve the assembly.

The dissolution of the First *Duma* on 21 July 1906 is documented in the extract below:

> We summoned the representatives of the nation … to the work of productive legislation … We confidently anticipated benefits for the country from their labours. We proposed great reforms in all departments in the national life. We have always devoted Our greatest care to … the removal of … burdens by improving the conditions of agricultural work.

A cruel disappointment has befallen Our expectations. The representatives of the nation, instead of applying themselves to the work of productive legislation, have strayed into spheres beyond their competence, and have been making enquiries into the acts of local authorities established by Ourselves, and have been making comments upon the imperfections of the Fundamental Laws, which can only be modified by Our imperial will. In short, the representatives of the nation have undertaken really illegal acts, such as the appeal by the Duma to the nation. The peasants … seeing no hope of the improvement of their lot, have resorted in a number of districts to open pillage and the destruction of other people's property, and to disobedience of the law and of the legal authorities. But Our subjects ought to remember that an improvement in the lot of the people is only possible under conditions of perfect order and peace. We shall not permit arbitrary or illegal acts, and We shall impose Our imperial will on the disobedient by all the power of the State.

Q

How does Nicholas' government justify its decision to dissolve the Duma?

How useful is this source for revealing that Nicholas had learned nothing from the events of 1905?

KEY ISSUE

Vyborg Manifesto.

Nicholas fell back on Article 87 of the Fundamental Laws, which provided for government by decree and appointed Petr Stolypin. However, the Kadets and most of the Labour group crossed into Finland where they issued the *Vyborg Manifesto* calling on the people to show passive resistance and refuse to pay taxes and to send recruits to the army. The people ignored this appeal and the deputies were arrested, tried and imprisoned for 3 months resulting in a loss of the *Kadets'* most able leaders.

The first *Duma* had appeared to end with no substantial results but in fact, Stolypin recognised the importance of agrarian reform and between 1906 and 1911 sponsored a number of reforms that met some of the peasants expectations before he was assassinated in 1911. However, the immediate aftermath of the collapse of the *Duma* was a resurgence of violence, terrorism, mutiny in the navy and assassinations, including a failed attempt on Stolypin's life that resulted in 27 dead and his daughter badly injured. He set up field courts martial that delivered the death sentence to 638 people. He tried to divide the opposition in the *Duma* by offering ministry posts to the Octobrists, but nothing came of these talks because their price for co-operation was too high.

The second *Duma* proved to be as stubborn and as short-lived as the first. Stolypin had hoped to get its support for his agrarian reforms but the new assembly had seen a shift in power away from the moderate liberal constitutionalist parties towards the extreme left. It proceeded to attack the army and encouraged by messages of support from 'True Russian Men all over Russia' expressing their fury at the 'disrespectful behaviour' of the *Duma*, 'Nicholas decided on its dissolution'. Police discovery of a supposed Social Democratic plot to assassinate the tsar provided the excuse. Not waiting for the *Duma* to carry out its own investigation, the assembly was closed and SD deputies arrested.

KEY ISSUE

Second Duma *2nd February–June 1907.*

WHAT HAD BEEN ACHIEVED BETWEEN 1904 AND 1907?

By 1907 the harsh repression associated with the reign of Alexander III had relaxed. Some improvements had been secured.

● Political parties had achieved legally recognised organisations throughout the country and the right to hold political meetings while membership of the *Duma* gave those parties who were represented contact with political power.
● Political issues could be discussed openly in the press since censorship had been relaxed and the main political parties had their own newspapers. Editors however could still be arrested if they offended the regime.
● There was greater freedom of expression.

However, repressive elements remained.

WHAT REMAINED UNCHANGED BETWEEN 1904 AND 1907?

● Agitators who incited people to violence still faced the risk of arrest and deportation to Siberia or to remote penal colonies in the Arctic.
● The army continued to be used against strikers killing and wounding in the process.
● The police continued to infiltrate Socialist organisations even placing agents on the editorial board of the Bolshevik *Pravda* and in key positions.

LATER *DUMAS* 1912–17?

Nicholas' alteration of the system of elections produced a large number of right-wing deputies though they not as easily managed as he might have wished. The *Duma* attempted to exercise its right to question ministers, particularly the role of Rasputin, to propose improvements in national defence, and to offer comment on the estimates of the Ministry of Navy. Nicholas, who regarded them as matters within his authority only, opposed these efforts. On the whole however, the composition of the *Duma* ensured that it would co-operate with the regime.

KEY ISSUE

Third Duma
November–June 1912.

The *Octobrists*, in alliance with the *Kadets*, formed a majority in the Centre supported on the whole by the Nationalists. Nicholas' chief minister and chairman of the upper chamber (Council of Ministers) Stolypin was willing to co-operate with the moderate centre and left of centre parties to achieve his economic and social reforms. Despite being a conservative and a narrow Russian nationalist, he established good relations with Guchkov, leader of the *Octobrists* and President of the *Duma*, for both were concerned to find new social stability for Russia. Guchkov optimistically claimed in 1907 that, 'if we are now witnessing the last convulsions of the revolution and it is undoubtedly coming to an end, then it is to this man (Stolypin) that we owe it'.

By 1910 co-operation between the regime and the *Duma* started to break down from May 1910 onwards when Nicholas' chief minister, Stolypin, encountered landlord opposition to proposed reform of local government. The land-owning majority in the upper chamber was alarmed that proposals to introduce *zemstva* institutions into the Western region would result in a loss of their authority. Stolypin persuaded Nicholas to discontinue the two chambers for 3 days so that the measure could be passed by an emergency imperial decree under Article 87 of the Fundamental Laws. This was a blatant misuse of the constitution and Stolypin was forced to visit the *Duma* to defend his action. He argued that Article 87 'gives the Monarch, according to the law, the right to create a way out of a hopeless situation'. The *Duma* rejected his argument and the *Octobrists* split into separate factions. The majority who had supported Stolypin now became his critics and withdrew their co-operation. He lost the confidence of Nicholas who felt he had been put in a difficult situation and his right-wing enemies increased their intrigues against him. Had he not been assassinated in 1911 Stolypin would probably have been dismissed in 1912. Support for the regime slipped away and it was the leaders of the fourth *Duma* who supervised the abdication of Nicholas in 1917.

During its term the *Duma* achieved two important reforms of its own:

1 Introduction in June 1912 of accident and health insurance for workers. This consisted of a 'hospital fund' in all firms employing more than 100 workers with smaller forms sharing a fund financed mainly by contributions from employers with workers paying only 2% to 3% of their wages. The latter received sickness benefits from the fund. Disputes were referred to an insurance board which were set up in each province.
2 Restoration of the office of justice of the peace whose judicial powers had been transferred to the land commandants.

Nothing was done to change the separate status of the peasants. They remained under the jurisdiction of the *volost* court and could be punished for drunkenness and a variety of vaguely phrased offences, such as insults to persons in authority, causing a disturbance, which carried physical punishment up to 30 strokes.

The fourth *Duma* revealed the divisions in Russia's upper classes. The Right increased its representation, the *Kadets'* vote remained stable while support for the *Octobrists* and the parties on the left and Nationalists declined. Both the Social Revolutionaries and the Social Democrats were weakened by internal quarrels.

After the death of Stolypin in 1911 Nicholas appointed conservative ministers who lacked the imagination to deal with a changing situation. The autocracy lost its traditional supporters, the landed nobility as well as the entrepreneurs and intelligentsia. In 1917 Guchkov observed with the wisdom of hindsight that (from Ben-Cion Pinchuk, *The Octobrists in the Third Duma, 1907–1912*, Seattle, 1974):

> ... even before the physical death of Stolypin, I had lost faith in the possibility of a peaceful evolution of Russia. As Stolypin was gradually dying politically it became increasingly clear to me that Russia would be forced ... to follow a different road, a road of violent change that would sever the ties with the past, that Russia would drift along the shoreless seas of political and social searching, without any compass or rudder.

KEY ISSUE

Fourth Duma *1912–17.*

See diagram 13 on page 152.

How useful is this source for those who argue that the collapse of the Tsarist regime was inevitable?

After 1912 the regime became increasingly isolated as it could only rely on the extreme right-wing groups, such as the *Black Hundreds* or *Union of the Russian People* along with the army and bureaucrats. Nicholas failed to appreciate this trend and to recognise that concessions were necessary if he was to broaden the basis of his appeal. The period of the fourth *Duma* witnessed the unravelling of the autocracy against a background of revived unrest along with a disastrous involvement in war, which culminated in the first Revolution of February 1917.

The period 1912–14 witnessed a revival of working class militancy starting with the Lena goldfields Massacre of 4 April 1912. The workers at this British owned company in Eastern Siberia had gone on strike because of the failure of the company to understand their needs. Troops were called out and opened fire on a crowd of 5000 killing 270 and injuring many more. The event not only provoked a wave of sympathy from fellow workers and students, but also started a new period of working class militancy in industrial regions. Despite the settlement of 1905, there had been little improvement in workers' conditions. Although there had been a growth in the number of trade unions they had not been successful in winning concessions. Unions were not sufficiently strong to protect their members against employers while the strike weapon remained illegal. Stolypin's reforms in the countryside had failed to solve peasant grievances.

Disaffected industrial workers and peasants showed their grievances in a number of ways:

- An increasing number, especially the young, joined the Bolshevik Party.
- Some workers showed growing interest in developing a legal and democratically led labour movement.
- Growth in collective bargaining by striking. There was a mounting political threat in the towns leading to a general strike in St Petersburg in July 1914. Disturbances followed the usual pattern of violent exchanges between police and strikers, although the events of 1914 did not pose the same threat to the regime as had occurred in 1905. No leaders from the intelligentsia came forward since their interest in revolution had declined since 1905, the army remained loyal, and the peasantry was relatively quiet. In the period from 17 July 1914 there were 265 peasant disturbances requiring troops to be called out on 35 occasions in contrast with a total of 5935 strikes in the towns. Estimates for the number of strikes in the towns vary depending on the sources consulted; those based on official police records are too low while figures provided by the socialist press exaggerate the numbers involved. Table 22 gives some indication of the unreliability of contemporary sources and the problems confronting historians in assessing the scale of political unrest in St Petersburg between 1912 and 1914. The opening shots in the revolution that eventually led to Nicholas' abdication started in St Petersburg.

Year	Authors	Police	Socialist press
1912	310 129	478 000	701 000
1913	478 777	438 913	764 604
1914	654 762	604 685	870 229

TABLE 30 *Political mass strikes in St Petersburg, April 1912 to July 1914 (population in 1914 = c. 2.2 million)*

Table 31 is an estimate of total strike activity, including political strikes, for the empire as a whole. It probably under-estimates the actual number.

The situation was prevented from escalating into a potential revolution with the outbreak of war in 1914, which was followed by a burst of patriotic feeling.

To what extent is it justified to claim that Stolypin had solved workers' grievances since 1905?

How did the balance of political strikes change?

Year	Total strikes	Political strikes
1905	13 995	6024
1906	6114	2950
1907	3573	2558
1908	892	464
1909	340	50
1910	222	8
1911	466	24
1912	2032	1300
1913	2404	1034
1914 (January–July)	3534	2401

TABLE 31 *Strike activity 1905–14*

DIAGRAM 14
Strike activity 1905–14

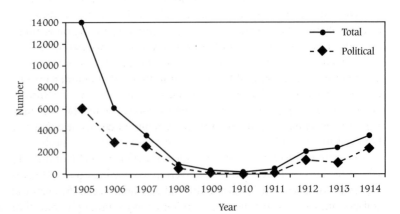

L. Haimson in The problem of social stability in urban Russia, 1905–1917 (*Slavic Review*, 23 (4), 1964) states that

> No demonstrations, no public meetings, no collective petitions, no expressions of solidarity even barely comparable to those that *Bloody Sunday* had evoked were now aroused. Thus, in the last analysis, the most important source of the political impotence revealed by the Petersburg strike was precisely the one that made for its 'monstrous' revolutionary explosiveness: the sense of isolation, of psychological distance, that separated the Petersburg workers from educated privileged society.

Q

To what extent did the events in St Petersburg in 1914 pose a threat to the regime?

CHURCH REFORM

The fourth *Duma* continued with its predecessor's attempts to reform the Orthodox Church by reducing state control, broadening education in Church schools and providing priests with a regular salary. Pobedonostsev who opposed these proposals resigned in 1905. The issue of reform was referred to a Commission in 1912, composed of bishops and university academics. It made a number of recommendations that would have made the Church self-governing. Nicholas delayed making any decisions apart from some vague promises. In 1914 the Church was still linked to the State and dependent on a civil bureaucracy. This proved to be a dangerous relationship for it shared in the collapse when Tsarism was abolished. The fourth *Duma* only achieved some improvement in the salaries of parish clergy but the latter remained a depressed group exercising a dwindling influence on the rural population. Despite attempts to the contrary the fourth *Duma* also failed to achieve religious toleration.

EDUCATIONAL REFORM

The fourth *Duma* showed continuing support for the law of 1908, which had provided for universal education including compulsory primary schooling for at least 4 years between the ages of 8 and 11 in the 3Rs. It was hoped that this provision would be complete by 1918. The law fixed the salaries and terms of work for teachers and provided for government funding for resources though local authorities would be responsible for school maintenance. Government spending on elementary education rose from 19 million roubles in 1905 or 1.8% of budget to 76 million roubles in 1914 or 4.2%. Education continued to be provided by the Church and *zemstva* although individual agreements were made between the Ministry of Education and *zemstva*. The success of the law can be seen from Table 32, which shows the increase in number and percentage growth of primary schools under the Ministry of Education.

Despite this increase, there was still a shortfall in 1914 of 167 542 schools needed to make education universal. The period up to 1914 also saw continuing growth in the number of secondary schools, technical colleges, universities and teacher training colleges although education

See Table 32 and Diagram 15 on page 160.

TABLE 32
Growth in the number of primary schools under the Ministry of Education, 1905–14

Year	Number of schools	Percentage growth
1905	43 551	–
1906	45 629	4.8
1907	47 838	4.8
1908	50 876	6.4
1909	54 726	7.6
1910	59 000	7.8
1911	64 318	8.9
1912	69 318	7.8
1913	76 416	10.2
1914	80 801	5.7

Q

By what percentage had the number of schools increased by 1914?

When did the largest growth take place?

DIAGRAM 15
Percentage growth in the number of primary schools under the Ministry of Education, 1905–14

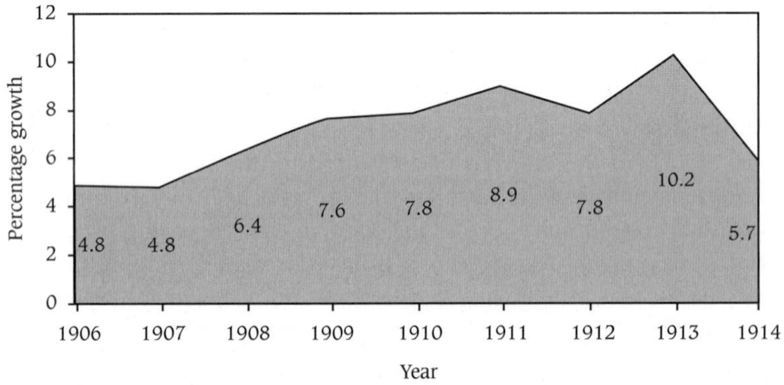

for girls lagged behind. Enrolment in secondary schools quadrupled and in higher education tripled between 1900 and 1914. The growth in education facilities reflected the change in government attitude to education compared with the beginning of the twentieth century. It was recognised that Russia needed a literate work force if she was to be a Great Power. In 1913 the education budget was 400% larger than it had been in 1900 though the Ministry of Education continued to be managed by unsympathetic conservatives who imposed restrictions on women and Jews. Despite this success Russia still lagged behind other countries of Europe in terms of the percentage of students in education at all levels as Table 33 indicates.

TABLE 33
Proportion of population attending educational institutions in 1910

Country	% Primary	% Secondary	% University
Britain	14.9	0.46	0.07
France	14.5	0.33	0.11
Germany	15.9	1.56	0.11
Austria-Hungary	14	0.46	0.10
Italy	9.7	0.47	0.08
Spain	7.7	0.24	0.10
Russia	5.2	0.39	0.07

The drive for a more literate population met with some success. It led to a 7% rise in literacy for the Empire as a whole, from 21% to 28%

City	1897	1910	1911	1912	1913
St Petersburg	52.6	66.9			
Moscow	52.3			64.0	
Kharkov	52.5			66.6	
Voronezh	52.1		61.2		
Baku	32.4				38.8

TABLE 34
Changes in urban literacy 1897–1912 (percentage literate according to years of census)

between 1896 and 1913 though this rise was higher in some of the major cities. St Petersburg and Moscow saw a rise in literacy rates between 10% and 12%, but only 6% in Baku.

The long-term effect of the growth in literacy was a rise in the proportion of children of peasants and workmen attending higher education from 15.7% in 1880 to 38.8% in 1914 and even higher in higher technical colleges. University teachers continued to be dismissed for holding socialist ideas and restrictions were placed on their meetings. There was an ongoing undercurrent of student conflict and protest that expressed itself in student strikes in 1909 and 1911. This bitter atmosphere led to open hostility between the government and educated classes and students came out in support of the striking workers between 1912 and 1914.

RELATIONS BETWEEN GOVERNMENT AND *ZEMSTVA*

The *zemstva*, who had been alarmed by the events of 1905, had become more conservative by 1912 and were prepared to improve relations with central government. The *zemstva* who attracted increased subsidies from central government concentrated their budgets on the provision of education and health, which accounted for 30% and 20%, respectively, of the total. Cities borrowed heavily to finance provision of facilities leading to increasing indebtedness – by 1914 the average deficit of a Russian city was twice its annual budget.

DRUNKENNESS

The fourth *Duma* expressed concerns about the health of the people especially the large consumption of vodka, which was an important state monopoly. A temperance movement had developed and the third *Duma* debated measures to introduce Prohibition. Nicholas expressed some sympathy for Witte's suggestion that half of the State's spirit revenues should be used to finance a campaign against drunkenness. However, attempts to curb drinking were defeated by disagreements over temperance propaganda while doubts were expressed whether the government could afford to lose revenue from its spirits monopoly or that peasants would be prepared to give up their drinking of vodka.

The fourth *Duma* had to deal with a deteriorating situation in foreign affairs, particularly continuing rivalry between Austria-Hungary and Russia for control of the Balkans. Russia, who continued with her ambition of gaining control of the Dardanelles Straits, took every opportunity to weaken Turkey, and prevent Austria increasing her influence. Within 2 years local warfare in the Balkans was to lead to World War I and Russia's involvement with disastrous consequences for the Tsarist regime.

KEY ISSUE

Fourth Duma *and a deteriorating foreign situation.*

KEY ISSUE

Role of the fourth
Duma in the war.

See page 175.

The *Duma* welcomed war and with the exception of Social Demo-crats voted war credits, before it was suspended. Thereafter they rarely met during the war but concerns at the management of the war led to the formation of a 'Progressive Bloc', which called for a 'government of confidence'. Nicholas' government rejected this and the *Duma* was again suspended. It met again briefly in 1916 and again in 1917 and some members started to discuss the possibility of Nicholas' abdica-tion. After being suspended yet again a secret committee was formed and this eventually organised Nicholas' abdication and became the Provisional Government.

5 ᔕ COULD STOLYPIN HAVE BEEN THE 'SAVIOUR' OF RUSSIA?

Stolypin introduced a series of constructive reforms to modernise agriculture, and a plan to achieve universal education of the masses by 1922.

Stolypin was concerned to stabilise Tsarism after the 1905 Revolu-tion and to this end he set out to win over the peasantry who had been its traditional supporters. He recognised that some of the grievances of the peasants stemmed from their long-standing resentment of the limi-tations of the 1861 Emancipation and the burden of the redemption payments. A recurring demand during the 1905 Revolution had been for more land and relief from their financial indebtedness. It had been proposed that land hunger should be solved at the expense of the 30 000 largest landowners whose land would be seized for redistribu-tion. Some landowners had been prepared to accept limited redistri-bution in 1905 in the hope of keeping part of their estates but once the danger of revolution had passed this idea ceased to hold any appeal.

Advised by Danish experts and other officials in his Ministry, Stolypin rejected the redistribution of land demanded by peasants in favour of a gradual dissolution of the *Mir* and the transference of land ownership from collective to individual peasant holding. This proposal:

- would give peasants a vested interest in preserving the *status quo* and help 'de-revolutionise' them
- was acceptable to the *Octobrists*, whose support he needed in the *Duma* against those parties who argued for redistribution of land-lords' land
- would help the most efficient peasants modernise agriculture to achieve increased productivity.

KEY ISSUE

Stolypin's proposals.

Three laws were passed between 1906 and 1911 – the 9 November 1906 Manifesto and two laws of 14 June 1910 and 29 May 1911 – which aimed to:

- create a class of prosperous independent smallholding peasants at the expense of the *Mir*

- reduce the power of the *Mir* which had been criticised for being economically inefficient and a 'seed-bed of socialist ideas'. In the long-term Stolypin planned for the *Mir* to be abolished
- improve the efficiency of agriculture by ending backward methods of farming practised by the *Mir*
- encourage the transfer of land from the inefficient unenterprising peasants to the prosperous peasants who were looking to set themselves up as big farmers
- promote colonisation of Siberia and the Steppes by those peasants who sold their land to their more prosperous neighbours
- redistribute land belonging to noble landowners, the state and Imperial lands to peasant owners.

The 1906 November Manifesto abolished collective ownership of land within the family by recognising the title of the head of each household, usually male. It allowed those who had acquired title to their land to demand that it be separated from the commune to become their personal property and that their strips could be consolidated into a compact holding. The government set up land organisation commissions composed of experts to supervise the process of land transfer. These existed at district and province level and included representatives elected by the peasants. A special Land Bank was set up to help fund transfer of land ownership. These reforms did not receive full legal recognition until they were approved by the third *Duma* in 1910.

Stolypin's measures achieved some success:

1. The authority of the *Mir* and of the land captains was reduced since peasants were free to leave the village.
2. Redemption payments ended in 1907 as promised in 1905.
3. There was a substantial amount of land transfer not only between landlords and peasants but also within peasant ranks. Poor peasants sold out to prosperous peasants who were developing large farms. The amount of land rented increased with peasants paying either money rents or paying through sharecropping and labour.

Year	Peasants		Nobles		State	
	m. ha	%	m. ha	%	m. ha	%
1877	127	31	102	25	181	44
1917	202	47	69	16	160	37

TABLE 35
Land held by Nobles, peasantry and State (millions hectares, m. ha)

4. Two main types of consolidated holdings appeared. The *otrub* whose owner lived in the village with all the other peasants but had his land in one place and the *khutor* whose owner lived on his land away from the village.
5. Colonisation of Siberia, the Steppes and Central Asia was a great success even though about a sixth returned. These new lands produced wheat, livestock, and diary products such as eggs and butter

See Table 36 overleaf.

Year	Number (out of an estimated total of 10–12 million households)
1907	48 271
1908	508 344
1909	579 409
1910	342 245
1911	145 567
1912	122 314
1913	134 554
1914	97 877

TABLE 36

Number of peasant households becoming independent 1907–14

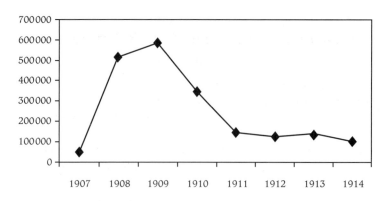

DIAGRAM 16 *Number of peasant households becoming independent 1907–14*

for export. The new settlers were drawn from peasant rather than noble ranks and gradually a new type of society developed composed of self-made men, farmers and merchants.

6 Farming methods improved, not only on the large estates but also on peasant holdings especially on the compact farms. Machinery and artificial fertilisers were introduced. In 1911 European Russia had 66 000 reapers and West Siberia 36 000. Co-operatives started to appear in villages, providing credit and savings facilities, loans to buy livestock, tools, fertilisers and land though there was limited progress in co-operative marketing. Russian agriculture produced grain for home consumption and for export, raw cotton, sugar-beet and tobacco.

It was impossible to 'solve' the underlying problems of rural over-population and poverty or to control the weather, which determined the harvest. Even so there were limitations to his reforms.

KEY ISSUE

Limitations of Stolypin's achievements.

1 Most of the land transfer occurred between 1908 and 1913 with a marked decline by 1914 suggesting that Stolypin had under-estimated the conservatism of the peasantry who wanted to keep the *Mir* since this offered collective security in bad times. This was particularly true of the densely populated central regions, which had witnessed most of the peasant disturbances 1905. By 1914 the strip system of farming still predominated with only 10% of land having been consolidated into compact farms.

2 Peasant poverty continued and tensions remained. A strong rural society with a vested interest in preserving the *status quo* did not develop as proved by the renewed peasant riots in 1917.

Historians in assessing Stolypin's rural reforms have disagreed over their impact both in terms of increasing agricultural productivity and creating a stable class of peasants. R.B. MacKean and Hugh Seton-Watson have taken a rather limited view of his success.

Historians' assessments of Stolypin's rural reforms

R.B. MacKean, *The Russian Constitutional Monarchy, 1907–1917,* **The Historical Association, 1977:**
The agrarian reforms stood little chance of developing a conservative capitalist peasantry. In the absence of class struggle in the Marxist sense in the countryside and in the face of peasant belief in collective ownership of land, the premises of the Stolypin legislation are false.

Hugh Seton-Watson, *The Russian Empire 1801–1917,* **OUP, 1967:**
The extravagant claims made by some on his (Stolypin's) behalf, that he was a statesman who placed Russia on the way to a peaceful happy future from which she was diverted only by a war forced on her by others, may be discounted …

In Stolypin's defence it should be noted that he had talked of needing 20 years before his reforms would take effect but this was not achieved as a result of his untimely death in 1911 and the outbreak of war in 1914.

6 ⌐ RUSSIA AND THE OUTBREAK OF WORLD WAR I, 1914

A *Events in the Balkans 1912–14*

As part of her strategy to gain control of the Dardanelles, Russia supported the efforts of the Balkan League, composed of Serbia, Bulgaria, Greece and Montenegro, when they declared war on Turkey in 1912. In the short war, which followed Turkey was reduced to a narrow strip of land around Constantinople, but the victor states could not agree on the division of the conquered territories, particularly the future of Macedonia, Albania and Salonika.

A second Balkan War broke out in 1913 when Bulgaria declared war on the rest of the Balkan League, supported by Romania and Turkey. Bulgaria lost Thrace to Turkey and a strip of Dobrudja to Romania, Macedonia was divided between Serbia and Greece, and Montenegro was enlarged. As a result of the two Balkan Wars, Turkey in Europe was greatly reduced, while Serbia was considerably enlarged to the dismay of Austria-Hungary who feared Serbian leadership of the Southern Slav peoples, many of whom were Austrian subjects. Bulgaria was left with a deep resentment of her former allies and waited for the opportunity to take revenge. These developments met with Russia's approval since they undermined the Austro-Hungarian Empire and led to unsettled conditions which could work to Russia's favour.

The next incident in the Balkans occurred on 28 June 1914, when Archduke Franz Ferdinand, heir to the Austrian throne, and his wife were assassinated while on a visit to Sarajevo in Bosnia (annexed and incorporated into the Austro-Hungarian Empire in 1908). The assassin was a young Serbian student, Gavrilo Princip. When the Serbian government rejected their humiliating demands, the Austrians prepared to invade their small neighbour. In spite of the internal chaos within Russia, the tsar was determined to protect Serbia, a country with which Russia had close ties. On 30 July, he ordered the mobilisation of his armies. Rasputin warned, 'Let Papa not plan for war, for with war will come the end of Russia and yourselves'.

B *Reasons for Russia's involvement in World War I*

During the years before the outbreak of war rivalry between the great powers of Europe resulted in the creation of two opposing power-bloc alliances – the Triple Alliance and the Triple Entente.

1 In 1879, Germany and Austria-Hungary decided to protect themselves from any possible Russian threat by forming a Dual Alliance. Both countries agreed to fight together if Russia ever attacked them. Three years later, in 1882, Italy joined them to form the Triple Alliance. Germany and Austria-Hungary agreed to support Italy if she was ever the victim of French aggression.

2 Both France and Russia saw this alliance as a threat and so, in 1894, those two countries came together in another Dual Alliance. France and Britain, who both feared the growing power and commercial rivalry of Germany, formed in 1904 the Anglo-French Entente popularly known as the 'Entente Cordiale'. In 1907, Britain and Russia settled their differences and joined to form the Anglo-Russian Entente. It seemed natural that the two ententes should merge and, in the same year, they formed the Triple Entente.

KEY ISSUE

Alliance system.

See Map 10 opposite.

Thus Europe was divided, with the Triple Alliance of Germany, Austria-Hungary and Italy, ranged against the Triple Entente composed of France, Britain and Russia. These were intended to be defensive alliances but they bound their members to military support of partners even when their interests were not directly involved. This is what happened in 1914 even though family and marriage connected the opposing powers. Nicholas II, tsar of Russia, was the cousin of Wilhelm II, Kaiser of Germany, while Edward VII of Britain, son of Queen Victoria, was the uncle of Wilhelm II. The German Kaiser's mother was Princess Victoria, sister of Edward VII and daughter of Queen Victoria; the mother of Alexandra, tsarina of Russia, was Princess Alice, also a daughter of Queen Victoria.

The Austrians held Serbia responsible for the assassination of Franz Ferdinand, and when the Serbian government refused the terms of the Austrian ultimatum, Austria-Hungary invaded Serbia. Germany then demanded that Russian preparations for war should cease, and when the Russians refused, Germany declared war. France's association

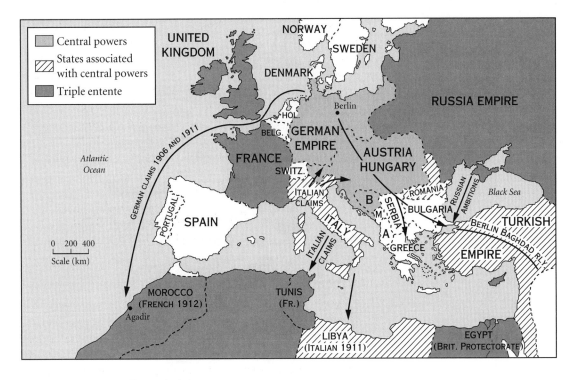

MAP 10 *European alliances before 1914*

with Russia in the Triple Entente meant that she was expected to support Russia in the face of German aggression. The French refused to give Germany a guarantee of their neutrality, and so Germany declared war on France. A few days later, Britain too became involved in the war.

C *Russia's readiness for war in 1914*

With Russia's declaration of war traditional loyalties to Tsarism came to the forefront and the social conflicts of the preceding 2 years were temporarily forgotten. There was a rush of patriotic feeling; the *Duma* and people expressed loyalty to Nicholas as they gathered outside the Winter Palace when war was declared.

Nicholas' first action was to change the name of his capital city from St Petersburg, which sounded too German, to Petrograd. In an effort to win popularity and prove her loyalty, the tsarina, Alexandra, German by birth, threw herself into hospital work. Declaration of war rescued the regime from another impending crisis but it represented dangers for the regime for war serves as a powerful engine for change. War creates new strains, a potential, which was recognised by only a few.

The Russian army, which only 10 years earlier had been beaten by the Japanese, now took on the military might of Germany and Austria-Hungary. In 1914 it numbered 1 400 000 men rising to four million after mobilisation and reaching a peak in January 1917 when it stood at 6.9

PICTURE 19

Austria: I say, my man, you've rather exceeded the speed, limit, Punch. The Russian steam-roller chases the aged Austrian Emperor, Franz Joseph, from the battlefield

KEY ISSUE

Condition of the Russian army.

See page 44.

million. To her allies the size of the Russian army appeared to be overwhelming. The British Prime Minister, Sir Edward Grey assured the French President, Poincaré that, 'Russian resources are so great that in the long run Germany will be exhausted without our helping Russia' (Richard Tames, *The Last of the Tsars: The Life and Death of Nicholas and Alexandra*, Pan, 1972). The Russian war machine was likened to a steamroller, it would move slowly at first but once into its step nothing could stop it.

Over the course of Russia's involvement in the war probably 15 million men were engaged. Such a large force raised problems not only of equipping and provisioning but also of finding sufficient numbers of educated and trained officers. The 1875 army reforms had reduced the number of officers as a result of the system of exemptions. By 1917 there was a higher proportion of officers over the age of 40 and the minimum physical qualifications had been reduced compared with the other powers (see Table 37). Generals were generally drawn from the ranks of the aristocracy and owed their position to favouritism rather than merit. Many were inefficient and errors were made at a great cost of life. Enlisted men lost confidence in their officers and by 1917 they were ignoring their orders and deserting.

Central to the apparent strength of Russian manpower were certain disadvantages:

● Frontier railway gauges deliberately made narrow to hinder German invaders meant that rolling stock halted at the frontier when Russian troops invaded East Prussia.

Country	Peacetime army	After initial mobilisation	At end of war	Total population	Percentage called
Russia	1.4	5.3	15.3	180	8.8
France	0.8	3.8	7.9	39	19.9
Britain	0.2	0.6	5.7	45	12.7
Germany	0.8	3.8	14.0	68	20.5

TABLE 37 *Number of men (in millions) conscripted according to country*

> **Q**
>
> *To what extent was Russia's military strength overestimated?*

- Between 1905 and 1913, hundreds of inefficient generals were dismissed, but lack of suitable replacements left Russian forces 3000 officers short. The Minister for War, General Sukhomlinov, boasted that he had 'not read a military manual for the last twenty-five years'. He favoured friendship with Germany and was half-hearted in his support for the war. His loyalty was suspect especially as one of his close associates was later shot as the spy who betrayed the armies' plans in 1915.
- Acute shortage of shells, 850 were required per gun, crippled Russian efforts. Sukhomlinov's promise in 1912 of 1000 per gun was not fulfilled. Russian losses were heavy, in 5 months of fighting, one-quarter of the mobilised Russian army had been killed, wounded or taken prisoner; their guns were reduced from six to four per battery. A report to the tsar from one Russian General in 1915 explained why courage and sheer numbers had not been enough, 'in recent battles a third of the men had no rifles. These poor devils had to wait patiently until their comrades fell before their eyes and they could pick up weapons. The army is drowning in its own blood' (Richard Tames, *The Last of the Tsars: The Life and Death of Nicholas and Alexandra*, Pan, 1972). On 7 July Nicholas wrote to Alexandra, 'Again that cursed question of shortage of artillery and rifle ammunition, it stands in the way of an energetic advance. If we should have three days of serious fighting we might run out of ammunition altogether. Without new rifles it is impossible to fill up the gaps. The army is now almost stronger than in peacetime; it should be (and it was at the beginning) three times as strong. This is the situation in which we find ourselves at present. If we had a rest from fighting for about a month our condition would greatly improve. It is understood, of course, that what I say is strictly for you only. Please do not say a word to anyone' (M. Christine Walsh, *Prologue: A Documentary History of Europe 1848–1960*, Cassell, 1968).

Nicholas wanted to assume command of the Russian armies himself but was prevailed upon to appoint his uncle, the Grand Duke Nicholas. A man of great energy and a good administrator, he had only limited experience as a military commander. Even so, as a soldier and strategist he was far superior to the generals who served him. The Russian Minister for War was Vladimir Sukhomlinov. A devious man, who flattered to win favours, he was corrupt and inefficient. Jealous of the Grand Duke, who despised him, Sukhomlinov was to be more responsible than any other for the disasters that lay ahead.

KEY ISSUE		Population size	Birth rate	Death rate
Condition of the Russian economy.	Russia	160.7	43	27
	Austria–Hungary	49.5	32	20
	Germany	64.9	27	19
	Britain	40.8	24	14
	France	39.6	18	18

TABLE 38 *Population size (in 1911, in millions), birth and death rates (in 1913, per 1000)*

National Income an economist's term for the total income of a country made up of the total goods and services produced in a year.

Gross National Product (GNP) an economist's term for the measurement of the total 'value' of the economy.

	National income	GNP (%)
Russia	101	30
Austria–Hungary	175	47
Germany	300	70
Britain	505	73

TABLE 39 **National Income** *(in gold roubles, 10 to the £) and contribution of industry to* **Gross National Product (GNP)**

	Coal	Pig iron	Steel	Raw cotton consumed 1910	Oil
Russia (rank)	36 (5)	4.6 (5)	4.8 (4)	0.36 (3)	9.1 (2)
Germany	190	16.8	18.3	0.38	0
Britain	292	10.4	7.8	0.74	0
France	40	5.2	4.6	0.16	0

TABLE 40 *Comparative production of major industries in 1914 (in millions of tons). Figure in brackets is Russia's rank in production of that product*

	Production of machines (%)	Electrical industry (%)	Value of foreign trade
Russia	3	2	190
Austria–Hungary	3	3	199
Germany	35	35	1030
Britain	12	16	1223
France	2	4	424

TABLE 41 *Comparative production as a percentage of world production and value of foreign trade (in millions £) in 1913*

	Agriculture (%)	Industry (%)	Growth rate (%)
Russia	58	28	3.5
Germany	25	43	3.75
Britain	6	34	1.0
France	30	36	N/A

TABLE 42
Proportion of National Product in agriculture and industry 1909–13 and growth rate per annum (1880–1913)

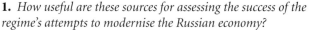

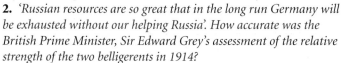

1. *How useful are these sources for assessing the success of the regime's attempts to modernise the Russian economy?*
2. *'Russian resources are so great that in the long run Germany will be exhausted without our helping Russia'. How accurate was the British Prime Minister, Sir Edward Grey's assessment of the relative strength of the two belligerents in 1914?*

7 ∽ RUSSIAN INVOLVEMENT IN WORLD WAR I

A *The Eastern Front*

The Eastern or Russian Front stretched from the Baltic Sea southward across East Prussia and the Russian province of Poland to Galicia in Austria-Hungary. Along this line, the armies of Tsar Nicholas confronted those of Austria-Hungary and Germany. The Germans, who placed greatest emphasis on winning a speedy victory in the West, hoped that the Austro-Hungarians would be able to hold a defensive line and counter any Russian moves in the East with minimum German support. Unfortunately German commander von Moltke's plans were disrupted by the failure of the **Schlieffen Plan** and the unexpected speed with which Russia mobilised her armies.

On the face of it, the Russians had one major advantage, they possessed near limitless manpower resources. The Russian regular army's pre-war strength was 1 400 000 men and mobilisation added a further four million. Behind these lay millions of peasants willing to die for 'Mother Russia'. On the other hand, their armies were badly equipped and lacked modem weapons. Whilst the Russians did reasonably well against the Austro-Hungarians, they fared badly against the Germans who soon showed the value of their superior military training and modern weaponry. Unlike the Russians, the Germans were able to benefit from a modern railway network, which allowed them to move troops speedily from one battlefront to another. In addition, they had the advantage of being alerted of their enemy's movements since they were able to intercept uncoded messages sent by the Russians on their radio transmitters. During the winter months, the harsh conditions on the Eastern Front would prove exceptionally demanding on the men of both sides. In response to an urgent appeal from France to relieve pressure on their own army, on 17 August the Russians launched

Schlieffen Plan was a German plan to defeat France quickly before Russia had time to mobilise so that Germany would be fighting on one front only. Germany would invade France through neutral Belgium and Luxemburg, across the lower Seine, wheel east and attack the French fortresses from the rear. It was estimated that France would be defeated in 6 weeks, while Germany mounted a holding operation against Russia. After France's defeat the whole of German forces would be directed against Russia. The plan failed in 1914 due to the French counter-attack on the Marne and as German forces withdrew some divisions from the Western Front to stop Russia's advance into East Prussia.

an offensive into East Prussia. There, Generals Rennenkampf and Samsonov won an unexpected victory, which caused the Germans concern. The response of the German High Command was to transfer units from the Western Front and send Generals Paul von Hindenburg and Erich von Ludendorff to take charge of their armies.

In the spring of 1915, the Russians continued to advance and were able fight their way across the Carpathian Mountains and towards the River Danube. Here, shortages of supplies and ammunition brought the Russian advance to a halt. Within the German High Command, there was some disagreement as to whether greater emphasis should be given to the Eastern or Western Fronts. Opposed views were held by Falkenhayn, who favoured an offensive in the West, and Hindenburg, who wanted to press home their advantage in the East and force Russia out of the war. The views of Hindenburg prevailed. In April 1915, the Germans, stiffened by the arrival of additional reinforcements from the West, launched an offensive that took the Russians by surprise. During a massive artillery bombardment in which 700 000 shells were fired in four hours, the Russian defences were shattered. With the Germans advancing along the whole front, the Russians risked being caught in a pincer movement between Austrian armies advancing from Galicia in the south and German armies advancing from East Prussia in the north.

They were forced to retreat and this allowed the Germans to move forward rapidly and capture first Warsaw and then Brest-Litovsk. The Russian army was seriously short of rifles and ammunition. Driven from Poland, the Russians retreated eastward and were now fighting on their own soil. Although they resisted stoutly, the Germans advanced nearly 500 km before the Grand Duke's armies were able to re-establish a new defensive line that extended from Riga on the Baltic Sea to the Romanian frontier in the Balkans. It was soon to become 600 contested miles of mud and horror. Up to this point, Russian casualties stood at two million with a further million taken prisoners. The suffering of the solders was appalling. Disastrous as the whole episode may have been, it should be remembered that the Russians had made it impossible for the Germans to concentrate their efforts on the Western Front. They had given the French and British sufficient breathing space to call up reservists, begin the training of new recruits and bring to Europe armies being raised in the British Empire. Now Russia was herself, in desperate need of help from her allies.

In spite of their superiority in numbers, during the early stages of the war the Russian army gained only limited success against the Austro-Hungarians in Galicia before being badly hammered by the Germans in East Prussia and forced to retreat. Her disasters were accompanied by catastrophic losses. What went wrong? In the first place, the soldiers of the so-called Russian 'steamroller' army lacked adequate training and were poorly led. Whilst the Grand Duke Nicholas was considered to have done as well as circumstances allowed, his subordinates were ineffective. Recruits drafted in as replacements for the losses were often without weapons and had to use agricultural

KEY ISSUE

Reasons for failures on the Eastern Front.

implements or wait to take rifles from the fallen. They were inadequately equipped, had insufficient artillery and very few aircraft. For their offensives, they still depended heavily on the success of cavalry charges and even such skilled horsemen, as the Cossacks were no match for German machine gunners. Of the slaughter, Hindenburg wrote, 'Sometimes we had to remove the mounds of enemy corpses from before our trenches in order to get a clear field of fire against fresh assaulting waves'. John Erickson in *The Eastern Front*, summed up the situation: 'the Russian infantryman ill-equipped and under-fed performed great feats of endurance and showed raw, unflinching courage, but manpower could not continually match the murderous enemy firepower: German superiority in artillery mangled the Russian army. Within a month of the opening of the war, Russian armies were chronically starved of ammunition and their gun batteries bereft of shells. The war minister, Sukhomlinov, an empty and disorderly man, bore most of the responsibility for this disgraceful state of affairs, but it was the regime itself, which allowed men like Sukhomlinov to remain in office in spite of obvious inefficiency. The Russian High Command was inept and allowed the army to take to the field inadequately trained, incompetently led, badly supplied – and for all this the peasant solder had to pay with his life. His back proved broad, but not unbreakable'.

VLADIMIR SUKHOMLINOV (1848–1926)

The Russian Minister of War was a friend of Nicholas II and one of the court favourites who kept himself in favour by avoiding serious and unpleasant matters. A former General, who had served in the Russo-Turkish War (1877–78), he was largely responsible for Russia's ill-advised entry into the war in 1914 and for the mobilisation of her armies. He assured the *Duma* that the Russian army was ready for war and that he could be relied upon to cope with any demands placed on him. From the start, his relationship with Grand Duke Nicholas was troubled and the two men grew to hate each other. The disasters of 1914 and 1915 were largely blamed on Sukhomlinov's incompetence. His leadership of the Russian War Office was considered so pathetic that some thought him to be secretly in the employment of the Germans. This was almost certainly not the case although he did have two German spies on his staff. He was even known to have borrowed large sums of money from one of them. He was dismissed in June 1915 following a report of a commission of enquiry that found him guilty of criminal incompetence. He was later tried and convicted of corruption and treason. Sukhomlinov was sent to prison but, on the recommendation of Rasputin, the tsar ordered his release. After 1917, he lived abroad and died in Berlin in 1926.

B *Russia's withdrawal from the war*

During the early months of the war, Russia had experienced mixed fortunes on the Eastern Front. Limited successes in East Prussia and Galicia turned to disaster during 1915 when the brave but ill-equipped and inadequately trained Russian solders proved no match for the superior firepower of the Germans. By the end of the year, the Russian armies were totally demoralised and at the point of collapse. In August 1915, Nicholas II took over command of his armies. It was a well intended if foolish act since the tsar could now be held personally responsible for any disasters that followed. His decision also meant that he spent most of his time at his army headquarters at Mogilev and could only exercise limited control over events on the home front. In Petrograd, these responsibilities largely felt to the tsarina and her trusted councillor, Grigory Rasputin. On his advice, she encouraged her husband to appoint corrupt and incompetent men to important posts in the government. The Russian people distrusted Alexandra and some went as far as to suggest that she was a German spy. Such rumours, which were unfounded, were widespread. In December 1916, Rasputin was murdered and the distressed tsarina found herself with no trusted friend to turn to for advice.

It took the Germans by surprise when, on 4 June 1916, the Russians launched a major offensive on the Eastern Front. The armies of General Alexei Brusilov broke through the Austrian lines and caused sufficient panic for the Germans to withdraw troops from the Western Front to reinforce their allies. The Russian advance into Galicia encouraged Romania, long sympathetic to the Allies, to enter the war. With some 375 000 prisoners taken and most of Galicia again in their hands, Brusilov's offensive proved to be the only truly successful Russian campaign of the war. Even so, without adequate supplies and reinforcements, Brusilov could not support the momentum of his advance and once again, success turned into disaster. This became only too apparent when the Germans launched a counter-offensive, which forced the Russian armies to retreat, and ended in their retreat. From the Russian viewpoint, the Brusilov offensive represented a last chance. With millions of casualties and the economic situation on the home front at crisis point, desperation born of their exhaustion and disillusionment drove the tsar's armies to mutiny. Russia's peasant soldiers and their families had suffered enough and the scene was set for revolution.

During the winter of 1916 the crisis worsened. At the front, earlier heavy losses meant that resentful peasant conscripts had replaced the loyal solders of the Russian regular army. To add to their misery, the winter of 1916–17 was bitterly cold with temperatures falling to 35 degrees below zero. As soldiers threw away their arms, disobeyed their officers, and deserted, so army units edged towards open mutiny. Rodzianko, the President of the *Duma*, telegraphed the tsar on the 26 February and begged him to return to Petrograd. He warned, 'the situation is growing worse. The capital is in a state of anarchy. The government is paralysed; the transport system has broken down the supply systems for food and

See Map 10 on page 167.

KEY ISSUE

Brusilov's offensive – events on the Eastern Front 1916–17.

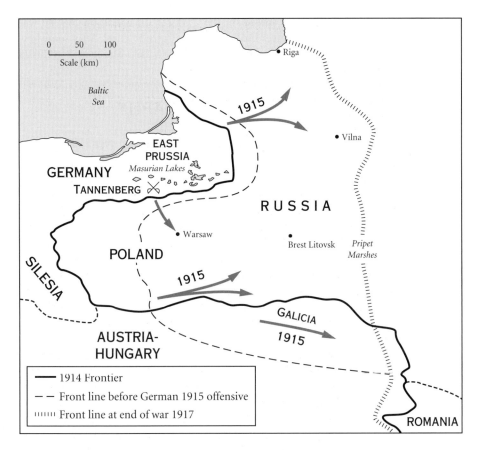

MAP 11   *Eastern Front 1914–17*

fuel are completely disorganised. General discontent is on the increase. There is disorderly shooting in the streets, some of the troops are firing on each other. It is necessary that some person enjoying the confidence of the country be entrusted with the formation of a new government. There can be no delay. Measures should be taken immediately, as tomorrow will be too late' (G. Vernadsky (ed.), *A Source Book for Russian History from Early Times to 1973*, Yale University Press, 1972). Nicholas commented, 'That fat bellied Rodzianko has written me a lot of nonsense, which I won't even bother to answer' (H. Seton-Watson, *The Russian Empire 1801–1917*, OUP, 1967). He then ordered forceful suppression of the disturbances in St Petersburg. Immediately the whole country was paralysed by a general strike. Public buildings were set on fire and inmates released from prisons. Solders refused to take action against the demonstrators and in many instances joined them. Everyone seemed aware that a dramatic upheaval was imminent. In an effort to try and restore order, Nicholas left the front and made his way home. On 1 March, his train was stopped and his military commanders advised him of the situation in Petrograd and told him that he had no choice but to abdicate. The tsar agreed on the 2 March on condition that he was succeeded by his younger brother, Grand Prince Michael. After some hesitation, the prince wisely declined the offer on the 3 March and so Russia became a republic.

8 ⌁ BIBLIOGRAPHY

A general bibliography for Imperial Russia appears on page 120. There are a number of specific textbooks on the events covered in this chapter: R. Charques, *The Twilight of Imperial Russia*, OUP, 1965; M. Ferro, *Nicholas II: The Last of the Tsars*, Penguin, 1991; David Floyd, *Russia in Revolt 1905: The First Crack in Tsarist Power*, Macdonald, 1969; M.T. Florinsky, *The End of the Russian Empire*, Collier Books 1961; G. Katkov & E. Oberlander (eds), *Russia Enters the Twentieth Century*, Methuen, 1971; L. Kochan, *Russia in Revolution 1890–1918*, Granada, 1966; M. McCauley, *Octobrists to Bolsheviks: Imperial Russia, 1905–1917*, Edward Arnold, 1984; R.B. McKean, *The Russian Constitutional Monarchy, 1900–1917*, The Historical Association, 1977; E. Radzinsky, *The Last Tsar: The Life and Death of Nicholas II*, Doubleday, 1992; Hans Rogger, *Russia in the Age of Modernisation and Revolution, 1881–1917*, Longman, 1983; R. Service, *The Russian Revolution, 1900–1927*, Macmillan Education; N. Stone, *The Eastern Front, 1914–1917*, Hodder & Stoughton, 1976; B. Williams, *The Russian Revolution*, Basil Blackwell Historical Association Studies, 1987; A. Ulam, *Russia's Failed Revolutions*, Weidenfeld & Nicolson, 1981; A. Wood, *The Origins of the Russian Revolution*, Methuen, 1987.

9 ⌁ STRUCTURED AND ESSAY QUESTIONS

A *This section consists of structured questions that might be used for discussion or written answers as a way of expanding on the chapter and testing understanding of it.*

1. (a) Explain briefly the events of *Bloody Sunday* 9/22 January 1905.
    (b) To what extent did the protestors achieve their demands?
2. (a) What were the main causes of the 1905 Revolution?
    (b) Why did it break out in 1905?
3. (a) Explain briefly the aims of those who took part in the 1905 Revolution.
    (b) To what extent did they achieve their aims?
4. (a) What do you understand by the term 'state *Duma*'?
    (b) How successful was the 1905 Revolution in achieving political reform in Russia in the period up to 1914?
5. (a) Explain briefly what Stolypin hoped to achieve for Russian agriculture.
    (b) To what extent were his policies a success?
6. (a) Explain why Tsar Nicholas II agreed to the October Manifesto.
    (b) How successful was the 1905 Revolution in achieving political reform in Russia in the period up to 1914?

7. (a) Why was there a build-up of a revolutionary movement in Russia from 1894 to 1914?
   (b) What had the revolutionary movement achieved by 1914?
8. (a) Why did Russia go to war in 1914?
   (b) How soon did it become clear that the decision to go to war was 'a foolish act'?
9. (a) What success did the Russian army achieve in 1914?
   (b) How close was Russia to military defeat by 1916?

B *Essay questions.*
1. To what extent would you agree that the events of *Bloody Sunday*, 1905 marked a turning point in the popularity of the Romanov dynasty?
2. 'Revolution in 1905 was the result not of insufferable conditions but of irreconcilable attitudes' (R. Pipes, *A Concise History of the Russian Revolution*, 1995). How far do you agree?
3. How far is it justified to describe the events of 1905 as a 'Revolution'?
4. 'The history of the *Dumas* from 1906 to 1916 was a history of lost opportunities by the tsar and his ministers'. Discuss this statement.
5. 'Short-sighted and mean-spirited'. Discuss this assessment of Nicholas II's responses in 1905–6 to the events of the 1905 Revolution within Russia.
6. 'From 1906 to 1914, there was much determined opposition to Nicholas II but no real threat to his authority'. How do you account for this?
7. How far was participation in the World War I responsible for bringing about the downfall of the Tsarist regime in Russia?

10 ∽ MAKING NOTES

Read the advice section about making notes on page ix of the Preface: How to use this book, and then make your own notes based on the following headings and questions.

A Bloody Sunday *9 January 1905*
1. What are the immediate events leading to *Bloody Sunday*?
2. Who were the petitioners?
3. What request had they made to their employers before the workers went on strike?
4. What had been the workers 'other demands'?
5. What complaints did the workers direct against Nicholas' officials?
6. What did the workers' regard as the solution to their grievances?
7. What does the tone of the Petition tell you about the attitude of the people to the tsar?
8. What were the main events of the day?
9. What was the significance of *Bloody Sunday* in terms of its impact of
   (a) the regime and its response?
   (b) attitude of the workers?

B *Development of a revolutionary movement January to October 1905*
1. What were the causes of the Revolution?
   (a) Long term.
   (b) Medium term.
   (c) Immediate or 'trigger' to events.
2. Outline the main chronology of events January to October 1905 noting the most important developments on the part of actions taken by each of the following:
   (a) Workers.
   (b) Revolutionary leaders – appearance of *Soviets* and role of Trotsky.
   (c) Liberals – *zemstva*.
   (d) Intelligentsia – academics and students.
   (e) Nicholas and the regime.
3. What was the outcome of the 1905 Revolution in terms of each of the following?
   (a) Granting of basic civil liberties and a *Duma*.
   (b) Peasant Gains.
   (c) Fundamental Laws of the Russian Empire, 23 April 1906.
4. Response of different groups to Nicholas' concessions:
   (a) Liberal response.
   (b) Peasant response.
   (c) Response of the rank and file in the army and navy.
   (d) Working class response.
5. Reasons for Tsarist survival and recovery.
6. What was the significance of the 1905 Revolution?

Main issue to consider
Did the 1905 Revolution show the strength of the Tsarist regime, or confirm that it was on the way to destruction?

C *The age of the* Dumas *1906–17*
1. What was the attitudes of each of the following towards the *Duma*: (a) Nicholas II, (b) Witte, (c) Political parties.
2. How did the electoral system for the third and fourth *Dumas* change compared with the first and second?
3. Why did the regime make this change?
4. What effect did the change have on the composition and attitude of the *Duma*?
5. What was the composition of the four *Dumas* 1906–17? Use the following chart to organise your evaluation.

Party/political grouping	First *Duma*	Second *Duma*	Third *Duma*	Fourth *Duma*

6. Identify the attitude of each political party towards the *Duma*, its leaders, aims and policies. Use the following chart to organise your evaluation.

Party/political grouping	Attitude towards *Duma*	Leaders	Aims	Policies

7. What were the main features of the *Dumas* 1906–14? Use the following chart to organise your evaluation.

Duma	Character (in terms of dominant parties)	Co-operative/ hostile to autocracy?	Issues discussed	Effectiveness/ Achievements	Reasons for success or failure?
First					
Second					
Third					
Fourth					

Main issue to consider
'The history of the *Dumas* from 1906 to 1916 was a history of lost opportunities by the tsar and his ministers'. Discuss this statement.

D *Stolypin – was he the 'saviour' of Russia?*
1. Revise Stolypin's character and attitude towards the autocracy
2. Stolypin's reputation amongst the
    (a) people, (b) revolutionaries, (c) Liberals.
3. Stolypin's proposals.
4. Stolypin's aims.
5. Stolypin's reforms.
6. Stolypin's achievements.
7. Limitations of Stolypin's achievements.
8. Historians' assessments of Stolypin's achievements.
9. Deterioration in social conditions between 1912 and 1914:
    (a) reasons for this.
    (b) Nicholas' response to the situation after 1912.

Main issue to consider
'Twenty momentous years for Russia'. To what extent is this a valid assessment of the period 1894–1914?

E *Russian involvement in World War I*
1. Events in the Balkans and reasons for Russia's involvement.
2. Events leading to the outbreak of war.
3. How ready was Russia for war?
    (a) Response of the people.
    (b) Condition of the Russian army.
    (c) To what extent was Russia's military strength overestimated?
    (d) Condition of the Russian economy – how prepared was it to fight World War I compared with the industrial strength of the other belligerents?

4. Summarise main events on the Eastern Front.
   (a) What was the 'Eastern Front'?
   (b) Quality of leadership.
   (c) Nicholas' reasons for assuming command of the Army and the implications of this decision.
   (d) Reasons for failures on the Eastern Front including the role of Vladimir Sukhomlinov.
5. Russia's withdrawal from the war.
   (a) Events of 1916–17.
   (b) Collapse of the Russian army.

F *Nicholas II's decision to abdicate*
Immediate background to the event.

11 ✑ SYNOPTIC QUESTION ON NICHOLAS II

Study Sources A–F and then answer Questions (a) and (b) which follow.

Central War Industries Committee This was set up in 1915 to help armaments production. It was a non-governmental body whose members were drawn from *zemstva*, industrialists and workers.

In the opinion of the spokesmen of the labour group of the **Central War Industries Committee** the industrial proletariat of the capital is on the verge of despair and it believes that the smallest outbreak, due to any pretext, will lead to uncontrollable riots, with thousands and tens of thousands of victims. Indeed, the stage for such outbreaks is more than set: the economic position of the masses ... is distressing.

Even if we assume that wages have increased 100%, the cost of living in the meantime has risen by an average of 300%. The impossibility of obtaining, even for cash, many foodstuffs and articles of prime necessity, the waste of time involved in spending hours waiting in line in front of stores, the increasing morbidity due to inadequate diet and insanitary lodgings (cold and dampness as a result of lack of coal and firewood) etc. all these conditions have created such a situation that the mass of industrial workers are quite ready to let themselves go to the wildest excesses of a hunger riot.

In addition to economic hardships the 'legal disabilities' of the working class have of late become 'intolerable and unbearable', the denial of the mere right to move freely from one factory to another has reduced labour, in the opinion of the Social-Democrats, to the state of mere cattle, good only for 'slaughter in the war'. The prohibition of all labour meetings ... the closing of trade unions ... and so on make the labour masses, led by the more advanced and already revolutionary-minded elements, assume an openly hostile attitude towards the Government and protest with all the means at their disposal against the continuation of the War ... A saying by one of the speakers at a meeting ... 'You must end the War if you do not know how to fight' has become the war cry of the Petrograd Social Democrats.

The close relations between the workers of Petrograd and the army also indicate that the atmosphere at the front is disturbing, not to say revolutionary. The high cost of living and the shortage of foodstuffs from which soldiers' wives are the first to suffer have been made known to the army by soldiers returning from leave.

Revolutionary circles, then, have no doubts that revolution will begin soon, that its unmistakable precursors are already here, and that the Government will prove incapable of fighting against the revolutionary masses, which are the more dangerous because they consist largely of soldiers or former soldiers

SOURCE A
From a Police Department report in October 1916, quoted by M. Florinsky, The End of the Russian Empire, *Collier Books, 1961.*

The situation is serious. The capital is in a state of anarchy. The government is paralysed; the transportation system has broken down; the supply systems for food and fuel are completely disorganised. General discontent is on the increase. There is disorderly shooting in the streets; some of the troops are firing at each other. It is necessary that some person enjoying the confidence of the country be entrusted immediately with the formation of a new government. There can be no delay. Any procrastination (delay) is fatal. I pray God at this hour the responsibility not fall upon the sovereign.

SOURCE B
From the Duma *leader Rodzianko's telegraph to Nicholas, 27 February 1917, quoted by David Christian,* Imperial and Soviet Russia: Power, Privilege and the Challenge of Modernity, *Addison-Wesley Longman, 1986.*

I think the Red terror has already made some people, and will make many others, reconsider the personal responsibility of Nicholas II for the horrors of his reign. I for one do not think he was the outcast, the inhuman monster, the deliberate murderer I used to imagine. I began to realise there was a human side to him. It became clear to me he had acquiesced in the whole ruthless system without being moved by any personal ill will and without even realising that it was bad. His mentality and his circumstances kept him wholly out of touch with his people. He heard of the blood and tears of thousands upon thousands only through official documents, in which they were represented as 'measures' taken by the authorities 'in the interest of the peace and security of the state'

From his youth he had been trained to believe that his welfare and the welfare of Russia were one and the same thing. So that 'disloyal' workmen, peasants and students who were shot down, executed or exiled seemed to him mere monsters that must be destroyed for the sake of the country and the 'faithful subjects' themselves.

SOURCE C
From the socialist member of the third and fourth Dumas, *and Prime Minister August to October 1917 Alexander Kerensky,* The Catastrophe, *published in 1929 (quoted by A. Mazour,* Rise and Fall of the Romanovs *1960) in which he describes a visit to Nicholas after his abdication.*

His character is the source of all our misfortunes. He is incapable of steering the ship of State into a quiet harbour. His outstanding failure is a lack of willpower. Though benevolent and not unintelligent, this shortcoming disqualifies him totally as the unlimited autocratic ruler of the Russian people.

The Emperor's character may be said to be essentially feminine ... His Majesty would not tolerate about his person anyone he considered

SOURCE D

From Count Sergei Witte,
Memoirs, *Heinemann, 1921, in*
which the former minister
Chairman of the Committee
of Ministers 1903–5 describes
Nicholas' character and
view of his role.

more intelligent than himself or anybody with opinions differing from those of his advisors...

(Nicholas II) I do what I please, and what I please to do is good. If people do not understand it, that is because they are ordinary mortals, while I am God's anointed.

If Nicholas was weak-willed and devious if he had so little confidence in his own judgement that he distrusted his ministers and failed to back them up, was this not as much an indictment of autocracy as of the autocrat?... Nicholas was not lacking in firmness or, depending on one's view, obstinacy... when it came to the integrity of his power or the defence of cherished prejudices... The problem was rather an excess than a want of firmness; more precisely, an inability to distinguish between flexibility and weakness, strength and mulishness.

Even more poorly prepared than his father for the burdens of kingship, Nicholas had no knowledge of the world of men, of politics or government to help him make the difficult and weighty decisions that in the Russian system the Tsar alone must make. His training was adequate only for the one role he would not play, the ceremonial one of the constitutional monarch. The only guides he recognised were an inherited belief in the moral rightness and historical necessity of autocracy, and a religious faith, bordering on fatalism, that he was in God's hands and his actions divinely inspired.

A simple man himself, he was convinced until the very end that the simple people were on his side and that this made him the best judge of the country's mood. Protest and dissent were temporary aberrations traceable to agitators, Jews or selfish politicians.

SOURCE E

From Hans Rogger, Russia in
the Age of Modernisation and
Revolution, *Longman, 1983.*

It is hard to imagine anyone less well equipped to steer Imperial Russia into the twentieth century than Nicholas II. A family man first and foremost... as an autocrat he was hopeless. He had not even had the benefit of proper preparation for his task. His education had essentially been that of a cavalry officer...

Nicholas' personality did not help him overcome the limitations of his education. A short neat figure of a man, five feet seven inches tall, he was timid, introverted and weak, in the sense that he was incapable of making up his mind and sticking to his decisions. However, it must be said that he always commanded great love and loyalty in his immediate entourage, together with a considerable amount of respect. He had great charm...

Yet despite his considerable majesty of manner, as an emperor he lacked stature and that taste for power... which is vital for an autocrat...

Yet weak though he may have been as a ruler he possessed that peculiar dogged obstinacy that sometimes accompanies weak men in power. On the rare occasions on which he made up his mind definitely he was impossible to move; no argument, however convincing, could reach him. Nicholas sincerely believed that he had received Russia from God, and was personally responsible for her well being. This meant he did not have the right to delegate or dilute his power in any way. It also meant that when he heard the voice of conscience advise a certain course nothing could dissuade him from taking it. Obstinacy, mysticism, and weakness combined to shape perhaps the most disastrous of all his characteristics: a deadly fatalism.

SOURCE F
From A. De Jonge, Life and Times of Rasputin, *1983.*

Answer both Questions (a) and (b)

(a) Using your own knowledge, and the evidence of Sources D–F, what do you consider to have been Nicholas II's deficiencies as a ruler?

(b) Using your own knowledge, and the evidence of all six sources, how far do you agree with the claim that 'Nicholas II was totally unfitted to deal with the many challenges facing Russia'?

From revolution to reconstruction: Russia 1917–24

6

INTRODUCTION

Reference was briefly made at the end of the preceding chapter to the immediate events leading to Nicholas II's abdication on 2 March 1917. These events are now explored in greater detail. The Revolution in Russia in 1917 has been universally viewed as a 'turning point in history and possibly the greatest event of the twentieth century' (E.H. Carr, *The Russian Revolution: From Lenin to Stalin 1917–1929*). However, any assessment of the causes and consequences of the revolution have run into two main problems.

1 ⌐ NATURE OF THE EVIDENCE ON THE RUSSIAN REVOLUTION

A *Limitations of the evidence*

The first problem arises from the limitations of the evidence since Russia retreated into virtually total isolation from world affairs from 1920 onwards. Little was published in the West except the memoirs of ex-Tsarist generals, such as A.I. Denikin's *The Russian Turmoil* published in 1922, or of extreme right wing historians. Mensheviks in exile added to the anti-Bolshevik view. Within Russia, and prior to Stalin's success in the late 1920s, Trotsky and other participants in the Revolution narrated their recollections in a number of pro-Bolshevik histories. Among the most prominent Bolshevik memoirs written before 1930, were those of Shliapnikov, Lenin's widow, Krupskaya, and the brothers Raskolnikov and Ilyin-Zhenevsky. The two most valuable eyewitnesses to the events were not members of Lenin's party, but Sukhanov, a member of the Menshevik Party whose memoirs were considered to be required reading in party circles and an indispensable source book for the study of revolution. However, it had become discredited by the end of the 1920s when Sukhanov became an early victim of Stalin's 1931 purge. The other famous eye-witness was the

American journalist, John Reed, whose *Ten Days that Shook the World* was recommended by Lenin, when it was published in 1919, as 'a truthful and most vivid exposition of the events'. Its praise of Trotsky and virtual neglect of Stalin led to it being banned after 1928. Stalin during his years of dictatorship suppressed the historical record, tampered with photographic evidence and 'edited' written accounts including Lenin's *Collected Works*, while Lenin's *Testament* was never published in the Soviet Union. Stalin's concern to establish the origins of his orthodoxy in Bolshevik theories of 1917 led to a further distortion, while histories written in the West were influenced by the advent of the Cold War. It was not until the publication of E.H. Carr's *The Bolshevik Revolution 1917–1921* in three volumes in 1956 that a real attempt was made to understand ideological and political aspects of Bolshevism and Lenin.

B *Viewpoint of historians and its change over time*

Since the Bolsheviks took power in 1917, the Russian Revolution has been the subject of fierce debate among historians, not merely between Soviet and western writers, or between opponents and sympathisers, but even within one school of thought.

- Pre-1960s liberal western historians tended to stress the role of a determined and ruthless Bolshevik Party and of particular individuals, such as Lenin or Trotsky, whether or not they agreed that the October Revolution had been a seizure of power by a minority rather than a popular revolution. They were influenced by the writings of anti-Bolsheviks commentators, of former Mensheviks, such as Sukhanov who was a member of the Executive Committee of the Petrograd Soviet, and of the prime minister of the Provisional Government from June to October 1917, Alexander Kerensky. Taking an optimistic view of events, these historians claimed that the Revolution was not inevitable. Had it not been for World War I and Lenin's seizure of power, Tsarist Russia would have developed along western lines, into a parliamentary system. Lenin came to power by force and due to better organisation rather than because of mass support from the people. He carried out a military style operation with little popular support and imposed a dictatorship on the people. Lenin and his successor Stalin were nothing more than 'Red Tsars'. Yet such a view has serious drawbacks. It is more indicative of the theories and opinions of those who put forward this interpretation since Western commentators were influenced throughout the 1950s by the tense relationship between Russia and the West, known as the Cold War. They were more concerned with condemning the Russian Revolution as a complete disaster, than assessing whether Tsarism in the late 19th and early 20th centuries was capable of meeting the demands of modernisation; or even willing to do so.

● Pre-1960s Marxist commentators, who sympathised with Russia, reflected the views of Soviet historians. They were uncritical in their praise of the Russian Revolution as a popular rising that would lead eventually to the historical stage of socialism.

● Since the 1960s, views in the west began to be revised as the Cold War declined and as a New Left developed which was critical of both liberal and communist interpretations of the Revolution. There was a move away from the mainly political interpretations into social history as western historians redirected their focus on the workers and the factories, and reduced their emphasis on the role of a tightly disciplined, elitist Party. The latter came to power only because they were able to direct the demands of the workers to their own advantage. Yet, even here there is debate on how important factory workers were in the labour composition of the Russian urban population. Other historians have looked again at the Bolshevik Party, stressing the ideological divisions and challenging the assumption that the Party was a single-minded organisation dominated by Lenin.

● The impact of changes in the Soviet Union since 1985, particularly under the policy of openness known as *GLASNOST* and the release of 'forbidden' material from the archives, has led to yet more revision. It has been more critical of the previous Soviet view of mass support for the Bolsheviks and their achievements. It has widened the focus from St Petersburg and Moscow to the rest of the Tsarist Empire, and from the Bolsheviks to other groups. Western historians reflected this wider view with the writings of Donald Raleigh, *Revolution on the Volga: 1917 in Saratov*, 1986, Ziva Galili, *The Menshevik Leaders in the Russian Revolution*, 1990, and Edward Acton, *Rethinking the Russian Revolution*, 1990.

However, certain crucial questions remain concerning the continuation of constitutionalism before World War I; the nature of social discontent; the influence of revolutionaries and the relationship between war and revolution. Robert Service believes that the opening up of Soviet archives may reveal fresh insights into Lenin's leadership, and help explain what Service sees as a gap between Lenin's actions in 1917 and the swift establishment of a secret police, the *Cheka*, in December 1917, not long after Lenin won power. Service's 1979 study of *The Bolshevik Party in Revolution: A Study in Organisational Change 1917–23* stressed that the Party in this period was radically different both from the Stalinist Party of the 1930s, and from the western view which saw Stalin as the inevitable successor to Lenin. Service focused on Lenin's stormy struggles in 1917 to win the Bolshevik Party over to his line. Clearly the history of the Russian Revolution of 1917 has gone through many revisions.

2 ∽ HISTORIANS' ASSESSMENT OF THE 1917 REVOLUTION

HISTORIANS'

DEBATE

Was the collapse of the Tsarist regime inevitable?

Pessimists

Some leading historians

Leopold Haimson, *The Problem of Social Stability in Urban Russia, 1905–1917, Slavic Review,* XXIII, December 1964.

D. Geyer, *The Russian Revolution: Historical Problems and Perspectives,* 1987.

T.H. Von Laue, *Why Lenin? Why Stalin? A Reappraisal of the Russian Revolution, 1900–1930,* 1964.

Diane Koenker, *Moscow Workers and the 1917 Revolution,* 1981.

Stephen Smith, *Red Petrograd: Revolution in the Factories, 1917–18,* 1983.

They argue that

● The fall of the Tsarist autocracy was inevitable; the outbreak of war only postponed revolution.

● Nicholas II's poor leadership meant that he was incapable of meeting the social and economic challenges arising from industrialisation intensified by his stubborn refusal to grant political reforms.

● War was a catalyst of the revolution.

The American historian, Leopold Haimson, was very pessimistic about the future of Tsarism on the eve of World War I. He focused on:

● The widespread nature of social grievances, pointing to a two-fold division in urban Russia between privileged society and the industrial working class on the one hand, and between privileged society and the Tsarist regime on the other.

Optimists

Some leading historians

G. Katkov, *Russia 1917: The February Revolution,* 1967.

G. Kennan, *The Breakdown of the Tsarist Autocracy,* in R. Pipes, *Revolutionary Russia.*

Robert McKean, *St Petersburg between the Revolutions: Workers and Revolutionaries June 1907–February 1917,* 1990.

Francis Weislo, in *Reforming Rural Russia,* 1990, Andrew Verner, *The Crisis of Russian Autocracy,* 1990.

They argue that

● Tsarism was developing a constitutional system and would have survived if war had not broken out.

● The monarchy was the victim of a conspiracy led by a small group of professional revolutionaries led by Lenin.

● War was a cause of the revolution since it placed significant strains on Russian society.

Kennan, McKean and Hugh Seton-Watson, argue that it was defeat in World War I that made Tsarism exposed to revolutionary attack rather than any fundamental structural failing. According to McKean:

● The strike movement was already dying down, before war was declared.

● Russia had been developing constitutionalism after the 1905 Revolution

(continued overleaf)

- The period 1912–14, was one of revolutionary crisis, with an increasingly politically motivated strike movement, which the outbreak of war only temporarily interrupted.
- The outbreak of war in 1914 put a brake on the revolutionary movement.
- Koenker and Smith who studied the working class in Moscow and in Petrograd (see above) focused on 'history from below'. They looked at the factory workers who were politically active in their own right and not simply controlled by the Bolsheviks.

- Tsarism was trying to reform itself, notably under Stolypin until his assassination in 1911. Weislo and Verner who have studied this period from the standpoint of the tsar and his bureaucracy, agree with McKean that under Stolypin, whom all three historians see as the last great statesman of Tsarist Russia, there was progressive legislation. However, all three accept that even before Stolypin's death, there were signs of collapse and that with his removal, the bureaucracy lost its reforming impetus. The conservatives and the provincial nobility regained the privileges and powers, which they had lost through the reforms. Thus, the long-term prospects for constitutionalism were bleak by 1911.
- McKean questions the significance of factory workers. He points out that they were in the minority among St Petersburg workers, and that there were more workers in the service sector than in the metal industry; indeed, that just over a third of the St Petersburg labour force in 1910 was in domestic service. McKean also insists that the socialist factions, the Bolsheviks, Mensheviks and Socialist Revolutionaries, and the trade unions were unable to offer effective leadership to the labour protest in 1917. In his view, the unsung heroes of the Petersburg labour movement were the shop-floor activists. Indeed, whereas Lenin was adamantly opposed to co-operation with other groups, the worker activists wanted unity in the labour movement. Thus, there was a gulf between the working class Bolsheviks in Petersburg and the intellectual Bolsheviks, mostly in exile. It was a distance paralleled by that between the skilled and the semi-skilled workers, most of whom were women.

They stress as the main causes
- Poor Tsarist leadership.
- Inherent structural weaknesses in the state, arising from rapid industrialisation, which disrupted traditional divisions of society and weakened the political structure.

They stress as the main causes
- A conspiracy by a small group of professional revolutionaries.
- The impact of war in terms of its interruption of constitutional developments and its creation of new problems.

- The impact of war in terms of the added strains it put on Tsarism, which was already in crisis.

It follows from what has been discussed above that historians' discussion of the causes of the Russian Revolution have focused on four main explanations.

3 ⌐ MAIN FEATURES OF THE FOUR HISTORICAL EXPLANATIONS

A *Tsarism in crisis*

The 1917 Revolution has been viewed as the failure of Russian liberalism to transform Tsarism into a constitutional monarchy. The movement for a constitution can be traced back to the reforms of the 1860s and the introduction of *zemstva*. The gentry dominated these in part as compensation for loss of control over their serfs in 1861. There is disagreement amongst historians over the extensiveness of *zemstva* reform. Most, however, agree that it at least encouraged the development of gentry liberalism especially among the increasing numbers of professionals employed by the *zemstva*. In addition, it led to increasing antagonism between local and central government. Yet liberalism, like Marxism, was a western concept; the nobility were divided over reform while the middle class were too few in numbers and, politically and socially weak. It seemed that constitutionalism had its best chance of success in 1905 when Nicholas lacked reliable support among conservative and liberal groups. Some commentators have argued that concern with getting a constitution led liberals to neglect the growing social problems in towns and villages. Another view is that the liberals became alarmed by the popular movement and concluded that reforms from above were the only alternative to further revolution.

Nicholas II has been held responsible for the failure of the moderates to achieve reform. He had no intention of surrendering any of his autocratic powers. Neither was he well suited to the challenges of steering Russia into a constitutional monarchy in the face of political, social and economic challenges arising from industrialisation. He clung to his autocratic powers, and rejected the attempts of Russian liberals to transform Tsarism into a constitutional monarchy by withdrawing his constitutional concessions after June 1907. From 1915 onwards when he assumed command of the army his wife Alexandra and the group of ministers who surrounded her were left effectively in charge. As we have already noted, this led to divisions and criticisms both within court circles and the country at large at the influence of Rasputin and the corruption and incompetence of ministers. Rumours were wide-

KEY ISSUE

The issue of constitutional government.

KEY ISSUE

The role of Nicholas II.

spread and ill feeling was directed against the German Alexandra. The latter was totally opposed to any lessening in Nicholas' autocratic powers. The conservative court clique, who surrounded his wife, influenced Nicholas and he refused to make any concessions. He became increasingly out of touch with what was going on in the country and refused to listen to the warnings of the *Duma.* In November 1916, the liberal *Duma* leader Milyukov declared that, 'the gulf between us and the government has grown wider and has become impassable … We are telling this government … We shall fight you; we shall fight with all legitimate means until you go … When the *Duma* insists that the rear must be organised for a successful struggle … the government … prefers chaos and disorganisation; what is this: stupidity or treason?' The deteriorating relationship between Nicholas and members of the *Duma* provoked the comment from Nicholas's brother-in-law, Grand Duke Alexander, in January 1917. 'The Government is today the body which prepared the revolution; the people do not want it; but the Government does everything it can to increase the number of discontented, and succeeds admirably. We are witnessing an unprecedented scene; a revolution not from below, but from above' (A.J. Halpern, *Revolution in Russia 1905 and 1917*, quoted in M. & L. Kochan (ed.), *Russian Themes*, Oliver & Boyd, 1967, page 124). Revolution took place in a country in which

- the vast majority of the population were peasants living in extreme poverty and for the most part illiterate
- all the social institutions were backward dominated by a small landholding aristocracy and a monarchy which insisted on its leading role
- initiative for industrial development had been provided by the State rather than the middle class
- revolutionaries and liberals were in a minority, isolated from the mass of the people.

To remain a great power the Tsarist regime needed to modernise but it wanted to retain traditional power structures. In the view of D. Geyer, the question should not be 'why was there a revolution in 1917' but 'how the Russian autocracy managed to survive as late as 1917, given the vitality of social change and economic development since the 1860s'.

B *Social strains*

The root causes of the 1917 Revolution have been seen to lie in the deterioration in the condition of life of the mass of the people and the failure to modernise society and economy under Tsarism. Some trace the roots back to the 1861 Emancipation of the Serfs and the subsequent disappointment with Alexander II's attempt at reform from above. As we have seen, despite the reforms of Stolypin many peasant grievances remained (see page 164). They were joined by a landowning nobility who felt that not only was their economic and social position being undermined by change, but that they were also being ignored by the Tsarist government. Their traditional place in society was being challenged by the rise of a new prosperous class of businessmen and industrialists. They became more critical of the regime, which found its support narrowing. Other commentators' point to the attempt to industrialise in the 1890s which burdened a weak, backward economy with a heavy foreign debt and concentrated a working class, labouring and living in appalling conditions, in the centres of political power.

The Russian Revolution of 1917 remains the only example of a successful revolution in which urban workers played a major role though questions remain over the role of the peasantry who still composed the great majority of the population. Whether the conditions of life improved or declined on the eve of World War I, they remained desperately hard for the bulk of the population.

C *A body of revolutionaries*

There has been some re-assessment of the part played by the revolutionary parties. They are now seen as having a minimal role in the events leading to the mainly spontaneous revolution in February. In the view of historian, 'it is difficult to subscribe to the theory of Bolshevik leadership. The Bolshevik party as a whole failed to react to the workers' strike movement quickly and imaginatively. The Russian Bureau was constantly behind the developing events and grossly underestimated the revolutionary potentialities of the movement' (Tsuyoshi Hasegawa, *The February Revolution: Petrograd 1917*, University of Washington Press, 1981). The contribution of the revolutionary movement that developed consisted of providing propaganda, which helped undermine people's traditional loyalty to Tsarism. There was a body of revolutionaries willing and able to lead a revolution, but most of them were in exile at the time of the first Revolution. Even Lenin's role in the second Revolution has undergone some re-assessment. The contribution of the revolutionary movement was more in its indirect impact. Its presence frightened the regime into a policy of repression which further alienated support for it.

D *Impact of World War I*

This explanation stresses the importance of involvement in World War I though interpretations differ as to its role:

> ### KEY ISSUE
> *How have views on the role war differed?*

1 One group argue that the war interrupted the development of a modern state along western, constitutional lines. In this view, the war rather than revolutionary forces caused the collapse of Tsarism as a result of its disastrous effects. Soldiers on the Eastern Front suffered from incompetent leadership, high mortalities and injuries, and inadequate provisioning while the civilian population experienced the social hardships of food shortages, high prices and increased demands in the workplace. Demoralisation and discontent spread. The *Duma* used war as an excuse to demand political concessions and a greater share in government.

2 Others deny that the war had any decisive impact on the timing of the revolution, except to hold it back for a time.

3 A variant of the role or war explanation is the presence of German agents in Russia, who were intent on knocking out a wartime enemy.

Whatever role war played in the downfall of Nicholas II, the fact that Russia remained an opponent of Germany after the February Revolution is seen as a key factor in bringing the Bolsheviks to power in October. They were the only party that had consistently criticised the war and called for an immediate peace.

E Assessment of the relative role played by each explanation

The sequence of events indicates that only three of the four explanations are relevant in interpreting why the first Revolution occurred. Starting with a strike, a not unusual event, and culminating in Nicholas' abdication, the February Revolution owed nothing to a body of revolutionaries. Even so, underlying weaknesses in Russian society and a government that had lost credibility in the eyes of the people were not sufficiently decisive. The same problems had been present in 1905, but Nicholas survived because he had retained the loyalty of the police, the cossacks, and the army. Under pressure from an able minister, Witte, he had been prepared to make concessions, which won over the moderate liberals. In 1917 Nicholas was again faced with similar conditions – humiliation in war, social and economic pressures, lack of reliable support among respectable groups in society, whether liberal or conservative, but this time he had no armed force to fall back on. He had lost the loyalty of the army as a result of disasters on the Eastern Front, incompetence, and Nicholas himself. In 1917 General Krymov wrote to the *Duma* members, 'the spirit of the army is such that news of a coup d'etat would be welcomed with joy. A revolution is imminent and we at the front feel it to be so. If you decide on such an extreme step, we will support you. Clearly, there is no other way' (L. Kochan & R. Abraham, *Making of Modern Russia*, Harmondsworth, Penguin, 1983; page 285). What started as a strike, was allowed to escalate into a popular rebellion outside the control or direction of revolutionary leaders who were still in exile.

F Could Tsarism have survived?

The Revolution of 1917 was not inevitable. Under a different man Tsarism could have survived. Had Nicholas accepted the constitutional demands of the Progressive Bloc in the *Duma* the privileged sections of Russian society might have rallied behind him. Could Tsarism have survived? They were aware of the dangers of the situation and its accompanying risk of social revolution. But the problem lay with the personality of Nicholas II rather than with Tsarism. In 1917 there was no Witte or his equivalent to force Nicholas to make concessions, though even if one had been present there was no certainty that Nicholas would have honoured any concessions he might have been forced to make. Concessions in 1905 had won over moderate liberals and this might have been possible again in 1917. A more able tsar might have prevented the situation from reaching a point of collapse but, as we have already noted, Nicholas was determined to 'maintain the principle of autocracy just as firmly and unflinchingly as it was preserved by his father'. He failed to recognise the dangers of the situation and that a divide had grown up between himself and the ruling class. Had he been prepared to give the constitutionalists in the *Duma* political power they had the expertise to improve management of the war effort. They would also have united to oppose any attempt from the people to change government. Nicholas appeared to be blind to the realities of the situation, a fact, which is reported by the British Ambassador Buchanan. According to Buchanan he had advised Nicholas in January 1917 that, 'Your Majesty ... has but one safe course open to you, namely to break down the barrier that separates you from your people and to regain their confidence'. Drawing himself up and looking hard at me, the Emperor asked, 'Do you mean that I am to regain the confidence of my people, or that they are to regain my confidence?' (R. Massie, *Nicholas and Alexandra*, Victor Gollancz, 1968, page 373). As far as Alexandra was concerned she dismissed the start of the Revolution as a 'hooligan' movement which 'will pass and become calm if only the *Duma* will behave itself'. Nicholas' refusal to allow peaceful constitutional reforms to develop meant that the moderate constitutional parties did not defend him when the crisis appeared. Both the *Duma* leadership and the High Command of the Army insisted that he abdicate. By February 1917 Russia had collapsed from within, the way having been prepared by war.

4 ∽ IMPACT OF WORLD WAR I

A *Impact on the Russian Army*

By the end of 1916 the impact of war on Russia's relatively untrained peasant conscript army had reached disastrous proportions. After the war the German general, Von Hindenburg, who had campaigned on the Eastern Front wrote that 'in the Great War ledger, the page on which the Russian losses were written has been torn out. No one knows the figure. All we know is that sometimes in our battles with the Russians we had to move the mounds of enemy corpses from before our trenches in order to get a clear field of fire against fresh assaulting waves. Imagination may try to reconstruct the figure of their losses, but an accurate calculation will remain forever a vain thing' (G. Hughes and S. Welfare, *Red Empire*, 1990). Estimates of the number of dead

Army	Number (in million)
Total size	14.6
In the field	6.9
In the rear	2.0
Unaccounted	?
Casualties	5.5
Prisoners of war	2.1
Dead, sick, wounded	3.4
Overall population	181.5

TABLE 43

Estimates of World War I casualties in the Tsarist Army at the end of 1916

and wounded have varied. Table 43 shows the estimates provided by A.K. Wildman in *End of the Russian Imperial Army* has provided on the number of casualties from Tsarist armies.

Other estimates have suggested 1.7 million dead, 8 million wounded and 2.5 million prisoners of war (D. Christian, *Imperial and Soviet Russia: Power, Privilege and the Challenge of Modernity*, Addison-Wesley Longman, 1986). Whatever the figures, the impact of war on the loyalty of the Imperial army was disastrous. Rapidly trained draftees were often peasants who were insufficiently trained and led by inexperienced officers drawn from the ranks of the intelligentsia. Poor morale was heightened by inadequate supplies, equipment, food and clothing. Turkey's entry into the war closed the Dardanelle Straits, which had been the major route for supplying Russia from the West. Russian industry and raw materials could not meet the army's demand for weapons, boots, clothing and munitions. Improvements in the organisation of industry led to some improvement in 1916 but reports from the Eastern Front continued to warn the government of the dangers of the situation:

The following extract details reports by government officials of conditions at the Front conditions, these are quoted by quoted by M. Florinsky in *The End of the Russian Empire* (Collier Books, 1961). Florinsky was a historian who fought in the Tsarist army.

> ...the atmosphere in the army is very tense, and the relations between the common soldiers and the officers are much strained, the result being that several unpleasant incidents leading even to bloodshed have taken place. The behavior of the soldiers, especially in the units located in the rear, is most challenging. They openly accuse military authorities of corruption, cowardice, drunkenness and even treason.
>
> ... Every one who has approached the army cannot but carry away the belief that complete demoralisation is in progress. The soldiers began to demand peace a long time ago, but never was this done so openly and with such force as now. The officers not infrequently even refuse to lead their units against the enemy because ...

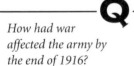

Q

How had war affected the army by the end of 1916?

KEY ISSUE

Attitude of the rank and file.

Despite these heavy losses the army at the front remained loyal and continued fighting, the disillusionment was felt more by those in the rear. Nicholas added to the problem by allowing a large number of exemptions amongst the more privileged groups in society – the educated, wealthy groups, and skilled industrial workers. This meant that most of the conscripts were peasants and they became increasingly responsive to revolutionary propaganda. By 1917 mass surrenders and desertions had become one sign of the army's demoralisation particularly among units stationed in the rear.

B *Impact on government finance*

The government was trapped between a fall in its revenues on the one hand and spiralling expenditure on the other. Part of the problem was the decline in foreign trade (Germany had accounted for half of the total), the export of grain stopped and an important route, through the Dardanelle Straits was closed. Apart from these factors, which were outside government control, Nicholas had contributed to a 30% drop in its revenues. As soon as war was declared he had made the decision to ban the production and sale of alcohol in an effort to avoid a repeat of the scenes in 1905 when the discipline of reserve troops had collapsed in drunken riots. Despite the advice of his Ministry of Finance and the *Duma*, which had relied on alcohol sales to part fund the war, Nicholas made the ban permanent. It was initially successful but eventually people by-passed it and organised an illegal production of vodka which defeated the policy but did not bring the government any financial advantage. Nicholas' decision on the ban was criticised by the *Duma* one member commenting 'never since the dawn of human history has a single country, in time of war, renounced the principal source of its revenue' (M.T. Florinsky, *The End of the Russian Empire*, Collier Books, 1961). Nicholas' ban, the first of many subsequent foolish decisions, brought discredit on his political reputation.

It was not until 1916 that the Ministry of Finance developed alternative sources of revenue, which included the introduction of an income and profits tax, borrowing but most disastrously of all printing more money.

This led to rapid inflation; money supply grew by 336%, but prices rose by 398% as producers increased their prices to take account of the fall in the value of money. Workers found that their standard of living was declining for although their wages had increased by 100% the cost of living had risen by an average of 300%. They complained of food shortages, food queues, cold damp living conditions and poor working conditions. By 1916 the police department was warning of that 'the proletariat of the capital is on the verge of despair … the mass of industrial workers are quite ready to let themselves go to the wildest excesses of a hunger riot … the labour masses, led by the more advanced and already revolutionary elements, assume an openly hostile attitude towards the government and protest with all the means at their disposal against the continuation of the war … The close relationship between the workers of Petrograd and the army also indicate that the atmosphere at the front is disturbing not to say revolutionary … The Government will prove incapable of fighting against the revolutionary masses, which are the more dangerous because they consist largely of soldiers' (M.T. Florinsky, *The End of the Russian Empire*, Collier Books, 1961).

KEY ISSUE

Evils of inflation.

A report by Petrograd secret police on the effect of inflation on living standards in Petrograd, October 1916, quoted by G. Vernadsky (*A Source Book for Russian History from Early Times to 1973*, Yale University Press, 1972) gives an insight into the problems of the times.

Despite the great increase in wages, the economic condition of the masses is worse than terrible. While the wages of the masses have risen fifty per cent, and only in certain categories 100 to 200 per cent (metal workers, machinists, electricians), the prices on all products have increased 100 to 500 per cent. According to the data collected by the sick benefit hind of the 'Triangle' plant, a day's wages for a worker before the war were as follows in comparison with current wages in roubles.

Type of worker	Pre-war wages	Present wages
Unskilled	1.00–1.25	2.50–3.00
Metal worker	2.00–2.50	4.00–5.00
Electrician	2.00–3.00	5.00–6.00

At the same time, the cost of consumer goods needed by the worker has changed in the following incredible way [in roubles]:

Item	Pre-war cost	Present cost
Rent for a corner of a room	2.00–3.00 monthly	8.00–12.00
Dinner in a tea room	0.15–0.20	1.00–1.20
Tea in a tea room	0.07	0.35
Boots	5.00–6.00	20.00–30.00
Shirt	0.75–0.90	2.50–3.00

Even if we estimate the rise in earnings at 100 per cent, the prices of products have risen, on the average, 300 per cent. The impossibility of even buying many food products and necessities, the time wasted standing idle in queues to receive goods, the increasing incidence of disease due to malnutrition and unsanitary living conditions (cold and dampness because of lack of coal and wood), and so forth, have made the workers, as a whole, prepared for the wildest excesses of a 'hunger riot'.

If in the future grain continues to be hidden, the very fact of its disappearance will be sufficient to provoke in the capitals and in the other most populated centres of the empire the greatest disorders, attended by pogroms and endless street rioting. The mood of anxiety, growing daily more intense, is spreading to ever wider sections of the populace. Never have we observed such nervousness as there is now. Almost every day the newspapers' report thousands of facts that reflect the extremely strained nerves of the people in public places, and a still greater number of such facts remains unrecorded. The slightest incident is enough to provoke the biggest brawl. This is especially noticeable in the vicinity of shops, stores, banks, and similar institutions, where 'misunderstandings' occur almost daily.

Q

What effect did inflation have on peoples' living standards?

What dangers existed in the situation?

What is the value of this source to a historian studying the impact of wartime inflation on the people?

C *Impact on the home front*

The war's disruption of communications added to the problem of supplying the cities with food and other essential products. They had been forced to take second place to the needs of the army and the war. The problem of supply was made worse by the rapid growth in population in the towns, especially Moscow and Petrograd, as workers from the villages were pulled into the towns to work in the war industries. They became increasingly discontented under the twin sufferings of food shortages and working conditions that deteriorated under the pressure to increase productivity.

The problem was not with food supply for harvests remained normal, and export of grain had ended, but with disruption to distribution and to production on the large commercial farms in the northern and central regions. Landowners, who farmed for the market, found it increasingly difficult to find labourers as peasants were either drafted into the army or were pulled into the factories in the towns.

The low prices paid by the government for its grain was a further disincentive since there was a discrepancy between their income from sales and the high prices they had to pay for industrial goods. In this situation the government found that supplies of grain to the cities declined from 25% of the grain harvest in 1914 to 15% in 1917, a situation which added to the hardships experienced by the civilian population.

KEY ISSUE

Problem of food supply.

D *Impact on Nicholas' position as tsar*

The incompetence shown by Nicholas II led eventually to a breakdown in the loyalty of his traditional supporters.

● He made a mistake in assuming the role of Commander-in-Chief of the army in 1915 for then he was held personally responsible for the army's defeats.
● Moreover, his presence on the Eastern Front increased his isolation pushing him to rely on the support and advice of his wife, rather than on his ministers.
● The presence of Rasputin, as we have already noted, added to the disrepute of the royal couple. Alexandra and Rasputin's influence proved disastrous for they advised Nicholas against making any concessions.

There followed a rapid succession of ineffectual ministers contributing to the government's instability. *Duma* and *zemstva* developed their own organisations to co-ordinate the war effort and to organise aid for those affected by war. Dominated by liberals and industrialists, these became the nucleus of an alternative government, which was a dangerous development for Nicholas II. The willingness of the recalled *Duma* to co-operate proved short-lived. By 1915 hostility to the regime had revived and expressed itself in a number of intrigues by its members. By 1916 it was clear that the regime was heading for a crisis which finally arrived in

February 1917. The build-up came from the gradual desertion of the regime by its liberal and conservative elements, though the final trigger came from 'below' in the form of a strike.

Kadets, Octobrists, and right-wing deputies formed a *Progressive Bloc*, which gained a majority in the *Duma*. The Progressive Bloc campaigned for traditional liberal demands of representative government, which had the confidence of the public. It wanted a ministry formed from majority groups in the *Duma* that would include Alexander Kerensky (a *Trudovik* and deputy to the fourth *Duma*), Pavel Milyukov (leader of the *Kadets*) and Alexander Guchkov (leader of the *Octobrists*). Nicholas not only rejected the demand 'but dismissed those ministers who showed any liberal tendencies and who had opposed his assumption of command of the army in 1915'. The incompetent advisers who replaced them were not prepared to impose advice on Nicholas. His enemies amongst the liberals gained ground and directed their attacks against Alexandra. There was also increased criticism of Rasputin's role at court, his assassination by Prince Yusupov can be interpreted as an indirect attack on Nicholas. In November 1916 Milyukov used his position in the *Duma* to accuse the government of treachery.

The mood of the times is documented *A Source Book for Russian History from Early Times to 1973*, edited by G. Vernadsky (Yale University Press, 1972).

KEY ISSUE
The Progressive Bloc.

> The present government has sunk beneath the level on which it stood during normal times in Russian life... And now the gulf between us and that government has grown wider and has become impassable...
>
>   Today we see and are aware that with this government we cannot legislate, any more than we can with this government lead Russia to victory... We are telling this government, as the declaration of the Bloc stated: 'We shall fight you; we shall fight with all legitimate means until you go... When the *Duma* with even greater persistence insists that the rear must be organised for a successful struggle, while the government persist in claiming that organising the country means organising a revolution and deliberately prefers chaos and disorganisation, then what is this, stupidity or treason?'

By August 1916 Alexander Guchkov began to intrigue with a group of young cavalry officers and members of the Petrograd garrison to depose Nicholas and set up a new government headed by another member of the Romanov family. Some generals were supportive but unwilling to commit themselves in advance. The coup was planned for the middle of March 1917 but it was postponed by Guchkov's illness until it was too late.

CASE STUDY – IMPACT OF WORLD WAR I ON RUSSIA
Study the collection of Sources A–E and then answer the questions which follow.

I consider that with the atmosphere which I have seen to exist in the army, and with the mood of the people which is heard of on all sides, we cannot fail to be victorious. Two things educate the people in an instant: revolution and, especially, victorious wars like this one. The people reaches an unprecedented high point and immediately displays its genius, and its leaders, as if independent of themselves, flourish and perform miracles ... I already see clearly the forerunners of the future – this soberness, and general love and goodwill.

SOURCE A
From a letter dated 29 December 1914 by V. Musin-Pushkin, a wealthy Moscow landowner and member of the Centre group in the fourth Duma, *quoted by M. McCauley*, Octobrists to Bolsheviks: Imperial Russia 1905–1917, *Arnold, 1984.*

Year 1915	Political strikes		Economic strikes	
	Number of strikes	*Number of strikers*	*Number of strikes*	*Number of strikers*
August	24	23 178	16	11 640
September	70	82 728	13	7470
October	10−	11 268	21	13 350
November	5	11 020	19	6838
December	7	8985	26	13 284
Total	116	137 179	95	52 582

Year 1916	Political strikes		Economic strikes	
	Number of strikes	*Number of strikers*	*Number of strikes*	*Number of strikers*
January	68	61 447	35	16 418
February	3	3200	55	53 723
March	51	77 877	16	11 811
April	7	14 152	48	25 112
May	3	8932	42	26 756
June	6	3452	37	15 603
July	2	5333	27	20 326
August	4	1686	18	6259
September	2	2800	33	24 918
October	177	174 592	12	15 184
November	6	22 950	24	18 592
December	1	1000	7	8798
Total	330	377 421	354	243 500

SOURCE B
Strikes in Petrograd, 1915 and 1916, adapted from I.P Leiberov, History of the Leningrad Working Class, *quoted by John Daborn*, Russia Revolution and Counter-Revolution, 1917–1924, *Cambridge University Press, 1991.*

Extract I
... the mass of the population is at present in a very troubled mood. At the beginning of September this year an exceptional heightening of opposition and bitterness of mood became very obvious amongst wide sections of the population of Petrograd.

Complaints were openly voiced about the corruption of the government, the unbelievable burdens of the war, the unbearable conditions of everyday life. The difficult material position of the ordinary people, living a half-starved existence and seeing no hope of improvement in the near future, made them look sympathetically and with a rare attention at any sort of plan based on a promise to improve the conditions of life. Calls from radical and leftwing elements on the need to 'first defeat the Germans here at home, and then deal with the enemy abroad' began to get a more and more sympathetic hearing…

As a result, a situation was created which was highly favourable to any sort of revolutionary propaganda and actions and which the active leaders of left wing and other anti-government groups correctly evaluated. It is difficult to discount the possibility that German secret agents were operating in such a favorable atmosphere.

In view of the fact that similar opinions are being heard at the moment in literally all sections of the population, including those which in previous years have never expressed discontent (for example, certain groups of Guards officers) one cannot but share the opinion of the *Kadet* leaders, who say, in the words of Shingarev, that 'we are very close to events of the greatest importance, in no way foreseen by the government, and which will be tragic and terrible, but are at the same time inevitable…

Extract 2

… The *Kadet* delegates paint no less sorry a picture of food purchase in Russia. In the words of one of them, 'there is absolute ruin everywhere': the peasantry, cowed by requisitions, unhappy with interference in trading deals by provincial governors and the police, has no desire to sell its grain and other stocks, fearing that they will get only the statutory price. They refuse to believe all assurances that they will get paid at the going rate. As a result of this the provinces are almost devoid of food.

The attitude of the countryside to the war has, right from the outset, been extremely unfavourable, for conscription had a much greater effect there than in the towns. Now in the country there is no belief that the war will be successful; in the words of insurance agents, teachers and other representatives of the 'rural intelligentsia', 'everyone wants the war to end, but no one expects that it will'. The peasantry willingly talks about politics, something that was hardly ever heard between 1906 and 1914.

In the words of other *Kadets*… 'across the whole of Russia the same thing is seen: everyone understands that under the old order the Germans cannot be beaten… that the nation itself must interfere in the war… This movement, which to begin with was purely economic, has become political and in the future could turn into a serious movement with a definite programme.'

SOURCE C

Extracts from Police Reports recounting the discontent in Petrograd October 1916, quoted by M. McCauley, Octobrists to Bolsheviks: Imperial Russia 1905–1917, *Arnold, 1984.*

When the *Duma* declares again and again that the home front must be organised for a successful war and the government continues to insist that to organise the country means to organise a revolution, and consciously chooses chaos and disorganisation – is this stupidity or treason? (Voices from left: treason).

We have many different reasons for being discontented with the government... But all these reasons boil down to one general one: the incompetence and evil intentions of the present government... we shall fight until we get a responsible government... Cabinet members must agree unanimously as to the most urgent tasks, they must agree and be prepared to implement the programme of the *Duma* majority and they must rely on this majority not just in the implementation of this programme, but in all their actions.

SOURCE D
From a speech on the 1 November 1916 to the fourth Duma by P. Milyukov, Leader of the Kadets, quoted by M. McCauley, Octobrists to Bolsheviks: Imperial Russia 1905–1917, Arnold, 1984.

In Bryansk county, Orel Province, there is no rye flour, salt, paraffin or sugar... Discontent is rife and more than once there have been strikes in the factories and plants with the demand for 'flour and sugar'. There is in Bryansk county a village called Star... Workers there struck on 8 October because they had not eaten bread for two weeks... they selected two spokesmen and sent them to the factory manager with a demand for flour and sugar...

From 13 to 16 November I stayed in the town of Zhizdra, Kaluga Province. There was an acute shortage of domestic items; at all times there was no flour, sugar or paraffin at all. No commodities other than hay were being brought in from the villages. I then travelled round the villages: grumbling, discontent and a vague apprehension all round

SOURCE E
From Alexander Shlyapnikov On The Eve Of 1917, in which a Bolshevik organiser in Petrograd reports on the food crisis in 1916, quoted by John Daborn, Russia Revolution and Counter-Revolution, 1917–1924, Cambridge University Press, 1991.

Q

1. Using the evidence of Sources A and D, show how the attitudes of members of the Duma *had changed towards World War I?*
2. Using your own knowledge, how do you account for this change in attitude?
3. Using the evidence of Sources C–E what were the causes of (a) rural and (b) urban discontent in Russia in October 1916?
4. What, according to Source E, was the cause of strikes in 1916?
5. How does the evidence of Source B confirm the views expressed in Sources C–E?
6. What is the value of Source B as evidence of the growth of revolutionary feeling in Russia during the war?
7. What does Source C reveal about the regime's attitude towards discontent?
8. What was the significance of this attitude in accounting for the collapse of the regime?
9. To what extent do Sources C and E support the view that 'the collapse of the Tsarist regime was due to spontaneous riot rather than organised revolution'?
10. Using the collection of sources and your own knowledge to what extent would you agree with the claim that 'war undermined the political stability of the regime'?

5 ∽ SEQUENCE OF EVENTS 22 FEBRUARY–3 MARCH 1917

Date	Masses	Revolutionary leaders and Petrograd Soviet	Government and security authorities	Duma and its committees	Military leaders Nicholas
February 22	Strike at the Putilov engineering works in Petrograd. Workers demanded pay rises and the re-employment of some sacked workers.				
February 23	Bolsheviks of the Vyborg district in Petrograd which had large industrial concerns, called a strike to coincide with International Women's Day. Large numbers of female textile workers went on strike and called on male workers in metal and munitions factories to join them.	Vyborg District Committee decided to expand the movement. Representatives of labour movement met.	Cossacks were reluctant to interfere.	*Duma* met and passed a motion to organise food supply.	
February 24	Strike spread to other districts in the city. It was followed by violent demonstrations, bread riots, and strikes caused by food shortages and inflation.	The gap widened between Bolshevik activists and Russian Bureau. Leaders of the labour movement continued to meet.	Cossacks continued to suppress the strikers and even forced some police to move away.	Concern increased in the *Duma*. Rodzianko pressed for a meeting with the government on the vital question of food supply crisis.	
February 25	A General Strike involving 240 000 workers affected factories, transport, banks, shops, restaurants and newspapers paralyses Petrograd. Slogans read 'Down with the war', 'Bread', 'Return our husbands from the front'.	There is a widespread call for Soviets to be established. Revolutionary intelligentsia met regularly.	A few soldiers started to defect. The police opened fire killing nine demonstrators. Two police chiefs were shot in retaliation. Police arrest 100 leaders.	*Duma* continued to discuss the problem of food distribution. A meeting took place between the *Duma* and government to decide the transfer of food distribution to city *Duma*.	The commander of the Petrograd garrison wired Nicholas of events in the city. Nicholas ordered his military commander, Khabalov, to suppress the disturbances.
February 26	Troops had started to fire regularly on demonstrators.	Revolutionary leaders expected the strike movement to collapse under troop fire.	Troops fired on demonstrators, but one troop company who tried to desert were arrested. The government felt sufficiently strong to end talks with the	Rodzianko wired Nicholas informing him that 'the situation was serious … the capital was in a state of anarchy' and that a ministry which had the confidence of the	Nicholas dismissed Rodzianko's telegram as 'nonsense' and ordered the army be used to put down disorders. His commanders were reluctant to take

Date	Masses	Revolutionary leaders and Petrograd Soviet	Government and security authorities	Duma *and its committees*	Military leaders Nicholas
			Duma and ruled by decree.	people should be appointed. Nicholas' reply was to suspend the *Duma* and the Council of Ministers.	action due to fear that soldiers would join the demonstrators. Nicholas' order was fatal since many of the troops now decided to side with the demonstrators.
February 27	170 000 soldiers revolted with the mutiny of the Volynsky regiment. Strikers seized rifles, took over prisons, and released prisoners. Anarchy spread and the rebels marched to the building where the *Duma* and government worked and began to arrest ministers.	Petrograd Soviet of Workers and Soldiers' Deputies was formed by a group of left wing socialist intellectuals and workers' deputies. Delegates from the suburbs and factories and from troop units joined it. It formed a potential second government and took over the Tauride Palace, the home of the *Duma*. Military Commission and Food Supply Commission was appointed and the first Soviet session began. An Executive Committee was elected.	More troops deserted and Government resigned and ministers were arrested. Khabalov, military commander of Petrograd, asked for re-enforcements	A Provisional Committee of the *Duma* is formed that 'corresponds to the wishes of the population and that can enjoy its trust'.	The General Headquarters of the Russian Army, the *Stavka*, received contradictory orders.

Nicholas refused advice from court circles, dismissed his War Minister, Khabalov, and made a new appointment. |
| February 28 | All military units joined the insurrection and rebels continued with their march to the *Duma*. Assembly building. A Workers' Militia was formed in Vyborg District and deputies were elected to the Soviet. | The Petrograd Soviet issued its first newspaper, *Izvestia*, which calls on people to take power. | Loyalty of troops collapsed and the War Minister, Khabalov was arrested. | The Provisional Committee of the *Duma* decided to take power and sanctioned the arrest of ministers. It took control of transport. Rodzianko ordered a city militia to be formed and argued for responsible government, which had the support of grand dukes. | *Stavka* decided on a policy of counter-revolution and called for re-enforcement.

Nicholas decided to join his family at his palace, Tsarkoe Selo, in Petrograd. |
| March 1 | Workers' militia was formed in parts of the city. Soldiers attended the Petrograd Soviet session that declared that the army was | The Executive Committee discussed the problem of power. Right wing forces pressed for a coalition government while the extreme | | Nicholas' train was stopped by two of his military commanders. *Duma* Committee plotted to secure Nicholas II's abdication. | *Stavka* learnt of the existence of the *Duma* Committee. *Stavka* was alarmed at the spread of revolution to Moscow, Kronstadt, *(continued overleaf)* |

Date	Masses	Revolutionary leaders and Petrograd Soviet	Government and security authorities	Duma *and its committees*	Military leaders Nicholas
	under its control. Order Number One was issued which called for soldiers' soviets thereby removing the authority of officers over men. Moscow followed the lead set by Petrograd.	Left called for a provisional revolutionary government. The Executive Committee accepted Order Number One that called for a surrender of weapons.		Rodzianko's influence declined while Pavel Milyukov's grew. The latter began to draw up a list of provisional government members.	and the Baltic fleet, General Alekseev, Chief of Staff presses for a responsible ministry. Nicholas tried unsuccessfully to return to Petrograd but was prevented by striking railway workers. He was advised by General Alekseev to resign if the army was to continue fighting at the front.
March 2	The masses were hostile to Milyukov's suggestion that monarchy continue. Attacks against officers by soldiers increased. Soldiers and the discontented embark on a campaign of seizing property.	Negotiations between the Provisional Committee and the Petrograd Soviet led to the formation of a Provisional Government with Prince Lvov at its head as prime minister, and commissars replacing the ministers who were mostly arrested.		*Duma* Committee negotiated with the Executive Committee for the transfer of power. Guchkov was charged with getting Nicholas' abdication. Milyukov announced the setting up of a Provisional Government with power transferred to Grand Duke Mikhail Alexandrovich. Milyukov was given the Ministry of Foreign Affairs, Guchkov was given responsibility for War while Kerensky had Justice.	Rodzianko, supported by military leaders, claimed that Nicholas's abdication was necessary. Nicholas on learning that the army refused to support him agreed to abdicate on both his, and his son's, behalf and in favour of his brother, the Grand Duke Mikhail.
March 3	The streets began to return to normal.	*Izvestia* printed both the Provisional Government and Soviet proclamations. Terms for the conditional support of the Petrograd Soviet were drawn up.		*Duma* Committee and Provisional Government met with the Grand Duke Mikhail who refused to become tsar. Prince Lvov issued his first proclamation as head of Provisional Government.	Military leaders accepted Nicholas' abdication and indicated their refusal to take any action on his behalf.

Okhrana Report, 26 February, just before it was shut down by the rioters, quoted by Richard Pipes, *The Russian Revolution 1899–1919*, Fontana Press, 1990.

Date	Strikes	Strikers
23	48	99 700
24	147	196 632
25	206	271 211
27	216	314 439

TABLE 44
Growth of the strike movement in Petrograd city 23–27 February 1917

The movement broke out spontaneously without preparation and exclusively on the basis of the supply crisis. In as much as the military units did not hinder the crowd and in individual cases even took steps to paralyze the actions of the police the masses gained confidence that they could act with impunity. Now after two days of unimpeded movement on the streets when revolutionary circles have raised the slogans 'Down with the war' and 'Down with the government' the people have become convinced that the revolution has begun, that the masses are winning, that the authorities are powerless to suppress the movement by virtue of the fact that the military units are not on their side, that the decisive victory is near because the military either today or tomorrow will come out openly on the side of the revolutionary forces that the movement which has begun will not subside but grow ceaselessly until ultimate victory and the overthrow of the government.

Q

What evidence is offered that the February Revolution was unplanned?

Why, according to Okhrana, did it succeed?

6 ⟋ MAIN FEATURES OF THE PROVISIONAL GOVERNMENT FEBRUARY–OCTOBER 1917

Following his abdication, Nicholas was taken to Petrograd with his family to be held at their country home at Tsarkoe Selo just outside the city. News of his abdication was received with enthusiasm throughout Russia. Moscow and other Russian cities and even those soldiers left on the Eastern Front followed the example of Petrograd and set up their Soviets, while in the countryside the peasants seized land. At the front thousands of soldiers deserted to rush back to their villages not to miss out in the their share of seized land. During the next 15 months Nicholas with his family, two servants and family doctor were held as 'prisoners' until they were shot and stabbed in a cellar in Ekaterinburg on the orders of the Bolshevik regime.

A *Formation of the 'Dual Alliance' or 'Dual Power'*

Two new revolutionary bodies, the first Provisional Government, and the Petrograd Soviet of Workers' and Soldiers Deputies took control. Tsarist autocracy, bureaucracy and police force were replaced by a confused variety of bodies, all claiming to represent the people, though in

KEY ISSUE

Composition of the Provisional Government.

fact protecting their own sectional and often conflicting interests. Professional revolutionaries were not in a position to take advantage of this discontent. Petrograd had taken the lead and the suddenness of events had taken many of the exiled leaders, including Lenin, by surprise.

As a result of the February Revolution, a Provisional Government representing a cross section of Russia's ruling elite was set up with:

- Prince George Lvov, a wealthy aristocratic landowner and *zemstva* liberal leader, was chosen as Prime Minister by Milyukov. He had done much to organise the war effort under the tsar. He supported the idea of a decentralised system of government in Russia.
- Pavel Milyukov was made Minister of Foreign Affairs and was the real force in government. He had initially wanted a British style constitutional monarchy but after he was forced out of government he looked for a military dictatorship to save Russia from the Soviet system. He emigrated to Paris, the home of many Tsarist emigrés.
- Alexander Guchkov was made Minister of War and Navy but resigned when his policy of war to victory was opposed by the Petrograd Soviet. He supported the pro-tsar Whites in the Civil War before emigrating to Berlin in 1921.
- Alexander Kerensky was first made Minister of Justice and then in July he became Prime Minister. A former member of the *Trudoviks* Party, he joined the Social Revolutionary Party at the time of the February Revolution and was elected to the executive body of the Petrograd Soviet. His appointment provided a link with the Petrograd Soviet. He eventually emigrated to America.
- The remaining posts were given to *Kadets* and *Octobrists*.

It had the support of army commanders, government officials, the police, landowners, and intelligentsia. It was to this body that Grand Duke Mikhail surrendered his powers as tsar 'until the Constituent Assembly ... shall by its decision on the form of government express the will of the people'. Although it had not been elected, the Provisional Government assumed responsibility for governing the Empire until a constitution was drawn up and elections held. As early as 9 March Guchkov was acknowledging that, 'the Provisional Government has no real force at its disposal and its decrees are carried out only to the extent that it is permitted by the Soviet of Workers' and Soldiers' Deputies'. It had to share power with the Petrograd Soviet whose representatives were drawn from moderate socialist parties, the Mensheviks and Social Revolutionaries and which had the support of the working class. The Soviet controlled railways, posts and telegraphs, the army and had more real power than the Provisional Government. In the absence of political parties the Soviets became the means whereby the views of the people could be represented. In June the First All Russian Congress of Soviets met in Petrograd attended by 1600 representatives from 350 local Soviets. At this stage Bolshevik influence was negligible – only 40 delegates attended.

The Petrograd Soviet could have seized power as early as June but decided against taking this action for a number of reasons:

KEY ISSUE

Attitude of the Petrograd Soviet.

1 It believed that it needed a middle-class bourgeoisie revolution first before the socialist stage could arrive.
2 It recognised that the Provisional Government was composed of men with the skill and experience to keep the economy running.
3 The Socialists, who were drawn from the class of educated elite, shared the same viewpoint as members of the Provisional Government that unless events were controlled a working class revolt would occur and anarchy would follow.

Kerensky negotiated the Soviet's co-operation on condition that the provisional Government agreed to grant: a general amnesty, civil liberties, removal of legal restrictions based on class, religion and nationality, the right of labour to strike and to organise. There was nothing new to these demands; they had been included in the programme of the revolutionaries in 1905 and in the demands of the Progressive Bloc. The Provisional Government agreed to these conditions relieved that the Soviet had not insisted on more radical changes, especially the redistribution of land or state control of industry. This short-lived alliance of the Provisional Government and the Petrograd Soviet became known as the 'Dual Power', which was based on co-operation between Russia's classes.

B *Policies of the Provisional Government*

During the 8 months of its life the Provisional Government introduced a number of sweeping reforms. It

● announced an immediate amnesty for all political and religious cases, including terrorist attacks, military uprisings, agrarian crimes
● replaced the police by a people's militia with an elected administration under the control of local self-government
● introduced independent judges, trial by jury and abolished capital punishment and exile
● removed restrictions on the right to free speech, press, union, assembly and strikes and extended political liberties to soldiers who were also given civilian rights
● abolished discrimination based on class, religion and nationality
● introduced local self-government elected on the basis of general, direct, equal and secret ballot
● prepared for the meeting of a Constituent Assembly, which would draw up a constitution and introduce general, equal, secret and direct voting. It would then be followed by a general election to secure a democratic government.

C *Policies of the Petrograd Soviet*

These policies had the support of the Petrograd Soviet but the latter body was also concerned to establish its own authority particularly over the army. The Provisional Government had to agree that the military units, which had taken part in the revolutionary movement, would not be disarmed or removed from Petrograd. More significantly the Petrograd Soviet issued in the 1 March edition of *Izvestia* Order Number One which gave it control of the army as a result of its power to reject military decisions passed by the Provisional Government.

Order Number One issued by the Petrograd Soviet, quoted by A.F. Golder, *Documents of Russian History, 1914–17*, The Century Company.

How did Order Number One challenge the authority of the (a) officers and (b) the Provisional Government?

The Soviet of Workers' and Soldiers' Deputies has resolved:
1. In all companies, battalions … committees from the elected representatives of the lower ranks … shall be chosen immediately …
4. The orders of the military commission of the State *Duma* shall be executed only in such cases as do not conflict with the orders and resolutions of the Soviet of Workers' and Soldiers' Deputies.
5. All kinds of arms, such as rifles, machine-guns, armoured automobiles, and others, must be kept at the disposal and under the control of the company and battalion committees, and in no case be turned over to officers, even at their demand.
6. In the ranks … soldiers must observe the strictest military discipline, but outside the service … soldiers cannot in any way be deprived of those rights which all citizens enjoy. In particular, standing at attention and compulsory saluting, when not on duty, is abolished.

A.W. Knox, *With the Russian Army, 1914–17*, 1921, Russia Observed Series, Ayer Co. Publications, 1971.

Major General Sir Alfred Knox, British Military Attaché reported to the British Ambassador in Petrograd April 1917 on the condition of the Russian army after Order Number One.

I returned to Petrograd from a visit to the Northern front on April 28. I gave you my opinion of the deplorable state of things at the front. Units have been turned into political debating societies; the infantry refuses to allow the guns to shoot at the enemy; parleying in betrayal of the Allies and the best interests of Russia takes place daily with the enemy who laughs at the credulity of the Russian peasant soldier. Many senior officers complained that the Government, to which every army has a right to look for support, has left all the burden of dealing with the agitation to the army. In Petrograd things are growing worse daily. The tens of thousands of able bodied men in uniform who saunter about the streets without a thought of going to the front or working to prepare themselves for the war, when every able bodied man and most of the women in England and France are straining every nerve to beat the common enemy, will be a disgrace for all time for the Russian people and its Government.

What was the impact of the Order on the condition of the Russian army?

The Provisional Government did not feel threatened by the Order Number One. Its members did not see themselves in conflict with the Petrograd Soviet; rather they were grateful for the success of the Soviets in restoring order including bringing the army under control.

D *Attitude of the Provisional Government to the war*

Contrary to German belief that the new government would ask for peace, the provisional Government remained loyal to the allies and declared its intention of continuing the war. One of the reasons for liberal desertion of Nicholas was their belief that a genuinely liberal regime, a government of public confidence, would be more capable of conducting the war and achieving victory. Milyukov, Minister for Foreign Affairs and leader of the *Kadets*, reported to the French ambassador, Paléologue, 'we didn't want this revolution to come during hostilities. I didn't even anticipate it, but it has taken place. Our business is now to save Russia by ruthlessly prosecuting the war to victory'. This view was shared by Kerensky who later recorded in his memoirs that his, 'words to the soldiers were: It's easy to appeal to exhausted men to throw down their arms and go home, where a new life has begun. But I summon you to battle, to feats of heroism – I summon you not to festivity, but to death; to sacrifice yourselves for your country!'(Alexander Kerensky, *The Kerensky Memoirs*, 1965). Continuation with the war was an absurd decision. Whilst some officers were prepared to continue the struggle against Germany, the troops, as Brusilov wrote, 'just did not want to fight any more'. According to one historian, 'the officer at once became the enemy in the soldier's mind, for he demanded continuance of the war; and in the soldiers' eyes represented a type of master in military uniform. To the average Russian peasant, his country was a hovel on the Volga, or perhaps the Urals, where he happened to born and to which he thought the Germans could never penetrate' (Alfred Knox, *With The Russian Army, 1914–17*).

E *Weaknesses of the Provisional Government*

Despite the inherent difficulties of the relationship, the Dual Alliance worked well for the short life of this phase of the Russian Revolution. As already noted, it had introduced a number of important reforms, but it was vital, if it was to survive, to win support among the different groups who had 'made' the February Revolution. This did not happen; it failed to achieve the hopes and expectations of different social groups.

Social group	Hopes and expectations	Provisional Government response
Peasantry	● Democratic Republic ● Action against the upper classes ● End to non-peasant holdings and transfer of land to the peasants	● Set up Land Committees in April 1918 to collect information on local land arrangements and land needs of the population

(continued overleaf)

Social group	Hopes and expectations	Provisional Government response
	● Regulation of the grain market to benefit producers ● End to the old system of local administration whereby peasants had been controlled by the land captains, police and officers of the Tsarist bureaucracy	● Armed force was used to suppress rural disturbances ● Government set up a state monopoly on grain whereby food committees administered fixed prices at 60% above the Tsarist level. However this was not linked to the price rises in consumer goods so that producers had no incentive to sell their grain ● The Government decided to retain existing administrative bodies, which were democratically elected, but dominated by local landowners. These bodies were unsympathetic to peasant demands
Working classes	● Improvements in living and working conditions ● Eight-hour day ● Wage rise ● Security of employment ● Supervision of management	● Set up conciliation chambers and factory committees but they were viewed by workers as a Government attempt to use them to maintain the *status quo* in the factories ● Government supported the efforts of employers to restore discipline in the factories, refuse the 8-hour day, and worker control of factories ● Failed to stop a further decline in living standards in the cities and increasing unemployment
Army	● Work towards peace ● Reform of the systems of control by aristocratic/privileged officers whereby control was passed to officers from the same social class ● Peasant conscripts wanted land	● In June a large offensive was unsuccessfully launched against Germany ● Government refused to consider signing a separate peace with Germany ● Fresh public demonstrations against involvement in war
Nationalities	● Greater self-rule ● Share in the concessions gained by Russian peasants and workers	● Recognised the independence of Poland which was behind German lines ● Other nationalities were ordered to wait for the decisions of the Constituent Assembly

The failure of the Provisional Government can be explained by a number of factors:

1 It refused to take the initiative until a fully democratically elected assembly was in place, but it was also torn by internal disagreements, party divisions and personality conflicts.

2 The concessions issued to meet the demands of the Petrograd Soviet rebounded on the Provisional Government. By lifting censorship restrictions it lost its power to mould public opinion to its favour. The decision to continue with the war proved to be very unpopular and much of the anti-war propaganda was directed against the Government.

3 It lost control of the countryside when it replaced provincial governors with elected *zemstva*. A system of peasant committees and later Soviets developed and showed independence.

4 Army discipline collapsed as soldiers elected their own Soviets, which ignored officers' commands. The unpopular decision to continue with the war led to an increasing number of soldiers returning to their villages concerned not to lose out if land was redistributed. Whereas there had been 195 000 desertions between 1914 and February 1917; this escalated to 365 000 between March and May.

Below are the minutes of a conference at which Russian military commanders reported to the Provisional Government and the Petrograd Soviet, May 1917.

The officers welcomed the Revolution. Had we not given the Revolution so friendly a reception it might not have been brought about so easily. But it turned out that liberty meant liberty only for the private soldier. The officer had to be content to be the social outcast of liberty. The granting of liberty has stupefied the masses who have little understood what has really taken place. Everyone knows that important rights have been granted but not what those rights are; nor are the masses interested in doing their duty. The officers are in a difficult position … The Provisional Government the *Duma* and especially the Soviet of Soldiers' and Workers' Deputies should spare no effort to assist us. They must do it without delay for the sake of the country … **Fraternisation** the newspaper *Pravda* widely circulated, and the proclamations of the enemy written in good Russian, – all alike result in depriving the officers of all influence although they themselves are willing to fight.

Report of General Headquarters of the Russian Army, October 1917.

The general feeling of the army continues to be one of highly nervous expectancy. Now as before, an irresistible thirst for peace, a universal desire to leave the front, and end the present situation somehow in

Q

What are the main complaints of military commanders of the army?

Why, according to the military commanders, was it necessary for the Government and Soviet to 'assist us … without delay'?

Fraternisation breakdown of formal relationship between officers and men.

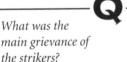

Q What was the condition of the Russian army?

Using the evidence of both sources, discuss the extent to which the condition of the Russian army proved to be a handicap to the success and survival of the Provisional Government.

Q What was the main grievance of the strikers?

the quickest possible manner constitute the main motives on which the attitude of most of our troops is based … The army is simply a huge, weary, shabby, and ill fed mob of angry men united by their common thirst for peace, and by common disappointment.

5 The government failed to control workers in the vital war industries so that supply broke down aggravating the situation on the Eastern Front. Workers became more radical as their living standards remained low, food shortages, and inflation continued, unemployment increased and goods became scarcer. The number of strikes rose considerably often accompanied by demonstrations and factory seizures.

1917	Number of strikes	Strike issues	Number of strikers involved in each strike issue
April	35 000	Wages	1 800 000
June	175 000	Hours	1 250 000
September	110 000	Rules	400 000
October	120 000	Political issues	250 000

TABLE 45 *Number of strikes and strikers (nationally) April–October 1917*

Workers became more organised forming Soviets, trade unions and factory committees, which negotiated with employers on issues of work contracts, working conditions, and management of the factory. In some cases workers' groups were powerful enough to undermine factory owners' control even though the Government had given permission for owners to dismiss workers and ban the committees from meeting during working hours. The same level of worker organisation was extended to living conditions as Soviets were set up to manage housing accommodation. A sense of class-consciousness developed out of these activities which benefited the Bolsheviks in their bid to represent themselves as representatives of working class interests. Loyalty to the Provisional Government faded away.

6 Following the resignations of Milyukov and Guchkov in April and their replacement by socialists from the Soviet, landowners, factory owners and army leaders lost faith in the Provisional Government. It was impossible for them to fulfill the expectations of all groups since these were often mutually contradictory. Property owners wanted protection of their property and social stability; workers and peasants looked for a reallocation of wealth. The Government had little chance of success. 'The conflict between the attitude of the masses and that of the educated classes … was fundamental, insoluble, fatal … There was no room for compromise between the two points of view and the conflict had to be fought out to its bitter end' (M.T. Florinsky, *The End of the Russian Empire*, Collier Books,

	March	April	May	June	July	August	September	October
Levels of rural unrest	1.9	7.1	11.6	16.6	17.1	13.1	16.0	16.6
Type of action								
Open land seizure	2.6	24.9	34.3	37.0	34.5	35.8	23.6	18.2
Destruction	51.3	8.0	6.7	3.6	4.3	10.0	19.7	23.4
Personal violence	7.7	12.7	10.6	9.1	7.1	11.2	12.3	7.5
Crop seizure	7.7	1.9	2.6	7.8	23.7	22.2	11.9	11.3
Seizure of timber	25.6	20.2	19.9	17.9	10.9	11.0	26.7	32.6
Seizure of inventory	–	4.7	8.6	10.1	9.6	6.0	3.9	5.1
Establish rental rates	2.5	5.6	3.8	1.0	0.8	0.7	0.2	0.2
Remove labour	2.6	22.1	13.4	13.5	9.1	3.2	1.6	0.2

TABLE 46 *Levels of rural unrest March–October 1917 (in terms of monthly share of all unrest) and the types of peasant action against landed property per month*

1961). In the towns factory owners complained that profits and productivity were falling due to the introduction of the 8 h day and factory committees. Its failure to deal with peasant disturbances in the countryside lost its upper class support as order broke down and property in the countryside was attacked and seized by the peasants.

Local government bodies proved incapable of controlling peasant actions while the People's Militia had no inclination to take action. Peasants defied state orders and refused to send their grain to the towns due to the low prices paid. Crop failure in the main European grain producing regions prevented the Government from importing grain to end the continuing food shortages in the towns. The replacement of liberals by socialists from April onwards led many property owners to agitate for a new strong unified government that would maintain the unity of the Empire.

7 Prior to April the Bolsheviks along with the other political parties had appeared to support the Provisional Government, but Lenin's return to Russia in April 1917 changed this. He had been helped by the German High Command, who planned to add to the chaos in Russia by secretly arranging for Lenin to be smuggled in a sealed railway carriage across their country and then taken, by way of neutral Sweden, to Petrograd. They expected Lenin, who was known to be opposed to Russian involvement in the war, to conclude peace once he was in power. Lenin arrived on 16 April and demanded peace and a transfer of power to the Soviets. Trotsky also returned in May and buried his differences with Lenin. They began to work together to overthrow the Provisional Government. Lenin issued a number of policy statements which came to be known as the '*April Theses*' which maybe summarised as follows:

● If the working classes and the army rank and file wanted to end the war quickly, they would have to overthrow capitalism in Russia. The capitalists had other interests besides the defence of the Russian people.

Q

Identify the period when the level of peasant unrest was at its highest?

What was (a) the most frequent type and (b) the least frequent type of peasant action?

KEY ISSUE

April Theses.

- The Provisional Government was middle class and must not be supported. It was now his task to educate the working class so that they could take over the revolution.
- Although the Bolsheviks were in a minority in most Soviets, it was essential that the people reject the Provisional Government and give their support to the Bolsheviks.
- It was necessary to replace the existing government with a system of Soviets.
- All land was to be confiscated and taken over by the state. The land would be re-allocated to the peasants by local Soviets.

The Bolsheviks worked to take advantage of the riots and strikes to stir up as much trouble as possible in the hope of achieving a second revolution. They were helped by the failure of the Provisional Government to meet the expectations of different social groups combined with its decision to launch a new offensive in June. By July 1917 the Provisional Government was noticeably in trouble and was confronted with two major challenges, the July Days and the Kornilov Revolt, though it managed to defeat these and to hold on to power until October.

7 ⌐ 'JULY DAYS'

The 'July Days' refer to the series of demonstrations in Petrograd between 3 and 6 July carried out by a crowd of 30 000 composed of soldiers, sailors from Kronstadt and workers against the war, low wages and hatred of the Provisional Government.

A *Historians' views*

> **KEY ISSUE**
>
> *Role of the Bolsheviks.*

Historians have debated whether these left-wing challenges were stage-managed by the Bolsheviks who then denied any involvement when the demonstrators failed, or whether they were a spontaneous protest. Those who have taken a sympathetic view of the Bolsheviks argue that Lenin was opposed to the events since he believed that it was too soon for the Bolsheviks to launch their bid for power until the Government had become completely discredited with the failure of the June offensive. In fact he was away from the capital when the demonstration started and quickly returned but he was too late to alter the course of events. Other historians have been more unsympathetic and claimed that the July Days were one of Lenin's worst miscalculations threatening the destruction of the Party and that failure led Bolshevik propagandists to lie about the event. In a bid to distance themselves they claimed that the initiative came from the Kronstadt naval base and factory workers. The Provisional Government, however, believed that Lenin was responsible and it was to escape arrest that Lenin fled to Finland for a restful holiday! The truth of the matter is that the men at Kronstadt, who had been influenced by Bolshevik ideas, feared being sent to the Front, while the Bolsheviks recognised that the base's removal would deny them an important potential power base for a later seizure of power.

B *Course of events*

The preliminaries to the demonstrations started when soldiers and sailors from the naval base along with factory workers were called out by activists of the Petrograd Soviet to overthrow the unpopular Government with the rallying call 'All Power to the Soviets'. The left Socialist Revolutionary Marie Spirdonova led some of the march, and although the Bolshevik leadership did not appear there were some Bolsheviks amongst the rank and file. The three days of demonstrations witnessed rioting and looting, some railway stations were seized and there was a great deal of confusion and panic. Lenin's failure to intervene, and the willingness of troops loyal to the Government to move against the demonstrators, meant that there was no general uprising. Lenin fled to Finland on the fourth day before the Government issued warrants for the arrest of the Bolsheviks on the grounds that they were traitors in receipt of German support.

C *Results of 'July Days'*

The immediate result of the July Days was a hardening of Government attitude towards the left whose leading figures, including Trotsky, were imprisoned. The Bolsheviks had received a setback: Lenin's reputation was damaged by his failure to take a positive lead while Bolshevik propaganda was banned from the Front and the offices of *Pravda* closed.

However, the Party continued to work at local level, amongst the radical factory committees and Soviets, to increase its support amongst the working class.

Within the Government, Prince Lvov resigned and was replaced by Kerensky. The latter appointed General Lavr Kornilov (1870–1918), the son of a peasant Cossack and a man renowned for his devotion to Russia, as Commander-in-Chief of the Army. He had been taken prisoner by the Germans during the war but had managed to escape. He was a hero-type figure, with a reputation as a tough leader and particularly popular amongst those groups who opposed the Bolsheviks. As a precondition to his acceptance, he insisted on the re-introduction of the death penalty and courts martial for the army to restore order and discipline. The regiments, which had taken part in the demonstrations, were disbanded and disarmed while Kronstadt was reduced to 100 000 men. The Kronstadt's community dislike of, and lack of trust in, Kerensky grew and it became a major force in the October Revolution. Fearing a right-wing reaction, Kerensky ordered the removal of Nicholas II and his family to Tobolsk in Siberia.

8 ⟿ THE KORNILOV AFFAIR

A *Significance of Kornilov's appointment as Commander-in-Chief of the army*

Kornilov was welcomed by both right-wing groups as wells as the Liberals and *Kadets* as the man who would rescue the Empire from collapse after the threats of the 'July Days' and introduce a new strong unified government. He became the focus for all counter-revolutionary forces. Kornilov's demand that he should also control industries vital to the war effort – armaments and railways – raised doubts in Kerensky's mind of Kornilov's personal ambitions and long-term intentions. However, he had no choice in July but to agree though he had no intention of surrendering his power to a military style dictatorship. In his evidence to the Extraordinary Commission of Enquiry after his attempt to seize power had failed, Kornilov claimed that he had reached an agreement with Kerensky that he would move a large military force to Petrograd so that Soviet inspired disturbances, if they occurred, could be suppressed. It was understood that the Soviets would be included in this counter-offensive, a 'pact' that Kerensky subsequently dismissed as pure invention.

KEY ISSUE

Support for Kornilov.

B *Kornilov's 'programme'*

Kornilov's programme was simple: 'the time has come to hang the German agents and spies, headed by Lenin' he told his aide-de-camp, 'to disperse the Soviet of Workers' and Soldiers' Deputies so that it can never reassemble'. It had the backing of Milyukov, Guchkov, Rodzianko and some industrialists, army and navy officers. Kornilov gained some support and sympathy from the Allies, which in the case of Britain extended to finance and transport though publicly the British Ambassador claimed that although he had known of their intentions he, 'would not give them either (his) countenance or support'. On the contrary he had urged them on 23 August, 'to renounce an enterprise that was not only foredoomed to failure but that would be at once exploited by the Bolsheviks. If General Kornilov were wise he would wait for the Bolsheviks to make their first move and then come and put them down'.

C *Details of the attempted 'coup'*

See page 208.

The Petrograd Soviet was hostile to Kornilov's appointment which threatened to undermine the Soviets' authority achieved under Order Number One. They refused to allow restoration of the death penalty in the army. Kerensky was in a difficult position trapped between his need to keep the support of the left under the Dual Alliance, the moderates and the army. German capture of the city of Riga and advance into Russian territory amid revived rumours of another proposed Bolshevik coup created panic in the capital. There is some uncertainty about subsequent events; did:

- Kerensky agree to the proposal of a right wing group led by Vladimir Lvov that he transform his Government into a military dictatorship but then change his mind?
- Kornilov and Kerensky plan to act together against the Bolsheviks but Kerensky then changed his mind when he feared he would be removed as well?
- Kornilov act alone?

In the event between 27 and 29 August troops moved towards the capital. On 27 August Kerensky ordered Kornilov to surrender his command and issued a press release accusing Kornilov of sending Vladimir Lvov to him with the demand that, 'the surrender by the Provisional Government of all civil and military power, so that he may form … a new government to administer the country … Perceiving, a desire of certain circles of Russian society to take advantage of the grave condition of the State for the purpose of establishing in the country a regime opposed to the conquests of the revolution … I order … General Kornilov to surrender the post of Supreme Commander … The city of Petrograd to be placed under martial law. I call upon all the ranks of the army and navy to carry on … their duty of defending the country against the external enemy' (Radiotelegram from Kerensky to the Nation, 27 August 1917, quoted in *The Kerensky Memoirs*). In retaliation Kornilov issued his own press release directed to all military commanders in which he counter claimed that:

General Kornilov declared the following in 27 August 1917 (from E.I. Martynov, *Kornilov*, 1927, quoted by Richard Pipes, *The Russian Revolution 1899–1919*, Fontana Press, 1990):

The first part of the Minister–President's telegram – is a complete lie. It was not I who sent Vladimir Lvov … to the Provisional Government but he came to me as the envoy of the Minister–President … A great provocation has thus taken place which puts the fate of the motherland in doubt. People of Russia! Our great motherland is dying. The hour of her death is near. Obliged to speak openly I General Kornilov declare that under the pressure of the Bolshevik majority in the Soviets the Provisional Government is acting in complete accord with the plans of the German General Staff and simultaneously with the imminent landing of the enemy force at Riga it is destroying the army and is undermining the very foundations of the country.

I General Kornilov son of a Cossack peasant declare to everyone that I want nothing for myself save the preservation of a Great Russia and I swear that my goal for the people is the convocation of a Constituent Assembly which will come about as a result of victory over the enemy.

Q

What arguments are used by Kornilov to justify his actions?

What promises does he make to attract support for his cause?

Which groups in Russian society were most likely to rally to his defense?

Despite a telegram from the representative of the Ministry of Foreign Affairs at Army Headquarters to Kerensky on 28 August that 'the entire commanding staff, the overwhelming majority of officers, and the best army units will follow Kornilov', the latter failed to get the support of the masses. As Kornilov's cavalry approached Petrograd, people began to see the 'Red Guards', armed bands of workers, as their defence against a military counter-revolution. The commander of the troops outside Petrograd made peace with Kerensky who had assumed the post of Commander-in-Chief of the army. Kornilov and his other generals submitted to arrest on 1 September and were sent to a barracks in Bykhov where they remained until their escape in December. They went south to join the new anti-Bolshevik Whites and Kornilov was killed the next year.

D *Significance of the 'coup'*

The Kornilov affair ended in a complete failure. The only real gainers from the event were the Bolsheviks. Right wing, Liberals, *Kadets*, Army who had all at one time or another supported Kornilov, were discredited. Kerensky's position as Prime Minister had been gravely weakened since he lost the support of the Petrograd Soviet and the army. In a secret letter to the Bolshevik Central Committee on 30 August Lenin instructed them to 'point out to the people the weakness and vacillation of Kerensky'. He went on 'the main thing now is to intensify our propaganda in favour of some kind of 'partial demands'. Keep up the enthusiasm of the workers, soldiers and peasants … urge them to demand the immediate transfer of land' … The Bolsheviks had appeared to be a shield against counter-revolution and throughout the country 'Committees to save the Revolution' appeared. The way was open for the October Revolution. The growth in their support became obvious in voting in local *Duma* elections in Moscow between June and December when the Bolshevik vote increased by 164% while that of the *Kadets* fell by 6%, the SRs by 85% and the Mensheviks by 79%. At the end of 30 August Kerensky released all Bolshevik prisoners which included Trotsky and by the beginning of September the Bolsheviks had a majority in both the Petrograd and Moscow Soviets. Lenin decided that the time was now ready for taking power to give the people 'peace, bread and freedom'.

E *Case study problems of the Provisional Government*

Study the collection of Sources F–L relating to the problems of the Provisional Government, February–October 1917 and then answer the questions which follow.

SOURCE F *From* Resolution of the Conference of the Petrograd Socialist Revolutionaries, 2 March 1917, *quoted by M. McCauley,* Octobrists to Bolsheviks, *Edward Arnold, 1984.*

The conference considers that support for the Provisional Government is absolutely necessary, whilst it carries out its declared programme: an amnesty, the granting of individual freedoms, the repeal of estate, religious and national restrictions and preparation for the Constituent Assembly. The conference reserves the right to change its attitude should the Provisional Government not adhere to the implementation of this programme.

All citizens should have confidence in this regime ...
Forget all your party, class, estate and national differences! The united Russian people should rise up and create conditions in which all citizens can live peacefully. Each class, estate and nationality should be able to express its opinions and achieve its aims. The most important slogan now is 'Organisation and Unity', organisation and unity for victory over the external enemy, organisation and unity in internal construction.

SOURCE G *From* Appeal of the Central Committee of the Kadet Party, 3 March 1917, *quoted by M. McCauley,* Octobrists to Bolsheviks, *Edward Arnold, 1984.*

Some soldiers then started to arrive home full of revolutionary ideas. They talked about freedom about the land and about how the Provisional Government had promised to divide up the land amongst all the peasants. What the peasants understood most from these conversations was 'land'.

SOURCE H *From the account of a visitor to Ufa Province recounting peasant recollections of the February Revolution, quoted by M. McCauley,* Octobrists to Bolsheviks, *Edward Arnold, 1984.*

Conference appeals to the whole revolutionary democracy of Russia to rally around the Soviets of Workers' and Soldiers' Deputies as organisational centres of the forces of democracy created by the Revolution. These soviets united with other progressive forces are capable of countering attempts at a Tsarist and bourgeois counter-revolution and of consolidating and increasing the gains of the revolution.

Conference recognises the necessity of gradually gaining political control and influence over the Provisional Government and its local organs so as to persuade it to conduct the most energetic struggle against counter-revolutionary forces, to take the most resolute steps towards a complete democratisation of all walks of Russian life, and to make preparations for universal peace without annexations and indemnities based on the self-determination of nations.

Conference appeals to democracy to support the Provisional Government without assuming responsibility for all the work of the Government as long as the Government steadfastly confirms and expands the gains of the revolution.

SOURCE I *From the Resolution of the All-Russian Conference of Soviets, 5 April 1917, quoted by M. McCauley,* The Russian Revolution and the Soviet State 1917–21, *Macmillan, 1975.*

SOURCE J

From a report by Major General Sir Alfred Knox, the British Military Attaché to the British Ambassador in Petrograd, April 1917, quoted by J. Daborn, Russia: Revolution and Counter-Revolution 1917–1924, Cambridge University Press, 1991.

I returned to Petrograd from a visit to the Northern front on 28 April. I gave you my opinion of the deplorable state of things at the front. Units have been turned into political debating societies; the infantry refuses to allow the guns to shoot at the enemy; parleying in betrayal of the Allies and the best interests of Russia takes place daily with the enemy who laughs at the credulity of the Russian peasant soldier. Many senior officers complained that the Government, to which every army has a right to look for support, has left all the burden of dealing with the agitation to the army.

SOURCE K

From Izvestia, the newspaper of the Petrograd Soviet, 16 May 1917, quoted by J. Daborn, Russia: Revolution and Counter-Revolution 1917–1924, Cambridge University Press, 1991.

The country is … in a dangerous position. Three years of war have exhausted her strength. Finances are disorganised; railways are broken down; there is a lack of raw materials and fuel, a need of bread at the front and in the cities – all these have brought on discontent and mental unrest which Tsarist tools are ready to make use of. The army is breaking up. In certain places a disorderly seizure of land is going on, a destruction of livestock and implements. Discontent is growing. No one pays any attention to the authorised agents of the Government … which feels itself powerless and helpless. Only a strong revolutionary government, enjoying the confidence of the people, can save the country, hold on to the conquests of the revolution, put an end to the split in the army, and keep it on a war footing …

This is the reason why the Executive Committee has submitted the terms on which the representatives of the Soviet would join the Provisional Government.

SOURCE L

From Proclamation by General Kornilov, 27 August 1917, quoted by M. McCauley, The Russian Revolution and the Soviet State 1917–1921, Macmillan, 1975.

I, General Kornilov, declare that under the pressure of the Bolshevik majority in the Soviets, the Provisional Government is acting in complete accord with the plans of the German General Staff … it is destroying the army and is undermining the very foundations of the country.

The heavy sense of the inevitable ruin of our country forces me to call upon all the Russian people in these terrible times to come to the aid of the dying motherland …

1. Using the evidence of Source L and your own knowledge explain Kornilov's motives behind his 27 August Proclamation.
2. What promises and expectations are revealed in Sources F and H?
3. To what extent was the Provisional Government successful in achieving these promises and expectations?
4. Using the evidence of Sources F, G and I, to what extent did the Social Revolutionaries, Kadets and the Soviets share a common attitude towards the Provisional Government?

5. *Using the evidence of Sources J–L, how serious were the problems facing the Provisional Government?*
6. *Using the evidence of all the sources and your own knowledge, to what extent would you agree with the claim that, 'what is surprising is not that the Provisional Government failed but that it lasted for so long'.*

9 ⌐ LENIN AND THE ESTABLISHMENT OF COMMUNIST GOVERNMENT IN RUSSIA 1917–24

A *The decision to seize power*

The weakness of the Provisional Government ensured that 'there would probably have been a socialist regime in Russia by the end of 1917 even without Lenin's intervention, though it was not certain that it would be Bolshevik' (Robert Service, *The Russian Revolution 1900–1927*, Macmillan, 1986, page 51). During the first phase of the Revolution, February to October, the Bolsheviks were not a tightly organised and disciplined party under the undisputed leadership of Lenin. He watched events unfolding in Russia from his voluntary exile in Finland where he remained until just before the revolution in October. He found it difficult to persuade his colleagues on the Central Committee to agree to a seizure of power since the Committee was composed of individuals who had their own views as to the best way of achieving power. Lenin had to rely on writing to the Central Committee but two prominent committee members, Zinoviev and Kamenev, opposed his call for a Second Revolution. They did not share Lenin's optimism that the time was ready following the upsurge in support for the Bolsheviks as a result of the Kornilov Affair and their success in gaining majorities in the Petrograd and Moscow Soviets. The Central Committee not only rejected Lenin's call for a seizure of power contained in a succession of letters throughout September and October, but also directed that measures be taken to prevent demonstrations of any kind amongst workers and soldiers who were taking the initiative from below. Lenin eventually succeeded, despite the opposition of Zinoviev and Kamenev, in persuading the Central Committee on 10 October, that 'an armed uprising (is) on the order of the day', though no decisions were taken on tactics or strategy. This was confirmed at another meeting on 16 October and a Military Revolutionary Centre, which included Trotsky and Dzerzhinsky, was set up to organise, and subsequently carry through the coup. Zinoviev and Kamenev distanced themselves from the events that followed. It follows from what has been said about the circumstances of seizing power in October that historians have debated for many years Lenin's role.

B *The role of Lenin*

HISTORIANS' DEBATE

Interpretation 1

E.H. Carr, *The Bolshevik Revolution 1917–23*, Macmillan, 1953, vol. 1.

E. Acton, *Rethinking the Russian Revolution*, Edward Arnold.

Lenin was the key influence in shaping the Revolution

- He was central to Bolshevik success being responsible for the change in strategy with the April Theses and adoption of the resolution to seize power at the 10 October meeting of the Central Committee.
- He had tremendous prestige within the Bolshevik Party and had a great gift for combining theory and practice. Only he could have succeeded in getting the item for a second revolution on the agenda of the 10 October meeting. Trotsky called him 'the greatest engine-driver of Revolution'.
- He increased public awareness of the party and was responsible for the rise in membership from 10 000 in February to 250 000 by October, which transformed it into a mass workers' party. According to Acton, 'its success in October came from its ability to articulate the masses' own goals, but it did not create either these goals or the mass radicalism which went with them'.
- Lenin was the central directing force and the main inspiration though the task of organising the workers was carried out by Party workers and officials while the seizure of power was the work of Trotsky and the Military Revolutionary Committee.

Interpretation 2

S.A. Smith, *Red Petrograd: Revolution in the Factories, 1917–18*, CUP, 1983.

D. Koenker, *Moscow Workers and the 1917 Revolution*, Princeton University Press, 1981.

Graeme J. Gill, *Peasants and Government in the Russian Revolution*, Macmillan, 1979.

There were limits to Lenin's importance

- These historians have concentrated on the social forces that made the October Revolution and have focused on the part played by the masses. Though they have not denied that Lenin had a role to play, they have stressed that this must be seen in context.
- He was not in Russia for most of 1917 and on his return he confined himself to Petrograd.

- They emphasised the contribution of forces outside his control. It was government failure to meet the increasingly radical demands of the people, which created the conditions for the Bolshevik seizure of power.
- Lenin responded to the people's demand for action on policies that they had devised. Their actions influenced him to adopt a more radical position in 1917 and to make the decision in September/October that the time was ripe for the second revolution.

C *Contribution of other Bolshevik leaders*

LEV DAVIDOVICH BRONSTEIN (LEON TROTSKY) (1879–1940)

PROFILE

The fifth son of a prosperous Jewish farmer from the Ukraine he was a brilliant and famous figure in the Bolshevik Movement. In his autobiography he referred to the 'intense hatred of the existing order, of injustice, of tyranny' from an early age. His father wanted him to become an engineer but stirred up by the self-sacrifice of a girl student in Petrograd in 1897, he decided to take up revolutionary politics. He formed a commune of students and workers but in 1898 they were betrayed to the Tsarist police and he, with many others, was imprisoned in Moscow and then exiled to Siberia. There he married for the first time, Alexandra Lvovna, a member of the South Russian Workers' Union. During his exile he embarked on a writing career and studied Marx, Engels, Plekhanov, and Lenin. In 1902 he escaped from the prison camp in which he was held, leaving his wife and two daughters behind, and fled to Europe using a false passport in the name of one of his prison guards, Trotsky. Known as the 'pen' for his brilliance as a writer, he worked for the revolutionary paper *Iskra*, arriving in London via Paris in 1902 where he met Lenin. He did not agree with Lenin's ruthless authoritarian methods that led to the division of the Social Democrats between Mensheviks and Bolsheviks and he remained apart from both groups maintaining his own Inter-District group. He returned briefly to Russia in 1905 to take part in the 1905 Revolution. He founded the first workers' council or Soviet in St Petersburg, was elected chairman and wrote three papers, *The Russian Gazette, Nachalo* (The Beginning) and editorials for *Izvestia*. The Soviets became the basis of a network of Bolshevik strongholds in Russia. It was during this time that he married his second wife, I.N. Sedova, another political activist.

Shortly afterwards he was again arrested with other members of the Soviet and spent the next 15 months in prison before he escaped in 1907 and left Russia via Finland for foreign exile.

After attending the Social Democratic Congress in London in 1907, Trotsky and his wife settled in Vienna for the next 7 years, mostly to keep in touch with the political situation. The Russian revolutionaries regarded the German Social Democratic Party as a model. In 1908 he began publication of *Pravda* in Vienna, which was smuggled into Russia by members of the underground Seamen's Union. He also travelled in the Balkans and continued to study economics and mingle with both Menshevik and Bolshevik factions of the Party. Immediately after the outbreak of World War I in August 1914, Trotsky and his wife moved to Zurich and entered into the life of the Swiss Socialist Party. In November 1914 he went to France as a war correspondent and settled down in a borrowed house at Sèvres, attending from there the conference at Zimmerwald. In 1916 Trotsky was deported from France. He spent a few weeks in Spain with his family, sailed for New York and arrived there on 13 January 1917. In New York he met Bukharin, but by 27 March, with news of the February revolution, he was on his way to Russia with his family as passengers on a Norwegian boat. But, at a request from the Provisional Government, they were held at a camp in Halifax in Canada for a month. Finally, in May, they arrived in Petrograd, where he was briefly imprisoned after the 'July Days' but when released made chairman of the Petrograd Soviet, as he had been 12 years earlier. His groups joined with the Bolsheviks in July 1917. Despite the Bolsheviks imprisoned by Kerensky, their numbers were growing in the Soviet and were increased by the threat of a right-wing coup headed by General Kornilov.

At the Congress of the Soviets on the evening of the October Revolution Trotsky, replying to Martov who was urging the revolutionary party to form a coalition with the Mensheviks and SRs, said 'Your part is over. Go to the place where you belong from now on – the trash bin of history.' He was the main practical co-ordinator of the Bolshevik seizure of power in October 1917. At the first meeting of the Party Central Committee, at Trotsky's suggestion, ministries in the newly formed government were called People's Commissars and the government the Soviet of People's Commissaries. Lenin proposed him as the chairman, which he rejected, as he also turned down the Commissariat of the Interior because of his Jewish origins, and the use that might be made from this by their enemies. Finally he accepted the post of Foreign Affairs. In doing so he became involved, much to the fury of the Western Allies, in separate armistice talks with the Germans and their allies at Brest-Litovsk.

The negotiations were complex and on 7 February Trotsky announced to the startled Germans and their allies that the Russian armies had been demolished. This was an expression of his 'neither peace nor war' policy. On 6 March under threat of Lenin's resignation the Treaty was signed.

Trotsky who was subsequently appointed Commissar of War and chairman of the Supreme War Council moved to Moscow with Lenin and the rest of the government. He reorganised the Red Army

See page 233.

that by 1920 numbered 5 500 000 men of who about 48 000 were former Tsarist officers and 214 000 non-commissioned officers. It developed into an efficient fighting force defeating the Poles and the Whites. Trotsky fitted out the armoured train which was to become his home for the next 2½ years and which included a squad of handpicked troops with machine guns and their own transport for deployment in the civil war. His arrogance made him unpopular among the other Bolshevik leaders who prevented him from succeeding Lenin in 1924. He was expelled from the Party in 1929 and murdered by a Stalinist agent in Mexico in 1940.

NIKOLAI BUKHARIN (1888–1938)

PROFILE

He became a Bolshevik in 1906 when he joined the Social Democrats and was forced to live abroad in Western Europe from 1911 where he met Lenin and Stalin. He became a close friend of Lenin, whom he first met when they were in exile in Cracow in 1912. He moved from country to country and was in the USA in 1917 prior to returning to Russia via Japan. He joined the October Revolution in Moscow, seeing it as the beginning of a world revolution and called for a 'holy war in the name of the proletariat'. He was on the extreme left of the party and opposed any divergence from what he considered true Marxism. He produced an easy guide, the *ABC of Communism* to understanding Communism and was editor of *Pravda* in 1917. Lenin regarded him as the 'greatest and most valuable thinker in the Party'. He supported Lenin's policy of 'War Communism' as a natural step to socialism but subsequently accepted the New Economic Policy and later became a supporter of Stalin's 'socialism in one country'.

FELIX DZERZHINSKY (1877–1926)

PROFILE

The son of a rich Polish-Lithuanian landowner, Dzerzhinsky joined the Social Democrats in 1895 and in 1897 was exiled to Siberia. He spent the next 20 years until the 1917 Revolution escaping, and being recaptured. Lenin used his skills on the Revolutionary Military Council and made him responsible for organising the *Cheka*, the political police of the new regime. This became the State Political Administration (GPU) in 1922 and then the OGPU in 1923 when it was brought under the unified control of the People's Commissariat for Internal Affairs (NKVD). It grew from 100 operatives in 1917 to 30 000 in 1921 and was composed of informers and guards including those from the nationalities. It was responsible for the 'Red Terror'. He was also Commissar for Transport in 1921 and director of the Economic Council from 1924 until his death in 1926. Harsh and incorruptible, he was strongly on the left. He opposed the Treaty of Brest-Litovsk and the principle of self-determination for nationalities, which led him to support Stalin's policy of *russifying* and occupying Georgia.

LEV BORISOVICH KAMENEV (1883–1936)

Kamenev was the son of a Jewish railway engineer and joined the Social Democrats in 1901. As a student radical he was arrested many times before the 1905 Revolution. In 1902 he visited Paris and met the *Iskra* group. In 1908 Lenin asked Kamenev to join him in Geneva to edit the Bolshevik paper, *Proletary*. He became a leading propagandist overseas until the 1914 War when he was arrested and in May 1915 deported to Siberia, where he met Stalin. He returned to Russia in April 1917 and took over editorship of *Pravda* in which he opposed Lenin's 'April Theses'. With Zinoviev he voted against the call for an armed uprising in October 1917, demanding conciliation and a coalition with socialists. Lenin's need for support led him to overlook Kamenev's opposition and he was appointed a member of Lenin's Politburo. He was with Trotsky at the negotiations for the Treaty of Brest-Litovsk but he played no real part in the Civil War. In 1922 during Lenin's illness, Kamenev was one of the three, with Zinoviev and Stalin, who opposed Trotsky. His political career ended in 1927 as Stalin, who took over the Party machine, eased him out of power. He was finally expelled from the Party in 1932 though he was eventually executed in 1936 after Stalin's Show Trials.

JOSIF VISSARIMOVICH DJUGASHVILY (STALIN) (1879–1953)

A Georgian, he was the son of a peasant turned cobbler and a washer-woman mother who spent his early years training for the priesthood in the Greek Orthodox Church. Georgia was socially backward and a centre for deported revolutionaries so that it became a breeding ground for radical ideas and movements. He joined a Social Democratic group in 1898 and was expelled from his seminary in 1899 for his activities. He became actively involved in the Social Democratic movement and in the years prior to the 1917 Revolution he was arrested, exiled to Siberia and escaped several times though this did not prevent him from continuing with his revolutionary activities. He supported Lenin when the Party divided though he disagreed with him over the issue of land nationalisation. He played a key role organising the Party's 'fighting squads' who raised money by robbing banks and hijacking treasury vans, and encouraged agitation amongst the oil workers in Baku. He became a member of the Central Committee in 1912 and visited Europe at the end of 1912 before he was again arrested and sent to Siberia where he remained throughout the war. He returned to Petrograd in 1917 with Kamenev and others, took over the editorship of *Pravda,* and presided over the All-Russian Conference of Bolsheviks where he supported a moderate position. He changed this with the publication of the 'April Theses' and the arrival of Lenin. As a member of the new Central Committee he organised the party groups in the various Soviets but he played a minor role in events of October. He became a member of the new government as Commissar for Nationalities and opposed the inclusion of other parties in government. He was responsible for drafting the new Constitution for a Russian Soviet Federative Socialist Republic and had no sympathy with nationalists. After Lenin's death, he rose to become the dictator of Russia. He is better known by the name Stalin.

GREGORY ZINOVIEV (1883–1936)

Of Jewish origin, he joined the Social Democrats in 1901 becoming a member of the Bolshevik Central Committee in 1907 until 1927. He was close to Lenin in exile from 1907 and returned with him in 1917 but then supported Kamenev in opposition to his leader's call for revolution. He was head of the Party's Petrograd organisation, 1918–26, and head of the Third International, the Comintern, 1919–26. After Lenin's death, he joined with Kamenev and Stalin to exclude Trotsky from the leadership, but subsequently became the leader of the United Left Opposition against Stalin 1926–7. He was expelled from the Party for this but was readmitted in 1928 before being finally expelled again in 1932. He was arrested in 1934 and sentenced to death in 1936 after Stalin's Show Trials.

See page 310.

D *Main events in the establishment of Bolshevik power October 1917–February 1918*

September

9	General Alekseev resigns as Chief of Staff in protest against the treatment of Kornilov.
20	A 'South-Eastern Union' of Cossacks is declared, pledging the independence of the various Cossack groups and hostility to the Bolsheviks.
21	The Bolshevik Central Committee decides to take part in Kerensky's 'Pre-Parliament'.
25	Trotsky becomes chairman of the Petrograd Soviet Praesidium, which now has a Bolshevik majority among the soldiers' delegates.

October	
6	The *Duma* and State Council are formally dissolved.
7	Kerensky organises a 'Pre-Parliament', ahead of the elected Constituent Assembly due in November. The 'Pre-Parliament' meets but its lack of purpose produces no effective action. In Petrograd the Bolsheviks collaborate with it, but Lenin in Finland urges them not to do so but to aim to seize power.
10	Lenin, who has secretly returned to Petrograd in September, attends a meeting of the Party Central Committee. He wins over a majority to his policy of taking power since now, unlike in July, the Bolsheviks have a majority. Two other leading Bolsheviks, Kamenev and Zinoviev, oppose a coup still hoping for a parliamentary victory, but the Central Committee approves of an uprising in principle.
20	Although he is aware of the Bolsheviks' preparations, Kerensky fails to take defensive preparations on the assumption that his troops will defeat a coup. The Bolsheviks set up a Military Revolutionary Committee, organised by Trotsky, with commissars appointed to military units who will issue orders and control stores of ammunition. There are 20 000 Red Guards, 60 000 Baltic sailors and 150 000 soldiers of the Petrograd garrison under the control of the Military Revolutionary Committee.
23–25	An armed rising is called by the Bolshevik Central Committee's Military Revolutionary Committee. Red Guard detachments occupy, without bloodshed, key points in Petrograd: the telephone exchange, the post office, and railway stations. Summoned by the committee, some 5000 sailors and soldiers from Kronstadt land in the city and a further 3000 land in the next four days. The Winter Palace, where the Provisional Government is in session, is threatened by the guns of the cruiser Aurora and of the Peter and Paul Fortress, used as military headquarters by the Revolutionary Committee. Red Guards, soldiers and sailors surround the Palace, which after a little resistance surrenders. The ministers are taken into custody but Kerensky had already left, looking in vain for military support. Petrograd remains outwardly calm, with restaurants and theatres open. Lenin issues a proclamation to the Russian people informing them that the Provisional Government had been deposed and that power had passed into the hands of the Petrograd Soviet of Workers and Soldiers' Deputies.
25	The 2nd All-Russian Congress of Soviets opens with a socialist, but not Bolshevik, majority. The newly proclaimed Don Cossack State boycotts it on the grounds that the Provisional Government is the only real authority. Lenin proposes a government composed solely of Bolsheviks but members of the Central Committee and Socialists reject this. Lenin reluctantly agrees to the formation of a coalition government that included the Left SRs only.
26	The All-Russian Committee for the Salvation of the Country and the Revolution is set up by the Praesidium of the Pre-Parliament. It is composed of representatives from the Mensheviks, Social Revolutionaries and others, including trades unions. The Congress of Soviets elects a Council of People's Commissars, or *Sovnarkom* with Lenin as its head and Stalin as Commissar for Nationalities. All 14 members are Bolsheviks,

	although Left Social Revolutionaries later join them. It becomes the effective, decision-making body ruling the nation.
27	The 3rd All-Russian Congress of Soviets issues two decrees. The Decree on Peace: calls for an immediate just peace without indemnities. Both the Western Allies and the Central Powers ignore it.
	The Decree on Land: all land is declared as the property of the people and is redistributed by village Soviets. This was Socialist Revolutionary rather than Bolshevik policy and although it had popular appeal, it tended to increase the ownership instincts of the peasants. It was issued on the 57th anniversary of Tsar Alexander II's decree emancipating the serfs. It announces the future direction of a socialist agricultural programme based on the collective rather than individual ownership of land.
29	Officer cadets, under orders from the Committee of Salvation, attempt a counter-rising but it fails with heavy casualties. Kerensky who has retreated to Pskov attempts to raise an anti-Bolshevik force.
30	Cossack troops are defeated in an attempt to move into Petrograd by a force of sailors, workers and Red Guards.

November

2	General Alekseev forms the first anti-Bolshevik 'White' army on the Don composed of Cossacks.
	Decree on the rights of nationalities is issued by the Petrograd Soviets.
3	Bolsheviks with 30 000 Red Guards take power in Moscow after several days' fighting and after reinforcements arrive from Petrograd. The majority of the troops stay neutral.
6	The Ukraine becomes an independent republic and enlists soldiers of Ukrainian origin into an army to enforce repressive measures against Bolsheviks.
10	The 2nd All-Russian Congress of Peasant Deputies meets in Petrograd. The delegates are divided equally between Social Revolutionaries, led by Victor Chernov and Bolsheviks in combination with the Left Social Revolutionaries, led by Spiridonova. The soldier deputies elect Spiridonova to the chair, rather than the popular Chernov, because they hate the war and Chernov's 'Defensist' position. The Congress breaks up and many of the Social Revolutionaries leave Petrograd; Chernov goes to Samara and later Ufa.
12	Elections, promised by the Bolsheviks, take place for the Constituent Assembly (see Table 47 and Diagram 17 overleaf). The results of the elections are bad for the Bolsheviks who attract less than a quarter of the votes cast. Their support comes from the cities and the working class while the peasantry remained loyal to the Social Revolutionaries who had an overall majority. The Bolsheviks believed that in the long term the peasantry would disappear and had limited understanding of the problems facing the peasants. The National Parties were anti-Bolshevik.
13	A Tartar Constituent Assembly takes power in the Crimea, led by the Tartar National Party and Kadets.
15	Estonia announces its independence. The Bolsheviks seize power in Byelorussia.
17	A weak coalition government is announced composed of Bolsheviks and Left SRs.

Party	Seats	Votes (%)
Right Social Revolutionaries	370	38
Bolsheviks	175	24
Left Social Revolutionaries	40	–
Mensheviks	16	3
Kadets	17	5
Other minority National groups	89	
Total	707	

TABLE 47

Results of elections to the Constituent Assembly, 12 November 1917 (41 million voted)

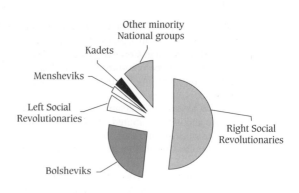

DIAGRAM 17

'20	Army headquarters is attacked and the general staff of the army are arrested and the acting Commander-in-Chief is shot when he refuses to open peace negotiations with Germany.
21	*Cheka*, the Commission for Combating Counter-Revolution and Sabotage, is set up in Moscow under the fanatical and ruthless Felix Dzerzhinsky. During 1918 it embarks on a purge of thousands of dissidents in a 'Red Terror'. Public meetings and all newspapers are banned, apart from those published by the Bolsheviks.
23	Finnish nationalists announce independence.
December	
6	Kornilov and the generals escape detention and arrive at the Don headquarters of the Volunteer 'White' army under General Alekseev.
8	Russo-German negotiations for a peace treaty open at Brest-Litovsk. Trotsky, the leader of the Bolshevik delegation, tries to use delaying tactics by declining to agree the terms. Their patience exhausted the German army resumes its advance towards Petrograd until Lenin instructs his representatives to accept any terms demanded no matter how harsh. The Russian withdrawal from the conflict comes as a great disappointment to the Allies who went as far as to offer support for the Bolshevik government in return for Russia's continued participation in the war.
13	Lenin publishes anonymously an article, '*Theses on the Constituent Assembly*', in *Pravda*, in which he argued a Constituent Assembly to represent workers' interests was no longer necessary since the Soviets, which were worker dominated now controlled Russia and would govern alone.
18	The Volunteer army agree to be under the military command of Kornilov while political relations with civil authorities and foreign powers remains with Alekseev.
1918 January	
4	An article in *Izvestia* warns that any attempt by individuals or institutions to challenge the power of the Soviets would be viewed as a counter-revolutionary act and would be crushed.
5–6	The Constituent Assembly opens, but the Bolsheviks and the Left Social Revolutionaries leave when their resolution that the

Assembly should have only limited power is defeated. This defeat is viewed as a counter-revolutionary act and Red Guards are used to stop delegates entering the Assembly. The latter disperses, never to meet again. The Red Guards kill a number of 'armed conspirators' who carried out protests in Petrograd. Over the next few months rival political parties, which had called for the overthrow of the Bolsheviks, are eliminated. The leaders of the *Kadets*, SRs and Mensheviks are arrested and their party presses are closed though they did not formally cease to exist until the introduction of Lenin's New Economic Policy 1921–2.

See page 245.

6   The All-Russian Congress of Soviets meets and proclaims the Russian Socialist Soviet Republic, a new federal structure based on the voluntary union of the peoples of Russia.

15   The Workers and Peasants Red Army is set up by decree.

26   An anti-Bolshevik provisional government is set up and claims to rule Siberia.

February

1   The Gregorian Calendar is introduced.
A new 'red Fleet' is introduced and sailors are removed from Kronstadt as the Black Sea fleet is re-organised.

March

19   Coalition government collapses when the Left SRs walk out in protest at the terms of the peace treaty with Germany, the Treaty of Brest-Litovsk.

July

3   A new Constitution – The Fundamental Law of the Russian Socialist Federal Soviet Republic – is issued declaring Russia to be a one party Republic with supreme power lying with the All-Russian Congress of Soviets. The Bolsheviks, renamed the Russian Communist Party after the March meeting the seventh All-Russian Congress of Soviets, elected the All-Russian Central Executive Committee, which in turn appointed the Council of People's Commissars. The Constitution guaranteed people freedom of speech, freedom from discrimination based on race, religion but also laid down certain obligations such as military service to protect the state. Local Soviets dealt with local issues while, controlled central committee legislated on national issues. The Bolsheviks controlled the executive committees of the Soviets resulting in their loss of independence and potential to challenge Bolshevik rule.

19   The Constitution of the Russian Socialist Federal Soviet Republic is published in Izvestia. The Bolsheviks have succeeded in consolidating their seizure of power in October, establishing a one party state, and eliminating opposition with virtually no widespread popular protest. They had not however, established sole control of the country as a whole.

This was further revised in 1923. The country became a federation of seven republics, the Union of Soviet Socialist Republics (USSR). Each republic was to be ruled by its own Soviet representing the workers and peasants and then send delegates to the All-Union Congress of Soviets in Moscow. The Communist Party now governed Russia and the most influential men were the party leaders, the members of the Politburo. The dreaded Cheka was replaced by the OGPU though this was only a change in name; its purpose remained the same.

E *Lenin's early reforms*

Between October 1917 and February 1918, a large number of decrees were issued in an effort to begin the work of transforming Russia into a communist society.

- An 8-hour day was introduced and a system of social insurance planned to cover old age, sickness, injury, unemployment, maternity and needs of widows and orphans.
- All titles and class distinctions were abolished and 'comrade' adopted as the normal style of address.
- All ranks were abolished in the army, and the wearing of decorations and the saluting of officers were abandoned.
- Workers took over the factories and the railways, the banks were nationalised and, in the countryside, the private ownership of land was forbidden. All estates were confiscated without any compensation to the former landlords, and the land was then shared amongst the peasants.
- All schools were taken over by the state.
- Church lands were confiscated and marriage became a civil, not a religious ceremony.

Lenin had promised 'peace, bread and land'. He realised that to keep these promises and ensure the success of the Revolution, he had to make peace with the Germans.

F *Russo-German negotiations for the Treaty of Brest-Litovsk 1918*

Early in November 1917 Lenin had issued a decree for peace in which he declared that 'the workers' and peasants' government, created by the Revolution … proposes to all the warring peoples and their governments that they immediately enter into negotiations for a just, democratic peace. A just or democratic peace, such as the majority of the workers and the toiling classes of the warring countries, exhausted, tormented and ravaged by the war, are yearning for … this sort of peace, in the opinion of this Government, would be an immediate peace without annexations and without indemnities'. Russian soldiers were ordered to stop fighting the Germans though the two countries remained formally at war. With the clear possibility of a civil war in Russia between the Bolsheviks and non-Bolsheviks, Lenin realised that he would have to make a formal peace treaty with the Germans. The German High Command indicated its willingness to agree terms for the war had reached a critical point and the Germans wanted to release armies for use on the Western Front against the French and British. Early in 1918, delegates assembled at Brest-Litovsk. The Germans imposed such severe terms that 'when the Soviet delegation heard the German terms, General Skalon, one of the Soviet experts, committed suicide on the spot. Another Soviet delegate, Professor Pokrovsky, said with tears in his eyes: 'How can one speak of peace without annexations if Russia has to be deprived of territories equal to the size of eighteen provinces?' General Hoffmann did not contradict him' (David Shub, *Lenin*, Penguin, 1966). The Germans retaliated by continuing their advance and, when negotiations were resumed, imposed even harsher terms. Lenin's reaction to the terms was to call a meeting on 21 January 1918 between the Bolshevik Central Committee and the Bolshevik deputies to the Third Congress of Soviets to discuss the German terms. Lenin spoke in favour of signing peace even at the cost of ceding considerable territory. Trotsky, on the other hand, recommended that war be declared at an end without signing peace terms. By this device of 'no peace, no war', he hoped that the German and Austrian armies, demoralised by inactivity and revolutionary propaganda, would revolt. The third suggestion was to wage a 'revolutionary war' against Germany and her allies. 15 voted for Lenin's recommendation, 16 for Trotsky's and 32 for a 'revolutionary war'. Three days later the Central Committee again took up the question of peace. Lenin again insisted on immediate acceptance of the German terms. In his *Collected Works* he justified his decision on the grounds that, 'our impulse tells us to rebel, to refuse to sign this robber peace. Our reason will in our calmer moments, tell us the plain, naked truth – that Russia can offer no physical resistance because she is materially exhausted by a three-years war … The Russian Revolution must sign the peace to obtain a breathing space to recuperate for the struggle. The central point of the world struggle now is the rivalry between English and German finance-capital. Let the Revolution utilise this struggle for its own ends'. He knew the Russian army was in no state to challenge the German military machine; Trotsky himself had seen that the Russian trenches were virtually empty of soldiers when he had crossed the front line on his way to Brest-Litovsk. Moreover, reports in December had suggested that the only reliable Russian forces were anti-Bolshevik and this might offer an opportunity for their left-wing opponents to weaken the Bolshevik hold. The Bolsheviks recognised that there was little likelihood of support from the west in the event of the renewal of hostilities. With these various considerations in mind, the Bolshevik regime signed the Treaty of Brest-Litovsk on 3 March 1918.

G *Terms of the Treaty of Brest-Litovsk 1918*

The terms were harsh, with Russia losing a quarter of its territory, a third of its population, over half of its industry and four-fifths of its coalmines. It was agreed that

- Russia was to surrender to Germany her part of Poland, which she had possessed since the Napoleonic wars and the Baltic States.
- Turkey took part of the Caucasus region.
- Finland, Georgia and the Ukraine, all previously Russian possessions, were to become independent.
- Reparations of six billion marks were to be paid by Russia to Germany.

Lenin justified his acceptance of these harsh terms on the grounds that Russia was exhausted. He added, 'it is true that there are people willing to fight and die in a great cause. But they are romanticists, who would sacrifice themselves without prospects of real advantage ...The Russian Revolution must sign the peace to obtain a breathing space to recover for the struggle'.

H *Consequences of the Treaty of Brest-Litovsk 1918*

Despite the harsh and humiliating terms imposed on Russia they gained greater benefit from the Treaty compared with Germany. Lenin's scheming tactics and temporary retreat brought their expected reward. They gave Soviet Russia the necessary time for consolidation at a critical stage. The economic gains the Central Powers had anticipated from the separate peace remained far below the expected levels and were not enough to make any appreciable difference to the war economies of Germany and Austria-Hungary. The treaty also meant defeat for the Central Powers in another and equally sensitive field. Thousands of prisoners returned to Germany after experiencing the revolution in Russia with very different values and concepts than those that they had held in 1914.

10 ⌢ CIVIL WAR

Initially the Bolsheviks were only in control of Petrograd followed seven days later by Moscow but elsewhere the country remained largely unaffected by these events. From the start, the Bolsheviks faced the threat of a counter-revolution. The elections of 12 November 1917 showed that, in the country as a whole, they did not have the massive support they expected. Lenin's decision to dissolve the democratically elected Constituent Assembly after one chaotic meeting showed that he was prepared to ignore the wishes of the Russian people. A number of anti-Bolshevik 'Provisional Governments' were set up following the Bolshevik success in October 1917. In January 1918 the Bolsheviks set out to gain control of these bodies leading to the outbreak of Civil War which lasted until 1920. This was a complex affair consisting of a number of uncoordinated campaigns fought over a vast distance. The anti-Bolshevik forces were numerous and included the Social revolutionaries, Mensheviks, *Kadets*, several generals, and the remaining loyal supporters of the tsar. Collectively, these forces were known as the 'Whites', a colour clearly opposite to the 'Red' Bolsheviks and one that is often associated with monarchist and loyalist movements. The 'Whites' received help from the involvement of allied troops but were weakened by divisions and hostilities, which benefited the Bolsheviks.

The Allies hoped for a White victory, since they had not forgiven the Bolsheviks for signing a separate peace with Germany in the treaty of Brest-Litovsk, that had seriously threatened their chances of winning the war. The Bolsheviks had confiscated property belonging to the

Allies and refused to repay loans made to the tsar's government. There was also a great deal of concern about the welfare of the tsar and resentment against the activities of the Cheka.

A *Composition of the rival armies*

In the south, General Denikin tried to set up a military dictatorship. He was supported by the Cossacks and French troops and was supplied through the Black Sea ports. In the east, Admiral Kolchak controlled a vast area. He set up a government at Omsk and gained some early victories over the Bolshevik Red Army. The Allies helped him, especially the Czech Legion, which at the start of the civil war numbered some 40 000. Mainly prisoners of war, they had asked to be taken to Vladivostock so that they could be sent back to Europe. Held up by the Bolsheviks, who hoped to recruit them for the Red Army, they became

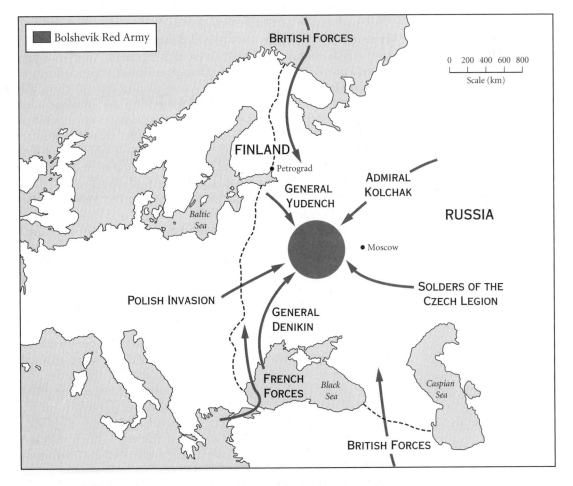

MAP 12 *Civil War 1918–20*

impatient and mutinied, and joined the White forces. Even further to the east, the Japanese seized Vladivostock and provided the Whites with a useful supply route. In the north, British, French and American troops landed at Murmansk and Archangel, while a White army under General Yudenich advanced to attack Petrograd. This threat forced Lenin to move his capital to Moscow and to develop an army of loyal Bolsheviks. He realised that his only chance of survival against such large forces lay in building up a loyal and well-trained army. The task of organising the Red Army fell to Trotsky. Short of trained officers, he took a risk and recruited many of the officers of the old Tsarist army and had them watched by 'political commissars'. The Cheka forced men to serve in the army and other soldiers were conscripted when there were insufficient volunteers ... Throughout the war, Trotsky directed operations from his famous armoured train that toured the battle areas.

B *Attitudes to foreign intervention*

The intervention of British, French, Czech and even American and Japanese forces in the civil war provided the Bolsheviks with a valuable propaganda weapon, which they were able to exploit. In 1918, Lenin issued a proclamation to the 'toiling masses of France, England, America, Italy and Japan: "Workers, like a vicious dog loosed from its chain, the whole capitalist press of your countries howls for the intervention of your governments in Russian affairs they have already started military operations. Anglo-French bandits are already shooting Russian workers ... They are cutting off the Russian people from their bread and force them to put their necks once more into the noose of the Paris and London stock exchanges ... In the interests of capital you are to be the executioners of the Russian workers' revolution" ... Down with the bandits of international imperialism.'

Intervention was also a burning issue among the various allied governments and this is well illustrated by the bitter disagreements, which raged within the British government at that time. Prime Minister David Lloyd George wrote to Winston Churchill, 'the main idea ought to be to enable Russia to save herself if she desires to do so and if she does not take advantage of opportunity then it means either she does not wish to be saved from Bolshevism or that she is beyond saving'. Churchill, strongly anti-Bolshevik, did not agree and did his utmost to press for a greater British intervention in Russia. He warned that, 'the overthrow of Bolshevism in Russia is indispensable to anything in the nature of a lasting peace'. Lloyd George became increasingly irritated and asked Churchill to 'throw off his obsession which, if you will forgive me for saying so, is upsetting your balance'. He then forcibly pointed out that, 'the various Russian enterprises have cost us this year between £100 and £150 millions ... Neither this Government nor any other Government that this country is likely to see will do more. We cannot afford it. The French have talked a good deal about anti-Bolshevism, but they have left it to us to carry out the Allied policy'.

C *Problems faced by the Red and White Armies*

Trotsky was alarmed at the rapidly deteriorating situation. In the west the Germans had occupied Poland, Lithuania, Latvia while the Ukraine had become an Austro-German colony. In the summer of 1918, Czech regiments in the Volga rebelled. The German High Command warned that if the Whites approached Moscow from the east, the Germans would come from the west to penetrate the formation of a new Eastern Front. The Bolsheviks were caught between two enemies. In the north, the French and English occupied Murmansk and Archangel, the Ural Mountains were plagued by bandits while there was an even greater rebellion on the Don. The civil war was moving more and more against the Bolsheviks. Lenin was very aware of the state of affairs and in a letter to the Central Committee, tried to reassure them that 'Kolchak and Denikin are the chief and the only serious enemies of the Soviet Republic. If it were not for the help they are getting from the allies, they would have gone to pieces long ago'. The Whites, too, had their problems. General Peter Wrangel, who took over command of Denikin's armies in 1920, reported that, 'the war is becoming a means of getting rich, requisitioning has degenerated into pillage ... Each unit tries to get as much as possible for itself. What cannot be used on the spot is sent to the interior and sold at a profit ... Many officers, absent from the front, are engaged in selling and trading loot. The army is completely demoralised and is rapidly turning into a bunch of traders and profiteers'. One of the major problems facing the Red Army was the need to ensure continued supplies of recruits and foodstuffs. To help cope with this, Lenin introduced 'War Communism'.

11 ⌁ WAR COMMUNISM

A *Definition of the term*

This is the term used to describe the policies adopted during the confusion, which verged on near anarchy during the first years of communist rule from mid-1918. In order to ensure that the Red Army was supplied with munitions and fed, Lenin introduced a decree of nationalisation, which established strong centralised control over all areas of production and distribution in the areas under his control.

B *Main features of War Communism*

This amounted to a command economy, which was influenced by the state, rather than by the laws of demand and supply.

> **KEY ISSUE**
>
> *A command economy.*

1 Because of the acute shortages, all factories and businesses were nationalised in November 1920, so that they could be geared to war production. The workers lost their freedom and were forced to work excessive hours without wages. Their reward was a meagre ration of food, some clothing and lodgings.

2   In rural areas, all grain had to be delivered to the state. Soldiers went into the villages and confiscated crops and livestock. Sometimes they failed to leave enough for the peasants' own needs. These measures were very unpopular and, as the peasants grew less and hid their crops, so food shortages grew even worse. Unrest increased and Lenin was forced to back his measures with the terror of the Cheka. Those who protested were arrested and strikes were considered acts of treason.

3   There was a ban on private trade and a rationing system was introduced on food and consumer. Food rationing in towns discriminated against the bourgeoisie.

4   Money lost all value and in many areas people stopped using money in favour of a system of barter. Wages and salaries were paid in kind. Inflation, multiplying some 1917 costs by four million in 1922 was welcomed by War Communism supporters as 'the dying out of money and the breakdown of society and its replacement by a communist society'.

C *People's response to War Communism*

KEY ISSUE

Use of the Cheka.

In areas occupied by the Bolsheviks, Trotsky used the Cheka to establish control and ensure the loyalty of the people. Within the Red Army, civilian commissars were attached to each unit to indoctrinate the soldiers with the theories of Marxism and ensure their political loyalty. It was a war in which it was impossible to be neutral. Russians found that they either had to be for or against one side or the other, and this was largely determined by which side controlled the area at any particular time. Hostages were taken and there were mass executions and other outrages by both the Reds and Whites. During the summer of 1918, the Reds began a period of indiscriminate murder and wholesale atrocities. The peasants did not give up their crops easily and the requisition of food and supplies often proved difficult. They disarmed the bands of men sent to the village to requisition the bread reserves. This refusal was usually met with the detachment of an armed force, but instead of quelling the villagers, weapons were seized.

D *Effects of War Communism*

War Communism involved ruthless treatment of the peasants. The peasants decided that it was not worth growing food for the Communists to steal and reduced their sowings. The result was an acute food shortage in 1920 and a terrible famine in 1921. It has been estimated by various sources that between 7 500 000 and 10 000 000 Russians died during the Civil War and very few were battle casualties. Hunger and disease, especially typhus were the main culprits caused by the constant movement of lousy troops, the absence of soap and hot water and medical supplies, combined with malnutrition. A Commissariat of Supplies, *Narkomprod*, was made responsible for the feeding of the cities and the army. In 1918, the immediate method was to organise committees of poor peasants in the villages and detachments of armed workers in the towns, both of whom were to exact grain from the kulaks. The confusion of requisitioning that ensued soon antagonised a large class of middle peasants and upset the partnership of proletariat and peasantry that Lenin was determined to create.

Townspeople fled to the country where they believed that starvation was less of a problem reducing the number of workers left in the towns. It is estimated that in December 1920 the population of 40 capitals had fallen by 33% compared with 1917 while that for Petrograd fell by 57.5% and 44.5% for Moscow. A black market flourished for all types of goods. This affected the total output of industry that fell while the number of strikes increased. The most famous and serious for the regime was the strike of sailors in the Petrograd naval base of Kronstadt. They had been loyal supporters of the 1917 Revolution and their rebellion was viewed as a serious criticism of Bolshevik policies and an expression of a sense of betrayal of the values of the 1917 Revolution.

12 ⌐ THE 'RED TERROR'

A *Events leading to its outbreak*

On 30 August 1918, after speaking at a labour rally in Moscow, Lenin was shot and seriously wounded by Fanya Kaplan. For reasons known only to her, she claimed that Lenin was a traitor to the revolution, she had earlier served 11 years in a labour camp for the attempt to murder a Tsarist official. She was executed three days after the assassination attempt on Lenin. On the same day as the attack on Lenin, the head of the Petrograd Cheka was murdered. These two events provoked a period of uncontrolled terror as Bolsheviks ransacked the streets looking for victims.

B *Main features of the 'Red Terror'*

During the 'Red Terror', the bourgeoisie were driven from their homes, deprived of food rations and forced to do degrading work. Sometimes they were indiscriminately shot. But as the civil war dragged on, the Red Army began to gain the upper hand. Felix Dzerzhinsky, much-feared founder of Lenin's secret police, the Cheka, had warned of the impending blood bath. He made it clear that he was intent on searching out, and eliminating, counter-revolutionaries. In August 1918, Lenin ordered the implementation of a ruthless mass terror against the kulaks, priests and White Guards by specially chosen men loyal to the Bolshevik regime. All suspicious persons were detained in concentration camps. There are various accounts of the horrors experienced during the period of the 'Red Terror'. Former officials, landlords and priests were executed and whole families wiped out for no other reason than they had once been rich. Any opposition to the Bolshevik authorities was dealt with by violence. Peasants who resisted the requisitioning of their crops or who hoarded grain were punished, often by shooting. Industrial unrest was similarly crushed. In many cases the class, educational experience and profession of the arrested person was sufficient to determine the fate of the accused. Inevitably these instructions were often ignored and ruthless men acted on the basis of 'why even ask those questions? I'll just walk into his house and look into his pots. If there is meat in them, then he is an enemy of the people and should be stood up against the wall'. One consequence of this period of the 'Red Terror' was the decision to murder the ex-tsar, Nicholas, and his family. During the summer of 1918, units of the Czech Legion fighting with the Whites closed in on Ekaterinburg, their place of confinement. As the Czechs approached, the local Bolsheviks panicked. They realised that, if the tsar was rescued, he would become a rallying point for the Whites. Without direct instructions from Moscow, they took matters into their own hands. At midnight on 16 July 1918, the royal family was shot, and an attempt was made to disguise their remains. Three days later, *Izvestia* published an official announcement of the execution of the former tsar, which stated that 'the wife and son of Nicholas Romanov were sent to a safe place'. Apparently the extermination of the former tsarina, the tsarevich, and his four sisters, was too unsavoury for the public. Moreover, no code of laws, even revolutionary justice, could admit the 'execution' of the former tsar's physician, cook, chambermaid and waiter. Later, Trotsky commented that 'under judicial procedures, of course, execution of the family would have been impossible'.

Q

Who were the victims of the 'Red Terror'?

13 ⌁ THE RUSSO-POLISH WAR 1920–1

A *Main features of the war*

As the civil war raged, the Poles, who were not satisfied with the terms of the treaty which determined their eastern frontier with Russia, decided to take advantage of the chaos. The problem of the eastern borders of Poland was a complicated one. In December 1919, the British foreign secretary, Lord Curzon, put forward plans for a boundary between Poland and Russia, which came to be called the 'Curzon Line'. As far as the Poles were concerned, the line was not generous enough and they wanted to see it put some 160 km further to the east. In April 1920, the Polish leader, Marshal Josef Pilsudski (1867–1935), ordered the invasion of Russia. Polish forces crossed the Curzon Line and, by June 1920, had captured Minsk and Kiev. With the civil war drawing to a close, the Red Army recovered sufficiently to launch a counter-attack. The Russians drove the Poles back to within a few miles of their capital, Warsaw. Here the Poles were saved by the intervention of France. At the Battle of the Vistula, the Poles, with French help, won a decisive victory and the following year the war was ended by the Treaty of Riga, 1921. This treaty established a new eastern frontier agreed some 160 km to the east of the original Curzon Line. The Poles were satisfied but the Russians felt humiliated and later, in 1939, were to gain their revenge.

KEY ISSUE

Polish grievances.

14 ∽ END OF THE CIVIL WAR

A *Victory for the Reds*

During the hard-fought and bitter civil war which witnessed the most appalling atrocities committed by both sides, the very survival of the new Bolshevik regime had been at stake and there were times when it was in doubt. The civil war had been fought along uncertain frontiers, which extended across Russia for some 6000 miles. Not only did the Red Army have to battle against the various White Armies of Denikin, Kolchak, Wrangel and Yudenich, but it also had to quell uprisings. In addition, it had to contend with the rebel Czech Legion, an invasion by the Poles and the intervention of Allied forces. At one stage, the Bolsheviks had lost control of nearly 75% of Russia and were opposed by armies numerically twice the size of their own. In his later autobiography, *My Life*, Trotsky, their brilliant Commissar of War, wrote, 'for two and a half years, I lived in a railway carriage. There I received those who brought orders, held conferences and dictated orders' ... Out of bands of irregulars, of refugees fleeing from the Whites ... of peasants ... detachments of workers ... we formed companies, battalions. ... When they were aware of the train just a few miles behind the firing line, even the most frightened units would summon up all their strength. ... Often a commander would ask me to stay for an extra half-hour so that news of the train's arrival might spread far and wide'. According to one of Trotsky's biographers, Isaac Deutscher, 'he found the front in a state of virtual collapse. ... From his train that stood within reach of enemy fire, he descended into panic-stricken crowds of soldiers, poured out on them torrents of passionate eloquence ... and personally led them back to the firing line. The local commissars proposed that he should move to a safer place ... but fearing the effect this might have on the troops, he refused' (Isaac Deutscher, *Trotsky: The Prophet Armed*, OUP, 1970). By the summer of 1920, the Red Army had defeated the main forces of the White counter-revolutionaries and the final defeat of Wrangel in the Crimea brought the civil war to an end. According to one Soviet historian 'the Socialist revolution had proved that it knew how to defend itself against aggression. The new social and political system had endured the most severe trials and had demonstrated its strength. Now it had to build a new society'.

B *Reasons for the success of the Red Army*

The reasons for the eventual victory of the Bolshevik Red Army may be summarised as follows:

● Although the Whites were numerically stronger, they were hopelessly divided. The Whites included Mensheviks and Social Revolutionaries who were Marxist, as well as *Kadets* who were Liberals, and right-wing elements such as supporters of the tsar. They could also depend on the support of the landowners, capitalist industrialists, the officer-class in the army and the Church. Few of these were sympathetic to the needs of the Russian working classes.

● The Red Army, though small, was better-trained and dedicated to the cause of the Revolution. Commissars ensured unity and loyalty.

● The Red Army leaders, Lenin and Trotsky, were men of considerable personality and organising skills. They were far more united in their aims.

● The Red Army used the railway system more effectively and was better able to move troops from one section of the front to another.

● The Reds were inspired by the idealistic promise of a fairer, socialist society, and popularised such slogans as 'Peace, bread and land'. The Whites were associated with privilege, corruption and the suffering caused by the war with Germany. The peasants and industrial workers wanted to retain the land, wealth and property gained from the middle and upper classes.

● The Reds controlled Petrograd and Moscow. The Whites were based on makeshift capitals – Omsk and Archangel.

● The intervention of British and French forces on the side of the Whites allowed the Reds the prestige of fighting for 'Mother Russia' against foreign, imperialist invaders.

15 ～ RUSSIA AFTER THE CIVIL WAR TO 1924

A *Economic chaos*

By the end of the civil war, Russia was in a state of economic collapse. With mines flooded and machinery smashed, its industries were producing little; the index of gross industrial output fell from 100 in 1913 to 31 in 1921 while the index for large-scale industrial output fell from 100 to 21 in the same period. This slowdown in industrial activity

Year	Number of workers
1917	3 024 000
1918	2 486 000
1919	2 035 000
1920–21	1 480 000
1922	1 243 000

TABLE 48 *Numbers in the industrial workforce 1917–22 (in Russia)*

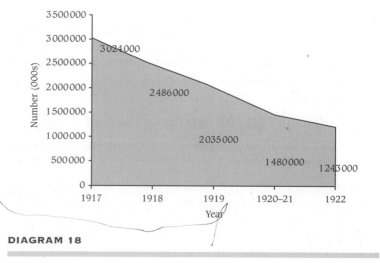

DIAGRAM 18

was reflected in the decline in the size of the industrial workforce as indicated in Table 40.

The railway system was at a near standstill. Towns and cities were depressed and infested with vermin so that there were epidemics of typhus that, in 1920 alone, caused the deaths of more than three million people. In rural areas, the peasants still worked only to provide sufficient for their own needs, so that agricultural production was just over half the pre-war level. Across the whole country there was widespread and acute famine, so that thousands died of starvation and cannibalism appeared in some parts with a trade in the sale of dead bodies to the starving. Russia's population fell from 170.9 million in 1913 to 130.9 by 1921 while the percentage of those who lived in the towns fell from 18% to 16% in the same period.

The Bolsheviks had assumed that the problem was basically one of distribution caused by the fact that the peasants would not part with their crops while, in fact, the truth was that they were no longer bothering to grow sufficient for the nation's requirements. The redistribution of land and the civil war had brought chaos to the countryside, but the main fault lay in the harshness of Lenin's 'War Communism'. As their plight worsened, some reached the limits of their endurance and in March 1921 there was an uprising at Kronstadt.

B *The Kronstadt Mutiny 1921*

The sailors and workers at Kronstadt, many of who were of peasant origins, had been amongst the determined supporters of the Revolution, but had grown tired of the ruthless years of War Communism. They demonstrated and made a list of demands – free elections, freedom of the press and of speech.

The following is from a newspaper article of the Kronstadt Temporary Revolutionary Committee, 8 March 1921, *Article What We Are Fighting For*, adapted from R. Daniels (ed.), *A Documentary History of Communism*, vol. 1, I.B. Taurus & Co., 1987.

> The power of the Tsarist police state has gone into the hands of the Communist-usurpers, who instead of freedom offer the toilers the constant fear of falling into the torture-chambers of the Cheka, which in their horrors surpass many times the gendarme administration of the Tsarist regime ...
>
> The glorious symbols of the workers and peasants – the sickle and hammer – have actually been replaced by the Communist authorities with the bayonet and the barred window, for the sake of preserving the calm, carefree life of the new bureaucracy of Communist commissars and officials.
>
> But the most hateful and criminal thing, which the Communists have created, is moral servitude: they laid their hands even on the inner life of the toilers and compelled them to think only in the Communist way ...

'**Third Revolution**' reference to rebels demand for greater power to trade unions, peasant organisations and other political parties such as Social revolutionaries and Mensheviks.

Q

What do you understand by the terms, 'Third Revolution' and 'the Constituent Assembly'?

Why, according to the article, did the Kronstadt rebellion break out?

How does the author of the article justify the actions of the Kronstadt sailors?

How useful is this article for understanding the problems facing Lenin's government between 1918–21?

To the protests of the peasants, expressed in spontaneous uprisings, and of the workers, who are compelled to strike by the circumstances of their life, they answer with mass executions and blood-thirstiness, in which they are not surpassed by the Tsarist generals.

In this sea of blood the Communists are drowning all the great and glowing pledges and slogans of labour's revolution.

There can be no middle ground. Victory or death!

Here the banner of insurrection has been raised for liberation from the three-year violence and oppression of Communist domination... Here at Kronstadt the first stone of the **Third Revolution** has been laid, to break off the last fetters on the toiling masses and open a new broad road for socialist creativity.

This new revolution will rouse the labouring masses of the East and of the West, since it shows an example of the new socialist construction.

The first step has been completed without a single shot, without a drop of blood. The toilers do not need blood. They will shed it only at a moment of self-defence. Firmness is enough for us, in spite of the outrageous actions of the Communists. We confine ourselves to isolating them from social life, so that their evil false agitation will not interfere with revolutionary work.

The workers and peasants unreservedly go forward, abandoning behind them the Constituent Assembly with its bourgeois element and its Cheka men, its state capitalism, its hangman's noose encircling the neck of the masses and threatening to strangle them for good.

This rebellion at last makes it possible for the toilers to have their freely elected soviets, working without any violent party pressure, and remake the state trade unions into free associations of workers, peasants and the labouring intelligentsia. At last the policeman's club of the Communist autocracy has been broken.

C *Response of the authorities*

A leading party member, Mikhail Kalinin, was sent to warn the people of Kronstadt and prevent any further embarrassment. His mission had little effect and on 15 March Trotsky sent them a menacing ultimatum. Two days later, the Red Army launched an assault on the garrison. The general who led the assault later said, 'I was in the war for 5 years, but I cannot remember such a slaughter. It was not a battle, it was an inferno ... The sailors fought like wild beasts. I cannot understand where they found the might-for such rage. Each house where they were located had to be taken by storm. An entire company fought for an hour to capture one house and when the house was captured it was found that it contained two or three soldiers at a machine-gun. They seemed half-dead, but they snatched their revolvers and gasped "Too little did we shoot at you scoundrels".'

Lenin claimed that it was just another bourgeois-inspired plot, 'the most characteristic feature of the Kronstadt events was precisely the indecision of the petty-bourgeois element. There was very little of anything that was fully formed, clear and definite. We heard vague slogans about "liberty", "free trade", "emancipation from serfdom", "Soviets without Bolsheviks" ... Both the Mensheviks and the Social Revolutionaries declared the Kronstadt movement to be "their own".' Bukharin said more honestly, 'who says the Kronstadt rising was White? No ... we were forced to suppress the revolt of our erring brother' ...

D *Significance of Kronstadt*

To Lenin, events at Kronstadt served as a warning. In many cases, the people had endured War Communism long enough and many had reached the end of their tether. At Kronstadt, rebels had carried slogans such as "Soviets without Communists", and had begun to demand greater political freedom. 'Kronstadt', said Lenin, 'was the flash which lit up reality better than anything else'. It was time to compromise and to recognise the failure of War Communism. To face the challenge of Russia's economic situation and avoid further rebellions like the one at Kronstadt, Lenin had to admit his errors, revise his policies and make a tactical retreat. It was central that he win over the Russian peasantry and he admitted, 'only agreement with the peasantry can save the socialist revolution in Russia'. In April 1921 he acknowledged that, 'the civil war of 1918–20 greatly increased the devastation of the country, slowed down the restoration of its productive forces, and bled the proletariat more than any other class. To this was added the failure of the harvest of 1920, the fodder shortage, the dying off of cattle, which still further retarded the restoration of transport and industry, because, among other things, it interfered with the employment of peasants' horses for carting wood, our main fuel' (Lenin's *Collected Works*, vol. 32, 1960).

16 ∾ NEW ECONOMIC POLICY (NEP)

A *Main features of NEP*

At the tenth Party Congress in March 1921, Lenin announced the details of a New Economic Policy. As with War Communism his central concern was to ensure adequate food supplies. Often shortened to NEP, the plan was as follows:

1 The requisitioning of crops was to cease and instead, peasants would be expected to hand over a fixed proportion of their harvests as a form of tax. They would then be allowed to sell the remainder, their surplus crops, for profit on the open market.
2 Private traders, who came to be known as Nepmen, were to be permitted to buy and sell goods for profit on the open market.
3 Small businessmen were to be permitted to own and run medium-sized firms and factories and to make a profit. Larger enterprises, 'the commanding heights of the economy' as Lenin called them,

were to remain under state ownership. The new private entrepreneurs also had to obey government legislation relating to working conditions and wage levels.

4 The old discredited currency was to be replaced by a new revalued rouble.

B *Significance of NEP*

NEP represented a retreat from Bolshevik policy of state control of the economy to a mixed economy where some private ownership was allowed to exist alongside state control. Lenin defended his policy as 'state capitalism' and reminded his critics that war and ruin had forced 'War Communism' on them, but it was only intended to be a temporary measure. He warned them that, 'we are still in such a state of ruin that we cannot give the peasant manufactured goods for all we require … Hence, it is necessary, to a certain extent, to help to restore SMALL industry … the effect will be the revival of the petty bourgeoisie and of capitalism on the basis of a certain amount of free trade. This is beyond doubt. However, he tried to re-assure his critics that, 'the proletarian regime is in no danger as long as the proletariat firmly hold power in its hands, as long as it firmly holds transport and large-scale industry in its hands. We must not be afraid of Communists 'learning' from bourgeois specialists, including merchants, small capitalist co-operation and capitalists' (V.I. Lenin, *Collected Works*, vol. 32, 1960).

He recognised that the time had come to 'construct everything in a new and solid manner'. Those devoted Bolsheviks, such as Bukharin, who saw these measures as a betrayal of their party and Communist principles were forced by the realities of Russia in 1921 to accept NEP. It provided a breathing space during which the country could begin an economic revival and concentrate more on important developments like electrification and starting industrial projects. Lenin also sought to re-establish trading links with the capitalist world. Even so, food supplies were slow to increase and even by 1928, industrial output was only just approaching that of 1914.

C *Success of NEP*

It was impossible for the government to legislate to prevent drought, and in the south, blizzards and plagues of locusts, which led to the failure of harvests. Even with the introduction of NEP, the peasants remained distressingly short of seed, implements, fertilisers and modern equipment or even beasts of burden. By the end of 1921, famine threatened over 36 million Russians, a condition, which had led him to condemn the earlier Tsarist regime.

By the spring of 1922, a million had died of starvation and the Central Committee struggled with plans to mobilise the nation's resources to provide for the worst affected areas before it was too late. The situation was so bad that as one area produced its first corn harvests, so they had to be requisitioned to provide seed for other areas. Even Party members and

Ownership of enterprises	Percentage of share of trade	Percentage of distribution of workforce	Average number of workers in each factory
Private	75	12	2
State	15	85	155
Co-operatives	10	3	15

TABLE 49

Distribution of economic activity

industrial workers went into the countryside to help with the sowing. Help also arrived from abroad. The United States, France, Britain, Germany and Italy sent food, medicine and clothing, while the American Relief Administration provided some £20 million worth of aid and help was also forthcoming from the International Red Cross which made available over 80 000 tonnes of food. By the end of 1922, the crisis began to ease. By 1923 production figures suggested that NEP was working. The amount of land under cultivation rose from 77.7 million hectares in 1922 to 91.7, which was higher than the 1921 figure of 90.3. This is reflected in the increase in the grain harvest from 37.6 million tons in 1921 to 56.6 in 1923. Coal, steel, finished cloth, electricity also saw a rise in output while the average monthly wage of urban workers rose from 10.2 roubles in 1921 to 15.9 in 1923. The state controlled industry while agriculture and trade remained largely in private hands as indicated in Table 41.

D *Limitations of success of NEP*

Industry did not keep pace with the growth in agriculture. The 'Nepmen' benefited but industrial workers were faced by high unemployment. This disparity in comparative rates of growth between agricultural and industrial growth led to what Trotsky described at the Twelfth party Congress in 1923 as the 'Scissors Crisis' (from a graph he devised to show rising industrial prices and falling agricultural prices. The two axes of the graph looked like the widening blades of scissors). This was caused by the revival of agriculture after the end of famine. By 1922–23 there had been an improvement in weather conditions and hence the harvest. The increase in the amount of land under cultivation had partly contributed to an increase in productivity that in turn had led to a fall in price. This was not accompanied by a fall in industrial prices since industry had found it more difficult to recover its position. Scarcity in factory goods pushed up prices at the same time as increased supplies were reducing the price of agricultural goods. This meant that farm producers had to sell their goods at too low a price too enable them to buy industrial goods. This situation ran the risk of discouraging peasants from producing anything more than their immediate domestic needs since they were not able to afford industrial goods. This had been the main problem facing Lenin in 1921 when he had introduced NEP to avoid an economic depression. The Central Committee set up a 'Scissors Committee' in October 1923 to consider incentives to improve industrial production. Critics of NEP formed a rival 'Platform of 46' composed of 46 party members, including Trotsky, who blamed the government

KEY ISSUE

The 'Scissors Crisis'.

Year	Industrial production	Agricultural production
1913	100	100
1921	31	60
1924	45	90
1925	73	112
1926	98	118
1927	111	121
1928	132	124

TABLE 50
Index of economic development under NEP (base year 1913 = 100)

for lack of a coherent economic plan and its tolerance of the 'Nepmen'. Economic recovery in 1923 leading to a fall in the price of industrial goods along with a good harvest averted a potential political crisis over the issue of NEP. The issue of private enterprise within the Communist State remained unresolved at the time of Lenin's death in 1924.

17 ⌐ DEATH OF LENIN

After the attempt on his life in 1918, Lenin's health worsened. In May 1922, he suffered a stroke, and several others followed this. During these years, his wife nursed him. He was only able to speak with diffi-culty and walk a few steps, but he still insisted on working at his office in the Kremlin. On 21 January 1924, at the age of 53, Lenin died of a brain haemorrhage. His death was mourned throughout Russia and over a million attended his funeral procession. His body was embalmed and placed in a mausoleum in Moscow's Red Square. Petrograd, birth-place of the Revolution, was renamed 'Leningrad' in his honour. Lenin's achievement was the creation of the first socialist state, Soviet Russia, ruled according to his application of the theories of Karl Marx, now called Marxism-Leninism.

Winston Churchill, outspoken opponent of Communism in any form, did not express sorrow at Lenin's death. According to him, 'the Russian people were left floundering. Their worst misfortune was his birth ... and their next worst was his death'. Historians have not been quite so harsh. A.J.P. Taylor, said of Lenin that, (he) 'did more than any other political leader to change the face of the 20th-century world. The creation of Soviet Russia and its survival were due to him. He was a very great man and even, despite his faults, a very good man'.

A *Perceptions of Lenin*

Views of a friend and fellow revolutionary, V Serge from *Memoirs of a Revolutionary*, translated and edited by Peter Sedgwick, OUP, 1963.

'He was neither a great orator nor a first-rate lecturer. He employed no rhetoric and did not try to rouse his audience. His vocabulary was that of a newspaper article and he was inclined to be very repetitive, all with the idea of driving ideas in thoroughly ... Here was a man of basic simplicity, talking to you honestly and with the sole purpose of convincing you'.

Views of the fellow revolutionary and successor to Lenin, Josif Stalin, from *Works*, Lawrence & Wishart, 1952.

'The greatness of Lenin lies above all in this, that by creating the Republic of Soviets he gave a practical demonstration to the oppressed masses of the world that the hope of deliverance is not lost ... He thus fired the hearts of workers and peasants of the whole world with the hope of liberation. This explains why Lenin's name has become the name most beloved of the labouring and exploited masses'.

Views of Lenin's biographer, David Shub, *Lenin*, Pelican, 1966. (Shub had joined the Social Democrat Party in 1903. He wrote this account in 1920.)

'Lenin might well have said, "I created the Bolshevik Party. I was the brain of the November Revolution. Several times, when our power seemed about to crumble, I saved it by bold improvisation, by signing an unpopular peace in 1918, by introducing NEP in 1921 ... " Lenin could rightfully have said all this, but never did, for no dictator in history was less vain. In fact, he was repelled by all attempts on the part of men around him to set him on a pedestal'.

Views of two historians:

Geoffrey Hosking, *A History of the Soviet Union*, Fontana, 1992

'Lenin shared with previous Russian revolutionaries the belief in a humane and democratic future society. Where he differed from them was in a hardheaded realism and the determination to achieve power at all costs. He craved a historical theory, which would provide absolute certainty, and in Marxism he thought he had found it'.

E. Acton, *Rethinking the Russian Revolution*, Edward Arnold, 1990

... 'he was in no position to impose policy upon the party. The stamp he set upon party policy reflected the close correspondence between his programme and the demands welling up from below ... the party was neither at the beck and call of Lenin nor was it an elite group of intellectuals divorced from the masses ... "Bolshevism" in 1917 did not flow from a single fount but embraced many different currents of

KEY ISSUE

Some views of Lenin.

thought ... Lenin therefore was not an all-powerful dictator, and if he is criticised, perhaps it should be on the grounds of ill-founded optimism rather than insincerity'.

18 ∽ BIBLIOGRAPHY

The following are some of the many books which have been written on the Russian Revolution: E.H. Carr, *The Bolshevik Revolution, 1917–23*, Macmillan, 1950; E.H. Carr, *The Russian Revolution from Lenin to Stalin, 1917–29*, Macmillan, 1979; John Laver, *Russia 1914–1941*, Hodder & Stoughton History at Source Series, 1991; T. Cliff, *Lenin*, Bookmarks, 1987; John Laver, *Lenin*, Hodder & Stoughton Personalities and Powers, 1994; M. McCauley, *The Soviet Union since 1917*, Longman, 19821; R. Pipes, *The Russian Revolution, 1899–1919*, Knopf, 1990 (Chapter 11); E. Mawdsley, *The Russian Civil War*, Allen & Unwin, 1987; Richard Pipes, *The Russian Revolution 1899–919*, Collins Harvill, 1990; J. Reed, *Ten Days that Shook the World*, Penguin Modern Classics, 1966; N. Rothie, *The Russian Revolution*, Macmillan Education Documents and Debates, 1991; D. Shub, *Lenin*, Penguin, 1966; L. Trotsky, *The History of the Russian Revolution*, 3 vols, Sphere Books, 1976.

19 ∽ STRUCTURED AND ESSAY QUESTIONS

A *This section consists of structured questions that might be used for discussion or written answers as a way of expanding on the chapter and testing understanding of it.*

1. (a) What were the aims of the Bolsheviks?
    (b) Why did the Bolshevik's succeed in October 1917?
2. (a) Who were the main members of the Provisional Government February–October 1917?
    (b) To what extent was its collapse due to the unpopularity of its policies?
3. (a) Explain what you understand by the terms 'White' and 'Red' armies.
    (b) Why were the White armies, despite support by the Allies, unable to win the Civil War?
4. (a) What was 'War Communism'?
    (b) To what extent did War Communism contribute to the success of the Bolsheviks during the Civil War?
5. (a) What was the New Economic Policy?
    (b) What had NEP achieved by 1924?

B *Essay questions.*

1. Was there any reason to suppose that in 1914 a major war would threaten the existence of Tsarism?
2. How valid is it to claim that it was the decision to continue in the war which was the main reason for the collapse of the Provisional Government during 1917?

3. How far was World War I responsible for the fall of Tsarism?
4. Why did the Provisional Government fail to maintain its seizure of power?
5. How valid is the claim that Bolshevik success in the Civil War owed more to the weakness of its opponents than to their own strengths.
6. To what extent did Lenin's economic policies, in the period up to 1924, attempt to solve the problems facing Russia in 1918?

20 ⌒ MAKING NOTES

Read the advice section about making notes on page ix of Preface: How to use this book, and then make your own notes based on the following headings and questions.

A *Impact of World War I*
1. What was the impact of the war on each of the following:
   (a) the Russian army
   (b) the Home Front
   (c) Nicholas
   (d) Government at home
2. What was the political impact of Russia's military defeats?
3. What signs were there of growing unrest before the events of 22 February–3 March?
4. What was the position of Tsarism in (a) 1914 and (b) 1917?
5. What problems faced Nicholas in 1917?
6. To what extent was Nicholas personally responsible for the challenges to his position in 1917?

B *Causes of the February Revolution*
This section requires you to use the information contained in this chapter but also to recall work covered in preceding chapters to assess the role of long-term, medium-term events and the immediate cause of the 1917 Revolution. Use the following to organise your summary:

Long-term	Medium term	Immediate 'trigger'
● Land question and grievances of the peasantry	● Nicholas II – his personality and attitude towards his role as tsar	● Events in 1916 – defeat on the Eastern Front
● Industrialisation and the grievances of the workers	● Divisions at the royal court – influence of Alexandra and Rasputin	● Mutiny in the army
● Growth of middle class including professionals – demand for modernisation of society and politics	● Instability in government – change of ministers and incompetence	● Events 2 February– 3 March by the masses – role of strikes demonstrations
		● Role of the liberals and *Duma*

(continued overleaf)

Long-term

- Growth of liberalism and socialism and their challenge to autocracy – alternative systems
- Abuses in autocratic system of governing – role of the police and army, reactionary royal court and Orthodox Church, censorship, controls on education, inefficiencies in bureaucracy and relationship with local government
- Economic and social changes affecting aristocracy and elite and their relationship with tsar
- Failure/limitations of reform
- Repression within the Empire
- Russification and discontent amongst Russia's nationalities – role they played amongst the revolutionaries

Medium term

- Legacy of 1905 Revolution
- Limitations to experiment in constitutional government
- Impact of participation in the World War I
- Activities of the Revolutionary parties
- Alienation of liberal and conservative parties by 1916

C *The Russian Revolution*

1. What are the main features of the four interpretations which historians have put forward to explain the events of February 1917?
    (a) Tsarism in crisis.
    (b) Social discontents reflecting deterioration in the condition of life for the mass of the people.
    (c) Impact of war.
    (d) Activities of a body of revolutionaries?
2. How well founded are each of these four explanations?
3. What were the terms of Nicholas's abdication?

D *Could Tsarism have survived?*

Using the evidence of this chapter and your own knowledge draw up evidence to argue for and against the claim that 'the collapse of Tsarism was inevitable'.

The collapse of Tsarism was	Arguments for
Inevitable	
Not inevitable	

E *Sequence of events 22 February–3 March 1917*

Using the evidence of Tables 47 and 48, what role was played by each of the following:

1. Masses.
2. Revolutionary leaders and Petrograd Soviet.
3. Government and security authorities.
4. *Duma* and its committees.
5. Military leaders.
6. Nicholas II.

F *Provisional Government*

1. What do you understand by the term 'Provisional Government'?
2. To what extent did the Provisional Government meet the hopes and expectations of each of the following groups:
   (a) Peasantry.
   (b) Working class.
   (c) Army.
   (d) Nationalities.
   (e) Elites.
3. What were the main aims of those who took part in
   (a) the 'July Days'.
   (b) the Kornilov Affair.
4. What contribution to the collapse of the Provisional Government was played by
   (a) the 'July Days'.
   (b) the Kornilov Affair.
5. To what extent was the Provisional Government a failure? In organising your evaluation consider the following areas of activity/ policies:

Reforms	*Failures*
● Civil liberties	● Continuation of war
● Censorship	● Failure to hold elections
● Police	● Loss of control of countryside
● Local Government	● Loss of support of army
● Factories	● Loss of support of landowners, industrialists
● Army	● Loss of support of workers
	● Lack of a coherent policy

G *The Second Revolution – Events of October 1917*

1. What factors contributed to growth in support for the Bolshevik Party?
2. Why did the Bolshevik Party decide to seize power in October 1917?
3. Identify the main stages in Bolshevik seizure of power.

4. What role was played by each of the following in consolidating Bolshevik rule:
   (a) Achievement of a one party state;
   (b) End to opposition by individuals and rival parties;
   (c) Elimination of the Constituent Assembly.
5. To what extent was Lenin central to the success of the Bolshevik Party in the seizure and consolidation of power?

G *Civil War*
1. Explain what you understand by the terms 'White' and 'Red' armies.
2. Why did the Allies intervene on the side of the 'Whites'?
3. What were the main stages to the Civil War campaigns?
4. What do you understand by the 'Red terror'?
5. What were its main features?
6. What role did it play in accounting for Bolshevik success?
7. Why were the White armies, despite support by the Allies, unable to win the Civil War?

F *War Communism*
1. Why was 'War Communism' introduced?
2. What were its main features?
3. To what extent was it successful?

G *Russia after the Civil War*
1. What was the impact of War Communism on agriculture and industry?
2. What was the impact of famine on society and attitudes towards the government?
3. How did the government respond?

H *The Kronstadt Mutiny*
1. What do you understand by the 'Third Revolution'?
2. How did the government respond to the rebels?
3. What was the significance of the Kronstadt mutiny?

I *New Economic Policy*
1. Why was NEP introduced?
2. What were its main features?
3. Why did it cause divisions amongst the Bolsheviks?
4. What was the 'Scissors Crisis?
5. How successful was NEP in achieving its aims?

21 ⌁ A2 DOCUMENTARY EXERCISE ON LENIN AND THE NEW ECONOMIC POLICY

Study the collection of Sources M–Q and then answer the questions which follow:

The most urgent thing at the present time is to take measures that will immediately increase the productive forces of peasant farming. Only in this way will it be possible to improve the conditions of the workers and strengthen the alliance between the workers and peasants, to strengthen the dictatorship of the proletariat.

This cannot be done without a serious modification of our food policy. Such a modification was the substitution of the surplus-appropriation system by the tax in kind, which implies free trade ... after the tax has been paid.

We were forced to resort to 'War Communism' by war and ruin. It was not, nor could it be, a policy that corresponded to the economic tasks of the proletariat. It was a temporary measure. The correct policy of the proletariat, which is exercising its dictatorship in a small-peasant country, is to obtain grain in exchange for the manufactured goods the peasant requires ... the last *possible* and only sensible policy is not to try to prohibit, or put the lock on the development of capitalism, but to try to direct it into the channels of *state capitalism*.

This is economically possible ...

Can the Soviet state, the dictatorship of the proletariat, be combined, united with state capitalism? Are they compatible? Of course they are ...

SOURCE M
From V.I. Lenin, The Tax In Kind, *April 1921, quoted by R. Daniels (ed.),* A Documentary History of Communism, *vol. 1, I.B. Tauris, 1985.*

He [Lenin] became finally convinced of the necessity of retreat and, true to his nature, he made of the necessity a set of basic principles ... He, Lenin, would [keep] the levers of political power firmly in the hands of a disciplined party. So it was not a coincidence that the beginnings of NEP were accompanied not only by the final ban on all political parties other than the Bolsheviks, but also, at the tenth party congress in March 1921, by a ban on factional organisation within the Bolshevik Party itself.

SOURCE N
From A. Nove, An Economic History of the USSR, *Penguin, 1969.*

These uncertainties and inconsistencies in the attitude of the party and of Lenin himself towards NEP reflected the persistent duality that lay behind it – the need at all costs to create a workable economy by way of agreement with the peasantry, and the desire to effect the long delayed transition to a Socialist order, which could be realised only through a radical transformation of the peasant economy. It involved the fundamental problem, which had dogged the Bolshevik revolution from the outset – the problem of building a socialist order in a country, which had missed the stage of bourgeois democracy and bourgeois capitalism.

SOURCE O
From E.H. Carr, The Bolshevik Revolution, *vol. 2, Penguin, 1952 (now Macmillan).*

In a few years the NEP restored to Russia an aspect of prosperity. But to many of us this prosperity was sometimes distasteful and often disquieting. A persistent anxiety took hold of us Communists. We had accepted all the necessities of the revolution ... Then immediately following the Kronstadt killings – our blackest memory – Lenin gave the signal for retreat saying: 'We must learn from the bourgeoisie.' ... And now the cities we ruled over assumed a foreign aspect: we felt ourselves sinking into the mire – paralysed corrupted ... Money lubricated and befouled the entire machine just as under capitalism. A million and a half-received unemployment relief – inadequate relief... There was gambling drunkenness and all the old filth of former times ... Classes were born under our very eyes ...

SOURCE P

Adapted from V. Serge, From Lenin to Stalin, *Monad Press (now Pathfinder Press), 1937 (V. Serge was a friend of Lenin and a fellow revolutionary).*

In terms of economic policy the problem was expressed by the relationship between industry and agriculture. The latter was recovering more rapidly than industry; the peasant accumulated reserves of grain because he was offered too low a price for it; and the low price of wheat resulted in high prices for manufactured goods whose quantity was not up to the demand.

Statistics relating to Soviet economic development

Sector	1913	1921	1923
Industrial production (million roubles)	10251	2004	4005
Coal (million tons)	29	9	14
Electricity (million kWh)	1945	520	1146
Pig iron (thousand tons)	4216	116	309
Steel (thousand tons)	4231	183	709
Cotton fabrics (million metres)	2582	105	691
Sown area (million hectares)	1500	903	917
Grain harvest (million tons)	80	38	57

SOURCE Q

Adapted from A. Nove, An Economic History of the USSR, *Penguin, 1992.*

1. *What, according to Source M, was Lenin's motives for introducing NEP?*
2. *What evidence is provided by Source N, which suggests that NEP had its critics within Bolshevik, ranks?*
3. *To what extent does the evidence of Sources M and O support A. Nove's claim in Source N that NEP marked a 'retreat'?*
4. *How reliable is the evidence of V. Serge in Source P of the impact of NEP on society and the economy?*
5. *To what extent does the statistical evidence of Source Q support the claims made in Source P?*
6. *In what ways and to what extent is Source Q useful as evidence of the success of NEP?*
7. *Using the evidence of Sources M–Q and your own knowledge why did NEP provoke controversy and opposition within Bolshevik ranks?*

The power struggle, 1924–8

INTRODUCTION

In May 1922, Lenin suffered the first of a series of strokes. Partly paralysed, his doctors ordered him to limit the amount of work he undertook each day. Following a more severe stroke in December, his workload was further reduced to the dictation of letters. Yet another stroke early in 1923 left him without speech. He died on 21st January 1924 at the age of 53.

As the Russian people mourned his passing, many were uncertain and feared for the future. Winston Churchill, a lifelong opponent of Bolshevism, summed up the situation – 'The Russian people were left floundering in a bog. Their worst misfortune was his birth … their next worse, his death.' It was certainly true that Lenin's death left a political vacuum since there was no one of his calibre available to replace him. Even before his death, leading members of the Political Bureau of the Communist Party, the Politburo, had been manoeuvring for position in readiness for the struggle to succeed. The one thing that held them together was the resolution passed at the Tenth Party Conference in 1921 which banned factionalism – the existence of groups within the Party that openly disagreed with official policy as dictated by the leadership. Anyone who dared show any independent line of thought was liable to be expelled from the Party and this even applied to members of the Central Committee.

1924	January	Death of Lenin. Stalin supervises funeral arrangements
	May	Thirteenth Party Conference. Party demands that Trotsky refutes his belief in permanent revolution
1925	January	Trotsky resigns as Commissar for Army and Navy
	April	Stalin puts forward theory of Socialism in One Country
1926	July	United Opposition formed. Trotsky and Zinoviev expelled from the Party
1927	October	Fifteenth Party Conference. Party decides on policy of collectivisation of agriculture. Trotsky expelled from the Party
1928	January	Trotsky exiled in Kazakhstan. Serious grain shortages. Campaign against peasants. Right Opposition challenges Stalin's policies
	November	Bukharin and Rykov expelled from Central Committee. Tomsky replaced as head of the trade unions

TABLE 51
Date chart of Stalin's rise to power, 1924–8.

1 ⌐ THE AFTERMATH OF THE DEATH OF LENIN

A *The leadership issue*

During the period that Lenin was incapacitated, Lev Kamenev, Grigori Zinoviev and Josif Stalin had led the Party. After his death and in the absence of a nominated successor, the same men formed a triumvirate – a three-man collective leadership. Although the real struggle, when it came, was to be between Stalin and Leon Trotsky, Kamenev and Zinoviev also joined the contest for the leadership. In addition, there was Nikolai Bukharin as well as the rank outsiders Andrei Rykov and Grigori Pyatakov.

See pages 223–227.

> **Lev Kamenev**, his real name was Rosenfeld, had joined the Social Democrats in 1901 and, at the time of the Party split, had sided with the Bolsheviks. Banished to Siberia in 1915 for his revolutionary activities, he returned after the March Revolution in 1917 and was appointed a member of the first Politburo of the Russian Communist Party. Like Kamenev, **Grigori Zinoviev** came from a Jewish background. Originally named Radomyslsky, he also first joined the Social Democrats in 1901 and then became a Bolshevik in 1903. During the revolution of 1905, he was active in St Petersburg and then elected to the Party's Central Committee. During a period abroad, Zinoviev collaborated with Lenin and returned with him to Russia in March 1917. Like Kamenev, he opposed Lenin's plan for the Bolshevik seizure of power in October 1917 because he thought it premature. In 1919, he was appointed head of the Comintern and a member of the Politburo. Described as 'the short, red bearded fanatic', **Nikolai Bukharin** was also a Bolshevik and the Party's leading political theorist. He spent the years 1911–17 abroad, mainly in the United States, where he edited the revolutionary paper *Novy Mir,* 'New World'. He returned to Russia to take part in the revolution of October 1917 and afterwards became editor of the newspaper, *Pravda,* Truth. He did not become a full member of the Politburo until 1924. **Andrei Rykov** and **Grigori Pyatakov**, both young men in their twenties, had impressed Lenin and were considered the rising stars of the Party.

Trotsky, a close associate of Lenin and leader of the Red Army during the Civil War, was a well-known national figure. He was popular, particularly with the military, and many regarded him as Lenin's obvious heir. However, behind the scenes it was Stalin who had managed to place himself in the most advantageous position. Since April 1922, he had been General Secretary of the Communist Party. It was a position that gave him control of the Party machine and he used his power to influence appointments, recommend promotions, arrange dismissals, place his own supporters in key positions and direct Party policy. Backed by such a powerful power base, he engineered himself into a position from which he could isolate and then eliminate those who stood in his way. As we shall see, the struggle for the leadership rapidly developed into a two horse race – Stalin versus Trotsky.

B *Lenin's political testament*

During the last months of his life, Lenin was well aware of the rivalry and intrigue that was going on behind his back. In December 1922, from his sickbed he dictated a letter to the Politburo that he wanted read at the Twelfth Party Congress in April. In the letter, he critically examined the structure of the Central Committee of the Communist Party and expressed his views regarding the personal qualities of the leading members of the Politburo. The letter came to be regarded as Lenin's political testament.

He first suggested a broadening of the membership of the Central Committee to lessen the chances of conflict based on sectional interests:

'I would urge strongly that at this Congress a number of changes be made to our political structure ... At the head of the list I set an increase in the number of Central Committee members ... I think this must be done in order to raise the prestige of the Central Committee and prevent small sections from acquiring excessive importance ... '

He was unsparing in his assessment of the leading members of the Politburo:

'Comrade Stalin, having become General-Secretary, has unlimited authority concentrated in his hands and I am not sure whether he will always be capable of using that authority with sufficient caution. Comrade Trotsky, on the other hand, is distinguished not only by an outstanding personality. He is personally perhaps the most capable man in the present Central Committee but he has displayed excessive self-assurance and excessive concern with the purely administrative side of the work. These two qualities of the two outstanding leaders of the present Central Committee can inadvertently lead to a split, and if our Party does not take steps to prevent this, the split may come unexpectedly. I shall not give any further appraisals of the personal qualities of the members of the Central Committee. I shall just recall that the October episode* with Zinoviev and Kamenev was, of course, no accident, but neither can blame be laid upon them personally ... Speaking of the younger members ... Bukharin and Pyatakov are the most out-standing. Bukharin is not only the most valuable, he is also rightly considered the favourite of the whole Party ... Pyatakov ... is unquestionably a man of outstanding will and ability but shows too much enthusiasm for the administrative side of work ... '

*In October 1917, Zinoviev and Kamenev had disagreed with Lenin when they thought his plans to seize power too risky.

A week later, after Stalin had been abusive to his wife, Krupskaya, during a telephone conversation, Lenin added a postscript to his letter:

> 'Stalin is too rude and this defect ... becomes quite intolerable in a General Secretary. That is why I suggest that comrades think about a way of removing Stalin from that post and appointing another man who differs from Comrade Stalin in being more tolerant, more loyal, more polite and more considerate to his comrades ... From the standpoint of safeguards against a split between Stalin and Trotsky, it is not a minor detail but it is a detail which can become extremely important.'

Stalin, using his customary cunning, was quick to present himself to the nation as Lenin's right-hand man and natural successor. Immediately after the Bolshevik leader's death, he came to the fore and took over the arrangements for the former leader's funeral. Against the wishes of Krupskaya, he turned the event into a staged ceremony as Lenin's embalmed body was placed in an impressive mausoleum in Red Square. In an emotional funeral oration, Stalin said:

> 'Leaving us, Comrade Lenin bequeathed to us the duty of holding high and keeping pure the great calling of being a member of the Party. We swear to you, Comrade Lenin, that we shall fulfil your commandment with honour ... There is no higher calling than being a member of the party whose founder and leader was Comrade Lenin ... Comrade Lenin ordained to us the unity of our Party ... We vow to you, Comrade Lenin, that we shall fulfil honourably your commandment ...'

2 ⌐ JOSIF STALIN

A *Childhood*

PROFILE

See Pictures 20 and 21 on page 261.

Josif Vissarionovich Djugashvili was born on 21 December 1879. His father, Vissarion (Beso), came from a family of former serfs and was a shoe repairer; his mother, Yekaterina (Keke), was of peasant stock. Keke was deeply religious, literate and loved music. She was also a hard-working woman who took in laundry and repaired clothes in order to earn extra money. The Djughashvili family were poor and lived in a run-down shack on the outskirts of a small town, Gori, in Georgia. There were rumours that the young Josif was illegitimate and that his real father was a Tsarist official in whose house his mother had once worked. Josif, known to the family as Soso, was their third child. Two children born to the Djugashvilis earlier, Mikhail and Georgi, had both died in infancy. Vissaion Djughashvili had the reputation of being a drunkard and a short-tempered lout. It was generally known that he regularly beat his wife and young son. Yekaterina, a devout Christian, was a loving mother who wanted her son to make something of his life. As a young boy, Josif suffered ill health and was prone to accidents. During his early years, he managed to survive smallpox, was badly injured when knocked down by a cart and suffered blood poisoning which caused his left arm to stiffen and become deformed. Once he became a public figure, Soviet photographers took great trouble to conceal his withered arm and the pockmarks left by smallpox. Eventually the family moved to Tbilisi where his father found work in a shoe factory. It was Keke's wish that her son should study to become a priest but her husband would have none of it. He was withdrawn from school and became an apprentice shoemaker. In 1890, Vissarion died after being knifed in a brawl. He was buried in a pauper's grave.

PICTURE 20
Stalin's father, Vissarion. No actual picture exists and this is a reconstruction which shows a likeness to Stalin. It was made posthumously

PICTURE 21
Yekaterina, Stalin's mother

B *Early years*

The death of his father meant that Josif could return to school. He studied hard but found that others teased him about the poverty of his family. Up to the age of ten, he only spoke Georgian but in school, because of Tsarist laws, he was forced to do his lessons in Russian.

Although he later mastered Russia, throughout his life he spoke with a strong Georgian accent. This he resented. It is also said that it was during this time that he first became aware of class distinctions and began to loathe those better off than himself. Nevertheless, in 1894, Josif appeared to be about to fulfil his mother's wishes when he won a scholarship to a seminary in Tbilisi and began to train for the priesthood. To start with, he was a clean cut, hard working student and things went well. As time passed, he came to reject the repressive regime imposed by the priests. It was during this time that he first began to read the works of Charles Darwin, Karl Marx and Lenin. Around him, the country was in uproar as men engaged in revolutionary activity and demonstrated. Locally, Tsarist officials were assassinated. Josif's character underwent a profound change and he became an atheist and began associating with revolutionary groups. In 1898, he joined the Georgian revolutionary group, *Mesame Dasi* or Third Group, and as time passed he became less a Georgian patriot and more a Marxist. The following year, he was expelled from the seminary for indiscipline.

PICTURE 22 *Stalin as a 14-year-old theological student in 1893*

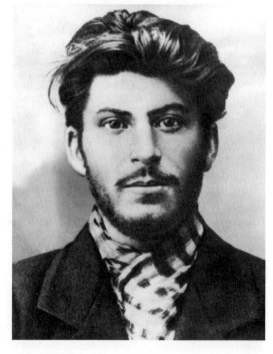

PICTURE 23 *A picture of Stalin taken from police files in 1902. Now aged 23, he is an established revolutionary*

C *Young revolutionary*

In 1904, Josif Djughashvili married the beautiful Keke Svanidze. They had a son, Yakov, but two years later she died of tuberculosis. The young revolutionary was devastated by his wife's death and at her funeral said to a friend, 'She was the only creature who softened my stony heart. She is dead and with her have died any feelings of tenderness I had for humanity.' Afterwards, he devoted himself totally to the cause of revolution. He first came into contact with Lenin in 1905 and he was much impressed by his brilliant mind and eloquence. Meanwhile, back in his native Georgia, he adopted the name Koba, a Turkish word that means courageous, and turned to terrorism in order to raise funds for the Party. His methods, which included murder, robbery, blackmail and protection rackets, attracted the attention and disapproval of Lenin. For a time, he assisted with the publication of a revolutionary newspaper, *Mnatobi*, 'The Torch'. Afterwards, his behaviour became more conventional although he still engaged in revolutionary activities and enjoyed being referred to as 'The Lenin of the Caucasus'. He wrote articles, printed and distributed revolutionary leaflets, spoke at gatherings of workers and encouraged and took part in strikes and demonstrations. As a result, he was continuously under police surveillance. He was frequently arrested and between 1901 and 1917 spent most of his time either in prison or in exile. During this time he took many aliases but the one that stuck was Stalin – 'Man of steel'. When World War I broke out in 1914, he was exiled at Kureika in Siberia north of the Arctic Circle and remained there until 1917. On hearing news of the March Revolution, he escaped and made his way to Petrograd. There he became editor of the Bolshevik newspaper, *Pravda*, 'Truth' and a co-opted member of the Party's Central Committee. Stalin played a relatively minor role in the events of October 1917 but still managed to commit errors of judgement that attracted his leader's displeasure. He accepted such criticism since there was no way he would dare take issue with Lenin. Following the successful Bolshevik *coup*, he was appointed Commissar for Nationalities and given responsibility for the non-Russian peoples living within the nation's borders. In 1922, he was elected General Secretary of the Communist Party.

D *Stalin and Trotsky*

Stalin took a dislike to Trotsky from their first meeting. Being a man of limited education and little personal charisma, it has been suggested that he was jealous of Trotsky's eloquence and intellect. He was certainly envious of the fact that Trotsky was a close confidante of Lenin. Stalin's loathing of Trotsky might also have been born of the anti-Semitism that was to become evident later. As the years passed their feud intensified and their dislike of each other became deep-rooted. When the opportunity arose, the two men quarrelled openly and, during the Civil War, Stalin had publicly criticised Trotsky's decision to recruit ex-Tsarist officers to serve in the Red Army. Trotsky considered Stalin a political lightweight and did not regard him as a threat. He accused him of seeking personal glory instead of supporting every means of securing a Bolshevik victory. Although Stalin was intellectually inferior to Trotsky, as we shall see, he was by far the more astute politician.

Meanwhile, following Lenin's death, the Party launched a campaign to increase membership. During what was called the 'Lenin enrolment', in less than two years the membership doubled and reached a million. The new members, the *Lenintsy*, were mainly young people who were poorly educated, inexperienced and politically naïve. The advantage to the Party was that they were more easily **brainwashed** by Bolshevik propaganda and did as they were told.

> **brainwashed**
> indoctrinated or subjected to pressure so that they will accept certain views.

3 ∽ STAGES IN THE POWER STRUGGLE

The struggle to be Lenin's successor was an unworthy spectacle involving behind the scenes scheming, unseemly infighting, all sorts of double-dealing and acts of treachery and betrayal. Although factionalism had been banned, members of the Politburo made alliances of convenience, changed sides and then formed new groupings. What emerged was a political free-for-all in which honesty and loyalty were disregarded. The main battlegrounds were the annual congresses of the Party.

A *The triumvirate against Trotsky*

The man most feared by the triumvirate was Trotsky. This was because he had a national reputation, had once been Lenin's right-hand man, had the support of the army and large sections of the workers and was considered by many to be Lenin's natural successor. Immediately Kamenev, Zinoviev and Stalin closed ranks to take advantage of his weaknesses and plot about his downfall. Trotsky was certainly vulnerable. It was never forgotten that he had once been a Menshevik and that he had openly disagreed with Lenin on matters of policy. In addition, he was his own worst enemy and his errors of judgement often played into his opponents' hands. A disclosure of the contents of Lenin's testament at the Twelfth Party Congress in 1923, a time when Lenin was critically ill but still alive, might have stopped Stalin in his tracks. Lenin's wife, Krupskaya, sent the documents to the Politburo but they were never read publicly. Much to Stalin's embarrassment they were read to the Central Committee in closed session but he was saved when Zinoviev rose to tell delegates that Lenin's fears regarding Stalin were unfounded. As the British historian Martin McCauley has written, 'The triumvirate held together and not even the dead pharaoh could prise it apart'. Earlier, Trotsky had made a bitter attack on the way the affairs of the Party were being managed and he was asked to attend the Congress to explain his views. He failed to turn up. In his absence, the triumvirate turned on Trotsky and accused him of factionalism. For the first time the term Trotskyist was used. A few months later he also failed to make an appearance at Lenin's funeral.

In May 1924, at the Thirteenth Party Congress, Zinoviev renewed the attack on Trotsky and called on him to refute his earlier claims. Six months later, Trotsky published *Lessons of October* that included blistering attacks on both Kamenev and Zinoviev. They responded with a torrent of abuse. As a result, Trotsky gave up his position as Commissar for Military and Naval Affairs. For him, this marked the beginning of the end of his influence in political affairs since he had surrendered his only power base without a fight. Throughout these exchanges, Stalin had taken a back seat. He was biding his time and playing a waiting game. As the situation worsened, so other disagreements arose.

B *Issues that divided the Party*

BUREAUCRACY OR THE RULE OF THE PROLETARIAT

Trotsky was opposed to the extension of bureaucratic government – centralised government by officials and departments at the top. He wanted a return to the ideals of the revolution with a broad-based government guided by the wishes of the proletariat. Stalin favoured a centralised bureaucracy that, as secretary of the Party, gave him the greatest influence. He denied vigorously that the Soviet Union risked becoming a one-man dictatorship.

PERMANENT REVOLUTION OR 'SOCIALISM IN ONE COUNTRY'

Trotsky believed that the Bolshevik revolution in Russia in 1917 was but a prelude to similar revolutions elsewhere in Europe. He said – 'We are building socialism in the USSR with the aid of the world proletariat in alliance with the main mass of our peasantry. We shall win final victory because revolution in other countries is inevitable'. Stalin disagreed. His view was that socialism should first be firmly established in the Soviet Union and that once its success was obvious, others would wish to follow their example.

THE ROLE OF THE PEASANTS AND THE DRIVE TOWARDS RAPID INDUSTRIALISATION

Stalin wanted to press ahead with a programme for the rapid industrialisation of the Soviet Union. He argued that the country was surrounded by enemies, the capitalist world beyond her frontiers, and needed to catch up with them and match their industrial and military might. To achieve this, it would be necessary for the peasants to produce sufficient food to feed the industrial workers in the towns and cities. The peasants were still enjoying the benefits of the New Economic Policy and some, the kulak class, had become prosperous. In 1924, a poor grain harvest led to price increases that further enriched the peasants. Because of this, increased pressure was placed on them to increase output and pay higher taxes. Within the Politburo, there were differences of opinion regarding the role of the peasantry and the speed with which the country needed to industrialise.

C *The United Opposition*

It was late in the day that Kamenev and Zinoviev realised that they had been outwitted and that Trotsky was not the real enemy. In July 1926, they formed an alliance with Trotsky, the United Opposition. In effect, it was an anti-Stalinist bloc aimed at opposing the policies of the Right. Lenin's widow, Krupskaya, backed them. Almost immediately, Kamenev and Zinoviev were removed from the Politburo and, with no voice in the government, the United Opposition took their case to the people by addressing public meetings and groups of factory workers. The Party Congress of October 1926 was stormy as Stalin and his ally, Bukharin, poured scorn on the United Opposition. Trotsky, making his last speech to the Congress, was heard in silence but when Kamenev and Zinoviev spoke they were booed and jeered. Stalin and his supporters also took the opportunity to embarrass their opponents. Kamenev was reminded of his **faux pas** of 1917 when, on the abdication of the Tsar Nicholas, he had sent a letter of congratulation to Grand Duke Nicholas on his accession to the throne and that later that year, he had opposed the Bolshevik coup. It was also recalled that Trotsky had once been a Menshevik and that after his conversion to Bolshevism, he had frequent differences of opinion with Lenin. Afterwards, Zinoviev lost his position as head of Comintern and was replaced by Bukharin.

faux pas a mistake or blunder

Trotsky next produced a document, the *Declaration of the 83*, which attacked the policies of the leadership and was severely critical of their failures in foreign policy. Stalin retaliated by accusing Trotsky of being a traitor. The summer of 1926 was a difficult time for the United Opposition. Without access to the press to put forward their case, they organised public meetings but everywhere they were pilloried and abused. A witness to these events recalled:

> Everywhere they were followed by Stalin's roughnecks ... Everywhere they were greeted with yells, catcalls and riots. Gangs that raced from hall to hall and factory to factory ahead of them ready to break up their meetings engineered this. Nowhere did any of them get the opportunity to speak freely to the ordinary Russian people. Bukharin, Rykov and Tomsky reacted by forming a Rightist group and looked for a chance to speak their mind. The majority of workers, having lived through years of terror, were in no mood to defend the rebels. A temporary increase in rations coupled with a promise of better living quarters lulled most of them into a state of apathy. Trotsky's long-winded arguments fell on deaf ears. At a factory meeting ... I saw Trotsky hissed, spat at, and all but kicked off the platform ... In less than a year the hero of the people had become an object of pity.

Matters came to a head at the Fifteenth Party Congress in December 1927 when Stalin finally came into his own and convinced the Congress of the need to expel Trotsky and Zinoviev from the Party. At the same time, Kamenev lost his seat on the Central Committee. Trotsky was first sent to Alma Ata in Kazakhstan close to the Chinese border and, in 1929, was finally deported to Turkey. An observer of these events wryly commented, 'An idol must never step down from his pedestal. If he does, his glory is dimmed forever.' And so it was with Trotsky.

KEY ISSUE

The stages by which Stalin outwitted his opponents.

D *The Right Opposition*

1927 was a difficult year. Although harvests had been reasonable, the peasants failed to produce the necessary surpluses. In many cases, they refused to hand over their grain and stockpiled it instead. During a campaign of terror orchestrated by the OGPU, they were victimised and their stocks requisitioned. Those who resisted were murdered. It was clear that those fighting for control of the Party were showing little concern at the plight of the Opposition. They demanded that the peasants be better treated and that there was a slackening in what they regarded as an unnecessary stampede into industrialisation. Their proposals were not unsound but Stalin would have none of it and declared that the peasants had to be dealt with once and for all. Two years previously, the Right had helped Stalin to overthrow the New Opposition but he felt no loyalty or obligation to them. One by one, they were demoted and removed. In 1928, Tomsky was replaced as leader of the trade unions and was not re-elected to the Politburo. Bukharin complained – 'Stalin will strangle us. He is an unprincipled schemer who subordinates everything to his lust for power.' The realisation came too late, he was forced to resign as the editor of *Pravda* and, together with Rykov, was expelled from the Central Committee. The purge complete, a group of pro-Stalinists replaced them – men such as Mikhail Kalinin, Vyacheslav Molotov and Kliment Voroshilov.

See Diagram 19 on page 268.

4 ⟿ HOW WAS STALIN ABLE TO WIN THE POWER STRUGGLE?

There was not one reason that explains Stalin's success in overcoming his opponents and coming to power in the Soviet Union. There were numerous factors that contributed and made it possible.

- Stalin's strength came from his broad power base. As General Secretary of the Communist Party he wielded immense power and influence and was able to place supporters in strategic positions. Within the Party bureaucracy, all the important positions were held by placements of Stalin.
- The Left wanted rapid industrialisation and the peasantry pressurised into producing more grain and paying higher taxes whilst the Right wanted to move forward at a more moderate pace and the peasants to continue to flourish under NEP. Stalin was a shrewd political operator and whilst his objectives were clear, in the short term he was happy to play one side off against the other and manipulate the changing alliances within the Politburo.

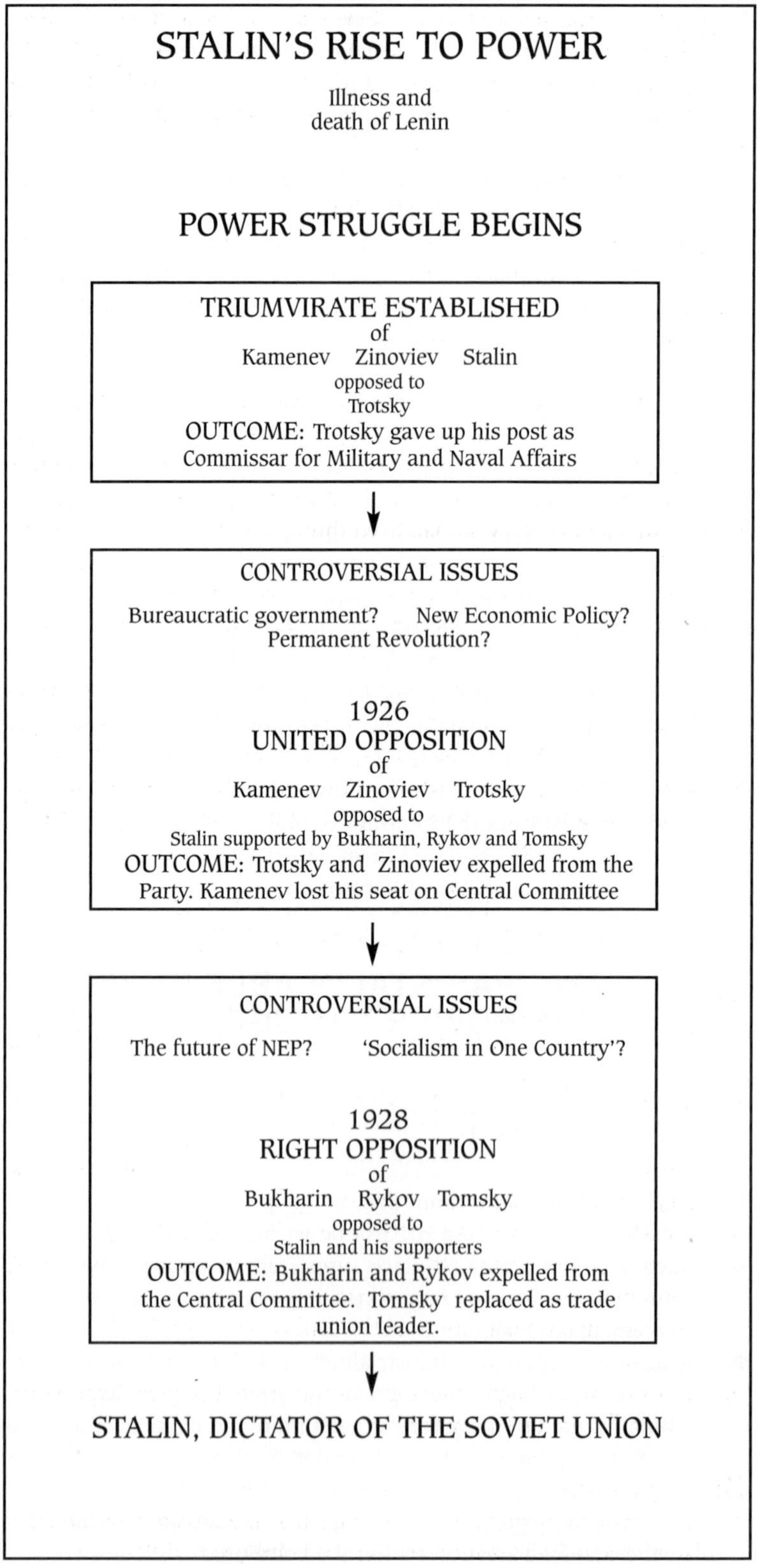

STALIN'S RISE TO POWER

Illness and
death of Lenin

POWER STRUGGLE BEGINS

TRIUMVIRATE ESTABLISHED
of
Kamenev   Zinoviev   Stalin
opposed to
Trotsky
OUTCOME: Trotsky gave up his post as
Commissar for Military and Naval Affairs

CONTROVERSIAL ISSUES

Bureaucratic government?   New Economic Policy?
Permanent Revolution?

1926
UNITED OPPOSITION
of
Kamenev   Zinoviev   Trotsky
opposed to
Stalin supported by Bukharin, Rykov and Tomsky
OUTCOME: Trotsky and Zinoviev expelled from the
Party. Kamenev lost his seat on Central Committee

CONTROVERSIAL ISSUES

The future of NEP?   'Socialism in One Country'?

1928
RIGHT OPPOSITION
of
Bukharin   Rykov   Tomsky
opposed to
Stalin and his supporters
OUTCOME: Bukharin and Rykov expelled from
the Central Committee. Tomsky replaced as trade
union leader.

STALIN, DICTATOR OF THE SOVIET UNION

DIAGRAM 19

*Stalin's rise to power (From
Years of Russia and the USSR,
1851–1991 by David Evans and
Jane Jenkins)*

- At every stage, he completely outwitted the intellectually brilliant Trotsky who many took to be Lenin's obvious successor. Trotsky made serious errors of judgement when he failed to exploit the condemnation of Stalin in Lenin's political testament and surrendered his power base as Commissar for the Army and Navy.
- Stalin's opponents underestimated him. He cunningly manipulated the various groups within the Politburo, took advantage of their differences and then turned them against each other. He outmanoeuvred Bukharin, Kamenev and Zinoviev and by the time they came to appreciate his true nature and the extent of his lust for power, it was too late. Their dislike of Trotsky blinded them to the ambitions of Stalin.
- The ban on factionalism meant that it was difficult to challenge the official Party line - Stalin's line! As can be seen by the Party's acceptance of the need for collectivisation and rapid industrialisation, Stalin came to have the final say in matters of policy.
- The Russian people, who had lived through war, revolution and civil war, looked for a respite and an improvement in their condition. To them, Stalin seemed a moderate and a man able to bring stability to the country. The severity of his proposed programme of economic change and his ruthlessness were not yet apparent.
- The increase in Party membership in the mid-1920s was to Stalin's advantage. The influx of new members included many who were young, poorly educated and easily influenced by Party propaganda.
- He was able to gradually win control of the press and other media. The opposition had no means of putting their case to the people.

5 ᔍ STRUCTURED AND ESSAY QUESTIONS

A *This section consists of questions that might be useful for discussion (or writing answers) as a way of expanding on the chapter and testing understanding of it.*

1. In what sense did the death of Lenin leave the Russian people 'floundering in a bog'?
2. What advantages did Stalin gain from being appointed General Secretary of the Communist Party?
3. For what reasons was the Party opposed to 'factionalism'?
4. To what extent might the revelation of the contents of Lenin's political testament have been damaging to Stalin?
5. Why did Stalin's activities in the Caucasus attract the disapproval of Lenin?
6. To what extent might it be rightly claimed that Trotsky largely contributed to his own downfall?

B *Essay questions.*

1. To what extent might it be claimed that the antagonism between Trotsky and Stalin was based solely on ideological differences?

2. 'He won control largely because his opponents underestimated him.' How valid is this assessment of Stalin's rise to power?

6 ⌐ MAKING NOTES

In order to help you be sure that you have a full understanding of the nature and the outcome of the power struggle between Trotsky and Stalin, complete the following chart:

	Trotsky	Stalin
Background		
Importance to the Party and part played in the Revolution in 1917		
Power base. On whom could they depend for support?		
Differences in policy and ideology		
Reasons for success or failure		

Stalin's economic policies, 1928–39

8

INTRODUCTION

Stalin had rejected Trotsky's theory of continuous revolution that would have meant committing much of the nation's resources to supporting revolutionary movements elsewhere abroad. Instead, in 1925, he proposed the policy of 'Socialism in one country'. His intention was to convert the Soviet Union, whose economy was then backward and largely agricultural, into a modern, industrialised state. It was to be a 'revolution from above'. Stalin told the Russian people 'We are fifty to a hundred years behind the advanced countries. We must make good this difference in ten years. Either we do it or we shall be crushed.' He hoped to make his country an example of Communist achievement and convince others that it was the path to follow. His proposals were far more attractive to the Russian people than those of Trotsky. After years of war, revolution and then civil war they had endured enough and looked forward to a period of stability. His intention was to bring about the rapid transformation of his country in stages – Five-Year Plans. Stalin said

> The fundamental task of the Five-Year Plan is to convert the USSR from an agrarian and weak country dependent on the **caprices** of the capitalist countries, into an industrial and powerful country, fully self-reliant and independent of world capitalism.

caprices changes of humour without reason.

However, such progress could not be sustained without the backing of an agricultural system able to feed the workers in the new industrial regions and also contribute largely to the nation's finances.

1 ⌐ THE END OF LENIN'S NEW ECONOMIC POLICY

See pages 245–8.

A *The opposition to NEP?*

The severity of War Communism led to a backlash. Popular discontent resulted in riots and anti-Communist demonstrations which came to a head in the Kronstadt mutiny of March 1921. Although the naval mutineers, who demanded 'Soviets without Communists', were ruthlessly crushed by the Red Army, the significance of the uprising was not lost on Lenin. He commented, 'This was the flash that lit up reality better than anything else.' It was time to compromise. At the Tenth Party Congress in 1921, he proposed a series of far reaching measures some of which were aimed at appeasing the peasants. Instead of having their crops and animals requisitioned, peasants were allowed to pay their taxes in kind – in agricultural produce. They were also allowed to sell any surpluses on the open market. Within limits, the peasantry was left to manage its own affairs. The measures disappointed hard-line Communists who saw them as a retreat from true Marxist principles and a return to bourgeois ways. To them, any step back towards capitalism was offensive. Some went as far as to complain that NEP was as significant a surrender as that at Brest-Litovsk! The Left-wing writer, Maxim Gorky, said to a French visitor:

'In the struggle which, since the beginning of the revolution, has been going on between the two classes, the peasants have every chance of coming out victorious ... The urban proletariat has been declining incessantly for four years ... The immense peasant tide will end by engulfing everything ... The peasant will become master of Russia, since he represents numbers. And it will be terrible for our future.'

For Lenin, NEP represented a compromise and only a short-term retreat. He thought it possible that the poorer classes of peasantry might be offended by the growing wealth of the rich peasants, the kulaks, and turn against them. This did not happen and all classes of the peasantry remained largely united.

B *The 'scissors' crisis'*

By 1923, there were signs that NEP was achieving its aims. The problem was that agriculture was recovering more quickly than industry and this created an imbalance in the economy.

As the peasants produced more crops so the price of food fell but, since factory-made consumer goods were still scarce, their price continued to rise. Trotsky used a diagram involving a scissors to illustrate what was happening and so the trend became known as the 'scissors' crisis'.

analogy indicating a likeness by reference to something that is otherwise different.

Using the **analogy** of a pair of scissors with one blade representing falling food prices and the other the increasing price of manufactured goods, Trotsky argued that as the blades opened and the income of the peasants fell, they would be unwilling to produce the extra food required.

If the blades were opened too far the scissors would break and by this Trotsky implied that the essential good relationship between the factory workers and the peasants would come to an end. In 1924, the government took steps to reduce the price of manufactured goods and so the gap between the blades of the scissors narrowed. The crisis was over although the problem remained. The peasants would only continue to produce food surpluses for as long as the price of consumer goods remained low.

KEY ISSUE

What led to the 'scissors' crisis'?

2 ⤳ THE COLLECTIVISATION OF SOVIET AGRICULTURE

A *The need to introduce collectivisation*

The plan to force the Soviet Union through a period of rapid industrialisation meant that money had to be found to purchase the necessary capital equipment, such as machinery, from abroad. Where was it to come from? Capitalist countries were unlikely to make loans available whilst, at home, there were few left with sufficient wealth to tax. The only alternative was to increase grain production and sell it abroad and, at the same time, increase the taxes paid by the peasantry. If the peasants resisted their grain could be requisitioned, as it had been during the period of War Communism, and in order to boost production, they could be forced into collective farms.

Q

Why was Soviet agriculture in need of urgent reform?

Lenin had always supported the collectivisation of agriculture but gradually and by argument and voluntary means. With Stalin in control, things changed rapidly. He wanted a return to Marxist principles and the Party's ideological objectives and felt it was time 'to guide peasant farming towards socialism'. Backed by the Politburo, Stalin decided to abandon Lenin's experiment in economic freedom. The problems he faced were enormous. The Soviet Union was a massive country extending to over 22 million square kilometres of land. In the east, much of this was barren tundra but elsewhere there were areas that were fertile and arable. One might ask, if the prairies of North America could produce sufficient grain to feed the people of the United States and millions besides, why not the steppes of Russia? What was wrong with Soviet agriculture? The truth was that Russian farming methods were primitive and inefficient. Machinery was seldom available, there was little knowledge of modern farming methods and the majority of smallholdings were too small to be run efficiently.

In 1928, some 75% of the Russian people were employed on the land and depended on agriculture for their living. At the top end of the scale were the prosperous kulaks and, at the other end, poor peasants struggling to grow enough for their own needs on their meagre smallholdings. However, the bulk of the peasants, over sixty-per-cent, were neither desperately poor nor kulak-rich. They were self-sufficient, enjoyed reasonable living standards and were proudly independent. The Bolshevik leadership was mainly urban in origin and their sympathies tended to be with the industrial workers in the towns and cities and not with the peasants who they thought ideologically unreliable. Stalin knew that the peasants would resist collectivisation but there was no longer any scope for compromise. It was time to bring the peasants to order.

B *Collectivisation – the theory*

The intention was to encourage the peasants to surrender their privately run smallholdings in order to create large farms or *kolkhozee. Kolkhoz* is the abbreviated form of *kollektivnoe khozyaistwo*, a collective farm. The pooling of land and livestock meant that farming would be based on much larger units and benefit from the economies of scale – the advantages of large-scale production. These advantages include increased output without a proportionate increase in costs and a greater division of labour that would allow individual workers to specialise in one aspect of the work done. In the long run the main advantage would be cheaper production costs and consequently lower prices. Stalin also promised to set up Mechanical and Tractor Stations, MTS, to make tractors and agricultural equipment available on hire. The peasants would surrender their independence to become wage-labourers. Families would live in village communities and eventually benefit from improved amenities – nurseries, schools, hospitals and clinics. In addition to collective farms, it was also intended to set up state farms or *sovkhozes*. These, described by Martin McCauley as 'factories without a roof', were established in areas where there had been little agricultural development. Those employed in *sovkhozes* were considered to be workers rather than peasants and they received a fixed wage. If a *sovkhoze* made a loss it was covered by the state whereas any loss made by a *kolkhoze* had to be made good by the peasants themselves. To start with, Stalin urged the peasants to form collective farms voluntarily but he was well aware that, in spite of the well advertised advantages, they would not surrender their independence willingly. The fiercest opposition came from the kulaks.

THE KULAKS

The word kulak means 'fist', a grasping fist (see pages 8 and 9). The kulaks first emerged after serfdom had been abolished in 1861. They were those who bought up common pastureland and woodland and took advantage of the peasantry who wanted grazing land for their cattle and firewood. During World War I it was claimed that some of the kulaks bribed local officials in order to avoid conscription into the army and then, at the first opportunity, bought up the land of those killed at the front. Their success can be seen by the fact that by 1917, they owned ninety-percent of Russia's most fertile land. The war

Q

Why did the kulaks oppose collectivisation?

brought acute shortages and, as food prices increased and so did the wealth of the kulaks. By the end of the war, the kulaks were a distinct class of prosperous farmers.

C *Collectivisation – the practice*

On 27th December 1929, just a few days after Stalin's 50th birthday, a Central Committee resolution officially ordered the start of enforced collectivisation. The methods Stalin intended to use to collectivise the peasants had nothing in common with the ideas of Lenin. Pressed by the urgent need for extra food, he sent Party officials into the country-side to organise the compulsory collectivisation of all farming land in the Soviet Union. Police and Red Army units ruthlessly confiscated grain and livestock to feed the towns and cities. 'They collectivised,' said Trotsky, 'not only horses, sheep, pigs, but even new-born chickens'. A foreign observer noted that they took everything 'down to the felt shoes, which they dragged from the feet of little children'.

The reaction of the peasants, and the kulaks in particular, who were determined not to hand over their stock to the *kolkhozee* was to sell their grain off cheaply, destroy their implements and slaughter their animals. Stalin told the Party:

'In order to oust the kulaks as a class, the resistance of this class must be smashed in open battle ... That is a step towards the policy of eliminating the kulaks as a class. Without it, talk of ousting the kulaks as a class is empty prattle ... without it, no substantial, let alone complete, collectivisation of the countryside is conceivable ... Hence, the Party's present policy is ... a turn away from the old policy of restricting the capitalist elements in the countryside towards a new policy of eliminating the kulaks as a class'.

On 30th January 1930, Stalin approved the resolution – On Measures for the Elimination of Kulak Households in Districts of Comprehensive Collectivisation.

D *'The red holocaust' – the elimination of the kulaks*

The kulaks were to be divided into three categories. The first, the most hostile and reactionary, were to be shot or imprisoned; the second, the families of the first, were to be deported; the third were to be settled in marsh and forest land where farming would be extremely difficult if not impossible. As the OGPU and Party activists moved into the countryside they were warned that they must make no concessions and show no mercy. The kulaks had to be found, isolated and eliminated. This extract from *Famine in Russia* by Brian Moynahan (1975) describes the times:

> So one family was deported because it owned a cow and a calf; another because it's mare had a foal; another because a woman helped a relative with the harvest. A peasant with eight acres was forced to clear the railway lines of snow. On his return, he found all his property seized apart from a kettle, a saucer and a spoon. He was then sent lumbering in the far North. In some villages, a Party activist would arrive from the city, produce a pistol, and say that any peasant who refused to join a *kolkhoz* would be sent immediately to Siberia.

Every kulak was rounded up and, as Alexander Solzenitsyn wrote, 'all had to go down the same road, to the same common destruction'. Whole families, even the youngest children, were herded into cattle wagons so tightly that their feet seldom touched the ground. Deported kulaks often took weeks to reach Siberia and, unfed and subject to sub-zero temperatures, thousands died during the journey. Those that reached their destination were placed in camps and used as slave labour. The camps were run by an OGPU agency, the Chief Executive of Corrective Labour Camps, usually known by the **acronym**, GULAG. In the camps, tens of thousands died of starvation, disease and exposure to severe weather conditions. Some of those who survived did so by living in holes in the ground and by scratching a living out of the earth with their bare hands. The guards referred to their prisoners as 'white coal' and a common saying was that 'Moscow does not believe in tears'. By 1931, there were over two million held in the camps.

acronym a word formed from the initial letters of other words.

As the process of collectivisation proceeded rapidly across the Soviet Union, Stalin called for a pause and a period of consolidation and blamed the excesses on over enthusiastic Party officials. In an article in *Pravda* in March 1930, he attempted to explain their behaviour:

> It is a fact that by February of this year 50 per cent of the peasant farms have been collectivised … it is a tremendous achievement … Such successes sometimes lead to a spirit of vanity and conceit: 'We can do anything!, 'There's nothing we can't do!' People become intoxicated by such successes; they become dizzy with success, lose all sense of proportion and the ability to understand realities.'

As a spur to the peasantry who had formed collectives, he offered a concession – each would be allowed to cultivate a small area of their own and even keep a number of animals. In fact it was a ploy to get them their spring seed. Afterwards, many could not resist the temptation to concentrate their efforts on their own plots and neglect the needs of the kolkhozee. It was a return to what Harold Sukman referred to as 'a kind of mini NEP'. It was only a temporary halt. The pressure to collectivise resumed in 1932 and was to coincide with a disastrous famine.

E *The consequences – famine*

In eliminating the kulaks, Stalin had deprived his country of its most productive farmers. The bulk of the other peasants, now experiencing a 'second serfdom' as enforced members of collectives, were in no mood to over exert themselves in the interests of the Communist state. As a result, seeds went unsown and crops went unharvested. With no kulaks left, the axe next fell on the peasants who were accused of being loafers and still influenced by the 'kulak spirit'. Even though agricultural output had fallen alarmingly, orders were sent from Moscow to the provinces increasing the quotas of grain demanded. Each district was ordered to produce their share of the quota and, in turn, the district made similar demands of each village. The quotas demanded were totally unrealistic and had no chance of being fulfilled. When they were not forthcoming, the OGPU and Communist officials from the towns and cities swarmed over the region confiscating all the food they could find. Anyone found guilty of hoarding was liable to be sentenced to terms of imprisonment or even shot. Stalin's plan was to starve the peasantry into submission and if necessary sentence them to death by hunger. Vasily Grossman, a Russian journalist witnessed the effects of the famine with his own eyes, documented in the following extract from his book *Forever Flowing* (1972).

> Fathers and mothers wanted to save their children and hid tiny amounts of grain, and they were told: 'You hate the country of socialism. You are trying to make the plan fail, you parasites, you kulak supporters, you rats.' The entire seed fund had been confiscated. Everywhere there was terror. Mothers looked at their children and screamed in fear. They screamed as if a snake had crept into their house. And this snake was famine, starvation, death... And here, under the government of workers and peasants, not even one grain was given them... Death from starvation mowed down the village. First the children, then the old people, then those of middle age. At first they dug graves and buried them, and then as things got worse they stopped. Dead people lay there in the yards and in the end remained in their huts. Things fell silent. The whole village died.

Starving peasants stood at railway stations and alongside railway tracks in the hope that food might be thrown from passing trains. This ended when soldiers dispersed them and passengers were forbidden to open carriage windows. In some areas, the peasants resisted but, lacking leadership and weapons, they were easily overcome. One of the main centres of resistance was the Ukraine that once produced vast harvests of grain and was regarded as 'the breadbasket of Europe'. The whole region was encircled by the military to ensure that no food entered the stricken area. At one stage, Stalin considered deporting the whole population of the region but was told there was no place to deport them to! It was as one woman claimed 'a war in which the weapons were not tanks, machine guns or bullets – but hunger.' In his book, *I Chose Freedom*, Viktor Kravchenko describes the extremes to which people would go to find even the smallest amount of food. He recalled, 'Yes, the horse manure. We fought over it. Sometimes there were whole grains in it.' In the Ukraine, the loss of life from starvation was greater than any country in World War I. The famine and systematic starvation of the peasantry was politically motivated. It was a reprisal for opposing Stalin and the enforced imposition of collectivisation by means of terror. Lev Kopelev, young Party activist involved who helped implement Stalin's policy, later wrote in his book *The Education of a True Believer* (1980).

> And I persuaded myself, explained to myself I mustn't give in to the weakness of pity. We were carrying out an historical necessity. We were performing our revolutionary duty. We were obtaining grain for the socialist fatherland, for the five-year plan. Some sort of rationalistic fanaticism overcame my doubts, my pangs of conscience and my simple feelings of sympathy, pity and shame … it was necessary to clench your teeth, clench your heart and carry out everything the Party and the Soviet power ordered. … How could all this have happened? How could I have participated in it?

Yet there were men who did show remorse for their actions even at the time. In *Black Famine in the Ukraine* (1977), Andrew Gregorovich provides an account of a meeting with a colonel in the OGPU. Close to tears, he said:

> I am an old Bolshevik. I worked in the underground against the Tsar and then I fought in the civil war. Did I do all that in order that I should now surround villages with machine-guns and order my men to fire indiscriminately into crowds of peasants? Oh no, no!

The confiscated grain was stockpiled and guarded by the military and OGPU. Later it was either exported to earn much needed foreign currency or simply allowed to rot. None was released to feed the starving masses. Abroad, an international relief committee was set up under the Archbishop of Vienna but it was barred from the Soviet Union because the government insisted there was no famine. It is impossible to calculate how many Russians perished during the terrible famine of 1932–3. Some claim that 10 million died but this may be a very conservative estimate. Whatever, it places Stalin high in the ranks of those responsible for mass murder and genocide – and there was even worse to come!

F *How successful was collectivisation?*

It is possible to consider the success of collectivisation from two points of view. Firstly there was the undoubted success of the extent to which collectivisation was implemented. After 1930, the speed by which it was carried through was impressive and by 1941, the second year of the Soviet Union's involvement in World War II, virtually all farming had been collectivised.

During this period some 25 million small peasant holdings were turned into a quarter of a million collective farms. However, if secondly we consider collectivisation from the point of view of production levels then it was a disaster. The elimination of the kulaks robbed the country of its most efficient farmers whilst the remaining peasants showed little enthusiasm to work as wage labourers on the land they had once owned. Some 19 million left the *kolkhozee* and headed for the industrial regions to work on Five-Year Plan projects. In the countryside, there was stagnation and production levels fell alarmingly. It took a full seven years before grain production recovered to reach 1928 levels whilst recovery in livestock production took even longer. By 1937, the output from the privately owned plots was greater than that of the collectives! Very gradually, as the *kolkhozee* were more efficiently managed, so production figures improved.

TABLE 52 *Progress towards collectivisation (% of land collectivised)*

1930	23.6
1931	52.7
1932	61.5
1933	66.4
1934	71.4
1935	83.2
1936	89.6
1941	98.0

TABLE 53 *Agricultural production in the Soviet Union 1928–35 (estimates based on Soviet statistics)*

	1928	1929	1930	1931	1932	1933	1934	1935
Grain (million tonnes)	73.3	71.7	83.5	69.5	69.6	68.6	67.6	75.0
Cattle (million head)	70.5	67.1	52.5	47.9	40.7	38.4	42.4	49.3
Pigs (million head)	26.0	20.4	13.6	14.4	11.6	12.1	17.4	22.6
Sheep and goats (million head)	146.7	147.0	108.8	77.7	52.1	50.2	51.9	61.1

Although each *kolkhoz* elected its own chairman, local Party officials still mainly dictated policy. Payment to the peasants was based on the productivity of their *kolkhoz* and, if no profit was made there was no payout. Generally the promised new schools and hospitals were slow to appear but there were showpiece collectives with modern amenities. Visitors to the Soviet Union were taken to see these models of socialist achievement. On the other hand, machinery leased by the Mechanical and Tractor Stations (MTS) became more readily available and the number of tractors and combine harvesters available increased considerably. Eventually agricultural output did increase sufficiently to support industrial growth but at what cost!

G *Collectivisation – an historical perspective*

The view held by the majority of historians is that Stalin sacrificed the Russian peasantry in order to bring about the industrial transformation of his country and that he overcame opposition to his scheme by approving the slaughter of millions of kulaks and peasants. In *Stalin and Stalinism*, Alan Wood comments, 'Collectivisation was in effect a civil war unleashed by the Party on the peasant population'. Alan Shukman agrees. In *Stalin*, he writes, 'Stalin chose a course that was bound to conflict with the peasants' basic instincts ... Thus, what began as an economic policy quickly turned the countryside into a scene of despair, bloodshed and terror.' K. Perry in *Modern European History* describes collectivisation as 'a tragedy for Russia ... Stalin, ignorant on economic matters, launched policies which brought economic disaster by the mad speed which characterised them.' Later, in 1942, when Winston Churchill, the British prime minister, questioned Stalin about these events he went as far as to admit – 'Collective farm policy was a terrible struggle ... Ten millions ... It was fearful. Four years it lasted. It was absolutely necessary ... '

On the other hand, some historians have questioned the extent of Stalin's responsibility. It has been argued that if he had not ended NEP it might well have undermined the revolution and led to a return to a capitalist system. Others have maintained that Stalin did not plan collectivisation but 'stumbled into it with neither planning nor foresight'. In *The Politics of Stalinism* (1986), J. Arch Getty argues that collectivisation was a panic measure and that Stalin 'went with the momentum and was influenced by an economic and political environment that he did not create.' Some go as far as to question if Stalin was really in charge and suggest that the situation simply 'ran out of control.' Then there are those who deny it ever happened. Ray Nunes, a leading New Zealand Communist, has written 'Nobody has any evidence. But that didn't stop the newspapers of the capitalist world from making totally unfounded assertions about the millions murdered, all attributed to Stalin.'

3 ⁓ STALIN'S FIVE-YEAR PLANS

With NEP abandoned, the last traces of capitalism disappeared as all industries were placed under state ownership. The Five-Year Plans were intended to bring about an economic miracle by transforming the Soviet Union into an advanced, industrialised socialist state in ten years. Five-Year Plans were based on forward planning which set production targets five years in advance and then followed a programme requiring an all out effort in order to achieve them. Each factory was set predetermined quotas – minimum amounts that had to be produced each year over a five-year period. Each year the quota was increased. Each man and woman was set a 'norm' – the amount they were expected to produce each week. The scheme was backed by a system of rewards and punishments. Workers who exceeded their norms became entitled to additional pay, extra allowances of food and even improved housing whilst those who failed forfeited some of the pay and food to which they were normally entitled. The OGPU was always at hand to deal with slackers and any that complained. Gosplan, the abbreviation for Gosudarstvenny Planovy Komitet, the State Planning Committee, was responsible for supervising all aspects of the Plans. Based in Moscow, Gosplan employed half a million officials whose job it was to set targets for every factory, works and mine and then check that the targets set were being achieved. Although workers were being forced to work extremely long hours for limited rewards, the majority entered into the task of modernising their country with enthusiasm. John Scott, an American, witnessed these events at first hand (this extract is from his book *Behind the Urals: An American Worker in Russia's City of Steel*)

> The hard life and sacrifices of industrialisation were consciously and enthusiastically accepted by the majority of workers. They had their noses to the grindstone, but they knew that it was for themselves, for a future with dignity and freedom for all workers. Strange as it may appear, the forced labour was a source not only of privation but also of heroism … Soviet youth found heroism in working in factories and on construction sites …

A *The First Five-Year Plan, 1928–33*

The Party adopted Stalin's First Five-Year Plan in 1928. It called for the rapid industrialisation of the country with the greatest emphasis to be placed on the development of heavy industry. The Plan aimed to build new steel works, dams to provide hydro-electric power, factories to make machine tools and tractors as well as expand into new areas of production – chemicals, motor vehicles, synthetic rubber, artificial fibres and electrical goods. It was intended to raise coal output from 35 million tonnes to 150 million tonnes annually and bring about significant increases in the production of iron and steel and in the generation of electricity. Overall, Stalin was looking for an expansion of over three hundred per cent in heavy industry! This would require the building of many new factories as well as the construction of new housing estates for the workers and thousands of kilometres of additional roads, railways and canals. Fear of a future war led Stalin to locate the new industries well inland and far from his country's frontiers. East of the Urals, they would be out of the reach of any invading armies. With the resources of the country being geared to the production of capital rather than consumer goods, in the short term the workers would gain little material benefit for their efforts and their living standards deteriorated. The regimented workers, many of them unskilled and only recently arrived from the countryside, endured appalling conditions. In the factories and mines, scant regard was given to safety regulations and the health of the workers. Piece-work, payment according to how much a worker produced rather than the number of hours he worked, was introduced as was a seven day working week with Sunday no longer considered a rest day. Continually pressurized to an even greater effort, workers were subjected to morale boosting speeches, advertisements and slogans. In *Stalin and Stalinism*, Alan Wood comments on the vocabulary of war used by Party propagandists to promote the Plan – they 'trumpeted of "industrial fronts", "shock troops", "storming fortresses", "creating bastions" and rooting out the enemy.' Factories displayed their latest production figures and challenged workers to improve on them. As the stamina of the workers began to suffer, for some, the strain became intolerable. Absenteeism, lateness and idleness were considered crimes and those found guilty lost their jobs and consequently their pay and factory housing. Those who complained were accused of being troublesome Mensheviks and sent to the gulags in Siberia. Industrial espionage merited the death penalty and there were instances when foreign specialists and engineers were accused of deliberately hindering production and were put on trial. Some factory managers who had failed to produce their quota were shot. In some factories, part of the workforce consisted of slave labour. Largely made up of peasants who had opposed collectivisation, they endured appalling conditions. In *I Was a Soviet Worker*, Andrew Smith, an American who worked in a factory in Moscow, recalled:

> The room contained approximately 500 narrow beds, covered with mattresses filled with straw or dried leaves. There were no pillows or blankets ... Some had no beds and slept on the floor or in wooden boxes. In some cases, beds were used by one shift during the day and by others at night. There were no screens or walls to give any privacy ... There were no closets or wardrobes because each one owned only the clothing on his back.

In other regions, workers froze to death living in tents in sub-zero temperatures or perished from starvation because food supplies failed to reach them. From the safety of his place in exile, Trotsky scathingly wrote the following (which appears in his book *The Revolution Betrayed*, 1929):

> 'State ownership of the means of production does not turn manure into gold and does not surround with a halo of sanctity the sweat-shop system, which wears out the greatest of all productive forces – man. As to the preparation for the change from socialism to communism that will begin at the exactly opposite end – not with the introduction of piece work payment, but its abolition as a relic of barbarism.'

In 1931, there were some who pleaded for a slowing down of the stampede towards industrialisation. Stalin's response was – 'No, comrades, the pace must not be slackened! On the contrary, we must quicken it as much as is within our powers and possibilities. This is dictated by our obligations to the workers and peasants of the USSR ... To slacken the pace would mean to lag behind and those who lag behind are beaten ... '. The unrealistic quotas set meant that not all targets were reached yet, in spite of errors and shortcomings resulting from dislocation and bad planning, the First Five-Year Plan was responsible for many noteworthy achievements. Among the 1500 new enterprises set up were some quite massive in their scale. These included industrial complexes at Dneproges, Magnitogorsk and Kutnetsk, a machine factory and chemical works in the Urals, impressive tractor factories at Chelyabinsk, Kharkov and Stalingrad and car factories in Moscow and Sormovo. The first stage of the Moscow underground was started with its impressive marble walls and chandelier-lit platforms. Canals were also built which connected Moscow with the River Volga and the White Sea with the Baltic Sea. In 1933, Stalin proudly told the people that the First Five-Year Plan had been completed in four years and that it was now time to start on the second stage of his programme of industrialisation. Although it is known that some factory managers produced inflated production figures and that those supplied by the Soviet government were unreliable, it should be remembered that these achievements came at a time when the capitalist countries were suffering the effects of a worldwide slump and mass unemployment.

KEY ISSUE

The impact of the Five-Year Planning on workers.

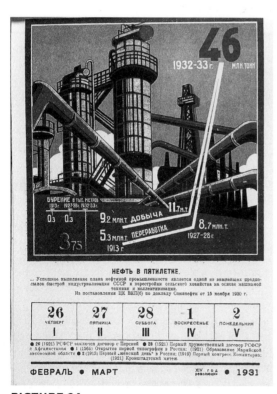

PICTURE 24

Soviet propaganda: the achievements of the First Five-Year Plan

PICTURE 25

Soviet propaganda. A top-hatted capitalist ridicules the plan in 1928 and later winces when faced by its achievements

B *The Second Five-Year Plan, 1933–8*

The planners had more realistic expectations when they set the quotas for the Second Five-Year Plan. With lower production figures demanded, the Second Plan was able to proceed more smoothly and build on the achievements of the First. There was an impressive increase in the manufacture of machinery and this made the Soviet Union less dependent on the import of foreign products. Levels of production of coal and electricity also continued to improve but the performance of the oil and textile industries was disappointing. Although promises of better living and working conditions were not fulfilled and life of the workers and their families remained grim, there were some marginal improvements. There was a small increase in the amount of consumer goods produced and food became more readily available. Early in 1935, bread rationing came to an end and, later in the year, the rationing of other foodstuffs – meat, fats, sugar and potatoes – was abandoned. Even so, Russian housewives often joined lengthy queues only to find all the available stock quickly sold out. With the emergence of Hitler and the Nazis in Germany in 1933, Stalin recognised a need to place greater emphasis on

	First Five-Year Plan (1928–32)	Second Five-Year Plan (1933–7)	Fourth Five-Year Plan (1946–50)
National income			
Official Soviet estimate			
(1926–7 prices)	91.5	96.1	118.9
Jasny estimate			
(1926–7 'real' prices)	70.2	66.5	
Bergson estimate			89.9
Nutter estimate			84.1
Industrial production			
Official Soviet estimate			
(1926–7 prices)	100.7	103.0	116.9
Jasny estimate	69.9	81.2	
Nutter estimate	59.7	93.1	83.8
Kaplan and Moorsteen			
estimate	65.3	75.7	94.9
Official Soviet estimate,			
producer goods			
(1926–7 prices)	127.6	121.3	127.5
Official Soviet estimate,			
consumer goods			
(1926–7 prices)	80.5	85.4	95.7
Agricultural production			
Official Soviet estimates			
(1926–7 prices)	57.8	62.6–76.9	89.9
Jasny estimate	49.6	76.7	
Nutter estimate	50.7	69.0	76.4
Johnson and Kahan			
estimates	52.4	66.1–69.0	79.4

TABLE 54 *Estimates of the extent to which the aims of the Five-Year Plans were fulfilled (From* Stalinist Planning for Economic Growth, 1933–52 *by E. Zaleski, 1980.)*

defence and during the period 1933 to 1938 the production of armaments trebled. A feature of the Second Five-Year Plan was the emergence of Stakhanovism.

See page 287.

The figures provided in Table 55 allow you to compare the official Soviet estimates with those of the Western economists Jasny, Bergson, Nutter, Kaplan, Moorsteen, Johnson and Kahan.

1. *How do the official soviet estimates compare with those of the Western economists?*
2. *In which areas are there major differences between the official Soviet estimates and the estimates of the Western economists?*
3. *Do the Soviet industrial or agricultural estimates appear to be closest to those of the West?*
4. *Which of the Western economists appears to be (i) closest to and (ii) furthest from the official Soviet estimates?*
5. *Suggest some reasons for the discrepancies between the Soviet and Western estimates.*

SOME ACHIEVEMENTS OF THE FIVE-YEAR PLANS

Agricultural
The creation of some 250 000 collective farms or *kolkhozee* which were eventually able to support the growing population of the industrial regions.

Industrial
Rapid growth that, by 1940, allowed the Soviet Union to rival and, in some cases even overtake, Europe's major industrial powers. Foremost amongst these achievements were:

Heavy industry

Chelisbinsk	A major tractor manufacturing centre.
Gorky	A major motor vehicle producing centre.
Magnitogorsk	A metallurgical complex built during the period 1929–31 on the River Ural in south-western Siberia. Close to rich iron-ore deposits it became a leading centre for the manufacture of steel and a symbol of Soviet industrial growth.
Novosibirsk	The administrative centre of Siberia that developed into a major industrial city specialising in the manufacture of machine tools.

PICTURE 26 *Magnitogorsk. An industrial centre founded in 1929, it contained the largest steel plant in the Soviet Union*

Stalingrad	Previously known as Tsaritsyn, this city on the River Volga became one of the Soviet Union's major industrial centres specialising in the manufacture of tractors, river vessels, iron and steel products and chemicals.
Stalino	Situated in a coalfield in the Donetz Basin, apart from its industries the town became the centre of an important railway network.
Transport Belomar canal	Built to connect the White Sea to the Baltic Sea.
Moscow	The construction of the Moscow underground or Metro. Under the supervision of Lazar Kaganovich, a workforce of 75 000 completed the first line in 1935. The complete network was finally opened in 1954. It was to become a showpiece of Soviet achievement.
Moscow–Donetz Railway	Important railway link connecting the capital with the Ukraine.

| Moscow–Volga canal | Completed a waterway that connected the Baltic Sea with the Black Sea. |
| Trans-Siberian Railway | Although originally constructed between 1891 and 1914, during the Second Five-Year Plan, the 7000 km of track were modernised |

Hydro-electric power

| Dneprostroi dam | Impressive dam built across the River Dneiper. |

ALEKSEI STAKHANOV AND STAKHANOVISM

PROFILE

Aleksei Stakhanov worked in the coalmines in the Donbass region. On 30–31 August 1935, as a result of a superhuman effort and the use of his intelligence to use new methods to increase his productivity, he managed to extract 102 tonnes of coal in one six-hour shift. In doing so, he achieved an output of 14 times his expected norm. Acclaimed by the Party for his achievement, he won fame and his example was used to motivate others through the encouragement of 'socialist competition'. Workers formed 'Shock brigades' and attempted to achieve equally remarkable production figures as Stakhanov. The young miner, together with other workers who had won similar distinctions, became known as Stakhanovites. They were given extra pay, free holidays and a chance to visit the Kremlin and receive the honour of either the Order of Lenin or Hero of Soviet Labour from the hand of Stalin, himself. Their achievements increased the pressure on other workers and, as a result, this elitist group attracted the resentment of others who were jealous of their achievements and their privileges. They were shunned, attacked and some, so it is claimed, even murdered. Some even doubt if Stakhanov really existed and suggest that he was an artificially created figure used to tour factories and assume the status of a workers' idol. For the record, another miner, Nikita Isotov, later claimed to have mined over twice as much as Stakhanov in a single shift!

See Picture 27 on page 288.

C *The Third Five-Year Plan, 1938–42*

Stalin's Third Five-Year Plan, approved at the Eighteenth Party Conference, started in 1938. The threat of war created the need to urgently develop the country's military potential and this meant that the production of armaments became the main priority. Plans to produce more consumer goods had to be abandoned and once again workers were pressurised to produce more. In June 1941, after only three years, the Third Five-Year Plan was interrupted by the German invasion of the Soviet Union and the country's involvement in the World War II.

PICTURE 27
The legendary Aleksei
Stakhanov

4 ∽ FIVE-YEAR PLANS – A SUCCESS OR FAILURE?

Soviet claims and statistics relating to the Five-Year Plans lost credibility because they were influenced by the needs of propaganda and by the inflated returns provided by Gosplan. Yet, even though we know that the Plans often failed to reach their targets and were affected by confusion, waste and inefficiency, there is no doubt that Stalin's industrialisation of the Soviet Union was a remarkable achievement. During a period in which rapid economic growth (see below) transformed the country into a modern industrial state, the population of the Soviet Union increased from 147 million to 170 million. In 1926, just 17% of the Russian people lived in towns; by 1939, this had risen to 33%. Stalin had changed the face of the Soviet Union. It was now a country of factories, iron and steel works, hydro-electric dams and much improved systems of transport and communications. By 1940 the USSR had overtaken Britain in iron and steel production and was within reach of Germany. The Russian people, themselves without foreign loans or investment, had financed all. It was true that hundreds of foreign technicians had been employed but an expansion in technical education meant that the country was now able to produce its own skilled workers. But then, against such progress there is the human cost to be considered. If the success of the Five-Year Plans is to be measured against any immediate increase in the prosperity of the Russian people then they were a resounding failure. On the other hand it might be argued that millions had died and the people forced to

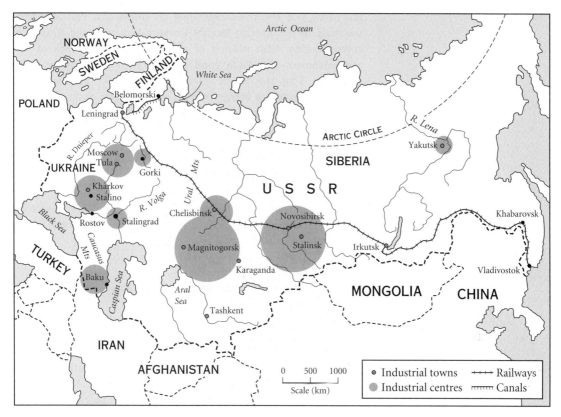

MAP 13 *Expansion of Soviet industry and communications*

endure hard labour, shortages, reduced living standards and the loss of their personal liberties in order to create a better life for future generations of Russians.

	1900	1928	1932	1938	
Coal	20	34	63	130	m. tonnes
Iron and steel	3	8	12	31	m. tonnes
Oil	4	12	22	31	m. tonnes
Electricity	0	1000	5000	11 000	m. watts

TABLE 55 *Five-Year Plans and industrial growth in the Soviet Union*

In *Stalin's Economic Policy* (1986) Malcolm Falkus writes:

> The Russian government was able to perform an economic miracle during the 1930s which, to the outside world, appeared scarcely credible. The country had been transformed from a backward, pre-dominantly agricultural society to a major industrial power. The secret of success lay partly in the supreme power of the state so that it was able to translate into reality its dream of an industrialised society.

But partly also the government met an enthusiastic response from the mass of the Russian factory workers and, after the turmoil of collectivisation, from millions of agricultural workers. Lack of skill and equipment was made good by hard work and reduced living standards. That the Soviet government was able to inspire this response is perhaps a better measure of the success of the plans than any number of cold statistical tables.

5 ⌐ STRUCTURED AND ESSAY QUESTIONS

A *This section consists of questions that might be useful for discussion (or writing answers) as a way of expanding on the chapter and testing understanding of it.*

1. Why did the Bolsheviks consider the peasants, particularly the kulaks, to be politically unreliable?
2. To what extent might collectivisation have allowed Soviet agriculture to benefit from the 'economies of scale'?
3. In what ways did a *kolkhoz* differ from a *sovkhoz*?
4. What did Stalin mean when, in 1930, he excused over zealous Party officials by claiming that they had become 'dizzy with success'?
5. What was the purpose of Mechanical and Tractor Stations (MTS) and how did they operate?
6. In what ways do 'capital goods' differ from 'consumer goods'?
7. What did the authorities hope to achieve by promoting the image of people such as Aleksei Stakhanov?

B *Essay questions.*

1. 'The human cost far outweighed the benefits'. Is this a fair assessment of Stalin's programme of collectivisation?
2. To what extent might the achievements of the Five-Year Plans be considered an economic miracle?
3. With what justification might it be claimed that during the 1930s Russian men and women made huge sacrifices in order to 'create a better life for future generations'?

6 ⌐ MAKING NOTES

In order to help you be sure that you have a full understanding of the nature of Stalin's economic policies, complete the following chart:

	Agriculture	Industry
What name was given to the policies Stalin adopted?		
For what reasons did he adopt these policies?		

What measures did Stalin take to enforce these policies?	
To what extent were these policies a success?	
To what extent were these policies a failure?	
Estimate the human cost of these policies.	

7 ⌐ DOCUMENTARY EXERCISE ON THE AIMS OF STALIN'S ECONOMIC POLICY

Study the sources and then answer the question based on them.

One feature of the history of old Russia was the continual beatings she suffered because of her backwardness... Do you want our socialist fatherland to be beaten and to lose its independence? If you do not want this, you must put an end to this backwardness in the shortest possible time... There is no other way. That is why Lenin said on the eve of the October Revolution: 'Either perish, or overtake and outstrip the advanced capitalist countries.' We are fifty or a hundred years behind the advanced countries. We must make good this difference in ten years.

SOURCE A
From a speech made by Stalin in 1931 to the First All-Union Conference of Leading Personnel of Socialist Industry

The rapid industrialisation drive of the First Five-Year Plan symbolised the grand and dramatic goal of building a new society. Promoted against the background of depression and mass unemployment in the West, the Soviet industrialisation drive did evoke heroic, romantic, and enthusiastic superhuman efforts. According to a contemporary, 'those days were a really romantic, intoxicating time'. 'People were creating by their own hands what had appeared a mere dream before and were convinced in practice that these dreamlike plans were an entirely realistic thing.'

SOURCE B
From H. Kuromiya, Stalin's Industrial Revolution, *1988*

Q

1. *In Source A, what did Stalin mean when he claimed that old Russia had suffered 'continual beatings ... because of her backwardness'?*
2. *In the same source, who were the 'advanced capitalist countries', and in what sense were they 'advanced'?*
3. *Bearing in mind the nature of his audience, what did Stalin hope to achieve by his speech (Source A)?*
4. *What, in Source B, is meant by 'a really romantic and intoxicating time'?*
5. *To what extent was Stalin's speech (Source A) likely to have contributed to the reaction of the Russian people described in Source B?*

Stalin's Russia 1928–39

INTRODUCTION

By the mid-1930s, most Russians were reasonably content because, although their living standards had improved little, they were conscious that in working to transform their country into a modern industrial state they were creating a better future for themselves and their children. However, apart from the changes in the countryside and the industrial regions, there were other significant developments taking place more generally. After the Revolution, Lenin worked to impose Marxist principles on the Russian people. In *Das Kapital*, Karl Marx had written, 'The evils of a capitalist society cannot be abolished by reform ... but only by the destruction of the whole capitalist economy and the establishment of a new classless society. In his struggle to achieve egalitarianism, the total equality of all Russian citizens, Lenin imposed measures intended to remove all bourgeois influences from everyday life. In forcing through his programme of industrialisation, Stalin soon discovered that Marxist idealism did not work when faced by the realities of the economic situation. Put simply, men were not prepared to study to gain qualifications and skills and then work for the same pay as an unskilled labourer. There had to be incentives in the form of pay differentials – greater rewards for those with the greater skills.

1 ↜ TOWARDS STALINISM

To start with, Stalin went along with the old Marxist–Leninist ideals but as his position became more secure, he encouraged changes in emphasis and approach to both economic and social life. These changes were not the result of any softening in his policies but were forced upon him by two considerations. Firstly, the achievements of the First and Second Five-Year Plans had been dependent on the use of foreign engineers and draughtsmen. Stalin wanted to provide educational facilities that would allow the Soviet Union to produce its own highly skilled technicians. Secondly, as Hitler's aggressive intentions became increasing obvious so did the prospect of a European war and consequently, part of the Third Five-Year Plan was designed to arm the nation in readiness for such an eventuality. As far as work and earnings were concerned, the Marxist principle of 'From each according to his ability, to each according to his needs' was no longer sustainable. Stalin recognised that incentives and bonus payments would have to be introduced to attract men and women of the right calibre into further education and then encourage them to employ their skills in industry. Marxists tended to pay less regard to the need for formal education but Stalin reversed this and ordered a return to traditional teaching methods in schools and a major expansion in the building of new technical colleges and universities. Stalin also encouraged changes in aspects of social and domestic life. He rejected the Marxist view that marriage was a bourgeois institution and therefore obsolete and supported a return to family traditions. Marriage was again encouraged, divorce made more difficult and abortion declared illegal. Marxist theory was that, as a result of the new social climate instilled by communism, crime would 'wither away'. The reality was that this forecast was far from the truth and the country had experienced something of a crime wave caused by the activities of its younger generation. To counter this, discipline and the wearing of school uniform was again enforced in schools and a new strict criminal code introduced. Immediately after the Revolution, the needs of egalitarianism meant that the use of all titles prohibited and the acceptable style of address when greeting others was 'comrade'. In the Red Army, all ranks and the wearing of insignia were abolished. As far as the nation's heritage was concerned, past history was regarded as irrelevant and former national heroes were dishonoured. Literature and the arts had to conform to strict Marxist principles and concentrate on extolling the achievements of the proletariat. A campaign was launched against all forms of religious belief and atheism encouraged. Stalin reversed much of this. Whilst he continued to pay lip service to egalitarianism, pay differentials were introduced in industry and rank and the wearing of insignia were restored in the army. The great figures of Russian history such as Ivan the Terrible, Peter the Great and Catherine the Great were rehabilitated and greater freedom of expression allowed to writers and artists – particularly if they extolled the virtues of collectivisation, the achievements of the Five Year Plans and the qualities of Stalin. A consequence of these developments was the emergence of a new middle-class that Party hard-liners considered as being a step back towards a return to old bourgeois ways.

> **KEY ISSUES**
>
> *To what extent did Stalin remain loyal to Marxist principles?*

MARXIST–LENINISM AND STALINISM – A COMPARISON

	The Marxist–Leninist regime	*The Stalinist regime*
Wages	Based on the Marxist principle of 'From each according to his ability, to each according to his need.'	Recognition of the need for wage differentials – 'From each according to his ability, to each according to his work.'
Education	Less regard paid to the need for formal education.	Return to formal education methods and the imposition of discipline.
The family	Marriage considered to be bourgeois and outdated.	Return to family values. Marriage again encouraged, divorce made more difficult and abortion declared illegal.

(continued overleaf)

	The Marxist–Leninist regime	*The Stalinist regime*
Law and Order	Under communism, crime expected 'to wither away'.	New strict criminal code introduced.
Heritage	Past history disregarded and heroes dishonoured.	Some rehabilitation of the great figures of the past.
Religion	Campaign against religion and atheism encouraged.	Some marginal increase in religious tolerance.
Art and culture	To conform to communist principles. Intended to illustrate the achievements of the proletariat.	Some greater freedom of expression but still expected to extol the achievements of the Five-Year Plans and the qualities of Stalinism.
Armed services	Rank and the wearing of insignia abolished.	Rank and the wearing of insignia restored.

A *The emergence of a new Russian bourgeoisie*

The new emphasis on further education and the introduction of pay differentials in the form of higher wages and bonuses resulted in the creation of a new middle class of citizens with all the trappings of the former bourgeoisie of Tsarist times. These men and women, the engineers, scientists, doctors and academics dressed well, owned cars and town flats, stayed at hotels, ate at restaurants and enjoyed holidays. Leading ballet dancers and artists also formed part of this new privileged group together with Party functionaries and bureaucrats – the administrators and officials who ran the Party machine. The historian Elizabeth Mauchline Roberts writes in her book *Stalin: Man of Steel* published in 1968:

By 1935, it was almost impossible for a man to attend a Government evening reception without wearing 'tails', once thought to be a symbol of the detested capitalist... Their homes were like those of wealthy middle-class Victorians with plush upholstered furniture, satin-covered cushions and lace antimacassars with the walls covered with pictures of scenes from Russian legends. The wealthy classes enjoyment of these material possessions was increased by the knowledge that, like the aristocracy of old, they could bequeath them to their children. This right made it possible for the new class to be self-perpetuating, as did Stalin's introduction of school fees, for they meant that only the children of the rich could afford the kind of education that in turn would entitle them to be members of the privileged class.

In 1936, Stalin granted the Russian people a new constitution. It was, he claimed, 'the only truly democratic constitution in the world'.

2 ↷ THE NEW CONSTITUTION OF 1936

In 1933, the republics that made up the Soviet Union totalled 11. Later, this was to grow to 15 following the annexation of the Baltic provinces, Estonia, Latvia and Lithuania as well as Moldova, formerly a region of Romania. In addition, there were smaller administrative units such as Oblasts, Okrugs and Rayons. The government of the country was based on a pyramid of Soviets. Stalin's new constitution which, replaced that of 1924, was largely the work of Nicolai Bukharin who had changed his views and been accepted back into the Party. The Supreme Soviet, the law making body of the USSR, was to consist of two houses of equal authority – the Soviet of the Union and the Soviet of Nationalities. The Soviet of the Union contained some 750 elected deputies representing the constituencies whilst the Soviet of Nationalities was composed of 630 members from the republics and other autonomous regions and the nationalities that made up the Soviet Union. The two houses elected the 33 members of the Presidium. The President of the Presidium was regarded as the head of state. Elsewhere, each republic elected its own Soviet and there were also Soviets to manage the affairs of the Oblasts and other smaller administrative regions. In reality, the Supreme Soviet existed mainly to approve the legislation placed before it by the secretariat of the Communist Party. The Communist Party of the Soviet Union was the only political party allowed to exist. The main decision-making body of the Party was the Political Bureau or Politburo and, since it controlled the actions of all government departments, it was here that the real power lay. The direction of Party policy lay in the hands of the Central Committee that included members and non-voting members or candidate members. The most influential position was that of General Secretary of the Party.

> **KEY ISSUE**
>
> *Just how democratic was the Soviet system of government?*

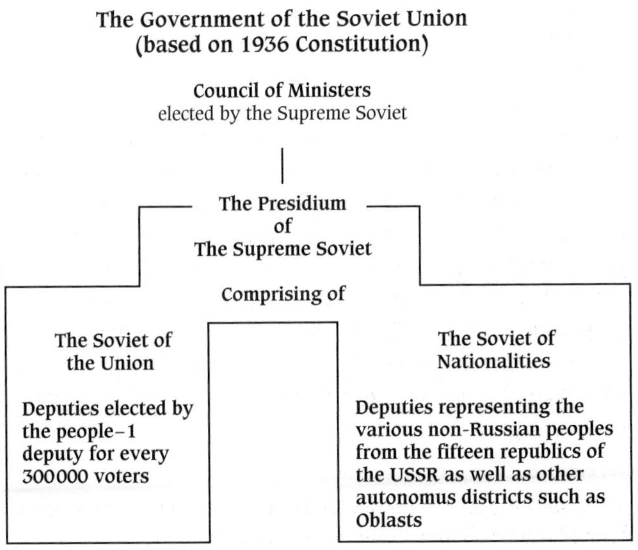

**The Government of the Soviet Union
(based on 1936 Constitution)**

Council of Ministers
elected by the Supreme Soviet

**The Presidium
of
The Supreme Soviet**

Comprising of

**The Soviet of
the Union**

Deputies elected by
the people–1
deputy for every
300000 voters

**The Soviet of
Nationalities**

Deputies representing the
various non-Russian peoples
from the fifteen republics of
the USSR as well as other
autonomus districts such as
Oblasts

DIAGRAM 20
The Government of the Soviet Union (based on 1936 Constitution)

DIAGRAM 21

The Organisation of the Communist Party of the Soviet Union (CPSU)

At election time, voting was by secret ballot and universal suffrage was extended to all men and women aged over 18 with the only exceptions being the insane and those serving prison sentences. However, candidates had to be nominated by Communist Party organisations. In effect this meant that, at election time, in each constituency the voters had to choose from a list approved by the Party so that the winning candidate was invariably a Communist. Everyone was expected to vote and this explains why the turn out in a Soviet election would be in the region of 98% to 99%. Elections were festive occasions and were used to rally support for and register appreciation of the achievements of the Communist Party.

The articles of the new constitution make interesting reading. The first dealt with the organisation of Soviet society:

Article 1. The Union of the Soviet Socialist Republics is a socialist state of workers and peasants.

Article 3. In the USSR all power belongs to the working people of town and country as represented by the Soviets of Working People's Deputies.

Article 4. The socialist system of economy and the socialist ownership of the means of production firmly established as a result of the abolition of the capitalist system of economy … and the abolition of the exploitation of man by man, constitute the economic foundation of the USSR.

Article 6. The land, its natural deposits, waters, forests, mills, factories, mines, rail, water and air transport, banks, post, telegraph and telephones … belong to the whole people.

A number of articles dealt with the rights to own property and to work:

> **Article 9.** Alongside the socialist system of economy … the law permits the small private economy of individual peasants and handicraftsmen based on their own personal labour and not involving the exploitation of others.
>
> **Article 10.** The right of citizens to personal ownership of their incomes from work and of their savings, of their dwelling houses, their household furniture and utensils and articles for personal use, as well as the right of inheritance of personal property, is protected by law.

Then there is the article that covers work and the payment for work. This includes a significant departure from previously held Marxist theory:

> **Article 12.** In the USSR work is a duty and a matter of honour for every able-bodied citizen in accordance with the principle – 'He who does not work, neither shall he eat'. The principle applied in the USSR is that of socialism – 'From each according to his ability, to each according to his work'.

As for the rights and duties of citizens, the constitution said:

> **Article 118.** Citizens of the USSR have the right to work …
>
> **Article 119.** Citizens of the USSR have the right to rest and leisure …
>
> **Article 120.** Citizens of the USSR have the right to maintenance in old age and also in case of sickness or loss of capacity to work.
>
> **Article 121.** Citizens of the USSR have the right to education.
>
> **Article 122.** Women in the USSR are accorded equal rights with men in all spheres of economic, state, cultural, social and political life.

Article 125 comprised of what was in effect is a bill of rights:

> **Article 125.** … citizens of the USSR are guaranteed by law:
> - a. freedom of speech;
> - b. freedom of the press;
> - c. freedom of assembly, including the holding of mass meetings;
> - d. freedom to hold street processions and demonstrations.

As you can see, the new constitution of the Soviet Union was democratic on paper but, in practice, fell far short of being 'the only truly democratic constitution in the world' if indeed it was democratic at all. Even though its membership only totalled one and a half million and it could hardly claim to be truly representative of the Russian people, the electoral system allowed the Communist Party to remain fully in control. In any case, the Supreme Soviet seldom met and had no real power. The Soviet Union remained effectively governed by the Presidium that was made up of leading members of the Communist Party and, above them, the imposing figure of Stalin. Even the freedoms promised in Article 125 never really materialised. No opposition parties were allowed and the secret police, who in 1934 changed their name from OGPU to NKVD, kept a close watch on the people and insured there was no open criticism of Stalin or his policies. The foreign press made much of reports that at elections the winning candidate, the only candidate, almost invariably gained 99% of the votes, that election results were sometimes declared before polling had taken place and that the number of votes cast often exceeded the total electorate!

3 ⌒ LIFE IN THE SOVIET UNION

A *The Soviet education system*

After the Revolution, there was a reaction against learning and scholarship. Children under the age of six were taught by *babushkas* or their grandmothers and the responsibility for providing schools was handed to the collective farms and industrial enterprises. These were short-term measures and some even spoke of the need for schools 'withering away'. Traditional teaching methods were abandoned and only the most elementary instruction given often by adults who were themselves barely literate. It was said that such education as was necessary should be achieved through 'a system of learning through productive labour'. In Moscow, the head of the Institute for Educational Research stated that the *metod proektov*, the project method, was the 'one and only Marxist and democratic method of teaching'. The project method involved sending children into factories where they worked alongside workers. Afterwards they prepared reports on what they had seen and done. Where schools existed, places were allocated on a quota basis according to class. The children of the proletariat were the most favoured whilst those of the former bourgeoisie were assigned only a minimal number of places. Some were denied access to any sort of education. The few universities provided instruction in a very limited range of practical subjects taught to a low level. With examinations scrapped, the quality of student achievement was poor and the drop-out rate extremely high with some three-quarters of all students failing to complete their courses. Teachers and academics were generally considered relics of the discredited bourgeoisie and were baited, humiliated and driven out of their profession.

Under Stalin, the Soviet education system changed radically. As the need for a sound education system was recognised, the project method was abandoned and plans were made to extend nursery, primary, secondary and further higher education across the country. By the mid-1930s, the Soviet Union had one of the most centralised education systems in the world. Experimentation was scrapped and traditional

Q

To what extent did the Soviet attitude to education change during the Stalinist period?

teaching methods restored as was strict classroom discipline and the requirement to wear school uniform. For girls, hair worn in plaits was compulsory. Nursery schools were provided for those under the age of three whilst those aged three to seven attended infant schools or kindergarten. This was followed by 8 years at secondary school where attendance was compulsory up to the age of 15. A range of subjects was taught as a common core and schools stressed the need for obedience, hard work and loyalty. Pupils were also subject to a degree of political indoctrination. With over a 100 different languages spoken across the Soviet Union, pupils were allowed to study in their own native tongue but the learning of Russian was made compulsory. A system of rigorous examinations was introduced and parents had to make some financial contribution during the final years at the secondary stage of education. The overall responsibility for the provision of education lay with the *Narkompros*, the People's Commissariat for Enlightenment, with policy decisions made by the Central Committee of the Communist Party. Amongst the pioneers of educational reform were Anatoly Lunarcharsky and Alexander Bubnov. The charismatic Lunarcharsky, known as the 'Poet of the Revolution', was an educated and cultured man as well as a dedicated Communist. He was to be responsible for turning the country's former stately homes into museums. Bubnov, a staunch supporter of Stalin's reforms, was responsible for ending the period of experiment and returning to traditional methods of teaching. Each of the republics of the Soviet Union had its own ministry and, in each locality, members of the local Soviet appointed a school board. The boards selected the headteachers who, in turn, appointed their own teaching staff. Advancement in the teaching profession often depended on one's standing in the Communist Party. With the status of teachers and lecturers restored, young people were encouraged to enter higher education and working men and women to improve themselves by joining adult education classes. *Rabfak*, the Workers' Faculty, which was created specifically to improve the level of education of working people, provided such opportunities. Amongst those to benefit were Nikita Khrushchev, the future Russian leader, and the aircraft designer, S.V. Ilyushin. In the new universities and technical colleges special emphasis was placed on the study of mathematics, science and technology. Entry to higher education was by competitive entrance examination, and with the restriction on students from non-proletarian families removed, there was a rush to secure places. To start with, a fixed percentage of places in higher education were allocated to women. This soon became unnecessary and by 1940, nearly 60% of all undergraduates were women. From a racial viewpoint, some 80% of students were ethnic Russians, Ukrainians and Jews. Russian Jews, who only accounted for two per cent of the population of the Soviet Union, showed their enthusiasm for learning by taking up 13% of the university places. By 1936, the country's higher education system was producing large numbers of well-trained engineers, scientists, doctors and teachers.

At all levels, the purpose of education was seen as preparing students to play their part in the life of a modern industrial state. As future citizens of a Communist state, they were expected to show a desire to work, patriotism in the form of love for Mother Russia, an appreciation of Party ideology, a rejection of religion and a hatred of capitalism. To help insure this, the Communist Party exercised tight control over textbooks and the curricula. The whole system was geared, as Stalin himself put it, to creating 'the new Soviet man' who thought and acted as instructed by the Party.

B *Soviet Youth Movements*

In common with all totalitarian regimes, the rulers of the Soviet Union tried to influence and indoctrinate its young people by encouraging them to enrol in one of the Communist youth organisations. The aim of all was to spread Communist ideology and prepare the young to be part of the next generation of Communists. For the very young there was the Little Octobrists. At the age of nine, they could transfer to the All-Union Lenin Pioneer Organisation. Organised into brigades, they now took part in politically orientated educational and recreational activities. At 14, they became eligible for membership of the Komsomol.

Komsomol is the abbreviated form of *Vsesoyuzny Leninsky Kommunistichesky,* the All-Union Leninist Communist League of Youth. The movement, which included young people aged between 14 and 28, first came into being in 1918. It was made up of members of various Communist youth groups that had been involved in the Revolution and were now brought together to form fighting groups needed to support the Red Army in the civil war. After 1922, it reverted to the more normal activities associated with youth movements and encouraged its members to engage in sporting, educational and health activities as well as industrial projects. Membership of Komsomol brought with it numerous advantages. Members were favoured in matters of employment and promotion and were more likely to be awarded educational scholarships. More important, active participation in the activities of Komsomol could become a major consideration when seeking much coveted membership of the Communist Party.

C *Women and the family in Soviet Society*

During the processes of collectivisation and industrialisation, Russian women and their children shared the same hard-ships as their menfolk. Whole peasant families endured hunger and death at the time of the famine whilst kulak women and children were not spared the horrors of transportation to Siberia and the tortuous existence of life in the labour camps. After the Revolution, the Bolsheviks applied Marxist philosophy to marriage and family life. Marriage, a bourgeois institution intended to exploit and degrade women, was not encouraged. Those who married did so at a civil ceremony. This was part of a general policy to downplay religion and reduce the significance of church ritual. The truth was that the employment of women was essential to Stalin's plans to industrialise the Soviet Union. Women were active at all levels of industry and child bearing did not absolve mothers from their commitment to work. Granted minimum maternity leave, mothers left their children with elderly relatives. Mothers also had to undergo the indignity of transferring the milk from their breasts to bottles so that the feeding of infants would not interrupt their work routine. Many children that were orphaned or abandoned took to the streets and engaged in criminal activities. In 1937, Stalin wrote:

'The triumph of socialism has filled women with enthusiasm and mobilised the women of our Soviet land to become active in culture, to master machinery, to develop a knowledge of science and to be active in the struggle for high labour productivity.'

Control of policy decisions relating to women was placed in the hands of the women's section of the Central Committee, the *Zhenotdel*.

THE *ZHENOTDEL*

The *Zhenotdel*, the Party's Women's Bureau, was set up to encourage Russian women to play a more active part in the political and economic life of the country. Its leaders included the eminent Party members and feminists Aleksandra Kollontai and Inessa Armand. Both originally from upper class families, Kollontai was the daughter of a general. Although married to an officer in the Tsarist army, she became an active revolutionary and was forced to live in exile in the United States. She returned to Russia in 1917 and, after 1920, became the first commissar for social welfare. Later she joined the diplomatic service and was the first woman to hold ambassadorial rank. Armand, twice married and the mother of five children, was a close friend of Lenin. She became the first director of *Zhenotdel*. Representatives of the Bureau toured factories to make sure that the laws intended to protect the rights of women were being enforced. *Zhenotdel* championed the cause of female emancipation and their campaigns contributed to the undermining of the influence of the family. They saw to it that divorce was made easier and that contraception and abortion were freely available to all women. By 1934, in Moscow, the capital city, 37% of all marriages ended in divorce whilst nationally the number of abortions was three times greater than that of live births. Believing that education provided women with the best chance of improving their status, they encouraged women to study and organised childcare facilities to enable them to do so. From the start, many men, including leading Party members and even groups of women workers, opposed their policies. Those who lived in the Soviet Unions Muslim provinces particularly resented their attempts to abolish **polygamy** and the traditions of the seclusion of women, purdah. Although the number of women in the nation's workforce increased rapidly, *Zhenotdel* was unsuccessful

PROFILE

polygamy marriage to more than one person at a time.

in its attempt to enroll them as Communist Party members. By 1930, less than 15% of women had applied for membership. In addition, there was no female representation on the country's ruling Presidium and very little on the Central Committee.

Stalin, concerned at the decline of the family in national life, recognised the need to bring about change in the Party's attitude to women. A propaganda campaign emphasised that the ideal woman was a good wife and mother as well as being a good worker. In 1930, the *Zhenotdel* was closed down since it was claimed that it had achieved its aims. Although the majority of women workers were employed in traditional female occupations – clerical work, nursing, teaching and the textile industries – a great many worked shoulder to shoulder with their male counterparts in the steel and engineering industries and were encouraged to become *stakhanovi*. Some worked in coalmines and they also contributed fully to the more menial jobs of street cleaning and refuse collection. In spite of the claim that women had the same pay, promotion prospects and status as men, in reality this was seldom the case. As the 1930s progressed so the authorities accepted that the family unit was central to national stability and traditional attitudes to women and family values began to reassert themselves. Marriage was again encouraged and promiscuity, contraception and abortion frowned upon. Women were once again expected to be central to family life. The happy family was once again fashionable in the Soviet Union. As Martin McCauley has written – 'Nowhere are the contradictions of Stalinism greater than in the reluctant acceptance of the family'. As for the extent of employment of women, the figures speak for themselves. During the period 1928–40, the number of working women rose from 3 to 13 million. During the World War II, this rose further to 16 million and women comprised 56% of the workforce. In addition, during the war, some 800 000 Russian women were recruited into the armed services and over 70% fought as combat soldiers. There is a legend that a husband and wife went as far as to secure Stalin's permission to obtain their own tank and fight together at the front!

D *Stalinism and religion*

In 1844, Karl Marx wrote 'Religion is the sign of the oppressed creature, the feelings of a heartless world and the spirit of conditions which are unspiritual. It is the opium of the people.' In equating religion with opium, Marx was expressing the view that religion, like a drug, allowed people to escape the pain of their everyday lives. He also believed that the ruling class used organised religion for their own purposes. It was a means of convincing the downtrodden working classes that they should accept their status in life since it was the station 'into which God had called them'. He pointed out that the Churches possessed considerable influence over the lives of the people, possessed great material wealth and were themselves part of the ruling class, a 'Pillar of the

PICTURE 28
Used for propaganda purposes, a Soviet cartoon identifies the enemies of socialism.

Establishment'. Lenin's views were identical. In his *Collected Works*, published in 1922, Lenin writes.

> 'Religion is one of the forms of spiritual oppression which everywhere weigh upon the masses of the people crushed by continuous toil for others, by poverty and loneliness... Religion teaches those who toil in poverty all their lives to be resigned and patient in this world and consoles them with the hope of reward in heaven.'

Although Marx favoured religious tolerance and was against the persecution of people for their religious beliefs, after the Revolution the Bolsheviks set out to eradicate religion. Their immediate target was the Russian Orthodox Church and other Christian sects in Russia but they also turned their attention to the Muslims and Buddhists who lived in their Asian republics. During the Civil War priests and their congregations fell victim to Bolshevik atrocities. In 1929, a law was passed which made it illegal to hold religious ceremonies outside church buildings and congregations could only gather if they had first been licensed. The situation worsened during period of collectivisation. Churches were closed and priests, often accused of being capitalist agents or of being in league with the kulaks, were arrested and murdered. They were **disenfranchised**, subjected to higher rates of taxation and their children barred from attending schools. Muslims were prohibited from practicing Islamic law. Fasting during the Holy Month of Ramadan was forbidden, women were encouraged to abandon the veil and men and women were not allowed to take part in pilgrimages to Mecca. In spite of the fact that many leading Party members – Trotsky, Bukharin, Kamenev and Zinoviev – were themselves Jews, Russian Jewry suffered the same persecution as others. Jewish schools, libraries and synagogues were closed and the study of Hebrew forbidden. As we shall see, many religious leaders

disenfranchised denied the right to vote.

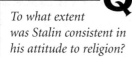

To what extent was Stalin consistent in his attitude to religion?

and high ranking priests became victims of the Terror. The campaign against religion was orchestrated by the League of Godless. As part of the attack on church institutions marriage became a civil ceremony, the wearing of wedding rings was frowned upon, the religious observance of Sunday was abolished, and religious teaching was abolished in schools and replaced by anti-religious teaching. Many churches were converted into anti-religious museums and those who persisted with their religious beliefs were openly ridiculed. Within the Party, a good Communist was expected to be an atheist. In 1935, the campaign against religion eased. Easter novelties and Christmas trees were sold, the children of priests allowed to attend school and a number of churches reopened. This respite did not last long and with the start of the Terror, Stalin renewed his attack on the Church which was estimated to be still actively supported by over half the people. To counter this, the Church went underground and priests survived by abandoning their clerical robes so that they were indistinguishable from the rest of the population. As concern about Nazi Germany and the prospect of war grew, so Stalin again relented. In 1941, in the needs of national unity, he went as far as to ask the Church to support the war effort.

E *The arts – a cultural revolution?*

Although many Russian artists, writers and musicians fled abroad in 1917, it was the hope of those that remained that the Bolshevik Revolution would allow them to enjoy greater freedom of expression. It was certainly true that the early 1920s witnessed a period of great creativity in all forms of the arts. Previously Lenin had expressed the view that access to the arts should be freely available to the masses and to help achieve this *Narkompros*, the People's Commissariat for Enlightenment, took over galleries and museums and arranged for new ones to be built. Once Stalin was in power, all forms of creative art were directed towards *partiinost* – serving the needs of the Party. His aim was to bring about a 'cultural revolution'.

LITERATURE

After the triumph of the Bolsheviks, many Russian writers emigrated and continued their work abroad. Those that remained had to adapt their talents to the needs of the new regime. In the 1920s, writers wishing to get their works published had to join the Association of Proletarian Writers (RAPP). The Association urged writers to concentrate on the lives and achievements of the proletariat and the needs of socialism. Consequently the period 1928–31 turned into what Martin McCauley has described as years of 'the glorification of the man in the street'. This situation was short-lived. Stalin demanded major changes and, in 1932, RAPP was abolished and replaced by the Union of Soviet Writers. The Union imposed the new political correctness on writers and greatly reduced their creative freedom. Andrei Zhdanov stated that the aim of writers should now be to achieve 'Socialist Realism'. It was a switch from writing about the masses to writing about the achievements of collectivisation, industrial developments, and to glorify Stalin. The change also marked the rediscovery of Russian history and the great national heroes of the past. Amongst the most famous Russian writers of the time were Maxim Gorki and Mikhail Sholokhov.

Maxim Gorki (1868–1936) was the pen name of Alexsei Peshkov. Orphaned at the age of nine, he was brought up by his grandparents and experienced hard times as he struggled to survive as a down and out or by taking part-time manual jobs. He first became famous as a writer in tsarist times but was arrested for his revolutionary activities and sent to live abroad. Gorki returned to Russia in 1917 and found his sympathy with the Bolsheviks strained by the unbridled violence of the Civil War. He had considerable influence with the Bolsheviks and tried to build a bridge between the old classical culture of tsarist times and the requirements of the Soviet regime. Between 1921 and 1928, he lived abroad in Italy but returned to the Soviet Union and helped to develop the idea of Socialist Realism. He died in 1936 whilst undergoing medical treatment but some suspect that he was murdered on Stalin's orders. In spite of his fame in Russia, few of his works became widely read in the western world. After his death, his birthplace, Nizhni Novgorod, was renamed Gorki in his honour.

Mikhail Sholokhov (1905–84) came from the Don Cossack region of Russia. Of mixed background, his father worked in many occupations whilst his mother was illiterate and of peasant stock. During the Civil War, Sholokhov joined the Red Army but, afterwards, was reduced to supporting himself by doing manual labour. His first book, *Tales of the Don*, an account of the strife within a family during the Civil War, was published in 1925. In 1932, Sholokhov joined the Communist Party and, in 1937, was elected to the Supreme Soviet. Party members thought his criticism of the treatment of the kulaks and the mass arrests in 1938 amounted to treason but Stalin saw to it that he was spared. By far his most famous book was *Quiet Flows the Don*, a novel that covered events in the Soviet Union between 1928 and 1940. In 1941, he was awarded the Stalin Prize for Literature. In his later years, Sholokhov invariably followed the official Party line of the day and by the end of his life, some 79 million copies of his works had been sold published in 84 languages. In later years, the dissident Russian writer, Alexander Solzhenitsyn alleged that *Quiet Flows the Don* had been **plagiarised** from the works of a little known Cossack writer.

plagiarised writing or ideas copied or stolen from another.

ART AND ARCHITECTURE
In 1920, Lenin proclaimed himself to be a 'barbarian who disliked Expressionism, Futurism, Cubism and all the other isms.' Referring to

the limited appeal of art, he said, 'it does not matter what art gives to hundreds, or even thousands, out of a total population numbering millions. Art belongs to the people.' For a while after the Revolution, a modernistic movement amongst artists was allowed to flourish in Russia. However, before the Ministry of Culture could impose the traditional styles of Socialist Realism, many of the country's greatest artists moved abroad. Art had to portray people, scenes and events as they really were and could not be abstract. The abstract artists that remained had their work condemned and it was never exhibited. Among the leading artists of the day were Georgi Nisski and Vera Mukina. Many others had to be content to produce paintings and posters that illustrated the achievements of socialism. Similarly in architecture early experimentation was soon brought to an end and Soviet architects had to concentrate on austere designs that were soon to produce functional high rise blocks of flats and offices. The exception was the so-called 'wedding cake' architecture used in the construction of the new Academy of Sciences in Moscow. One of the country's most noted architects was Alexei Shchusev who designed the Lenin mausoleum in the Red Square.

MUSIC

At the time of the Revolution in 1917 some of the country's greatest composers and musicians chose to leave Russia. These included Nicolai Medtner, Sergei Rachmanivov, Igor Stravinsky, Nicolai and Alexander Tcherepnin and Sergai Prokofiev. Prokofiev worked in the United States until the mid-1930s when he chose to return to the Soviet Union. The Association of Contemporary Music, established in 1923, supported experimentation and modern music but in the 1930s, in common with other art forms, music had to conform to the Stalinist requirement of Socialist Realism. Music considered modern or *avant garde* was no longer acceptable. Composers had to belong to Composers' Union and new works had to have 'a socialist content and be expressed in a musical language that ordinary people could easily understand'. It was also supposed to 'rejoice in the glorious potential of life under Communism' and extol the country's industrial achievements. Typical of this was the symphony, the *Iron Foundry*, written by Alexander Mossolov, a composer later removed from the Composers' Union for being drunk and behaving lewdly. He spent the next eight years in a Siberian *gulag*. Among the greatest composers of the 1930s were Sergai Prokofiev and Dmitri Shostakovich and Aram Khachaturian.

PROFILE

Sergai Prokoviev (1891–1953), whose mother was a gifted pianist, was excused military service during the World War I in order to continue his musical studies. After he returned home from self-imposed exile in 1935, he composed his most famous work, *Peter and the Wolf*, as well as the score for the film *Alexander Nevsky*. Because he slavishly complied with the requirements of the Soviet authorities, his work was criticised elsewhere for being too simple and naïve. **Dmitry Shostakovich** (1905–84) was criticised for failing to uphold the principles of Socialist Realism and had to adjust his style so that it was more cheerful and less complicated. His Fifth Symphony (1937) proved acceptable to the authorities and helped him to re-establish his reputation. He wrote many symphonies, concertos and choral works. The Armenian, **Aram Khachaturian** (1903–78) whose *Song of Stalin* (1937) won him great popularity, still tended to go his own way and this irritated of Soviet officialdom. His most famous work was his *Sabre Dance* that many years later made the pop charts in Britain.

THE CINEMA

When Lenin came to power in 1917, he quickly recognised the propaganda value of the cinema in indoctrinating the largely illiterate masses with socialist principles. Although the cinema was still in its infancy and the films made were silent and in black and white, to him the cinema presented a unique opportunity of encouraging the Russian people to share his ideals. The Bolshevik leader went as far as to describe the cinema as 'the most important art'. As a film historian has written in the book *Idols and Icons. A Survey of Russian and Soviet Cinema* by Mike Hertenstein, 1999.

The Bolsheviks gained power by quickly seizing all possible means of communication. Their Revolution sent the Russian film establishment fleeing the country and vanishing into history's dustbin. The Soviets had to rebuild with a younger generation – one imbued with, and eager to share, the Communist vision.

The new Soviet film industry followed the official style imposed by Socialist Realism. An outstanding Russian filmmaker and a man subsequently acclaimed as one of the greatest film directors of all time was Sergei Eisenstein.

PROFILE

Sergei Eisenstein (1881–1948) was born in Riga in Latvia. He first trained as a civil engineer and architect before serving in the Red Army during the Civil War. He first made his mark in the cinema as a stage designer but, after 1917, was one of those given the task of re-establishing the Soviet film industry. His first film, *Strike*, made in 1924 established his reputation. The film, that told the story of a strike that was brutally put down by the authorities, was considered a brilliant piece of Communist propaganda. Eisenstein soon proved himself one of the great masters and innovators of the silent film era. His most famous film was *The Battleship Potemkin* made in 1925. Now considered a cinema classic, it covered an episode in the 1905 revolution. In 1948, an international panel judged it to be the best film ever made. His later films included *Alexander Nevski* (1938) and *Ivan the Terrible* (1945). His main rival was another

Russian, **Vsevoled Pudofkin** (1893–1953). His films were largely based on the exploits of heroic characters.

There were also other art forms that flourished under Stalin largely because of the appeal to the Soviet proletariat. Classical ballet had been popular in Russia since the mid-eighteenth century. The most famous companies in the Soviet Union were the Bolshoi, in Moscow, and the Academic Theatre in Leningrad. In 1935, it was renamed the Kirov Ballet following the assassination of the city's Party leader. Being even more egalitarian in its appeal, the circus was considered to be on a par with ballet and opera. An Englishman, Philip Astley, first introduced the circus to Russia in the late eighteenth century. In Stalinist Russia, the leading company was the Moscow State Circus.

See page 309.

4 ⌐ THE TERROR AND THE PURGES

After the near bloodless Revolution of October 1917, the country suffered civil war, famine, imposed collectivisation and industrialisation, mass murder and class genocide. Terror was not new to the Russian people. Between 1928 and 1934, during the First Five-Year Plan, there were a series of staged show trials intended to make engineers and technicians the scapegoats for any mechanical breakdown or failure to reached specified production targets.

A *The Shakhty and other trials*

In 1928, at the coal-mining town of Shakhty in the Donets Basin, 53 engineers were arrested and accused of being German agents and sabotaging production. They were found guilty and 11 shot whilst the remainder were sent to the labour camps. This, the first show trial, was followed by the first executions for economic crimes. It triggered a period of terror against so-called bourgeois specialist workers the majority of which had acquired their professional qualifications in Tsarist times and were now discovered to be dangerous Trotskyist agents. By 1930, political leaning was considered more important than skill in qualifying to be a specialist technician. In 1933, six British engineers employed by the Metropolitan Vickers Electrical Company were arrested by the secret police. This led to a crisis in Anglo-Soviet relations. In the same year, eight members of a so-called Industrial Party were put on trial and charged with being involved with foreigners in a plot to sabotage industry. The charges made against individuals were absurd. A scientist investigating the use of chemicals to destroy weeds was accused of plotting to ruin the Soviet harvest; a marine biologist was charged with planning to pollute Russian rivers and so destroy the nation's fish stocks. During this time, the main instrument of terror was the secret police who frequently changed their name but never their function. They were the watchdogs of state security that kept an eye on the Russian people and weeded out dissidents and malcontents.

KEY ISSUE

The Terror – the role of the Soviet secret police.

TIMELINE

The Soviet Secret Police

1917–22	Cheka (The All-Russian Commission to Fight Counter-Revolution, Sabotage and Speculation)	Felix Dzerzhinsky
1922–34	OGPU (The Department of Political Police) established as GPU in 1922 but changed its name to OGPU the following year	Felix Dzerzhinsky, Genrikh Yagoda
1934–43	NKVD (The People's Commissariat of Internal Affairs)	Genrikh Yagoda, Nikolai Yezhov (sometimes spelt Ezhov) Lavrenti Beria

After arrest, the victims of the secret police were beaten and tortured, interrogated under bright lights and forced to endure sleeplessness. In the end, although innocent of absurd charges, they signed confessions in order to escape further punishment.

B *The Riutin affair*

In 1934, Mikhail Riutin and his supporters were arrested. Riutin, who had once been a member of the Central Committee, was at that time Party secretary for a district of Moscow. He had dared to write a 200-page document that was highly critical of Stalin. In it, he described the Soviet leader as 'the evil genius of the Russian revolution who, motivated by personal desire for power and revenge, had brought the revolution to the brink of destruction'. In his document he claimed that the dictatorship of the proletariat would perish unless Stalin was liquidated and the entire Party leadership replaced. He also called for an end to all *kolkhozes* that he claimed had been created by force and the restoration of limited capitalism. An outraged Stalin claimed that Riutin and his supporters were planning to assassinate him and demanded the death penalty for all. The Politburo did not agree and only expelled Riutin from the Party. Another aspect of the case that troubled the Soviet leader was that many Party members had been aware of the existence of the offending document and had not reported it. In fact, Bukharin, who had admitted his earlier errors and been restored to the Party, and numerous others had secretly approved it! Stalin soon exacted his revenge. In a massive purge of the Party, over a million members considered unreliable were expelled. He still, however, feared for his own position. If dissidents in the Central Committee were planning to remove him, who would be his leading challenger? Popular within the Party was his close friend, the Party leader in Leningrad, Sergei Kirov.

C *The assassination of Kirov*

On 1 December 1934, Sergei Kirov was gunned down in Leningrad. A popular and charismatic Party member, at the Seventeenth Party

Congress, the so-called 'Congress of Victors', he had stood against his leader in the election of Party Secretary, a position that Stalin had held since 1923. Kirov actually won but this was covered up and the result fixed to allow Stalin to continue. The assassin was Leonid Nikolaev, a disillusioned Party member. It had also been suggested that Kirov, a well-known womaniser, was having an affair with his assassin's wife. Stalin immediately placed the blame on oppositionists – 'Those comrades who do not always confine themselves to criticism and passive resistance but threaten to raise revolt in the Party'. In more recent times, it has been claimed that Stalin himself was involved in Kirov's assassination. In 1953, a high ranking KGB defector, Alexander Orlov, claimed that Stalin had masterminded the killing but this has never been proved with any certainty. It should be remembered that whilst Kirov might have been regarded as a potential replacement for Stalin, he was himself a hard line Party man. The so-called 'Leningrad dictator' did not represent a clear-cut alternative to the Soviet leader. Under cross-examination, Nikolaev claimed to have acted alone and was executed together with 13 alleged accomplices. In addition, 103 others, who had no apparent connection with the crime, were also shot and this was only the beginning. The assassination of Kirov provided Stalin with the necessary excuse to remove all those in the Party whose loyalty he doubted and many others besides. There followed a massive nation-wide purge of the Party that extended from leading members of the Central Committee down to minor officials in the distant republics of the Soviet Union. By the time it ended, 1108 out of a total of 1966 delegates to the Party Congress of 1934 had been arrested whilst a similar fate befell 98 of the 139 members of the Central Committee. By any standard, it had been a massive clear out of unreliable and unworthy members of the Party.

KEY ISSUE
The aftermath of the assassination of Kirov.

D *The purges and show trials*

The first major show trial – trials to which the public and the overseas press were invited – began in August 1936 following the arrest of Kamenev and Zinoviev. Like Bukharin, both had made their peace with Stalin and been allowed to rejoin the Party. Both were accused of being in league with Trotsky and being responsible for murders and stirring up discontent. The notorious Andrei Vyshinsky prosecuted them. On trial, Kamenev admitted that for 10 years 'I waged a struggle against the Party, the government and against Stalin personally.' During the trial, an attempt was made to get the accused to implicate other prominent Party men including Rykov, for whom Lenin had forecast a bright future, Tomsky, once a trade union leader, and Bukharin. Although an investigation into their activities was called for, neither Rykov nor Bukharin would confess to the ludicrous charges made against them. Lack of evidence meant that their trial had to be called off – at least for the time being. Loyal to Stalin's wishes, Vyshinsky found both Kamenev and Zinoviev guilty and ordered them to be shot.

ANDREI VYSHINSKY
(1883–1954)

Andrei Vyshinsky was born in Odessa in the Ukraine. Active in politics, in 1903 he sided with the Menshevik faction of the Social Democrat Party and did not become a member of the Communist Party until 1920. In 1913, he qualified as a lawyer and after a period during which he taught at Moscow State University, he began practicing law as a prosecuting attorney. He gradually gained a reputation as a legal scholar and, in the late 1920s, proved himself a successful prosecutor at a series of trials involving people accused of industrial sabotage and counter-revolutionary activity. In 1931, he was appointed deputy prosecutor of the Soviet Union and attracted attention when he became involved in the trial of British engineers accused of wrecking hydro-electric installations. As a prosecuting lawyer, he earned the reputation of being aggressive, vengeful and cunning. He approved of confessions being obtained by torture and sentenced people to death on **uncorroborated** evidence. He played a leading role in the great purge trials (1934–38). Later he was to become a member of the Party's Central Committee and prominent in Soviet foreign affairs.

uncorroborated
not certain,
unconfirmed.

The head of the NKVD, Genrikh Yagoda, had been a close associate of Stalin but this meant nothing. His failure to secure the confessions of Rykov and Bukharin led to his replacement by Nikolai Yezhov.

NIKOLAI YEZHOV
(1895–1939)

Nikolai Yezhov, an alternative spelling of his name is Ezhov, was born in a poor working class family in St Petersburg. After an elementary education, he worked in a factory until he was drafted into the Russian army during World War I. He deserted, became an active revolutionary and, in 1917, joined the Bolsheviks. Another Bolshevik said of him, 'In my whole life, I have never known a more repellent personality than Yezhov'. During the civil war, he served as one of the dreaded political commissars and afterwards worked for *Komsomol* and the Party. On meeting Stalin, he fell completely under his spell and joined the OGPU. Promotion came quickly. In 1934, he was elected to the Central Committee and, in 1936, replaced Yagoda as head of the secret police, now renamed the NKVD. It is claimed that Stalin raised him to power with the specific purpose of setting up a blood bath. A man who delighted in excessive cruelty, he was nicknamed the 'Iron Commissar' whilst behind his back, his lack of stature earned him the name the 'bloody dwarf'. Those who knew him claimed he was dependent on drugs. Yezhov was head of the NKVD at the height of Stalin's purges and was responsible for the execution of thousands and death by torture or starvation of millions. A new word entered the Russian language, *Ezhovshchina* – 'the evil times of Ezhov (Yezhov)'. His entry in the *Who's Who in Russia and the Former USSR* describes him as 'a bloody hangman, one of the most repulsive figures of the Stalin era'. The full extent of his crimes did not become evident until after the death of Stalin in 1953. It has been claimed that Yezhov's evil reputation as a sadistic degenerate is at least partly due to the fact that he took the blame for many of Stalin's crimes and that he was merely his agent.

The second major show trial began in January 1937. This time the leading victims were Grigorii Pyatakov, arrested because of his supposed involvement in explosions in Siberian mines, Karl Radek, the industry chief, and the former secretary of the Central Committee and Commissar of Finance, Grigorii Sokolnikov. Accused of being Trotskyists, Vyshinsky denounced them as 'vipers' and 'liars, and clowns, insignificant pigmies'. Radek was accused of meeting Trotskyist agents in a hotel in Copenhagen that had been demolished before World War I! All admitted to their crimes and pleaded for their lives. Radek, Sokolnikov and two others who were sentenced to 10 years imprisonment, but the rest were shot. Radek had formerly been an assistant of Grigorii Ordzhonikidze, Commissar of Heavy Industry. Despairing at the turn of events in his country, including the execution of Radek and his own brother, and possibly feeling that the net was closing in on him, Ordzhonikidze took his own life. Soviet propagandists tried to convince the people that what was happening was in their interests. Were acts of **industrial espionage** really occurring in the Soviet Union at the time? An American engineer, John D. Littlepage, working in the mines in the Urals at the time wrote in his book *In Search of Soviet Gold* published in 1939.

industrial espionage
the use of spies to gain secret information about or to disrupt industry.

'Of course its all for their own good, say the Communists. But many of the people can't see things that way, and remain bitter enemies of the Communists and their ideas, even after they have been put back to work in State industries. From these groups have come a considerable number of disgruntled workers who dislike Communists so much they would gladly damage any of their enterprises if they could.'

Next it was the turn of the Soviet Union's military leaders to be purged. Amongst the first to be arrested was Marshal Mikhail Tukhachevsky. From an aristocratic background and formerly an officer in the Tsarist army, Tukhachevsky had joined the Bolsheviks in 1918 and held important commands in the Civil War. He had been responsible for suppressing the Kronstadt mutiny in 1921 and had overseen the modernisation of the Red Army. The best known officer in the army, he had been scheduled to travel to London to represent the Soviet government at the coronation of King George VI but it was not to be. Accused of being part of a 'gigantic conspiracy', he and several other generals were found guilty of treason and espionage and shot. In need of total control over the armed services, Stalin sanctioned the arrest of over 35 000 serving officers.

The following is from Philip Longworth's *Purges and Trials:*

> … security officers descended on military establishments and carried off officers by the lorry load. Entire staffs disappeared. Within two years all eleven vice-commissars for war and all but five of the eighty members of the Supreme Military Soviet had been eliminated. Three out of five marshals, fourteen out of sixteen army commanders, 167 out of 280 corps and divisional commanders and nearly half the brigadiers had disappeared. Though the blow fell heaviest on the senior ranks, the purge bit deep into the command structure. About a third of the entire officer establishment were arrested. It was the same in the air force, and only one senior commander survived the navy purge.

The last of the great show trials began in Moscow on 2 March 1938. At last Nikolai Bukharin's time had come and amongst the others arrested were Andrei Rykov and the former head of the secret police, Genrikh Yagoda. Mikhail Tomsky, who would have most certainly been included, had committed suicide. In listing the charges against the accused, Vyshinsky reached new heights of fantasy. Quite incredibly it was claimed that in 1918 they had been part of a plot to kill Lenin and had recently been involved in a conspiracy with German and Japanese agents to partition the Soviet Union and then restore capitalism. In his summing-up, Vyshinsky showed his most **vitriolic** form. He accused the 'bloc of Rights and Trotskyists' of not being merely a band of 'felonious criminals' but of also being 'the basest, lowest, the most contemptible, the most depraved of the depraved' and demanded that they 'be shot like dirty dogs!'

vitriolic scathing, showing ill-will.

Standing before the court, Bukharin confessed and made one last statement – 'I am perhaps speaking for the last time in my life… I am kneeling before the country, before the Party, before the whole people… As I await the verdict… what matters is not the personal feelings of a repentant enemy, but the flourishing progress of the USSR.' After being condemned to death, Rykov wrote a letter to the Supreme Soviet asking for clemency – 'I ask you to believe that I am not a completely corrupt person. In my life there were many years of noble, honest work for the Revolution. I can still prove that even after having committed so many crimes, it is possible to become an honest person and to die with honour. I ask that you spare my life.' It was all to no avail. In fact, Yezhov, with Stalin's approval, had decided on the sentences beforehand and they were shot. What puzzled foreign observers that attended the trials was that obviously innocent people, some of them Old Bolsheviks

Q

Why did obviously innocent people plead guilty to crimes they could not possibly have committed?

denunciation – to criticise or volunteer to give evidence against another person.

and still dedicated Communists, pleaded guilty to crimes they could not have committed. Undoubtedly they did so to save themselves from further torture or to protect their families. One or two pleaded guilty because they believed their sacrifice was in the interest of the Soviet Union. In the dock, some appeared drugged and disorientated. Immediately after the verdicts were reached, the unfortunates would be taken to the cellars of nearby Lubyanka prison and shot in the back of the head. Those who could not be broken were tried in secret. It was claimed that anyone who survived torture by the NKVD was unlikely to walk or even stand upright again. It was said that in the Soviet Union there were no such things as innocent and guilty people but just lucky and unlucky ones!

The Moscow trials were but the tip of the iceberg. Similar trials occurred throughout the Soviet Union and thousands were purged and eliminated. The situation threatened to get out of hand as Party members denounced each other and, in order to save their own skins revealed the treachery of others. **Denunciation** became a convenient way of acquiring another Party member's position, property or wife and, in some instances, a means of settling an old score. By the end of 1938, the Party had lost a third of its members. The executions were not limited to Russians alone but also embraced foreign Communists who had sought refuge in the Soviet Union. Gradually, after what Martin McCauley has described as 'a catalogue of methodical madness', the

PICTURE 29
A statue raised in honour of Pavlik

PICTURE 30 *Six-year-old Engelsina Chezkova embraces Stalin. He later ordered her parents to be shot*

nightmare came to an end. Afterwards Stalin remained unrepentant and, in 1939, told the 18th Party Conference that the purge was 'unavoidable and its results, on the whole, beneficial'. He did however admit that mistakes had been made but, much to the relief of those that remained, declared that he would not be resorting to another mass purge. In the meantime, Lavrenti Beria had replaced Yezhov. The architect of the terror suffered the same fate as so many of his victims. After being tortured he was secretly tried and shot. Even so, it was not quite all over. Stalin had one more score to settle.

E *The assassination of Trotsky*

After being expelled from the Soviet Union in 1929, Trotsky had lived in Turkey, France and Norway before finally settling in Mexico. From his various places of exile, he wrote books and articles and gave lectures and interviews that poured scorn on Stalin and denounced the debased Communist system he had imposed on the Russian people. He claimed that Stalin had ignored the interests of the proletariat and was simply out to further his own interests. Undoubtedly Trotsky and his agents remained in contact with sympathisers still in the Soviet Union. During the period of the great purges, among the charges made against the accused was that they were Trotskyists. Trotsky referred to the trials as 'the greatest frame-up in history'. Meanwhile, Stalin bided his time and waited for his chance. In 1938, Trotsky's son, Leon Sedov, was murdered whilst receiving treatment in a Paris hospital. Shortly afterwards, the headless body of one of his close friends and collaborators, Rudolf Klement, was found floating in the River Seine. Well aware that he would be a target of NKVD assassins, Trotsky lived with his family in a fortified house on the outskirts of Mexico City. There he continued to write books and care for his rabbits. In May 1940, men broke into his home and sprayed his bedroom with bullets but Trotsky was unharmed. Three months later, on 20th August, Ramon Mercador, a man who had gained access to Trotsky by pretending to show an interest in his political views, entered his study and plunged an ice-axe into the top of his head. In spite of attempts to save his life, he died the following day. Mercador was sentenced to 20 years imprisonment but in Moscow, his mother received the Honour of Lenin on his behalf from Stalin.

F *The victims of the purges*

Date	Victims	Accused of	Punishment
1928	Engineers at Shakhty	Treason and sabotage	Shot or sent to labour camps
1934	Supporters of Riutin	Treason and plotting against Stalin	Expelled from the Party
1936	Zinoviev and Kamenev	Being Trotskyists and being involved in the murder of Kirov	Shot

(continued overleaf)

Date	Victims	Accused of	Punishment
1937	Pyatakov and Serebryakov	Espionage and being German agents	Shot
	Yagoda, head of the NKVD	Treason and murder	Shot
	Marshal Tukhachevsky and the majority of the army's senior officers	Treason	Shot
	The junior army officers – an estimated 35 000	Treason	Shot or sent to the labour camps
	All the admirals of the Soviet navy	Treason	Shot
	Radek and Sokolnikov	Espionage and being German agents	Shot
1938	Bukharin, Rykov numerous other Party leaders and members of the Soviets of other republics	Treason	Shot
		Various crimes including treason	Shot or sent to the labour camps
1939	Yezhov, head of the NKVD	Treason – being a British agent	Shot
1929–39	An estimated 24 million people	Treason, being kulaks, having bourgeois views, and many other crimes	Sent to the labour camps where some 13 million died
1940	Trotsky	Long time critic of Stalin	Murdered at his home in Mexico City.

G *The purges – some considerations*

A) WHY DID THE PURGES TAKE PLACE?

There is no simple answer to this question. Some historians believe that Stalin plotted the assassination of Kirov in 1934 in order to provide himself with an excuse for the blood-letting that followed. He would certainly have been taken aback by the fact that some delegates to the Seventeenth Party Congress asked Kirov to stand against him in the election of General Secretary. It would have left Stalin in no doubt of the popularity of the man from Leningrad or that he was a potential rival. It would also have made him mindful that, with many members prepared to vote against him at the 'Congress of Victors', he was not in total control. There were certainly policy differences within the Party mainly over the speed of the changes that were taking place. On such issues, Stalin usually sat on the fence and flayed one faction off against the other. He was also keen to cleanse the Party of Old Bolsheviks, members who had joined before 1917 and whose first loyalty had originally been to Lenin, and replace them with younger men dedicated to him. He was also aware that Party bureaucrats were hindering economic progress and there were also corrupt Party officials who used their position for personal gain. Did Stalin possibly believe the purges were necessary to protect his Communist state? Again, Stalin saw the influence of Trotskyists everywhere and it was certainly true that Trotskyist sympathisers existed and they were active in smuggling their leader's literature into the country. Were the purges necessary to eliminate the Trotskyists once and for all or were Stalin's purges merely a continuation of the terror started by Lenin after the Revolution and an unavoidable consequence of Bolshevik thinking? There is, of course, a much more simple explanation. Was Stalin, as Harold Shukman has written 'paranoid by nature' or as Alan Wood claims, driven by '**paranoid machinations**' of a criminally deranged psychopath'? In *Stalin: Man of Steel*, Elizabeth Roberts expresses the view – 'It is doubtful if a truly sane man would have done as Stalin did.'

> **paranoid machinations** suspicion based on a delusion that causes a person to plot and scheme.

B) WAS STALIN SOLELY RESPONSIBLE?

There is no doubt that Stalin was mainly responsible for the terror that ravaged the Soviet Union during the 1930s. The issues of whether he instigated it in the first place and was solely responsible for what followed are still strongly debated by historians. In spite of the evidence by a KGB defector whether or not he plotted the assassination of Kirov remains unproven. Even if Stalin triggered the purges, is it possible, as some suggest, that as Party members competed to denounce each other, matters went beyond his control? Were the leaders of the secret police, Yagoda and Yezhov, who were responsible for the most appalling crimes and the deaths of tens of thousands, the real culprits? Before taking these theories too seriously, bear in mind that in 1938 alone, Stalin personally sanctioned 366 death warrants that led to the execution of over 44 000 people. He did not even spare his own family the trauma of the purges. It is not known if Stalin was responsible for the deaths of his relations but he certainly did nothing to protect them. Finally, is it possible that Yagoda and Yezhov were themselves both liquidated to prevent them from revealing the truth?

C) WHAT WERE THE REPERCUSSIONS OF THE PURGES?

One repercussion of the purges and show trials was their impact on public opinion both at home and abroad. Obviously, the Russian people could not register their disapproval at what was happening in their country but the foreign press had a field day with lurid accounts, mostly true but some imagined, which horrified the outside world. Amongst the 20 million people murdered or sent to the labour camps were many of the Party's bureaucrats and administrators. Their replacements were younger men appointed and promoted by Stalin which meant that he could depend on their total loyalty. They did not have the experience of their predecessors and, for a time, administration at both national and local levels suffered disruption. Many of the victims of the purges were also academics and teachers and this had an impact on the quality of state education. Equally damaging was the fact that the removal of so-called bourgeois managers and engineers meant that industry suffered a shortage of suitably skilled people. Very often, newcomers did not possess the same skills as those they had replaced. The removal of so many of the nation's military commanders and the near elimination of the officer class meant that the armed services lacked experienced leadership as it faced up to the prospect of a war with Germany. With the Red Army unprepared, Stalin had to appease Hitler and, in 1939, entered into a pact with Nazi Germany. The short comings of the Soviet armed

See Chapter 10.

services were short lived and, as we shall see, the Red Army recovered and played a major role in the defeat of Germany.

5 ⇝ STRUCTURED AND ESSAY QUESTIONS

A *This section consists of questions that might be useful for discussion (or writing answers) as a way of expanding on the chapter and for testing the understanding of it.*

1. Why did Stalin conclude that the old Marxist dictum 'From each according to his ability, to each according to his needs' was no longer sustainable?
2. To what extent might it be claimed that the real power in the Soviet Union lay with the Communist Party?
3. To what extent did the Constitution of 1936
   (i)   allow citizens the right to own private property?
   (ii) safeguard women's rights?
   (iii) guarantee the individual rights and freedom of citizens?
4. In what sense was the Soviet education system geared to creating 'the new Soviet man'?
5. For what reasons did the policies of *Zhenotdel* attract opposition?
6. What did Marxists mean when they referred to religion as
   (i) 'the opium of the people'?
   (ii) 'a Pillar of the Establishment'?
6. Why might the assassination of Kirov in 1934 have been engineered by Stalin?

B *Essay questions.*
1. To what extent did developments in Stalin's Russia represent a retreat from the ideals of the Revolution?
2. How justifiable is the claim that Stalin's Constitution of 1936 was the 'only truly democratic constitution in the world'?
3. To what extent might it be claimed that during the 1930s Soviet women became fully emancipated?
4. 'Simply to eliminate his rivals'. Is this a valid explanation of the Stalinist purges during the late 1930s?

6 ⇝ MAKING NOTES

Read the advice given about making notes on page ix of the Preface: How to use this book, and then make your own notes based on the following headings and questions.

A *The Soviet education system and youth movements*
1. For what reasons was there a reaction against learning and scholarship during the years following the Revolution?
2. How did the *Method Proektov* work?

3. What major changes took place in Soviet education during the 1930s?

4. What advantages were to be derived from membership of *Komsomol*?

B *The role of women in Soviet society*

1. What was the attitude of the Bolsheviks towards marriage and the family during the years after the Revolution?

2. What were the aims of *Zhenotdel*, the Party's Women's Bureau?

3. Why was the employment of women essential to Stalin's programme of industrialisation?

4. For what reasons might Stalin's attitude to the family be considered contradictory?

C *Religion in the Soviet Union*

1. For what reasons did the Bolsheviks set out to eradicate religion?

2. To what extent were the Jews persecuted in Stalin's Russia?

3. How was it that, in spite of the measures taken against it, the Church managed to survive?

D *The Cultural Revolution*

1. What was the aim of Socialist Realism?

2. Use the following chart to list some of those who were famous in literature and the arts in the Soviet Union during the 1930s.

Literature	
Art	
Architecture	
Music	
Cinema	

7 ⁓ DOCUMENTARY EXERCISE ON STALIN'S PURGES

Study the sources and then answer the questions based on them.

The investigation … has established that on the instructions of the intelligence services of foreign states hostile to the USSR the accused organised a conspiratorial group named the 'bloc of Rights and Trotskyites', the object of which was to overthrow the Socialist social and state system existing in the USSR and to restore capitalism and the power of the bourgeoisie in the USSR.

SOURCE A
The indictment against the accused

President of the court: Do you plead guilty to the charges brought against you?

Bukharin : Yes, I plead guilty to the charges brought against me.

Rykov : Yes, I do.

Yagoda : Yes, I do.

Krestinsky: : I plead not guilty. I am not a Trotskyite. I was never a member of the bloc of Rights and Trotskyites, of whose existence I was not aware. Nor have I committed any of the crimes with which I am personally charged ...

The 'bloc of Rights and Trotskyites', the leading members of which are now in the prisoners' dock, is not a political party ... but a band of felonious criminals, and not simply felonious criminals, but criminals who have sold themselves to enemy intelligence, criminals whom even ordinary felons treat as the basest, the lowest, the most contemptible, the most depraved of the depraved ... The whole country, from young to old, is awaiting and demanding one thing: the traitors and spies must be shot like dirty dogs. Our people are demanding one thing: crush the accursed reptile!

Q

1. *According to Source A, what were the aims of the 'bloc of Rights and Trotskyists'?*
2. (a) *For what possible reasons did Bukharin, Rykov and Yagoda plead guilty to the charges made against them (Source B)?*
   (b) *Suggest some reasons why Krestinsky chose to deny the charges.*
3. *What impact was the summing-up of Vyshinsky, Source C, likely to have had on the People's Court?*
4. *What do the sources reveal about the nature of Stalin's show trials?*

Stalin's foreign policy: the Soviet Union and World War II

INTRODUCTION

In some areas, the aims of Soviet foreign policy was a mixture of the old and the new and had much in common with those of Tsarist times. Both sought to protect the country from outside, that is Western, influences and both sought to extend Russian power in the Middle and Far East. Even so, the aftermath of revolution and Civil War together with the economic upheavals that followed meant that Russia's Communist regime had little time for involvement in foreign affairs. What foreign policy decisions were made reflected the country's isolation and her hostility to the capitalist world around that had earlier opposed the overthrow of the tsar and supported the Whites during the Civil War? The head of the Commissariat for Foreign Affairs was Georgi Chicherin, an able diplomat of noble birth. His deputy, Maxim Litvinov, had taken an active part in the revolution of 1905 and afterwards lived in exile in Britain. Neither were members of the all important decision-making Politburo and, prior to 1925, they were not even represented on the Party's Central Committee. Lenin had hoped that the revolution in Russia would be followed by similar insurrections elsewhere in Europe. For a time it seemed that it might be possible since, during the immediate post-war years, there were uprisings in Germany and Soviet Republics declared in Bavaria and Hungary. In Germany, the unrest culminated in an attempted Spartacist *coup* in January 1919 and a successful if short lived attempt by Bela Kun to set up a Communist regime in Hungary. After both were crushed, enthusiasm for revolution died away and Europe settled to a more stable period. In 1920, Lenin seemed to indicate a change of attitude when he said – 'We have entered a new period in which we ... have won the right to our international existence in the network of capitalist states.' Did this mean that the Soviet Union was about to adopt traditional methods of diplomacy and abandon her subversive activities and give up her stated aim of working to overthrow capitalism?

1 ⌐ SOVIET FOREIGN POLICY DURING THE 1920s

The leaders of the Soviet Union appreciated that with the failure of attempted Communist *coups* in Europe and a general decline in revolutionary zeal, their chance had gone. They realised that the interests of their new Communist state would now be best served by reaching agreement and co-operating with the capitalist countries. This was intended to be only a short-term measure. In the meantime, they would continue to work behind the scenes to infiltrate, subvert and use revolutionary propaganda as a means of overthrowing democratic institutions in other countries. Their main means of achieving this was through Comintern.

KEY ISSUE

The aims of Soviet foreign policy.

A *The Third International – Comintern*

Comintern, the abbreviated form of Communist International, was founded in Moscow in 1919. It was intended to be more revolutionary in outlook than its immediate predecessor, the Second Socialist International, and its declared aim was to sponsor and support world revolution. At its Second Congress held in 1921, it laid down 21 conditions for membership. These conditions effectively gave the leadership of Comintern to the Soviet Union. It insisted that Communists now went ahead alone and not, as previously, as part of a left-wing grouping which included moderate socialists. Its members had to accept all Comintern policy decisions as binding and they were instructed to infiltrate the political systems of other countries and, whenever possible, to take advantage of democratic institutions and use them to overthrow governments. As we shall see, the activities of Comintern infuriated foreign governments particularly since the Soviet Union persisted with the view that it was only a member of Comintern and it did not control the organisation's activities. As the situation in Europe stabilised, so the influence of Comintern lessened. Even so, the policy of the Soviet Union remained **ambiguous** since, although it sought to establish diplomatic relations with the capitalist nations, it remained dedicated to the cause of world revolution. Its achievement would remain the corner stone of Soviet foreign policy.

ambiguous doubtful, having more than one meaning.

KEY ISSUE

Comintern and subversion.

B *The Soviet Union and Germany – the 'pariah nations'*

Even though the Bolsheviks had openly supported the post-war attempted Communist *coups* in Germany, the new German government, the Weimar Republic, had a great deal in common with the Soviet Union. Lenin summed this up and was unusually prophetic when he said:

> 'Germany wants revenge and we want revolution. For the moment our aims are the same … but when our ways part, they will be our most ferocious enemies. Time will tell whether German authority or Communism is to arise out of the ruins of Europe.'

Both were considered **'pariah nations'** – countries that were outcasts from main stream European affairs. Both had been denied membership of the League of Nations, both faced major economic problems and both countries resented the fact that, as part of the post-war settlement, they had lost territory to re-create Poland. These considerations, together with the fear of a possible Western anti-Soviet alliance, caused the Russian leaders to look for closer ties with Germany. This came about when the two countries signed the Treaty of Rapallo in 1922.

> **pariah nations**
> undesirable or outcast.

C *The Treaty of Rapallo, 1922*

The Treaty of Rapallo brought about a restoration of diplomatic relations between the Soviet Union and Germany. Both countries agreed to drop any outstanding reparation or other financial claims they had against each other and pledged economic co-operation. Since both had been forced to give territory towards the re-creation of Poland, they agreed to a common policy towards that country. Links were established between the Red Army and the German *Reichswehr* and, although forbidden by the Treaty of Versailles, secret arrangements were made for German troops to take part in exercises on Soviet soil and for German engineers to manufacture and test new weapons. It was during this time that many German pilots, later to fly with the bombers of the *Luftwaffe*, received their training. From a Russian viewpoint, this gave them the added advantage of having access to German military technology. (Take care not to confuse this treaty with another Treaty of Rapallo also signed in 1920 which settled outstanding differences between Italy and Yugoslavia.)

Relations between the Soviet Union and other major European and world powers did not run so smoothly.

2 ∾ SOVIET DIPLOMACY IN THE 1920S

During the 1920s, an effort was made to rehabilitate the Soviet Union and bring her back within the European family of nations. The Soviet Union was also keen to resume trade with the capitalist countries since she needed to import modern machinery and find markets for her exports in order to earn urgently required foreign currency. In 1920, the first to establish diplomatic relations with the Communist regime were Russia's immediate neighbours, the Baltic provinces, Estonia, Latvia and Lithuania, and they were soon to be followed by Finland. In 1921, the Treaty of Riga finally settled the border between Russia and Poland and this allowed diplomatic relations to be resumed between the two countries. At the Genoa Conference in 1922, the Western powers offered credit and loans to the Soviet government but they also made demands that included the settlement of debts remaining from Tsarist times and the restoration to their owners of foreign property and businesses that had been confiscated. These demands, Chicherin refused even to consider.

A *Soviet relations with other powers*

Anglo-Soviet relations proved tricky. Even though a trade treaty was agreed between the two countries in 1921, it failed to achieve anything worthwhile largely because the British remained suspicious of Russian intentions particularly since Soviet propaganda was encouraging unrest in British India. Even so, early in 1924, the first British Labour Government led by Ramsay MacDonald officially recognised the Soviet government. In October of the same year, at the height of an election campaign, the British press published a letter allegedly signed by Zinoviev, Chairman of Comintern, ordering Communists to encourage acts of mutiny in the British army. The letter, which may have been a forgery, led to a **'Red Scare'** and contributed largely to the failure of the short-lived Labour government to win re-election. In spite of this, in 1925, Mikhail Tomsky was invited to address the British Trades Union conference and arrangements were made to set up an Anglo-Russian committee. At the time of a General Strike in Britain in 1926, Comintern agents were suspected of being involved in subversive activities. Then, in May 1927, Anglo-Soviet relations hit rock bottom when police raided the offices of *Arcos*, a Russian trading organisation in London, and there claimed to have found subversive material. As a result, the British government broke off diplomatic relations with the Soviet Union and these were not resumed until 1930. In addition, the Anglo-Russian committee came to an end. French relations with the Soviet Union were soured by the continued Russian refusal to repay Tsarist debts. Between 1894 and 1914, some two million French people had invested in Russian bonds which, under the Communist regime, had become worthless. In spite of this, France finally recognised the Soviet Union in 1924 and, in 1932, the two countries concluded a non-aggression pact. The United States continued to withhold her recognition until 1933.

> **Red Scare** fear of Communist inspired subversive activities.

> **KEY ISSUE**
>
> *Difficulties in Anglo-Soviet relations.*

B *Soviet involvement in the Far East*

Beyond Europe, the country that appeared to offer the Soviet Union the greatest opportunities to extend her influence was China. In 1911, Chinese nationalists, known as the *Kuomintang* or KMT, overthrew the Manchu dynasty that had ruled China since 1644. The leader of the *Kuomintang*, Sun Yat-sen, turned China into a republic. After his death in 1925, the leadership of the movement fell to Chiang Kai-shek. From the start, his rule was challenged by the Chinese Communists led by Mao Zedong who set up a communist republic in the distant province of Kiangsi. The Soviet Union played a cunning game and backed both sides. Whilst, on the one hand, aid was sent to Mao's Communists, on the other, Communists were encouraged to infiltrate the KMT and Mikhail Borodin, a Comintern agent, was sent to serve as a military adviser to Chiang Kai-shek's armies. Trotsky warned against becoming too involved in Chinese affairs in case it attracted the attention of other major powers and possibly encouraged the involvement of Japan. In 1927, at the Party Congress in Moscow, Stalin told delegates that he regarded China as 'the second home of world revolution' and confided secretly to others that he intended to use Chiang Kai-shek's nationalists to his own advantage and 'squeeze them out like a lemon' before throwing them away. He had badly underrated the KMT leader. Stalin's scheme collapsed when in April 1927 after the capture of Shanghai, Chiang Kai-shek ordered the massacre of all the Communists in the city. What was left of Mao Zedong's men had to escape to the hills. Continually harassed by the KMT, in 1934 they embarked on a 13 000 km 'Long March' and finally found refuge in distant Shensi province. Stalin's policy in China had ended in disaster. In Moscow, this led to much soul searching as members of the Politburo sought to allocate blame. Trotsky and the Left placed the responsibility for the disaster fully on Stalin and Bukharin. As we have seen, this was the time when Stalin expelled his critics from the Party.

> **Q**
>
> *In her relations with China, why did the Soviet Union appear to back both sides?*

See page 266.

C *Stalin begins his search for collective security*

In the late 1920s, there were attempts to improve the prospect of a lasting peace in Europe. At the Locarno Conference in 1925, the German representative, Gustav Stresemann, agreed to accept Germany's Western frontiers with France and Belgium as final but not those in the East with Poland and Czechoslovakia which he wanted renegotiated in the future. The Soviet Union was not party to these decisions but, the following year, managed to further improve her own relations with Germany by signing the Treaty of Berlin. Overall, 1927 was a bad year for Soviet diplomacy. Apart from Britain, Canada too broke off diplomatic relations whilst in Warsaw, the Soviet ambassador to Poland was assassinated. The problem was that whilst Stalin wanted to be more involved in European politics, the activities of Comintern and his own utterances meant few would trust him.

3 ⌐ SOVIET DIPLOMACY IN THE 1930S

In 1933, the rise to power of Hitler and the Nazis in Germany changed the situation completely. The new German leader had been outspoken in his condemnation of Soviet Communism. 'Bolshevism', he said, 'was the arch enemy of civilisation' and in *Mein Kampf*, he had openly stated that the additional living space, *Lebensraum*, needed by Germany could only be obtained at Russia's expense. Litvinov now, more than ever, appreciated that his country's best guarantee of safety from possible German aggression was collective security. That is to join together with other nations in a series of pacts and so achieve safety in numbers. In part of what became known as the 'Litvinov Protocol', the Soviet Union entered into a series of non-aggression pacts with France, Poland, Finland and Estonia, in 1933, with Italy and, in 1936, with Czechoslovakia. Britain, however, had recently agreed to a treaty with Germany, the Anglo-German Naval Treaty and this made Stalin suspicious of Britain's long-term intentions.

From the start, the Soviet Union had been hostile to the League of Nations. Lenin had referred to it as 'a band of robbers' and Chicherin always spoke of it in the most sarcastic terms. Gradually, as she became involved in some of the League's projects, her attitude changed. In 1927, Russian delegates attended an economic conference organised by the League and, in 1927, Litvinov took part in disarmament talks held at Geneva. As a further indication of her new found respectability, in 1934 the Soviet Union finally joined and was elected member of the all important Council which met when there was an emergency and prompt action was needed.

Stalin was not only worried about the intentions of Hitler in Europe, but he also had good cause to be once again concerned about the turn of events in the Far East. When the Japanese first made moves against Outer Mongolia and Manchuria, he tried to buy them off by offering mineral and fishing rights and selling them the Chinese Eastern Railway. This was only successful for a time and, by 1937, clashes between Russian and Japanese forces along the Manchurian border were threatening to develop into a full-scale war. In Europe, the years 1934 and 1935 proved a watershed in international relations. It saw a reshuffle in alliances that brought about a major and dangerous shift in the balance of power. In 1934, Hitler concluded a German–Polish Non-Aggression Pact aimed, so he claimed, to encourage the 'peaceful development of their relations'. This, in effect, ended the period of good relations with Germany brought about by the Treaty of Rapallo. In a stampede to enter into alliances that offered collective security, in 1935 the Soviet Union made pacts of mutual assistance with France and Czechoslovakia. In October of that year, Italian armies invaded the African kingdom of Abyssinia, present-day Ethiopia. Severely criticised by the League of Nations and her former allies, Britain and France, the reaction of the country's Fascist dictator, Benito Mussolini, was to resign from the League and seek closer ties with Nazi Germany. Mussolini spoke of 'the Rome–Berlin line … an axis, around which can revolve all those European states with a will to collaboration and peace'. Afterwards, Nazi Germany and Fascist Italy became known as the Axis powers. Stalin's concern at these developments increased further when, in 1936, first Germany and Japan and then Italy agreed to an Anti-Comintern Pact.

> **Q**
> *How successful was the Soviet Union in improving relations with other European powers?*

A *The Anti-Comintern Pact, 1936*

The Pact, first agreed between Germany and Japan, was signed in Berlin on 25 November 1936. Italy joined a year later. The aims of the Pact were clearly stated as being 'to mutually keep each other informed concerning the activities of the Communist International' and 'to confer upon the necessary measures of defence'. It was also agreed to invite other nations 'menaced by the disintegrating work of the Communist International' to join the Pact. Whilst the purpose of the Pact was to counter the activities of Comintern, there can be no doubt it was also specifically aimed against the Soviet Union. Since coming to power Hitler had continually raged against the Bolshevik–Jewish plot to achieve world domination whilst the Japanese were angered by a Soviet–Chinese Non-Aggression treaty of August 1936 and the fact that the Soviet Union was selling aircraft and munitions to China. According to Mussolini, Italy joined the Pact in order to 'defend Western values against the threat of Soviet Communism'.

The problem faced by the Soviet Union was that although she had appeared to have abandoned her revolutionary aims and introduced a constitution which, on the face of it, matched Western democratic standards, fear remained. Was the change of attitude genuine? Could the Soviet Union really be trusted? France was uncertain whilst Britain thought not. Somewhat late in the day, the Soviet leadership abandoned its opposition to socialism and urged communists and socialists to come together and form 'popular front' governments. In July 1936, a civil war broke out in Spain.

B *Soviet involvement in the Spanish Civil War*

Earlier that year, Spanish voters had elected a left-wing Popular Front government that promised the people a much needed programme of social reform. The election result concerned conservative elements within the country and Spanish Fascists, the Falange, reacted by organising riots and carrying out murders. In July, the Spanish army in Morocco mutinied and crossed to the Spanish mainland with the aim of overthrowing the government. The civil war that followed became a clash of ideologies. On the one side, the Republicans, were the supporters of the Popular Front government backed by the socialists and communists and most urban and agricultural workers; on the other, the Nationalists, were most of the upper and middle classes together with the landowners and those with industrial and commercial interests, the Church, the Falange and the Spanish army. From the start, there was outside intervention. General Francisco Franco's Nationalist armies received military aid from Italy and Germany. The Italians sent 50 000 men and large amounts of weapons and the Germans, squadrons of aircraft. Stalin had to play his hand carefully. To become directly involved might tempt France and Britain to follow suit and he certainly did not want to risk any confrontation with Germany. To counterbalance the German and Italian involvement, he sanctioned the use of Comintern. It was Comintern that helped to recruit the International Brigades, units made up of overseas volunteers, and also arranged for Soviet military advisers to assist the Republican army. The Comintern involvement was organised from Odessa, a Russian port on the Black Sea. Stalin used Comintern's Communist agents to influence the conduct of the war and become involved in Republican politics. The Communists took measures against Spanish socialists and Trotskyists and organised executions and reprisal killings that appalled their socialist and republican allies. During 1938, the Soviet Union gradually withdrew from its involvement in Spain but, by this time, the activities of Comintern had created divisions in the ranks of the Republicans that contributed to the ultimate victory of Franco's Nationalists during the following year. For the Soviet Union, the outcome of the Spanish Civil War was another setback but for the Fascist powers it had provided an opportunity to measure the effectiveness of their new weapons and tactics. It was formerly held that Soviet involvement in the Spanish Civil War was only marginal and far less than that of the Fascist powers, Italy and Germany. More recent research has shown this to be untrue.

TABLE 56 *Foreign involvement in the Spanish Civil War (in addition, an estimated 35 000 volunteers fought with the various units of the International Brigade and some 10 000 served as non-combatants)*

	Men	Tanks	Artillery	Planes
Italy	75 000	150	1000	660
Germany	17 000	200	1000	600
Soviet Union	3 000	900	1550	1000

In March 1936, German troops defied the terms of the Treaty of Versailles and occupied the demilitarised Rhineland. Stalin watched anxiously as Hitler's bluff worked. France, who had wanted to act, would not do so without Britain. For their part, the British tended to sympathise with the Germans who, after all, were only 'going into their own back garden'. In March 1938, Hitler ordered the completion of the *Anschluss* and German forces occupied Austria. In the summer of that year, the German *Fuhrer* turned his attention on Czechoslovakia.

C *The Soviet Union and the Czech crisis*

In April 1938, the leader of the Germans living in the Sudeten region of Czechoslovakia demanded their independence from Czech rule. Rumours of German troop movements along the Czech frontier led to a panic and it seemed that a European war was imminent. Although it was France and the Soviet Union that had entered into agreements to guarantee the independence of Czechoslovakia, it was the British Prime Minister, Neville Chamberlain, who took the lead in trying to resolve the situation. In a series of meetings held with Hitler during September of that year, the Nazi leader gradually increased his demands. In an agreement reached at Munich, Chamberlain gave way and Hitler's demands were imposed on Czechoslovakia. His **appeasement** of the German leader came to be regarded as an act of betrayal. Uninvolved in the discussions, the Soviet government repeatedly proposed international action to deter Hitler's aggression but this went unheeded. Litvinov's attempt to form alliances and bring his country within a protective framework of collective security had failed. In May 1939, Stalin replaced him with Vyacheslav Molotov.

Ignored by Britain and France and with grave doubts about the ability of those countries to stand up to Hitler, Stalin was faced with a choice of alternatives. He could continue to press for what now seemed like an unlikely alliance with Britain and France or he could reach an agreement with Hitler. He said, 'Let every country defend itself against

appeasement
willingness to give in and grant concessions.

the aggressor as it will and can, our interest is not at stake, we shall bargain with the aggressors …' On 23 August 1939, the foreign ministers of the Soviet Union and Nazi Germany signed a non-aggression pact.

Vyacheslav Molotov (1890–1986)

Born Vyacheslav Skriabin and related to the famous Russian composer Alexander Skriabin, he became involved in revolutionary activities and joined the Bolsheviks in 1909. He took the name 'Molotov' which means 'hammer'. After working on the newspaper, *Pravda*, in 1921, he became the youngest member of the Politburo. After the death of Lenin, he became a staunch supporter of Stalin and was rewarded for his loyalty by being appointed chairman of the Council of People's Commissars, Prime Minister of the Soviet Union, a position he held until 1941. In May 1939, he was chosen to replace Litvinov as Soviet Commissar for Foreign Affairs.

TIMELINE

Years of Pacts and Treaties – The Soviet search for collective security

1922	Treaty of Rapallo
1925	Trade treaty agreed with Germany
	Treaty of friendship with Turkey
1926	Treaty of friendship with Lithuania
	Terms of Rapallo confirmed with Germany together with a non-aggression pact
1927	Treaty of friendship with Persia
1928	Litvinov Protocol
1931	Non-aggression pact with Afghanistan
1932	Non-aggression pacts with Finland, Latvia, Estonia, Poland and France
1933	Diplomatic relations established with the USA
1934	Soviet Union joined the League of Nations
1936	Pacts of mutual assistance with France and Czechoslovakia
1939	German–Soviet Non-Aggression Pact

D *The German–Soviet Non-Aggression Pact of August 1939*

It was the Soviet foreign secretary, Molotov, who first contacted the Germans about the possibility of an agreement in May 1939. When the German delegation arrived in Moscow, an Anglo-French mission was already there trying to reach an agreement with the Russians. Suddenly they were told that the talks were to be adjourned and were sent packing. Instead Molotov opened negotiations with the Germans. The Pact, which is also sometimes referred to as the German–Soviet Pact or, after the foreign ministers who were its signatories, the Ribbentrop–Molotov Pact, consisted of two agreements. The first, which dealt with

PICTURE 31

*A cartoon of August 1939 shows
Hitler and Stalin involved in a
three-legged race*

economic matters, was agreed on 19 August and the second, a non-aggression pact, was signed four days later. The economic agreement provided for the exchange of Russian food products and raw materials for German manufactured goods and machinery. The non-aggression pact publicly stated that the two countries would never attack one another and that any problems arising between them would be settled amicably.

The pact between two countries of such totally opposed ideologies was intended to last for 10 years. It amazed the world but few thought it would last since it was recognised as nothing more than a **marriage of convenience**. In real terms it meant that if Germany invaded Poland then the Soviet Union would not come to the aid of the Poles. If, although Hitler thought it unlikely, Britain and France went to war as a result of the German invasion of Poland, the Soviet Union agreed not to become involved in the war. From the German viewpoint, it meant that if she invaded Poland, even with Anglo-French intervention, she would not have to face the prospect of fighting on two fronts. From a Soviet viewpoint, it meant at least some respite from the threat of a possible German invasion, the creation of a buffer-state between herself and her uncertain neighbour and time to prepare for a war which now seemed inevitable. A secret protocol or addition to the pact was the agreement for the future partition of Poland between the two countries along the Rivers Narew, Vistula and San. As a reward for agreeing not to become involved in a future war, Germany agreed that the Soviet Union could occupy the Baltic states.

marriage of convenience a union brought about because it was convenient at the time.

Sir Fitzroy Maclean, who was in Moscow at the time, later wrote in his book *Eastern Approaches* published in 1949.

> Stalin was being offered on the one hand by Hitler what he hoped meant peace, which he needed very badly to pull the Soviet Union together, plus very considerable territorial gains, the Baltic states, half of Poland, Finland, odd bits of the Balkans, all for keeping out of the war, which he wanted to do anyway. We were offering him a front-line position in the nastiest war there'd ever been. And that didn't appeal to him at all.

Even so, who made the greater gains from the pact was an issue still to be decided.

On 1 September 1939, Germany invaded Poland. Two days later, Britain and France declared war on Germany and so World War II began. As earlier agreed, on 17 September Soviet troops entered Eastern Poland and advanced to the line agreed in the secret protocol. That part of former Poland now became Western Ukraine and Western Byelorussia.

Behind them came the political commissars of the Red Army and the NKVD to begin the process of the Sovietisation of the people. Many atrocities were committed against the Polish people. The worst of these was at Katyn, near Smolensk, where thousands of Polish army officers were executed and buried in a nearby wood. As Molotov later boasted

THE TWO CONSTRICTORS

"I don't know about helping you, Adolf, but I *do* understand your point of view!"

PICTURE 32

A Punch cartoon of November 1939 shows Hitler and Stalin as two snakes swollen by their territorial gains

to the Supreme Soviet, the Red Army had wiped out 'all remains of the misshapen offspring of the Versailles Treaty'. Ten days later, Molotov and Ribbentrop signed a new friendship treaty that formalised the partition of Poland and finalised the demarcation line between the two countries. Arrangements were also made for Germans living in what had formerly been Eastern Poland to return to Hitler's *Reich*. Under duress, during the weeks that followed the Baltic states each signed treaties which allowed Soviet troops to be stationed within their borders. This marked the beginning of the end of their independence. Finland, however, refused to agree to a request for territory on the Karelian Isthmus. The Russians wanted this land in order to protect the approaches to the port of Leningrad and make it less vulnerable to a German attack. They also demanded the demilitarisation of the Mannerheim Line, a line of fortifications across the Karelian Isthmus, a 30-year lease of Hanko as a naval base and the surrender of several islands in the Gulf of Finland. The Finnish refusal to accept Soviet demands was an affront to Stalin. On 27 November 1939, the Soviet leader scrapped the non-aggression pact between the two countries. The next day the Russians accused the Finnish army of firing on a village close to the frontier and broke off diplomatic relations with their neighbour. On 30 November, Soviet forces invaded Finland and Molotov declared the country to be under the control of a new Finnish People's Government under the leadership of the Russian puppet, Otto Kuusinen. He was speaking prematurely!

E *The Russo-Finnish War, 1939–40 – 'The Winter War'*

In invading Finland, the Soviet Union had taken on more than they had bargained for. Amazingly, the tiny state held more than its own against the Russian colossus. The Red Army, short of experienced officers following the recent purge, failed to win its easy victory and, much to Stalin's annoyance, 'the Russian steamroller army failed to roll'. The Finns were superior to the Russians in winter warfare and from their defensive positions behind the Mannerheim Line they were able to check the advance of the Red Army. The League of Nations denounced the Soviet Union as an aggressor and expelled her from membership. The bravery of the Finns attracted the admiration of the world and whilst Sweden and Norway sent volunteers, Britain and France made supplies available. Although the Russians made little headway and suffered over 200 000 casualties, in the end the Finns had to give way against overwhelming odds and their resistance collapsed. Russian newspapers claimed their victory to be 'a deed without parallel in the history of war'. By the terms of a peace treaty signed in Moscow, Finland handed to the Soviet Union a part of the Karelian Isthmus, the port of Vyborg (Viipiri) and other territory including the Petsamo region in the north. This gave the Soviet Union a common frontier with Norway.

As we shall see, the war between Finland and the Soviet Union was far from over. Later, in June 1941, Finland was to ally herself with Hitler's Germany and join the invasion of Russia. In April 1940, when the Germans invaded Denmark and Norway, Stalin excused Hitler's action by claiming it was a defensive measure against the possibility of a British invasion. Two months later, he increased the pressure on the Baltic provinces and insisted that they appointed governments which 'coincided with Soviet interests'. The states became Soviet-style republics and, in August 1940, were embraced into the Soviet Union.

Meanwhile, in Europe, the war was going badly for the Anglo-French allies. In turn, the German armies had successfully invaded Denmark and Norway as well as Belgium, the Netherlands and Luxembourg. In addition but not unexpectedly, Italy had entered the war on Germany's side. On 22 June 1940, France agreed an armistice with Germany and this left Britain to fight on alone. The following month, Stalin, not to be outdone by Hitler's conquests in the West, demanded that Romania surrendered the provinces of Bessarabia and Bukovina. When Romania refused, the Red Army occupied these regions. In spite of their pact of 1939, relations between the Soviet Union and Germany began to worsen. Even so, every German victory in the war brought a letter of congratulation from Molotov. There was some irony in the fact that even as Hitler and his generals were making their plans for the invasion of the Soviet Union, Russian grain and raw materials continued to reach Germany. This continued right up to June 1941! In November 1940, Molotov travelled to Berlin in search of new territorial gains. He wanted to complete the invasion of Finland and, in addition, occupy Romania and Bulgaria. The Germans would have none of this and fobbed him off with vague promises of parts of the British Empire once the British had been defeated. On the chessboard that was the map of Europe, Hitler held all the major pieces and Stalin only a handful of pawns. Barely a month later, the Nazi leader signed Order Number 2 which sanctioned preparations for the invasion of the Soviet Union.

As the Soviet armaments industry was working flat out to equip its standing army of four million men in readiness for war, so Molotov intensified his search for allies. It was an act of near desperation that led him to agree a treaty of neutrality with Japan, which finally agreed the frontiers of their territories in the Far East. It also guaranteed that, when war came, the Soviet Union would not have to fight on two fronts. Meanwhile in Europe Stalin was alarmed when, in April 1941, Hitler unexpectedly ordered the invasion of Yugoslavia and, unknown to him, delayed his plans to attack Russia. In Germany, military preparations were intensified and by mid-June all were ready.

Although Stalin appeared to accept the inevitability of a war with Nazi Germany, he refused to believe that such a war was about to begin. He had ample warning. Winston Churchill, the British Prime Minister, told him that a German invasion was imminent as did his own agent, Richard Sorge.

PICTURE 33
*A Soviet postage stamp honours
the achievements of Sorge*

STALIN'S ACE SPY – RICHARD SORGE

Born at Baku in the Caucasus in 1895, Richard Sorge had a German father and a Russian mother. The family moved to Berlin before the outbreak of World War I and during that war Sorge served in the German army. After the war, he went to university and there joined the German Communist Party. A master linguist, he returned to the Soviet Union and became a member of their espionage network. He worked in Britain and the United States before being posted to the Far East. From time to time, he ventured back to Germany and even became a member of the Nazi Party and a correspondent for the German newspaper, *Frankfurter Zeitung*. Back in Japan, he worked as a press attaché at the German embassy and, at the same time, set up a very successful spy network. He was able to keep his masters in Moscow informed of all Japanese plans and discovered the intended dates of the German invasion of the Soviet Union and the intended Japanese attack on Pearl Harbor. Unfortunately Stalin did not accept his information as genuine and preferred to believe that Hitler would never go back on their treaty. Sorge was finally arrested by the Japanese in 1941 but was not executed until 1944.

In addition, German reconnaissance aircraft flew openly over Soviet territory. It is even claimed that a sympathetic German soldier, Private Alfred Liskow, went over to the Russians and told them the actual day of the impending German attack. He was shot for spreading rumours! Stalin persisted in his belief that Hitler would not betray the agreement reached in 1939. The final meetings between the representatives of both countries were very tense affairs:

The following extract is from *Ribbentrop* by Michael Bloch, 1992.

As soon as Dekanozov (the Soviet ambassador) walked through the door, Ribbentrop adopted his 'most freezing manner'. The Ambassador began by complaining about German violations of Soviet air space but Ribbentrop cut him short with the words: 'That is not the question now. The Soviet Government's hostile attitude to Germany and the serious threat represented by Russian troops on Germany's eastern frontier have compelled the Reich to take military counter measures.' He then read a list of alleged Soviet misdemeanours, concluding 'I myself have come to the conclusion that, in spite of serious endeavours, I have not succeeded in establishing reasonable relations between our two countries.' The Russian expressed regret ... and left without shaking hands. At the same time in Moscow, Molotov ended a similar interview with the German ambassador, Count Schulenberg, with the words: 'Surely we have not deserved this.' Then Goebbels broke the news in a broadcast and Ribbentrop read a formal statement declaring war.'

At 4.15 a.m. on Sunday 22 June 1941, German armies invaded the Soviet Union.

WHY DID HITLER INVADE THE SOVIET UNION IN JUNE 1941?

- Directly opposed to National Socialism, Hitler made no secret of his loathing of Bolshevism and considered it to be an ideology that had to be destroyed. In *Mein Kampf*, he described Bolshevism as 'an infamous crime against humanity' and later in a speech, he told his audience – 'Bolshevism is the doctrine of the people who are lowest in the scale of civilisation'. In 1940, Hitler showed his increasing impatience when he said – 'Russia's destruction must be made part of the struggle … The sooner Russia is crushed the better'.
- Hitler had no long-term belief in Stalin's good faith. Since there was to be a war, it was essential for Germany to strike first.
- The invasion of the Soviet Union would bring about the territorial expansion needed to gain much-needed *Lebensraum* – adequate living space for the German people. Hitler quite openly stated 'If new territory is to be acquired, it must be mainly at Russia's cost.' The regions he sought to annex were White Russia (present-day Byelorussia) and the Ukraine.
- Regions of western Russia would provide many of the raw materials needed for Germany to achieve *autarky* or self-sufficiency. The grain-growing Ukraine, Hitler described as 'Germany's bread basket' whilst the oil of the Caucasus would be essential to the German armed forces in any future war. The German *fuhrer* put it bluntly when he said – 'We will acquire soil for the German plough by use of the German sword and thus provide the nation with its daily bread.'
- The invasion was part of Hitler's campaign against the Jews. He regarded Marxism as being part of a Judaish plot to achieve world domination. In a speech made in 1937, he claimed that as 'a fact proved by irrefutable evidence, Communism was part of a Jewish world conspiracy'. He further claimed that 'the Jews had established a brutal dictatorship over the Russian people'. Earlier, he had emphasised the need to oppose Marxism and the Jews and warned – 'Either they will pass over our bodies or we over theirs'.
- Hitler calculated that the invasion of the Soviet Union would ultimately bring about the collapse of Britain. In 1939, he said – 'Britain's hope lies in Russia … If Russia drops out of the picture, all is lost for Britain …'

THE GREAT PATRIOTIC WAR, 1941–5

1941 June	Operation Barbarossa. German invasion of the Soviet Union Finland declares war on the Soviet Union Katyn Forest atrocities

TABLE 57
Date chart of the Soviet Union's involvement in World War II

July		Stalin announces 'scorched earth' policy
		Germans cross R. Dnieper and advance into the Ukraine
		German advance on Leningrad
September		German offensive to capture Moscow
		Siege of Leningrad begins
		Start of Lend-Lease
		Babi Yar. Mass murder of Soviet Jews
1942		Failure of Russian spring offensive
		Germans reach the River Don
November		Start of the Battle of Stalingrad
		Germans advance to within 30 km of Moscow
1943 January		Germans surrender at Stalingrad
		Major Russian advances along front
July		Battle of Kursk
		Russian offensive in the Ukraine
		Stalin recognises Russian Orthodox Church
1944 January		Red Army enters Poland
		Siege of Leningrad finally lifted
1945 January		Red Army captures Warsaw
April		Red Army takes Vienna
		Russian troops in Berlin
		Soviet and US troops meet at Torgau
May		Germany surrenders unconditionally to the Allies

4 ∽ OPERATION BARBAROSSA

The code name Hitler gave to his plans for the invasion of the Soviet Union was Operation Barbarossa. He took the name from the former Holy Roman Emperor Frederick I, a legendary German hero who was known as Barbarossa, the Italian for 'red beard'. The Nazi leader said – 'When Operation Barbarossa is launched, the world will hold its breath.' The ease with which his armies had won victories in the West and the poor performance of the Russians against the Finns led Hitler to be confident of a quick and easy victory. He boasted 'We will only have to kick in the front door and the whole rotten edifice will come tumbling down'. On the morning of 22 June 1941, more than 3 million German troops backed by Panzer units consisting of some 3350 tanks and massed formations of aircraft of the *Luftwaffe* began the invasion of the Soviet Union. In a massive *blitzkrieg* offensive, the Germans advanced along a 2300 km front that stretched from the Baltic Sea in the north to the Black Sea in the south.

The same day, the Soviet foreign minister, Molotov, spoke to the Russian people on the radio. The following is an extract from a speech of Vyacheslav Molotov on 22 June 1941 [adapted].

Citizens of the Soviet Union:
Today, without any claims having been presented to the Soviet Union, without a declaration of war, German troops attacked our country …
This unheard of attack upon our country is a betrayal unparalleled in

the history of civilised nations. The attack on our country was carried out despite the fact that a treaty of non-aggression had been signed between the USSR and Germany... Entire responsibility for the attack falls fully and completely upon the German Fascist rulers. The war has been forced upon us, not by the German people, not by German workers... but by the clique of bloodthirsty Fascist rulers of Germany. It is not the first time that our people have had to deal with an attack of an arrogant foe. At the time of Napoleon's invasion of Russia... he suffered defeat and met his doom. Our entire people must now stand solid and united as never before. The government calls upon you to rally closely around our glorious Bolshevik party, around our great leader and comrade, Stalin. Ours is a righteous cause. The enemy shall be defeated. Victory will be ours.

On 26 June, Finland declared war on the Soviet Union and, on the following day, Hungary followed. In July, Britain and the Soviet Union signed an agreement on mutual aid and both countries agreed not to make a separate peace with Germany.

5 ⌐ THE COURSE OF THE WAR

1941

At the start of Operation Barbarossa, the German land forces, which included Romanians, Hungarians and Italians, were organised into three Army Groups. Each was to be part of a three-pronged drive deep into the Soviet Union. Army Group North was to advance from East Prussia north-eastward through the Baltic States towards Leningrad; Army Group Centre was to advance due East to take Minsk and Smolensk before moving towards Moscow; Army Group South was to advance through the Ukraine, cross the River Dnieper and then move towards Kharkov. Although the Russian troops fought admirably, the German advance was impressive. Their Panzers swept aside Soviet resistance as they raced forward across the full length of the front. At the end of 3 weeks, Army Group Centre alone had taken over 300 000 Russian prisoners, 2500 tanks and masses of vehicles and military equipment. By early August, all former Polish territory occupied by the Russians had been taken, Leningrad was encircled and the people began the horrors of a 900 day siege, Minsk and Smolensk were in German hands, the River Dnieper crossed, and Odessa was besieged by the Romanians. At the end of September Hitler launched Operation Typhoon, an all out offensive to capture Moscow. Although units of the German army entered the suburbs of the city, they were driven back by ferocious Russian counter-attacks and forced to retreat. During this time, the Soviet government moved from Moscow to the safety of Kuy-byshev in the East but Stalin chose to stay in his capital city. As German forces advanced through the Baltic States and the Ukraine, many greeted the invaders as liberators from the oppressive rule of Stalin. Thousands were soon to volunteer to collaborate with the Germans. However, the onset of winter meant that the impetus of the German advance slowed. With Leningrad and Moscow still in Russian hands, it was clear that Hitler's plan to win an outright victory by the end of 1941 had failed.

When, before the end of the year, the war lapsed into a stalemate, it was more to the advantage of the Russians than the Germans. On 7 December, the Japanese attacked the American naval base at Pearl Harbor and, without hesitation, Hitler declared war on the United States. It was a decision that was to greatly influence the outcome of the war.

MAP 14 *'Barbarossa', the initial onslaught*

Barbarossa – what went wrong?

Three main reasons are usually given to explain the German failure to win an outright victory against the Soviet Union in 1941. Firstly, Hitler's decision to embark on the invasion before he had defeated Britain meant that he was, after all, committed to fighting on two fronts. Secondly, the German army had been weakened by the need to divert units to other fronts – the Balkans and North Africa. Thirdly, the 5-week postponement of the invasion that meant that the German army had less time to achieve its objectives before the Russian winter set in. But there were also other important reasons. It is claimed that Hitler was over confident and paid too little regard to the need to gather military intelligence about the deployment of the Red Army. Further, the information he received, he chose to ignore. Hitler was certainly surprised by the bravery and tenacity of the Russian soldiers – 'They fight with truly stupid fanaticism,' he said, 'with the primitive brutality of an animal that sees itself trapped.' The Russian soldiers certainly fought with unexpected ferocity. Discipline in the Red Army was strictly enforced and, behind the front line, there were always units of NKVD ready to deal with deserters or those whose morale was flagging. It was said that defaulters were sometimes sent forward to clear minefields with their feet! As the Germans advanced deeper into the Soviet Union, so their supply lines lengthened and shortages of munitions and food occurred. The gauge of Russian railway lines was different to that of Germany and this meant that German rolling stock could not be used to bring supplies to the front. To make things worse, as the Russians retreated, Stalin ordered them to carry out a 'scorched earth policy' in order to destroy everything which might help their survival. 'Do not leave a single house a single animal or a single grain of food,' he ordered. Behind the front line, Russians formed groups called 'partisans' to attack the invader from the rear. The morale of German soldiers was also affected by rumours of what might befall them if the Russians took them prisoner. The Russians were more used to and better able to cope with the severity of the weather. In the summer, the German soldiers had to contend with the scorching heat of the Ukraine. In the winter came sub-zero temperatures in which transport and weapons became useless and the men were liable to suffer frostbite and even freeze to death. In the spring came the heavy rain that clogged machinery and made the already poor Russian roads impassable.

A *The siege of Leningrad*

The Germans and their Finnish allies completed the encirclement of Leningrad on 8 September 1941 and the city was to remain under siege until 27 January 1944 – a total of 872 days. The three million Leningraders together with 200 000 Red Army soldiers were determined to hold on to their city, considered to be 'the birthplace of the Revolution', and there was never any question of surrender. All able-bodied men, women and children helped to dig anti-tank ditches and reinforce the city's defences. With no heating, water supply, almost no electricity and very little food, the defenders withstood continuous German shelling and bombing. The only means of contact with the outside world was across Lake Ladoga. In summer, limited supplies reached the beleaguered city by barge; in winter, the *Doroga Zhizni*, 'The Road of Life' across the frozen lake was used. Quite incredibly, during the length of the siege, the city's factories still managed to produce munitions. Starvation-level rations that included a mere 125 g of bread a day, exposure to sub-zero temperatures, disease and enemy action took its toll. In 1942, during the months of January and February alone, some 200 000 Leningraders died of cold and starvation. It was during this time that Dmitry Shostakovich composed his Seventh 'Leningrad' symphony and it was first performed in the besieged city. When the siege was finally lifted in January 1944, something approaching 800 000 people had died and been buried in mass graves. After the war, the city was awarded the Order of Lenin and had the title Hero City of the Soviet Union bestowed on it.

1942

In the spring of 1942, an early Russian offensive was unsuccessful. A German counter-attack led to the encirclement and annihilation of a Soviet army. The disgraced commander, General Efremov, took his own life. The German summer offensive that started late in June aimed to make up for the failures of the previous year, take the city of Stalingrad on the River Volga and pass around the Sea of Azov and then advance south to the oilfields of the Caucasus. Again, the Germans made impressive gains and advanced deep into the northern Caucasus. During this time, the Red Army suffered over 4 000 000 dead, wounded or taken prisoner. German losses were a relatively modest 1 150 000. On 19 November, the Battle of Stalingrad began.

See Map 14 on page 338.

B *The Battle of Stalingrad*

It was on Hitler's orders that, in June, a German army of 330 000 under General Friedrich Paulus was diverted to take Stalingrad, an industrial city on the banks of the River Volga. The German leader's intention was to capture the city, cross the river and then sweep southwards towards the Caucasus and the Caspian Sea. By the end of August, German troops had reached the River Volga and begun fighting their way into the city. In a battle that was to witness some of the fiercest hand-to-hand fighting of the war, the Red Army under Marshal Georgi Zhukov contested every street and every house. Nevertheless, the Germans succeeded in taking 80% of the city and there seemed the chance that the Red Army might be pushed to the Volga. At this moment of crisis, Zhukov devised 'Operation Uranus'. Realising that the German army

MAP 15
The German offensive in the south – the advance on Stalingrad

formed the spearhead of the advance and that their extremities were protected by less fanatical troops drawn from Italy, Romania and Hungary, he secretly assembled a large army to attack what he considered to be the weaker flanks. His plan was successful and, as the enemy's line collapsed, he used a pincer movement from north and south to encircle von Paulus's army of 330 000 men. During the months of December 1942 and January 1943, the Germans fought valiantly to hold their ground. Paulus asked for permission to fight his way out but Hitler ordered the German armies to stay and fight to the bitter end – to the death. In the knowledge that no rescue attempt was to be made and with food supplies and munitions running low, Paulus had no choice but to surrender. During the battle, the Germans lost 147 000 men with a further 91 000 taken prisoner. Zhukov's victory, which coincided with a British victory over the Germans at El Alamein in North Africa, proved to be major turning points in the war. It proved that the Germans were not invincible and gave the Allies a new confidence. On the Eastern

Front, it marked the beginning of a slow advance that would finally expel the German invaders from the Soviet Union.

1943

In spite of the humiliation at Stalingrad, the German armies were still strong enough to launch an offensive in February 1943 which held the Red Army advancing towards the River Dnieper and then forced it to retreat. However, to the north the German armies facing Moscow withdrew to a shortened and more easily defended line between Smolensk and Orel. To the south, between Orel and Kharkov, was a salient or bulge based on Kursk that extended 160 km into the German lines. In order to remove this salient and eliminate much of the Red Army's strength, the Germans made plans for 'Operation Citadel'.

KEY ISSUE

Stalingrad – a turning point in the war?

C *The Battle of Kursk*

For the coming battle, the Germans massed 900 000 men and some 3000 tanks, many of them formidable Tiger tanks. The offensive was to be supported by 1800 aircraft of the *Luftwaffe*. Hitler told his commanders, 'A victory at Kursk must shine like a beacon to the world.' It was a victory that never came! The Russians knew of the German plans and thought it best to wait for the enemy to attack first. The Red Army, under Marshal Rokossovsky, concentrated on building defensive positions on an unprecedented scale. Altogether over 400 000 mines were laid in front of the Russian positions which were 170 km in depth. Although the Germans were aware of the extent of the defences facing them, on 5 July they launched a massive tank-led offensive. In spite of suffering heavy losses they managed to force the Russians to retreat 30 km. On 11 July, the Russians counter-attacked and succeeded in destroying 40% of what remained of the German tanks. Within three days, the German offensive had been brought to a standstill. What came to be regarded as 'the greatest tank battle in history', the Germans lost 2900 tanks and 70 000 men killed. From that point on, the initiative on the Eastern Front firmly passed to the Russians.

See Map 16 on page 343.

After the Battle of Kursk, the Soviet army continued to advance steadily. Kharkov was taken and by the end of August, they had reached the River Dnieper and cut off the German forces trapped in the Crimea.

1944

During the early months of 1944, the Russian advance westward gathered pace and in April Soviet forces captured the Black Sea port of Odessa. In the summer came a major Russian offensive along the whole front. In the West, the Allied invasion of Normandy on D-Day had opened a long-awaited 'second front' against Germany and Allied troops were also fighting their way through Italy. Early in July, the Russians captured Minsk and by the middle of the month, their forces were again in Poland and advanced to the banks of the River Vistula. In anticipation of liberation, Polish resistance in Warsaw rose against the Germans and briefly took over sections of the city. The Red Army did not move and

MAP 16
*The Russian advance and
the Battle of Kursk*

watched as the Germans put down the revolt. It was later claimed that Stalin declined to help the Warsaw uprising in order to allow the Germans to eliminate Poles that might have caused him difficulties during the post-war period. In fairness, the Warsaw uprising had occurred without first consulting the Russians and the speed of their advance, over 700 km in five weeks, had exhausted the Red Army. The Soviet forces remained on the River Vistula for six months. In September, Finland surrendered and Russian troops were able to sweep through Estonia, Latvia and Lithuania. Units of the Red Army entered Romania and Bulgaria in August and, in October, they crossed into Yugoslavia and, with the aid of partisans led by Marshal Tito, liberated the country.

1945

At the start of 1945, the Russians prepared their final assault into the heart of Germany. Hitler refused to believe the size of the Soviet build-up and commented – 'It's the biggest lie since Genghis Khan! Who is responsible for producing all this rubbish.' The offensive opened on 12 January 1945. Pouring through a bridgehead in the German defences, Khukov's forces finally captured Warsaw. Next his armies pressed on through central Poland until the first units of the Red Army were on the River Oder. Once on German soil, the behaviour of some units of the Red Army left much to be desired and there were mass killings and rape. By the end of January, Russian tanks were barely 60 km from Berlin whilst, in the west, in March Allied forces had crossed the River Rhine and were advancing across Germany. The Red Army entered Austria in late March and on 13 April captured Vienna. A week later, the first Russian units entered the outskirts of Berlin. On 25 April 1945, Russian and American patrols met at Torgau on the River Elbe,

MAP 17

The Red Army's advance into eastern Europe and the heart of Germany

40 km to the south of the German capital. Defended by over a million troops and units of the *Volkssturm*, a type of home guard, the Germans fought ferociously for their capital. The Red Army used tanks and multiple rocket launchers to clear the city street by street. On 30 April, with Russian troops only a few hundred metres away, Adolf Hitler took his own life. That day, two Red Army sergeants, Kantariya and Yegorov, famously hoisted the Soviet flag above the *Reichstag* building. On 7 May, Germany surrendered unconditionally to the Allies.

The war was over but what of its impact on the Soviet Union and the Russian people?

The following extract is taken from *Stalin and Stalinism* by Alan Wood, 1990.

Apart from the physical mutilations, masses of Soviet citizens were left psychologically scarred for life. Indeed, the shocking slaughter left a deep and irremovable trauma in the mind and soul of the Soviet people ... The sheer scale of the human suffering and material destruction is unimaginable. Complete cities, towns, villages and settlements were obliterated, leaving around twenty-five million homeless. In Stalingrad, 90 percent of the city was flattened. In Leningrad, more people died through shelling, cold or starvation than were killed by the American atomic bombs on Hiroshima and Nagasaki. The victory was therefore bought at a terrible price, not only for the fighting men but also for the civilian population.

PICTURE 34 *The Soviet flag being raised on the Reichstag building on 30 April 1945*

6 ⌁ THE USSR UNDER GERMAN OCCUPATION

As the Germans advanced across the Western regions of the Soviet Union, they set up new provinces of the German empire. The Baltic provinces became *Reichskommisariat* Ostland and was placed under a civilian administration whilst the Ukraine became *Reichskommisariat* Ukraine under a military administration. Once victory had been achieved, the Germans intended to create a state beyond the Urals for Russians of ethnic Slav origin. Wherever possible and when the racial origins were suitable, the people were either to be 'Germanised' or resettled. The rest were to be gradually exterminated.

A *Atrocities and the treatment of the Soviet people*

The first atrocities against Russian civilians were not committed by the Germans but by the Soviet authorities themselves. As they withdrew ahead of the German advance, agents of the NKVD shot all political detainees held in Ukrainian prisons. Later during the war, the NKVD, under the supervision of Ivan Serov moved into areas where minorities were thought to be unreliable. Tartars living in the Crimea and ethnic Germans living along the River Volga were among the first to be targeted. Entire villages were wiped out and thousands sent in cattle wagons to the east – to Siberia and Kazakhstan. Few survived the journey. The first victims of the Nazis were Soviet political commissars. Guidelines issued before the invasion stated:

From a German Staff Command Secret Document issued in June 1941.

> In the fight against Bolshevism it is not expected that the enemy will act in accordance with the principles of humanity or international law. In particular, the political commissars of all kinds, who are the real bearers of resistance, can be expected to mete out treatment to our prisoners that is full of hate, cruel and inhuman. In this battle it would be mistaken to show mercy or respect … towards such elements. Action must be taken immediately, without further consideration, and with all severity. Therefore, when they are picked up … they are, as a matter of principle, to be finished immediately with a weapon.

As Hitler's New Order was imposed, so the country was exploited for its raw materials and slave labour and Nazi racial policy applied. The Soviet Union had a Jewish population of 2 100 000 and these together with the ordinary Russian Slavs, said to be *Untermensch* or sub-human became the tragic victims of the *Einsatzgruppen*, Special Task Forces, and the *Ordnungspolizei*, the Order Police. Four mobile killing groups of *Einsatzkommandos* operated across German-occupied

Russia. Their purpose was to eliminate 'undesirables' – Communists and their political commissars and those of inferior race, Slavs and Jews. From the first day of the war, the *Einsatzkommandos* followed behind the German army and were responsible for appalling atrocities as they carried out the Nazi programme of systematic **ethnic cleansing**. Jewish men, women and children were either massacred openly or sent to out-of-sight mobile gassing installations referred to as 'slaughter-houses on wheels'. The worst atrocity occurred at Babi Yar near Kiev where 33 000 Jews were murdered in two days.

> **ethnic cleansing**
> exterminating a
> racial group.

Babi Yar, September 1941

ANALYSIS

Before the war, Kiev had a Jewish population of 175 000. During 29–30 September 1941, 34 000 Jews were brought to a ravine in the outskirts of the town close to the Jewish cemetery. The ravine was known as Babi Yar. There in a two-day orgy of murder, all – men, women and children – were machine-gunned. The Germans were helped in their work by Ukrainian collaborators. In spite of their wounds, a few of the victims were able to crawl away and find hiding places. After the war they gave evidence against the perpetrators of the crime. For the remaining years of the war, the site was converted into an extermination camp to which Jews were sent from other regions of the Ukraine.

TABLE 58   *Some wartime atrocities in the Soviet Union*

1939–40	Katyn Forest	Some 14 500 Polish army officers shot by NKVD. At first Soviet authorities blamed the Nazis but 50 years later, in 1990, admitted responsibility.
1940–1	Baltic states	Over 229 000 Jews murdered during the first months of the German occupation of Estonia, Latvia and Lithuania.
1941	Ukraine	An estimated 10 000 Ukrainian political prisoners murdered by NKVD as Red Army retreated before the German invaders.
	Babi Yar	Mass murder of Jews (see above).
	Nicolaiev	Over 35 000 people, the majority were Jews, were murdered by the SS in the region of Nicolaiev.
	Chartsysk	370 children murdered by the NKVD. They were killed because they were exhausted and could not keep up with the general Russian retreat.
1941–4	Ponary	70 000 people, mainly Jews, murdered at an extermination site at Ponary, near Vilna in Lithuania.
1942	Kortelisy	Because of their support of local partisans, the entire population of the Ukrainian village of Kortelisy, 2892 men, women and children were murdered by Einsatzgruppen. Afterwards the village was razed to the ground. For similar reasons, the same fate befell at least 27 other Ukrainian villages.
1944	Korsun	During a blizzard, 20 000 German troops were slaughtered by Cossacks of the Red Army as they attempted to make their escape. None were taken prisoner.

During the years of German occupation, over one and a half million Russian Jews perished – 71% of the countries pre-war Jewish population. To these must be added Russian prisoners-of-war and others who were sent to Germany as forced slave labourers. There an estimated 3 million died as a result of being bullied, overworked and starved to death in labour camps. Within the Soviet Union, the Germans used Russian civilians as slave labourers. The Nazi view was summed up by SS chief Heinrich Himmler when he said, 'If ten thousand Russian families die of exhaustion digging an anti-tank ditch, that interests me only in so far as the ditch was dug for Germany.'

ANALYSIS

The Footballers from Kiev who defied the Nazis

In his book, *Dynamo: Defending the Honour of Kiev* (2001) Andy Dougan tells of the remarkable bravery of the players of Dynamo Kiev football team. Those that survived and were captured were reunited as slave workers in a bakery. In order to prove the theory of Aryan racial superiority, these badly treated and underfed men were forced to play matches against teams of Russian collaborators and Germans. In one match played against German stormtroopers, they were warned that they had to lose. In spite of the fact that a young SS fanatic refereed the match, the Russian players won 5–3. On their return to the bakery, they were arrested by the Gestapo and sent to a death camp. Years later, Leonid Brezhnev saw to it that a monument was raised in their honour.

B Collaboration and resistance

When the Germans first invaded the Soviet Union they were astonished to find that large numbers of Russians welcomed them as liberators from Stalinist oppression. This was particularly true of the Baltic states, Byelorussia and the Ukraine. Ukrainians still retained bitter memories of Stalin's enforced famine and German troops were offered the traditional gifts of bread and salt. It soon became clear that thousands were prepared to collaborate with the invaders and even serve in the German army. Some agreed to serve as *Hilfswillige* or volunteers and were used as labourers or to carry supplies to front-line soldiers. A number of Ukrainians formed a unit within the *Waffen-SS* known as the Galacia Division. The obvious leader of such men was Andrey Vlasov.

PROFILE

ANDREY VLASOV (1900–45)

Born in 1900 in the Vladmir province of Russia, Andrey Vlasov was the son of a kulak. In 1919, at the time of the Civil War, he was conscripted into the Red Army. He joined the Communist Party in 1930 and promotion soon followed when he was sent to China to act as a military adviser to Chaing Kai-shek's Nationalists. Promoted General in 1941, during the Great Patriotic War he distinguished himself in the defence of both Kiev and Moscow. He became a Hero of the Soviet Union and was awarded the Order of the Red Banner. In 1942, during the siege of Leningrad, he was taken prisoner. He blamed Stalin for the disaster that had befallen himself and his men and, as a captive, agreed to work for the Germans. From amongst Russian prisoners-of-war and Red Army deserters, he was able to recruit members of his Russian Liberation Movement. His declared aim was 'to fight as Germany's ally for a socialist Russia and rid the country of Stalin's system of terror.' 'Vlasov's army', as it became known, grew to total 50 000 men and towards the end of the war was allowed to go into battle against their former comrades in the Red Army.

Vlasov's men were not the only Russians to fight for the Germans. Eventually over a million swore oaths of loyalty to Hitler and enlisted in the German army. Although German generals accepted the volunteers with enthusiasm, Hitler opposed the idea of sub-human Slavs fighting alongside Aryan Germans. Consequently many were only allowed to perform menial tasks and quickly became disillusioned.

In July 1941, the Central Committee of the Party called upon all Soviet citizens to take up arms. As a result, thousands of Russians continued to oppose their German invaders even after their lands had been overrun. Stalin said, 'Insufferable conditions must be created for the enemy' and Red Army soldiers left behind by the speed of the retreat and local patriots formed units of resistance fighters known as partisans. They used guerrilla tactics to harass the enemy and, as the war progressed, they became better organised and were helped by officers and arms supplied by the Red Army. From time to time uprisings were

Q

Why did many Russians chose to collaborate with the Germans?

PICTURE 35

General Vlasov inspecting a group of Russians who have volunteered to serve in the German army

attempted and this caused the Germans to carry out extensive anti-partisan sweeps across the country that involved thousands of men. The penalty for those partisans captured was inevitably death by hanging. There were also occasions when partisan activity led to German retaliation. Hostages were taken and shot and whole villages raised to the ground and their inhabitants slaughtered. By the end of the war, an estimated million or more partisans were creating havoc behind the German lines.

7 ⌐ THE SOVIET WARTIME ECONOMY

Hitler assumed that his sudden invasion of the Soviet Union would ensure that the industries based in western Russia would soon be within his grasp. To some extent, this was true. By the end of 1941, the territories occupied by the Germans accounted for 63% of the county's coal production, 68% of her iron, 58% of her steel, 45% of her railways and 41% of her arable land. However, as we have seen much of the industrial development that occurred during the Five-Year Plans took place to the east of the Urals and were well away from the Nazi *blitzkrieg*. Even so, a great deal of industry essential to the Soviet Union's survival remained in the west.

A *The evacuation of Soviet industry*

On the first day of the German invasion, the Supreme Soviet issued a decree, 'On the Military Situation' which made plans for the mobilisation of the nation's resources for the war effort. It was imperative that Soviet forces had the necessary armaments to fight a prolonged war. An Evacuation Council was set up together with a State Defence Committee under the direction of Stalin. People's Commissariats were set up to supervise the various sections of war production such as tanks, guns and aircraft. Additional labour was to be recruited by committing the entire able-bodied urban population to war production. This included all men aged 16 to 55 and women aged 16 to 45. White-collar workers were switched to munitions factories, pensioners encouraged to return to work and students asked to undertake part-time work. There was a major redistribution of national expenditure so that by the end of 1942, the military share of the budget rose from 29% to 57%. The most staggering achievement came with the introduction of a Military/Economic Plan. Its aim was to evacuate factories from the West and reconstruct them in the east. This involved operations of gigantic proportions. In spite of enemy action intended to disrupt their movement, between July and November 1941, 1503 industrial units had been moved. Such a massive achievement was not brought about without hitches but the Russian people were aware that the Red Army was involved in a fight to the death and without adequate munitions, the war would be lost.

The following is from *Stalin's War Machine* by G.S. Kravchenko quoted in Purnell's *History of the Second World War.*

> Workers, office employees, engineers and technicians worked like heroes and displayed initiative in the restoration work – for example, it took two and a half years to erect a blast furnace in the south of the country before the war, but new furnaces at Magnitogorsk were built in eight months, and in Chusovaya in seven months. The Engels plant in Zaporozhye started production twenty days after it had been moved to a new place, while the Moscow military plant of the Armaments Commissariat was loaded on to 12 trains in the middle of October 1941, was on the move for 11 days, and started production in the first week of December. From that moment, it turned out 50% more production than before the evacuation.

The evacuation had largely been completed by the summer of 1942. By the end of that year, the manufacture of munitions accounted for 76% of all production. Recruitment for the armed services led to labour shortages but retraining women solved this problem. Once they had acquired the necessary industrial skills, they replaced their husbands and brothers so urgently needed as soldiers at the front. The employment of outstanding engineers and designers also meant that the quality of the weapons produced became superior to those of the Germans. The T-34 tank, Katyusha rocket launcher and Yak-1 fighter aircraft were recognised as amongst the best produced during the war.

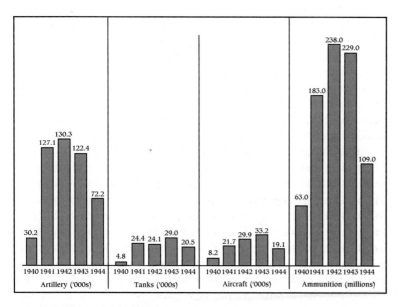

DIAGRAM 22   *Soviet military production, 1940–4*

B *Foreign aid*

During the course of the war the Soviet Union sought and received considerable aid from her partners in what was now called the Grand Alliance. Ships of the British Royal Navy and merchant fleet risked German submarines and air attack as they carried their cargoes of war materials across the icy waters of the Arctic Ocean to the port of Murmansk. Other aid from Britain and the United States reached the Soviet Union overland by way of Iran. By the Lend-Lease Act of 1941, the American Senate approved the sending of war materials to nations 'whose defence was considered vital to the defence of the United States'. As a result of Lend-Lease, the USA supplied the USSR with 6430 planes, 3734 tanks, 104 ships, 210 000 vehicles as well as essential raw materials and 5 million tonnes of food. By the end of the war, 427 000 of the 665 000 motor vehicles used by the Russians came from overseas. During the course of the war, the Soviet Union received over $11 billion in American aid. Stalin never acknowledged this and took steps to ensure that the Russian people were unaware of the help they were receiving from their capitalist allies. Instead, he criticised Britain and the United States for not opening a 'second-front' in western Europe. He paid scant regard to the fact that both those countries were fighting campaigns against the Germans in North Africa and, after 1943, in Italy. Both were also engaged in a war against Japan in the Far East – a conflict in which the Soviet Union was not yet involved.

> **KEY ISSUE**
>
> *How important was foreign aid to the Soviet war effort?*

8 ⌐ 'THE GREAT PATRIOTIC WAR' – SOME CONSIDERATIONS

A *Why was the Soviet Union able to defeat the German invasion?*

When Hitler ordered the invasion of the Soviet Union in June 1941, he had the advantage of tactical surprise but failed to appreciate the enormity of the task facing his armed forces. Hitler failed to pay sufficient regard to the geographical size of the country his troops were invading and the severity of its climate. He also under-estimated the ability of Josif Stalin as a war leader, the fighting qualities of the Red Army and the potential of the Russian economy once it was fully geared to the needs of war. Much of the credit for the Soviet survival and ultimate victory of the USSR must be attributed to the leadership of Stalin. After the initial onslaught of the German *blitzkrieg* in 1941 and the speedy occupation of much of western Russia, the German advance lost momentum. During the months that followed, the German armies failed to capture Leningrad and Moscow and, in 1942–3, were annihilated at Stalingrad. Stalin achieved centralised control of the Soviet war effort through the State Defence Committee and through his military headquarters, Stavka, which was based on the Tsarist idea of a military high command.

To some extent, the Soviet economy was already mobilised by the needs of Five-Year Planning. Following the evacuation of much of Russian industry to the east, it was able to resume full-scale war production which rapidly caught up with and then overtook that of Germany. As Hitler had assumed his *blitzkrieg* offensive would produce a speedy victory, the Germans had to re-think their economic strategy and were only able to fully mobilise for total war by 1943. This meant that the Soviets were able to replace their heavy losses more easily than the Germans. In spite of the purges of the 1930s, the Red Army was able to produce a new generation of able generals including Konev, Malinovsky, Rossakovsky, Tomoshenko and the man considered by many to have been the outstanding general of the Second World War, Zhukov. The fighting qualities and the ferocity of Red Army soldiers also took the Germans by surprise and they came to hold the 'Ivans' as they called them, in high regard. It should be remembered that Russians were fighting on their home ground and for their very existence. Those likely to preach defeatism or show cowardice were eliminated by units of the NKVD stationed behind the front line. Following the capture of his own son, Yakov, Stalin declared surrender a crime and refused state support to the families of those taken prisoner. The Soviets were also assisted by the tactical errors made by Hitler particularly at Stalingrad and Kursk. Unlike the Nazi leader, Stalin listened to his generals and planned his campaigns accordingly and was prepared to learn from his mistakes. He also worked tirelessly to maintain the morale of the Russian people. Taking the title 'Generalissimo' and defining the conflict as a 'Great Patriotic War', he was able to bring about a massive patriotic response as he constantly urged the people to greater effort. On the face of it, Stalin also appeared to abandon some of his ideological goals. In 1943, he announced his recognition of the Russian Orthodox Church, a move that pleased millions who, in spite of earlier persecution, had secretly retained their religious faith. He also encouraged glorification of Russian heroes of the past – men such as the warrior Tsar Peter the Great, Alexander Nevsky, thirteenth century victor over the Swedes and Mikhail Kutusov, who forced Napoleon to retreat from Moscow. But all this was no more than expediency and part of his drive to create a strong patriotic sentiment?

Another major error of judgement by Hitler was his refusal to take advantage of the enthusiastic support shown by millions of non-ethnic Russians at the time of the German invasion. In fact, the atrocities committed by such as the *Einsatzgruppen* undermined this initial good-will. Instead they switched their loyalty and joined the thousands of partisans who committed acts of sabotage and wrought havoc behind the German lines. Although Stalin would not admit it, aid received from his allies as part of the Lend-Lease programme contributed to the Soviet success as did the fact that Hitler had to divert divisions to North Africa and Italy as well as maintain a sizeable army in France in readiness for an Allied invasion.

See pages 347 and 348.

D How significant was the Soviet contribution to the final allied victory in 1945?

One set of statistics alone is sufficient to indicate the significance of the Soviet contribution to the final allied victory in 1945.

TABLE 59 *Soviet contribution to the final allied victory in 1945 (The figures relating to the Soviet Union are only estimates since the exact numbers are not known. The number of civilian dead includes the millions of Russian Jews murdered during the years of the German occupation.)*

	Military dead	Civilian dead
Soviet Union	11 000 000	7 000 000
Britain	264 443	92 673
United States	229 131	6 000
Germany	3 500 000	780 000

Of course, a consideration of the contribution made by the USSR must bear in mind the fact that in September 1939, the country entered into an alliance with Nazi Germany and consequently took part in the invasion of Poland and an attack on Finland. The Soviet Union did not willingly engage in a war with Germany and only became involved when their country fell a victim of Nazi aggression. A Soviet historian might argue that the German–Soviet Treaty was a result of his country's concern at the Anglo-French decision to appease Hitler in 1938 at the time of the Czech crisis and that the Pact was Stalin's means of buying time to prepare for war.

Once the Soviet Union became involved, its armed forces bore the brunt of the fighting in Europe and sustained massive losses. Unlike Britain and the United States, large tracts of its territory were occupied by the Germans and its people subject to great brutality. By comparison, whilst Britain suffered heavy bombing and shortages, the United States survived the war unscathed.

There is no doubt that the Battle of Stalingrad (1942–3) was not only a turning point in the war on the Russian Front but also a turning point in the war generally. No other battle was fought with such ferocity or produced such heavy losses. To describe it as 'the Verdun of World War II' is, if anything, an understatement and it certainly proved that the Germans were not invincible. Even after the formation of the Grand Alliance between Britain, the United States and the Soviet Union, relations between the leaders of the powers was always strained. Stalin achieved a better working relationship with Roosevelt, the American President, than with the British Prime Minister, Churchill. Even though Stalin dissolved Comintern in 1943, the Western powers remained suspicious of his long-term intentions. For his part, Stalin repeatedly urged Roosevelt and Churchill to open a second front in the West and feared that their reluctance to do was an indication that they were content to stand by as Germany and the Soviet Union fought each other to a standstill. He was also concerned that his allies might seek a separate peace with Germany and leave the USSR to fight on alone. Post-war Russian historians had a different view of World War II to that of their British and Americans counterparts. There was a tendency to play down the significance of Anglo-American aid and it was even claimed that the tanks supplied by the British were obsolete and inferior. They also considered the campaigns fought by Allied forces in North Africa and Italy to be mere sideshows and no mention was made of the fact that Allied forces were also involved in a war with Japan. They also claimed that the Allies were slow to open a second front and when they did, in June 1944, it was far too late. In fact, in 1941–2, it was true that 80% of German forces were active on the Russian Front but by early 1944 this had dropped to only 65%. Nevertheless, it is certainly true that compared with that of the Soviet Union, the loss of life amongst British and American servicemen was minimal. Apart from her military involvement in the war in Europe and the Far East, the United States made the major financial contribution to the winning of the war. It can rightfully be claimed that for the bulk of the war the United States was the main source of armaments and money. Of the three powers, Britain was the only one to oppose Nazi aggression by declaring war on Germany. Further, during 1940 and most of 1941 she fought on alone when the odds seemed very much against her survival.

9 ⁓ STRUCTURED AND ESSAY QUESTIONS

A *This section consists of questions that might be useful for discussion (or writing answers) as a way of expanding on the chapter and for testing the understanding of it.*

1. What advantages did the Soviet Union gain as a result of the Treaty of Rapallo (1922)?
2. Why did the activities of Comintern create difficulties in the Soviet Union's relations with other powers?
3. In what sense was the German–Soviet Non-Aggression Pact of 1939 'a marriage of convenience'?
4. To what extent might the Russo-Finnish War of 1939–40 be considered a set-back for the Soviet Union?
5. What was the purpose of the Russian 'scorched earth' policy?
6. To what extent might the Battle of Stalingrad be considered a major turning point in World War II?

B *Essay questions.*

1. How successful was the Soviet Union in its search for collective security during the 1920s and 1930s?
2. 'The need to gain control of Russia's natural resources was the main reason for the German invasion of the Soviet Union in June 1941.' How valid is this assessment?
3. To what extent might Stalin's leadership be considered the main reason why the Soviet Union successfully withstood the German invasion?

10 ⌐ MAKING NOTES

Read the advice given about making notes on page ix of Preface: How to use this book, and then make your own notes based on the following headings and questions.

A *Soviet foreign policy*
1. For what reasons were Germany and the Soviet Union considered 'pariah nations'?
2. What advantages did the Soviet Union gain as a result of the Treaty of Rapallo (1922)?
3. What led to the breakdown in Anglo-Soviet relations during the 1920s?
4. What difficulties did Stalin face in his relations with China?
5. For what reasons did the Soviet Union agree a Non-Aggression Pact with Nazi Germany in 1939?

B *Comintern*
1. What were the aims of Comintern?
2. What part did Comintern play in the Spanish Civil War?
3. Why did Stalin decide to dissolve Comintern in 1943?

C *The Soviet Union and World War II*
1. For what reasons did Germany invade the Soviet Union in 1941?
2. Why were the German armies able to advance so quickly across Russia during the early months of the war?
3. What factors helped Leningraders to survive an 872-day siege?
4. What was the purpose of Stalin's 'scorched earth' policy?
5. Why was the Soviet Union able to maintain such a high level of arms production during World War II?

11 ⌐ DOCUMENTARY EXERCISE ON THE BATTLE OF STALINGRAD

Study the sources and then answer the questions based upon them.

SOURCE A
From an entry in the diary of the German General Hermann Hoth on 7 August 1942.

The company commander says that the Russian troops are completely broke, and cannot hold out any longer. To reach the Volga and take Stalingrad is not so difficult for us. The *Fuhrer* knows where the Russians' weak spot is. Victory is not far away.

Lorry-loads of infantry and tanks tore into the city. The Germans obviously thought that the fate of the town had been settled, and they all rushed to the centre and Volga as soon as possible and grabbed souvenirs for themselves ... we saw drunken Germans jumping down from their lorries, playing mouth organs, shouting like madmen, and dancing on the pavements ...

SOURCE B
A Russian eye-witness account of the behaviour of German soldiers on 14 September 1942

September 16. Barbarism...not men but devils.
September 26. Barbarians, they use gangster methods.
October 27. The Russians are not men but some kind of cast-iron creatures; they never get tired and are not afraid of fire.

SOURCE C
From a series of entries in the diary of the German soldier, Kurt Hoffman in 1942

SOURCE D
Hitler's response to von Paulus' request to allow the German army to withdraw from the Volga in November 1942

I am not leaving the Volga. The Sixth Army will do its historic duty at Stalingrad until the last man.

We have fought during fifteen days for a single house ... And imagine Stalingrad – eighty days and eighty nights of hand-to-hand struggles. The street is no longer measured in metres but in corpses ... Stalingrad is no longer a town. By day it is an enormous cloud of burning, blinding smoke. The nights of Stalingrad are a terror ... animals flee this hell; the hardest stones cannot bear it for long; only men endure.

SOURCE E
From an account written by the Russian General Vasili Chuikov

Q

1. *Compare Sources A and C. To what extent do they represent different views of the fighting qualities of the Russian soldier?*
2. *To what extent do Sources A and B suggest that, at one stage, the Germans thought they had won the battle for Stalingrad?*
3. *What evidence is there in Sources C, D and E that might help to explain why the Germans were defeated at Stalingrad?*
4. *How useful are the sources to an understanding of the Battle of Stalingrad?*

11

Stalin – the final years 1945–53

INTRODUCTION

When World War II came to an end in Europe in May 1945, the prestige of the Red Army, the Soviet Union and the nation's leader, Josif Stalin, had never been higher. There were victory parades in Moscow's Red Square and elsewhere in other Russian towns and cities. On 24 May, Stalin held a victory reception in the Georgevsky Hall in the Kremlin for over a thousand officers. Whilst the Soviet leader took the title supreme commander or generalissimo and delighted in the adulation of his people, he appeared to accept the lion's share of the credit for winning the war. He played down the roles of his generals, many of whom were appointed to distant commands well away from Moscow and some even demoted. He also seemed reluctant to acknowledge the valour of the Soviet people and made little mention of the achievements of this largely peasant Red Army or the important part played in the war by Soviet women. As might have been expected, he made no reference to the contribution of the Soviet Union's wartime allies. It was a period during which propaganda was used to promote Stalin's prowess and achievements to new dimensions. His 'cult of personality', as the historian Alan Wood has written, 'was not just hero-worship, it was **deification**'. Even so, the global war was not yet over. On 6 August, the Americans dropped the first atomic bomb on the Japanese city of Hiroshima. Two days later, the Soviet Union declared war on Japan, a move that would ensure that they had some say in the post-war treaties in the Far East. The following day, a second atomic bomb fell on Nagasaki and on 15 August Japan surrendered. The war was finally at an end.

deification to worship as a god.

1 ↝ POST-WAR RECONSTRUCTION

A *Industry*

In addition to the massive loss of life, with a quarter of her industry destroyed, the Soviet Union had suffered far greater material damage than the other Allied powers. In the areas fought over and then occupied by the Germans, villages, towns and cities had been razed to the ground and nearly 100 000 collective farms had been completely destroyed and their livestock slaughtered and machinery seized.

Thousands of kilometres of rail track and much of the country's rolling stock had been destroyed. Industry had been left devastated with factories destroyed and mines flooded, something approaching 70% of the nation's industrial production had been lost. Once demobilised, workers returning from war had to readjust to civilian life whilst a great many of those wounded or mentally scarred by their experiences would never work again. In 1946, Stalin announced the introduction of a Fourth Five-Year Plan aimed at national reconstruction. Although American Lend-Lease came abruptly to an end and there was a shortage of skilled labour, the Russian people showed enthusiasm and a willingness to continue the self-sacrifice shown during the war. Their vigour was such that industrial recovery came at an amazing pace as, across the war-torn country, factories and steel works were rebuilt, mines reopened and production resumed. By the end of 1947, the hydro-electric power station on the Dneiper Dam was back in operation and coal production in the Donets Basin had overtaken that of 1940. Soon the production of coal and steel nationally had passed the pre-war figure. The very speed of Soviet recovery produced its own problems – **bottlenecks** in production and distribution and shortages of component parts and raw materials. Whilst there was some very small increase in the production of consumer goods – clothing, furniture and radios – other items remained as scarce as ever. Industrial progress was aided by the seizure of machinery, rolling stock and other materials from the defeated countries as reparations and the use of prisoners-of-war and their own political prisoners as slave labour.

> **bottlenecks** situations where movement is difficult because of congestion.

B *Agriculture*

The attempts to revive Soviet agriculture proved far less successful. During the 1930s, the needs of agriculture had taken second place to those of industry. Now as then, the way forward was seen to be continued industrial development and expansion. As far as agriculture was concerned, memories of peasant opposition to collectivisation lingered and many in the Party hierarchy considered rural workers to be still bourgeois in outlook. During the war, many had turned their backs on the *kolkhozes* and concentrated on the cultivation of their own plots. During the immediate post-war years, Soviet agriculture faced many problems. Since the peasantry had been the backbone of the Red Army, the heavy loss of life meant that there was now an acute labour shortage in the countryside. In addition, much of Russia's arable land had been left uncultivated, livestock slaughtered and machinery destroyed. In the occupied regions, the Germans had returned the collectives to private ownership. As in the 1930s, in the post-war situation Stalin regarded agriculture as important only as a means of feeding the urban workers. As Martin McCauley has written, farms were 'the milch cows of the cities and industry'.

Immediately after the war attempts were made to once again enforce collectivisation and restock the *kolkhozes*. Unfortunately, a shortage of labour and machinery, lack of motivation amongst the peasantry and severe droughts hampered progress. Consequently the grain harvest of 1946 was barely half that of 1940. Procurements, the amounts of produce allocated to the state, accounted for up to 70% of the harvest yield and this left barely enough to sustain the peasants and their stock animals. Reduced once again to near serf status, the peasants were subject to strict control, confined to their regions and subject to ever increasing demands to produce more. Increases in taxation made it difficult for families to survive and as food became scarce so many suffered malnutrition and the threat of famine returned. If production targets were not achieved, the blame was not placed on the faulty planning by the centralised administration. Instead, the leader of the *kolkhoz* became the scapegoat and was dismissed. Eventually, those who worked on the land lost their entitlement to food rations and were expected to be self-sufficient and fend for themselves. In 1946, all those who continued to work their own plots had their land confiscated and they were forced to return to labour on the collectives. The following year, quotas were increased and private trade, selling at market stalls, was forbidden. In 1948, Stalin introduced his plan for the 'transformation of nature'. This involved the extensive planting of trees to prevent erosion, the construction of irrigation canals, and the adoption of the crackpot ideas of the controversial agricultural scientist and biologist, Trofim Lysensko.

> ### KEY ISSUE
>
> *Reasons for the USSR's recurring agricultural problems.*

PROFILE

> ## TROFIM LYSENKO
> ## (1898–1976)
>
> Born in the Ukraine in 1895, Trofim Denisovich Lysenko took a degree in agricultural science and, until 1929, worked at an experimental station. He was then appointed head of the department of physiology at the Ukrainian All-Union Institute of Selection and Genetics in Odessa. On the basis of crude and unproven experiments, he claimed to be able to increase crop yields using methods other scientists thought impossible. His view was that the quality of a crop depended on environmental influences and not on genetics. According to his theory of vernalisation – crops and animals could acquire new characteristics through modification – enforced change. For example, he claimed that grain intended for spring sowing could be changed to grain suitable for winter sowing if it was subject to moistening and refrigeration. He went further and expressed the view that wheat raised in the appropriate environment could produce the seeds of rye. A critic has likened this to claiming that dogs brought up in the wild could give birth to foxes! During Stalin's regime, Lysenko's views became accepted Marxist theory and he rose to become the controlling influence in Soviet agriculture. After the Soviet leader's death in 1953, his views were rejected and he was subject to ridicule and removed from office. In fairness it must be mentioned that some scientists have not totally dismissed Lysenko's theories.

During this period the First Secretary of the Moscow Party and rising member of the Politburo, Nikita Khrushchev, became involved in planning Soviet agricultural policy. He was bold enough to put his plans to Stalin. Known as *agrogorods* and based on the idea of amalgamating *kolkhozes* into larger units, Khrushchev wanted to establish town-like settlements in the countryside each with its own range of utilities – community centres, hospitals, clinics, nurseries and schools. The peasants would live in blocks of flats with water, electricity and sanitation provided. Rural workers did not like the idea and, at the Party Congress in 1952, Georgy Malenkov spoke against Khrushchev's scheme describing it as too expensive and a mistake. Consequently, plans to establish *agrogorods* were abandoned. Agriculture was to remain the most vulnerable aspect of Soviet economic planning with its problems continuing to defy solution.

2 ⌐ YEARS OF STALINIST TYRANNY

A *Stalin – 'an unbalanced psychopath'?*

During the immediate post-war years, Josif Stalin, who had earlier appeared to be an astute and rational wartime leader, became increasingly morose and destructive. Appearing to be unbalanced and emotionally unstable, his paranoid behaviour was evident in his irrational suspicion of those around him. He made few public appearances and lived in near seclusion in his dacha, country house, or Black Sea residence. Few people were allowed access to him and his fear of imaginary enemies led him to have his meals tasted for poison, the rooms of his house regularly searched and, when he travelled, his route changed in order to thwart any possible assassination attempt. There was an instance when a youth was shot for daring to catch a glimpse of the train in which he was travelling! Party leaders lived in constant fear of his mood swings since they knew that a person who appeared to be a friend one day was liable to be arrested and disappear the next. Sometimes he organised social functions for his colleagues that involved heavy drinking and crude horseplay that often included ridiculing his guests. Later, Nikita Khrushchev said, 'When Stalin said dance, a wise man danced'. Some historians have argued that Stalin did not undergo a personality change and that all his abnormalities of character were apparent in the 1930s. It was simply that old age and senility had made him even more morose and vindictive. Even so, the Soviet propaganda machine continued to promote their all-powerful *Vozhd* as a great leader and spoke of the 'solidarity of the Soviet peoples under their leader of genius, J.V. Stalin.'

> **KEY ISSUE**
>
> *Stalin's mental condition. Had he become paranoid and psychopathic?*

B *'Hysterical isolationism'*

The Russian historian, Yuri Levada, has described the years 1945–53 as a period of 'hysterical isolationism'. During this time, Stalin took every possible measure to ensure that the Russian people were denied access to the outside world and particularly Western influences. The Soviet leader claimed that such steps were necessary to ensure the security of their country which, he claimed was threatened by the capitalist powers who were plotting to overthrow their Communist regime. People were warned to be on their guard and denounce any 'hidden agents of Western imperialism'. Russians were not allowed to travel abroad and even needed special permission to travel widely within their own country. Few foreigners were allowed to enter the Soviet Union and those that did were kept under constant surveillance. In truth, these measures had nothing to do with national security but were aimed at ensuring that Stalin's rule would continue unchallenged and that his policies would be accepted without question. For these reasons, the Russian people had to be isolated and those who might be tempted to challenge or question the Soviet system eliminated. Amongst those considered a risk were men being demobilised or repatriated. These included returning Red Army servicemen who had fought their way across eastern Europe into Germany and come into contact with Western influences. One Russian soldier reacted by saying – 'the standard of living was incomparable with the standard of living in Russia ... the shops had a great many things we had long forgotten about'. Such an observation made in the Soviet Union would have been considered subversive. Consequently, returning soldiers were carefully screened and many were arrested and deported to the labour camps. Even more suspect were returning prisoners-of-war. Although officially declared to be either traitors or collaborators, all had endured the appalling conditions in German labour camps and some had managed to escape and fight with local resistance groups. Those liberated by British and American forces were forcibly repatriated. Some aware of their probable fate chose to commit suicide rather than return to their homeland. Clearly those that had served with Vlaslov's Russian Liberation Army had little or no chance of survival. Former prisoners-of-war were either executed or sent in their tens of thousands to slave labour camps, the *gulags*. During the immediate post-war years, some 2 272 000 Russian citizens were returned to the Soviet Union to face the wrath of Stalin. An eye-witness described the reception of Russian prisoners-of-war at Odessa:

The following quotation is in *Victims of Yalta* by Nikolai Tolstoy, 1977.

The disembarkation started at 1830 hrs and continued for four and a half hours. The Soviet authorities refused to accept any stretcher cases as such and even the patients who were dying were made to walk off the ship carrying their own baggage ... The prisoner who had attempted suicide was very roughly handled and his wound opened up and allowed to bleed. He was taken off the ship and marched behind a packing case; a shot was heard ... The other 32 prisoners were marched or dragged into a warehouse some fifty yards from the ship and after a lapse of fifteen minutes, automatic fire was heard ... They were not the only victims. Altogether about 150 Russians were separated from the rest and marched behind sheds on the quayside.

> They were massacred by executioners, many of whom appeared to be
> youths aged between 14 and 16.

At whatever cost, Stalin was determined to ensure that Western culture
and political ideas would not contaminate the Russian people. He
set out to eliminate every vestige of independent thought and remove
anyone, both within and outside the Party, who stood in his way or
posed a threat. Within Russia, even the relatives of those who had spent
some time outside direct Soviet control, remained permanently suspect
and it was extremely risky to know or communicate with anyone from
the West. In *American in Russia* (1950), Harrison Salisbury described
his experiences as a journalist in the Soviet Union the previous year:

> I returned in 1949... I had many friends in Moscow that I had met
> during the war. I telephoned several of them... when they heard my
> voice they hung up... As I walked down Gorky Street, not infre-
> quently I met someone whom I had met during the war. At first I
> tried to speak to them, but they looked right through me and go
> straight ahead without speaking. I quickly understood it was too
> dangerous to talk to me... for any Russian to have a contact with me
> was the equivalent almost certainly to arrest and possibly a one-way
> ticket to Siberia.

> **Q**
> *Why did Stalin*
> *fear Western influences?*

What followed were years of violence when fear and intimidation
permeated every aspect of Soviet life. In such a climate, Russians
regarded each other warily looking for the opportunity to curry favour
by unearthing a dissident and living in fear that they themselves would
be denounced. There were secret police and informers everywhere and
people were liable to be arrested for careless slips of the tongue, a hint
of independent thought and behaviour considered inappropriate.
Then, subjected to interrogation and even torture, they would invariably be found guilty and sent to the labour camps. Life in the camps
was extremely harsh and although sent to serve a specified number of
years, many had their sentences extended over and over again for no
valid reason. An estimated 12 million men and women were sent to the
camps to endure grim conditions which included long working hours,
near starvation rations and appalling living conditions. One of those
sent to the *gulags* was Aleksandr Solzhenitsyn who later became a leading Russian writer of his generation. In his book, *One Day in the Life of
Ivan Denisovich* (1970), he describes life in the camps:

permeated pervaded or
spread through

> They had given Kilgas twenty-five years. Earlier, things had been
> better: ten years without exception to everybody... The law can be
> turned any way you want. You serve your ten years, and perhaps
> they'd give you another ten... So you went on living like this with
> your face on the ground, and there was no time to be thinking how
> you got in and how you'd get out.

> Shukhov began to eat the cabbage in what was left of his gruel. He came across a small piece of potato … an average sort of piece, frostbitten of course, and somewhat hard and sweet. But there was very little fish – an occasional bit of bare backbone. But you had to suck away at every bit of backbone or fin – to get the juice out of it, for the juice was nutritious … Your belly is a cruel master – however well you've treated it one day, it'll be singing for more the next.
>
> They looked around – should he take his coat? But they'd only take it away from him, and leave him with only his jacket … 'Well, good-bye brothers,' he said and nodded in a confused way … He followed the warder out. A few voices shouted after him: 'Keep cheerful. Don't let them get you down'. The men knew the cells, they'd built them themselves: stone walls, cement floor, no windows, a stove lit only to melt the ice on the walls … You slept on bare boards, and if your teeth did not fall out from chattering, 300 grams of bread to eat a day – and gruel on every third day. Ten days in the cells meant that your health was ruined for life … Fifteen days – and you were a dead man!

The system of terror was supervised by the secret police, the NKVD, under the leadership of Beria. Well known national figures who disappeared were subject to even further indignity. Stalin not only took their lives, he also took steps to erase their names from the pages of history. All references to them in books, especially the massive volume of Russian biography, the *Great Soviet Encyclopedia* were removed and, in what the historian David King has called 'pictorial genocide', their pictures were crudely deleted. As far as the Russian people were concerned, it was as if these people had never lived. It has been suggested that the obvious forgeries were intentional and meant to warn others that they were liable to be eliminated.

NOW YOU SEE HIM, NOW YOU DON'T.
SOME EXAMPLES OF 'PICTORIAL GENOCIDE'

PICTURE 36
(a) Lenin, supported by Trotsky, making a speech in 1917

PICTURE 36
(b) an effort to discredit Trotsky and to play down his earlier friendship with Lenin, Trotsky has been removed from his position at the side of the platform

PICTURE 37 *(a) Stalin and Yezhov beside the Moscow–Volga Canal. (b) After Yezhov had fallen from favour, he was removed from the photograph*

LAVRENTI BERIA (1899–1953)

Born in 1899 in the Georgian town of Mingrelia, Lavrenti Beria first qualified as an architect before joining the Communist Party and serving in the secret police. It is said that he first met Stalin when he saved the Soviet leader from an assassination attempt. Others think that he staged the plot himself in order to enhance his reputation. In 1938, he was appointed head of the NKVD. A highly intelligent man, able to get things done, he was unscrupulous and able to manipulate those around him. He came to exercise immense power and was feared by all. Beria was largely responsible for the development of the system of labour camps, the *gulags*. Sinister and a known paedophile, Beria is described by Jonathan Lewis and Phillip

Whitehead as 'a man of unbridled appetites and ambitions, with terror at his beck and call', he was responsible for the murder and imprisonment of millions. His excesses and crimes even excelled those of his predecessors Yagoda and Yezhov.

PICTURE 38
Svetlana, Stalin's daughter sitting on Beria's knee. As she grew older, she came to hate him

In *Twenty Letters to a Friend* published in 1967, Stalin's daughter, Svetlana Alliluyeva, said of Beria:

> Beria was more treacherous, more practised in perfidy and cunning, more insolent and single-minded than my father. In a word, he was a stronger character... He (Stalin) was simpler and could be led up the garden path by someone of Beria's craftiness... He flattered my father... He extolled and flattered him in a way that caused old friends, accustomed to looking on my father as an equal, to wince with embarrassment... The spell cast by this terrifying evil genius on my father was extremely powerful and it never failed to work.

C *Zhdanovism – the purge of Soviet culture*

Clearly, if freedom of thought was considered a threat to the Stalinist regime then those most likely to express unacceptable views were the educated, the intelligentsia – lecturers, teachers, writers and those involved in the arts. In 1946, Andrei Zhdanov began what amounted to a cultural purge when he began a campaign to bring all creative arts under his own strict political control.

ANDREI ZHDANOV (1896–1948)

Born in the Ukraine in 1896, after the October Revolution of 1917, he rapidly rose through the Party ranks. A close friend and loyal supporter of Stalin, in 1934 he was appointed head of the Party in Leningrad and, in 1939, became a member of the Politburo. In World War II, he played a leading role in the defence of his city during the lengthy siege of 1941–44. After the war, he strongly supported an aggressive anti-West policy and, in 1947, was instrumental in setting up Cominform. He then turned his attention to establishing ideological guidelines to which intellectuals and those engaged in cultural activities had to conform.

Under *Zhdanovshchina* or Zhdanovism all forms of artistic and intellectual activity had to conform to Communist ideals and promote Stalinist achievements and the cult of Stalin. Above all, they had to reject and abandon Western influences which Zhdanov regarded as bourgeois and decadent. Directives were issued and those who declined to accept Socialist Realism risked ending their careers and even put their lives at stake. Zhdanov's campaign, which aimed to portray Soviet culture as superior to the decadent West, began with a vicious attack on two highly regarded Leningrad writers, Anna Akhmatova and Mikhail Zoshchenko. Akhmatova, an eminent poet whose husband and son were already exiled in Siberia, he denounced as being 'half nun and half whore'; the satirist Zoshchenko, who in 1946 published *The Adventures of a Monkey*, had his book condemned as being 'malicious and insulting to the Soviet people'. Both were expelled from the Union of Soviet Writers and their works were banned. After Stalin's death, Akhmatova and Zoshchenko were rehabilitated and regained their former popularity. In 1965, Akhmatova was able to travel to Britain to receive an honorary degree from Oxford University. Others who became victims of Zhdanov's rigid censorship were the world famous composers Shostakovich and Prokofiev. They were accused of 'following bourgeois ideology fed by the influence of West European and American music' and failing to 'use the wealth of popular melodies of which the USSR is so rich'. In order to be able to continue to work both recanted. Shostakovich at first resisted but then confessed – 'I know the Party is right … and that I must search for creative paths which lead me to Soviet realistic popular art'. Zhdanov's purge of the free-thinking intelligentsia was limited to prominent academics who were openly criticised and humiliated. Scholars were denounced if they even hinted that Western writers such as Shakespeare, Rousseau, Moliere or Dickens had in any way influenced Russian literature. As Zhdanov's campaign continued, it became broader in its scope and more severe in its application so that academics could only survive by accepting the Party line and avoiding sensitive questions. This was the time when the theories of Trofim Lysenko were promoted as official Party line and scientists had to pay lip service to his false theories. A most bizarre aspect of Zhdanov's anti-West stance was the attempt made by Soviet propagandists to claim that most Western inventions and scientific advances were really of Russian origin. The period 1946–53, which created a barrier between the normal exchange of ideas between Russia and the West, came to be regarded as a time of stagnation in Soviet artistic and cultural development when few works of merit appeared.

> ### KEY ISSUE
> *The impact of Zhdanovism on Soviet culture.*

Zhdanov died unexpectedly in 1948. He had been one of Stalin's closest confidantes and supporters but he may have become too influential. It has even been suggested that he was murdered at Stalin's instigation. He was not the first leader of the Leningrad Party to be regarded as a threat and die this way – the murder of the popular Kirov in 1934 also occurred in suspicious circumstances.

D The 'Leningrad Affair' and the purge of the Party

> **euphoria** a feeling of well-being.

During the immediate post-war period, the **euphoria** of victory together with resurgence of a spirit of national revival led to a new enthusiasm for the Communist Party. Many ambitious newcomers joined looking for the opportunity of advancement and a chance to join in Zhdanov's campaign against Western influences. As a result, by 1950 membership of the Party had risen to over five and a half million. This new vanguard of staunch supporters, gave Stalin a chance to rid himself of those who he feared might emerge as possible rivals as well as those who had served the Party but whose enthusiasm had waned and were now no longer needed. A few months after the death of Zhdanov, Stalin began a sudden and wide-ranging purge of the Soviet Communist Party. It began in Leningrad where numerous high ranking Party and government officials were arrested including many of Zhdanov's former associates. They were either executed or imprisoned. The purge then became nationwide as thousands of Party officials and managers were sent to the labour camps. Charges of conspiracy and treason made against victims of the purge were baseless and many of those sent to the *gulags* had been long serving and loyal Party members. The purge even threatened the Party hierarchy. Amongst those arrested was Molotov's Jewish wife, Polina Zhemchuzhina. She was accused of being a spy after being overheard talking in Hebrew to Israel's first ambassador to the Soviet Union, Golda Meir! Now in his seventies, the aging Stalin had groomed no obvious heir apparent and, living in constant fear, leading Politburo members sought to win favour with the leader by discrediting the others. In a grotesque game of political musical chairs, Party leaders jockeyed for position. Stalin enjoyed playing one off against the other. They well knew that to win the temporary friendship of the Soviet leader one day might result in their arrest the next. Historians are uncertain about the reasons for the purge. Some feel that it was further evidence of Stalin's paranoid suspicion of those around him, particularly the rising young leaders of the Leningrad Party. Others suggest that the purge was part of a power struggle within the Party between a group led by Malenkov and Beria and the former supporters of Zhdanov.

E *Stalin – the family man*

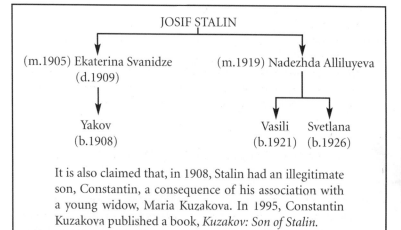

JOSIF STALIN

(m.1905) Ekaterina Svanidze (d.1909)

(m.1919) Nadezhda Alliluyeva

Yakov (b.1908)

Vasili (b.1921)　Svetlana (b.1926)

It is also claimed that, in 1908, Stalin had an illegitimate son, Constantin, a consequence of his association with a young widow, Maria Kuzakova. In 1995, Constantin Kuzakova published a book, *Kuzakov: Son of Stalin*.

PICTURE 39
Yakov, a prisoner of the Germans. He was the only child of Stalin's first marriage

During these years, Stalin's family suffered in much the same way as any other. His elder son, Yakov, who had been taken prisoner by the Germans, died in captivity. Afterwards Stalin imprisoned Julia, his Jewish daughter-in-law. In 1948, Stalin's deceased wife's sisters were sent to the camps because, according to him, 'they talked a lot and knew too much'. Vasili, his younger son who was a notorious alcoholic and womaniser, died of his condition in 1962.

His daughter, Svetlana, who first married a Jewish scholar without her father's blessing, survived these terrible times and, after her father's death, chose to live in the West and write her own account of these events. Altogether, Stalin had eight grandchildren but only three ever met their grandfather.

F *Stalin and the 'cult of personality'*

Meanwhile, Stalin's cult of personality now reached ridiculous proportions as those around him went to great lengths to foster the 'synthetic adulation' of the brooding old man. Treated as near god-like and infallible, across the country, towns sought the honour of carrying his name – Stalingrad, Stalino, Stalinsk, Stalinabad, and Stalinogorsk. In 1949, his seventieth birthday celebrations became an orgy of adulation and flattery. Massive crowds assembled in Red Square beneath a gigantic portrait of their leader suspended from a large balloon and

PICTURE 40
*Stalin with Vasili and Svetlana,
the children of his second
marriage*

illuminated by searchlights. Church leaders thanked God for giving the country a 'pillar of social justice' and in a speech given in the Bolshoi theatre, Nikita Khrushchev, newly appointed Party leader in Moscow, said (from Thomas P. Whitney, (ed.), *Khrushchev Speaks*, 1963):

implacability absolute
refusal to accept

> He (Stalin) has taught and is teaching us the Bolshevik mode of work and sharp **implacability** towards the slightest manifestation of alien bourgeois ideology, bourgeois nationalism, rootless cosmopolitanism and servility before decadent bourgeois culture.

Later, the same man said that Stalin's cult of personality transformed him into 'a superman possessing supernatural characteristics, akin to those of a god. Such a man supposedly knows everything, thinks for everyone, can do anything, is infallible in his behaviour. Such a belief about Stalin was cultivated among us for many years.' There is no greater support for Khrushchev's view than the poem that appeared in *Pravda* which had all the attributes of a hymn or even a prayer:

The following is quoted in Alan Wood's *Stalin and Stalinism*, 1989.

> O great Stalin, O leader of the peoples,
> Thou who broughtest man to birth,
> Thou who fructifiest (made fruitful) the earth,
> Thou who restorest the centuries,
> Thou who makest bloom the spring,
> Thou who makest vibrate the chords of music …
> Thou, splendour of my spring, O Thou,
> Sun reflected by millions of hearts.

G Stalinist anti-Semitism

It is perhaps strange that, although Karl Marx was a German Jew and many Old Bolsheviks including Trotsky, Kamenev and Zinoviev were of Jewish origin, anti-Semitism was never far beneath the surface in Stalin's Russia. In the 1930s, although Jews only accounted for 2% of the population, they were dominant in many of the professions and represented 4% of Party members. During World War II, an Anti-Fascist Jewish Committee was set up and thousands of Jews served in the Russian armed forces. After World War II, discrimination against the Jews was commonplace as anti-Semitism became increasingly a feature of the Stalinist regime. In 1948, the Committee was dissolved and most of its members arrested and shot. Stalin's distrust of the Jews arose from the fact that earlier thousands of Russian Jews had emigrated to the United States and many now held positions of influence in their adopted country. It was also unacceptable that a great many Russian Jews had relatives in the West and it was thought that their loyalty might be more to international Jewry than to the Soviet Union. Although the Soviet Union had been amongst the first to recognise the state of Israel, Stalin considered the country to be closely aligned with the West. This meant that the Jews that remained in Russia were suspect and Stalin feared that their number might include agents and saboteurs working for the West. Accused of being 'rootless cosmopolitans', following a wave of anti-Semitic propaganda, many were arrested by Beria's secret police and accused of being part of an American-backed Zionist conspiracy. In addition, Jewish synagogues, schools and libraries were closed and the teaching of Yiddish forbidden. In 1953, Stalin's campaign against the Jews reached its climax with the unearthing of proof of a Zionist conspiracy, the 'Doctors' Plot'.

H The 'Doctors' Plot'

On 13 January 1953, Soviet newspapers carried banner headlines announcing the arrest of nine doctors. They were medical specialists who had previously been caring for leading Party and government officials. They were accused of poisoning Zhdanov and army administrator,

Alexander Shcherbakov, and the attempted murder of several other marshals in the Soviet army. Of the nine doctors arrested, six were Jews and two died during their interrogation. It was claimed that they had confessed to their crimes and admitted that they had been working for the British and American intelligence services. Under the headline 'Vicious Spies and Killers under the Mask of Academic Physicians', a newspaper account in *Pravda* on 13 January 1953 read:

> This terrorist group, uncovered some time ago by organs of state security, had as its goal shortening the lives of leaders of the Soviet Union by means of medical sabotage. Investigation established that participants in the terrorist group, exploiting their position as doctors and abusing the trust of patients, deliberately and viciously under-mined their patients' health by making incorrect diagnoses, and then killed them with bad and incorrect treatments. Covering themselves with the noble and merciful calling of physicians, these fiends and killers dishonoured the honour of scientists... The majority of the participants of the terrorist group were bought by American intelli-gence. They were recruited by... the international Jewish bourgeois nationalist organisation called 'Joint'. The filthy face of this Zionist spy organisation, covering up their vicious actions under the mask of kindness, is now completely revealed.

Across the Soviet Union, there were anti-Semitic outbursts as people stopped attending the surgeries of their Jewish doctors in case they were poisoned. There were even rumours that Jewish doctors were infecting healthy Russians with cancer tumours and that all Jews were going to be deported to Siberia. The charges made against the doctors were completely false and it now appears certain that Stalin intended to use their trial as an excuse to intensify even further his campaign against Russian Jews and launch a new and extensive purge of the Communist Party. This was not to be. On 5 March 1953, Josif Stalin died.

I *The death of Josif Stalin*

On the night of 1–2 March, Stalin suffered a stroke and lost his power of speech. On the morning of 5 March, a radio bulletin told the Russia people – 'the life of the wise leader and leader of the Communist Party and Soviet people, Lenin's comrade and brilliant disciple, J.V. Stalin, is over.' There is some confusion about the circum-stances of his death. It appears that there was some lapse of time between his nurse's discovery of him in a collapsed state and the arrival of medical assistance. Beria was first on the scene and, although it was clear that his leader was close to death, it is claimed that he sent everyone away claiming that Stalin was only sleeping. The best part of a day passed before a doctor arrived and diagnosed a stroke. Very briefly, Stalin showed signs of recovery and it is said that Beria grovelled at his bedside seemingly forgetful of the fact that closeness to his leader was no guarantee of survival. In *Twenty Letters to a Friend*, his daughter provides an emotive account of her father's last hours:

> When we were through the gates and Khrushchev and Bulganin waved my car to stop outside, I thought it must be all over. They were both in tears. ... There was a whole crowd of people jammed into the big room where my father was lying unconscious ... There was only one person who was behaving in a way that was nearly obscene. That was Beria. He was extremely agitated. His face, repulsive enough at best, now was twisted by his passions, by ambition, cruelty, cunning and a lust for power ... As the end was approaching, Beria suddenly caught sight of me and ordered: 'Take Svetlana away!' But no one moved ... I was sitting at my father's side holding his hand and he looked at me. I kissed his face and hand. There was no longer anything more for me to do ... My father died a difficult and terrible death. It was the first and so far the only time I have seen somebody die. God grants an easy death only to the just.'

When news of Stalin's death reached the people there were spontaneous demonstrations and widespread grief across Russia. People cried openly in the streets and it is even claimed that some of those in the *gulags* wept. It would be more realistic to assume that for the majority they were tears of joy. In Moscow, some were crushed to death as people struggled to pay homage as his body lay in state in the Hall of Columns. Finally, on 9 March, the coffin bearing his embalmed body was carried to its final resting place by Malenkov, Beria, Khrushchev, Molotov, Voroshilov and his son, Vasili. He was placed beside Lenin in the mausoleum in Red Square.

Stalin left no obvious heir. As the Russian people mourned the passing of a man they considered their Supreme Leader and Father of the People, they were concerned about the future. Would the inevitable power struggle result in the emergence of a leader the equal of Stalin or someone even worse?

3 ↭ THE RULE OF JOSIF STALIN – SOME CONSIDERATIONS

A *What is meant by Stalinism?*

The term 'Stalinism' refers to the style of government and policies adopted by Josif Stalin during the years he ruled the Soviet Union between 1928 and 1953. After the Revolution, the official ideology of the

Soviet Union was Marxism–Leninism. This was based on the theories of socialism put forward by the German political philosopher, Karl Marx (1818–83), and then adapted by Lenin to the needs of Russia at that particular time. Lenin used the promise and appeal of Marxism as a stimulus to stir the Russian peasants, workers and soldiers to rise against the injustices of Tsarist rule. Stalin also made a contribution and for a time, the official ideology was known as Marxism–Leninism–Stalinism.

Stalinism was not a fixed ideology and, during the period 1928–53, it changed significantly. Stalin took different stances during the years he struggled to overcome his rivals and again later when his political and economic plans went through different phases of development. However there was much in Stalinism of which Marx and Lenin would not have approved and, during the 1930s, it followed significantly different lines and so came to be considered a distinct ideology. Whereas Marx claimed that the state would wither away as socialism developed and Lenin wanted the Russian example to inspire world revolution, Stalin took an opposite point of view. He argued that before he could realise Lenin's dream of a classless society, the state had to be strengthened in order to oppose the enemies of socialism within the Soviet Union and be secure from the threat posed by the country's capitalist neighbours. He won the support of the people for his policy of 'socialism in one country' and then began what amounted to an imposed 'revolution from the top'. Using the revolutionary spirit and nationalistic fervour of the Russian people, he began a programme of industrial development aimed at converting the Soviet Union into a modern industrial state.

To achieve his aims, Stalin had to be sure that he could meet the needs of his industrial workers and this required the collectivisation of land. To overcome the opposition to his scheme, he declared war on the kulaks and millions were either murdered or exiled in Siberia. Since his economic policies were imposed on what was still a largely backward and rural economy, it would need to be rigidly controlled and centrally directed. Whilst Lenin was no slouch when it came to the use of terror, Stalin was prepared to go further. During the 1930s, he used the entire apparatus of a police state – purges, show trials, deportations and mass murder – in order to remove any possible challenge to his authority. Even the Old Bolsheviks, those revolutionaries who had taken part in the events of 1917, were not spared. In the end, Stalinism led to the total personal dictatorship of one man based on the rule of terror. A campaign to promote a 'cult of personality' won him recognition as being infallible and the sole interpreter of Party ideology. All aspects of private, social, cultural and intellectual life became subject to Stalin's authority. Stalin had little regard for religion, was even prepared to backtrack and recognise the Orthodox Church. When it suited his needs. The uneasy compromise reached with the Church continued up to his death. As leader, he dominated the Russian Communist Party. He manipulated the members of the Central Committee and, later, the Politburo, by playing them off against each other. He permitted the emergence of an elite that enjoyed privileges and some exercise of power. It was made up of leading Party members, functionaries and careerists with each only too aware that he was liable to be removed suddenly and for no obvious reason. No one was safe from the vagaries of Stalin's moods. Even so, to the Russian people Stalin appeared to be a father figure and miracle worker incapable of any error or indiscretion. In reality, Stalinism came to represent legalised barbarity and subservience achieved by the bullet. Some historians have argued that the brutality of Stalin's rule was necessary in order for him to achieve his aims and an inevitable phase in the country's development; others regard Stalinism as a betrayal of the ideals of the Revolution. Today there are those who look back on the years of Stalin's totalitarian rule with nostalgia and affection. Some even long for its return. However, it is now usual to use the term Stalinism in a negative sense and most consider it to be synonymous with terror based totalitarianism.

Stalinism as Revolution from Above by Robert Tucker, 1977.

> Stalinist 'socialism' was socialism of mass poverty rather than plenty; of sharp social stratification rather than relative equality; of constant fear rather than emancipation.

Stalinism by Graeme Gill, 1975.

> A highly centralised economic system characterised by mass mobilisation and an over-riding priority on the development of heavy industry. A personal dictatorship resting upon the use of terror as an instrument of rule and in which political institutions are little more than the instrument of the dictator.

Bolshevism and Stalinism by Stephen F. Cohen, 1980.

> Stalinism was not simply nationalism, bureaucratisation, absence of democracy, censorship, police repression … These phenomena have appeared in many societies and are rather easily explained. Instead Stalinism was excess, extraordinary extremism … a holocaust by terror that victimised tens of millions of people.

B *What was Stalin's legacy to the Russian people?*

When Stalin died in March 1953, he had ruled the Soviet Union with unlimited power for over 25 years. Did the achievements of these years outweigh the suffering? What was Stalin's legacy to the Russian people? To evaluate these years, it is necessary to make estimates from two contrasting viewpoints. Firstly, it has to be remembered that Stalin came to power following a period of revolution, civil war and famine and during a leadership crisis. In his funeral oration following the death of Lenin, Stalin promised 'we shall not spare our lives to strengthen and broaden the alliance of the workers of the whole world'. However, once in power he appealed to the Russian people by promising them the benefits of bringing about 'Socialism in one country'. He also made clear his aim of modernising Russia – 'We are fifty years behind the advanced countries. We must make good this difference in ten years. Either we do it, or we shall be crushed'. To achieve this he embarked on a programme of industrial expansion – Five-Year Plans – backed by the collectivisation of agriculture. Did he succeed? Reference to the statistics indicating Soviet industrial growth and achievements between 1928 and 1939 shows quite clearly that he did. The industrialisation of the Soviet Union must be regarded as the most formidable of his achievements. It was during this period that the spadework was done that allowed Russia to emerge as one of the world's leading industrial powers. In addition, the scientific and technological advances that came after Stalin's death would have been impossible without these earlier achievements. However, the human cost was quite massive as contemporary Russians literally worked themselves to death in the interests of their country and future generations. The high industrial output was concentrated on capital goods rather than consumer goods and this meant that ordinary Soviet citizens enjoyed little material benefit as a result of their efforts. In addition, much of the industrial development was haphazard and created environmental problems for the future. Agricultural policy, which Stalin considered important only because the urban workers had to be fed, was far less successful and, in some ways, a disaster. The collectivisation of land proved even more expensive in human terms and largely failed in its aim of achieving self-sufficiency. Even today, Russian agriculture remains plagued by seemingly insoluble problems.

Stalin's other great accomplishment was his leadership of the Soviet Union during World War II. Whilst it should be remembered that his country first entered into a pact with Germany in 1939, apologists would argue that this was born of the Russian leader's frustration with Anglo-French appeasement of Hitler. Against this, it should be noted that Stalin blundered when he ignored warnings of an impending invasion of his country in 1941. Whatever, the Soviet Union played a major role in the Allied victory over Nazi Germany in 1945 and it was a war from which Stalin emerged as a national hero.

Josif Stalin probably wielded more power than any other tyrant in history. He ruled by means of terror and through a government apparatus that he dominated. He tolerated no threat to his power, real or imaginary, and his leadership went unquestioned. The severity of his regime brought death and suffering to millions. He imposed his policies on every aspect of the nation's life and robbed the Russian people of the ability to think for themselves. Stalin's totalitarian rule was based on a style of government that was elaborate, heavily bureaucratised and over which he exercised dictatorial power. This meant that when he died, he left the country with no durable form of government. His dominance of the Politburo also meant that there was no obvious heir apparent. Historians, almost without exception, have regarded Stalin in a bad light. Robert Tucker has described him as 'a twentieth century Ivan the Terrible' and George Kennan as 'a great man, but one great in his incredible criminality'. In *Twentieth Century World Affairs* (1974), Jack Watson has written – 'Lenin had been ruthless when he thought it was necessary, but he never sought personal glory nor lost sight of the ultimate goal. Stalin, it seemed, found glory and power sufficient in themselves.' Barely 50 years after the dictator's death, is it too early to make an objective assessment of his legacy to the Russian people? As the historian John Keep has written in *Last of the Empires* (1995) – 'In the mid-1990s, the defects of the Stalinist regime looms larger than its successes. The perspective may change in decades to come.'

4 ∽ STRUCTURED AND ESSAY QUESTIONS

A *This section consists of questions that might be useful for discussion (or writing answers) as a way of expanding on the chapter and for testing understanding of it.*

1. What difficulties faced the Soviet economy immediately after World War II?
2. For what reasons might the views of the agriculturist Trofim Lysenko be considered 'crackpot'?
3. With what justification might the years 1945–53 be considered a period of 'hysterical isolationism' in Soviet history?
4. What evidence was there to suggest that during the post-war years Stalin became an 'unbalanced psychopath'?
5. What impression of life in the gulags is given in the extracts from Solzhenitsyn's '*One Day in the Life of Ivan Denisovich*'?
6. What was the significance of the 'Leningrad Affair'?

B *Essay questions.*

1. Was the seizure of machinery and materials from the defeated countries the main reason for the speed of the Soviet Union's post-war economic recovery?
2. 'An absolute tyrant, he tightened his hold on the Russian people and wielded more power than ever before.' How valid is this judgement of Stalin's rule during the period 1945–53?
3. 'He suspected their loyalty.' To what extent was this the main reason for the measures Stalin took against Russian Jews?

5 ∽ BIBLIOGRAPHY

There is a mass of academic material published about the Stalinist period of Russian history. In addition, there are numerous novels that are well worth reading as well as useful television programmes and films. The three books by John Laver, *Joseph Stalin* (one of the Personalities and Powers series), *Russia 1914–41* and *The USSR 1945–90* (two of the

Access to History series and all published by Hodder & Stoughton in 1991, 1993), provide an excellent background to the period and include a great deal of useful advice on revision and examination technique. Also very popular are the books by Martin McCauley, *The Soviet Union Since 1917* and *Stalin and Stalinism* (both published by Longman in 1983 and 1998). *Stalin's Russia* by Martyn Whittock (Collins Educational 1997) is concisely written and excellent for revision whilst Stephen J. Lee's *Stalin and the Soviet Union* (Routledge 1999) follows an analytical approach and contains a wide range of sources. Brief and easy to read is *Stalin* by Harold Shukman (Sutton Publishing 1999) whilst other recent books on the Soviet dictator include the lengthy but absorbing *Stalin* by the Russian historian, Edvard Radzinsky (Hodder & Stoughton 1996), *Stalin and Stalinism* by Alan Wood (Routledge 1990), *Stalinism* by G. Gill (Macmillan 1990) and *Stalin: Triumph and Tragedy* and *The Rise and Fall of the Soviet Empire* both by Dmitri Volkogonov (Harper Collins 1991 and 1998). An excellent collection of documents relevant to the Stalinist period is contained in Philip Boobbyer's *The Stalin Era* (Routledge 2000). *Stalin: A Time for Judgement* by Jonathan Lewis and Phillip Whitehead (Methuen 1990) is easy to read and includes an interesting collection of pictures as does *Red Empire: The Forbidden History of the USSR* by Gwyneth Hughes and Simon Welfare. Useful books covering specialist topics include *Life and Terror in Stalin's Russia, 1934–41* by Robert W. Thurston (Yale University Press 1996) and Anthony Beever's highly acclaimed *Stalingrad* (Penguin 1998). If time permits, interesting comparisons between the two dictators are made in *Hitler and Stalin: Parallel Lives* by Alan Bullock (Harper Collins 1991). Also well worth reading are the books written by Stalin's daughter, Svetlana Alliluyeva, *Twenty Letters to a Friend* (World Books 1968) and sections from the novels of Alexander Solzhenitsyn – *One Day in the Life of Ivan Denisovich, Cancer Ward* and the *Gulag Archipelago*.

Soviet foreign policy, 1945–53

12

INTRODUCTION

During World War II, a series of conferences took place between the leaders of the Allied powers. At first, they were only attended by the British Prime Minister, Winston Churchill, and the American President, Franklin D. Roosevelt. These were held mid-Atlantic (1941) and Casablanca and Quebec (1943). They were mainly concerned with plans for bringing about the final defeat of Germany and Japan. Josif Stalin did attend the conference held in Teheran late in 1943 where the main issues discussed included the opening of a second front in the west against Germany and the possibility of the Soviet Union's entry into the war against Japan. More important were the meetings attended by the so-called 'Big Three' at Yalta and Potsdam in 1945.

TIMELINE

Timeline of events in Soviet foreign policy, 1945–53

1945 February	Yalta Conference	
March	Unconditional surrender of Germany	
June	UN Charter signed	
July	United States successfully tests first atomic bomb	
	Potsdam Conference	
August	US ends Lend-Lease Programme	
	Surrender of Japan	
October	Soviet Union, Belorussia and Ukraine join as founder members of the UN	
1946 March	Churchill's 'iron curtain' speech at Fulton, Missouri	
	Truman Doctrine proclaimed	
June	Marshall Plan announced	
September	Cominform set up	
1948 February	Communist *coup* in Czechoslovakia	
June	Western powers introduce new currency in their zones. Start of the Berlin blockade and airlift.	
	Yugoslavia expelled from Cominform	
1949 January	Comecon set up	
April	NATO established	
May	End of Berlin blockade	
September	Formation of the German Federal Republic. Successful test of Soviet Union's first atomic bomb	
October	Formation of German Democratic Republic	
1950 January	Soviet Union ceases to participate in UN Security Council and UN agencies	
June	Start of Korean War. Soviet Union fails to use veto to prevent use of UN forces in Korea	
1951 June	Cease fire in Korea	

1 ⌐ THE YALTA AND POTSDAM CONFERENCES

A *The Yalta Conference*

In February 1945, with the war still in progress, a conference was held at Yalta in the Crimea. There it was confirmed that the war would continue until Germany surrendered unconditionally. Plans were also made for the post-war division of Germany into four zones of occupation (American, British, Russian and French) under a control commission based in Berlin.

It was decided that, after the war, the only responsibility of the Allies to the German people would be to ensure that they were minimally provided for. It was also agreed that Germans guilty of war crimes would be brought to trial. The future of the other defeated and liberated countries was considered and it was agreed, and accepted by Stalin, that at the earliest opportunity such countries would 'establish through free elections ... governments responsive to the will of the people.' Most difficult was the consideration given to the future of the Soviet Union's immediate neighbour, Poland. During the course of the war, two Polish governments in exile had emerged – the Lublin government backed by Stalin and a London-based Polish government in exile supported by the Western Allies. It was agreed that the two would be brought together and organised on a 'broader, democratic basis'. The issue of Poland's future frontiers was not decided. Stalin insisted that all Soviet citizens taken prisoner or interned during the war and subsequently liberated by Anglo-American forces should be returned to the USSR. The Russian leader agreed that the Soviet Union would enter the war against Japan within two or three months of Germany's surrender. In return, he was promised certain territorial gains – the South Sakhalin and Kurile Islands as well as a zone of occupation in Korea. In addition, territory lost during the Russo-Japanese War of 1904–5 including Port Arthur was to be restored to the Soviet Union. All three leaders agreed to support the founding of the United Nations Organisation. For this purpose, a meeting was arranged at San Francisco on 25th April of delegates from the 50 nations currently at war with Germany. Stalin wanted all 16 Soviet republics to be admitted as full members of the United Nations but, after an agreement had been reached about voting rights, this was finally set at two – the Ukraine and Belorussia (Belarus). The United States and Britain also undertook to recognise the autonomy of Outer Mongolia.

A feature of the conference was the differing attitudes to Stalin taken by Roosevelt and Churchill. Whilst the American President seemed prepared to accommodate the Soviet leader, the British Prime Minister clearly distrusted him and doubted if he would keep his word. Roosevelt was later accused of playing into Stalin's hands by agreeing to terms that would allow much of Eastern Europe to fall under Communist domination.

> **KEY ISSUE**
>
> *Decisions about the future of Germany.*

"AND HOW ARE WE FEELING TO-DAY?"

B *The Potsdam Conference*

The war barely over, during July–August 1945 'the Big Three' gathered
for a conference in a suburb of Berlin, Potsdam. Since Yalta President
Roosevelt had died and had been replaced by Harry S. Truman and
whilst Churchill, who attended at the start of the conference, lost a general election at home and was replaced by Clement Attlee. In other
words, Stalin was now dealing with two relatively inexperienced national
leaders. Truman said of his first impressions of the Soviet leader – 'I
think I can do business with Stalin ... He's very honest but he's also
smart as hell'. Although the contents of possible peace treaties were discussed, these issues were put aside and left to a Council of Ministers. As
agreed at Yalta, Germany was divided into four zones of occupation and
it was decided that Berlin, in the Soviet zone, would be split into four
sectors.

THE POST-WAR DIVISION OF GERMANY

Similar arrangements were agreed for Austria and its capital city Vienna.
An Allied Control Council was to deal with matters affecting Germany
and Austria. Its policies were based on what became known as the 'five
Ds' – demilitarisation, denazification, democratisation, decentralisation
and deindustrialisation. Since most German industry was located in the
Western zones, the issue of reparations proved difficult. In the end it was
agreed that whilst each power could claim reparations from its own
occupied zone, the Soviet Union would receive additionally 10–15% of

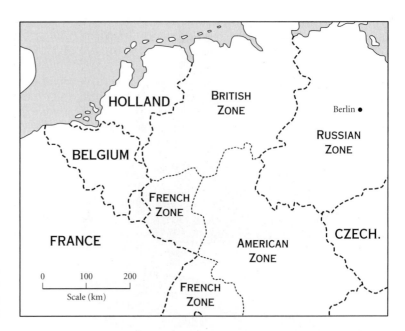

MAP 18

*The division of Germany
into four zones*

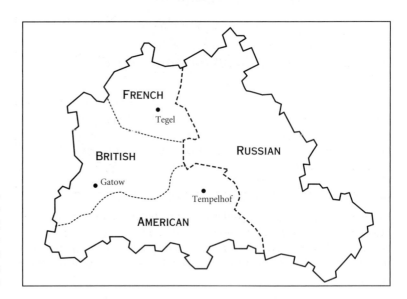

MAP 19

*The division of Berlin into four
sectors. Tegel, Gatow and
Tempelhof were the airports
that were to become important
in view of subsequent events*

the industrial plant and machinery from the Western zones in exchange
for agricultural produce from its own zone. A major territorial change
was brought about when it was agreed that the Soviet Union would gain
large areas of what had been eastern Poland and that Poland would be
recompensed by having her borders moved eastward into Germany to
the banks of the Rivers Oder and Neisse. This necessitated the wholesale
evacuation of millions of Germans who had lived in those areas.

MAP 21 *Soviet territorial gains following World War II. Note how Poland's frontiers were moved westward to the Rivers Oder and Neisser to allow for substantial Russian gains in the East*

THE SOVIET UNION'S TERRITORIAL GAINS

Whatever goodwill had existed at Yalta five months earlier evaporated at Potsdam. The differing aims of the Western powers and the Soviet Union became increasingly evident as it became clear that Stalin was determined to prevent any outside interference in the affairs of countries liberated by the Red Army and now under Communist control. Matters were not improved when President Truman informed Stalin of the successful testing of the first atomic bomb in New Mexico and of his intention of using the weapon against Japan. This gave the president an ace that Stalin would not be able to counter until Soviet scientists had developed their own atomic weapons. In the meantime, Truman steadfastly refused to share American nuclear secrets with the Russians. It also became increasingly clear that the Soviet Union would receive little of reparations promised from the Western zones of Germany! As the American historian Walter LaFeber wrote – 'Potsdam marks the point at which Truman and Stalin do not have a lot to say to each other anymore.'

2 ⌒ POST-WAR DEVELOPMENTS

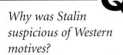

Why was Stalin suspicious of Western motives?

Ideas about providing relief for the war-torn regions of Europe were considered long before the end of the war. In 1943, the United States sponsored the United Nations Relief and Rehabilitation Administration (UNNRA) which was to provide food and medical supplies to the worst affected people. At the Bretton Woods Conference in 1944, the US oversaw the setting up of the International Monetary Fund and World Bank. Their aim was to encourage the expansion of world trade and provide loans. The General Agreement on Tariffs and Trade (GATT), which was not finally agreed until 1948, was intended to encourage trade by preventing the crippling effects of high tariffs. Stalin regarded all these initiatives as capitalist inspired and would have no part in them. He did however agree for the Soviet Union to be one of the signatories of the United Nations Charter in July 1945.

A *Broken promises and the end of the wartime alliance*

At the time of the Potsdam Conference, it was already clear that the wartime alliance of Britain, the United States and the Soviet Union was breaking down. The final defeat of Germany meant that they no longer had a common aim and doubt and suspicion replaced wartime cooperation. Both sides returned to promoting their rival ideologies of capitalism and communism. Stalin failed to keep his promise to allow free elections and representative government in the countries under his control but instead, by using diplomatic pressure, infiltration, intimidation and subversion, began consolidating communist rule across much of Eastern Europe.

B *Stalin's imposition of communist rule over Eastern Europe*

In *Romania*, King Michael had to accept a communist Democratic Front government and, in 1947, he was forced to abdicate when the country became a People's Republic under Nicolae Ceausescu. After forcing King Peter into exile, the communist and former partisan leader, Marshal Tito, came to power in *Yugoslavia*. Free elections held in

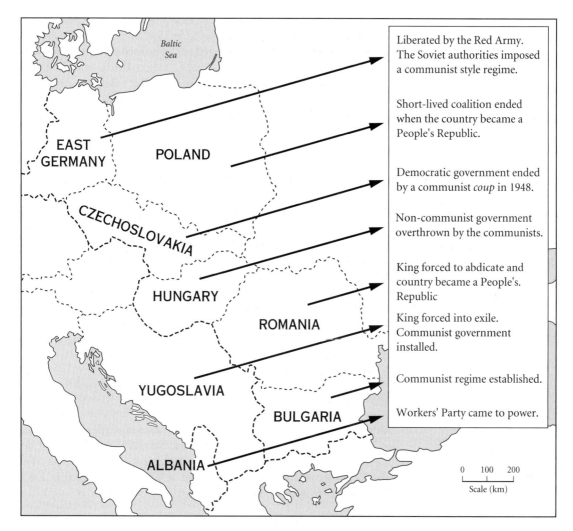

Liberated by the Red Army. The Soviet authorities imposed a communist style regime.

Short-lived coalition ended when the country became a People's Republic.

Democratic government ended by a communist *coup* in 1948.

Non-communist government overthrown by the communists.

King forced to abdicate and country became a People's. Republic

King forced into exile. Communist government installed.

Communist regime established.

Workers' Party came to power.

MAP 20 *The Soviet domination of Eastern Europe. Although ruled by a Communist Government, Tito's Yugoslavia followed an independent line and continued to enjoy good relations with the West*

Hungary saw the return of a non-communist Smallholders' Party. This was short lived and, in 1946, the communist United Workers' Party came to power under Matyas Rakosi. Similarly, a communist regime was established in *Bulgaria* under Georgi Dimitrov. In *Poland*, the merging of the London and Lublin based governments in exile into a provisional Government of National Unity proved an uneasy and short-lived alliance. The President, Boleslaw Bierut, was a hard line Stalinist who saw to it that representatives of the London-based Polish government in exile were arrested on their arrival. By 1952, he had turned the country into a People's Republic. Enver Hoxha, leader of the Workers' Party, came to power in *Albania* where he established one of the most severe communist regimes in Eastern Europe and remained so even after Stalin's death! Soviet expansion was not solely dependent on subversion. Peace treaties finally agreed in 1947 even worked in Stalin's favour and the Soviet Union emerged as the only country to make substantial territorial gains. The Baltic States, Estonia, Latvia and Lithuania, that had been forcibly incorporated into the USSR failed to regain their independence whilst the Soviet Union gained Bessarabia and Northern Bukhovina from Romania and Karelia and Petsamo from Finland.

Stalin did not get it all his own way. Since 1942, a civil war had raged in Greece between the rival resistance groups, the Greek Democratic National League and the communist National Liberation Front. When the Germans withdrew from Greece in 1944, Giorgios Papandreou came to power as head of a Greek Government of National Unity. His regime was backed by the presence of British military units. As the civil war intensified in turn the British and Americans supported the Greek army. This ensured that the Communists were defeated and that Greek democracy survived. On the other hand, Stalin must have been pleased by the growth of large and well organised communist parties in France and Italy. In both countries it appeared possible that they might gain power by democratic means.

3 ⌐ THE COLD WAR

The term Cold War describes the period of hostility that existed between the Soviet Union on the one hand and the United States and other Western democracies on the other during the years after 1947. Although confrontations between the two sides sometimes led to crises, in Europe they led to a war of words and threats that fell short of an armed conflict – a Hot War. It might be claimed that the Cold War developed because the conferences held at Yalta and Potsdam in 1945 failed to deal with the major post-war issues.

A *The 'iron curtain' and the onset of the Cold War*

Excluded from their affairs, the Western powers found it increasingly difficult to communicate with countries under Soviet domination. Not only the Soviet Union but now all the countries under communist control in Eastern Europe had become subject to Zhdanov's 'hysterical isolationism' and avoided what they considered to be contamination by Western ideology and culture. Winston Churchill had earlier indicated his fears in a letter to President Truman in May 1945:

> What is to happen about Russia? An iron curtain is drawn down upon their front. We do not know what is going on behind... It is vital now to come to an understanding with Russia, or see where we are with her, before we weaken our armies mortally or retire to our zones of occupation.

In March 1946, he was under no illusions about East–West relations when, in a speech made in Truman's hometown, Fulton, Missouri, he famously declared:

> From Stettin in the Baltic to Trieste in the Adriatic, an iron curtain has descended across the continent. Behind that line lie all the capitals of the states of central and eastern Europe – all are subject in one form or another not only to Soviet influence but to a very high and increasing measure of control from Moscow.

Stalin reacted to Churchill's 'iron curtain' speech with an article in *Pravda*.

> The influence of the Communists grew because during the hard years of the mastery of fascism in Europe, communists showed themselves to be reliable, daring and self-sacrificing fighters against fascist regimes for the liberty of peoples ... Of course, Mr. Churchill does not like such a development of events ... he did not like the appearance of the Soviet regime in Russia after the First World War ... I do not know whether Mr. Churchill and his friends will succeed in organising ... a new military expedition against eastern Europe. But if they succeed in this, which is not very probable, since millions of common people stand on guard over the peace ... they will be beaten ...

PICTURE 42 *A* Daily Mail *cartoon – 'Churchill takes a peep under the iron curtain'*

There was clearly no way in which the Russian leader was going to relax his grip on eastern Europe. Why was this? What were the basic causes of Stalin's antagonism towards the West?

The reasons for Soviet antagonism towards the West

● Stalin, like all Bolsheviks, had never forgotten or forgiven the hostility of the West to the Revolution in 1917 or their involvement in the subsequent civil war.

● He remained unhappy about and suspicious of the reasons for the failure of the Allies to open a second front in Europe before 1944.

● He considered the sudden end of Lend-Lease in 1945, his country's exclusion from the administration of Japan and American unwillingness to share atomic secrets an indication of West's continued hostility to the Soviet Union.

● He feared that Western capitalist propaganda might influence the Russian people and undermine Communist ideology and even his own position.

● He thought that if he could convince the Russian people that their country was under threat from the West they would be more willing to accept his domestic policies and make a greater effort to achieve his economic aims.

● It is even possible that he genuinely believed that the capitalist world was heading for collapse and would try to survive by preparing for an imperialist/anti-Communist war.

Soviet influence did not always go unchallenged. In Yugoslavia where local partisans were largely responsible for bringing about the liberation of their country independently of the Red Army, Tito was prepared to follow an independent line. During the post-war years, he annoyed Stalin by refusing to allow Moscow to interfere in his country's affairs and by permitting a greater degree of decentralisation and liberalism than other Communist countries. His acceptance of economic aid from the United States caused the Soviet leader to rage – 'I will shake my little finger and there will be no more Tito. He will fall.'

In the United States, President Truman, like Roosevelt before him, faced increasing criticism for not taking a stronger line against Stalinist expansionist policies. In what amounted to a change in the direction of American foreign policy, Truman recognised that it was time to shoulder the responsibility of defending the free world from Soviet expansionism. It was simply time to get tough with Stalin.

B *The Truman Doctrine and the Marshall plan*

On 12th March 1947, in a speech made to the US Congress, President Truman pledged American support for 'free peoples who are resisting attempted subjugation by armed minorities or by outside pressures.' The Truman Doctrine, as it became known, carried an implicit warning that the United States would assist countries resisting outside interference in their affairs. The immediate effect was for American aid to be dispatched to the two countries currently resisting such pressures, Greece and Turkey. Stalin's initial reaction appeared to be moderate.

He told George Marshall, the American Secretary of State, that 'compromises were possible on all the main questions, including demilitarisation, the political structure of Germany, reparations and economic unity. It was necessary to have patience and not become pessimistic.'

Three months later, in June 1947, in a speech made at Harvard University, George Marshall made an offer of American financial aid to assist European economic recovery. The offer was conditional on the recipient European governments being willing to take steps towards greater economic cooperation. Churchill described the European Recovery Programme, better known as the Marshall Plan, as 'the most unsordid act in history'. Stalin and his Foreign Minister, Molotov, saw things very differently. They regarded it as a devious dollar-backed scheme to loosen the communist grip on Eastern Europe. They refused such aid and ordered the Soviet Union's satellites to do likewise. Tito's Yugoslavia declined to follow the instruction and the Czechoslovak government also showed interest.

PICTURE 43 *An American cartoon shows Stalin's reaction to the Truman Doctrine*

The Russians regarded both the Truman Doctrine and the Marshall Plan as provocative measures. Zhdanov wrote in a report:

> The Truman Doctrine, which provides for the rendering of American assistance to all reactionary regimes which actively oppose the democratic people, bears a frankly aggressive character ... The vague and deliberately guarded formulations of the Marshall Plan amount in essence to a scheme to create a block of states bound by obligations to the United States ...

C *Cominform*

In September 1947, a conference of Communist parties that included representatives from France and Italy, decided to establish an Information Bureau of the Communist and Workers' Parties. Better known as the Communist Information Bureau or Cominform, it was the product of Zhdanov's unbridled hatred of the West and, although its headquarters was established in Belgrade, it was controlled from Moscow. After the split between Tito and Stalin, Yugoslavia was expelled from Cominform and the seat of the Bureau was moved to Bucharest in Romania. From a Western point of view, Cominform was seen as a Soviet reaction to the Truman Doctrine and the Marshall Plan and really the recreation of the former Comintern. In fact, the activities of Cominform amounted to little more than publishing propaganda material aimed at encouraging solidarity amongst the east European communist states and their continued acceptance of the Stalinist line. Cominform was intended more to enforce Soviet policy than stir international revolution.

D *The fate of Czechoslovakia: the Cold War intensifies*

During 1948, the iron curtain became a reality as barbed wire and minefields were placed in position to separate the Russian zone of Germany from those of the Western powers. The Western sectors of Berlin, isolated and out on a limb in the Russian zone, were particularly vulnerable. During the same year came the first challenge to the Truman Doctrine when the communists brought off a *coup* in Czechoslovakia. For a while, the fate of Czechoslovakia appeared to hang in the balance. Free elections held after the war resulted in a close finish between parties of the right and left but with the Communists doing surprisingly well gaining 114 of the 300 seats. As a result, a coalition government led by the communist, Klement Gottwald, ruled the country. Any hope of the survival of Czech democracy ended when, in February 1948, Gottwald masterminded a communist *coup*. With the media rigorously censored, there followed a purge of the members of the opposition. Jan Masaryk, a leading anti-Communist, was found dead in the courtyard beneath his apartment. It was claimed that he had fallen from a window! The Western powers attempted to raise the issue of

Czechoslovakia at the UN but the Soviet Union vetoed the move. In the end they could do nothing as the country was declared a people's democratic republic and fell totally under Russian domination.

During this period there were regular conferences of foreign ministers at which they struggled to agree the terms of the proposed peace treaties with Germany and Austria. At the first, held in London in September 1945, issues were discussed but no agreement reached. The second held in Moscow two months later also achieved nothing. At the third held in November 1946, Molotov rejected all the proposals put forward by the other ministers. During 1947 there were four further conferences held. In February, peace treaties with Italy, Romania, Bulgaria, Hungary and Finland were finally settled and in March, the issue of reparations was also agreed. However, after days of discussions there was still no agreement on the terms to be imposed on Germany and Austria. It was the failure of these talks that first made the Western powers begin to discuss the possibility of going it alone and uniting their zones. In June 1948 came the first major crisis that threatened to turn the Cold War into an East–West conflict of arms, the Berlin blockade.

E *The Berlin blockade of 1948*

Whilst the Soviet authorities had denied their zone of Germany Marshall Aid, the American, British and French zones had benefited significantly. This meant that they had recovered more quickly from the war and their prosperity stood in stark contrast to the poor living standards and unrepaired war damage evident in the Soviet sector. Nowhere was this comparison more obvious than in Berlin. There the situation proved an embarrassment to Stalin since, in the Western sectors of Berlin situated in the heart of Communist controlled Germany, stood a glittering example of the achievements of capitalism. To make matters worse, during 1947, the Western powers finally united their zones of Germany for economic purposes and were making plans to reform the currency. These moves, undertaken without Soviet approval, angered Stalin and the Russians began to harass Western transport passing through their zone to Berlin. Trains, barges and vehicles were held up and long queues developed at the checkpoints. It was the Allied decision to go ahead and introduce a new common currency throughout their zones of Germany that led to a crisis. When discussions broke down, the Allies tried to avoid difficulties by not introducing the new *Deutschmark* in their sectors of Berlin. The Soviet authorities were not appeased and retaliated by introducing a new currency of their own intended for use in all sectors of the city. The Allies reacted by making their new currency available to Berliners.

Stalin was determined to show the West that their sectors of Berlin existed only on Soviet sufferance. It is also likely that he hoped that he might be able to force the Western powers to withdraw permanently from the city. On 24th June, he ordered the closure of all land and water routes into Berlin. All trains, barges and vehicles were stopped and turned back. There were those in the United States who wanted to use the military to force the land routes to the city, a move that might well have triggered a full-scale war. Instead the Americans and British decided to supply the two million beleaguered Berliners in their sectors from the air. During the ten months of the Berlin airlift, transport aircraft of the RAF and USAAF flew sufficient food, fuel and medical supplies to maintain the city. Even so, Berliners living in the Western sectors suffered acute shortages and the Russians tried to take advantage of this by offering rations to those willing to register with the Soviet authorities for that purpose. Less than 2% of the population took up the offer! Russian fighters tried to harass or 'buzz' the transport aircraft but never attempted to shoot them down. In the spring of 1949, Stalin escalated the crisis when he refused to enter into any further talks regarding the Berlin situation and matters took an even more serious turn when President Truman ordered American B-52 bombers to Britain. The Soviets had to be careful, they did not yet possess the atomic bomb. On 12 May 1949, the blockade was finally lifted.

Q *Why did the Berlin crisis of 1948 not lead to war?*

The failure of the Berlin blockade represented a moral defeat for Stalin. It proved that it was possible for the West to resist Soviet moves by peaceful means, it made the Western powers even more mindful of the communist threat. In April 1949, the United States, Canada and most of the countries of Western Europe signed the North Atlantic Pact that established the North Atlantic Treaty Organisation (NATO). It was a defensive arrangement aimed at taking joint action in the event of a Soviet attack. Stalin denounced NATO as an aggressive alliance and claimed that he had evidence that America and her allies were preparing for another war. It was six years before the Soviet Union joined with her East European satellites to form their own alliance when they agreed the Warsaw Pact. In September 1949, the Russian news agency TASS announced the explosion of the first Soviet atomic bomb. In the same month, the Western powers merged their zones of Germany to form the Federal Republic of Germany (FDR). Three weeks later the Russians transformed their zone into the German Democratic Republic (DDR).

F *The Council for Mutual Economic Assistance (COMECON)*

Earlier in January 1949, the Soviet Union set up the Council for Mutual Economic Assistance, COMECON, with its headquarters in Moscow. The aim of the Council was to co-ordinate the economic growth of the countries that were part of the Soviet bloc – the Soviet Union, Bulgaria, Czechoslovakia, Hungary, Poland and Romania. Albania joined soon after the Council was established and the German Democratic Republic and the Mongolian Peoples' Republic in the 1960s. Later Cuba and North Vietnam also became members. COMECON organised trade agreements between members and was also involved in arranging credit and preventing the overproduction of goods. This was achieved through a series of Five-Year Plans. Since the governments of individual members continued to set the prices of commodities, price differences made trading difficult. To some extent this was overcome through

bilateral trade agreements and barter. COMECON was also successful in establishing a railway network and an electricity grid across Eastern Europe. The Council did have other purposes. The Soviets hoped that it would discourage member states from having economic ties with the West and, at least to some limited extent, compensate for Marshall Aid.

bilateral trade agreements trade agreements that bring a shared advantage to the two countries concerned.

G *The Soviet Union – a nuclear power*

Soviet scientists had started working on an atomic research in 1940, a year before the United States. When, on 24 July 1945 at the Potsdam Conference, Truman told Stalin that the United States possessed 'a new weapon of unusual destructive force', the Soviet leader said that he was glad to hear of it and hoped that the Americans would make good use of it against Japan. Later on, on the same day, he said to Molotov – 'Let them. We'll have to talk it over with Kurchatov and get him to speed things up.' Yuri Kurchatov was the leading Soviet atomic scientist. Once back in Moscow, Stalin called his atomic scientists together and told them – 'A single demand of you comrades. Provide us with atomic weapons in the shortest possible time … it will remove a great danger to us.' Afterwards the scientists worked tirelessly to develop the first Soviet atomic bomb and successfully tested such a weapon on 22 September 1949.

TREACHERY – THE ATOMIC SPIES

Their progress was greatly helped by the treachery of a number of Western nuclear scientists. The greatest contribution was probably made by Klaus Fuchs. The German-born scientist had fled from Nazi Germany in the 1930s and taken British nationality. He went to the United States and there worked on the Manhattan Project at Los Alamos. During this time, he passed a great deal of important information to the Russians. After his arrest in 1950, he confessed to his betrayal. Another British scientist, Allan Nun May, was part of a Soviet spy ring operating in Canada. He too pleaded guilty when his treachery was exposed. Italian-born Bruno Pontecovo emigrated to the United States and, whilst working on atomic projects, passed information to the Russians. For a time, he then worked in Britain. At the point of being discovered he managed to avoid arrest and escaped to the Soviet Union. Americans who spied for the Russians included Harry Gold, David Greenglass, Morton Sobell and the husband and wife Julius and Ethel Rosenberg. It should be mentioned that some of the traitors were themselves betrayed by Soviet embassy officials who defected to the West. Most of those who spied did so for ideological reasons and not for financial gain. Fuchs claimed that his crime was not treason since the USSR was not an enemy. In a statement, May said – 'I gave and had given very careful consideration to the cor-rectness of making sure that the development of atomic energy was not confined to the USA.' They believed that the world would be safer if atomic secrets were shared by all the major powers. Recent revelations indicate that most of the information passed by the spies was already known to Russian scientists and that their betrayal advanced Soviet research by months rather than years. Greater damage was done by the betrayal of the British diplomats Guy Burgess and Donald Maclean in

1951 and Kim Philby in 1962. The information they passed to the Soviet Union was of political and not technological significance.

H *Soviet reaction to the Korean war*

In 1950, another major crisis occurred in the Far East when troops of the Soviet-sponsored Peoples' Democratic Republic of North Korea invaded their southern neighbour, the American-backed Republic of Korea. Previously, Stalin had turned down attempts by the United Nations to hold elections in both countries prior to creating a unified state. At the UN, the United States condemned North Korean aggression and put forward a resolution calling for an international force to be sent to the South to help repel the invaders. The Soviet delegate at the Security Council, Jacob Malik, was absent from the meeting and consequently there was no Russian veto. At the time it was thought that Malik's absence was part of the Russian boycott of the Security Council brought about by the UN's refusal to offer a seat to the Chinese communists. Years later, the Soviet foreign minister at that time, Andrei Gromyko, stated in his memoirs, *Memories* (1989) that the Russian delegate's absence was on Stalin's direct orders. Clearly the Russian leader hoped that the conflict would result in the Chinese, who backed North Korea, and the American-led UN forces becoming involved in a costly war that would be fought to a standstill. As it was, the war lasted for three bloody years and cost the UN some 160 000 lives whilst the Chinese and North Korean losses came to an estimated four million.

As we shall see, the death of Stalin in 1953 did bring about some relaxation in East–West relations but the Cold War was far from over.

4 ⌐ STRUCTURED AND ESSAY QUESTIONS

A *This section consists of questions that might be useful for discussion (or writing answers) as a way of expanding on the chapter and testing understanding of it.*

1. What is meant by the following terms:
   (a) subversion?
   (b) satellite state?
   (c) ideology?
   (d) *coup?*
2. To what extent did Churchill and Roosevelt disagree in their views of Stalin?
3. What difficulties were faced in deciding the future of Poland?
4. What was the basis of the disagreement between Tito and Stalin?
5. For what reasons was Stalin concerned over the presence of the Western powers in Berlin?
6. What were the consequences for East–West relations of the Berlin blockade?
7. For what reasons did some men and women chose to betray the West's atomic secrets to Russia?

B *Essay questions.*
1. To what extent was Stalin's fear of Western influences the main reason for Stalin's antagonism towards his former wartime allies?
2. Why did Berlin become such a sensitive issue in East–West relations?
3. 'To create a buffer between the Soviet Union and the West.' Was this the main reason why Stalin was determined to dominate Eastern Europe?

5 ⌐ MAKING NOTES

Complete the chart below in order to build up a picture of the stages by which the Soviet Union gained control of most of Eastern Europe.

Country	Year it fell under Communist control	Circumstances	Leader of the Communist regime
Baltic provinces			
Poland			
Hungary			
Romania			
Bulgaria			
Albania			
Czechoslovakia			

6 ⌐ DOCUMENTARY EXERCISE ON THE COLD WAR

Study the sources and then answer the questions based on them.

SOURCE A (PICTURE 44)
A French cartoon of 1948 shows Stalin dancing on the top of a table

SOURCE B

John Hamer in The Twentieth Century, *1980.*

There is another way of looking at Stalin's actions after the war. That is not to see them as the beginnings of a Communist takeover, but as part of a policy ensuring Russia's safety. If Russia was surrounded by friendly countries, any invasion from the west, like that of Hitler in 1941, would be less likely to succeed. Whatever Stalin's motives, within two years he had established a block of countries in eastern Europe dominated from Moscow.

SOURCE C

Christopher Culpin in Making History: World History From 1914 to the Present Day, *1986.*

Stalin turned the countries of eastern Europe into satellites of Russia. That meant that they were little more than provinces of Russia. Cominform, set up in 1947, made sure that the Communist Parties were controlled from Moscow. By 1948, Russia was in control of half of Europe... As commander of the victorious Red Army, he (Stalin) may have felt that he had the right to do what he liked in order to rebuild Russia. To Westerners, this Russian advance exceeded their worst fears.

1. *Study Source A:*
   (i) *What is the cartoonist indicating by the knives already thrown into the table top?*
   (ii) *What does the cartoonist imply about the future of his own country, France?*
2. *To what extent does the cartoon share the fear of Westerners mentioned in Source C?*
3. *Compare Sources B and C. To what extent do they share the same view of the reasons for Stalin's actions?*
4. *How useful are the sources towards an understanding of Stalin's motives for overrunning most of Eastern Europe?*

Post-Stalinist Russia: The years of Nikita Khrushchev

INTRODUCTION

Following the death of Stalin in March 1953 there was much speculation about his successor. There was talk of a collective-style of leadership based on a triumvirate comprising of Georgy Malenkov, who held both the important posts of chairman of the Council of Ministers and Party secretary, Lavrenty Beria, much loathed security chief, and Stalin's foreign secretary, Vyacheslav Molotov. Whilst they were the obvious front runners, there were other outsiders in the reckoning. These included Anastas Mikoyan, an astute politician who had used great skill to survive and stay at the top, the former Red Army General, Kliment Voroshilov, Lazar Kaganovich, one of Stalin's more ruthless subordinates who, although himself a Jew, was antisemitic and Nikita Khrushchev. In truth, Molotov, Voroshilov and Kaganovich had little chance since they had all been Stalin's men and had little influence in their own right.

1 ⌐ THE MALENKOV INTERLUDE

The first to emerge from the pack was Malenkov.

GEORGY MALENKOV (1901–88)

From an obscure, middle-class background, Georgy Maksimilianovich Malenkov was born in Orenburg in 1901. He was conscripted into the Red Army in 1919 and served as a political commissar. The following year, he joined the Communist Party. During the early 1920s, he studied at a technical institute in Moscow. A background figure, he worked as an administrator for the Central Committee and became head of their personnel department. As a friend of both Stalin and Beria, he was able to progress rapidly through the ranks of the Party and played a major role in the purges of the late 1930s. By 1939, he was a member of the Central Committee and, in 1946, was appointed to the Politburo. Within the Party, his arch-enemy was Andrei Zhdanov who plotted against him and finally brought about his dismissal. In 1948, it was Malenkov who helped Beria to organise the Leningrad Affair that led to a savage purge of the Party. In 1953 he was restored to the Politburo, now renamed the Presidium. In March of that year, with the support of Beria, he became Party secretary and Prime Minister.

In an effort to win popularity, Malenkov promised the Russian people that he would improve their living standards by encouraging the increased production of consumer goods. He also undertook to reduce the compulsory deliveries made to the State from private plots and increase the prices paid for the product delivered. This move away from the traditional emphasis placed on heavy industry did not please many of his Party colleagues. He was also unpopular because of his continued close friendship with Beria.

A *The removal of Beria*

It was evident that before his death, Stalin had turned against his security chief and that Beria's position was under threat. Beria, described by Martin McCauley as 'highly intelligent, a master of intrigue and as deadly as a viper' had made many enemies. He was feared by other members in the Party **hierarchy**, disliked by the army and unforgiven by the families of the millions he had sent to the gulag labour camps. After Stalin's death, Beria went out of his way to court popularity by suddenly appearing to be something of a liberal. In a sudden and complete **volte-face**, he hinted that he favoured legal reforms that included making the penal code less severe and taking steps to protect the individual rights of citizens. He declared a general amnesty for all non-political prisoners sentenced to less than five years. This gamble was not a shrewd move since many of those released quickly returned to their former ways and this led to a nationwide crime wave. He went further and admitted that the 'Doctors' Plot' had been a set-up and that the doctors' confessions had been obtained under torture or, as he put it, by 'inadmissible methods'. His apparent change of heart came too late in the day and failed to save him. Even his friend, Malenkov, turned against him and with Khrushchev also plotting against him, his downfall was assured. In July 1953 he was arrested together with many of his henchmen. Charged with scheming to seize power himself and of being a capitalist agent, he was shot hours after his arrest and without a trial. The speed with which he was executed suggests that he had refused to confess to the charges made against him. In addition, the leadership of the regional parties where Beria's influence was the greatest were removed. Under the new regime, the majority of those purged were not, as in the past, murdered. Afterwards, national security was made the responsibility of the Committee of State Security, more popularly known as the KGB. Like its predecessors, the KGB used repressive measures but these fell short of the pattern of institutionalised terror used by the NKVD.

B *The Virgin Lands Scheme*

In 1954, the Central Committee finally approved a scheme proposed by Khrushchev that was intended to solve the Soviet Union's chronic food shortages. His aim was to develop previously uncultivated areas of the Soviet Union so that they would come to rival the North American plains in grain production. To achieve this, he planned to cultivate over

hierarchy those in control at the top.

Volte-face a change of mind.

See pages 371–2.

KEY ISSUE

The reasons for Beria's unpopularity.

28 million hectares of new and previously unused 'virgin and idle' lands beyond the Urals in Siberia and Kazakhstan. Tens of thousands of enthusiastic Russians, mainly young Party members and Komsomol volunteers, were encouraged to go east and become the pioneers of Khrushchev's plan. The prospect of regular employment and the promise of guaranteed wages motivated much of their enthusiasm. Once at their destination, they were organised into state farms, *sovkhozes,* of between 20 000 and 40 000 hectares. Between 1954 and 1958, they had some success as grain production increased from 81 to 144 million tonnes but then things went badly wrong.

WHY DID THE VIRGIN LAND SCHEME FAIL?

- Basically, Khrushchev's plan was unrealistic in its aims. There was no way the Russian steppes could be developed to rival the grain production of the North American plains.
- Much of the land to be used was barely marginal – only on the very edge of what might be considered profitable to cultivate.
- The scheme was badly planned. Enthusiasm for the project meant that much was undertaken with undue haste and inadequate forward planning. As Martin McCauley has written – 'haste took precedence over contemplation'.
- After the first year, in many regions the topsoil became arid and subject to wind erosion. This created dust bowls.
- Much of the land brought under cultivation was liable to drought.
- It was not a good idea to replace traditional crops with crops such as maize and melons.
- The amount of fertilisers made available was inadequate and this meant that much of the land rapidly became exhausted.
- The scheme suffered excessive interference from management that was both ineffective and inefficient.
- Inadequate preparations were made to house and otherwise provide amenities for the young people who had volunteered to work in Siberia and Kazakhstan.
- The severity of the living and working conditions caused the early enthusiasm of the workers to give way to despondency. As a longing for the comforts of urban life returned many drifted back to the towns and cities.

Whilst Malenkov made some useful contributions to Soviet foreign policy by helping to arrange the peace treaty that ended the Korean War (1953) and finally agreeing a peace treaty with Austria, at home his position was becoming increasingly insecure. His promise of a 'New Course' that would bring with it an increased supply of cheap consumer goods failed to satisfy the demands of the Russian people. The truth was that the lower prices meant that demand outstripped supply. In addition, those who were dismayed by his disregard of the needs of heavy industry became increasingly vocal in their criticism. Khrushchev attacked Malenkov's policies describing them as 'a belching of Rightist deviationist views'. In February 1955, he was removed from office and replaced by Nikolai Bulganin. In his resignation speech, Malenkov blamed his inexperience and accepted the responsibility for the plight of Soviet agriculture. In 1957, he was well and truly demoted when he was made responsible for running a hydro-electric station in Kazakhstan. However, as we shall see, he was not yet finished.

C *Khrushchev's speech at the 20th Party conference*

Q

To what extent did the disclosures of Khrushchev's speech on 24 February 1956 take the Russian people by surprise?

See page 259.

On 24 February 1956, Nikita Khrushchev addressed a closed session of the Twentieth Congress of the Soviet Communist Party held in Moscow. His address, made to an audience of 1500 delegates, was an intended report 'On the Cult of Personality and its Consequences', but turned out to be a most remarkable speech which took everyone present by surprise. Over 20 000 words long, he used the occasion to launch a scathing attack on Stalin and accused him of flagrant abuses of power, gross acts of brutality and developing his own cult of personality. He spared the delegates little as he gave details of the purges, the terror and the torture inflicted on victims in order to get them to confess to fabricated crimes. He detailed the mass arrests, unjustified executions and told them of the millions still suffering in the *gulags*. He claimed that Stalin's conduct had caused 'tremendous harm to our country and to the cause of socialist progress'. He quoted the contents of Lenin's Testament as evidence of their founder's distrust of Stalin. He blamed the former dictator for the murder of Kirov and even questioned his reputation as a war leader. He called for the rehabilitation of Trotsky and others who had been eliminated and claimed that now all had been revealed, it would again be possible for the Soviet Union to progress 'along the Leninist path to new success, new victories'. In his speech, he took great care to blame Stalin for the betrayal of Leninist principles and not the Party. He did however imply that Malenkov and Molotov were Stalin's accomplices rather than his victims. At the conclusion of a speech in which he had completely destroyed the myth of Stalin, he sat down to tumultuous applause. Although the text of Khrushchev's speech was supposed to be secret and was not officially published in the USSR until 1988, illicit copies became immediately available and were passed around. Reuters, the press agency, quickly obtained a copy of the speech and its contents were quickly flashed around the world. The Soviet people were staggered that the infallible hero they had once worshipped had been so openly vilified. There were those who did not believe it but there were millions who, from their personal experiences, knew that Khrushchev had spoken the truth. Of course, his speech was a selective criticism and it is significant that, he made little mention of the treatment of the deported minorities and said nothing of Stalin's crimes before 1934! At the conference there were delegates who demanded that those responsible for the crimes should be brought to justice. Particularly outspoken were the head of the Young Communists, a 31-year-old Mikhail Gorbachev, and Alexander Shelepin, the newly appointed head of the KGB. Another delegate,

Leonid Brezhnev, praised Khrushchev for his 'magnificent example' whilst Alexei Kosygin warned that in future there must be 'no place for the cult of personality in the building of Communism'.

Not all were impressed by Khrushchev's disclosures. In the leadership there were those who thought that his criticism of Stalin had gone too far and not only threatened the position of the Party but the stability of the country. In Georgia, Stalin's birthplace, many of the local people regarded the defamation of their former hero as an insult whilst in Tbilisi students demonstrated as they prepared to send a letter of protest to Molotov. Order was only restored by the use of force that resulted in some loss of life. Far more serious was the reaction to the denunciation of Stalin in Eastern Europe where some saw it as a signal to turn against their own repressive Communist regimes. Later, Khrushchev did backtrack a little by making some more generous if only fleeting references to Stalin.

2 ↶ BULGANIN AND KHRUSCHEV

NICOLAI BULGANIN (1895–1975)

Nicolai Bulganin was born in Nazhi-Novgorod in 1895. During World War I, he had served in the ranks of the Tsar's armies. He joined the Bolsheviks in 1917 at the time of the Revolution and worked for the Cheka, Lenin's secret police. Promotion came rapidly and from 1931 to 1937, he was chairman of the Moscow Soviet. During World War II, he helped to organise the defence of Moscow and was appointed Marshal of the Soviet Union. After the war, he served as Soviet Minister of Defence and, in 1948, was promoted to membership of the Politburo. As a politician, he was regarded as a lightweight.

Although, after 1955, Bulganin was nominally leader of the Soviet Union, he lacked **dynamism** and was little more than Khrushchev's mouthpiece. On the face of it, they appeared to work well together, but there was no doubt that the real power lay with the Party secretary. Unusually for Russian leaders, they travelled abroad and visited Yugoslavia, India, Burma and Afghanistan. In 1956, they came to London and met Queen Elizabeth and Winston Churchill. Meanwhile, behind the scenes, new members were being added to the Presidium – all of them Khrushchev's men! Even so, Khrushchev's position was not totally secure. In 1957, a bitter Malenkov attempted a political comeback and tried to force Khrushchev's resignation. He, together with Kaganovich, Molotov, Voroshilov and Bulganin who had formed an Anti-Party Group, were opposed to the Party having the greatest say in the management of the economy and openly criticised Khrushchev's domestic and foreign policies. A vote of the Presidium went against the leader but Khrushchev took the issue to the full membership of the Central Committee. There he won the day largely because the Committee

dynamism *driving force or energy.*

was packed with his supporters conveniently flown to Moscow by Marshal Zhukov. Afterwards, Malenkov was expelled from the Party and spent the next 27 years of his life living in obscurity. He died in 1988. Molotov was dispatched to the Far East as Soviet ambassador to Mongolia whilst the other supporters of Malenkov were labelled an Anti-Party Group and dismissed. In March 1958, Bulganin, his position weakened, resigned as Prime Minister and Khrushchev added this position to that of Party secretary. He was now master of the Soviet Union.

PROFILE

NIKITA SERGEYEVICH KHRUSHCHEV (1894–1971)

Like Stalin but unlike the majority of the Communist hierarchy whose origins were middle class, Nikita Khrushchev's background was truly working class. Born in Kalinovka in 1894 the son of a coal miner, his grandfather had been a serf. He received an elementary education at the local village school before his family moved to Yuzovka in the Donets Basin. There he worked as a pipe fitter. Even before 1917, he became active in workers' organisations and in 1918, he joined the Communist Party. He fought in the Red Army during the Civil War and, afterwards, was admitted to a *Rabfak*, a workers' school which provided him with a secondary education. It was during this time that his first wife, Galina, died. In 1924, he married for a second time, Nina Petrovka, a schoolteacher. For some time, he worked as a Party administrator in Moscow before becoming its secretary. In 1938, he was placed in charge of the Ukraine Party and remained there until 1949. In 1939, he was appointed to the Politburo. After the Russian invasion of eastern Poland in 1940, he was made responsible for integrating the newly occupied territory within the Soviet Union. He also worked to eliminate the nationalist movements in Poland and the Ukraine. During the war, he was given the responsibility of overseeing the transfer of Ukrainian industry to the safety of the east. Then, attached to the Red Army, he helped to encourage civilian resistance in German occupied Russia and, as a political advisor, he was present during the defence of Stalingrad and the Battle of Kursk. The years 1949–53 were difficult for Khrushchev as, in Kremlin politics, he tried to avoid Stalin's displeasure in order to survive and still maintain his position in the Soviet hierarchy. He succeeded because he managed to remain unobtrusive. He regarded himself as something of a specialist in agriculture but his reputation suffered when his *agrogorod* proposals were rejected in 1951. In 1953, he replaced Malenkov as Party secretary. He was far from being the run-of-the-mill type of Soviet leader.

See page 361.

Described by the historians Gwyneth Hughes and Simon Welfare as 'The little man with baggy trousers from the Ukraine', he could nevertheless be ruthless and, during the years when he had been a zealous supporter of Stalin, had been involved in the purges of that time. Jonathan Lewis

PICTURE 45
Nikita Khrushchev in a jovial mood

and Phillip Whitehead regard him as '... a mixture of raw courage and blundering insensitivity which made him the right man to tackle Stalin's legacy.' In *Last of Empires* (1995), John Keep writes:

> In appearance he (Nikita Khrushchev) had the rough earthiness of his peasant origins, which he liked to emphasise, rotund and rubicund, with several warts on his face, irregular teeth and sharp, alert brown eyes. His speech was full of folksy **aphorisms**, proverbs, and metaphors ... He was temperamental and irascible, prone to fits of anger. He judged people capriciously, just as he decided complicated problems on impulse without having made a thorough preliminary study of the pros and cons. For him it was results that counted.

aphorisms sayings with significant meanings.

3 ᔐ THE SOVIET UNION UNDER NIKITA KHRUSHCHEV

Nikita Khrushchev, seldom polished in his behaviour or sophisticated in his utterances, was nevertheless an astute politician. More than was usual with politicians, he was willing to admit his mistakes and learn from them. There were times when he was unrestrained and appeared a buffoon but he was, when in the right humour, a quick-witted man who could inspire goodwill. Few would argue that he was very sincere in his political beliefs. In 1955, he commented on the possibility of the Soviet

Union abandoning Communism – 'Those who wait for that must wait until a shrimp learns to whistle.' The following year, in a very different frame of mind, he warned Western diplomats – 'Whether or not you like it, history is on our side. We will bury you.' Khrushchev was no liberal. He had a dark side to his character and could be ruthless. Nevertheless, he was a difficult man not to like and a dangerous man to underestimate.

A *'Reform Communism' and 'The Thaw'*

Khrushchev embarked on a policy of 'Reform Communism' which was intended to moderate and humanise the Soviet system by improving living standards and making life generally easier for the Russian people. As the people began to enjoy greater personal freedoms so life became more rewarding. For the first time in living memory Russians could express their feelings freely, read foreign literature and even listen to overseas radio stations. 'The Thaw' is the name sometimes given to the relaxation of the stringent conformity imposed on artistic and cultural activity during the years of Zhdanovism. The term comes from the title of a novel *Ottepel* (The Thaw) by Ilya Ehrenburg that was published in 1954. Khrushchev was pleased to promote the new freedom particularly when it was critical of the Stalinist period and served his own political ends. The composer, Shostakovich, and the writers Akhmatova, Babel, Pilnyak and Zoshchenko were rehabilitated. Alexander Solzhenitsyn, a long time prisoner in one of Stalin's labour camps, was released and allowed to publish *One Day in the Life of Ivan Denisovich* which provided a stark account of life in the camps and denounced Stalinist oppression. Books by Western authors such as Graham Greene, Ernest Hemingway and A.J. Cronin appeared in Russian bookshops. Even so, there was a limit to the new freedom of expression. The Jewish poet Boris Pasternak was severely criticised for his novel, *Doctor Zhivago*. Completed in 1955 and published abroad in 1957, it did not appear in the Soviet Union until 1988. Criticised and then expelled by the Soviet Writers' Union, the Soviet newspaper, *Pravda*, described Pasternak as 'a self-infatuated **Narcissus** marooned in a literary backwater, a weed on Soviet soil.' In 1958 he was refused permission to travel abroad to collect the Nobel Prize for Literature. Other so-called 'dissident writers' such as Ivan Dzyuba and Paul Litvinov who dared to criticise the Soviet system were arrested and imprisoned.

A limited number of Russian citizens were allowed to travel abroad whilst the tourist agency, *Intourist*, arranged for overseas tourists to visit the Soviet Union. Cultural and sporting exchanges were arranged with capitalist countries. The Moscow State Circus, the Bolshoi and Kirov Ballet companies, the Red Army Choir and football teams such as Moscow Dynamos became particularly popular. These changes in attitude meant that it became increasingly difficult to prevent the Russian people from being influenced by Western culture particularly styles of dress and popular music. There was also a noticeable increase in lawlessness and anti-social behaviour. In spite of the relaxation, Russian Jews were not allowed to emigrate and settle in the new state of Israel.

See pages 336–7.

Narcissus a person who loves himself.

B *De-Stalinisation*

Across the country there was an immediate reaction to Khrushchev's speech at the Twentieth Party Congress. In some of the *gulags* there were riots and the Soviet leader received masses of personal appeals from Party members who had been wrongfully convicted and from the families and friends of other victims. The release of thousands of prisoners from the labour camps added to the strong reaction against Stalin and Stalinism. Statues and portraits of the former dictator were pulled down and the towns and cities named in his honour given new titles – the battle famous city of Stalingrad was renamed Volgograd, Stalinsk became Novokuznetsk whilst Stalino and Stalinabad changed to Donetsk and Dushanbe respectively. Even before the end of the Congress, Stalin's body was removed from its place of honour next to Lenin in the Red Square mausoleum and buried in an ordinary cemetery plot.

C *Khrushchev's anti-religious campaign*

During the latter years of Stalin's rule, the various Russian churches suffered less persecution and enjoyed something of a revival. Khrushchev, however, led a vitriolic campaign against religion and renewed the victimisation of the clergy and churchgoers. During the period 1960–4, the number of Russian Orthodox Church monasteries and convents was greatly reduced and virtually all seminaries closed. The number of churches, estimated to be around 20 000 in 1960, fell to less than 8000. Many were turned into museums and community centres. Steps were taken to limit the authority and influence of priests and those that protested were arrested and imprisoned. One of the worst examples of religious persecution occurred at Uspensky monastery. There the buildings were confiscated, the monks dispersed and sent to labour camps, the novices beaten and the nuns raped. There were instances of children being removed from their families so that they would not be influenced by the religious beliefs of their parents. Other Christian sects suffered in a similar way, as did those of the Islamic faith. Atheism was introduced as a subject in the school curriculum and it became difficult for those with religious beliefs to enter further education or gain promotion in government employment. Foreign reaction to these measures did help to lessen the persecution.

D *Economic policy*

From the view of the average Russian citizen, Khrushchev made a more than valid point when he commented, 'it is no use everyone having the right ideology if they have to walk around without any trousers'. Later, he pulled no punches when he said:

> 'We must help people to eat well, dress well and live well. You cannot put theory into your soup or Marxism into your clothes. If after forty years of Communism, a person cannot have a glass of milk or a pair

> of shoes, he will not believe that Communism is a good thing, no matter what you tell him.'

The truth was that, in spite of the drain on the economy caused by high military spending, there had been some improvement in Russian living standards. Even so, they still lagged well behind those of the capitalist countries. During the early 1960s, consumer goods in the form of radios, televisions, refrigerators and other domestic appliances became more readily available but they were costly and of poor quality. More cars also appeared but they were prohibitively expensive and generally reserved for leading Party officials.

AGRICULTURE

Khrushchev introduced his Virgin Lands Scheme before he assumed the leadership of the Soviet Union in 1958. Once in control, he pressed ahead with other measures which were more successful and the country's agriculture began to enjoy one of its better periods. He was responsible for merging together the collective farms, *kolkhozes,* into his preferred state farms, *sovkhozes.* Workers on the *sovkhozes* enjoyed benefits denied to those on the *kolkhozes* since they received guaranteed, fixed wages and did not depend for their earnings on their share of the varying profits of a collective farm. In addition they received social benefits, not least the prospect of a pension. With the produce of the *sovkhozes* flooding into the industrial towns and cities and those working private plots no longer having to make compulsory deliveries to the State, the living standards of rural workers improved considerably. Khrushchev also set about decentralising the Soviet system of agriculture by granting greater **autonomy** to local Party administrators. By allowing the *sovkhozes* to purchase their own agricultural machinery, he freed the state farms from their dependence on the Motor Transport Stations.

autonomy the right to self-government.

INDUSTRY

Khrushchev also extended his policy of decentralisation into industry by abolishing Moscow-based ministries and replacing them with *sovnarkhozy* (not to be confused with *sovkhozes*). A *sovnarkhoze* was largely independent of central control and was free to regulate industrial activity within an area. Each *sovnarkhoze* covered an area of one of the administrative divisions of the country. Altogether there were 105 and, in 1962, a national *sovnarkhoze* was set up to replace the long established *Gosplan* and become responsible to the management of the Soviet economy. The local *sovnarkhoze* were, in part, politically controlled since they were intended to allow local Party leaders to have a greater say in the running of Soviet industry. Khrushchev also wanted the Party to gain the credit for the improved living standards of the Russian people. In 1959, the Sixth Five-Year Plan introduced in 1956 was abandoned in favour of a Seven-Year Plan (1959–65). It was intended to expand the manufacture of chemicals, fertilisers, man-made fibres and plastics and increase the production of oil and natural gas. It was also intended to increase the level of production of consumer goods.

The following is adapted from *Khrushchev and After* by J.N. Westwood in Purnell's *History of the Twentieth Century*.

Ownership of cars and household appliances per thousand of the population.

	1955	1966
Cars	2	5
Radios	66	171
Refrigerators	4	40
Washing machines	1	77
Sewing machines	31	151
Television sets	4	82

Increase in the availability of consumer goods in the Soviet Union, 1955–66

Although there was some improvement in the standard of living of the Russian people, they still lagged well behind the Western world.

In order to solve the chronic housing shortage, factories were to produce sections of prefabricated buildings that would lead to the construction of some 15 million new flats. The problem with Khrushchev was that he was full of well-intentioned schemes which, whilst they looked attractive on paper, were much more complex than he seemed to appreciate. His simple ideas too often showed his lack of understanding of the economic realities of the situation.

TECHNOLOGY AND THE SPACE INDUSTRY

A most impressive aspect of the Khrushchev years was the progress made in technology and the achievements of the Soviet space industry. After World War II and in common with the United States, the Soviet Union forcibly recruited German technicians to work on scientific projects. In addition, a new emphasis was placed on technology and science so that by 1965, the Soviet Union possessed over 4700 scientific establishments and employed more scientists in various forms of research than any other country. These developments, which placed Russia's technological mastery beyond dispute, allowed her to become the first country to enter the 'Space Age'.

In October 1957, the Soviet Union launched the first artificial satellite into space, *Sputnik*. Its designer was Sergei Korolev. Korolev was one of thousands of scientist intellectuals who Stalin had sent to the labour camps in the 1930s. Released and rehabilitated by Khrushchev, he became the country's leading rocket designer. In the same year the Russians launched *Sputnik II*. This took the dog, Laika, into space and provided Soviet scientists with information about the body's reaction to weightlessness. Unfortunately, the spacecraft was not equipped to re-enter the Earth's atmosphere and the mongrel perished. There followed exploratory missions to the moon, *Luna I* (1959), to Venus, *Venera I* (1961) and to Mars, *Mars I* (1962). The most historic flight occurred on

12 April 1961 when Yuri Gagarin became the first man in space when he orbited the planet in *Vostok I*. Launched from Baikonur in Central Asia, his flight took 108 minutes before he returned to Earth a national hero. On 16 June 1963, Valentina Tereshkova became the first woman in space. The following year, *Voskhod* became the first multi-manned spaceship to be launched. In 1965, Alexei Leonov on *Voskhod II* became the first man to successfully complete a 'walk' outside his space capsule. Her space achievements added greatly to the prestige of the Soviet Union and placed her well ahead of the United States. Unfortunately competition in space technology, particularly rocketry which provided the capacity to deliver atomic weapons, became an integral part of the Cold War. It has more recently been revealed that the Soviet space programme was blighted with numerous disasters that claimed the lives of many would be astronauts. Although the period 1955–66 witnessed some improvement in the living standards of the Russian people, they still lagged well behind the Western world. In the United States in 1966 there were 398 cars per thousand of the population, 1300 radios, 293 refrigerators, 259 washing machines, at the time, the authorities kept this a secret.

In 1959, in a speech made at the Twenty-first Party Congress, Khrushchev declared that socialism had now been achieved in the

---

KEY ISSUE

Why did the Soviets place a new emphasis on technology?

PROFILE

SOVIET SPACE HEROES – YURI GAGARIN AND VALENTINA TERESHKOVA

Yuri Gagarin was born in 1934 in Klushino, a small village near Moscow. The third of four children, both his parents worked on a *kolkhoz*, his father as a carpenter and his mother as a milkmaid. During World War II, his family suffered at the hands of the Germans but afterwards he attended secondary school before working in a steelworks as a foundry man. He then attended a technical school and there had the opportunity to join a flying club. In 1955, he qualified as a pilot and, in 1957, joined the Soviet air force. On 12th April 1961, he became the first man in space. On his return, he became a national hero and travelled world-wide. In 1963, he was killed in a plane crash. Valentina Tereshkova was born in 1937. On leaving school, she worked in the textile industry. She joined a parachute club and was selected for cosmonaut training. On 16th June 1963, she became the first woman in space. On her triumphant return, she, like Gargarin, was much honoured. She also fell victim to Khrushchev and Soviet propagandists who pressurised her into marrying a fellow cosmonaut, Adrian Nikolayev. The Soviet leader himself attended the marriage ceremony that took place in Moscow. The marriage was short-lived and with it ended the Soviet leader's idea of a propaganda scoop – a 'space family'. Afterwards, Tereshkova became a prominent member of the Communist Party and, in 1974, was elected to the Supreme Soviet.

Soviet Union and that it was now time to press ahead with a new drive to communism. The programme for the transition to communism was discussed at the next Party Congress, the Twenty-Second, held in 1961.

4 ᐧ SOVIET FOREIGN POLICY, 1953–64

As we have seen, the reaction of the West to the imposition of Communist ideology on many of the countries of Eastern Europe and the threat of further Soviet expansion led to a Cold War. The crisis over Berlin, 1948–9, the creation of two Germanys – the German Federal Republic (FDR) backed by the West and the Communist dominated German Democratic Republic (DDR) – together with the establishment of the North Atlantic Treaty Organisation (NATO) further intensified the hostility between the Western powers and the Soviet Union. The Russian leadership regarded NATO as an anti-Soviet alliance and accordingly increased their military spending. In May 1955, the Soviet Union sponsored the setting up of an Eastern European Mutual Assistance Treaty.

See Chapter 12.

Signed in the Polish capital and usually referred to as the Warsaw Pact, its members included the Soviet Union, Albania, Bulgaria, Czechoslovakia, the German Democratic Republic, Poland and Romania. Finland was invited to join but declined on the grounds that it preferred to remain non-aligned. In reality, the Warsaw Pact was the Russian response to NATO. Each member state undertook to assist any other faced by an armed attack by a foreign power. It provided for a unified military command under a Soviet commander-in-chief and their armies agreed to take part in joint manoeuvres annually. The headquarters of the Warsaw Pact was in Moscow. Khrushchev also tried to repair the rift in Soviet relations with Yugoslavia. In 1955, he travelled with Bulganin to Belgrade to apologise to Tito for Stalin's earlier highhanded behaviour. The Yugoslav leader, however, showed no willingness to return to the Communist fold. Another feature of Khrushchev's diplomacy was his courtship of Third World powers. In an effort to dislodge Western influence, he offered technical aid and loans to support projects in such countries as Afghanistan, Burma, India, Iraq, Morocco and the North Yemen. It was his offer to help finance the construction of the Aswan Dam in Egypt that indirectly contributed to the Suez Crisis.

Q

To what extent was the Warsaw Pact a Soviet response to NATO?

1955	May	USSR signs a peace treaty with Austria
		Warsaw Pact agreed
	July	Big Four summit in Geneva
	November	Soviet leaders visit India, Burma and Afghanistan
1956	February	Khrushchev declares peaceful co-existence to be the cornerstone of Soviet foreign policy
	April	Khrushchev and Bulganin visit Britain
	October	Hungarian uprising
1959	September	Khrushchev visits the United States. Meets Eisenhower at Camp David
1960	May	U-2 incident. Paris summit cancelled
	August	Soviet technicians withdrawn from Communist China

(continued overleaf)

TABLE 60
Date chart of the main developments in Soviet foreign policy, 1953–64

1961 June	Khrushchev and Kennedy meet in Vienna
1962 October	Cuban missile crisis
1963 October	USSR and USA sign nuclear test ban treaty (SALT)

A *Détente and peaceful co-existence*

In many ways the foreign policy aims of Nikita Khrushchev differed little from those of Stalin. He was determined to ensure that Eastern Europe remained under Soviet control and retained their Communist regimes. Like Stalin, he also wanted to force the Western powers to leave Berlin. He considered West Berlin as a Western peephole in the Iron Curtain and described it as 'a bone stuck in the throat of Communism'. Even so, if his aims were much the same as those of Stalin, Khrushchev differed in his approach. Instead of supporting the traditional view that war between the Capitalist and Communist powers was inevitable, he looked for *détente*, some relaxation in East–West relations, and put forward his own theory of 'peaceful co-existence'. In a speech made in February 1956 in Moscow he said:

> 'The principle of peaceful co-existence is gaining wider recognition … And this is natural, for in present-day conditions there is no other way out. Indeed there are only two ways: either peaceful co-existence or the most destructive war in history. There is no third way.'

At the Twenty-First Party Congress in 1959 he told delegates that 'We offer the capitalist countries peaceful competition' and, in the same year, he went to the United States and met the American President, Dwight D. Eisenhower at Camp David in Maryland. Plans were made to call a major summit conference in Paris in 1960 but this came to nothing when, a fortnight before the meeting was due to begin, an American U-2 spy plane was shot down over Soviet territory.

THE U-2 INCIDENT

Unknown to the Russians, the American Central Intelligence Agency had long been involved in sending high-flying reconnaissance aircraft on spying missions over the Soviet Union. On 1 May 1960, a U-2 aircraft, piloted by Gary Powers, was shot down near Sverdlovsk in the Ural mountains. The aircraft had flown from Peshawar in Pakistan and its intended destination was Bodo in Norway. Outraged by the incident, in a speech to the Supreme Soviet Khrushchev described the flight as an 'aggressive act' and decided to place the issue before the UN Security Council. Making available film taken from a camera on the plane as evidence that it was on a spying mission, he also protested most vigorously to Washington and demanded an apology from President Eisenhower and the punishment of those involved. With no apology forthcoming, Khrushchev refused to attend a summit conference in Paris arranged between the leaders of the United States, the Soviet Union, Britain and France and also withdrew an invitation made earlier for Eisenhower to visit Russia. Powers, who appeared on Russian television, was tried and sentenced to ten years' imprisonment. He served less than two years and, in 1962, was exchanged for the captured Soviet spy Colonel Rudolf Abel. Khrushchev used the propaganda value of the U-2 incident to good effect. Even the exchange of Powers for Abel was to his advantage – Powers was merely a pilot whilst Abel was an accomplished Soviet spy.

Q *How damaging to Soviet–US relations was the U-2 incident?*

Later in the year, the Soviet leader led the Soviet delegation to the UN General Assembly. He caused something of a sensation when he rudely interrupted the speeches of other delegates and then made a point by hammering the desk with his shoe. In November, John F. Kennedy was elected President of the United States. In a letter of congratulation to the American President-Elect, Khrushchev seemed remarkably conciliatory when he wrote the following which is from *American Foreign Policy: Current Documents, 1960*:

'We hope that while you are at this post the relations between our countries will again follow the line along which they were developing in Franklin Roosevelt's time, which would meet the basic interests not only of the peoples of the USSR and the United States but all mankind which is longing for deliverance from the threat of a new war. I think that you will agree that the eyes of many people are fixed on the United States and the Soviet Union because the destinies of world peace depend largely on the state of Soviet–American relations … We are convinced that there are no insurmountable obstacles to the preservation and consolidation of peace. For the sake of this goal we are ready, for our part, to continue efforts to solve such a pressing problem as disarmament, to settle the German issue through the earliest conclusion of a peace treaty and to reach agreement on other questions…'

In June 1961, Khrushchev met the new American president in Vienna. There he tried to browbeat the young and inexperienced Kennedy by demanding an immediate settlement to the Berlin problem. Kennedy refused to be bullied and the meeting achieved nothing. On 13th August 1961, the East German government used barbed wire to seal the border between East and West Berlin and, five days later, the construction of the Berlin Wall began.

B *Unrest in Eastern Europe*

The relaxation brought about by Khrushchev's more liberal policies at home had repercussions in the Soviet Union's East European satellites still largely under Stalinist-type regimes. In East Germany, forced to pay quite massive reparations to Russia in the form of machinery, railway rolling stock and other equipment, the people continued to endure acute shortages. Little post-war reconstruction had taken place and stretches of the roadways, the *autobahns*, were still impassable because of bomb craters! The staunch Stalinist, Otto Grotewhol, who urged the people to accept their hard-ship, ruled the country. In 1953, he caused outrage when he increased workers' norms. There were strikes and demonstrations in East Berlin and the hated Communist secret police, the *Volkspolizei*, lost control. Order was only restored when Russian tanks appeared in the streets. There were also strikes in other East German towns including Brandenburg, Halle and Magdeburg.

ANALYSIS

The Berlin Wall

It was in November 1958 that Khrushchev first publicly challenged the rights of the Western powers to remain in Berlin when he stated 'all of Berlin lies in the territory of the GDR. The Western powers no longer have any legal, moral, or political basis for their continued occupation of West Berlin.' He then demanded that within six months West Berlin should become a demilitarised, free city. The Western powers ignored the Soviet leader's ultimatum and nothing happened. In East Germany, the Communist authorities pressed ahead with unpopular measures – the enforced collectivisation of land and increased norms for workers – and this led to an even greater stampede to leave the country. The total number of refugees seeking asylum in the West rose from 199 000 during 1960 to 207 000 in the first six months of 1961 alone. The problem for the new East German leader, Walter Ulbricht, was that the exodus included a high proportion of highly qualified and professional people. Ulbricht first tried to encourage Khrushchev to forcibly enter and occupy West Berlin but the Soviet leader was only too aware of the risks involved. He then urged Khrushchev to agree a peace treaty between the Soviet Union and the GDR that would give the East Germans sovereignty over the access routes into West Berlin. As a safer alternative, Khrushchev agreed to the building of a wall and, on 13 August 1961, the East Germans began to take the necessary steps to isolate West Berlin. The Berlin Wall, which divided a city and cruelly separated families and friends, came to represent the face of Communist tyranny. There were still those prepared to attempt to escape the 'Wall of Shame', as it became known, by crossing the 'death strip' of mines and barbed wire and then attempting to scale the wall. Some succeeded but the majority failed and were shot by East German frontier guards. To counter the fear of West Berliners that they might be abandoned by the Western powers, in June 1963, President Kennedy visited the city. He said that if people wanted to see the real face of Communism 'Let them come to Berlin'. On the steps of the Schoneberg town hall, he told his German hosts that to be a citizen of West Berlin was the proudest boast of a free man and added – 'As a freeman I take pride in the words *Ich bin ein Berliner*' (I am a Berliner).

Poland, strongly nationalist and with a predominantly Roman Catholic population, was ruled by Wladyslaw Gomulka. Less willing to accommodate Stalin, Gomulka stated that he wanted Poland to follow an independent road to socialism and, as a result, was removed from office and imprisoned. After Stalin's death, he returned to power and released a large number of political prisoners. In 1956, serious riots broke out in Poznan as workers protested against their low wages and living standards. There was a stormy meeting between Gomulka and Khrushchev and, once again, Russian tanks were used to clear the streets. In the same year came the biggest challenge to a Communist regime in Eastern Europe, this time in Hungary.

The Hungarian Revolution, 1956

Since 1945, Hungary had been under the oppressive rule of a Communist regime led by the hard-line Stalinist, Matyas Rakosi. He steadfastly refused any relaxation in his policies or to limit the activities of his secret police. In 1953, Rakosi was removed from office and replaced by a reformer, Imre Nagy, who promised to give priority to improving living standards. Nagy was only in power for two years before he was forced to give way to the unpopular Rakosi. In 1956, during a year in which poor harvests coincided with acute shortages of food and fuel, students took to the streets of Budapest and dismantled a statue of Stalin. As the unrest spread across the country, Khrushchev gave way to pressure and allowed the hero Nagy to return. It even seemed that Soviet forces were preparing to leave the country. There were further demonstrations as the people demanded reforms and the release of political prisoners. More daringly, there was a move to withdraw Hungary from membership of the Warsaw Pact. For Khrushchev, this proved the last straw and with his army reinforced, he ordered Russian tanks back into Budapest. This led to a full-scale uprising with savage street fighting during which the Hungarian army fought alongside the country's freedom fighters. Soviet aircraft strafed the city as, in their unequal struggle against Russian tanks, over 20 000 Hungarians were killed. As their revolt crumbled, Nagy appealed for outside help but his request was ignored. During the course of the uprising some 200 000 Hungarians took advantage of their open frontiers with the West and sought asylum. Afterwards, Janos Kadar replaced Nagy, who sought asylum in the Yugoslav embassy. Promised safe passage, the Soviet authorities saw to it that he was arrested and then secretly executed.

In a letter to Khrushchev, the British prime minister, Anthony Eden, wrote: 'The world knows that for the past three days Soviet forces in Hungary have been ruthlessly crushing the heroic resistance of a truly national movement for independence, a movement which, by declaring its neutrality, proved that it had been no threat to the security of the Soviet Union.'

ANALYSIS

Q

Why did the Western powers fail to go to Hungary's assistance?

Khrushchev's decision to crush the Hungarian uprising badly damaged his reputation. Across the world, Soviet embassies were besieged by angry crowds and thousands of Communists resigned from their party in protest. The situation might have even been worse for the Soviet leader had international attention not been distracted by another event – the Suez crisis caused by the Anglo-French decision to intervene in Egypt when President Nasser nationalized the Suez Canal Company. Nevertheless, there were significant consequences. The Hungarian people began to enjoy greater freedom whilst Khrushchev became even more aware of the unreliability of his Warsaw Pact allies.

C *The Cuban missile crisis, 1962*

As disturbing as the Hungarian uprising had been, an even bigger crisis was to occur in 1962 when the world came close to a nuclear war. Khrushchev was aware that the Soviet Union was well behind the United States in the arms race, particularly the production of long-range nuclear weapons. Whilst Russian missiles were capable of striking any target in Europe, the United States remained well out of range. In April 1962, the Soviets sought to remedy this by building sites in Cuba capable of launching intermediate-range rockets. In 1959 following an insurrection, Fidel Castro came to power in Cuba, an island barely 300 km off the United States coast. As head of a Communist-type regime, Castro offended the United States when he went out of his way to court the friendship of the Soviet Union and Communist China. In 1961, an American inspired attempt to invade the island and overthrow Castro, the Bay of Pigs incident, led Castro to seek even closer ties with Russia. Khrushchev's offer of missile sites appealed to the Cuban leader since it provided him with a way of defending his island from any future attack by the US. The crisis began on 15th October 1962 when American reconnaissance aircraft returned with photographs showing missile sites under construction in Cuba. A week later, President Kennedy spoke to the American people on television and advised them of his intentions:

> All ships of any kind bound for Cuba from whatever nation or port will, if found to be carrying cargoes of offensive weapons, be turned back ... Our resolution (to the Security Council) will call for the prompt dismantling and withdrawal of all offensive weapons in Cuba, under the supervision of UN observers ...

Acting in this way to prevent the arrival of any more Soviet missiles and imposing a naval blockade on Cuba was a calculated act of 'brinkmanship'. He went further and warned Khrushchev that any nuclear missile attack launched from Cuba would be regarded as an attack on the United States by the Soviet Union. The world waited anxiously as American warships prepared to intercept Russian rocket-bearing cargo ships off the coast of Cuba. In a series of messages from Khrushchev, the Soviet leader first agreed to remove the missiles if the United States would

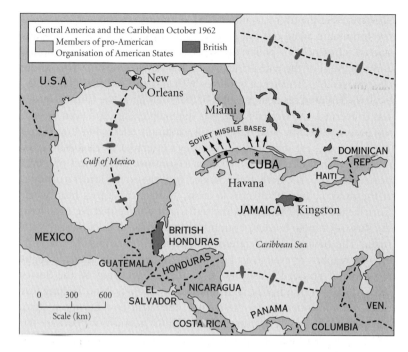

MAP 22
The Cuban crisis of 1962

guarantee not to invade Cuba and then went a step further in a second letter by demanding the removal of all NATO missiles in Turkey. The Americans ignored the second letter but agreed to the first and by early November the missiles had been dismantled. During this trial of strength between Khrushchev and Kennedy there seemed a grave risk of the outbreak of a nuclear war. Kennedy's firmness in dealing with the crisis certainly enhanced his prestige in the United States but, in the Soviet Union, Khrushchev faced criticism for backing down in the face of American threats. The view of most historians is that the Russian leader's action was equally an act of considerable statesmanship since it saved the world from the possibility of a nuclear war.

There were two immediate consequences of the Cuban missile crisis. Firstly a 'Hot Line' was established between Moscow and Washington in order to provide a direct means of communication between the leaders of the Soviet Union and the United States at a time of crisis. Secondly, Khrushchev and Kennedy agreed a Strategic Arms Limitation Treaty (SALT) which banned the testing of nuclear weapons in the atmosphere, outer space and under the sea.

D *The rift between the Soviet Union and Communist China*

In the mid 1950s, Nikita Khrushchev made several visits to Mao Zedong's Communist China, the Soviet Union's rival for the leadership of the Communist world. From 1959, there was a progressive deterioration in the relationship between the two countries. The main reasons for the rift were differences in ideology. Mao Zedong persisted with his insistence that the ultimate aim of the Communist movement was world revolution and an all out war against the capitalist imperialists. He considered Khrushchev's policy of peaceful co-existence to be revisionist and a betrayal of the true principles of Marxist–Leninism. Mao Zedong disapproved of Khrushchev's policies both at home and abroad and particularly deplored his denunciation of Stalin. As far as the Chinese leader was concerned, the United States was the main enemy and even though she possessed atomic weapons, he still scathingly referred to the USA as 'a paper tiger'. He deplored Khrushchev's attempts to establish better relations with the Americans in order to improve the chances of world peace. He was particularly unimpressed with the Soviet leader's conduct at the time of the Cuban missile crisis. Matters came to a head when Khrushchev refused to discuss the settlement of disputed regions along the Russo–Chinese border or support China in her border dispute with India. The Soviet leader's refusal to provide Communist China with atomic weapons or even assist her with her nuclear programme brought a torrent of abuse. Khrushchev responded by recalling all the Soviet technicians working in China. In matters of ideology, Mao Zedong was dogmatic and inflexible. In the dispute, the small East European state, Albania, sided with Communist China. This was said to be because the Albanian leader, Enver Hoxha, believed that Khrushchev was prepared to allow Tito to incorporate his country within Yugoslavia.

> **KEY ISSUE**
>
> *The ideological differences between Khrushchev and Mao Zedong.*

5 ⌐ THE END OF KHRUSHCHEV

Although there were many who disagreed with Khrushchev's policies, it was only after the Cuban crisis that members of the Presidium began to seriously consider his replacement. When, in October 1964, they decided to act, they moved quickly. Only six months earlier, Leonid Brezhnev, the secretary of the Central Committee, had delivered the main speech on the occasion of Khrushchev's seventieth birthday and loudly praised his achievements but now he was one of a group orchestrating his removal.

A *Khrushchev's resignation*

On holiday at Sochi on the Black Sea, the Soviet leader first rejected an urgent call to return home to attend a meeting of the Presidium. When told that the meeting would be held in his absence, he quickly made his way to Moscow. There, Mikhail Suslov, the Party theorist who had always tolerated rather than agreed with Khrushchev, read a prepared statement that catalogued his leader's shortcomings. Khrushchev listened in silence. Afterwards, no one spoke in his favour. Denied access to the media and the chance to put his case to the Russian people, he had no choice but to resign. At the time, the official reasons given were 'advanced age and ill health' but this did not prevent *Pravda* from accusing him of 'harebrained scheming, hasty conclusions, rash decisions and actions based on wishful thinking'. There remains some confusion regarding the role played by

Brezhnev in these events. There is the view that he played no part at all and that Suslov was the driving force behind the plot. But then there is the legend that he had earlier suggested poisoning Khrushchev!

The main reason given for Khrushchev's dismissal was declining health but, as we have seen, the real reasons were dissatisfaction with his policies and his one man-style of government. Those about to take over the leadership of the Soviet Union faced the problems of a declining economy, particularly in the agricultural sector, the future of *détente* and relations with the United States and the crisis in relations with Communist China. One thing was certain – many of Khrushchev's reforms would be difficult to reverse and there would be no going back on the new liberties enjoyed by the Russian people.

Criticisms of Khrushchev's policies

- His overbearing attitude had often offended senior Party members. He often declined advice and was inclined to make arbitrary decisions.
- His attempt to decentralise the structure of the Party upset many of his supporters. The Party had also lost ground to a *nomenkratura* – a civil service of bureaucrats and managers. The granting of autonomy to local Party leaders and Regional Economic Councils had weakened the Party's control of the economy.
- His agricultural policies, including his failed Virgin Lands Scheme, had led to a shortfall of foodstuff. The Soviet Union once again found it necessary to import grain from the United States and Canada.
- His decision to promote the production of consumer goods upset those who thought that he was failing to give adequate priority to the further development of heavy industry.
- He had offended the military by wanting to reduce expenditure on conventional weapons and concentrate more on nuclear weapons.
- His foreign policy was subject to a great deal of criticism. There was considerable disapproval of his handling of the Cuban missile crisis and he was held responsible for the rift with Communist China.

The removal of Nikita Khrushchev was a bloodless *coup* carried out by those who had earlier supported him and whose careers he had promoted. Chief amongst those who plotted his downfall was Leonid Brezhnev, his protégé and deputy. Retired from private life, he lived in obscurity outside Moscow where he later began to work secretly on his memoirs. Although they did not appear in the Soviet Union, in 1970 they were published in Europe and the United States. After his death at the age of seventy-seven in 1971, he was denied a state funeral or even a resting place for his ashes in the Kremlin wall amongst the famous and heroes of the Soviet Union.

B *Nikita Khrushchev – an assessment*

exposé making generally known a crime or scandal.

Although he was always liable to be outrageous and even exhibitionist and irrational in his behaviour, Nikita Khrushchev was responsible for changes that affected both the Soviet Union and the world-wide Communist movement. Following his **exposé** of the myth of Stalin, the face of the Soviet Union changed as the introduction of more liberal ideas allowed the Russian people to enjoy greater personal freedoms. Some went as far as to question the worth of Lenin's teachings and their application to the Soviet Union. His greater emphasis on creating a consumer-based economy led to an improvement in living standards and, in relaxing the rigid controls on cultural life, he went some way towards allowing Russian art and culture to flourish again. He set in motion changes in Soviet attitudes that his successors would find impossible to reverse. Relaxation only whetted the appetite of the Russian people for more and his was the spadework that later encouraged the introduction of the policies of *perestroika* (restructuring) and *glasnost* (openness) by Mikhail Gorbachev in the 1980s. His acceptance that it was possible to follow 'different roads to socialism' influenced events in Hungary (1956) and Czechoslovakia (1968). Across Eastern Europe generally, it sparked a demand for greater independence and more tolerant regimes.

See page 454.

In foreign affairs, his introduction of the doctrine of 'peaceful co-existence' marked a major break with traditional Communist teaching. It was his appreciation of the devastating consequences of a nuclear war that brought to an end the Cuban missile crisis in 1962. Afterwards he was willing to negotiate with the United States on limiting the spread and testing of nuclear weapons. In his memoirs, he wrote, 'I'll always remember the late president (Kennedy) with deep respect because, in the final analysis, he showed himself sober-minded and determined to avoid war.' Many of his policies failed and because of his stance on major issues, he made enemies both within the Soviet Union and abroad.

Writing retrospectively, most historians have been generous in their assessment of Nikita Khrushchev:

Fred Coleman writing in the *Washington Post*, 1966.

> 'As a direct result of Khrushchev's efforts, the losers in the Kremlin struggles no longer got arrested and shot. Instead, they were retired on pensions... Never again would the Soviet Union suffer another blood purge. Khrushchev's twilight years on a pension thus became a living symbol of the historical change he had bought to Russia. In that sense, they were his crowning achievement.'

N. Low in *Modern World History*, 1982.

> 'Khrushchev was a man of outstanding personality... He deserves to be remembered for his foreign policy reservations, for the return to comparatively civilised politics and for the improved living standards of the masses.'

John Keen in *Last of the Empires*, 1995.

> 'His greatest accomplishment was to end the reign of fear ... Millions owed him their release from the camps.'

The view of his son, Sergei Khrushchev in *Khrushchev on Khrushchev*, 1990.

> 'N.S. Khrushchev is a part of our history, and, in my opinion, far from the worst part.'

Yet, in spite of all his eccentricities, 'The little man in the baggy trousers from the Ukraine' proved himself a politician of substance and a world statesman.

6 ⌐ STRUCTURED AND ESSAY QUESTIONS

A *This section consists of questions that might be useful for discussion (or writing answers) as a way of expanding on the chapter and for testing understanding of it.*

1. What criticisms did Khrushchev make of Stalin in his speech to the Twentieth Party Conference?
2. Why would some Russians be (i) surprised and (ii) not surprised by Khrushchev's disclosures?
3. What measures did Malenkov take in an effort to win popularity?
4. Why did the attempted *coup* by the Anti-Party Group fail in 1957?
5. Give some examples of occasions when Khrushchev's behaviour might have been considered erratic or insensitive.
6. In what sense did Soviet–American competition in space technology become part of the Cold War?
7. To what extent did relations between the Soviet Union and the West improve during the Khrushchev years?
8. What did Mao Zedong mean when he referred to the United States as 'a paper tiger'?

B *Essay questions.*

1. 'Above all else, his handling of the Cuban crisis was the main reason for his downfall.' Is this a fair assessment of the reasons why Khrushchev was removed from office in 1964?
2. To what extent did the policies of Khrushchev affect the everyday lives of the Russian people?
3. 'His greatest accomplishment was to end the reign of fear'. How valid is this judgement of Khrushchev?

7 ⌐ SINGLE-SOURCE DOCUMENTARY EXERCISES ON THE U-2 INCIDENT AND HUNGARIAN UPRISING

SOURCE A

From US State Department papers

In another long speech to the Supreme Soviet on the next day, 7th May, Khrushchev said … that the pilot was still alive and that the Soviet authorities had recovered parts of the plane. He also displayed samples of the developed film allegedly taken from the camera equipment installed on the plane … In response to the speech, the American State Department issued a statement on 7th May admitting that as far as the authorities in Washington were concerned there was no authorization for the flight described by Mr Khrushchev … but that such a flight over the Soviet Union to gather information was justified as necessary 'given the state of the world today' …

1. *What was the mission of the plane to which Khrushchev refers?*

2. *To what extent does the State Department appear to deny responsibility for the flight?*

3. *What is meant by 'given the state of the world today'?*

4. *How full an understanding does the source provide of the events surrounding the U-2 incident?*

SOURCE B

From a letter sent by Nikita Khrushchev to President Kennedy on 26 October 1962

'Mr President, we and you ought not to pull on the ends of the rope in which you have tied the knot of war, because the more the two of us pull, the tighter that knot will be tied. And a moment may come when that knot will be tied so tight that even he who tied it will not have the strength to untie it, and then it will be necessary to cut the knot, and what would that mean is not for me to explain to you, because you yourself understand perfectly of what terrible forces our countries dispose.'

1. *What does Khrushchev mean when he refers to:*
   (i) 'the knot of war'?
   (ii) 'the more the two of us pull, the tighter the knot will be tied'?

2. *Explain the relevance of the source to the Hungarian uprising that was taking place at that time.*

3. *What were 'the terrible forces our countries dispose'?*

4. *To what extent might Khrushchev's letter to Kennedy be considered a warning?*

The Soviet Union 1964–82: the years of Brezhnev and Kosygin

14

INTRODUCTION

With Khrushchev removed, the Central Committee elected Leonid Brezhnev as Secretary of the Party and Aleksei Kosygin as Prime Minister. A one time rival of Brezhnev, Nikolay Podgorny was appointed to the less influential position of Chairman of the Presidium of the Supreme Soviet which made him nominally head of state. The three men were the first of a generation of Soviet leaders to be born in the twentieth century and were too young to have taken an active part in the Revolution of 1917. They had also made their way to the top by progressing through the Party's ranks as *apparatchiks* – full time officials working in the state bureaucracy. In an attempt to ensure that the leadership remained 'collective', it was agreed that, in future, no person could be head of the Party and head of the government at the same time.

1 ⌐ THE COLLECTIVE LEADERSHIP OF BREZHNEV AND KOSYGIN

LEONID BREZHNEV (1906–82)

Born in Kamensyoye in the Ukraine in 1906, Leonid Ilych Brezhnev was one of the three children born to an iron foundry worker. In 1921, the family moved to Kursk and there the young Brezhnev began to work in the same ironworks as his father. As a youth, he had ambitions to become an actor and took part in local amateur dramatics. He attended a technical school and there studied land management. Afterwards, he worked locally before being sent to the Urals. There he met his future wife, Victoria Petrona, and they married in 1927. In 1931, he joined the Communist Party and began studying metallurgy. He divided his time between his studies and Party work. After the German invasion in 1941, Brezhnev became involved in the evacuation of factories, machinery and civilian workers to the east. Then, much decorated and with a reputation for leadership, he served with distinction as a political commissar, on the Caucasian and Ukrainian

PROFILE

fronts. He ended the war with the rank of major-general. During the post-war years, he worked closely with Nikita Khrushchev. He served, in turn, as head of the Party in Moldavia and Kazakhstan and, in 1950, was elected to the Supreme Soviet.

At the Nineteenth Party Congress in 1952, he was elected to both the Central Committee and the Politburo. Following the death of Stalin, he suffered a setback when he fell out of favour and was dropped from the Politburo. Brought back by Khrushchev in 1957, he sided with his leader when an Anti-Party group tried to depose him. After playing an important part in implementing the Virgin Lands Scheme, in 1960 he was appointed President of the Presidium of the Soviet Union and in 1963, became secretary of the Central Committee.

Brezhnev now played his cards carefully. Although close to Khrushchev, indeed he might have been considered his **prodigy**, he distanced himself from his leader's policies. He also showed the political skills of a populist by appearing to be all things to all men. In order to avoid taking sides and causing resentment, he tended to take up a central position and 'sit on the fence'. It was a ploy that worked since his low-key approach and moderation appealed to Party members who did not want a return to the terror of Stalin or the volatile and unreliable ways of Khrushchev. A hard working and able administrator, he appeared to be safe. In reality, he was far more astute and ambitious than people realised. In October 1964, Brezhnev was appointed first secretary of the Party and Aleksei Kosygin became Prime Minister. To start with, their joint leadership had the appearance of being collective. In spite of being considered the best dressed of the Soviet leaders, he lacked the flamboyance and personal charisma of his predecessor. Seemingly humourless and gaunt in appearance, he was always considered a good if unspectacular committee man. As we shall see, this view of Brezhnev was not entirely accurate since it was not by personal charm but by stealth that he managed to consolidate his power base and become undisputed Soviet leader. His partner in the Soviet leadership, Kosygin, also lacked a sparkling personality but he was a capable administrator.

See pages 416–17.

prodigy an exceptionally gifted young person.

PICTURE 46
Leonid Ilych Brezhnev

PROFILE

OTHERS IN THE PARTY LEADERSHIP

Aleksei Kosygin (1904–80) was born in St Petersburg. Aged only fifteen, he joined the Red Army in 1919 and fought in the Civil War. After joining the Communist Party in 1927, he progressed through the lower ranks and was elected to the Supreme Soviet in 1938 and held a number of administrative posts in industry. The following year, he became a member of the Central Committee. During World War II, he was involved in the evacuation of Soviet industry to the east and played a part in the defence of his home city, Leningrad. Briefly, he held the positions of Chairman of the

State Economic Planning Committee and, together with Anastas Mikoyan, first deputy Prime Minister. Following the removal of Khrushchev, he became Chairman of the Council of Ministers. Although he supposedly shared the leadership with Brezhnev, he gradually lost ground and it was the latter who finally emerged as the central figure. The third lesser important figure in the hierarchy was **Nikolay Podgorny** (1903–83). From Karlovka in the Ukraine, he graduated from Kiev Technical Institute and worked as an engineer in the sugar industry. Within the Party he made a name as an able administrator in the food processing industry. During the war, he played a prominent role in the economic reconstruction of the Ukraine. After being appointed first Secretary of the Ukrainian Party, he progressed to membership of the Politburo in 1960 and became Secretary of the Central Committee in 1963. After the downfall of Khrushchev, he unsuccessfully challenged Brezhnev for the leadership. Afterwards, he was removed from his position as Secretary of the Committee and appointed to the far less influential post of Chairman of the Presidium. In effect, he was nominally the head of state and this allowed him to travel widely. Another person waiting in the wings for his opportunity was the Party's ideologist **Mikhail Suslov** (1902–82). Earlier he had been opposed to Khrushchev's de-Stalinisation measures and had played a major part in plotting his leader's downfall.

For a time, Brezhnev appeared to play a secondary role to Kosygin who took the lead in both economic and foreign policy matters but gradually Brezhnev's authority increased and by 1972 he was clearly in charge and 'the number one *apparatchik* in the Soviet realm'.

2 ➝ BREZHNEV'S RUSSIA

The years of Brezhnev's leadership are remembered for, on the one hand, continued scientific achievement and the emergence of the Soviet Union as a major world nuclear power and, on the other, for the reversal of most of Khrushchev's policies, the decline of the Soviet economy, a step back towards Stalinism where art and literature were concerned, the erosion of social standards and rampant corruption.

Brezhnev's main aim was to bring about stability in Soviet politics. He believed that the staff and officials, the **cadres**, in state organisations should be permanent appointments. To achieve this, he appointed his own supporters to leading positions in the government. The men he appointed tended to be reliable and mature and, once in position, they remained secure for as long as they carried out their responsibilities satisfactorily. There were few reshuffles at the top let alone purges! Typical Brezhnev men were Yuri Andropov, head of the KGB, Marshal Andrei Grechko, the defence minister, and the foreign minister, Andrei Gromyko. The austere and humourless Gromyko, who had not been

cadres highly trained and influential groups.

highly rated by Khrushchev, was to become the Soviet Union's longest serving foreign minister. Whilst Brezhnev's administration may have brought stability, it prevented the promotion of younger men of ability and lacked dynamism. At one stage, all but one of the members of the Politburo were aged over 60! His period in office has been variously referred to as 'a cult without a personality' and 'years of stagnation' whilst his policies have been described as 'an ideology without a target'. The result was that Brezhnev was able to rule the Soviet Union for the best part of 18 years without facing any real opposition. Although he took no positive steps to rehabilitate Stalin, there was less mention of the crimes perpetrated by former Soviet dictator and the process of de-Stalinisation slowed down. The appearance of Aleksandr Solzhenitzyn's *One Day in the Life of Ivan Denisovich* in 1963 caused alarm since some felt that it would encourage anti-Soviet attitudes. In 1966, Brezhnev took the former Stalinist title of general secretary of the Party rather than first secretary whilst the Presidium reverted to its former name, the Politburo. Brezhnev accepted that the achievement of communism would take longer than Khrushchev had promised. Instead, he proposed an interim stage of 'developed socialism' that would increase national prosperity and improve living standards and would be based on new technological and scientific advances. The decentralisation introduced by Khrushchev came to an end. The powers earlier extended to the regions were now restored to Moscow and this led to the growth of many new government ministries, departments and agencies. In an age of red-tape and officialdom, the Soviet *nomenklatura* came truly into its own.

A *The* nomenklatura – *privilege, nepotism and corruption*

Long before this time, the old Marxist dictum of 'From each according to his ability, to each according to his needs' had been abandoned. Now the technological and administrative skills needed to change the country would require the services of highly qualified men and women and the people who possessed these skills would have to be more than adequately rewarded. This meant that the existing system of pay differentials would have to be extended further. By 1970, nearly 19% of the total labour force in the Soviet Union were specialists or working in positions of responsibility and a quarter of Party members were university graduates. Their reward was not limited to their salaries. The system encouraged privilege, **nepotism** and corruption. The privileges came mainly to those at the top who were able to enjoy better city housing, out-of-town *dachas*, the best medical and educational facilities and chauffeur-driven cars. Nepotism usually appeared in the form of patronage – ensuring that family members were able to find well-paid jobs in government departments. Brezhnev's family was not above this. His son was a senior official employed in the foreign ministry whilst his unscrupulous son-in-law, who had gained rapid promotion in the

nepotism looking after the interests of one's relations.

army, was a known embezzler who had links with the Moscow criminal underworld! It was also widely accepted that promotion could be obtained through the payment of bribes and back-handers. Hotels, restaurants and nightclubs were set aside for use by the privileged *nomenklatura* and the Party bureaucracy, the *apparatchik*, as were certain retail outlets. Ordinary Russians knew what was going on and jokingly said of such shops – 'You'll find everything there except birds' milk'! Certain activities were enjoyed by more than the privileged few. There was a flourishing 'black market' where virtually any goods could be obtained – at a price. These included clothing and audio-cassettes of Western pop music. Some of the goods were illegally made, some smuggled into the country and some stolen. Stealing from the state was barely considered a crime! Amongst the illegally made goods was illicitly distilled vodka – *samagon.*

This source of income was documented by John Keep in *Last of the Empires* (1995) and an extract is given below.

> In the late 1970s, the average annual consumption of spirits was put at 15 litres a head; total consumption quadrupled during Brezhnev's rule. *Samogon* was easy to produce and extremely profitable. Sold at 4.5 to 5 roubles a litre (in the mid-1970s), it could bring a full-time 'speculator' an income of ten to fifteen times the average wage. Much liquor was also stolen from state depots, where security was lax, or in transit. Excessive drinking became one of the USSR's gravest social problems.

Other items available on the thriving 'black-market' included cars, stolen or forged antiques and religious icons. There was also a 'black economy', or as the Russians called it, *navelo* – work done on the side for higher than usual payment. The corruption was not limited to Moscow but was widespread amongst Party members throughout the Soviet Union. The ideologist of the Party, Mikhail Suslov, did question the correctness of some of the practices and protested strongly against the corruption amongst the bureaucracy. His criticisms went unheard. Brezhnev did not stand aloof from these excesses. To foster his own particular cult of personality, he awarded himself numerous medals, took the title Hero of the Soviet Union and received the Lenin Peace Prize. Like Stalin, he enjoyed the praise that was lavished upon him. Episodes in his life were embellished and films made about him. He also enjoyed the high life – he entertained lavishly, owned a fleet of cars and lived in sumptuous town residences and country *dachas.*

At the start of Brezhnev's period in office there were rumours that an attempt would be made to rehabilitate Stalin. And, in 1969, there was talk of celebrating the ninetieth anniversary of the former dictator's birth. The opposition of Soviet scholars and writers and the leaders of many East European states ensured that this did not come about. There was, however, some effort made to repair his tarnished image and open criticism of the former dictator was curbed. A feature of the Brezhnev years was the restoration of the authority of the secret police, the KGB. It did not, however, revert to the terror of the Stalinist period and the organisation's head, Andropov, was not of the same mould as Yezhov or Beria. He worked to change the image so that it became more like its Western counterparts, the CIA and MI5 and Soviet film producers went as far as to make films about the adventures of a James Bond-like KGB hero. In addition to dealing with dissidence and state security, it was also involved in anti-corruption activities. No longer were victims arrested and dragged of to Lubyanka prison to be tortured or shot. Instead they were liable to be placed under KGB surveillance and, if suspect, subject to interrogation. Even for those convicted and sent to the remaining camps, physical violence was rare. In the camps, prisoners were much more aware of their legal rights and were liable to protest or go on hunger strike. If arrested on a minor charge, the offender might be simply warned about his behaviour and sent on his way. Matters relating to internal security were the concern of the *Ministerstvo Vnutrennikh*, the MVD. By using the most modern methods of surveillance including 'bugging' and phone tapping, this counter-intelligence service trapped many Western agents.

Brezhnev, who had little sympathy for modern music, **avant-garde** art or literature that criticised the Soviet system, spoke of the need 'to tighten the screws … where culture was concerned'. Those that were concerned that he might attempt to curb the freedoms in the arts and culture tolerated by Khrushchev protested vigorously.

B *The dissidents*

The threat to cultural freedom led to dissent as writers and scholars defied the limitations imposed upon them and continued to express their views freely. Many were expelled from the Union of Writers and with it impossible for them to get their works published, they resorted to either *samizdat*, having their works copied and circulated secretly, or *tamizdat*, sending their work abroad for publication. The regime indicated its concern by attempting to intimidate writers and scholars. Those that persisted, the so-called dissidents were arrested and imprisoned. Some were placed in mental institutions. Psychiatric wards contained men and women said to be emotionally unstable, politically immature or distanced from reality.

SOME LEADING DISSIDENTS

Josif Brodsky Of Jewish parents, his poetry upset the Soviet authorities and he was arrested and accused of being a 'social parasite'. After serving six years hard labour, in 1972, he was allowed to leave the Soviet Union and he settled in the United States. In 1987, he was awarded the Nobel Prize for Literature.
Vladimir Bukovsky A student who, in 1963, was convicted for circulating anti-Soviet literature. He spent some years in a psychiatric hospital. After his release, he was again arrested on several

occasions until, in 1976, he was expelled from the Soviet Union. He settled in Britain.

Yuri Daniel A former Red Army soldier, he wrote satirical anti-Soviet books which were published abroad under a pseudonym. He was arrested and, convicted on crudely contrived evidence, he was sent to a labour camp. After his release, he continued to protest and was sentenced to a further period of hard labour. Gorbachev released him in 1988.

Aleksandr Ginzburg A writer and champion of the right to free expression, he was frequently arrested and spent many years in Soviet labour camps. Finally released in 1979, he was allowed to go to the West.

Vladimir Klebanov A trade union leader who wanted to establish free trade unions in the Soviet Union. He was detained in a mental institution and then sentenced to 20 years detention in the camps.

Viktor Nekrasov As a soldier, he served in the Red Army and fought at the Battle of Stalingrad. Afterwards he became a writer and was outspoken in his criticism of the treatment of Soviet intellectuals. He was eventually expelled from his homeland and lived in Paris.

Andrei Sakharov A Soviet scientist who played a major role in the development of his country's atomic weapons. Afterwards, he became a leading dissident and openly opposed the testing of nuclear weapons. He also became a supporter of East–West co-operation and an outspoken campaigner on human rights issues. In 1975, he won the Nobel Peace Prize. Arrested, he was banished to Gorky. In 1986, he was restored to favour and allowed to return to Moscow. Three years later, he was elected to the Congress of Peoples' Deputies.

Anatoly Sharansky The founder of the Jewish movement who became involved in underground Zionist activities. In 1977, he was arrested and, charged with treason, it was claimed that he was an American spy. He was sentenced to 13 years hard labour. Released in 1986, he emigrated to Israel.

Andrei Sinyavsky A writer and close associate of Daniel, he was arrested in 1965 for publishing anti-Soviet material. He was also a staunch supporter of Boris Pasternak. After spending six years in a labour camp, he was released in 1971 and made his home in France.

Aleksandr Solzhenitsyn One of the most famous of the dissidents, as a writer he dared to criticise Stalin and the Soviet system. His most famous books include *One Day in the Life of Ivan Denisovich*, *Cancer Ward* and the *Gulag Archipelago*. He was arrested on several occasions and spent many years in the labour camps. In 1974, he was arrested yet again and charged with treason. There was worldwide condemnation of the Soviet action and he was finally released and sent into exile.

Petr Yakir A writer who, in 1969, published a letter demanding that Stalin be posthumously tried for his crimes. At his trial, he pleaded guilty and was one of the few dissidents to repudiate his earlier view and apologise.

Anatoly Kuznetsov   A Ukrainian-born lecturer who wrote a controversial novel *Babi Yar* which was scathingly critical of the activities of both the Germans and Soviet authorities in his country. In 1969, during a visit to the West, he defected and made his home in London.

Brezhnev was furious when, in 1967, Stalin's daughter, Svetlana Alliluyeva, left the Soviet Union to live in the West. Her book, *Twenty Letters to a Friend*, which she dedicated to her mother, was written when she was still in Russia and later published abroad. In it, she described her childhood, her relationship with her father and gave an insight into the personalities of leading Soviet figures. Russian writers, who already had numerous martyrs to their cause including Anna Akhmatova, Mikhail Zoshchenko and Boris Pasternak, demanded freedom of expression and the full implementation of the Universal Declaration of Human Rights that guaranteed such freedom and which the Soviet Union had signed. One of the agreements reached at the Helsinki Conference (1975) concerned the need to respect human rights. Afterwards, a group of Russian dissidents formed a Helsinki Human Rights Group to make sure that these rights were being observed. Their leaders, including Sakharov, Ginzburg and Sharansky were arrested and imprisoned. The outspoken Sakharov said that Soviet society represented 'Maximum lack of freedom, maximum ideological rigidity and … maximum pretensions about being the best society, though it certainly is not that … .' Severe sentences were also imposed on Roman Catholic members of the group in Lithuania and the Ukraine. This repression led to worldwide protests that embarrassed the Soviet authorities. These events, particularly the decision to stage the public trials of Daniel and Sinyavsky, hinted at a return to the worst features of Stalinist repression. This alarmed Soviet writers and scholars and, more importantly, foreign Communist parties and world opinion. The result was some moderating of the campaign against Russian intellectuals.

See page 367.

Q

What were the main demands of the dissidents involved in the human rights campaign?

3 ⌐ RELATIONS BETWEEN THE RUSSIAN SOVIET FEDERATIVE SOCIALIST REPUBLIC (RSFSR) AND THE OTHER REPUBLICS OF THE USSR

With planning once again centralised in ministries and government departments based in Moscow, the Russian Republic gained even more dominance over the other autonomous republics that made up the USSR. Even so, the peoples of these republics remained strongly aware and fiercely proud of their individual national identities. None more so than the Ukrainians and the peoples of the Baltic provinces, Estonia, Latvia and Lithuania. Of the total population of the USSR (some 241 million in 1971), 54% were ethnic Russians and 17% Ukrainians. Of the remaining 29%, the Uzbeks, Belorussians, Kazaks and Tartars contributed a goodly number whilst the Armenians and Georgians represented less than 2%. There were also small racial groupings – the Crimean Tartars and Volga Germans – who had earlier been forcibly evicted from their lands and now wished to return home. Brezhnev was content with the Russian dominance of the country and wanted to eliminate the differences between the republics so that the Soviet Union would become a 'new historical community of people.' To help achieve this, the teaching of the culture, literature and history of the various non-Russian republics was reduced to a minimum whilst the Russian language was promoted as the main medium of learning. At the same time, the publication of non-Russian language newspapers and books was restricted. The emphasis placed on Russian meant that non-speakers had little chance of gaining promotion in their field of employment. The outcome was the reverse of what Brezhnev had intended since it led to the stirring of nationalist sentiments particularly in the Ukraine, Georgia and the Baltic states.

ANALYSIS

The problem of the racial minorities

The Crimean Tartars   The Crimean Tartars were the remnants of a Turkish people who had settled in the Crimea in the fifteenth century. By religion, they were Muslims. In the eighteenth century, Catherine II ordered the annexation of the Crimea and the Crimean Tartars were forced to live under Russia rule. An attempt was made to russify them and those that resisted were forced to emigrate. By the time of the Bolshevik Revolution in 1917, only 300 000 remained. To start with, they were well treated and Crimean Tartar was made the official language of the region along with Russian. Once they fell under the oppressive rule of Stalin, thousands were arrested and charged with being kulaks. Stalin also forced them to change their alphabet from their traditional Arabic script to Cyrillic (Russian-style). Most of their leaders perished during the purges of the 1930s. Although their able bodied men were serving in the Red Army, in May 1944, Stalin decided that they could not be trusted and ordered their mass deportation to remote central Asia. It was ironic that whilst their menfolk were fighting for Russia, their families were being sent to their deaths. In fact, some living in isolated areas were overlooked and when they were later discovered, they were put on a boat that was then sunk in the Sea of Azov. Red Army machine gunners were ordered to ensure that none survived. Under Khrushchev, the Crimean oblast became a part of the Ukraine and, in 1956, the Crimean Tartars were freed but, since others had occupied their former lands, they were not allowed to return to the Crimea. This led to the creation of the Crimean Tartar National Movement that campaigned for the right to return of their lands. In 1967, they were officially exonerated for any wrong doing during World War II and the first Crimean Tartars began to return to the Crimea and tried to resettle there. Some were arrested and were once again deported from the region. Some Crimean Tartar leaders and activists were arrested and tried in Tashkent in 1969. The expectations of the Crimean Tartars rose when Mikhail Gorbachev became leader of the Soviet Union but, today, the issue of whether they should once again be allowed to live in an autonomous state remains unsolved.

The Volga Germans   In 1763, during the reign of Catherine the Great, a number of Germans were invited by the Empress to settle in the Volga region. There they took up farming. During World War I, they faced great hostility and, in 1915, the Laws of Liquidation were passed which were intended to bring about their annihilation. Fortunately, the laws were not enacted. After the Bolshevik Revolution in 1917, the Volga Germans were persecuted because of their staunch religious faith and their clergy were sent to labour camps. In the widespread famine in the region during the early 1920s, a third of them perished. Their plight increased with the introduction of collective farming that denied them the right to farm their own land. Following the German invasion of the Soviet Union in 1941, they were considered unreliable and deemed to be the 'enemies of the state'. Afterwards, their young men were drafted into the Red Army and the remainder banished to the East. It was not until 1955 that their whereabouts was discovered and the remaining Volga Germans, now no more than a million, were granted an amnesty. On their release from captivity, they were asked to agree not to attempt to return to their former settlements. In 1964, the Soviet Union admitted its guilt in their persecution and they were declared innocent of the charges earlier made against them. However, like the Crimean Tartars, when they tried to return home they faced the hostility of those who had, in the meantime, occupied their lands.

Russian Jews   The migration of the Jews across the world, the *diaspora*, began in the first century AD. Many made their way to Europe. The *Ashkenazim*, the Jews who settled in Poland and Russia, were regarded as outsiders and not well received. Many such Jews became involved in commercial activities, travelled widely and established businesses as merchants, bankers and moneylenders. They also lived apart and established their own prosperous communities. Jealous of their achievements, the Jews had to endure persecution and many were murdered and their homes were ransacked. Even so, the plight of Jews living in Germany and Poland was even worse and many crossed into Russia looking for sanctuary! They bought with them a dialect that was a mixture of Hebrew and German – Yiddish. In 1880 and 1905, the authorities encouraged anti-Semitic violence in the form of pogroms and thousands fled abroad. Many made their home in the United States. After the Revolution in 1917, the remaining Russian Jews continued to be persecuted. Collective farming and industrialisation meant that they had to give up their traditional occupations to take up manual work in the new mines and factories. Many were well educated and were able to become doctors and engineers. Those who had been employed in agriculture were given their own autonomous region in the Far East close to the Chinese frontier, Birobidzhan. The enforced settlement ended in failure. Gradually many Jews were assimilated into Soviet society. During World War II, the Russian Jews were allowed to form the Jewish Anti-Fascist Committee to encourage support for the war effort. The popular Jewish actor, Solomon Mikhoels, chaired the Committee. Members of the Committee toured Britain and the United States and raised large sums of money. After the war, Stalin, suspicious of the loyalty of the Russian Jews, resumed his campaign against them. Accused of being 'rootless cosmopolitans' and being unpatriotic, in 1948 the Jewish Anti-Fascist League was dissolved and its leaders, including Mikhoels, murdered. In 1952, 25 leading Jewish writers were executed in Lubyanka prison and the following year Stalin's anti-Jewish campaign culminated in the 'Doctors' Plot'. At the time of Stalin's death in 1953, the total number of Russian Jews was some two and a half million. During the Khrushchev years, there was a renewed campaign against all forms of religion. As part of this, most of the remaining Jewish institutions were closed and even their cemeteries desecrated. For some Jews, the only means of survival was to abandon their religious customs and culture and seek anonymity within the populace. The Jewish state of Israel had existed since 1948 but few Russian Jews had managed to emigrate to their new homeland. The Six Day War of June 1967 made matters worse as the Soviet government scathingly attacked Zionism and Israel. This led to even greater pressure to emigrate but applications were refused and many were arrested and accused of 'parasitism'. Those refused exit visas, the *refuseniks*, demonstrated openly against human rights violations in Moscow and other Russian cities. Mounting overseas pressure led to a re-think and between 1971 and 1975 some 113 000 Russian Jews were allowed to leave the Soviet Union although they first had to pay an 'emigration tax' to cover the cost of their education in the Soviet Union.

4 ∽ BREZHNEV'S NEW CONSTITUTION OF 1977

In October 1977, to mark the sixtieth anniversary of the Revolution, Brezhnev planned a new Soviet constitution. It replaced Stalin's

See pages 295–8.

constitution of 1936. In a long-winded preamble (as given in the following extract from the *Constitution of the USSR* adopted at the Seventh Session of the Supreme Soviet, October 1977), it stated:

> The Great October Socialist Revolution, made by the workers and peasants of Russia under the leadership of the Communist Party headed by Lenin, overthrew capitalist and landowner rule, broke the fetters of oppression, established the dictatorship of the proletariat and created the Soviet state… Humanity thereby began the epoch-making turn from capitalism to socialism…. Continuing (after the Second World War) their creative endeavours, the working people of the Soviet Union have ensured rapid, all-round development of the country and steady improvement of the socialist system… The aims of the dictatorship of the proletariat having been fulfilled, the Soviet state has become the state of the whole people. The leading role of the Communist Party, the vanguard of all the people, has grown. In the USSR, a developed socialist society has been built. At this stage, when socialism is developing on its own foundations, the creative forces of the new system and the advantages of the socialist way of life are becoming increasingly evident, and the working people are more and more widely enjoying the fruits of their great revolutionary gains… It is a society in which the law of life is the concern of all for the good of each and the concern of each is for the good of all… The supreme goal of the Soviet state is the building of a classless communist society… to lay the material and technical foundation of communism, to perfect socialist social relations, to mould the citizen of communist society, to raise the people's living and cultural standards… The Soviet people… hereby affirm the structure and policy of the USSR, and define the rights, freedoms and obligations of its citizens…

The details of Brezhnev's new constitution extended over a hundred articles and sub-sections. It roughly followed the same lines of Stalin's constitution of 1936 but there were significant differences in content. It formally acknowledged the right of the people to cultivate their own private plots and hints at guaranteed freedoms of speech, assembly, the press and conscience. The value of a constitution is not what it contains but the extent to which it is carried out. For an example, Article 28 declared the aim of Soviet foreign policy would be to 'support the struggle of people seeking national liberation.' Yet, in 1979, Soviet forces intervened in a civil war in Afghanistan and occupied the country. Article 52 guaranteed the Soviet people 'freedom of conscience, that is the right to profess any religion or none.' Yet, two years after the constitution was adopted, members of an organisation formed to protect believers' rights were arrested and charged with spreading anti-Soviet propaganda.

5 ⁓ ECONOMIC PROBLEMS

Some terms used in economics

To help you understand the phrases used in the sections of Chapters 14 and 15 dealing with economic developments in the Soviet Union, their explanations are given below:

black economy   that part of the nation's economy in which scarce goods and services are provided at prices above the controlled price. It is a form of illegal trading.

black market   a situation in which people are prepared to deal with illegal traders and pay high prices for scarce goods and services.

capital goods   goods made to assist in the production of other goods such as machinery, factory buildings etc. Such goods are not usually available for retail in shops.

command economy   an economy that is planned and controlled from the centre. Targets are set from above for the various sectors of the economy to achieve.

consumer goods   goods that are made for use by the public – the consumers. They are available for purchase in shops and include such as food, clothes, furniture etc.

decentralisation   a move away from the situation where economic activity is controlled from the centre – government departments in the capital city – so that decision making is passed to regions or the local management of industrial units.

hard currency   a stable currency that retains its value. The American dollar and most Western currencies would have been considered 'hard'.

inflation   a situation in which the amount of money in circulation is increasing at a faster rate than the quantity of goods and services produced. As a result, prices rise.

market economy   a situation in which market forces (the supply of and the demand for a commodity) decide the price. (See **supply and demand** below.)

supply and demand   supply is the amount of a commodity that manufacturers are prepared to make and offer for sale at a particular price during a period of time. Demand is the quantity of a commodity that people are willing to buy at a particular price during a particular time. Demand and supply are called market forces and they decide the price of commodities.

gross national product   the GNP is the money value of all the goods and services produced in a country during one year. It is a means of measuring a country's prosperity.

minimum wage the lowest wage that can legally be paid to workers. It is intended to provide a minimum standard of living.

subsidising a subsidy is money paid by the government to part cover the cost of a commodity. It is a means of artificially keeping the price down and makes items more affordable. Subsidies help keep down the cost of living and check demands for higher wages. Their removal means higher prices and can make a government unpopular.

A *Slowdown and stagnation*

Q

What major economic problems faced the Soviet Union during the Brezhnev years?

During the Brezhnev years, three Five-Year Plans were introduced – an Eighth, 1965–70, a Ninth, 1971–5, and a Tenth, 1976–80. It was, however, a period during which the Soviet economy suffered serious setbacks in both industry and agriculture. In 1966, at the Twenty-Third Party Congress, the aims of an Eighth Five-Year Plan were outlined. Khrushchev's earlier plan to begin the next step forward in the transition from socialism to communism and his unrealistic dream of matching the productivity of the United States were abandoned. For the first time, Soviet economic planners signalled their intention of raising living standards by concentrating more on the production of consumer goods than capital goods. Another aim was to raise the living standards of the peasants to something approaching that enjoyed by industrial workers. For the Soviet people generally there was even talk of the prospect of being able to buy colour television sets and of the possible private ownership of cars. The senior figure in economic planning was Aleksei Kosygin. It was his aim to modernise the Soviet economy and rid it of the doctrinal straight jacket imposed by Party ideologists. In this, the Ukrainian professor, Evsey Liberman, supported him and, in an article in *Pravda* entitled 'Plan, Profit and Bonuses suggested wide ranging reforms which included the decentralisation of planning and greater independence for the managers of industrial enterprises. He also emphasised the importance of the profit motive and the need to give regard to demand and supply in the market. This was all too much for the traditional Marxist loyalists in the Party who sensed a move back towards capitalism and they also disapproved of what they regarded as the needs of heavy industry. Later, another Soviet economist, Vasili Nemchinov, proposed an alternative programme that also called for greater independence for management. The adoption of Liberman's policies in 1965 was an important victory for Kosygin's programme of economic reforms. Although decentralisation was approved, it was agreed that the Party would keep a close eye on economic developments. The financial implications of being a military super-power proved costly. A major problem facing the Soviet economy was the fact that so much of the national income was spent on the armaments industry and subsidising food, heating and housing. The continuing Cold War, together with Soviet involvement in Czechoslovakia in 1968, worsening relations with Communist China, military support for North Vietnam after 1965 and supplying arms to Syria, the United Arab Republic and numerous other countries required heavy military expenditure. To remove the long established subsidies enjoyed by the Russian people would have led to across the board price rises and unpopularity. As in the past, agriculture lagged well behind industry. During the years of the Eighth Five-Year Plan, the situation was not helped by poor harvests in 1965 and 1967. It was a time when, with living standards falling, an estimated 38% of the peasantry lived below the poverty line. In the hope that it would improve matters, there was a call for all collective and State-owned farms, the *kolkhozy* and *sovkhozes,* to be made individual enterprises outside centralised control. The Ninth Five-Year Plan was a lean period for both industry and agriculture. The further poor harvests of 1972 and 1975 meant that large quantities of grain had to be imported from the United States. The years of the Tenth Five-Year Plan proved even bleaker than the others. With industrial output slowing down, much attention was given to exploiting the Soviet Union's recently discovered additional reserves of coal, oil and natural gas. However, one quite spectacular achievement was the construction of the 3500 km long Baikal-Amur railway across Siberia. Although the harvest of 1978 was unexpectedly good, the poor returns of the following year meant that once again the country had to depend on grain imports from the United States. Of all agricultural output, a quarter came from privately owned plots.

To compare the level of industrial growth of the Brezhnev period with that of the Stalinist years is not comparing like with like. The impressive increases in production of Stalin's Five-Year Plans were measured against a very low starting point and were therefore relatively easier to achieve. For Brezhnev's economic planners to maintain that rate of growth would have been impossible. Even before 1964, the rate of growth of the Soviet economy had begun to decline and as this trend continued so the nation's economy entered a period of stagnation. However, the black economy flourished and came to account for some 25% of the country's gross national product. The Soviet newspaper, *Izvestia,* estimated that business carried on within the black economy was worth 7 000 000 000 roubles annually! With better off Soviet citizens able to pay over-the-odds for scarce goods and better and more immediate services, it was not surprising that they were prepared to deal on the black market.

As industrial growth fell, so the targets set by the Five-Year planners proved impossible to achieve. However, in a corrupt society, managers found that it was possible to hide their deficiencies by bribing officials to falsify their returns. The Kosygin economic reforms, based on the ideas of Liberman and Nemchinov that put greater emphasis on profitability and encouraged a more professional and scientific approach by management, were not working. Much of this was the fault of the apathy and lack of motivation shown by management and workers alike.

KEY ISSUE

Kosygin's economic reforms.

TABLE 61 *Levels of production in heavy industry 1965–85*

	1965	1975	1985
Iron (million tonnes)	66	103	110
Steel (million tonnes)	91	141	155
Coal (million tonnes)	577	701	726
Tractor's (thousands)	355	550	585

Whilst the period 1975–85 continued to show an increase in levels of production, the rate of increase had fallen dramatically compared with the period 1965–75. For an example, between 1965 and 1975, the output of iron increased by some 56% but between 1975 and 1985 by less than 7%. Similarly, in comparing the two ten-year periods, the increase in the output of tractors fell from 55% to a little over 6%.

By 1980, the condition of the Soviet economy was edging towards crisis point. According to estimates, the Soviet Union's gross national product had fallen from 5.2% in 1970 to 2.2% in 1980. During the same period, industrial growth fell from 6.3% to 2.6% and growth in agriculture from 3.7% to just 0.8%. The poor performance in both heavy industry and agriculture was not caused by simply by lack of motivation but also by the continued use of out-of-date machinery and technology and by excessive red-tape and intervention.

However, due to the work of scientists and cosmonauts, there were areas in which the Soviet economy continued to flourish. These were in the space and defence industries which both benefited from considerable investment and ongoing advances in military technology. 1970 and 1971 were remarkable years. In September 1970, the Soviet space probe, *Luna 16, landed* on the moon and collected fragments before returning safely. Two months later, *Luna 17*, successfully placed a vehicle on the moon, *Lunokhod 1*, which could be operated from earth. Finally, in December, *Venus 7* landed on that planet and transmitted information back to its base. In April 1971, the space station *Salyut 1* was sent into orbit and, two months later, three cosmonauts in a space capsule, *Soyuz 11*, docked with the station and remained in space for 23 days. Another space probe landed on Mars and briefly sent back signals. Nine years elapsed before, in April 1980, Leonid Popov and Valery Ryumin spent 185 days in space before safely returning to earth. The Soviet armaments industry also continued to expand. Short, medium and long range rockets with nuclear warheads were produced as well as nuclear submarines which patrolled Russia's coastal waters and well beyond. In the air, MiG fighters and Tupolev and Ilyushen bombers were considered formidable aircraft. The Russian army was equipped with *Klashnikov* sub-machine guns. These weapons, invented by Mikhail Klashnikov, became the most widely used weapon in the world. Used by the armies of more than 50 countries and much prized by terrorists and criminals, their sales exceeded 40 million.

B *Standards of living*

In 1968, for the very first time, the rate of growth of consumer goods marginally exceeded that of heavy industry. Although wages were rising, there remained wide discrepancies in the earnings of various sections of the community. With the basic minimum wage set at 60 roubles a month, a skilled worker might earn more than twice that amount. Whilst professional people such as doctors and schoolteachers earned 130–140 roubles monthly, the manager of a large industrial enterprise might earn up to 600 roubles a month or more. The top earners included government ministers who were paid 625 roubles monthly and senior Party officials whose monthly earnings might top 800 roubles. After 1967, the lot of workers on the collective farms was improved when they at last received a guaranteed monthly wage. Those operating within the black economy made considerably more than any of these. With food, heating, lighting and housing still heavily subsidised by the state, people could afford many of the consumer goods now appearing in the shops. Between 1965 and 1980, the production of television sets increased from 3 655 000 to 7 528 000 with a third of them being coloured. Whilst car manufacturers increased their output from 201 200 in 1965 to 1 327 000 in 1985, this was barely a third of that of Britain, France or Germany. However, there was large increase in the manufacture of more affordable motorcycles and scooters. There was also an impressive increase in the number of household appliances made available. The output of refrigerators, only 1 675 000 in 1965, reached 5 925 000 in 1980 whilst the number of sewing machines available nearly doubled. Some Russian manufactured goods were exported abroad – cars, photographic equipment and radios. Their appeal was that they were relatively cheap but they were also unreliable. It was said that after vodka, the most famous Soviet export was the *Autovaz* or *Lada* saloon car. Based in design on the old Italian Fiat 124 and manufactured in the Soviet Union under license, the quality of the *Lada* became the butt of much unkind humour. It was said that the value of the car doubled when its tank was filled with petrol! Another comment was that the *Lada* User's Manual included bus and train timetables! Other Soviet vehicles exported included *Moskvitch* cars and *Zil* lorries. The quality of Russian-made radio and camera equipment was considered to be of a higher standard. The *Zenit* camera had a fine lens but was unwieldy to use.

C *Environmental issues*

Dating back to Stalinist times and throughout the period of industrialisation, Soviet authorities paid scant attention to environmental issues. With factories and chemical plants allowed to contaminate and poison the environment, the pollutants released by fossil fuels in industrial processes, now known as acid rain, took a dreadful toll on the Russian forests. Untreated sewage, industrial waste and oil spillage was allowed to pollute the rivers and waterways so that marine life was badly affected and sometimes totally destroyed. One of the most severely contaminated rivers was the Volga, home of the sturgeon fish whose salted roe was sold abroad as caviar. Even Lake Baikal, the world's largest freshwater lake, and the coastal waters of the Black Sea became terribly polluted. In order to assist the growing of rice and cotton, an irrigation project was introduced which involved damming the rivers flowing into the Aral Sea. As a result, the water level of the lake fell and this reduced its size by nearly a half. The fishing industry in the region was ruined and one former fishing harbour, Aralsk, found itself 40 km from the sea! Even worse, the water that remained became extremely salty and harmful deposits from the dry area were carried some 400 km by the wind and endangered the health of people over a widespread area. Elsewhere in the Soviet Union, pollutants affected the quality of life of the people and, in some areas, reduced the life expectancy of the people. They were held responsible for major increases in the incidence of various forms of cancer, tuberculosis and emphysema. The reactors of nuclear power stations were not as well constructed as those in the West and it was later claimed that the Chernobyl disaster of 1986 was 'less an accident than a predictable catastrophe'.

TIMELINE

Soviet foreign policy, 1964–82

1965	Start of war in Vietnam
1967	Arab-Israeli 'Six Day War'
1968 August	Soviet and Warsaw Pact troops invade Czechoslovakia and suppress the 'Prague Spring'
1969	Dispute with China over Damansky Island followed by frontier clashes
1971	War between India and Pakistan over Kashmir
1972 May	US President Nixon visits Moscow SALT I signed
1973	Brezhnev visits West Germany and the United States. The end of war in Vietnam
1974	Brezhnev visits Cuba, Poland and France
1975	Helsinki Conference and Accord
1978	Brezhnev visits West Germany
1979	Soviet invasion of Afghanistan
1980	Troubled Moscow Olympics

6 ⌐ THE SOVIET STRUGGLE TO RETAIN THE LEADERSHIP OF THE COMMUNIST WORLD

During their early years in office, Brezhnev and Kosygin set out to prove to the world that the Soviet Union was a reliable and well-managed country capable of conducting a rational and responsible foreign policy. They continued to follow Khrushchev's policy of *détente* and peaceful co-existence with the West. Even so, there were occasions when they seemed eager to confront the United States by supporting left-wing subversion whenever and wherever it appeared. This was usually done in the form of military aid and not the direct involvement of Soviet forces. They were also concerned at the possible challenge of Mao Zedong for the leadership of the Communist world and the increasing influence of Communist China in the Far East and amongst Third World countries. The war in Vietnam presented the Russian leadership with particularly difficult problems.

A *Soviet involvement – the war in Vietnam, 1965–73*

Before World War II, Vietnam, together with Cambodia and Laos, had been the French colony of Indo-China. After the war, the French became involved in a war against the Viet-Minh, an army fighting for independence from colonial rule, led by Ho Chi Minh. The war was brought to an end in 1954 by the Geneva Agreement that partitioned the country into the Communist Republic of North Vietnam and the non-Communist Republic of South Vietnam. The Americans believed in the 'domino theory'. This theory suggested that similar to a line of dominos being knocked over by the first to fall, so the loss of one country to the Communists would cause the others in the region to fall under Communist control. As a result, the United States strengthened South Vietnam so that it would act as a barrier against further Communist expansion in South-East Asia. As the Vietcong, a guerrilla army dedicated to uniting the country under Communist control, became increasingly active in South Vietnam, so the United States became more committed to defending the country's independence. The civil war rapidly developed into a major conflict involving American forces. Under Khrushchev, the USSR kept a relatively low profile in events in Vietnam. The situation changed once US bombers started bombing North Vietnam. Afterwards, the Russians started supplying the Vietcong with large quantities of weapons and military advisers. Their aim was not only to bring about the defeat of the American-backed South Vietnamese but to also ensure that the Chinese Communists did not intervene and replace Russian influence in the area. The war ended in 1973 with a Communist victory and the withdrawal of US troops.

During the Arab–Israeli War of 1967, the so-called Six-Day War, the Soviet Union backed the Arabs but only provided them with limited military assistance. It did, however, result in a backlash against Russian Jews. During a second Arab–Israeli War of 1973, the *Yom Kippur* War, the Russians again supported the Arabs. This conflict might have developed into something more serious since rumours that Soviet troops were being sent to the Middle East caused the American President, Richard Nixon, to place US forces on alert. Afterwards, relations between Egypt and the Soviet Union became increasingly strained. As a result of differences, the Egyptians ordered 7000 Russian military and other advisers, from their country. Earlier, in 1971, the Russians and Americans had supported opposite sides during a war between India and Pakistan over the disputed region of Kashmir. It was Kosygin who prevented the war escalating when he acted as a mediator and arranged a peace treaty to be signed at Tashkent. The Soviet Union also became involved in civil wars in Africa and Central America. In 1961, the Russians sided with the People's Movement for the Liberation of Angola (MPLA) against the American-backed National Union for the Total Independence of Angola (UNITA); in Mozambique, the Soviets supported the Frelimo against the Portuguese. After independence in 1974, the country became the People's Republic of Mozambique and was soon involved in ongoing skirmishes with her neighbours Rhodesia and South Africa. Both Russians and Cubans supported Somali and Eritrean guerrillas in a war that brought chronic famine to Ethiopia in the 1970s whilst in Nicaragua, the Soviet Union backed the Sandinista Liberation Front trying to overthrow the oppressive rule of Anastasio Somoza.

B *Relations between the Soviet Union and Communist China*

See pages 414–15.

The Khrushchev period revealed major differences in the ideologies of the Soviet Union and Communist China. In 1965, the Soviet leaders went to the Chinese capital, Beijing, but rather than considering help for North Vietnam, the Russians annoyed their hosts by wanting to discuss Communist unity. Further embarrassment was caused when a crowd of Chinese students attacking the US embassy in Moscow had to be restrained by Soviet police and soldiers. Meanwhile, in 1966, Mao Zedong began a 'Cultural Revolution', a campaign against revisionism aimed at restoring the enthusiasm of the Chinese for revolution and Marxist doctrine. During this time, the Soviet Union was vigorously attacked in speeches made by Chinese leaders and in the press. The situation became so bad that relations between Moscow and Beijing virtually ceased to exist. The Russians responded by using radio broadcasts to encourage the Chinese to turn against their leaders. Even more serious were the border clashes. In 1969, disagreement over the ownership of Damansky Island in the Ussuri River led to fighting between Russian and Chinese troops and there were skirmishes along the Sino-Soviet border. The Chinese press claimed victories over the Soviet army and the criminal rule of the 'Soviet revisionist clique'. Although steps were taken to settle their differences, the Russians still reinforced their armies along their common border with China. The hostility between the two countries eased when, on his return from Ho Chi Minh's funeral in Hanoi, Kosygin visited Mao Zedong in Beijing and the following year, diplomatic relations were restored.

C *The 'Prague Spring' – the Czech crisis, 1968*

In Czechoslovakia, up to then a model Soviet satellite, there was growing discontent at the severity of the regime of Antonin Novotny. In

January 1968, he was replaced as First Secretary of the Czech Communist Party by Alexander Dubcek. The Soviet authorities approved the change. Once in power, Dubcek introduced a series of major reforms intended to create a more liberal society. Freedom of the press and civil liberties were restored, political prisoners of the Novotny years released and rehabilitated and it was even suggested that opposition parties would be tolerated. This 'socialism with a human face' enjoyed the popular support of the Czech people. However, in Moscow, the so-called 'Prague Spring' gave rise to concern. Dubcek went to great lengths to reassure Brezhnev that he was still a loyal Communist and friendly to the Soviet Union and that his reforms were an internal matter. Following a series of informal meetings, it appeared that the Soviet leadership was prepared to accept this. When unfounded rumours began to circulate that the Czech leadership was planning to leave the Warsaw Pact, the Russian attitude hardened. After much deliberation and consultation with her Pact allies, military manoeuvres were staged along the Czech border. Brezhnev told the Politburo that he had received an appeal for help from a group of leading Czech Communists who had asked him to 'repel the forces which are clearly a serious danger for the future of socialism in the Czechoslovak Socialist Republic'. He also claimed that he had proof that American agents were active in that country. On 20th August, the 'Prague Spring' came to an end when Russian and other Warsaw Pact forces invaded the country. Dubcek and other Czech reformist leaders were flown to Moscow and there made to accept Brezhnev's demands. As in Hungary 12 years earlier, the Czech people took to the streets but, this time, they only offered passive resistance by protesting and chanting slogans. There were instances when villages changed their name to Dubcekovo – 'belonging to Dubcek'. On his return from Moscow, Alexander Dubcek made a tearful speech and admitted that much of what he had hoped to achieve had been lost. The following year, he was demoted, expelled from the Party and sent to work as forestry official. The Soviet move against Czechoslovakia was widely condemned by the West as well as other Communist countries including Romania, who had refused to join the invasion, Yugoslavia, Albania and Communist China.

PICTURE 47
A street poster shows Lenin's dismay at the Soviet invasion of Czechoslovakia

See Map 23 on page 442.

D *The Brezhnev Doctrine*

Brezhnev was unrepentant. He claimed that socialist states had only limited sovereignty and that the Soviet Union had the right to intervene in the affairs of other socialist countries. In what became known as the Brezhnev Doctrine, he declared:

> When internal and external forces hostile to socialism attempt to turn the development of any socialist country in the direction of the capitalist system, when a threat arises to the cause of socialism in that country, a threat to the security of the socialist commonwealth as a whole – it already becomes not only a problem for the people of

MAP 23

The invasion of Czechoslovakia by Soviet and Warsaw Pact forces in August 1968

that country, but also a general problem, the concern of all socialist countries ... There is no doubt that the actions of the five allied socialist countries in Czechoslovakia directed to the defence of the vital interests of the socialist community ... will be increasingly supported by all those who have the interest of the present revolutionary movement ... at heart.

The Brezhnev Doctrine served as a stark reminder of what might befall other Communist bloc countries tempted to follow the same line as Czechoslovakia. Even so, both Romania and Albania cunningly courted the friendship of Communist China and continued to go their own way whilst in Poland, the Solidarity Movement was about to come into being. Even in Czechoslovakia, the popular demand for change that brought Dubcek to power still remained but now went underground. The following year when the Czech ice hockey team beat the Soviet Union in the World Championships in Sweden, there were widespread celebrations across the country and Soviet troops and buildings were attacked.

In spite of the hiccups in American-Soviet relations, representatives of both countries took part in a series of meetings aimed at limiting the arms race. In 1969, these Strategic Arms Limitations (SALT) talks finally reached agreement on limiting defensive anti-ballistic missile systems and a range of other matters. SALT 1 also sought to prevent the further spread of nuclear weapons to countries not yet possessing them. An agreement to co-operate in space exploration was later agreed when President Nixon visited Moscow in 1972. The improvement in American-Soviet relations was so marked that some spoke of a 'new era of *détente*'. There were even those who thought that the years of the Cold War were over. During all these pleasantries and comings and goings, Brezhnev had hoped to win official acceptance of terms of a treaty with West Germany that would confirm as final the existing European frontiers, particularly those of the German Democratic Republic, East Germany. At long last, the status of Berlin was finally agreed in a treaty signed in 1972 by the USSR, the USA, Britain and France. In 1974, arrangements were made for a second round of SALT talks to begin and, the following year, there was a symbolic link-up in space of Soviet and American spacecraft that attracted favourable publicity in both Russia and the West. In the same year, delegates from 35 nations assembled in Helsinki to take part in a European Security Conference.

KEY ISSUE

The significance of the SALT agreements.

E *The Helsinki Conference and Accord, 1975*

In July 1975, delegates from 35 countries gathered in the Finnish capital, Helsinki to discuss European security, means of reducing international tension, increasing economic co-operation between the Communist bloc countries and Western Europe and to settle human rights issues. Some progress was made towards preventing crises arising between the two power blocs and bringing about closer economic and technological collaboration. The Final Act of what became known as the Helsinki Accords set out details of the agreement reached on human rights. The clauses included:

> 'The participating States will respect human rights and fundamental freedoms, including freedom of thought, conscience, religion or belief, for all without distinction as to race, sex, language or religion.'

> 'They will provide and encourage the effective exercise of civil, economic, social, cultural, and other rights and freedoms all of which derive from the inherent dignity of the human person and are essential to his free and full development.'

> 'Within this framework the participating States will recognise and respect the freedom of the individual to profess and practice ... religion or belief acting in accordance with the dictates of his own conscience.'

> 'The participating States on whose territory national minorities exist will respect the right of persons belonging to such minorities to equality before the law ... and full freedoms.'

> 'The participating States recognise the universal significance of human rights and fundamental freedoms. Respect of which is an essential factor for peace ...'

Within the Soviet Union the acceptance of these clauses presented some difficulty and no little embarrassment. They were to form the basis of the demands made by Russian dissidents and human rights activists.

F *The invasion of Afghanistan, 1979*

Q

Why did the Soviet Union invade Afghanistan in 1979?

The Soviet Union had kept a close watch on events in Afghanistan. The country was close to the strategically important oil producing states of the Middle East and it was also an area from which Islamic fundamentalists might infiltrate into the Soviet Republic of Turkestan. In 1978, the republican regime of General Mohammed Daoud was overthrown by pro-Russian Army Forces Revolutionary Council. Immediately, Afghan nationalists and the Islamic Majaheddin began to harass the new government. Whilst government forces had little trouble in holding on to the major towns and cities, large areas of the inhospitable interior region were soon in the hands of the rebels. In December 1979, Soviet forces moved into Afghanistan to help the government forces regain control. The West and the country's Islamic neighbours, Iran and Pakistan immediately denounced the Russian involvement in Afghanistan. The United States and Britain, now led by the strongly anti-Communist President Ronald Reagan and Prime Minister Margaret Thatcher respectively, urged a boycott of the Twenty-Second Olympic Games due to be held in Moscow in the summer of 1980. They also brought to an end the SALT II discussions then taking place. In addition, the US placed an embargo on the export of grain and high technology to the Soviet Union and began to deploy intermediate ballistic missiles in Western Europe. For the Soviets, the decision to invade Afghanistan proved disastrous. Described as 'Russia's Vietnam', as the situation worsened so more than a million Soviet servicemen were sent to the country. Even with the use of aircraft and modern ground weapons, they could not contain the Majaheddin guerrillas who received outside help from the Islamic world and Communist China.

In a speech made to the Central Committee in June 1980, an ailing Brezhnev complained bitterly:

'Not a day goes by when Washington has not tried to revive the spirit of the Cold War, to heat up militarist passions. Any grounds are used for this, real or imagined. One example of this is Afghanistan. The ruling circles in the USA and China stop at nothing, including armed aggression, in trying to keep the Afghans from building a new life in accord with the ideals of the revolution of liberation of April 1978. And when we helped our neighbour Afghanistan, at the request of its government to give a rebuff to aggression, to beat back bandit formations mainly from the territory of Pakistan, then Washington and Beijing raised an unprecedented uproar. Of what do they accuse the Soviet Union? They accuse us of hoping to break out to warm waters, and the intention of grabbing foreign oil? ... In the Soviet act of assistance there was not a grain of greed. We had no choice other than the sending of troops.'

The 50 000 casualties and the financial cost of the war added to the economic problems facing the Soviet Union. On their return, young conscripts were nicknamed 'Zinky Boys' since their dead comrades had been sent home in zinc coffins. Many of the demoralised young men turned to drug abuse and crime. In addition, the Russians lost important friends amongst Arab, Third World and non-aligned countries. The war was to continue for eight years until, between 1986 and 1989, Mikhail Gorbachev gradually withdrew Soviet troops from Afghanistan.

7 ↜ BREZHNEV'S DECLINING YEARS

Even in the 1960s, there were signs that Leonid Brezhnev's health was beginning to fail and in 1975 and 1977, he suffered two serious strokes. On one occasion he was declared clinically dead but his doctors managed to revive him. Afterwards he retired from public life for some months but on his return he still appeared unwell. His slurred speech and slow and ungainly walk made him the subject of both sympathy and crude humour. Reluctantly, he was forced to delegate his responsibilities to other members of the Politburo, mainly Konstantin Chernenko. In March 1982, Brezhnev had an accident at Tashkent when the gantry on which he was walking during a visit to an aircraft factory collapsed. He broke his collarbone and was severely shaken. On 28th October, he was able to make a speech to Soviet army commanders in the Kremlin and a week later stood for hours on the mausoleum in Moscow's Red Square to watch the parade and processions arranged to commemorate the 65th anniversary Revolution. During the night of 10th November, he suffered a final, fatal stroke and died in his sleep. He was aged 75. The Soviet press referred to his 'inspiring example of loyalty to the Communist Party and the Soviet people' and commented that he would be 'forever remembered by history as a passionate fighter for peace and the safety of nations'. Yet within weeks, the first criticisms of Brezhnev were made at a Central Committee meeting and across the country his portraits disappeared and newspapers ceased to quote him.

8 ↜ LEONID BREZHNEV — AN ASSESSMENT

Leonid Brezhnev has been referred to as 'a stagnation age leader' but is this evaluation of him entirely fair? It should be remembered that he led the Soviet Union for 18 years and during that time the country emerged as one of the world's two great superpowers. It might be fairly asked – if he was such a poor leader, how did he manage to survive for so long?

Even though he lacked the authority of Stalin and the flamboyance of Khrushchev, he knew how to manipulate the Party machine. In truth, Brezhnev never intended to be part of a collective leadership and gradually, in stages, he was able to edge out Kosygin, Podgorny and Suzlov. By 1972 he was clearly in charge. His style of government was based on ongoing firmness and reliability – the 'stability of cadres'. He also used patronage to create a privileged class of administrators, the *nomenklatura*. This meant that opposition to his rule was minimal although Suslov did dare to speak out against the corruption. Nepotism and corruption became rife and Brezhnev, who himself enjoyed the good life, did nothing to prevent it. The example at the top led to a lowering of the morale of Soviet workers and a great deal of cynicism. His much-acclaimed new constitution of 1977 was not far removed from Stalin's of 1936. It promised much but in terms of civil rights produced little and did not prevent the harassment and imprisonment of dissidents.

Brezhnev wanted to improve the living standards of the Russian people but was soon made aware that the rigid demand-style economy of Stalin was not suited to a new situation in which advanced technology and sophisticated management were needed. Although he went some way towards introducing the measures advocated by Liberman, the steps he took were insufficient to deal with the problems of the Soviet economy and were often no more than pointless meddling.

On the industrial front, rates of increase in levels of industrial production continued to fall. In agriculture, where a series of bad harvests did not help, private plots flourished but a goodly number of the *kolkhozy*-based peasantry continued to live below the poverty line. By 1972, the country had to depend on imports from the United States to supplement its grain harvest. There was an increase in the production of consumer goods but with better off Russian workers able to spend more freely, this led to shortages. Bureaucratic interference, administrative incompetence and the high expenditure on the military and expensive subsidies contributed to the growing economic stagnation. Often the extent of the corruption and the acceptance of inflated returns hid the true state of the economy. Skilled workers came to consider that their education had been a waste of time since it had provided them with a wasted talent. The despondency of the Russian people turned to despair and encouraged them to become part of the black economy and indulge in crime and excessive drinking. The impact of alcoholism on the health of the people was such that it caused the government to stop publishing life expectancy figures!

In foreign policy, Brezhnev tried to remain on good terms with the United States and the West and continue with Khrushchev's policy of *détente*. Yet, at the same time, he gave his support to left-wing revolutionary groups and twice faced worldwide condemnation for his invasion of Czechoslovakia in 1968 and Afghanistan in 1979. By 1979, Brezhnev's health had declined to such an extent that he no longer took part in decision making. To what extent he approved of or was even aware of the abandonment of *détente* and a return to the politics of the Cold War is uncertain. The assessment of Brezhnev by historians varies but is largely critical:

The following was written by by the Russian dissident Andrei Sinyavsky (from *The Makepeace Experiment*, 1977).

> Daniel and I were not physically tortured or beaten, and therefore we did not confess to being guilty … In Stalin's time we would have been shot. Khrushchev's regime took three steps forward with the exposure of Stalin and two steps back with the Hungarian invasion … During Brezhnev's time two more backward steps were taken and history wavered on the edge of returning us to full Stalinism … but stopped short.

From Ian Derbyshire, *Politics in the Soviet Union*, 1987.

> The Brezhnev era had been one of caution and conservatism in which there was a constant search to compromise with and 'buy off' potential institutional opponents rather than radical, risk-taking initiatives. This had some advantages at home where a new stability was given to the state-party political system. The conservative Brezhnev approach to political affairs had, however, significant costs to Soviet society … Firstly, it entailed a continuation of centralised political and ideological control … Secondly, there were only tinkering attempts to inject new efficiency into the Soviet economy … Thirdly, the party leader's concern to maintain harmonious relations with the *apparatchiki* … led to the stultifying of the state and party bureaucracies and a growth in corruption …

From Gwyneth Hughes and Simon Welfare, *Red Empire. The Forbidden History of the USSR*, 1990.

> Leonid Brezhnev was in the forefront of the partial rehabilitation of Stalin and the establishment of stable Party rule … Functionaries could breath easily again. After the terror of Stalin's reign and the chaos of Khrushchev's, the Soviet Union was in for a period of stability, and that meant everyone kept their job and their perks for life.

The Russian historian Dmitri Volkogonov wrote the following in *The Rise and Fall of the Soviet Empire*, 1998.

> Brezhnev's image was not only as the harbinger of the collapse of the system, but also as the symbol of the decline of Bolshevik power, towards which the people had long become indifferent. The regime no longer inspired fear or respect. If Lenin and Stalin, and to some extent even Khrushchev, were able to enliven the moribund ideology of Communism, it was quite beyond Brezhnev …

9 ∽ STRUCTURED AND ESSAY QUESTIONS

A *This section consists of questions that might be useful for discussion (or writing answers) as a way of expanding on the chapter and for testing understanding of it.*

1. What do you understand by the terms
    (a) *apparatchiks* and
    (b) *nomenklatura*?
2. What steps did Brezhnev take to bring greater stability to Soviet politics?
3. Why did a 'black economy' flourish in Brezhnev's Russia?
4. In what ways did Andropov's KGB differ from its predecessors, the OGPU and NKVD?
5. Why did the outcome of the Helsinki Conference (1975) prove an embarrassment to the Soviet authorities?
6. To what extent did Brezhnev's new constitution of 1977 increase the civil liberties enjoyed by the Russian people?
7. In what ways did the Brezhnev Doctrine (1968) differ from the Truman Doctrine (1947)?

B *Essay questions.*

1. 'A period of political and economic stagnation.' How valid is this assessment of the Brezhnev years?
2. How successful were the Soviet authorities in dealing with the problems created by dissidents and racial minorities?
3. 'Brezhnev had no solutions to the economic problems facing the Soviet Union.' How valid is this judgement?
4. To what extent would it be accurate to claim that Brezhnev's foreign policy during the period 1964–82 was as aggressive as at any other time in Soviet history?

10 ∽ MAKING NOTES

Read the advice given about making notes on page ix of the Preface: How to use this book, and then make your own notes based on the following headings and questions.

A *Brezhnev – his background and the stages by which he assumed power*

1. Describe Brezhnev's role during World War II.
2. What was the relationship between Brezhnev and his predecessor Khrushchev?
3. How did Brezhnev manage to eliminate his possible rivals?
4. Would it be accurate to claim that Brezhnev
    (i) lacked a sparkling personality and

(ii) was a capable administrator.

B *Life in Brezhnev's Russia*
1. What was Brezhnev's attitude to
   (i) Khrushchev's policy of decentralisation?
   (ii) Western influences?
   (iii) the rehabilitation of Stalin?
2. How corrupt did Soviet society become during the Brezhnev era?
3. Why were racial minorities such as the Crimean Tartars and Volga Germans not allowed to return to their former homelands?
4. What was Brezhnev's reaction to Russian Jews who wished to emigrate to Israel?

C *Economic problems*
1. What economic reforms did Liberman and Neminchov suggest?
2. Which overseas involvements proved a drain on the Soviet economy?
3. To what extent did the standard of living of the Russian people improve during the Brezhnev years?
4. What efforts did the Soviets make to compete in the world's export markets?
5. What environmental problems affected the Soviet Union at this time?

D *The dissidents*
1. What were the demands of the dissidents?
2. Why did the activities of Andrei Sakharov prove particularly embarrassing to the authorities?
3. Why was Brezhnev furious by Svetlana Alliluyeva's decision to live in the West?
4. To what extent did Brezhnev return to the old Stalinist-style of repression in dealing with the Russian dissidents?

E *Soviet foreign policy, 1964–82*
1. What was the Soviet attitude to the war in Vietnam?
2. Why did Soviet relations with China further deteriorate during this period?
3. What were the implications of the Brezhnev Doctrine for the West?
4. Outline the events that led to
   (i) the Soviet involvement in Czechoslovakia in 1968.
   (ii) the Soviet invasion of Afghanistan in 1979

11 ⌐ DOCUMENTARY EXERCISES BASED ON LEONID BREZHNEV AND THE 'PRAGUE SPRING'

1. Single-source exercise
Study the source and then answer the questions based upon it.

Words of a song written by the American folksinger, Joan Baez.

> Happy birthday, Leonid Brezhnev
> What a lovely seventy-fifth
> We watched the party on TV
> You seemed to be taking things casually
> What a mighty heart must beat in your breast
> To hold forty-nine medals on your chest
> Think of all the gifts you've got
> Some were acquired and some were not
> Like a natural talent for marionettes
> Who do your dirty work and cover your bets
> So with one hand waving free
> The other one crushed a budding democracy

1. *What occasion does the song celebrate?*
2. *Explain what the singer meant by*
   'Think of all the gifts you've got
   Some were acquired and some were not'.
3. *What does she imply when she says*
   *'Like a natural talent for **marionettes***
   Who do your dirty work ... '?
4. *To what events is she referring to when she says*
   'The other one crushed a budding democracy'?
5. *What overall impression does Joan Baez give of Brezhnev?*

A **marionette** is a puppet moved by strings.

2. Multi-source exercise

Study the sources and then answer the questions based upon them.

SOURCE A

Part of a broadcast message to the Czech people in August 1968

Our brothers, Czechs and Slovaks!
The governments of the Bulgarian People's Republic, the Hungarian People's Republic, the German Democratic Republic, the Polish People's Republic and the Union of Soviet Socialist Republics appeal to you! Responding to requests for help received from leading Party and State leaders of Czechoslovakia who have remained faithful to socialism, we instructed our armed forces to go to the support of the working class and all the people of Czechoslovakia ... threatened by plots of reactionary forces.

SOURCE B

Part of an official statement made by the Czech Central Trade Union council in August 1968

During the night 20–21 August 1968, the Republic was occupied ... This action was taken without the knowledge of the government. This groundless, treacherous occupation of our peace-loving homeland is contrary to international law and to the Charter of the United Nations.

The Czech Radio had reported that the occupation troops are a few yards away from the radio station. Several hundred people are trying to stop the advancing tanks with their bodies... The Czech Radio asks the people to try and engage the troops in conversation. It is our only weapon.

SOURCE C
From a report in a Czech newspaper on 21 August 1968

1. In order to ensure the protection of working people from the actions of extreme and hooligan elements, I appeal to all citizens not to leave their homes between 10 p.m. and 5 a.m...
2. Until further notice public meetings are banned...
3. Radio and television broadcasting and publishing is subject to the approval of the relevant authorities.

SOURCE D
From orders issued by the commander of the Warsaw Pact forces in Prague

1. *Study Sources A and B. To what extent do these sources contradict each other?*
2. *Why in Source C does the Czech Radio advise its listeners that conversing with the occupying troops is 'our only weapon'?*
3. *Study Source D. For what reasons did the commander of the Warsaw Pact forces issue these orders?*
4. *What evidence is there in Sources B–D that the Czech people were against the invasion?*
5. *How valuable are the sources to an understanding of the events in Czechoslovakia in August 1968?*

15 Epilogue – the collapse of Communism and the end of the Soviet empire. The Putin years

INTRODUCTION

moribund in a state of decay or decline.

When Leonid Brezhnev died in 1982, both the political and the economic situation in the Soviet Union were close to crisis point. The administration was not only riddled with corruption but it also seemed **moribund** and incapable of finding solutions to the nation's problems.

ANALYSIS

The economic and social problems inherited by Brezhnev's successors

- Whilst the increase in the GNP (gross national product) of the developed countries was growing rapidly, that of the Soviet Union was falling.
- The management of agriculture and industry was still based on the 'command economy' of Stalin's day and was directed by a central planning authority – Gosplan.
- The country was also lagging behind in the use of modern technology and more sophisticated management techniques. Although the Soviet education system produced men and women with the required skills, they were given little opportunity to use them.
- The arms race that was part of the Cold War was a drain on the economic resources of the country. Too much was being spent on the military, supporting members of the Warsaw Pact, left-wing regimes in countries such as Cuba and revolutionary movements generally.
- Agricultural output was erratic. Most arable land was still collectively farmed and a large percentage of the peasantry lived below the poverty line. The situation was not helped by poor harvests that made it necessary to import grain from North America.
- Exports were declining and this meant that there was a shortage of the hard currency needed to buy Western technical know-how.

- Prices were rising and industry was failing to produce the quantity of consumer goods promised.
- Years of communist rule meant that there were no wealthy individuals able to invest in enterprises.
- The morale of the workers was low. Obvious corruption amongst the country's elite led to cynicism. Consequently, many opted to work and deal in unofficial economic activities and became part of the so-called black economy.
- Alcoholism had reached epidemic proportions and was affecting the health and life expectancy of the people.

The Politburo was dominated by failing old men. Whilst Kosygin, Mikoyan and Podgorny had passed from the scene, there remained Andropov and Shelepin, in their late sixties, Chernenko and Gromyko, both in their seventies, and 89-year-old Kaganovich who, although ousted in 1957, was still available to give interviews to the foreign press! Although Brezhnev would probably have chosen Konstantin Chernenko as his successor, the Central Committee opted for Yuri Andropov.

TIMELINE

Leaders of the Soviet Union and the Russian Federation, 1982–2007

1982–84	Yuri Andropov
1984–85	Konstantin Chernenko
1985–91	Mikhail Gorbachev
1991–99	Boris Yeltsin
2000–	Vladimir Putin

1 ⌐ RUSSIA'S AILING LEADERS – YURI ANDROPOV AND KONSTANTIN CHERNENKO

PICTURE 48
Yuri Andropov

PICTURE 49
Konstantin Chernenko

YURI ANDROPOV (1914–84)

Son of a railway worker, Yuri Vladimirovich Andropov was born at Nagutskoye and later worked in the shipyards at Rybinsk on the upper Volga. A relative newcomer to politics, he joined the Communist Party in 1939 and after World War II moved to Moscow to work for the Party's Central Committee. In 1954 he was appointed Soviet ambassador to Hungary and there he took a leading role in suppressing the revolution in 1956. From 1967 he was head of the KGB and was largely responsible for the measures taken to curb the activities of Russian dissidents and this enhanced his reputation. Realising that Brezhnev was a sick man, in 1982 he gave up his position in order to be better placed to compete for the leadership. Held in high regard by the Party's hierarchy, in spite of being considered a strict ideologist and austere in comparison with Brezhnev, he was also known to be a determined if cautious reformer. In 1982, he was chosen to succeed Brezhnev.

Andropov began his brief period in office by attempting to tackle some of the problems facing his country. He took steps to reduce the privileges enjoyed by the ***apparatchiks*** (bureaucrats unquestioningly loyal to the Soviet system), he tried to reduce the prevalent corruption and widespread alcoholism and he did his best to ensure that workers conformed to a strict code of discipline. He even went as far as to order the arrest of Brezhnev's son-in-law, Yuri Churbanov. Notoriously corrupt and known for his acceptance of bribes, Churbanov had used his father-in-law to try and realise his own political ambitions. Andropov also continued to clamp down on dissidents and, although many were confined to psychiatric hospitals, in an attempt to appease world opinion, a few were allowed to emigrate abroad. His attempts at reform achieved little, largely because the Soviet Union was already too far along the road towards total economic collapse. He did, however, have the good sense to appoint a number of energetic younger men, including Mikhail Gorbachev, to prominent positions.

In foreign policy, Andropov ordered work to cease on space-based weapons, but he lost face following a crisis in September 1983 when a Russian fighter shot down a South Korean airliner that had accidentally strayed into Soviet air space. 269 men, women and children were killed and this led to an increase in tension between NATO and the Soviet Union.

An act that earned Andropov much favourable publicity was his response to a letter he received from a young American girl, Samantha Smith. An extract from her letter is quoted below:

apparatchiks full-time officials of the Communist Party and state bureaucracy.

> Dear Mr. Andropov,
> My name is Samantha Smith. I am ten years old. I have been worrying about Russia and the United States getting into a nuclear war … God made the world for us to live together in peace and not to fight.

In his reply, Andropov wrote:

> Dear Samantha,
> It seems to me – I can tell by your letter – you are a courageous and honest girl, resembling Becky, the friend of Tom Sawyer in the famous book ... Yes, Samantha, we in the Soviet Union are trying to do everything so that there will not be a war on earth. This is what every Soviet man wants ... I wish you all the best in your young life.

He also invited her to visit the Soviet Union and this she did. Afterwards Samantha Smith became a child peace campaigner until her untimely death at the age of 13 when she was killed in an air crash.

Suffering from an acute kidney condition and needing regular dialysis, in 1983 Andropov was confined to hospital on a permanent basis. He died the following year after holding office for only 15 months. In spite of his hard-line stance on Hungary in 1956 and his treatment of dissidents, Andropov is regarded by some historians as a humane reformer.

KONSTANTIN CHERNENKO (1911–85)

PROFILE

Konstantin Ustinovich Chernenko was aged 72 and already terminally ill when he succeeded Andropov in 1984. Born in Bolshaya Tes in 1911 into an impoverished peasant family, he joined the Communist Party in 1931 and over the years was appointed to numerous local posts. A close associate of Brezhnev, he became a member of the Politburo in 1978 and was considered a rival of Andropov for the leadership. Chernenko was too incapacitated to take a major role in the nation's affairs but his brief period in power witnessed a return to the ways of Brezhnev with an increase in privilege and corruption. During his lengthy periods of sick leave, Chernenko was away from Moscow and the country was run by Mikhail Gorbachev and the Soviet Minister of Defence, Dimitri Ustinov. Suffering from **emphysema**, his health further deteriorated and he died following a heart attack in 1985. Chernenko's tenure as head of state was the briefest in Russian history, just 13 months.

emphysema an infection of the lungs that causes breathing difficulties.

2 ～ THE ERA OF MIKHAIL GORBACHEV

A *Background*

The historian, Michael McCauley, has written 'If Lenin was the founder of the Soviet Union, then Gorbachev was its grave digger.' Mikhail Sergeyevich Gorbachev (1931–) was born at Provolone, the son of an agricultural mechanic who worked on a collective farm. Unusual at that time, as a child he was baptised in the Russian Orthodox Church. During the later 1930s, his grandfather was arrested by the NKVD and, charged with being a Trotskyist, spent several years in a labour camp; during World War II, his home village was occupied by the Germans. Gorbachev was to claim that these events had a dramatic impact on his life. As a boy, he worked on a collective farm before studying law at Moscow University, and it was during his years as a student that he first joined the Communist Party. He graduated in 1952 and the following year married Raisa Maksimovna. For some years Gorbachev worked for the Young Communist League, *Komsomol*, and then moved gradually upwards within the Party. In 1970 he became the Party leader in Stavropol and was elected to the Supreme Soviet. Ten years later, as a **protégé** of Yuri Andropov, he joined the Politburo as its youngest member and became Secretary for Agriculture. His management of Soviet agriculture was far from successful but useful in the sense that it made him aware of the flaws in the collective system. He did, however, establish a good reputation as an opponent of corruption and inefficiency and in 1985 succeeded Chernenko as General Secretary of the Communist Party. From the start, Gorbachev's main aims were to revitalise the flagging Soviet economy and introduce measures that would make government more democratic and improve the efficiency of the bureaucracy.

protégé one whose career benefits from the support of a patron or person of influence.

PICTURE 50
Mikhail Gorbachev

To what extent did Gorbachev's reforms represent a break with the past?

B *Glasnost and perestroika*

Glasnost, which means openness, was the term used by Gorbachev to describe the series of measures he intended to introduce to combat corruption, prevent the abuse of privilege and allow greater freedoms – freedom of speech, freedom of the press, freedom to criticise the government and freedom of dissent. By encouraging intellectual and cultural openness, he hoped to reduce the influence of the *apparatchiks*.

Although still dedicated to the Soviet system, Gorbachev realised that to achieve his economic aims it would be necessary to push ahead with a programme of modernisation that would involve the greater use of modern technology, encourage much needed increased worker productivity and prune the bureaucracy to make it more efficient. Though there was some marginal progress, it was slow and ponderous. Gorbachev therefore decided on a comprehensive range of political, economic and social reforms based on the ideas of *glasnost* and *perestroika*. By *perestroika*, he meant restructuring and, in particular, a system of restructuring that would make the Soviet economy more efficient. Yet again, the response to his reforms was negative, so he decided to press ahead with a range of even more fundamental changes. A new administrative system was set up that allowed management greater freedom, the media was allowed to report and comment without restraint, and political prisoners were released. Amongst those allowed to return home was Andrei Sakharov.

See page 427.

A scientist, Sakharov was a civil rights campaigner who was strongly opposed to the testing of nuclear weapons. Earlier, in 1975, the Soviet authorities had refused him permission to travel to Oslo to receive the Nobel Peace Prize and five years later he was arrested and sent into exile. On his release in 1986, he urged the Soviet leader to proceed with his *perestroika* reforms more speedily.

Gorbachev next introduced measures to make the parliamentary system more democratic by allowing a choice of candidates and secret ballots for elections to posts in the Party and government, but matters did not rest there. Following his election as chairman of the Supreme Soviet in 1989 and backed by Boris Yeltsin (see below), he ended the Communist Party's monopoly of power and set about changing the structure of the old Soviet system, replacing it in stages with democratic, representative government based on a free multi-party system.

Even so, the old economic problems persisted. Although Gorbachev had sanctioned measures intended to make Russia a more democratic country, he still held firm to his belief in a **command economy** and resisted any moves towards creating a capitalist-style market economy. As the economy spiralled out of control, so there were further falls in productivity, inflation rose, prices increased and, fearful of food shortages, people began to hoard goods. Seemingly against his better judgement, Gorbachev recognised that the restructuring he planned would require granting greater freedom to those involved in the management of industry and he agreed to encourage a limited introduction of a free enterprise market economy by placing the ownership of some areas of Soviet industry and agriculture in private hands. Measures were passed that decentralised aspects of the country's economy and permitted individual enterprises to enter into trade agreements with foreign countries. This was to lead to the start of the dismantling of the Soviet-style command economy.

command economy an economy planned and centrally controlled by the government.

C *Gorbachev's revision of Soviet foreign policy*

One of Gorbachev's most ill-conceived decisions was to counter alcoholism by ordering the destruction of the prosperous vineyards in the Crimea. He seemed unaware that vodka was distilled from rye or potatoes!

Gorbachev also announced changes in Soviet foreign policy. With some 40% of government expenditure spent on the military, it became obvious to him that greater economic progress would be made if the Soviet Union was not involved in an expensive arms race that was part of the country's Cold War strategy. As a result, he set out to improve relations with the United States and the West and to encourage foreign trade and travel. At the end of 1987, he reached an agreement with the

American President, Ronald Reagan, to destroy all stocks of intermediate-range nuclear weapons. He also made it clear that he had no intention of interfering in the affairs of Eastern European countries and, two years later, announced the withdrawal of Soviet troops from Afghanistan. Gorbachev also recognised the need for European co-operation. In 1987, he wrote:

> Europe is indeed a common home where geography and history have closely interwoven the destinies of dozens of countries and nations. Of course, each of them has its own problems and each wants to live its own life, to follow its own traditions. Therefore, one may say the home is common, that is true, but each family has its own apartment, and there are differences too.

In 1990, Gorbachev was awarded the Nobel Peace Prize.

D *The collapse of the Soviet Union's satellite empire*

KEY ISSUE

The stampede to escape Communist rule.

Events in the Soviet Union affected the attitude of peoples in the Communist bloc countries of Eastern Europe. Over the years there had been numerous revolts against Soviet domination of their satellite states – East Germany (1953), Poland (1956) and, more famously, Hungary (1956) and Czechoslovakia (1968).

Now Gorbachev championed the reformist movements in these countries and consequently, as democratically elected governments came to power, so the Communist regimes collapsed. In October 1989, the East Germans overthrew their much hated hard-line leader, Erich Honecker, and on 9 November began to dismantle the Berlin Wall. By the end of 1990, the two Germanies were reunited. In Poland, Lech Walesa's *Solidarity* movement, backed by the predominantly Roman Catholic people, forced the resignation of the Communist General, Wojciech Jaruzielski; in Czechoslovakia, mass demonstrations against the oppressive Communist regime forced Gustav Husak to stand down. He was replaced by the dissident dramatist, Vaclav Havel, who became prime minister, whilst the not forgotten Alexander Dubcek was recalled to become Chairman of the Czech parliament. Similar bloodless revolutions occurred in all the former Communist countries and by the end of 1990 Poland, Czechoslovakia, Hungary, Bulgaria and Albania all had democratically elected governments. In Romania, the personal rule of the hated Communist Nicolae Ceausescu came to an end in 1989 when he was desposed, put on trial and executed. In all these countries, arrangements were made for the staged withdrawal of Russian troops.

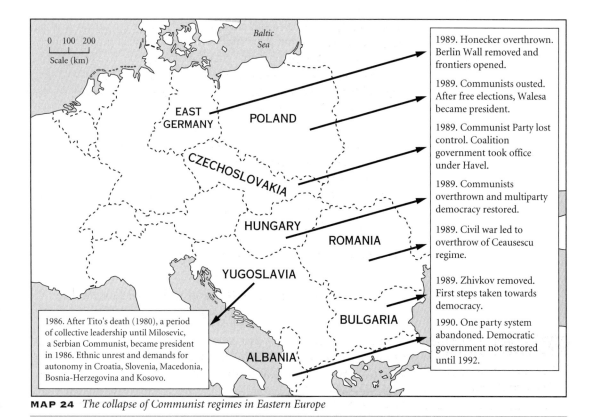

MAP 24 *The collapse of Communist regimes in Eastern Europe*

E *1989, 'The year that freedom broke out'*

Abroad, Gorbachev's policies won him friendship and admiration. With the identifying feature of a crimson birthmark on his bald head, 'Gorbie', as he was popularly known, travelled widely with his attractive, fashion-conscious wife, Raisa. He met the US President Reagan on several occasions; in London, he dined with the Queen at Buckingham Palace and made a good impression on Prime Minister Margaret Thatcher.

At home, however, the economic situation continued to decline and there were now strikes in various parts of the country. Whilst dissidents praised his policy of *glasnost*, they complained that there was still much to be done in the field of human rights. Then, to add to his problems, came the Chernobyl disaster.

THE CHERNOBYL DISASTER, 1986

Early in the morning of 26 April 1986 an explosion occurred at a nuclear power plant at Chernobyl, in the Ukraine, releasing radio-active material into the atmosphere. The fallout left the vicinity immediately uninhabitable and made necessary the evacuation and resettlement of over 336 000 people. Contamination was wide-spread and affected regions of the Soviet Union, Europe and even North America. The disaster was blamed on a flawed reactor, inadequately trained personnel and a lack of regard for safety; it also raised concerns about the overall safety of the Soviet nuclear power industry. During the months that followed, some 56 people died from radiation sickness and thermal burns; but how many have subsequently died from radiation-related conditions such as leukaemia and thyroid cancer will never be known for certain – estimates run into tens of thousands. The reactor was enclosed in a large concrete shelter and many people have now returned to live in the contaminated zone. The secrecy and misinformation circulated by the Russian authorities to the world's media regarding details and the extent of the disaster represented a backward step from the openness promised by *glasnost*.

Gorbachev's failure to stimulate the country's sluggish economy and bring about an upturn led to a rapid decline in his popularity. The Russian leader was in a no-win situation. After six years in office the radical reformers felt that his attempts at reform were too slow and the aims of *glasnost* and *perestroika* were not being achieved, whilst the Communist Party hard-liners felt victims of a sell-out as he was moving both too fast and in the wrong direction. Their privileges had been removed, the country was moving away from being a one-party state with a command economy and, because of Gorbachev's policy of *glasnost*, the Party had lost its control of the media and so was no longer able to cover up the country's economic and social problems. With production targets still not being met and projects left unfinished, Gorbachev's critics claimed that his economic reforms were no more than **cosmetic**. Rising inflation brought with it price increases, shortages and long queues for basic necessities and this led to a rapid decline in the quality of life of the Russian people. Some even made fun of *perestroika*, referring to it as 'katastroyka'. All in all, the hard-liners had had enough and in August 1991 were ready to act.

Rumours of a possible attempted *coup* had been rife for some time. Then, on 18 August 1991, a delegation visited Gorbachev, who was holidaying with his family at Foros in the Crimea, and demanded his resignation and that he agree to be replaced by Gennady Yanayev, the vice president.

When Gorbachev refused, the *coup* leaders announced that an Emergency Committee had assumed power and claimed that Gorbachev had been obliged to resign for reasons of ill health. In fact, he and his family had been placed under house arrest. At this point, Boris Yeltsin arrived in Moscow, declared the attempted *coup* illegal, appealed for public support and called for the release and return of Gorbachev. With many of the military supporting Yeltsin, after three days of uncertainty the *coup* collapsed. It failed because of the intervention of the military, the incompetence of the plotters, the apparent lack of support of the Russian people and the opportunism of Yeltsin, who had made the most of the occasion by challenging the *coup* leaders in a speech made to a crowd gathered outside the parliament building from the turret of a tank. Although Gorbachev survived the attempted *coup*, he was destroyed politically.

cosmetic only superficial and having no real substance.

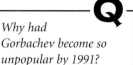

Why had Gorbachev become so unpopular by 1991?

F *The disintegration of the Russian empire*

MAP 25 *The break-up of the USSR*

For some time there had been agitation for independence in some of the republics of the USSR. Now fear of another possible *coup* that might succeed and restore Communist centralised control caused some of the republics openly to claim their independence. In August 1991, the first were the Baltic States of Estonia, Latvia and Lithuania. Armenia followed and then Azerbaijan, Belarus (formerly Belorussia), Moldavia, the Ukraine and Uzbekistan and finally Tajikistan and Turkmenistan, whilst what was left of the Soviet Union became the Russian Soviet Federated Socialist Republic (RSFSR). An attempt was made by the presidents of the Ukraine and Belarus to retain close ties between the former republics of the USSR through the formation of the Confederation of Independent States (CIS), but the Baltic States declined to join and Georgia withdrew. With other member states tending to go their own way and some showing strong nationalistic tendencies, it proved a very fragile alliance. In addition, the Volga Germans and the Crimean Tartars, who had been sent into exile by Stalin, were allowed to return to their homelands, though in the event only a small proportion did since their properties had long been taken over by Russians.

See pages 429 and 430.

3 ⌐ EXIT GORBACHEV, ENTER YELTSIN

The *coup* foiled and the situation restored, Gorbachev was allowed to continue as Soviet president but, with his position weakened, he had no choice but to play second fiddle to Yeltsin. He resigned from the Communist Party, took steps to disband the Central Committee of the Party and removed both the KGB and the army from Party control. On 25 December 1991, he finally resigned as President and, with the Russian rather than the Soviet flag flying over the Kremlin, the Soviet Union ceased to exist. At the end, Gorbachev may not have been highly rated in his homeland, but abroad he was held in high regard, as can be seen in the following quotations.

US President George Bush snr

> History will be very generous to you … With *glasnost* and *perestroika* your far-sighted vision paved the way for arms reductions, for ending the Cold War, and for bringing to your country a democracy and a market economy that will serve Russia well for years to come.

British Prime Minister Margaret Thatcher

> President Gorbachev is undoubtedly one of the great men of our time. His reforms marked the first significant steps to bringing freedom and democracy to Russia … These measures were undertaken in the face of fierce resistance by hard-liners and bureaucrats which would have daunted lesser men.

Israeli Prime Minister Shimon Peres

> Gorbachev did something no one before him dared to do, or at very least, gave it a chance. He threw open all the windows and all the doors, allowing fresh air flowing through the pores, throwing into disarray all the bureaucrats who were used to hiding behind barred windows and locked doors.

PROFILE

BORIS YELTSIN (1931–2007)

A man with numerous human frailties and unsound health, Boris Yeltsin's presidency covered a traumatic period in Russian history, during which his country suffered a series of political and economic crises. Weaknesses he may have had in plenty, but the man with a **titanic ego** also possessed one outstanding quality, courage. Born in 1931 in the village of Butka in the Sverdlovsk region of the Soviet Union, Boris Nikolayevich Yeltsin was the son of a building worker and a seamstress. In 1934, his father was arrested for anti-Soviet activities and spent three years in a *gulag*. The young Yeltsin was educated locally and then at the Ural Polytechnic in Sverdlovsk, where he excelled at sport and finally graduated in construction engineering. For some years he worked near home in the construction industry and in 1968 joined the Communist Party. Promotion came rapidly in both work and within the Party ranks so that, thanks to Gorbachev, by 1985 he was a member of the Politburo and First Secretary of the Moscow branch of the Party and was given the task of dealing with the corruption evident in the local Party organisation.

Yeltsin proved himself an able and determined reformer and was popular with Muscovites, but he quarrelled with Gorbachev. For some time he had been one of his leader's most severe critics and claimed that *perestroika* was moving too slowly. In 1987, at a meeting of the Moscow Party Committee attended by Gorbachev, he was accused of political immaturity and was forced to resign from his high ranking posts. The following year he also lost his position in the Politburo. Although humiliated, Yeltsin was far from finished and continued to criticise his leader's slow pace of reform. In 1989, at the time of the first elections to the new Soviet parliament, he was elected by a considerable majority to represent Moscow and the following year, much against Gorbachev's wishes, he stood against his leader's preferred candidate, Nikolai Ryzhkov, to become the first democratically elected president of the Russian Federation. Then, as we have seen, in spite of his differences with Gorbachev, he was still prepared to support him at the time of the 1991 attempted *coup*. Yeltsin now openly championed the right of the Soviet republics to declare their independence and supported demands for a multi-party political system and a free market economy – the scene was set for major changes.

titanic ego a great opinion of oneself.

Q *In what ways did the policies of Yeltsin differ from those of Gorbachev?*

A *Yeltsin at the helm*

As president, Yeltsin faced many formidable challenges as he tried to transform the country's failed command economy and replace it with one based on capitalistic free enterprise. Early in 1992 he ended the government's price subsidies and encouraged the growth of free markets. Increased interest rates, higher taxes and a reduction in government subsidies and welfare spending created an austere economic regime, which further reduced living standards. With the country facing the prospect of a major economic slump, many of his former supporters began to distance themselves from his policies. Opposed by both the Supreme Soviet and the Congress of People's Deputies, Yeltsin struggled to remain in control until, early in 1993, he announced that he was going to **rule by decree**. He dissolved the Congress of People's Deputies that was part of the Soviet-era Russian constitution and called for parliamentary elections. Meanwhile, appallingly low and still declining living conditions led to mounting civil unrest and mass demonstrations. Again, the former Communist Party hard-liners had had enough and attempted a *coup*, but

rule by decree to rule arbitrarily without reference to the government.

this was suppressed by troops loyal to Yeltsin after he had ordered tanks to shell his opponents meeting in the parliament building. During the months that followed, Yeltsin proved himself an authoritarian president as he appointed and then sacked a series of vice presidents, prime ministers and ministers, and by the end of the year a new constitution had been approved and come into force.

B *The rise of the oligarchs*

As part of his plans to dismantle the former Soviet-style economy, Yeltsin urged the privatisation of former state-run enterprises. In order to give his plans a flying start, he issued vouchers with a value of 10 000 roubles to all Russian citizens to invest in the new private companies. Most Russians took advantage of the offer by selling their vouchers at relatively low prices to those in a position to buy them; the latter were able to accumulate massive numbers of shares and became a breed of men described as **oligarchs**. Consequently, these new fat-cat moguls came to control the country's major industries and businesses – manufacturing industries, power and energy in the form of the gas, oil and coal industries, commercial enterprises, banking, telecommunications and the media. In order to cope with his country's mounting foreign debts, in 1996 Yeltsin tried to win the support of leading businessmen by offering shares in exchange for bank loans. Eminent oligarchs who took advantage of his offer included Boris Berezovsky, Anatoly Chubais, Mikhail Fridman, Vladimir Gusinsky, Mikhail Khodorkovsky, Vladimir Potantin and Roman Abramovich (later to become famous as the owner of Chelsea Football Club). In effect, the 'loans for shares' scheme turned the beneficiaries into overnight multi-millionaires. During this period over 10 000 enterprises employing 11 million workers were privatised as a result of voucher auctions. Of Yeltsin's 'loans for shares' scheme, Chrystia Freeland, in *Sale of the Century*, wrote:

oligarch one of an exclusive body of men who hold supreme power.

> The loans for shares scheme was a naked scam ... it is tempting to dismiss the rapacious oligarchs who instigated it as just plain evil ... The oligarchs did what any red-blooded businessman would do. The problem is that the state allowed them to get away with it.

To further his foreign policy objectives, Yeltsin travelled the world, and US President Bill Clinton and British Prime Minister John Major were amongst world leaders to visit Moscow. In 1994, Yeltsin joined a meeting of **G7** leaders in Naples. Towards the end of the year Queen Elizabeth II became the first British monarch to visit Russia since 1908. However, the Russian leader made a very controversial decision when, in December 1995, he ordered the invasion of Chechnya.

G7 Group of 7, the leaders of the world's seven richest countries.

C *The issue of Chechnya*

MAP 26
Chechnya

Chechnya is a small republic located in the mountainous Caucasus region of Russia. Covering an area of about 15 000 square kilometres and with a population of just over 1 100 000, by religion it is predominantly Muslim. During 1940, the Chechens had rebelled against Soviet rule and as a result Stalin had ordered the deportation of the people to Siberia. It is claimed that the few Chechens that remained carried out guerrilla warfare and assisted the Germans. It was not until 1956 that Nikita Khrushchev allowed the Chechens to return to their homeland.

In 1991, in common with other republics anticipating the collapse of the Soviet Union, the Chechen National Congress was formed with the aim of claiming independence. Yeltsin opposed this, claiming that Chechnya had never been an independent republic within the USSR; but the real reason for his opposition was the immense oil resources to be found in the region.

When, in 1994, Chechnya finally asserted its independence, Yeltsin ordered the invasion of the country and the capital city, Grozny, was occupied. The Chechens proved no pushover during the First Chechen

> **KEY ISSUE**
>
> *The justification of the Chechen demand for independence.*

War and the bloody campaign resulted in an estimated 70 000 casualties. When the Russians bombed Grozny, the Chechen President, Dzhokhar Dudayev, called for a *jihad*, a Muslim holy war, against Russia, thus giving rise to a series of Muslim-inspired acts of sabotage and hostage taking in Chechnya and Russia. In 1996, a ceasefire was agreed and Russian troops were withdrawn from the country.

D *Yeltsin – the final years*

Q

What were the causes of the economic problems that faced Yeltsin?

As a result of economic chaos, falling living standards and the Chechen wars, public opinion polls indicated that Yeltsin's popularity had plummeted. Since Yeltsin's policies had produced neither prosperity nor peace, many Russians recalled Soviet times when, from a domestic viewpoint, social and economic affairs were better ordered and, on the world stage, their country's prestige was much higher.

In 1996, when Yeltsin stood for election to a second period in office, few fancied his chances but with control of the media and the support of the oligarchs he won 54% of the vote. He was narrowly, if surprisingly, re-elected. However, his problems were not over and in 1998 a financial crisis arose when money received from an American loan was squandered, with most of it finding its way to Swiss banks. As the markets panicked, so the rouble fell to an all-time low and lost 75% of its value. Yeltsin tried to save the day by sacking and reshuffling his ministers but clearly his days were numbered.

There had long been rumours that Yeltsin had suffered bouts of ill health and that he was an alcoholic. From time to time his poor health had caused him to be hospitalised and disappear from the public eye for lengthy periods. Prone to heavy drinking, on several occasions he had appeared drunk in public and behaved erratically. Whilst attending a concert in Berlin, he had grabbed the conductor's baton and tried to sing with the orchestra; on another occasion he had climbed on the stage and danced at a rock concert. Unexpectedly, on 31 December 1999, he made a surprise appearance on television and announced his decision to resign and in an emotive speech asked the Russian people to forgive for him for his errors and for having failed to justify their hopes. He said, 'I cannot shift the blame for Chechnya … I made the decision, therefore I am responsible,' and added, 'Russia must enter the new millennium with new politicians, with new personalities, and with new, smart, strong and energetic people'. He advised the people that Vladimir Putin would take over as acting president until the next elections.

After Yeltsin's death in 2007, newspapers in the West showed a mixed reaction:

The *Washington Post*, April 2007

He did more than anyone to raze the rotting communist superstructure of the former Soviet Union and build from the ruins the framework of a newly democratic and capitalist country.

The *Daily Telegraph*, April 2007

> ... in office two very different Yeltsins etched themselves on the world's consciousness. There was Yeltsin the fighter, who climbed on the top of a tank to raise the standard of liberty against Soviet putschists who wanted to restore Communism. And there was another version ... puffy-cheeked, paralysed by heart disease and a fondness for the bottle.

Perhaps Mikhail Gorbachev, the man he backed and then outmanoeuvred, was the most accurate when he said that Yeltsin was responsible for 'many great deeds for the good of the country and serious mistakes.'

> **Q**
>
> *To what extent might Gorbachev's estimate of Yeltsin be considered accurate?*

4 ∽ THE UNKNOWN VLADIMIR PUTIN

Virtually unknown to the Russian public and considered only a stop-gap appointment, Vladimir Vladimirovich Putin (1952–) was the first Russian leader to have been born during the post-war period. Born in Leningrad (now St Petersburg) in 1952, he was the sole surviving child of three boys. His father, Vladimir, had once served in the Soviet navy and the NKVD, whilst his mother, Maria, was a factory worker. After graduating in law at Leningrad University, Putin was assigned to the KGB and from 1985 to 1990 worked in the German Democratic Republic, East Germany. Promotion through a chain of local government positions came quickly and in 1998 Yeltsin appointed him head of the FSB, the Federal Security Service of the Russian Federation and successor to the former KGB. The following year he was appointed First Deputy Prime Minister. Putin, a practising member of the Russian Orthodox Church, is a talented linguist and is able to speak both German and English. Considered to be something of a fitness fanatic, he is a judo black belt.

PROFILE

PICTURE 51
Vladimir Putin

Three months after being appointed his successor by Yeltsin in 1999, Putin won the elections to become president in his own right. Amongst his first acts were to make Yeltsin immune from public prosecution and to change the Russian national anthem to the former Soviet anthem but with different words. Then, in 2000, he was embarrassed by the *Kursk* disaster. The *Kursk*, a nuclear submarine, went missing on a training exercise in the Barents Sea. The Russians had no underwater craft capable of reaching the submarine and NATO's offer of help was declined. President Putin was subsequently criticised for his apparent lack of concern when the submarine's crew of 118 perished.

In 2004, Putin won re-election with a resounding 71% of the vote. The immediate problem he faced was dealing with the ongoing Chechen crisis. With the Chechens still refusing to accept Moscow's authority, in

1999 the Russians began the invasion of neighbouring Dagestan. Chechen terrorists reacted with terrorist attacks on apartment blocks in several Russian cities including Moscow, providing Putin with the excuse to launch a Second Chechen War. Better organised than the first, the Russian forces virtually destroyed Grozny and drove the Chechen fighters into the hills. Putin immediately claimed a victory but Chechen resistance was far from over. In 2002, actors and an audience totalling some 900 attending the opening night of a musical, *Nord-Ost*, were held hostage by Chechen terrorists in a Moscow theatre. Armed with **Kalashnikovs** and with explosives strapped to their bodies, they sustained the siege for two day before gas was used to storm the building. This resulted in the deaths of 130 people. Early in 2004, mid-air explosions destroyed two domestic airliners and claimed 90 lives. Only a week later, a suicide bomber blew up the Rizhskaya metro station in Moscow. These atrocities were thought to have had **Al-Qaeda** involvement. Then came the Beslan school crisis.

Kalashnikov Russian assault rifle.

Al-Qaeda ('the base') a terrorist organisation aimed at ending foreign influence in Muslim countries.

THE BESLAN SCHOOL HOSTAGE CRISIS

On 1 September 2004 gunmen burst into a school in Beslan and in an appalling act of terrorism held 1 300 children and teachers hostage. After some 50 hours the siege of the school ended when men of the FSB stormed the building; during the ensuing gunfight at least 330 people were killed, more than half of them children. Afterwards the Russian authorities were severely criticised for their management of the tragedy.

PICTURE 52

A woman cries in the ruins of the school gymnasium in Beslan

During Putin's second term as president, he imposed limits on the freedom of the media and there were hints that he was returning to the censorship of Soviet times. Television networks are in the hands of those who toe the Putin line. During this time, attention has also focused on the deaths of some 14 journalists, many of whom had been critics of Putin's regime and died in mysterious circumstances.

SOME RUSSIAN JOURNALISTS WHO DIED IN MYSTERIOUS CIRCUMSTANCES

Yuri Shchekochikhin, a journalist who exposed the extent of organised crime and corruption in the Russian government. In 2003, he died suddenly of an illness linked to thallium poisoning and there is good reason to believe that he was the victim of a politically motivated assassination.

Anna Politkovskaya, born in the United States to Ukrainian parents, she was a fearless critic of the Chechen Wars and the Putin administration. In October 2006 she was found dead in the elevator of her apartment building.

Alexander Litvinenko was a former KGB agent who worked for military counter intelligence. In 1998, he publicly accused senior FSB officers of the assassination of the multi-millionaire oligarch, Boris Berezovsky, and was arrested. On his release, he fled to Britain where he was granted political asylum and citizenship but, in 2006, Litvinenko fell ill. It was discovered that he was suffering from polonium-210 radiation poisoning and he died three weeks later.

Ivan Safronov, a journalist who disclosed classified information about Russian intercontinental ballistic missiles, was questioned by FSB agents. In 2007 he died after falling from the fifth floor of his Moscow apartment. People are sceptical about the Russian claim that he committed suicide.

A 'A system meant to serve one master'?

It cannot be denied that after the economic chaos of the Yeltsin years, Putin has brought much needed stability, based largely on petroleum-fuelled economic growth. His critics claim that his own political party, the United Russia Party, resembles the former Communist Party, that his reputation has been enhanced by the **spin doctors** of the Kremlin and that the Russian parliament merely rubber-stamps his proposals. As the *Washington Post* put it – 'Russia's fledgling democracy has been transformed into a system meant to serve one master.'

spin doctors those who give a favourable impression of people or events in order to manipulate public opinion.

In foreign policy, Putin's aim was to restore the Russian Federation to the superpower status once enjoyed by the Soviet Union and, in 2006, Russia became a member of G7, thus making it G8. He has called for 'a fair and democratic world that would ensure security and prosperity not only for the select few, but for all.' Backed by massive oil and natural gas resources, he has always stood his own ground against the United States. He strongly opposed the US-led invasion of Afghanistan and the action taken against Saddam Hussein's Iraq without United Nations approval. Putin has also taken steps that suggest that, if necessary, he is prepared to resume the Cold War. Criticised both at home and abroad for his style of autocratic rule, the future direction to be taken by Putin and the Russian Federation remains uncertain.

5 ⤳ STRUCTURED AND ESSAY QUESTIONS

A *This section consists of questions that might be useful for discussion (or writing answers) as a way of expanding on the chapter and testing your understanding of it.*

1. What is meant by the following terms?
   (a) GNP (gross national product)
   (b) a command economy
   (c) oligarchs
2. What methods did Andropov take to deal with Russian dissidents?
3. Why did Andropov's response to Samantha Smith's letter win him favourable publicity?
4. What changes did Gorbachev intend when he introduced *perestroika*?
5. Why did the attempted *coup* of 1991 fail?
6. To what extent might Yeltin's 'loans for shares' scheme be considered a 'naked scam'?
7. What criticisms have been levelled against Putin's domestic policies?

B *Essay questions.*

1. To what extent might Gorbachev be considered the 'grave digger' of the Soviet Union?
2. How successful were Gorbachev's policies of *glasnost* and *perestroika* in bringing about reform in the Soviet Union?
3. How significant were events in Chechnya to domestic affairs in Russia during the period 1991–2004?
4. To what extent would you consider it fair to claim that Yeltsin's years in power were disastrous for the Russian people?

6 ⤳ MAKING NOTES

Complete the following table to show the stages in which the Soviet Union's satellite empire in Eastern Europe broke up.

Country	Year that the Communist regime was overthrown	Last Communist leader	First democratically elected leader
Poland			
Czechoslovakia			
Hungary			
Romania			
Albania			

7 ↔ BIBLIOGRAPHY

Although many of the events described in this chapter occurred in the recent decades, there is already a wealth of published material available relating to the post-Stalin years. Amongst the most popular are the two books by John Laver – *The USSR 1945–90 (History at Source series)* and *Stagnation and Reform: The USSR 1964–91 (Access to History series)* both published by Hodder & Stoughton in 1991 and 1997. Ian Derbyshire also provides a concise and detailed account of much of this period in *Politics in the Soviet Union – From Brezhnev to Gorbachev* (Chambers 1987). Chapters 6 and 7 of Martin McCauley's *The Soviet Union since 1917* give a detailed and very readable account of the post-1953 years as do Chapters 3–7 of *The Rise and Fall of the Soviet Empire* by the Russian historian, Dmitiri Volkogonov (HarperCollins 1999).

More difficult are *Last of Empires. A History of the Soviet Union, 1945–1991* by John Keep (OUP 1995), *Soviet Politics – Struggle with Change* by Gordon B. Smith (Macmillan 1992) and Richard Sakwa's *Soviet Politics – An Introduction* (Routledge 1989). Detailed studies of the individuals involved include *The Khrushchev Era* by Martin McCauley (Macmillan 1987), Nikita Khrushchev's own *Khrushchev Remembers* (Andre Deutsch 1971) and *Khrushchev on Khrushchev* written by his son, Sergei Khrushchev (Little Brown 1990). There is also *Andropov* by Z. Medvedev (Blackwell 1983), *Gorbachev and After* by S. White (CUP 1992) and J. Morrison's *Boris Yeltsin* (Penguin 1991). Also interesting and extremely well illustrated are *Stalin. A Time for Judgement* (Chapter 10 – *The Stalin Legacy*) by Jonathan Lewis and Phillip Whitehead (Methuen 1990) and Chapters 6 and 7 in *Red Empire. The Forbidden History of the USSR* by Gwyneth Hughes and Simon Welfare (Weidenfeld & Nicolson 1992).

Recently published books covering aspects of Putin's rule of the Russian Federation include *Blowing up Russia* by Alexander Litvinenko and Yuri Felshtinsky, Gibson Square, 2007; Andrew Jack's *Inside Putin's Russia*, Granta Publications, 2004; *Putin's Russia* by Anna Politkovskaya, The Harvill Press, 2004; and *Sale of the Century* by Chrystia Freeland, Abacus, 2000. Litvinenko and Politkovskaya were amongst authors who subsequently died in mysterious circumstances.

8 ⌒ ANSWERING SYNOPTIC QUESTIONS

Synoptic questions require you to show your understanding of a topic by presenting an overview covering an extended period and by considering how it was influenced by political, economic, cultural, social and religious aspects. You are required to consider evidence of change and continuity, as well as provide historical explanations, make judgements and evaluate evidence. Some topics covered in this book that might be used as a basis for synoptic questioning include:

- agricultural developments and the condition of the peasantry
- the industrialisation of Russia, the Soviet Union and the Russian Federation
- Russia and the Soviet Union under repressive regimes
- Russian expansionism and foreign policy
- Church–State relations
- opposition and the role of dissent.

Let us consider a response to a synoptic question based on opposition and dissent.

To what extent can it be claimed that, during the period 1860–2000, every regime that ruled Russia faced opposition and dissent?

The Tsars	
Alexander II	Populist movement, the Narodniks. 'Young Russia' Manifesto. Socialist Revolutionaries. Assassination.
Alexander III	Opposition to reactionary policies. Russification and alienation of the Jews.
Nicholas II	Growth of various revolutionary groups – Social Revolutionaries, Social Democrats, Octobrists. 'Bloody Sunday' and 1905 Revolution. Revolutions of 1917. Murder of Tsar and family.
Lenin	Civil War. Kronstadt mutiny. Assassination attempts.
Stalin	Power struggle, Trotskyists. Kulak opposition to collectivisation. Anti-religious measures, enforced standards of culture. Baltic States/Ukrainian collaboration with Germans during World War II. 'Doctors' Plot' and possibility of murder.
Khrushchev	Opposition to many of his policies. Forced resignation.
Brezhnev	Opposition to nepotism and corruption. Growing number of dissidents.
Gorbachev	For different reasons, opposition from both hard-liners and reformers. Attempted *coup*.
Yeltsin	Unpopular economic policies. Unexpected resignation.

Glossary

Index